Information and Efficiency in Economic Decision

ADVANCED STUDIES IN THEORETICAL AND APPLIED ECONOMETRICS
VOLUME 4

EDITORIAL BOARD

THE SPECIAL SCOPE OF THE SERIES

The fortress of econometrics has often been laid siege to from one or a few sides only. According to their inspiration or inclination, authors have laid stress on model specification, parameter estimation, testing and prediction or more generally the use of models (prediction in particular being a rare bird in econometric literature). Special topics, such as errors in the variables, missing observations, multi-dimensional data, time-series analysis, dynamic specification, spatial autocorrelation, were dealt with as and when the need arose.

No econometric exercises will ever be complete. Nevertheless, in setting up such an exercise as part of an operational economic investigation, one may reasonably be expected to try and encompass in it as many aspects of econometric modelling as may present themselves. This series is devoted to the publication of work which, as far as possible, addresses all aspects of a "complete econometric modelling" approach; for instance, spatial econometrics or policy optimisation studies which account explicitly for the specification, estimation or analysis of components of those models in the widest sense, including any complementary components from the environment in which the economic model must operate.

The very objective of the series may limit its extensions; but as André Gide put it (Les faux monnayeurs), "il est bon de suivre sa pente, pourvu que ce soit en montant".

All correspondence should be addressed to A.J. Hughes Hallet or to J.H.P. Paelinck at the Erasmus University, PO Box 1738, 3000 DR Rotterdam, The Netherlands.

Information
and Efficiency in
Economic Decision

by

Jati K. Sengupta

1985 **MARTINUS NIJHOFF PUBLISHERS**
a member of the KLUWER ACADEMIC PUBLISHERS GROUP
DORDRECHT / BOSTON / LANCASTER

Distributors

for the United States and Canada: Kluwer Academic Publishers, 190 Old Derby Street, Hingham, MA 02043, USA
for the UK and Ireland: Kluwer Academic Publishers, MTP Press Limited, Falcon House, Queen Square, Lancaster LA1 1RN, England
for all other countries: Kluwer Academic Publishers Group, Distribution Center, P.O. Box 322, 3300 AH Dordrecht, The Netherlands

Library of Congress Cataloging in Publication Data

Sengupta, Jatikumar.
    Information and efficiency in economic decision.

    (Advanced studies in theoretical and applied
econometrics ; v. 4)
    1. Decision-making--Mathematical models.
2. Economic policy--Mathematical models.
3. Uncertainty--Mathematical models. 4. Stochastic
processes. I. Title. II. Series.
HD30.23.S458 1985   330'.0724   84-18958
ISBN 90-247-3072-4

ISBN 90-247-3072-4 (this volume)
ISBN 90-247-2622-0 (series)

Copyright

To Krishna

Preface

Use of information is basic to economic theory in two ways. As a basis for optimization, it is central to all normative hypotheses used in economics, but in decision-making situations it has stochastic and evolutionary aspects that are more dynamic and hence more fundamental. This book provides an illustrative survey of the use of information in economics and other decision sciences. Since this area is one of the most active fields of research in modern times, it is not possible to be definitive on all aspects of the issues involved. However questions that appear to be most important in this author's view are emphasized in many cases, without drawing any definite conclusions. It is hoped that these questions would provoke new interest for those beginning researchers in the field who are currently most active.

Various classifications of information structures and their relevance for optimal decision-making in a stochastic environment are analyzed in some detail. Specifically the following areas are illustrated in its analytic aspects:

1. Stochastic optimization in linear economic models,
2. Stochastic models in dynamic economics with problems of time-inconsistency, causality and estimation,
3. Optimal output–inventory decisions in stochastic markets,
4. Minimax policies in portfolio theory,
5. Methods of stochastic control and differential games, and
6. Adaptive information structures in decision models in economics and the theory of economic policy.

Stochastic processes have been increasingly used in recent times in models of rational expectations, stochastic control and other adaptive behavior in economics. We have attempted to illustrate some very simple applications of the following kinds of processes in economics: (a) Wiener processes (b) Markov processes and (c) multidimensional diffusion processes. These applications include a broad range from the applied aspects of stochastic stability to those of stochastic equilibrium characterized in rational expectations models. Although problems of classical statistical estimation belonging to the domain of conventional economet-

VII

rics have not been dealt with, we have considered some recent topics from an informational viewpoint as follows:

1. Estimation of parameters from outcomes of behavior revealed in two-person differential games,
2. How to estimate an "expectational parameter" and use it in rational expectation models?
3. What are the costs due to lack of full information for implementing any optimal decision?
4. How are the concepts of robustness and risk aversion related to adaptive information structures in optimal economic decisions?

The book can be used in graduate courses in mathematical economics, applied econometrics and quantitative economics in business schools. It would also be useful as a supplement for courses in economic theory, operations research and systems science. The mathematical and statistical requirements have been kept at an elementary level in the earlier chapters, while more advanced problems, of interest to researchers are treated later.

The book is not a textbook in the conventional sense, as it includes numerous results and concepts arising from the author's own research. Some of the results and ideas reported in the book have been published in the professional journals before and I would like to thank the following journals in particular: International Journal of Systems Science, Journal of Economic Dynamics and Control, International Journal of Mathematical Modeling, Applied Economics, and Journal of Policy Modeling.

We hope the book will stimulate economics students to consider economic problems without neglecting the stochastic point of view. We emphasize, however, that we have stressed in this book only those operational aspects of information structures and stochastic optimization, which are applicable to economic models and related fields.

We believe this book offers considerable flexibility for use in any subject which deals with methods for applying stochastic optimization in the form of (a) stochastic control, (b) efficient decision-making under uncertainty, (c) stochastic differential games and (d) problems of economic policy and planning.

Systems scientists and industrial engineers will perhaps find here some ideas and approaches which might be helpful in their own fields. The point of view taken in this book, that econometric estimation should be viewed as a part of decision theory should come very naturally to them, although it might not seem so to an economist. They would perhaps be most interested in the discussion of examples on rational expectations and self-tuning control, adaptive models in economics, value of alternative information structures in different economic systems e.g., futures market, competitive markets with agents having heterogenous information and adaptive control models with learning.

I have been very fortunate in having many gifted research students, who through interaction and cooperative research have contributed significantly to my knowledge and understanding of stochastically optimum systems in economics, operations research and control engineering. I take this opportunity to express my appreciation of them.

Finally I am most deeply indebted to my wife for her utmost support, which was readily available when I needed it most. My two children gave me support through their understanding and patience, when I was unstable to provide time for them., It is indeed a real pleasure to record my appreciation of their love and concern.

Contents

I. Introductory problem

1. Stochastic optimization: examples and applications

1. Introduction

Problems of optimization, both static and dynamic have occupied a central role in economic theory. The optimization behavior of economic agents, be they households or firms have provided the economists with a set of normative decision rules that can be tested against the observed behavior at the market place, which may be competitive, regulated or otherwise. The theory of economic policy, as applied to macromodels has postulated implicit normative behavior by assuming as decision maker such agents as the government, the central bank or the national planning authority. The process of optimization is thus basic to economic modeling at three levels: the specification, estimation and control. The specification, viewed as a set of equations in economic variables may or may not include a normative hypothesis. Thus, a production relation $y \leqslant f(x_1, x_2)$ between one output y and two inputs x_1, x_2 includes the case of a production frontier when an optimizing assumption is introduced. The estimation problem, conditional as it is on the specification, starts as soon as one makes a distinction between the parameters and the variables. The above production relation, for instance appears as $y \leqslant f(x_1, x_2; \theta)$, where θ denotes a set of unknown parameters. If the parameters θ are unknown but observations on variables (y, x_1, x_2) are available, then in suitable cases θ may be estimated by following a suitable method of estimation e.g. least squares (LS) or, maximum likelihood (ML). In spite of their differences, various methods of estimation share two basic points: each involves an optimizating objective like maximizing the likelihood, and each involves the probability distribution of the random elements or errors generating the observed variables (y, x_1, x_2), which are then called sample observations. Estimation thus provides, in suitable cases a statistic or estimate $\hat{\theta}$ of θ, from the observed data set generated by a probability mechanism, called stochastic process; the latter describes a family of random variables. The control problem may precede or succeed estimation. The latter is more conventional. Thus, in the theory

3

of the firm, the inputs x_1, x_2 are the control variables, which are optimally chosen so as to maximize profits

max $\quad z = py - q_1 x_1 - q_2 x_2$

subject to $\quad y \leqslant f(x_1, x_2, \hat{\theta})$ $\qquad\qquad\qquad\qquad\qquad$ (1.1)

where the prices (q_1, q_2, p) of inputs and output are assumed known or given. If the response function $f(\cdot)$ is linear in its arguments and the inputs and outputs are required to be nonnegative, we have then in (1.1) a stochastic linear programming (LP) problem. Let x^* denote the optimal control vector and the associated output and profit by y^*, z^*. Then, these are dependent on $\hat{\theta}$ i.e. $x^* = x^*(\hat{\theta})$, $y^* = y^*(\hat{\theta})$ and $z^* = z^*(\hat{\theta})$. Note that the probability distribution of $\hat{\theta}$ induces a distribution for x^*, y^*, and z^*, which, of course gets truncated when the nonnegativity requirement on x and y is added. Sometimes, the constraints of the form $a \leqslant x \leqslant b$ may be imposed by way of policy requirement. Then, the truncation of the distribution of profits or output alters the probability of attaining a target level of profits e.g., the convergence of $x^*(\hat{\theta})$ to x^0 or, $z^*(\hat{\theta})$ to z^0 may be blocked, where x^0, z^0 denote the unconstrained optimal solution and the associated optimal profit.

A second approach to estimation, often used in the linear decision rule approach solves for optimal control as a function of the state variable and then apply estimation. To illustrate this situation assume the production function in (1.1) as an equality and in a Cobb-Douglas form:

$$y = f(x, \theta) = a_0 x_1^{a_1} x_2^{a_2}, \quad \theta = (a_0, a_1, a_2)$$ $\qquad$ (1.2)

where the parameter vector θ denotes unknown constants. The optimal controls $\tilde{x}^* = (\tilde{x}_1^*, \tilde{x}_2^*)$ must satisfy

$$\tilde{x}_i^* = \alpha_i y, \quad \alpha_i = a_i p / q_i, \quad i = 1, 2$$ $\qquad$ (1.3)

If the vector of observations on $(\tilde{x}^*, y)$ is such that the conditional expectation of $\tilde{x}_i^*$ given y is a linear function of y

$$E(\tilde{x}_i^* \mid y) = \text{linear in } y$$ $\qquad\qquad\qquad$ (1.4)

Then (1.3) can be used as a valid equation for estimating the feedback parameter α_i. Two difficulties may arise however. The first is the problem of identification between the two input demand equations of (1.3); we have two equations but one explanatory variable y. Also, if returns to scale is constant or diminishing, which is the condition required for a proper maximum of profits, then we would have implicit constraints on the parameters i.e.

$$\sum a_i = \left(\sum \alpha_i q_i \right) / p < 1$$

The second problem is due to lack of information to test whether the specification (1.4) or (1.2) holds. Hence it is possible to conceptualize situations when either of them holds. For instance, Klein (1953) used cross-section railway data of 81 companies to estimate a_i by the geometric average of the ratio of cost of the factor to total revenue i.e.

$$\hat{a}_i = \frac{1}{n} \sum_{j=1}^{n} \left(\log(q_i x_{ij}) - \log(py_j) \right); \quad i = 1,2$$

where $n = 81$ and x_{ij}, y_j denote the observation on inputs and output for company $j = 1, 2, \ldots, 81$. Since the industry was regulated, revenue was demand determined, hence the problem for each railway company was to choose the optimal levels of inputs, given output and prices. Note that Klein's methodology here is not ordinary least squares but a direct estimate of the mean value of the parameters in the sample.

A dynamic example of linear decision rules, often arising in production-inventory models in microeconomic theory and in macrodynamic Keynesian models of stabilization policy may be more appropriate for purpose of illustrating the problem of jointness of estimation and control. Consider a simple discrete time control model with a fixed horizon: $y(t)$ is the state variable $u(t)$ is a control variable and t is time:

$$\text{minimize} \quad J = \frac{1}{2} \sum_{t=0}^{N-1} \left[y^2(t) + u^2(t) \right] \qquad (2.1)$$

subject to $\quad y(t+1) = \hat{a}y(t) + \hat{b}u(t)$

$$y(0) = y_0 \,(\text{fixed}), \, N \text{ fixed} \qquad (2.2)$$

Here $\hat{a}$, $\hat{b}$ are the ordinary least squares type estimates of the linear stochastic system

$$y(t+1) = ay(t) + bu(t) + \epsilon(t)$$

$$\epsilon(t) \sim N(0, \sigma^2), \text{ independent of } u(t) \text{ and serially uncorrelated} \qquad (2.3)$$

where the parameters a, b are unknown constants to be estimated. A second method of estimation is to use (2.3) in (2.1) and minimize the expected value of J to arrive at the optimal equations for $t = 0, 1, 2, \ldots, N-1$

$$y(t) + a\lambda(t+1) - \lambda(t) = 0, \qquad u(t) + b\lambda(t+1) = 0 \qquad (2.4)$$

$$y(t+1) - ay(t) - bu(t) = 0$$

where $\lambda(t+1)$ is the Lagrange multiplier associated with the state equation: $ay(t) + bu(t) + \epsilon(t) - y(t+1) = 0$. On eliminating $\lambda(t)$ in (2.4) and a little algebraic manipulation, one can express optimal control $u^*(t)$ as a function of current and past states as follows:

$$u^*(t) = \theta_1 y(t) + \theta_2 y(t-1), \qquad \theta_1 = (1+b^2)/(ab), \quad \theta_2 = -1/b \quad (2.5)$$

Alternatively, optimal control can also be expressed as

$$u^*(t) = \beta_1 u^*(t-1) + \beta_2 y(t-1) \qquad \beta_1 = (1+b^2)/a, \quad \beta_2 = b \quad (2.6)$$

With additive errors on the right-hand side of (2.5) or (2.6), one could again estimate the parameters $\hat{\beta}$ or $\hat{\theta}$, from which the structural parameter estimates $\hat{a}$, $\hat{b}$ can be recovered. Note that this method, which has been widely used in empirical analysis of industry output behavior (Belsley 1969, Hay and Holt 1975) has several differences from the direct method used in (2.2) For one thing, it assumes, like Klein's estimation of the parameters of the Cobb-Douglas production function from cross-section railway data, that the observed data on the variable $u(t)$ are structured around the central value $u^*(t)$. Second, the estimates of the structural parameters $\hat{a}$, $\hat{b}$ by these two methods are in general different. However, under certain situations the two estimates may be asymptotically equivalent. In control theory this is called the property of self-tuning (Wittenmark 1975, Astrom 1980) that will be analyzed later.

It is clear that by combining (2.3) and (2.6) one could define another method of estimation

$$\begin{pmatrix} u(t) \\ y(t) \end{pmatrix} = \begin{pmatrix} \beta_1 & \beta_2 \\ b & a \end{pmatrix} \begin{pmatrix} u(t-1) \\ y(t-1) \end{pmatrix} + \begin{pmatrix} \epsilon_1(t) \\ \epsilon_2(t) \end{pmatrix}$$

where the asterisk has been dropped from $u(t)$. It will be shown later that this view of simultaneous estimation and control may be profitably exploited to build cautions elements into an optimal control policy based on the dynamic model (2.2). The difference in loss functions (2.1) due to the two methods of estimation may be analyzed in terms of an iterative process involving estimation and control in successive steps. Thus one may estimate first the control equation (2.6) for $\hat{u}(t)$ given observations on $u(t-1)$ and $y(t-1)$. The second step consists in estimating $\hat{y}(t+1)$ from (2.2) using the regressors $\hat{u}(t)$ and $y(t)$. If the process converges in a few iterations, then this provides favorable evidence of robustness of either method of estimation. For econometric policy models, several applications made by Chow (1975), Klein and Su (1980), Prescott (1975), and Sengupta (1982) suggest that robustness may be the rule rather than an exception. This of course holds good, if there are no inequality restrictions on control or the state variables and the planning horizon is not too short.

The interactive nature of the estimation and control problems, which arise very naturally in dynamic economics leads to various methods of simulation and algorithmic computation. Besides the two-step iterative process mentioned above, simulation methods are required for two other reasons. First, the econometric model (2.2) may only hold as an approximation, where nonlinearities of various types and departures from a normal error structure are completely ignored. Thanks to the advent of new generation computers, various simulation techniques can now be applied to test the seriousness of the problems of nonlinearity and nonnormality which are assumed away in most policy applications of econometrically estimated models. Second, simulation may be used as a problem-solving tool for choosing between alternative specifications of a model, through their performance tested against artificial data. Methods of adaptive control, which have had a tremendous advance in recent years with significant applications in physical systems like chemical process control, digital and numerical control in power systems and nuclear fields have utilized simulation methods as a powerful tool for analyzing alternative modeling structures e.g., bilinear control models, models with variable coefficient structures, unstable dynamic systems where the errors are not stationary and systems dynamics specified by a set of jointly dependent partial differential equations, which are technically called distributed parameter systems.

2. Examples and Applications

Our objective here is to provide a selected set of examples and applications of stochastic optimization in economic fields. The selection is made primarily on the basis of two criteria: how useful is it in applied work? And, does it provide a computable solution that can be easily interpreted and updated with more information, if necessary? Since the field of application of stochastic optimization is very wide, we would limit ourselves to the following areas:
A. Production and allocation problems
B. Portfolio models in finance
C. Optimizing models in estimation
D. Control theory models in economic policy

A. Production and Allocation Problems

We consider here three simple examples derived from the production model (1.1) in order to illustrate the impact of randomness on the probability distribution of solutions, on the shape of the constraint set and on the robustness of any solution considered to be optimal in some sense. The examples make simplifying assumptions, both implicit and explicit but the points illustrated are very general, mostly applicable to multivariable models.

EXAMPLE 1 (Distribution Problem): Assume the production function to be cubic in one input x and the decision-maker (DM) maximizes profit $z = py - qx$, $y = f(x) = a_0 + a_1 x - \frac{1}{2} a_2 x^2 - \frac{1}{3} a_3 x^3$ to determine optimal input and output. If the parameter set $\theta = (a_0, a_1, a_2, a_3)$ contains elements, some or all of which are random, how would the DM select the optimal input? What would be its distribution, if the joint distribution of the elements of θ is known? How useful to the DM is the knowledge of the optimal input distribution?

It is clear that if θ were not random, the optimal input x_0 must satisfy the first and second order conditions for a maximum:

$$x_0^2 - \beta_1 x_0 + \beta_2 = 0 \qquad \beta_1 = -a_2/a_3, \quad \beta_2 = (a_3 p)^{-1}(q - a_1 p) \qquad (2.1)$$

$$pa_3(\beta_1 - 2x_0) \leqslant 0 \qquad (2.2)$$

where p, q are known quantities assumed to be positive. If the coefficients a_i, $i = 0, 1, \ldots, 4$ are positive then there must exist a real positive solution of the quadratic equation (2.1), which defines the economically relevant optimal input, if the associated output $y_0 = f(x_0)$ is positive. In practical situations however, the coefficients a_i, β_i are rarely known e.g. they may be subject to a joint probability distribution. Randomness in the coefficients may be due to two reasons in particular. One and perhaps the most important reason is the lack of complete information on the output response curve, hence the cubic response function is only an approximation to the true production function, where the approximation could be sequentially improved with more complete information. Second, the realized coefficients $\beta_i = \bar{\beta}_i + b_i$ may be viewed as stochastic perturbations around their mean values $\bar{\beta}_i$, so that the equations (2.1), (2.2) may hold at the mean:

$$x_0^2 - \bar{\beta}_1 x_0 + \bar{\beta}_2 = 0, \quad p\bar{a}_3(\bar{\beta}_1 - 2x_0) \leqslant 0 \qquad (2.3)$$

Let $R(\beta)$ denote the set of points $\beta = (\beta_1, \beta_2)$ defined by the variations β_i and $R_0(\beta)$ be a subset satisfying (2.3). Then, for all β not belonging to $R_0(\beta)$ i.e. $\beta \notin R_0(\beta)$ the input level x_0, found to be optimal in the deterministic case is no longer optimal e.g. if the second inequality of (2.3) fails to hold, the choice of x_0 may tend to minimize rather than maximize profits. Hence there arise two types of distribution problems:

one when $\beta \in R_0(\beta)$ and the other when $\beta \notin R_0(\beta)$. The latter case may be subsumed in the unconstrained case $\beta \in R(\beta)$. The first case i.e. $\beta \in R_0(\beta)$ is called the constrained distribution problem, since the stochastic variations are so structured around the mean that the feasibility and optimality conditions defined by (2.3) are maintained or preserved. The second case i.e. $\beta \in R(\beta)$ generates the unconstrained distribution problem, which of course is much easier to solve.

Taking the unconstrained case first, the probability $P(\text{Re})$ of real roots must satisfy the condition

$$P(\text{Re}) = \text{Prob}\left(\beta_2 \leqslant 1/4\beta_1^2\right) \tag{2.4}$$

where, on using the bivariate density $f(\beta_1, \beta_2)$,

$$P(\text{Re}) = \int \int f(\beta_1, \beta_2) d\beta_1 d\beta_2 \qquad \beta_2 \leqslant 1/4\beta_1^2$$

Hence the pdf of the two real roots x_1, x_2 of the quadratic equation

$$x_0^2 - \beta_1 x_0 + \beta_2 = 0 \tag{2.5}$$

is given by

$$g(x_1, x_2 | \text{Re}) = f(x_1 + x_2, x_1, x_2) | J | P(\text{Re}) \tag{2.6}$$

for all $x_1 \geqslant x_2$ and $|J| = (x_1 - x_2)$ is the Jacobian of the distribution. Thus, if the pdf $f(\beta_1, \beta_2)$ is bivariate normal with means $\bar{\beta}_i$, standard deviations σ_i, $i = 1, 2$ and correlation ρ, the pdf of the two real roots turns out to be

$$g(x_1, x_2 | \text{Re}) = \left[(x_1 - x_2) \exp\left(-\frac{Q}{2(1 - \rho^2)} \right) \right]$$

$$\times \left\{ \left(2\pi \sigma_1 \sigma_2 \sqrt{1 - \rho^2} \right) P(\text{Re}) \right\}^{-1}$$

where

$$Q = \left(\frac{x_1 + x_2 - \bar{\beta}_1}{\sigma_1} \right)^2 - 2\rho \left(\frac{x_1 + x_2 - \bar{\beta}_1}{\sigma_1} \right) \left(\frac{x_1 x_2 - \bar{\beta}_2}{\sigma_2} \right) + \left(\frac{x_1 x_2 - \bar{\beta}_2}{\sigma_2} \right)^2$$

In the constrained case, the term $P(\text{Re})$ has to be redefined to include $x_0 \geqslant \frac{1}{2}\beta_1$ where x_0 is a root of the random equation (2.5). For economic applications, it may be more appropriate to assume that β_1, β_2 have nonnegative domains. For instance, if $f(\beta_1, \beta_2) = \exp(-\beta_1 - \beta_2)$, $\beta_1 \geqslant 0$, $\beta_2 \geqslant 0$ then the pdf of the two real roots is:

$$g(x_1, x_2 | \mathrm{Re}) = \frac{x_1 - x_2}{0.24} \exp\{-(x_1 + x_2 + x_1 x_2)\}$$

where 0.24 is the approximate value of $P(\mathrm{Re})$ and $x_1 \geqslant x_2 \geqslant 0, 0 \leqslant x_1 < \infty$. These results, originally derived by Hamblen (1956) have been extended in several directions for multivariate cases (Bharucha-Reid 1970). For stochastic LP models (Sengupta, 1972, 1982) we have the simpler case of a set of random linear equations, instead of (2.5) which is quadratic.

For the decision-maker two specific advantages follow if he is able to specify the joint density $g(x_1, x_2 | \mathrm{Re})$ in (2.6) either exactly or approximately. First, he may be able to place a confidence limit on the so called mean solution (2.3).

Thus, the speed of convergence of x_i to its expected value $E(x_i)$ determined from (2.6) may determine which of the two optimal inputs x_1, x_2 may be preferable. Also, since the density $g(x_1, x_2 | \mathrm{Re})$ is unlikely to be symmetric, the probability of large derivations $|x_i - E(x_i)|$ from the mean solution $E(x_i)$ may indicate its unreliability. Thus, trade-off analysis between expected profit and its variance due to the standard error of any specific input policy may be performed. The examples of different input policies are $E(x_i)$ determined by (2.6), the solution x_0 of the mean equation (2.3) and the mode of x_i estimated from (2.6).

Second, a robustness analysis may be developed on the basis of the marginal densities $g_1(x_1 | \mathrm{Re})$, $g_2(x_2 | \mathrm{Re})$:

$$g_1(x_1 | \mathrm{Re}) = \int_{-\infty}^{x_1} g(x_1, x_2 | \mathrm{Re}) dx_2$$

$$g_2(x_2 | \mathrm{Re}) = \int_{x_2}^{\infty} g(x_1, x_2 | \mathrm{Re}) dx_1$$

from which the probabilities of x_i exceeding a preassigned level x_{i0} (e.g. this may be the solution of (2.3)) may be evaluated.

Thus, in a certain domain D the cumulative distribution $G_2(t) = \mathrm{Prob}(g_2(x_2 | \mathrm{Re}) \leqslant t)$ may dominate over $G_1(t = \mathrm{Prob}(g_1(x_1 | \mathrm{Re}) \leqslant t)$ in a stochastic sense i.e. $G_1(t) \geqslant G_2(t)$ for all $t \in D$. If D is the decision region for selecting a policy, then this property of robustness may be most desirable to preserve, when the production function is only incompletely known.

EXAMPLE 2 (Active Approach): Consider the LP model with two outputs y_1, y_2 as decision variables:

$$\begin{aligned}
\text{max} \quad & z = y_1 + y_2 \\
\text{subject to} \quad & a_{11}y_1 + a_{12}y_2 \leqslant b_1 \\
& a_{21}y_1 + a_{22}y_2 \leqslant b_2 \\
& y_i \geqslant 0, \quad y_2 \geqslant 0
\end{aligned} \tag{3.1}$$

The input availabilities b_i and the production coefficients a_{ij} are random as follows:

$$\begin{aligned}
a_{ij} &= \bar{a}_{ij} + \alpha_{ij} \\
b_i &= \bar{b}_i + \beta_i
\end{aligned} \tag{3.2}$$

where bar denotes mean values and the errors α_{ij} and β_i are assumed for simplicity to be mutually independent with zero means and finite variances.

As in Example 1, one may replace a_{ij}, b_i by their mean values $\bar{a}_{ij}$, $\bar{b}_i$ and solve LP model (3.1) at the mean. Let y_0 denote the optimal solution vector in this case and z_0 be the optimal profits at the mean. The risk associated with this policy y_0 measured e.g. by variance or other characteristics is unknown however. In default of this knowledge, the active approach to stochastic LP introduces allocation ratios u_{ij} to decompose the original problem and analyzes the implications of selecting them at alternative levels. Thus, the constraints of (3.1) would appear as:

$$a_{11}y_1 \leqslant u_{11}b_1, \quad a_{12}y_2 \leqslant (1 - u_{11})b_1$$

$$a_{21}y_1 \leqslant u_{21}b_1, \quad a_{22}y_2 \leqslant (1 - u_{21})b_2 \qquad y_i \geqslant 0, \quad i = 1, 2, \quad u_{11}, u_{21} \geqslant 0$$

$$\tag{3.2}$$

Now assume that the errors α_{ij}, β_i are so constrained that the following equations preserve feasibility and optimality for the allocation ratios u_{11}^0, u_{21}^0:

$$\begin{aligned}
y_1 &= \{(\bar{b}_1 + \beta_1)u_{11}^0\}/(\bar{a}_{11} + \alpha_{11}) \\
y_2 &= \{(\bar{b}_2 + \beta_2)(1 - u_{21}^0)\}/(\bar{a}_{22} + \alpha_{22})
\end{aligned} \tag{3.3}$$

We can write these as

$$y_i = \frac{\bar{b}_1 u_{11}^0}{\bar{a}_{11}} \left(1 + \frac{\beta_1}{\bar{b}_1}\right)\left(1 + \frac{\alpha_{11}}{\bar{a}_{11}}\right)^{-1}$$

$$y_2 = \frac{\bar{b}_2\left(1 - u_{21}^0\right)}{\bar{a}_{22}} \left(1 + \frac{\beta_2}{\bar{b}_2}\right)\left(1 + \frac{\alpha_{22}}{\bar{a}_{22}}\right)^{-1}$$

(3.4)

On expanding the right hand sides, taking expectations and assuming for simplicity that errors α_{ij}, β_i are symmetric in the sense that all odd moments are zero,

$$E(y_1) = \frac{u_{11}^0 \bar{b}_1}{\bar{a}_{11}} + \frac{u_{11}^0 \bar{b}_1 \sigma_{11}^2}{(\bar{a}_{11})^3}\left(1 + \frac{3\sigma_{11}^2}{(\bar{a}_{11})^2} + \ldots\right)$$

$$E(y_2) = \frac{\left(1 - u_{21}^0\right)\bar{b}_2}{\bar{a}_{22}} + \frac{\left(1 - u_{21}^0\right)\bar{b}_2 \sigma_{22}^2}{(\bar{a}_{22})^3}\left(1 + \frac{3\sigma_{22}^2}{(\bar{a}_{22})^2} + \ldots\right)$$

(3.5)

where σ_{ii}^2 is the variance of a_{ii}. When each of the random error components α_{ij}, β_i is identically zero, we have the solutions y_{10}, y_{20} at the mean:

$$y_0 = \frac{u_{11}^0 \bar{b}_1}{\bar{a}_{11}}, \quad y_{20} = \frac{\left(1 - u_{21}^0\right)\bar{b}_2}{\bar{a}_{22}}$$

Since the last expression in parenthesis on the right hand side of each equation (3.5) is strictly positive, we must have

$$E(y_i) > y_{i0} \quad \text{and} \quad E(y_i) + E(y_2) > y_{10} + y_{20}$$

Thus, the expected solutions $E(y_i)$ obtained from the random equations (3.4) results in higher profits. Thus it pays to have information on the pdf of y_1 and y_2, which can always be calculated in principle by the approximate method above.

Several features of this active approach are most important in practical applications. First, note that if the errors α_{ij}, β_i are not assumed to be symmetric, then the expected value solutions $E(y_i)$ in (3.5) would contain skewness and kurtosis coefficients involving third and fourth moments. Thus, the impact of asymmetry in the sense of third and fourth moments of the relevant random variables on $E(y_i)$ and on the associated profit $E(y_i) + E(y_2)$ may be analyzed. If this impact is very small, then the solution or policy may be said to be robust or insensitive to departures from symmetric normal-like distributions. Second, the confidence limits could be set up on the optimal outputs by using the approximate distribution of y_i. For instance, the asymptotic variance $\text{var}(y_1)$ of the optimal output y_1 in (3.5) can be approximately computed as

$$\text{var}(y_1) \simeq (\bar{a}_{11})^{-2} \{ c_{20} - 2dc_{11} + d^2 c_{02} \}$$

$$+ (\bar{a}_{11})^{-4} \{ 3c_{20}c_{02} + 5c_{11}^2 - 16dc_{11}c_{02} + 8d^2 c_{02}^2 \}$$

where

$$d = u_{11}^0 \bar{b}_1 / \bar{a}_{11}, \quad c_{st} = E\left\{ \left(u_{11}^0 \beta_1 \right)^s (\alpha_{11})^t \right\}$$

Likewise for $\text{var}(y_2)$. Under suitable conditions analyzed in the theory of stochastic linear programming (Kolbin 1977), the random variable ($y_i - E(y_i))/(\text{var}\, y_i)^{1/2}$ is known to converge asymptotically to a unit normal $N(0,1)$ distribution. Using this asymptotic result, any tentative solution say y_{i0} can be statistically tested in relation to $E(y_i)$ by the standard t-test. Lastly, the most important implication of the active approach in (3.3) is that the pdf of y_1, y_2 and of the profit $z = y_1 + y_2$ depends on the conditioning variables $u_{11} = u_{11}^0$ and $u_{21} = 1 - u_{22} = u_{21}^0$ – that can be suitably selected by the DM. Any such selection affects the mean and variance of outputs and profit and hence their pdf. Denote the set of allocation matrices $u = (u_{ij})$, $0 \leqslant u_{ij} \leqslant 1$, $\Sigma_j u_{ij} = 1$ by U and a specific allocation by u^0. Optimal profits then may be viewed as a scalar function of vector $y = x$ and matrix u: $z = z(u, x)$, $u \in U$, $x \in X$ where X is the set of constraints of the original LP problem. By varying u in U the whole set of conditional distributions $F(z \mid u^0 \in U)$ of profits may be specified and on comparing these distributions the truly optimal allocation matrix may be finally selected. One could also apply a stochastic version of two-person nonzero-sum game which has a stochastic payoff function. Player one is nature, who selects an $x^0 \in X$ from the feasible set X generated by the appropriate variations of the random elements of the problem. Given such an x^0, player two, the decision-maker selects an appropriate $u^0 \in U$. Note that the DM's decision problem is to choose between several conditional distributions of profits $F_k = F(z \mid u^0 = u(k) \in U)$, where $u(k)$ is the k-th selection. Since player one can choose the worst for player two, the latter can choose a policy of playing safe by choosing the best of the worst i.e. for each selection k, the worst possible x^0 is presumed in the first stage and then in the second stage a best u^0 is chosen over different selections. Thus, a minimax class of strategies can be characterized. Such minimax and gametheoretic strategies have been emphasized in recent developments of stochastic LP theory (Kolbin 1977, Sengupta 1982).

14

B. Portfolio Models in Finance

The traditional and widely used approach to the problem of portfolio choice has been the so-called mean variance approach, whereby the investor is assumed to be maximizing the expected value of a utility function that depends only on the mean and variance of the rate of return of the investment.

One important development of modern portfolio theory is the separability hypothesis, which specifies conditions for the optimal portfolio containing both riskless and risky assets such that the ratios of the amounts invested in both the risky asset and the riskless asset are fixed and independent of initial wealth. Our next two examples illustrate some stochastic aspects of these developments.

EXAMPLE 3 (Mean-variance model): Consider an investor who has to allocate optimally a proportion of his wealth, x_i in a risky asset i, where $x_i \geq 0$, $\sum_{i=1}^{n} x_i e_i = e'x = 1$ and the return $\tilde{r}_i$ is random. If the return vector $\tilde{r}$ is distributed with constant parameters $\theta = (m, V)$, m being the mean and V the variance-covariance matrix, then the traditional solution solves the following quadratic programming (QP) problem:

$$\min_{x \in R} \sigma^2 = x'Vx \tag{4.1}$$

where

$$R = \{x \mid m'x \geq w, \quad e'x = 1, x \geq 0\}$$

where w is initial wealth, which is net of cash, since money as a riskless asset is not introduced here. By varying w parametrically, the whole set of optimal or efficient portfolios $\{x^*(w)\}$ can be determined. Assume for simplicity that there is no nonnegativity constraint on x (i.e. short sales are permissible) and $m'x = w$ and under these assumption let x_* be the optimal solution or portfolio and σ_*^2 be the associated variance. Then, by Kuhn-Tucker theory it follows that

$$x_* = (\alpha\gamma - \beta^2)^{-1} V^{-1}[(m\gamma - e\beta)w + (e\alpha - m\beta)]$$
$$\sigma_*^2 = (\alpha\gamma - \beta^2)^{-1}(\gamma w^2 - 2\beta w + \alpha) \tag{4.2}$$

where $\alpha = m'V^{-1}m$, $\beta = m'V^{-1}e$ and $\gamma = e'V^{-1}e$. Note that the vector $y^* = x_*(w)/w$ of optimal asset proportions can be computed from (4.2) by dividing $x_* = x_*(w)$ by the nonnegative number w. Further, let $x^{(1)}$,

$x^{(2)}$ be two wealth-independent vectors in the set R (i.e. $x^{(1)}$, $x^{(2)}$ do not depend on w) defined as

$$x^{(1)} = (V^{-1}e)/\gamma, \quad x^{(2)} = (V^{-1}m)/\beta \qquad (4.3a)$$

$$x_* = k(w)x^{(1)} + [1 - k(w)]x^{(2)} \qquad (4.3b)$$

$$k(w) = (\alpha\gamma - \beta^2)^{-1}(\alpha\gamma - \beta\gamma w) \qquad (4.3c)$$

The optimal portfolio x^* or, equivalently y^* is said to exhibit the property of global separation, if and only if there exist such vectors $x^{(1)}$, $x^{(2)}$ in the constraint set R with $w = 1.0$ such that (4.3b) holds for all positive values of w. The property of separation is called local, if (4) holds for some finite interval $a \leqslant w \leqslant b$. The vectors $x^{(1)}$, $x^{(2)}$ belonging to the set R with w set equal to unity are called mutual fund and the relation (4.3b) expresses the efficient portfolio x^* as a weighted average of the two mutual funds, where the weights $k(w)$ may depend on the form of the utility function used by the investor in his optimization process. For example, the expected utility function $Eu(x)$ implicit in the derivations (4.2) is:

$$Eu(x) = -x'Vx + \lambda_*(m'x - w) = \lambda_* m'x - x'Vx - \lambda_* w$$

where λ_* is the optimal positive value of the Lagrange multiplier. Maximizing $Eu(x)$ subject to $e'x = 1$ leads to the optimal solutions x_*, σ_*^2 in (4.2). Thus, it is clear that the separability property may be more generally defined in terms of the following specification:

$$\max_{x \in R_w} Eu(\tilde{r}'x) = Eu(z)$$

where

$$R_w = \{x : e'x = w\}, \quad R_1 = \{x : e'x = 1\} \qquad (4.4)$$

where the utility function $u(\cdot)$ is assumed to be strictly concave and twice continuously differentiable in an open set (u_0, ∞), where u_0 is a natural lower bound for the domain of u in the sense that the marginal utility $M(z) = \partial u(z)/\partial z$ evaluated at $z = u_0$ is infinite. Following the work of Cass and Stiglitz (1970), Vickson (1975) has proved that a necessary condition for global separation of the optimal portfolio problem (4.4) without money as a riskless asset is that the marginal utility function $M(z)$ have one of the following forms:

$$M(z) = a + bz \text{ (quadratic utility)} \tag{4.5a}$$

or

$$M(z) = bz^c \text{ (constant relative risk aversion)} \tag{4.5b}$$

where a, b, c are scalar constants. These two conditions are also sufficient if $a < 0$, $b > 0$ for (4.5a) and $b > 0$, $c < 0$ for (4.5b). Thus, on applying the form (4.5a) to the objective function of (4.4) and applying the usual Kuhn-Tucker conditions one obtains for the optimal asset proportions $y^* = x^*/w$:

$$y^* = y^*(w) = k(w)y^{(1)} + [1 - k(w)] y^{(2)} \tag{4.6}$$

where

$$y^{(1)} = (V^{-1}e)/(e'V^{-1}e), \quad y^{(2)} = (V^{-1}m)/(e'V^{-1}m)$$

$$k(w) = 1 + (bw)^{-1}(ae'V^{-1}m)$$

Two important features of the separation property may be noted. First, this property divides the investor's optimal decision problem into two subproblems: (i) the determination of the wealth-independent mutual funds $x^{(1)}$, $x^{(2)}$ belonging to R_1 in (4.4), and (ii) the determination of investment in each mutual fund as a function of wealth. In general, there may be s mutual funds $x^{(1)}$, $x^{(2)}$, ..., $x^{(s)}$ depending on the problem and one may easily incorporate the nonnegativity condition for them. Thus, there may be s-fund separability, where for example s equals two in (4.6). Second, for the case when one of the assets is riskless i.e. money the traditional mean-variance approach still implies a two-stage separation of the optimal decision process. In the first stage, an efficient portfolio or fund of risky assets could be chosen and in the second, the investor's risk attitude could be introduced to determine the optimal allocation of wealth between the riskless asset and the efficient portfolio of risky assets. The separation hypothesis implies that all efficient portfolios are simply combinations of the same fund of risky assets and money. Ross (1978) has shown that the concept of s-fund separability may be restated in terms of stochastic dominance and this makes it very useful in a practical setting, since the probability distribution of returns is not required to be known.

Next we consider a simplier model due to Bertsekas (1976) where the constraint $e'x = \Sigma x_i = 1$ is dropped but a single riskless asset called money is introduced. This model is amenable to dynamic analysis and the dropping of the normalization constraint $e'x = 1$ is not much loss of generality.

EXAMPLE 4 (Dynamic Portfolio Separation): With an N-period planning horizon the investor maximizes $E\{u(w_N)\}$, the expected utility of his terminal wealth w_N, when the wealth w_{k+1} in period $(k + 1)$ follows the system equation:

$$w_{k+1} = d_k w_k + \sum_{i=1}^{n} \left(\tilde{r}_i^k - d_k \right) x_i^k \qquad k = 0, 1, 2, \ldots, N-1 \qquad (5.1)$$

containing one riskless asset with a sure rate of return d_k during the k-th period and n risky assets with random returns $\tilde{r}_i^k$. What is the consequence to the investor, if he adopts a myopic policy by ignoring the N-period character of the problem and solving instead, one period static problems in a recursive fashion? The latter proceeds as follows: For period one, he solve the problem

$$\max_{x^0} E\{ u(w_1) \}, \, w_1 = d_0 w_0 + \sum_{i=1}^{n} \left(\tilde{r}_i^0 - d_0 \right) x_i^0 \qquad (5.2)$$

by choosing the vector $x^0 = (x_i^0)$, when his initial wealth w_0 is given. It is assumed that the utility function depends only on w_{k+1}, $k = 0$, 1, 2,...,$N - 1$, is well defined and finite for all w_0 and x_i^k. It is also concave and twice continuously differentiable in an open set D. Under these conditions, an optimal portfolio $(x^0)^*$ exists and the associated optimal value $w_1^* = w_1(w_0,(x^0)^*)$ of w_1 is determined. In period two, the value w_1^* is known and the investor solves the new static problem

$$\max_{x^1} E\{ u(w_2) \}, \, w_2 = d_1 w_1^* + \sum_{i=1}^{n} \left(\tilde{r}_1^1 - d_1 \right) x_i^1$$

where the utility function satisfies the regularity conditions above. Let the optimal solution profile be denoted by $\{(x^1)^*, w_2^*\}$. Thus, the sequence of myopic policies may be denoted by $\{((x^0)^*, w_1^*), ((x^1)^*, w_2^*),\ldots,((x^{N-1})^*, w_N^*)\}$. In contrast the dynamic model (5.1) solves for the whole profile $(x^0, x^1,\ldots,x^{N-1})$ optimally, given the level of initial wealth w_0 and the probability characteristics of the random vectors $(\tilde{r}^1, \tilde{r}^2,\ldots,\tilde{r}^{N-1})$.

The purpose of this example is to demonstrate that under a certain class of utility functions $u(w)$, $w = w_j$ ($j = 1, 2, \ldots, N$) satisfying a linear property for the reciprocal of the Arrow–Pratt measure r_A of absolute risk aversion:

$$\frac{1}{r_A} = -\dot{u}(w)/\ddot{u}(w) = a + bw, \quad \text{for all} \quad w \tag{5.3}$$

where a dot over $u(w)$ denotes its derivative with respect to wealth level $w - w_j$ and a, b are scalar constants, the difference between the myopic policy and the n-period optimal policy may be nil or negligible. For in such cases, the investor when faced with the opportunity to reinvest his wealth sequentially over an N-period horizon, may use a policy similar to that of the single period case.

Consider first the single period model (5.2), where for convenience we drop the superscript zero over x and $\tilde{r}$. Denote the optimal solution by $x^* = x^*(w_0)$ with its typical element $x_j^* = x_i^*(w_0)$ dependent on the initial wealth w_0. The portfolio $x^*(w_0)' = (x_1^*(w_0), x_2^*(w_0), \ldots, x_n^*(w_0))$ is then said to be partially separated if it holds that

$$x_i^*(w_0) = \alpha_i h(w_0), \quad i = 1, 2, \ldots, n \tag{5.4}$$

where α_i, $i = 1, 2, \ldots, n$ are fixed constants and $h(w_0)$ is a function of w_0 which does not depend on i. Now assume that the utility function of (5.2) satisfies the linearity condition (5.3) for the reciprocal of the Arrow-Pratt measure of risk aversion, then by following the usual first order condition of maximization, one obtains for the optimal portfolio $x^*(w_0)$ and the associated value of the objective function:

$$x_i(w_0) = \alpha_i(a + bw_0), \quad i = 1, 2, \ldots, n$$

and

$$-\dot{J}(w_0)/\ddot{J}(w_0) = (a/d_0) + bw_0, \quad \text{for all} \quad w_0 \tag{5.5}$$

where

$$J(w_0) = \max E\{u(w_1)\}$$

$$= E\left\{ u\left[d_0\left\{1 + \sum_{i=1}^{n}(\tilde{r}_i - d_0)\alpha_i b\right\}w_0 + \sum_i (\tilde{r}_i - d_0)\alpha_i a\right]\right\}$$

Note that $h(w_0)$ of (5.4) takes the form $(a + bw_0)$ in (5.5), which is independent of i and α_i's in (5.5) are suitable scalar constants depending on i, involving for instance the parameters like mean and variance of the distribution of the random elements. Thus, if partial separation holds, we must have

$$x_i^*(w_0)/x_j^*(w_0) = \alpha_i/\alpha_j, \quad \alpha_j \neq 0$$

Further, if the parameter a in the linearity condition (5.3) is zero, then the optimal portfolio is said to be completely separated in the sense that the ratio of the amounts invested in both the risky asset and money are fixed and independent of initial wealth.

In the following are some examples of the class of utility functions satisfying the linearity condition (5.3) for the inverse of r_A:

exponential: $-e^{-w/a}$ for $b = 0$

logarithmic: $\log(w + a)$ for $b = 1$

power: $\dfrac{(a + bw)^{1-(1/b)}}{b - 1}$ for $b \neq 0, \quad b \neq 1$

Now in the N-period investment problem (5.1), we apply the dynamic programming algorithm to characterize the optimal portfolio, when the utility function $u(w_j)$ satisfies the linearity condition (5.3) for $j = 1, 2, \ldots, N$. Let

$$J_k(w_k) = \max_{\{x^k\}} E\left\{ J_{k+1}\left[d_k w_k + \sum_{i=1}^{n} (\tilde{r}_i^k - d_i) x_i^k \right] \right\}$$

and assume that we are at the beginning of period $(N - 1)$ and we have only one period to go. Then, from the solution (5.5) of the one-period problem we know that the optimal solution vector $x_{N-1}^* = x_{N-1}^*(w_{N-1})$ takes the form

$$x_{N-1}^* = \alpha_{N-1}(a + bd_{N-1}w_{N-1})$$

where α_{N-1} is an appropriate n-dimensional vector. Also, from (5.5) it follows:

$$-\dot{J}_{N-1}(w)/\ddot{J}_{N-1}(w) = (a/d_{N-1}) + bw$$

Using this result for the next to the last period we obtain by dynamic programming the optimal policy

$$x_{N-2}^* = x_{N-2}^*(w_{N-2}) = \alpha_{N-2}\left[(a/d_{N-1}) + bd_{N-2}w_{N-2}\right]$$

where α_{N-2} is again an appropriate n-dimensional vector containing parameters like the mean and variance of the joint distribution of the random rates $\tilde{r}_i^k$ of return. Proceeding similarly for the k-th period one obtains

$$x_k^* = x_k^*(w_k) = \alpha_k \left[(a/d_{N-1} \ldots d_{k+1}) + b d_k w_k \right] \tag{5.6a}$$

where as before α_k, $k = 0, 1, \ldots, N-1$ are suitable n-dimensional vectors that depend on the probability distribution $\tilde{r}_i^k$ and are determined by the optimal "cost-to-go" principle of dynamic programming

$$-\dot{J}(w)/\ddot{J}_k(w) = (a/d_{N-1} \ldots d_k) + bw \qquad \text{for} \quad k = 0, 1, 2, \ldots, N-1$$

$$\tag{5.6b}$$

On comparing (5.5) and (5.6) it becomes clear that the investor, when faced with the opportunity to reinvest his wealth w_k sequentially over future periods, uses a policy similar to that of the single period case. Further, if the parameter a is zero in the utility function, we obtain from (5.6) that the investor acts at each stage k as if he were faced with a single-period investment problem characterized by the rates of return d_k, $\tilde{r}_i^k$, $i = 1, 2, \ldots, n$ and the objective function $E\{u(w_{k+1})\}$. Also, it is clear from (5.6) that even when $a \neq 0$ only a small amount of foresight is required on the part of the investor to change from the myopic to the N-period control policy.

C. Optimizing Models in Estimation

Econometric estimation, viewed as a method of summarizing observed data is usually based on an optimization objective e.g., the least squares or the maximum likelihood. If the parameters are unknown constants, the estimators for these, by different methods of estimation are judged by several desirable properties like unbiasedness, minimum variance, consistency etc. Besides, there are qualitative properties like robustness or sensitivity to departures from the assumption of a specific distribution, sensitivity to outlier observations or truncations. While the conventional properties like unbiasedness, standard error and consistency, which apply to point estimates only are discussed in standard textbooks in econometrics, situations affecting the quality of an estimate are mentioned only rarely, if at all. Yet, the purpose of estimation in economic models goes beyond the need for summarization. Frequently, uses for control purposes e.g. macroeconomic policy are envisaged and the econometric criteria of identification explicitly recognize such need.

The next two examples illustrate some important modifications needed to the conventional least squares (LS) method, when the objective of estimation is not purely one of summarizing. Regulation or control in an implicit sense may also be another subgoal.

EXAMPLE 5 (Modified LS model): Consider the problem due to Whittle (1963), of forming a linear LS estimate of a scalar variate y from a finite set of n explanatory variables $x_1, x_2, \ldots, x_n$:

$$\hat{y} = \sum_{j=1}^{n} a_j x_j \tag{6.1}$$

where the coefficients a_j are to be chosen so that $E(\hat{y} - y)^2$ is a minimum. Write (6.1) in a vector form

$$\hat{Y} = AX \tag{6.2}$$

and assume that the vector variables X, Y have nonzero means as:

$$E(X) = \sum_{j=1}^{q} \beta_j G_j = G\beta \tag{6.3a}$$

$$E(Y) = \sum_{j=1}^{q} \beta_j H_j = H\beta \tag{6.3b}$$

where the β_j are unknown regression coefficients forming a q-by-one vector β, while G and H are matrices, whose columns, G_j and H_j are known sequences. The problem is: how to estimate the parameters in A and β by applying the logic of linear LS theory?

A variety of economic models can be fitted into this framework, where it is clear that the parameters A and β enter nonlinearly, since $\hat{Y}$ can be written as

$$\hat{Y} = A(G\beta + \epsilon), \quad X = E(X) + \epsilon \tag{6.4}$$

where ϵ is a zero-mean stationary process with known autocovariances. First, consider the usual model of autoregressive least squares:

$$y_t = ax_t + \epsilon_t$$

$$\epsilon_t = \rho\epsilon_{t-1} + \zeta_t$$

where $E\zeta_t = 0$, $\text{cov}(\zeta_t, \zeta_s) = \delta_{ts}\sigma^2$, $\delta_{ts} = 1$, if $t = s$ and zero otherwise, ϵ_t independent of x_t and $|\rho| < 1.0$ for stationarity. For any given ρ, say $\hat{\rho}$ the data may be transformed as $y_t^* = y_t - \hat{\rho} y_{t-1}$, $x_t^* = x_t - \hat{\rho} x_{t-1}$ and then a linear regression estimate made of the model $E(y_t^*) = aE(x_t^*)$. As a second example, assume (6.1) to be a production function, linear in logarithms of a n inputs and one output; there are N cross-sectional observations on agricultural farms from which to estimate a_j. But some inputs like management and technical innovation are not directly observable; the representation (6.3a) specifies this situation, where the vectors G_j may only denote indicator variables. Alternatively, the N farms may be divisible, on the basis of a priori knowledge or information, into two groups, one being more efficient than another. Our purpose is to estimate the response coefficients a_j for the efficient group, which has for its strategic inputs the relation (6.3a). As a third example, assume that $n = 1$ in the model (6.1), which is still supposed to be a logarithmically linear production function to be estimated from N agricultural farms, which are so divided into three groups that $p_i = N_i/N$, is the proportion of farms in each group $\sum_{i=1}^{3} p_i = 1$. Let the distribution of the single input, say land be represented by a normal density function $N(\mu_i, \sigma_i^2)$ with means μ_i and variances σ_i^2, $i = 1, 2, 3$ for each of the three groups, where the distributions are assumed for simplicity to be mutually independent. Let a_i denote the response coefficient when group i is sampled. Then, the probability density function of the random variable y is easily obtained by taking weighted sums over samples of the density functions of individual groups times their probability of occurence:

$$P = \frac{1}{2\pi} \sum_{i=1}^{3} \left\{ \frac{a_i p_i}{\sigma_i} \exp\left[-\frac{(y - \mu_i)^2}{2\sigma_i^2} \right] \right\} \tag{7.1}$$

We have $N = N_1 + N_2 + N_3$ sample observations and the problem is to find estimates of the parameter vector $\theta = (a_i, p_i, \mu_i, \sigma_i, i = 1,2,3)$. If we follow the maximum likelihood method of estimation, then we maximize the logarithm of the likelihood function $\ln L$, over the N sample observations:

$$\max_{\theta} \quad \ln L = \sum_{k=1}^{N} \ln P_k = f(\theta_1, \theta_2, \ldots, \theta_{12})$$

$$\text{subject to} \quad p_i \geqslant 0, \quad \sum_{i=1}^{3} p_i = 1, \quad \sigma_i \geqslant 0$$

It is clear that the estimation problem is no longer linear and some numerical methods like sequential unconstrained minimization techniques (Bracken and McCormick 1968), or conjugate gradient methods have to be adopted. It is apparent from this example that it would be a wrong specification to impose conditions such as $p_1 = p_2 = p_3 = N/3$ and $a_1 = a_2 = a_3$ unless we have prior information that they are so; likewise we cannot assume homogeneity of variances $\sigma_1^2 = \sigma_2^2 = \sigma_3^2$, since the real world may be heteroscedastic. However, a robustness analysis can be performed on the divergence of the two estimates, one constrained to be equal between groups and the other unconstrained.

One solution of the problem defined by (6.2) and (6.3), when we restrict ourselves to the linear predictor (6.2), is to apply a minimax criterion as follows:

$$E(\hat{Y} - Y)(\hat{Y} - Y)' = \min_A \max_\beta E(AX - Y)(AX - Y)' \tag{7.2}$$

The right hand term can be written as:

$$J = E(AX - Y)(AX - Y)'$$

$$= AV_{xx}A' - AV_{xy} - V_{yx}A' + V_{yy} + (AG - H)\beta\beta'(AG - H)' \tag{7.3}$$

where $E(xy') = V_{xy}$, $E(xx') = V_{xx}$ (assumed positive definite). The last term in (7.3) is the square of a scalar, $|(AG - H)\beta|^2$. Hence the maximum of J with respect to β will be indefinitely large unless

$$AH = G \tag{7.4}$$

Evidently this side condition (7.4) must be imposed, if the minimiax solution defined by (7.2) is to be finite. Hence the quantity to be minimized can now be taken as

$$AV_{xx}A' - AV_{xy} - V_{yx}A' + V_{yy} + (H - AG)K + K'(H - AG)' \tag{7.5}$$

where K is a vector of Lagrange multipliers. Minimizing this expression with respect to A leads to the modified LS estimator

$$A = \left(V_{yx} + K'G'\right)V_{xx}^{-1} \tag{7.6}$$

Evaluating K by substitution of (7.6) for A into (7.4) and substituting the resulting value of A into (6.2) one obtains the modified linear LS estimate Y as

$$\hat{Y} = H\hat{\beta} + V_{yx}V_{xx}^{-1}(X - G\hat{\beta}) \tag{7.7}$$

where

$$\hat{\beta} = \left(G'V_{xx}^{-1}G\right)^{-1}G'V_{xx}^{-1}X \tag{7.8}$$

The minimax criterion then has the following interpretation. Define

$X^* = X - G\hat{\beta}$, $Y^* = Y - H\hat{\beta}$ and then the linear regression of Y^* on X^* is the relation (7.7). Thus, the estimate $\hat{\beta}$ in (7.8) is just the maximum likelihood (ML) estimate of β, based on the sample vector X, if the vector is assumed normally distributed. This is so, because the equation (6.4) may be transformed as

$$QX = QG\beta + Q\epsilon \tag{7.9}$$

where, since $V_{xx} = V_{\epsilon\epsilon}$ is positive definite there exists a nonsingular matrix Q such that $QV_{xx}Q' = I$, I being the identity matrix. Hence the transformed equation

$$X^* = G^*\beta^* + \epsilon^*, \quad X^* = QX, \quad G^* = QG, \quad \epsilon^* = Q\epsilon$$

satisfies all the conditions of an LS model i.e. $E\epsilon^* = 0$, $\mathrm{var}(\epsilon^*) = E(\epsilon^*\epsilon^{*\prime}) = \sigma^2 I$, σ^2 being a scalar which may be set equal to one. Hence the estimate $\hat{\beta}^*$, which is identical with $\hat{\beta}$ given in (7.8) has the best linear unbiasedness property i.e. it is unbiased, linear and has the minimum variance in this class.

Although it has considerable appeal, the minimax criterion as applied in (7.2) has to be understood with some caution. First of all, the objective of maximizing rather than minimizing with respect to β in (7.2) is adopted due to either reasons of robustness or, wider representation and applicability. In game theory language, the criterion is based on choosing the best (i.e. $\max_\beta$) out of the worst. A degree of pessimism is built into the criterion. Second, if there is prior information on β in the form of a convex bounded set B:

$$B = \left\{ B : (\beta - \beta_0)'T(\beta - \beta_0) \leqslant k \right\} \tag{8.1}$$

where T is a known square matrix of order q, β_0 is the known center of the ellipsoid and k is a nonnegative constant term, then a natural interpretation of the minimax criterion can be given in terms of k. For instance, the larger k, the less binding is the constraint in (8.1). If $k \to \infty$, then the constraint vanishes altogether. Thus, the minimax criterion, interpreted in terms of the prior information set (8.1) defines three domains of an estimate $\hat{\beta}$ according as it equals β_0, or the inequality sign in (8.1) holds either as strict equality or strict inequality. Another special type of prior information, namely the component by component restriction on β is also frequently presumed in economic models i.e.

$$a_j \leqslant \beta_j \leqslant b_j, \quad j = 1, 2, \ldots, q \tag{8.2}$$

where the limits a_j, b_j are assumed known. Note that in this case the minimin criterion based on the simultaneous minimization with respect to A and β may be clearly defined. Again the estimates of β_j have now three domains, according as they do or do not hit the two limits. A Bayesian interpretation of revision of the prior information, either in the form of (8.1) or of (8.2) can be easily incorporated.

The next example shows that the minimax criterion, though more general is closely related to the class of biased estimators known as "ridge regression" proposed by Hoerl and Kennard (1970) and generalized by others. If a small amount of bias can be traded for a large gain in efficiency, measured by the reciprocal of standard errors, then ridge regressions may be naturally justifiable.

EXAMPLE 6 (Minimax Estimate and Ridge regression model): Consider the classical linear regression model with an n-element vector y of observations and a q-element vector β of parameters

$$y = X\beta + \epsilon, \quad \epsilon \sim N(0, \sigma^2 I), \quad \text{rank } X = r \leqslant q \tag{9.1}$$

The ordinary LS estimator (OLSE) denoted by $\hat{\beta}_0$, where

$$\hat{\beta}_0 = (X'X)^{-1}X'y \tag{9.2}$$

is unique, if $r = q$, so that the inverse of $X'X$ exists and by Gauss-Markov theorem the estimator is linear unbiased and within this class it is the best in the sense of minimum quadratic risk $R(\tilde{\beta}, I) = E(\tilde{\beta} - \beta)'(\tilde{\beta} - \beta)$ i.e.

$$R(\hat{\beta}_0, I) \leqslant R(\tilde{\beta}, I)$$

where $\hat{\beta}$ is another linear unbiased estimator. Two basic questions arise in this framework for many economic applications. One is the problem of multicollinearity between different x_j variables included in X, due to which the rank of X may be less than q, the number of parameters. The inverse of $(X'X)$ then does not exist and in default of a unique estimate several choices crop up. Second, if we do not restrict to the class of unbiased estimators, the property of best in the sense of minimum quadratic risk or, minimum variance in this case loses much of its usefulness. As a matter of fact, for any estimator $\hat{\beta}$ of β, unbiased or not, the mean square error MSE $(\tilde{\beta})$ where

$$\text{MSE}(\tilde{\beta}) = E(\tilde{\beta} - \beta)(\tilde{\beta} - \beta)'$$

$$= \text{variance} + (\text{bias})^2 \text{ in matrix form} \tag{9.3}$$

provides a better criterion for comparing alternative estimators, whether biased or not. An estimator, $\hat{\beta}$ unbiased or not, is said to dominate an estimator $\tilde{\beta}$ with respect to MSE, if

$$D = \text{MSE}(\tilde{\beta}) - \text{MSE}(\hat{\beta}) \geqslant 0, \qquad \text{for all} \quad \beta$$

and (9.4)

$$D = \text{MSE}(\tilde{\beta}) - \text{MSE}(\hat{\beta}) \neq 0, \qquad \text{for some} \quad \beta$$

where $D \geqslant 0$ is the notation used if D is a nonnegative definite matrix. In terms of this MSE criterion, the ridge-estimators may prove better. We may consider therefore the ridge estimators, as another form of modification of the OLSE.

The ridge estimator of β as proposed by Hoerl and Kennard (1970) is defined by

$$b(k) = (X'X + kI)^{-1} X'y \tag{9.5}$$

clearly, $b(0) = \hat{\beta}_0$ in (9.2) if it exists. Since

$$b(k) = G_k X'y,$$

where

$$G_k = (X'X + kI)^{-1}, \quad G_k X'X = I - kG_k$$

therefore

$$Eb(k) = G_k X'X\beta = \beta - kG_k\beta$$

so that

$$\text{bias } b(k) = -kG_k\beta$$

var-cov. matrix of $b(k) = \sigma^2 G_k X'X G_k$

$$\text{MSE}[b(k)] = G_k(\sigma^2 X'X + k^2\beta\beta') G_k$$

Using the MSE $(\hat{\beta}_0)$ of the OLS estimate one can show that the condition

$$2\sigma^2 I - k\beta\beta' \geqslant 0 \tag{9.6}$$

is sufficient for $b(k)$ to dominate over $\hat{\beta}_0$ in the sense

$$D = \text{MSE}(\hat{\beta}_0) - \text{MSE}[b(k)] \geqslant 0$$

It is interesting to note that the ridge estimator $b(k)$ in (9.5) can be interpreted as a minimax linear estimator, if we assume that there is prior information on the length of β as

$$\beta'\beta \leqslant h^2 \tag{9.7}$$

as in (8.1) before with $T = I$ and β_0 being zero. For then the value of β which minimizes

$$\sigma^2(y - X\beta)'(y - X\beta) \qquad \text{subject to} \quad \beta'\beta \leqslant h^2$$

is given by

$$b(\lambda) = (X'X + \sigma^2\lambda I)^{-1}X'y$$

where λ is the Lagrange multiplier satisfying

$$b'(\lambda)b(\lambda) = h^2$$

It has been shown by Swamy and Mehta (1977) that the ridge estimator $b(\lambda)$ dominates the OLSE $\hat{\beta}_0$, if and only if

$$\beta'\left[(2/\lambda)I + \sigma^2(X'X)^{-1}\right]^{-1}\beta \leqslant 1$$

However, since σ^2 is unknown for most applied problems, replacing it by its unbiased estimator s^2 leads to the approximate ridge estimator

$$\hat{b}(k) = (X'X + s^2kI)^{-1}X'y, \quad \lambda = k$$

Two features of this minimax linear estimator may be noted. First, the prior information constraint given either in the form (9.7) or, as (8.1) before may be interpreted in terms of a multivariate distance measure, known as the Mahalanobis distance. Thus, if β has a prior distribution which is normal with mean μ and variance covariance matrix Ω, then the square of the Mahalanobis distance is given by

$$D^2(\beta, \mu; \Omega) = (\beta - \mu)'\Omega^{-1}(\beta - \mu) \tag{9.8}$$

If μ is zero and $\Omega = I$ we get back the form (9.7). Several multivariate tests can therefore be developed on the basis of this distance statistic interpretation. For instance, if h^2 is large, then the constraint $\beta' \leqslant h^2$ is less binding and hence λ will be small. Coversely, choosing a small λ and setting up the estimator $b(\lambda)$ corresponds to using a large h in the prior information set (9.7). Second, a parametric variation of λ leading to the so-called ridge trace or plot of $b_j(\lambda)$ against λ may be examined to see if there is a certain value λ_0 of λ at which the plots tend to stabilize. Thus, the empirical notion of a stabilizing value may be utilized, provided it is consistent with other sign restrictions on the coefficients required by economic theory.

EXAMPLE 7 (Outlier Problem): In the classical model (9.1) of linear regression, it is assumed that the n observations $y_1, y_2, \ldots, y_n$ on the scalar random variable y are independently drawn from a normal population $N(\mu, \sigma^2)$ with mean μ and variance σ^2 by repeated sampling. Sometimes, however, there may occur a value y_{max} say, which differs sharply from the others. The problem is whether to reject such an observation and if so by what criterion.

The problem is important for the applied researcher for two reasons: one is that the LS estimate which has to pass through the mean is greatly affected by such an outlying observation. Hence methods of estimation based on other criteria e.g. minimizing the absolute sum of deviations are often recommended as more robust than LS. Second, there may be departures from normality, which may be large or small and one should be able to apply some test to detect large departures. There exist several test statistics for detecting outliers when they are significantly large (Dixon 1962), Hawkins 1980). We will discuss here two methods which are perhaps the easiest to apply.

The first statistic, a student-type ratio of extreme deviations is of the form:

$$v = (y_{max} \bar{y})/s \tag{10.1}$$

where $\bar{y}$, s^2 are the unbiased estimates of the parameters μ, σ^2 of the normal distribution $N(\mu, \sigma^2)$. The distribution of this statistic has been tabulated by Grubbs (1950) for values of sample size $n = 3, 4, \ldots, 25$ and probability levels $\alpha = 0.01, 0.025, 0.05$ and 0.10. Thus, for a given sample size n and a given significance level say $\alpha = 0.05$, a number $v_{n,\alpha}$ can be read off from the table such that

Prob $[v \geqslant v_{n,\alpha}] = 0.05$

If the observed value, y_{max} is such that the observed v computed from (10.1) exceeds the tabulated value i.e. $v > v_{n,\alpha}$ for given n and α, then y_{max} should be rejected as an outlier. But if $v \leqslant v_{n,\alpha}$ the y_{max} can be retained.

A comparative simulation of performance of a set of other statistics based on range, chi-square and modified F-tests, reported by Dixon (1962) showed that the statistic v in (10.1) has the best performance measured by MSE, if a single location error is present.

Assuming the existence of an outlying observation vector, the second method, applicable to multivariate observations detects the outlier vector in terms of a univariate metric or distance measure. Thus, let $y_1, y_2, \ldots, y_n$ be a random sample of n observations of a p-component normal vector y drawn from a multivariate normal $N(\mu, V)$ population. The outlier is defined by some vector y_i, such that

$$E(y_i) = \mu + a, \quad a \neq 0, \quad \text{some } i$$

$$E(y_j) = \mu, \quad j \neq i \tag{10.2}$$

and

$$Var(y_j) = V, \quad j = 1, 2, \ldots, n$$

where $Var(y_j)$ denotes the variance-covariance matrix of the sample vector y_j. Thus, in this case there is contamination in the location parameter only. If the population parameter V is known, then the likelihood of the sample $y_1, y_2, \ldots, y_n$ under the null hypothesis of no contamination is proportional to

$$|V|^{-n/2} \exp\left(-\tfrac{1}{2} \sum_{j=1}^{n} D_j^2\right)$$

where

$$D_j^2 = D^2(y_j: \mu, V) = (y_j - \mu)' V^{-1}(y_j - \mu)$$

The maximized log-likelihood, apart from a constant factor is given by

$$L(y|V) = -\tfrac{1}{2} \sum_{j=1}^{n} (y_j - \bar{y})' V^{-1}(y_j - \bar{y})$$

where $\bar{y}$ is the sample mean vector. Under the alternative hypothesis of a single outlier, the corresponding maximized log-likelihood is

$$L_A(y|V) = -\tfrac{1}{2} \sum_{j \neq i} (y_j - \bar{\bar{y}})' V^{-1}(y_j - \bar{\bar{y}})$$

where $\bar{\bar{y}}$ is the sample mean of the $(n-1)$ observations excluding y_i and the index i is chosen to maximize

$$L_A(y\,|\,V) - L(y\,|\,V)$$

thus, we have to declare as the outlier $y_{(n)}$ that observation vector y_i for which the distance statistic $D^2(y_i;\ \bar{y},\ V)$ is a maximum. In case of unknown V, this method has to be appropriately modified. Note that the probability ellipsoid

$$\text{Prob}\Big[(y-\mu)'V^{-1}(y-\mu) \leqslant c^2\Big] = \alpha$$

has considerable appeal, since the statistic D_j^2 defined before is closely related to the Hotelling's T^2-statistic, which is well tabulated. Hence, a multivariate generalization of the test (10.1) may be performed. These and other cases of contamination e.g. in the variance-covariance matrices are discussed by Barnett and Lewis (1978) and Hawkins (1980).

D. Control Theory Models in Economic Policy

The concept of control can be visualized in two different ways, that are not always compatible. Thus, in engineering and applications in statistical design of experiments, control is a physical input which affects the output or the state. The input-output relation may be deterministic or stochastic and the performance objective may be known completely or incompletely. Experimentation in this framework comes very naturally, if the input-output relations or the performance function are incompletely known. In this context the problem of predicting outputs or state variables appears only as incidental and the central problem is one of regulation i.e. of using past values to determine present action such that the future course of the process is as close as possible to the desired one.

A second and somewhat conflicting view of control is that it is an exogenous variable in an econometric model containing both endogenous and exogenous variables. Thus, in a Keynesian macromodel, with government assumed to be the policymaker, the monetary and fiscal instruments are the control variables, while national income and employment are the state or output variables. Note however the following sources of potential conflict of this approach with the first one. First, econometric models are viewed in this context as prediction models based on macrotheory e.g. Keynesian theory, the problem of regulation in the sense described in the first approach is very incidental. Control variables are never predicted or optimally chosen, as in the first approach, but conditional predictions of state, given the control variables are usually reported for judgemental purposes. Second, the example of the macropolicy model never allows any experimentation with any physical system;

i.e. the observed data on the endogenous and exogenous variables are behavioral and not experimental. Hence no new data can be generated by any experiment, since the latter cannot be performed under controlled conditions in a free market system. Third, the economic theory is seriously incomplete in two respects: one, it does not have the power of discriminating between a number of competing models and second, it does not have a complete and well specified theory about how the policy makers like the government and other non-market organizations behave. We lack a generalized general equilibrium theory. The closest approximation to this theory is perhaps provided by game theory, where there are so many variations of solutions (e.g. zero-sum, noncooperative, Stackelberg and others) that no statistical tests from the observed behavior can prove the validity of one solution against the other. Thus, in the macropolicy example, if the private business sector is a second player, with government as the first, the optimal policy of the first player would depend on those chosen by the second and hence the impossibility of specification of a true optimal policy.

The differences in the two approaches to control have been obliterated however by two recent developments. One is the possibility of simulation, thanks to the advance of the new computer technology. Thus, a large-scale econometric model may be analyzed in terms of imaginary policy-making in the sense of local perturbations around the mean values of the exogenous control variables and its impact on the state variables like national income and employment. This is the spirit of application behind the earlier work by Theil and others reported by Fox, Sengupta and Thorbecke (1972) detailing how to specify optimal economic policy. Second is the possibility of learning and adjusting, which are so much a part of modern methods of adaptive control. For instance, if the economic agents' behavior can be modeled as one of learning through the economic environment, and this part of modeling could be made a part of the specification of an econometric model, then the dichotomy between pure regulation and pure prediction can be resolved to a great extent. Various distributed lag models which allow the adjustment of control variables to their desired levels have thus offered a framework of harmony between learning (estimation) and control.

Our next three examples illustrate the above developments as follows: the first considers a physical example of temperature stabilization, a pure regulation problem due to Whittle (1963), the second is an example of Kalman filter, a pure forecasting problem, and the third is a rational expectations model due to Muth (1961), which provides a link between regulation and forecasting through modeling of price expectations.

EXAMPLE 8 (Temperature stabilization model): Let Y_t be the temperature of an oven at time t, measured in suitable units and X_t be the rate of fuel supply to the oven in the interval $(t-1, t)$ measured in such units that we can write

$$Y_t = aY_{t-1} + X_t + \epsilon_t \tag{11.1}$$

where ϵ_t is a random disturbance term and the parameter a represents the heat retention factor lying between 0 and 1. Suppose we observe past values of output, $Y_{t-j}, j = 1, 2, \ldots$ to determine present action or control X_t in such a way that the future output is as near as possible to the desired output level denoted by Y^*. The problem is how to choose optimal control X_t, by utilizing the past values of outputs. One possible solution by Whittle (1963) is to let the input or control X_t depend linearly on past values of Y.

$$X_t = c + \beta(D)Y_t = c + \sum_{j=1}^{\infty} \beta_j Y_{t-j} \tag{11.2a}$$

in such a way so as to minimize a criterion closely related to MSE:

$$\min J = E\left[(Y_t - Y^*)^2 + \lambda(X_t - \bar{x}_t)^2 + 2\alpha\bar{x}_t \right] \tag{11.3}$$

where $\bar{x}_t$ is the mean value of X and the terms in the loss function (11.3) represent costs due to temperature deviation, fuel supply variations and the average fuel rate. The parameters a, λ, α are assumed known.

Note that the control rule (11.2) defines inputs x_t as the sum of deterministic and stochastic components and if the latter is nonstationary, the control x_t may not have mean zero. On using the operator notation: $D^j Y_t = Y_{t-j}$ and $\sum_{j=1}^{\infty} \beta_j D^j y_t = (\sum_{j=1}^{\infty} \beta_j D^j)Y_t$ it is clear that the term $\beta(D)$ denotes the polynomial $(\sum_1^{\infty} \beta_j D^j)$. Let $Y_t = \bar{y}_t + y_t$ and $X_t = \bar{x}_t + x_t$ where $\bar{y}_t$, $\bar{x}_t$ denote the mean values. Then the unknown scalars c and $\beta_j's$ in $\beta(D)$ are to be so determined that the expected loss function defined in (11.3):

$$J = E\left(y_t^2 + \lambda x_t^2 \right) + \left(\bar{y}_t - Y^* \right)^2 + 2\alpha\bar{x}_t \tag{11.4}$$

is minimized by setting to zero the expressions $\partial J/\partial c$ and $\partial J/\partial \beta_j$. However, the second equation i.e. $\partial J/\partial \beta_j = 0$ may be highly nonlinear, if the polynomial term $\beta(D)$ involves higher order terms. Note also that we have not made any assumption about the stochastic component ϵ_t in (11.1). To obtain specific results, we now make some simplifying assumptions as follows:

$$E(\epsilon_t) = 0 \text{ forall } t, \qquad X_t = c + \beta_1 Y_{t-1} \tag{11.5}$$

The rationale behind the first-order lag assumption in (11.5) is two fold. First, even if we use (11.2a) in (11.1), we obtain

$$(1 - aD)Y_t = c + \beta(D)Y_t + \epsilon_t$$

which, in deviations forms becomes

$$(1 - aD)y_t = \beta(D)y_t + \epsilon_t, \text{ i.e. } [1 - aD - \beta(D)]\,y_t = \epsilon_t \qquad (11.6)$$

and we require the term $[1 - aD - \beta(D)]$ to take the value of unity, since the regulated system must now have only the residual uncertainty ϵ_t, which by assumption is not controllable. Hence $\beta(D) = \beta_1 D$. A second reason is that the impact of the remote past beyond $j > 1$ may be less significant, as the distributed lag models in economics show in their empirical applications.

Thus, on using (11.5) in (11.1) we obtain

$$(1 - a)\bar{y}_t = \bar{x}_t, \qquad \bar{x}_t = c + \beta_1 \bar{y}_t \qquad (11.7)$$

On substituting (11.7) into (11.4) and minimizing with respect to $\bar{y}$ we find that under optimum running we must have

$$\bar{y}_t = Y^* - (1 - a)\alpha$$

from which the optimal values of $\bar{x}$ and c can be determined on using (11.7). If we assume that the stochastic process $\{\epsilon_t\}$ is not only zero-mean but also uncorrelated with constant variance σ_ϵ^2, which is also termed 'white-noise', then in deviation form one could write for the optimal control:

$$x_t = (b - a)y_{t-1} \qquad (11.8)$$

where obviously $-\beta_1 = a - b$ and (11.1) becomes

$$y_t = by_{t-1} + \epsilon_t$$

from which the variances $\text{var}(y_t)$, $\text{var}(x_t)$ are readily found as:

$$\text{var}(y_t) = \sigma_\epsilon^2 (1 - b^2)^{-1}, \qquad \text{var}(x_t) = \sigma_\epsilon^2 (b - a)^2 (1 - b^2)^{-1}$$

Let $a = 0.98$, $\sigma_\epsilon^2 = 1.0$ and $-\beta_1$ change from 0.0 to 0.08, which means a change of b from 0.98 to 0.90. Then it follows that the variance of y_t changes from 25.25 for the unregulated system (i.e. $-\beta_1 = 0.0$) to 5.26 for the optimal regulated system. If b is raised to 0.80, $\text{var}(y_t)$ reduces to 2.78. The increase in $\text{var}(x_t)$ is very modest from 0.0 to 0.034 and 0.090.

It is thus clear that the heating system, when unregulated ($\beta_1 - 0.0$), is only just stable, quite a modest amount of regulation can bring about a remarkable reduction in var(y_t).

The remarkable nature of this impact can be better understood, if initially, without regulation, the system were not stable. Thus, assume that the parameter a lies outside the range $(-1,1)$. Then the unregulated system

$$y_t = ay_{t-1} + \epsilon_t, \quad |a| > 1$$

is explosive since $\lim_{t \to \infty} y_t \to \infty$. What would be the impact of regulation or control in this case when it is of the simple form (11.8)? To evaluate this, we substitute the linear rule $x_t = \beta_1 y_t$ into the objective function (11.4) and set the derivative $\partial J / \partial \beta_1$ equal to zero. This leads to the quadratic equation

$$\lambda a \beta_1^2 - \left[1 - \lambda(1 - a^2)\right]\beta_1 - a = 0$$

from which the optimal value of β_1 can be computed. Since $\beta_1 = b - a$, and we have to take the positive root, one gets

$$b = (2\lambda a)^{-1}\left[1 + \lambda(1 + a^2) - \left\{1 + 2\lambda(1 + a^2) + \lambda^2(1 - a^2)^2\right\}^{1/2}\right]$$

$$\lim_{\lambda \to \infty} b = \begin{cases} a, & \text{if } |a| < 1 \\ 1/a, & \text{if } |a| > 1 \end{cases}$$

The limiting values of $-\beta_1$ in the two cases are therefore

$$\lim_{\lambda \to \infty} (-\beta_1) = \begin{cases} 0, & \text{if } |a| < 1 \\ a - a^{-1}, & \text{if } |a| > 1 \end{cases}$$

Thus, if the original system, when unregulated were unstable (i.e. $|a| > 1$). then a modest amount of regulation will be required to secure stability, even when asymptotically the cost of regulation tends to be infinitely expensive. The fact that in the limit b does not take the value of 1.0 (but less than one), when the system was intrinsically unstable shows very clearly that attaining a greater degree of stabilization will in fact be cheaper.

Similar regulatory models has been considered by Whittle (1963) for stabilization of national income by government expenditure in a Keynesian model and for the linear decision rule approach to optimal output inventory decisions due to Holt, Modigliani, Muth and Simon (1960).

EXAMPLE 9 (Kalman filter): Let the system dynamics with a scalar input u_t and a scalar output x_t be given as

$$x_t + ax_{t-1} = u_{t-1} + e_t + ce_{t-1} \qquad (12.1)$$

where it is assumed that for all time points $t = 1, 2, \ldots$, the stochastic process $\{e_t\} \sim \text{NID}(0,1)$ is normally independently distributed with zero mean and unit variance and the parameters a, c where $|c| < 1$ are known. The problem is to choose a control law $\{u_t\}$ which minimizes the variance of output, Ey_t^2 at each t in the future. Alternatively, the problem may be stated as a case of pure prediction or forecasting for the system

$$x_t + ax_{t-1} = e_t + ce_{t-1} \qquad (12.2)$$

Consider the time point t when the set $X_t : \{x_t, x_{t-1}, \ldots, x_1, x_0\}$ of observation on the state x_t is available. We have to forecast or estimate a value $\hat{x}$ of x_{t+1} at the future time point $(t+1)$, such that $\hat{x}$ is a linear function of the available observation set X_t and it has minimum variance or prediction error. Whereas the first specifies a control-theoretic view, linear quadratic Gaussian (LQG) to be exact, the second describes the linear least squares (LS) view of the Kalman filtering techniques. The duality in interpretation is sometimes called the separation principle, which is more generally applicable e.g. inputs and outputs may be vectors, time may be continuous and even the Gaussian assumption may be somewhat relaxed.

Note that by setting $\epsilon_t = e_t + ce_{t-1}$ one would get back a dynamic model very similar to the one (11.1) considered before, except that the control variable has a lagged impact on x_t i.e. control today, u_t affects output tomorrow x_{t+1}. This type of model is called *causal*, in the sense that the cause variable (u_t) precedes the effect variable (x_{t+1}). Hence the conditional argument of linear LS theory is applicable e.g.

$$E[x_t \,|\, x_{t-1}, u_{t-1}] = -ax_{t-1} + u_{t-1}$$

In econometric theory, x_{t-1} and u_{t-1} are called predetermined rather than exogenous variables. Hence the ideal conditions of linear LS theory, which require x_{t-1}, u_{t-1} to be truly exogenous and independent of $\epsilon_t = e_t + ce_{t-1}$, and ϵ_t to satisfy $\{\epsilon_t\} \sim \text{NID}(0,1)$ are not exactly fulfilled. However, methods like Cochrane-Orcutt procedure discussed in standard econometric texts may be adopted to modify the LS procedure slightly in order to obtain unbiased and consistent estimates of the relevant parameters at least asymptotically.

For the minimum variance control problem (12.1), it is clear that

$$Ex_{t+1}^2 \geqslant E\left(e_{t+1}^2\right) = 1$$

Since e_{t+1} is assumed to be independent of x_t, u_t and e_t. Hence the best control law can only make the variance of output greater than or equal to unity. It is clear that if we choose

$$u_t = ax_t - ce_t \tag{12.3}$$

then $x_{t+1} = e_{t+1}$ which gives the smallest possible variance of x_{t+1}. If this control law is used in every time point, one would get $u_t = ax_t - cx_t = (a - c)x_t$, since $e_t = x_t$ under this control law. Hence the dynamic equation (12.1) becomes

$$x_{t+1} + cx_t = e_{t+1} + ce_t \quad \text{or} \quad \left(x_{t+1} - e_{t+1}\right) = -c\left(x_t - e_t\right)$$

Solving this difference equation with initial value $x_{t_0} - e_{t_0} = \tau_0$ we get

$$x_t = e_t + \tau_0(-c)^{t-t_0}$$

thus

$$x_t \to e_t \text{ as } t_0 \to -\infty, \quad \text{since} \quad |c| < 1 \tag{12.4}$$

Hence, if the above control law (12.3) is used, the output in the steady state has the smallest possible variance of unity.

Some interpretations of this minimum variance control law are in order. The quantity $\hat{x} = (-ax_t + bu_t + ce_t)$, where of course $b = 1.0$ in this simple example can be interpreted as the best estimate in the sense of minimum MSE of output at time $t + 1$ based on the data available up to time t. The prediction error is e_{t+1}. By choosing the optimal control law according to (12.3) we thus make the predicted value of x_{t+1} equal to the desired value of zero. Second, one could obtain the same result, if the normality assumption on the e_t is dropped but the admissible control laws are still restricted to be linear functions of available observations. We should then assume that $e_t's$ have zero mean and unit variance for all t, e_t, e_s are uncorrelated for all $t \neq s$ and that u_t is a linear function of the information set $X_t: \{x_t, x_{t-1}, \ldots, x_0\}$. Third, if one interprets x_t as deviations from some fixed targets x^* say, then we have a "tracking problem": the optimal control rule minimizes a measure of closeness to the target.

Now consider the alternative specification of the linear dynamics (12.3), which in operator notation $D^j x_t = x_{t-j}$ becomes

$$x_{t+1} = \frac{1+cD}{1+aD} e_{t+1} = e_{t+1} + \frac{c-a}{1+aD} e_t \qquad (12.5a)$$

but

$$e_t = \frac{1+aD}{1+cD} x_t \qquad (12.5b)$$

On eliminating e_t between (12.5a) and (12.5b) one gets:

$$x_{t+1} = e_{t+1} + \frac{c-a}{1+cD} x_t \qquad (12.5c)$$

Now let $\hat{x} = \hat{x}_{t+1\mid X_t}$ be any prediction of x_{t+1} as a linear function of the available observations contained in the set X_t defined above. It is assumed that the future error, e_{t+1} is statistically independent of the observations $(x_t, x_{t-1}, \ldots, x_1, x_0)$ i.e.

$$e_{t+1} \mid X_t, \qquad \text{for all} \quad t \qquad (12.6)$$

Hence we have

$$E[x_{t+1} - \hat{x}_{t+1\mid X_t}]^2 = E(e_{t+1}^2) + E\left[\frac{c-a}{1+cD} x_t - \hat{x}_{t+1\mid X_t}\right]^2$$

therefore

$$E[x_{t+1} - \hat{x}_{t+1\mid X_t}]^2 \geqslant E(e_{t+1}^2) = 1.0$$

where the inequality reduces to equality, if the forecast value $\hat{x} = \hat{x}_{t+1\mid X_t}$ satisfies

$$\hat{x}_{t+1\mid X_t} = \frac{c-a}{1+cD} x_t$$

which is nothing but the difference equation

$$\hat{x}_{t+1\mid X_t} + c\hat{x}_{t\mid X_{t-1}} - (c-a)x_t = 0 \qquad (12.7)$$

Under this optimal forecast (12.7), the minimum value of the MSE $(\hat{x})$ is

$$\mathrm{MSE}(\hat{x}_{t+1\mid X_t}) = E[x_{t+1} - \hat{x}_{t+1\mid X_t}]^2 = Ee_{t+1}^2 = 1.0$$

this result is identical with that of (12.3) and (12.4).

Now consider a two-step predictor denoted by $\hat{x}_{t+2|X_t}$ which is optimal in the sense of minimum MSE of forecast. In this case the observation set X_t is as before: we are at point t. We want to predict the future value x_{t+2} by a two-step predictor $\hat{x}_{t+2|X_t}$, which, as before must be a linear function of the available observations in the set X_t and minimize the MSE: $E[x_{t+2} - \hat{x}_{t+2|X_t}]^2$.

By following procedures analogous to (12.5), we obtain

$$x_{t+2} = e_{t+2} + (c-a)e_{t+1} - \frac{a(c-a)}{1+cD}x_t \tag{12.8}$$

By the assumption (12.6), the error terms e_{t+1} and e_{t+2} are independent of the observations in the set X_t, hence we have

$$E[x_{t+2} - \hat{x}_{t+2|X_t}]^2 = E(e_{t+2}^2) + (c-a)^2 E(e_{t+1}^2)$$

$$+ E\left[\hat{x}_{t+2|X_t} + \frac{a(c-a)}{1+cD}x(t)\right]^2$$

therefore

$$E[x_{t+2} - \hat{x}_{t+2|X_t}]^2 \geq 1 + (c-a)^2$$

where the equality sign holds for the optimal forecast $\hat{x}_{t+2|X_t}$ which must satisfy

$$\hat{x}_{t+2|X_t} = -\frac{a(c-a)}{1+cD}x_t$$

The two-step optimal predictor thus satisfies the difference equation

$$\hat{x}_{t+2|X_t} + c\hat{x}_{t+1|X_{t-1}} + a(c-a)x_t = 0$$

if $\eta_{t+2|t}$ denotes the error of the two-step optimal predictor i.e. $\eta_{t+2|t} = x_{t+2} - \hat{x}_{t+2|X_t}$, then it follows from (12.8):

$$\eta_{t+2|t} = e_{t+2} + (c-a)e_{t+1}$$

i.e. the two-step optimal prediction error is a moving average of second order. In this notation, the one-step predictor is a moving average of first order, since from (12.5c) and 12.7)

$$\eta_{t+1|t} = e_{t+1}$$

A more general result giving a k-step ahead optimal predictor $\hat{x}_{t+k|X_t}$, where the latter is a linear function of the available observations X_t and minimizes the MSE: $E[x_{t+k} - \hat{x}_{t+k|x_t}]^2$ is available in Box and Jenkins (1976), Gelb (1974) and Bierman (1977). Two points about the k-step optimal predictor ($k > 1$) are worth noting. First, it is a moving average of order k, hence the averaging process of future errors $e_{t+1}, e_{t+2}, \dots, e_{t+k}$, if correctly done is bound to improve the forecast. This updating process may not always be exactly realized in real life situations, since the parameters a, c, σ_e^2 which are assumed to be known here are rarely known. Besides, if the inputs and outputs are vector variables and not scalars, the updating process may involve substantial computations. This will be shown in the next section. Second, the most critical assumption in all these optimal k-step forecasts is that of independence of future errors $e_{t+1}, e_{t+2}, \dots, e_{t+k}$ mutually and from the observations $x_t, x_{t-1}, \dots, x_1$, x_0. Due to this assumption one gets $E\eta_{t+k|t} = 0$ and $E(\eta_{t+k|1}, \eta_{t+j|t}) = 0$ for $k \neq j$ i.e. the successive one-step ahead optimal forecast errors are unbiased and uncorrelated. hence under the given conditions, no better forecasts can be constructed. But how can one test if assumption of independence of future conditional errors holds or not? This is discussed in the example on rational expectations.

Now consider the system dynamics (12.1) in a vector-matrix form, where x_t and u_t are now n-element and m-element column vectors, A, B, C are matrices assumed for simplicity to be time-independent and v_t is measurement noise for outputs x_t:

$$x_{t+1} = Ax_t + Bu_t + e_{t+1} \tag{13.1}$$

$$y_t = Cx_t + v_t \tag{13.2}$$

where $Ee_t = 0$, all t, independent over time and $E(e_t e_t') = R_1$, $Ev_t = 0$, all t, independent over time and of e_t and $Ev_t v_t' = R_2$, where R_1 and R_2 are constant positive definite matrices. Also, the initial value x at $t = 0$ is assumed for simplicity to be normally and independently distributed $N(m, R_0)$ with known mean m and covariance matrix R_0. The problem again is to make an optimal prediction $\hat{x}_{t+1}$ of x_{t+1}, given the observations $(y_t, y_{t-1}, \dots, y_0)$, which of course has additive noise components. Note that this model (13) is causal in the sense that the control vector u_t precedes x_{t+1}; however x_t is not directly observable except through noisy measurements by vector y_t. Thus, economic models with permanent and transitory components fit this specification.

Let $\hat{x}_{t+1}$ denote the prediction of x_{t+1} constructed by the following linear decision rule (LDR):

$$\hat{x}_{t+1} = A\hat{x}_t + Bu_t + K_t[y_t - C\hat{x}_t] \tag{13.3}$$

where K_t is a matrix to be determined below. Denote $x_t - \hat{x}_t$ by $\tilde{x}_t$ and then from (13.1) through (13.3) one could derive

$$\tilde{x}_{t+1} = (A - K_t C)\tilde{x}_t + e_{t+1} - K_t v_t \tag{13.4}$$

which has the mean

$$E\tilde{x}_{t+1} = (A - K_t C)E\tilde{x}_t \rightarrow \text{zero}$$

if the initial condition is set such that $\hat{x}_0 = m$ and the matrix $(A - K_t C)$ has all its eigenvalue less than unity in absolute value. Let V_{t+1} be the variance-covariance matrix of $\tilde{x}_{t+1}$. Then it follows from (13.4) that V_{t+1} satisfies the linear difference equation

$$V_{t+1} = (A - K_t C)V_t(A - K_t C)' + R_1 + K_t R_2 K_t', \qquad V_0 = R_0 \tag{13.5}$$

Now we choose the matrix K_t, which is sometimes called the Kalman gain, by a MSE criterion. That K_t is chosen which minimizes the variance of the scalar product $w'\tilde{x}_{t+1}$ i.e. $w'V_{t+1}w$ where the vector w of nonzero weights is arbitrary. Since the variance of prediction error is now a matrix, this scalar version of the MSE criterion gives determinate results. On using (13.5) in the scalar MSE criterion $x'V_{t+1}w$ and minimizing with respect to K_t gives the optimal value of K_t as

$$K_t = AV_t C'(R_2 + CV_t C')^{-1} \tag{13.6a}$$

when

$$V_{t+1} = AV_t A' + R_1 - (AV_t C')[R_2 + CV_t C'](CV_t A') \tag{13.6b}$$

Several features of this optimal gain matrix K_t are to be noted. First, it is independent of the weights w used to define the scalar MSE criterion. Hence the result would hold even if we use a different set of weights. Second, the solution for K_t involves the variance covariance matrix V_t, which has to be solved from (13.6b), which is a set of quadratic matrix equations, which are sometimes called Riccati equations. These equations (13.6) can only be solved recursively through an iterative process and this may impose great computational burden, if the size of the square matrix V_t which is of order n is large. Moreover, the requirement from (13.4) that $E\tilde{x}_{t+1}$ tends in the limit $t \rightarrow \infty$ to zero depends on the fact that the eigenvalues of the matrix $(A - K_t C)$ are all less than unity i.e. this ensures asymptotic stability of the mean. Thus, for every t, K_t should be positive definite and the limit $\lim_{t \rightarrow \infty} K_t$ must be finite. If K_t becomes singular or, nearly so there arise additional computational difficulties.

Note that if the system is asymptotically stable and $\bar{V}$ denotes the steady state value of V_t, then $\bar{V}$ can be solved from the algebraic matrix equation:

$$\bar{V} = A\bar{V}A' + R_1 - (A\bar{V}C')[R_2 + C\bar{V}C]^{-1}(C\bar{V}A)$$

and the stady state value of K_t becomes

$$\bar{K} = (A\bar{V}C')(R_2 + C\bar{V}C')^{-1}$$

Using this approximation, the updating LDR (13.3) becomes

$$\hat{x}_{t+1} = A\hat{x}_t + Bu_t + \bar{K}[y_t - C\hat{x}_t] \tag{13.7}$$

which shows that the gain matrix $\bar{K}$ allows an adjustment of the first stage forecast denoted by $(A\hat{x}_t + Bu_t)$ by exploiting the difference $(y_t - C\hat{x}_t)$ between the actual measurements and their predictions. Note further that since we view Kalman filter as a pure prediction problem here, the coefficient B or, u_t do not appear anywhere in the optimal equations (13.6a) and (13.6b). Note however that once the optimal K_t is known, optimal control u_t can be chosen as a function of $\tilde{x}_t$. In capital stock adjustment models, the flexible accelerator principle showing investment to be proportional to the difference between actual and desired capital stock has been frequency used in this form (13.7). The Kalman gain helps to provide an optimal interpretation of the distributed lags in the adjustment cost theory, which has been used most frequently in economic models e.g. aggregate production – inventory models, monetary-fiscal policies under a macrodynamic model and commodity stabilization policies. Some other important economic applications include price adjustment in a Marshallian market (Aoki 1976), exponentially weighted forecasting rules (Bierman 1977) and various types of adaptive control policies in commodity markets.

One more point about the variance equation (13.6b) which must be recursively solved for computing optimal Kalman gain matrices K_t in (13.6a). Note that this variance, which is a matrix measure of the errors of prediction is a sum of three terms: the first i.e. $AV_t A'$ shows how the error propagates to stage $(t + 1)$ through system dynamics (i.e. if A is not known exactly, this would contribute to additional noise), the second term R_1 shows the increase of error variance due to the disturbances e_t and the third term shows how the error variance decreases due to information available from current measurements of the system.

EXAMPLE 10 (Rational Expectations Model): Consider a simple model, due to Muth (1961) of short-period price variations in a competitive market for a nonstorable good with a fixed production lag:

$$d_t = -\beta p_t \quad \text{(demand)} \tag{14.1a}$$

$$s_t = \gamma p_t^* + u_t \quad \text{(supply)} \tag{14.1b}$$

$$d_t = s_t \quad \text{(market equilibrium)} \tag{14.1c}$$

Here all variables, d_t (demand), price (p_t), s_t (supply quantity) and p_t^* (market price expected to prevail in period t, on the basis of information available through the $(t-1)$-th period) are measured as deviations from equilibrium values. u_t is an error term, representing say variations in yields due to weather and β, γ are parameters assumed to be positive. The error term u_t is unknown and unobservable at the time the suppliers make the output decisions but it becomes observable and hence known at the time demand is revealed and the market clears by the equilibrium condition (14.1c). The problem is: how to estimate from the information available through the $(t-1)$-th period the equilibrium price equation

$$p_t = -(\gamma/\beta)p_t^* - (u_t/\beta) \tag{14.2}$$

when the expectational variable p_t^* is not observable? How to interpret the stochastic equilibrium (14.2), when the unobserved variable p_{t+1}^* may represent a future anticipated price?

The answer provided by Muth (1961) to these questions contain the basic logic of the rational expectations (RE) theory. He argued that if the errors have zero mean and have no serial correlation, one obtains from (14.2)

$$Ep_t = -(\gamma/\beta)p_t^* \tag{14.3}$$

where E is expectations over the errors u_t. If the economic theory underlying the market model (14.1) provided substantially better predictions than the expectations of the suppliers, then there would be opportunities for the "insider" to profit from this knowledge. But such profit opportunities would be zero, if the suppliers' price expectations satisfy the condition

$$Ep_t = p_t^* \quad \text{(rationality assumption)} \tag{14.4}$$

On substituting this RE assumption (14.4) into (14.3), it follows that if γ/β is not equal to one, $p_t^* = 0$ or, that expected price equals equilibrium price.

Again, if instead of the situation $Eu_t = 0$, we consider the case when the shocks are predictable from the past, then the expected price p_t^* following from (14.2) under the RE assumption (14.4) becomes:

$$p_t^* = -(\gamma + \beta)^{-1} E u_t \tag{14.5}$$

The case when the shocks are serically correlated can also be handled in a similar way. For instance, let us assume

$$u_t = \sum_{i=0}^{\infty} w_i \epsilon_{t-i}, \quad E\epsilon_i = 0, \quad E(\epsilon_i, \epsilon_j) = \begin{cases} \sigma^2, & \text{if } i = j \\ 0, & \text{if } i \neq j \end{cases} \tag{14.6a}$$

i.e. that the shocks are a linear combination of the past history of normally and independently distributed random variables ϵ_t with zero mean and constant variance σ^2, where w_i are suitable weights to be determined. Market price p_t would then be a linear function of the same independent disturbances

$$p_t = \sum_{i=0}^{\infty} W_i \epsilon_{t-i} = W_0 \epsilon_t + \sum_{i=1}^{\infty} W_i \epsilon_{t-i} \tag{14.6b}$$

where the weights W_i would of course be different from w_i in (14.6a). Denote the information available through the $(t-1)$-th period by Ω_{t-1}, then the RE postulate (14.4) implies

$$p_t^* = E(p_t \mid \Omega_{t-1}) = E\left[W_0 \epsilon_t + \sum_{i=1}^{\infty} W_i \epsilon_{t-i} \mid \Omega_{t-1} \right] = \sum_{i=1}^{\infty} W_i \epsilon_{t-i},$$

$$\text{since} \quad E\epsilon_t = 0 \tag{14.6c}$$

Note the $E(p_t \mid \Omega_{t-1})$ is the one-step optimal linear predictor of p_t discussed in Example 9 of Kalman filter theory. On substituting (14.6a), (14.6c) into the market equilibrium equation (14.2) we get

$$W_0 \epsilon_t + \left(1 + \frac{\gamma}{\beta}\right) \sum_{i=1}^{\infty} W_i \epsilon_{t-i} = -\frac{1}{\beta} \sum_{i=0}^{\infty} w_i \epsilon_{t-1} \tag{14.7a}$$

This is an identity in the variables ϵ_t. Hence, on equating coefficients on both sides:

$$W_0 = -w_0/\beta, \quad W_i = -(\beta + \gamma)^{-1} w_i \quad i = 1, 2, \ldots, \infty \tag{14.7b}$$

Hence the relation (14.6c) becomes

$$p_t^* = -(\beta + \gamma)^{-1} \sum_{i=1}^{\infty} w_i \epsilon_{t-i}$$

which expresses the unobservable price expectation term p_t^* in terms of the past history of independent shocks. To express p_t^* as a function of observable prices we proceed as follows: we assume a form

$$p_t^* = \sum_{j=1}^{\infty} \alpha_j P_{t-j}$$

and solve for the undetermined weights α_j in terms of the weights W_j, resulting from (14.6b) and (14.7a):

$$W_i = \sum_{j=1}^{i} \alpha_j W_{i-j}, \quad i = 1, 2, 3, \ldots \tag{Z14.8}$$

This is a system with a triangular structure that can be solved recursively for the coefficients α_1, α_2, α_3 and so on. If the disturbances are independently distributed, as we assumed before, then $w_0 = -1/\beta$ and all the others are zero i.e. exogenous shocks affects supply one period ahead. Then (14.8) implies

$$p_t = 0 \quad \text{and} \quad p_t = p_t^* + W_0 \epsilon_t = -\epsilon_t/\beta$$

If, on the other extreme we assume that an exogenous shock affects all future conditions of supply, instead of only one period, then we would get instead of $w_0 = 1$, $w_i = 0$, $i = 2, 3, \ldots$ the following structure

$$u_t = \sum_{i=0}^{\infty} w_i u_{t-i} = \sum_{i=0}^{\infty} u_{t-1}, \quad w_i = 1, \quad \text{all} \quad i$$

From (14.7a)

$$W_0 = -1/\beta, \quad W_i = -(\beta + \alpha)^{-1}$$

Hence it follows from (14.8) that the unobservable expected price p^* is a geometrically weighted moving average of past prices:

$$p_t^* = \left(\frac{\beta}{\gamma}\right) \sum_{j=1}^{\infty} \left(\frac{\gamma}{\beta + \gamma}\right)^j p_{t-j} \tag{14.9}$$

One should note however that the logic behind substituting (14.9) in place of p_t^* in the equilibrium price equation (14.2) and then estimating the parameters of the resulting equation is not dependent on the demand-supply model alone. It can be applied to any econometric model in which expected or anticipated values of certain endogenous variables are included. For instance consider a reduced form version of any econometric model containing two sets of endogenous variables y_{jt}, y_{jt}^* and a set of exogenous variables u_t say:

$$y_{1t} = C_{11}y_{1t}^* + C_{12}u_t + v_{1t}, \qquad y_{2t} = C_{21}y_{1t}^* + C_{22}u_t + v_{2t} \qquad (15.1)$$

where the variable y_{1t}^* is given as the expectation of y_{1t} implied by the model, conditional on information Ω_{t-1} available at time $t-1$, i.e. $y_{1t}^* = E(y_{1t} | \Omega_{t-1})$. Here y_{jt} may be suitable vectors and C_{ij} may be suitable matrices and the error terms v_{jt} are here assumed for simplicity to be with zero mean, serially uncorrelated and uncorrelated with past values of the exogenous variables u_t. Taking conditional expectations of the first equation of (15.1) and denoting $E(u_t | \Omega_{t-1}) = \hat{u}_t$ one gets:

$$y_{1t}^* = (I - C_{11})^{-1} C_{12} \hat{u}_t \qquad (15.2a)$$

where $(I - C_{11})$ has been taken to be nonsingular. Using (15.2a) in (15.1) we get the observable reduced form:

$$y_{1t} = P_{11}\hat{u}_t + P_{12}u_t + v_{1t}, \qquad y_{2t} = P_{21}\hat{u}_t + P_{22}u_t + v_{2t} \qquad (15.2b)$$

This leads to

$$y_{1t} - y_{1t}^* = C_{12}(u_t - \hat{u}_t) + v_{1t} \qquad (15.3)$$

To complete the stochastic specification we may postulate the following vector autoregressive moving average (ARMA) model for u_t:

$$\left[I + A_1 D + A_2 D^2 + \ldots + A_p D^p\right] v_t = \left[I + B_1 D + \ldots + B_q D^q\right] \epsilon_t$$

where $D^j x_t = x_{t-j}$ and ϵ_t is a white noise process independent of v_t. Then, following the method of Example 9, we compute the optimal one-step forecast $\hat{u}_t$ as

$$\hat{u}_t = A_1 u_{t-1} - \ldots - A_p u_{t-p} + B_1 \epsilon_{-1} + \ldots + B_q \epsilon_{t-q} \qquad (15.4)$$

Thus it is clear that the lag structure of the polynomials $A(D) = I + A_1 D + \ldots + A_p D^P$ and $B(D) = I + B_1 D + \ldots + B_q D^q$ affect the conditional forecasts $\hat{u}_t$, which are then used in the observable reduced form (15.2b) at the second step. Note that this two-step method is readily extended to the case when the expectations variables y_{1t}^* relate to a future period or periods as of time t. As Wallis (1980) has shown, the reduced form system corresponding to (15.1) may be taken in a general form as

$$y_{1t} = \sum_{j=0}^{\tau} C_{11,j} y_{1,t+j}^* + C_{12} u_t + v_{1t} \qquad (15.5a)$$

$$y_{2t} = \sum_{j=0}^{\tau} C_{21,j} y_{1,t+j}^* + C_{22} u_t + v_{2t} \qquad (15.5b)$$

Taking conditional expectations of (15.5a) we see that the rational expectations variables $y_{1,t+j}^* = E(y_{1,t+j} | \Omega_{t-1})$ satisfy

$$(I - C_{11,0}) y_{1t}^* = \sum_{j=1}^{\tau} C_{11,j} y_{1,t+j}^* + C_{12} \hat{u}_t \qquad (15.6)$$

where $\hat{u}_t = E(u_t | \Omega_{t-1})$. The system (15.6) is a multivariate τ-order difference equation which, if stable yields a solution for y_{1t}^* in terms of $\hat{u}_{t+j} = E(u_{t+j} | \Omega_{t-1})$, $j = 0, 1, 2, \ldots$. The observable reduced form now involves all future u forecasts.

The RE models have been most frequently applied in macrotheory for specifying equilibrium equations on the money market , in which expected inflation plays a crucial role. Thus in logarithmic terms the money market model is:

$$m_t^d - p_t = \alpha(p_{t+1}^* - p_t) \quad \text{(real money demand)}$$

$$m_t^s = \tilde{z}_t \quad \text{(nominal money supply)}$$

where m_t^d is the logarithm of the nominal money demand at date t, p_t is the logarithm of the price level and p_{t+1}^* is the subjective expectation at date t of the price in period $(t + 1)$. The nominal money supply (m_t^s) is given by the stochastic process $\tilde{z}_t$. Under the RE assumption, the money market equilibrium yields

$$p_t = a E_t(p_{t+1}) + z_t, \qquad z_t = (\alpha - 1)^{-1} \tilde{z}_t, \qquad a = \alpha(\alpha - 1)^{-1} \qquad (16.1)$$

where $E_t(p_{t+1}) = E(p_{t+1} | \Omega_t)$ is the conditional expectation of p_{t+1} given the information Ω_t at date t. Viewed as an estimation problem, (16.1) is analogous to (15.5) considered before. Besides estimation, there is another problem: how to compute the solutions of the model (16.1) in terms of the current and past values of the k given random processes $\{ p_t \}$ i.e. $\{ p_t^1, p_{t-1}^1, \ldots; p_t^2, p_{t-1}^2, \ldots, p_t^i, p_{t-1}^i, \ldots), i = 1, 2, \ldots, k$ and z_t, where z_t

is a given random process such that for any t, $E_t z_t = z_t$? It has been shown by Gourieroux, Laffont and Monfort (1982) that there is an infinity of solutions of form

$$y_t = y_t^0 + (1/a^t) M_t$$

where y_t^0 is a particular solution of (16.1) and the stochastic process M_t is a martingale in the sense that $M_t = E_t(M_{t+1})$. They introduced several selection criteria e.g. (a) boundedness in mean, (b) stationarity of the solution, (c) high predictive power to reduce the infinite set of solutions.

Besides the problem of nonuniqueness, the RE models share two other basic problems associated with the market equilibrium condition. One is the possibility that at date $t - 1$, all traders in the market do not have the same information about the various stochastic factors which determine price and output in Muth's model (14.1) for example. Such expectations by different traders creates an incentive for the opening of the futures market to earn profits. Lucas (1972) and Grossman (1981) have shown that the notion of an equilibrium price under asymmetric information needs to be more general than the model (14.1) implies. To see this, consider the demand-supply market model (14.1) once again but presented in a different form. Let q_t be the output of a single firm in period t with a cost function $C(q_t)$. Assume there are N firms. Let the market demand for the firm's product be

$$\tilde{p}_t = D(S_t, \tilde{\epsilon}_t)$$

where $\tilde{\epsilon}_t$ is a random variable summarizing all the stochastic factors affecting total demand at t and p_t is the price at which total output $S_t = \sum_{t=1}^{N} q_t$ is demanded. Muth's model (14.1) assumes that firms acting as price takers maximize expected profit $E\tilde{\pi}_t = E\tilde{p}_t q_t - C(q_t)$, where q_t must be chosen at time $t - 1$, since production has one-period lag. Then the optimal output $\bar{q}_t$ for the firm will be a function of $E\tilde{p}_t$, say $\bar{q}_t = h(E\tilde{p}_t)$, where $h(\cdot)$ is the inverse of the marginal cost function. If the firms are identical, then total supply is $S_t = N\bar{q}_t$. From the condition of demand-supply equilibrium we get

$$\tilde{p}_t = D(Nh(E\tilde{p}_t), \tilde{\epsilon}_t) \tag{16.2}$$

Now suppose there exists a number p^* each that

$$p^* = ED(Nh(p^*), \tilde{\epsilon}_t) \tag{16.3}$$

where the expectation E in (16.3) is taken with respect to the distribution of the stochastic process $\tilde{\epsilon}_t$. If $p^* = E\tilde{p}_t$ solves (16.3) i.e. p^* is a fixed point of the mapping in (16.3), then it is called by Muth the rational expectations equilibrium price. This equilibrium price, as it should be clear from (16.3), is a random variable with a probability distribution. Here of course, all the firm are alike and all traders at time $t - 1$ have the same information about the stochastic factors summarized by the catch-all term $\bar{\epsilon}_t$. If the information available is not the same to all the traders, then an individual producer may have more information about the demands of his own customers and the productivity of his own inputs than he has about those of other producers. In such a case there may be incentives to open speculative markets and an equilibrium price in the sense of p^* in (16.3) may be either nonexistent, or not relevant for defining a stochastic equilibrium price.

A second difficulty of the RE equilibrium price, which follows form above is when the notion of equilibrium is one of many-person game theory. Since the notion of equilibrium solutions is more general in game theory models, depending on cooperation or noncooperation, complete or incomplete information we may again lack uniqueness of solutions resulting from RE-type equilibrium assumptions. Chow (1981) has considered such problems for an economy with two players, the first being the private business sector and the second is the government. The model of the economy is

$$y_t = Ay_{t-1} + C_1 u_{1t} + C_2 u_{2t} + b_t + e_t \tag{17.1}$$

where y_t is a state variable, u_{it} are the two control variables of the two players and e_t is a random error. Each set i of players selects its control variables u_{it} to maximize a quadratic objective function

$$-E\left[\sum_{t=1}^{T} (y_t - a_{it})' K_{it} (y_t - a_{it})\right], \quad i = 1, 2 \tag{17.2}$$

and derives its optimal behavior equation

$$u_{it} = G_{it} Y_{t-1} + g_{it}, \quad i = 1, 2 \tag{17.3}$$

The decision problem is how to specify an optimal policy for government, the second player. Clearly the model specified by (17.1) through (17.3) has to be viewed as a two-person differential game. Clearly, Cournot-Nash equilibrium, Stackelberg leader-follower and other types of solutions can be invoked in such a situation and the equilibrium solution for player two is not meaningful, unless it is consistent or compatible with the other player's decision rule and objective. If one were to have the a priori information as to which type of game theory solution prevailed, then it is possible in principle to statistically test such a hypothesis from the observed sequence of outcomes $\{y_t, u_{1t}, u_{2t}\}$. Short of such information, there exist varieties of plausible solutions that are reasonable. The RE hypothesis needs to be more detailed in such framework. Much more research work is needed in this case.

3. Concluding Remarks

In our discussion of optimization in dynamic models we have restricted ourselves to discrete-time models, where the disturbance terms of errors were assumed to follow continuous distribution functions like the normal. This is done for the sake of simplicity and convenience, since most economic data arise through discrete-time processes and are easier to handle. Also, the random components have stayed in the background, i.e. mostly as additive errors to a model, whose exact specification must follow from economic theory. An opposite view is to treat economic data as basically stochastic and then let the economic and statistical theory explain so to say the various transition probabilities from one state to another. This stochastic view has led to remarkable results in genetics, biology, physics, and electrical and chemical engineering. Tintner and Sengupta (1972) have applied this basic view of stochastic process theory to economic development in order to explain the diffusion of growth, changes in productivity and the effect of government policy. The next example is a simple application of their approach.

EXAMPLE 11 (Diffusion Process model): Let $X(t)$ be a state variable, say national income, at time t, defined by a continuous process $\{X(t), t \geqslant 0\}$ of the Markovian type satisfying the transition probability density

$$f(\tau, x; t, y) = \text{Prob}\left[X(t) = y; x(\tau) = x\right] \qquad 0 < y, x < \infty \qquad (18.1)$$

Consider the coefficients $b(t, x)$ and $a(t, x)$, the infinitesimal mean and variance of the change in $X(t)$ during a small interval Δt of time that characterize a simple process of diffusion as:

$$b(t, x) = b_t x, \quad a(t, x) = a_t x^2 \qquad (18.2)$$

where b_t, a_t are functions of time. For convenience we take $b_t = b_0$, $a_t = a_0$ as constants with a_0 positive. This means that we assume that the expected change and its variance in national income are proportional to its instantaneous size. This assumption (18.2) leads to a diffusion process which satisfy the following backward and forward Kalmogorov equations (Bharucha-Reid 1960; Tintner and Sengupta 1972) respectively

$$-\frac{\partial f}{\partial \tau} = \tfrac{1}{2} a_0 x^2 \frac{\partial^2 f}{\partial x^2} - b_0 x \frac{\partial f}{\partial x}$$

$$\frac{\partial f}{\partial t} = \tfrac{1}{2} a_0 y^2 \frac{\partial^2 f}{\partial y^2} + (2a_0 - b_0) y \frac{\partial f}{\partial y} + (a_0 - b_0) f$$

(18.3)

where f is the transition probability given in (18.1). Solving these diffusion equations one obtains the following log-normal density function for the transition probability f:

$$f(\tau, x; t, y) = \left[y \{ 2\pi\gamma(t - \tau) \}^{1/2} \right]^{-1} \exp(-Q)$$

where

(18.4)

$$Q = \{ 2\gamma(t - \tau) \}^{-1} \left[\log y - \log x - \beta(t - \tau)^2 \right]$$

$$\gamma = a_0 \quad \text{and} \quad \beta = (b_0 - a_0/2)$$

Two types of questions can be posed for this diffusion process model: how to estimate the parameters β and γ from observations $x(t)$ of the process $\{ X(t), t \geqslant 0 \}$ at times $t_0, t_1, t_2, \ldots, t_n$? Second, if some parameter like β depends on a control variable u_t representing government expenditure, then how to evaluate its impact on the stochastic environment represented by (18.3) and (18.4)?

The estimates of the parameters β and γ and hence of a_0 and b_0 by the method of ML are obtained as follows: let the joint probability of n observations be L. Then its natural logarithm is $\ln L$ where

$$\ln L = -\frac{n}{2} \ln(2\pi\gamma) + \sum_{j=1}^{n} \left(-\tfrac{1}{2} \right) \{ \ln x_j + \ln(t_j - t_{j-1}) \}$$

$$- \tfrac{1}{2} \{ \gamma(t_j - t_{j-1}) \}^{-1} \left[\ln x_j - \ln x_{j-1} - \beta(t_j - t_{j-1})^2 \right]$$

The ML estimates $\hat{\beta}$, $\hat{\gamma}$ obtained by solving the equations $\partial \ln L / \partial \beta = 0 = \partial \ln L / \partial \gamma$ are:

$$\hat{\beta} = \sum_{j=1}^{n} \left(\log x_j - \log x_{j-1} \right) / \sum_{j=1}^{n} \left(t_j - t_{j-1} \right)$$

$$\hat{\gamma} = \frac{1}{n} \sum_{j=1}^{n} \left[\frac{\{ \ln x_j - \ln x_{j-1} - \hat{\beta}(t_j - t_{j-1}) \}^2}{(t_j - t_{j-1})} \right]$$

If we assume that the n observations are such that $t_j - t_j = 1$ and $t_0 = 0$, then the ML estimates and their sampling variances are

$$\hat{\beta} = \frac{1}{n} \sum_{j=1}^{n} \left[\ln x_j - \ln x_{j-1} \right], \qquad \hat{\gamma} = \frac{1}{n} \sum_{j=1}^{n} \left(\ln x_j - \ln x_{j-1} \right)^2 - \hat{\beta}^2$$

$$V(\hat{\beta}) = \frac{\gamma}{n} \cdot \frac{1}{t} \to 0 \quad \text{as} \quad t \to \infty, \qquad V(\hat{\gamma}) = 2\gamma^2/n$$

For the control problem let us assume a linear effect of government expenditure u_t on the parameter β_t as:

$$\beta_t = \beta_0 + \beta_1 u_j \quad \text{for} \quad t_{j-1} \leqslant t \leqslant t_j, \qquad j = 0, 1, 2, \ldots, n \qquad (18.5)$$

where $b(t, x) = (b_0 + b_1 u_j)x$, $a(t, x) = a_0 x^2$, $a_0 > 0$ and $\gamma = a_0$, $\beta_0 = (b_0 - a_0/2)$ and $\beta_1 = b_1$. The probability density function of $X(t)$ with $t_0 = 0$ and $\text{Prob}[x(0) = x_0] = 1.0$ is given by

$$f(x_0; t, x) = \left(x\sqrt{2\pi\gamma t} \right)^{-1} \exp\left[-\frac{1}{2\gamma t} \left\{ \ln x - \ln x_0 - \beta_0 t - \beta_1 \sum_{j=1}^{t} u_j \right\}^2 \right]$$

$$(18.6)$$

where we have set equally spaced observations i.e. $t_j - t_{j-1} = 1$. The moments of this probability density function can be easily calculated from

$$E[X(t)]^k = X_0^k \exp\left\{ k\left[\left(\beta_0 - \frac{k\gamma}{2} \right)t + \beta_1 \sum_{j=1}^{t} u_j \right] \right\}, \qquad k = 1, 2, 3, \ldots$$

Hence

$$\text{mean} = E[X(t)] = X_0 \exp\left(b_0 t + b_1 \sum_{j=1}^{t} u_j \right)$$

$$(18.7)$$

$$\text{variance} = V[X(t)] = X_0^2 \exp\left[2\left(b_0 t + b_1 \sum_{j=1}^{t} u_j \right) \right] \cdot [\exp a_0 t - 1]$$

Thus, if a particular profile of expenditure $(u_1, u_2, \ldots, u_t)$ is considered as optimal, the conditional probability density function (18.6) would specify its distribution. Alternatively, any two profiles of expenditures can be compared in terms of the mean and variance of national income given by (18.7). Thus, if a separate loss function is introduced for the policy maker in the form:

$$h = E\left[X(t) - x^*\right]^2 = V\left[X(t)\right] + \left(E\left[X(t)\right] - x^*\right)^2$$

where x^* is a fixed desired target of the policymaker, then the profile of control variables $\{u_j\}$ can be specified by minimizing this loss function. The problem of joint estimation of parameters and of control of the diffusion process can also be posed in this framework (Astrom 1980).

Two aspects of this transition probability example are to be noted. In the policy application here, we obtain for the optimal control, the entire transition probability density, which can then be used to apply standard statistical tests. Thus, if in the limit $t \to \infty$, the transition probability remains will defined, we would obtain a steady state view of transition probability. In control theory language, this is the frequency-domain representation of the control problem, where Examples 9 and 10 are time-domain specifications. Second, these transition probability models are widely applied in queuing and marketing. A simple example is provided by the brand-loyalty model due to Lee, Judge and Zellner (1977):

$$y_j(t) = \sum_{i=1}^{m} p_{ij} y_i(t-1) + \epsilon_j(t), \qquad i, j = 1, 2, \ldots, m \tag{18.8}$$

where $y_j(t)$ is the quantity sold at time t brand j, as a proportion of total industry sales, $\sum_{i=1}^{m} y_i(t)$ and it is explained by customers switching from brand i to j with a transition probability p_{ij}, which is assumed to be constant for simplicity. The component $\epsilon_j(t)$ is the random disturbance with zero mean. Since p_{ij} is a probability we must have

$$p_{ij} \geqslant 0, \quad \sum_{j=1}^{m} p_{ij} = 1 \tag{18.9}$$

Given the observations on $y_j(t)$, $y_i(t-1)$ for $i, j = 1, 2, \ldots, m$ and $t = 1$, $2, \ldots, T$ one could estimate the parameters p_{ij} of the transition probability matrix, subject to the linear restrictions (18.9), by ordinary or generalized LS method.

A policy variable can be introduced in this set-up either by making the transition probabilities depend on the proportions $u_1, u_2, \ldots, u_m$ of total advertisement expenditure on the different brands or by including u_j as a separate explanatory variable in (18.8):

$$y_j(t) = \sum_{i=1}^{m} p_{ij} y_i(t-1) + \beta_j u_j(t-1) + \epsilon_j(t) \tag{18.10}$$

Note that the first approach would be in the frequency domain, while the second is in time domain. Thus, if profit $\pi(t)$ is viewed as a function of $y_1, y_2, \ldots, y_m$ and the advertisement costs $u_1, \ldots, u_m$ one could optimally choose the sequence of control variables by maximizing the terminal period expected profits $E\pi(t)$ subject to (18.10). Such problems are best solved by dynamic programming routines.

In demographic problems the transition probabilities are extensively used to characterize the growth of population indexed by size, skills, age etc. Family planning and other methods are frequently applied as deliberate policies in many less developed countries so as to change the transition probabilities to a desired level. Likewise the diffusion of technical innovation by research and development (R & D) methods, due to shortage of energy provides a useful field of application.

References

Aoki, M., Optimal Control and Systems Theory in Dynamic Economic Analysis. Amsterdam: North Holland, 1976.

Astrom, K.J., "Self-tuning Regulators: Design Principles and Applications, in K.S. Narendra and R.V. Monopoli eds., Applications of Adaptive Control. New York: Academic Press, 1980.

Barnett, V., and T. Lewis, Outliers in Statistical Data. New York: John Wiley, 1978.

Belsley, D.A., "Industry Production Behavior: The Order Stock Distinction." Amsterdam: North Holland, 1969.

Bertsekas, D.P., "Dynamic Programming and Stochastic Control." New York: Academic Press, 1976.

Bharucha-Reid, A.T., Elements of the Theory of Markov Processes and Applications. New York: McGraw Hill, 1960.

–, Probabilistic Methods in Applied Mathematics, Vol. 2. New York: Academic Press, 1970,

Bierman, G.J., Factorization Methods for Discrete Sequential Estimation. New York: Academic Press, 1977.

Box, G.E.P. and G.M. Jenkins, Time Series Analysis: Forecasting and Control. Revised ed., San Francisco: Holden Day, 1976.

Bracken, J. and G.P. McCormick, Selected Application of Nonlinear Programming. New York: John Wiley, 1960.

Cass, D. and J.E. Stiglitz, "The Structure of Investor Preferences and Asset Returns and Separability in Portfolio Allocations: A Contribution to the Pure Theory of Mutual Funds." Journal of Economic Theory. 2 (1970), 122–160.

Chow, G.C., Analysis and Control of Dynamic Economic Systems. New York: John Wiley, 1975.

–, Economic Analysis by Control Methods. New York: John Wiley, 1981.

Dixon, W.J., "Rejection of Observations," in A.E. Sarhan and B.G. Greensberg eds., Contributions to Order Statistics. New York: John Wiley, 1962.

Fox, K.A., J.K. Sengupta, and E. Thorbecke, The Theory of Quantitative Economic Policy with Applications to Economic Growth Stabilization and Planning. 2nd ed. Amsterdam: North Holland, 1972.

Gelb, A. ed. Applied Optimal Estimation. Boston: MIT Press, 1974.

54

Gourieroux, C., J.J. Laffont, and E. Monfort, "Rational Expectations in Dynamic Liner Models: Analysis and Solutions. Econometrica 50 (1982), 409–426.

Grossman, S.J., "An Introduction to the Theory of Rational Expectations Under Asymmetric Information." Review of Economic Studies. 48 (1981), 541–559.

Grubbs, F.E., "Sample Criteria for Testing Outlying Observations." Annals of Mathematical Statistics. 21 (1950), 27–58.

Hamblen, J.H., "Distribution of Roots of Quadratic Equations with Random Coefficients." Annals of Mathematical Statistics. 27 (1956), 1136–1143.

Hawkins, D.M., Identification of Outliers. London: Chapman and Hall, 1980.

Hay, G.a. and C.C. Holt: "A General Solution for Linear Decision Rules: An Optimal Strategy Applicable Under Uncertainty." Econometrica, 43 (1975), 231–260.

Hoerl, A.E., and R.W. Kennard, "Ridge Regression: Biased Estimation for Nonorthogonal Problems." Technometrics 12 (1970), 55–82.

Holt, C.c., F. Modigliani, J.F. Muth, and H.A. Simon, Planning Production Inventories and Workforce. Englewood Cliffs, NJ: Prentice Hall, 1960.

Klein, L.R., A Textbook of Econometrics. Evanston: Row, Peterson, 1953.

–, and V. Su, "Recent Economic Fluctuations and Stabilization Policies: An Optimal Control Approach," in Klein, L.R., Nerlove, M., and S.C. Tsiang, eds., Quantitative Economics and Development. New York: Academic Press, 1980.

Kolbin, V.V., Stochastic Programming. Dordrecht, Holland: Reidel Publishing, 1977.

Lee, T.C., G.G. Judge, and Z. Zellner, Estimating the Parameters of the Markov Probability Model from Aggregate Time Series Data. 2nd ed., Amsterdam: North Holland, 1977.

Lucas, R.E., "Expectations and the Neutrality of Money." Journal of Economic Theory. 4 (1972), 103–124.

Muth, J.R., "Rational Expectations and the Theory of Price Movements." Econometrica. 24 (1961), 315–335.

Prescott, E.D., "Adaptive Decision Rules for Macroeconomic Planning," in S.E. Fienberg and a. Zellner, eds. Bayesian Econometrics and Statistics. Amsterdam: North Holland, 1975.

Ross, S.A., "Mutual Fund Separation in Financial Markets: The Separating Distributions." Journal of Economic Theory. 17 (1978), 254–286.

Sengupta, J.K., Stochastic Programming: Methods and Applications. Amsterdam: North Holland, 1972.

–, Decision Models in Stochastic Programming, New York: North Holland, 1982.

Swamy, P.A.V.B., and J.S. Mehta, "A Note on Minimum Average Risk Estimators for Coefficients in Linear Models." Commun. Statist. Theor. math., 6 (1977), 118–1186.

Tintner, G. and J.K. Sengupta, Stochastic Economics. New York: Academic Press, 1972.

Vickson, R.J., "Separation in Portfolio Analysis," in W.T. Ziemba and R.G. Vickson, eds., Stochastic Optimization Models in Finance. New York: Academic Press, 1975.

Wallis, K.F., "Economic Implications of the Rational Expectations Hypothesis." Econometrica. 48 (1980), 48 = 9–73.

Whittle, P., Prediction and Regulation. New York: van Nostrand, 1963.

Wittenmark, B., "Stochastic Adaptive Control Method: A Survey," International Journal of Control. 21 (1975), 705–730.

2. Stochastic optimization in linear economic models

1. Introduction

Linear economic models containing variables x, y and parameters θ, that may be subject to a stochastic generating mechanism pose two basic problems of optimization. One is the problem of estimation of parameters θ from observations on x and y. This is dealt with in econometrics. The second is the problem of optimal decision-making under uncertainty under the stochastic environment. Two most basic questions in this theory are: how to select an optimal decision and how to update the solution if the information structure is changing? For instance, the model may be specified by a set of linear equations

$$f(x, y, \theta) = 0 \tag{1.1}$$

in state variables y control variables x and the stochastic components θ entering linearly. Then one type of selection problem is: how to choose the control vector x, if the objective is to reach a target level y^0? An alternative form of the objective is to minimize the expected value $EL(y - y^0)$ of the loss function $L(y - y^0)$ defined as a scalar convex function of the deviations of y from y^0. Some conventional loss functions used in economics and other applied decision models are quadratic as a sum $\sum \epsilon_i^2$ of squared errors $\epsilon_i = y_i - y_i^0$, or linear as a sum $\sum |\epsilon_i|$ of absolute deviations. These functions are symmetric and to that extent, asymmetry of information structure, if present in the stochastic generating mechanism may not be well captured here. Hence the need to evaluate the impact of changing information structure on the solution vector.

As a second example one may consider the portfolio model, which considers an investor who has to optimally invest a proportion of his wealth, x_i in a risky asset i, where $x_i \geqslant 0$ for $i = 1, 2, \ldots, n$ and $\sum x_i = 1$ and the return $\tilde{m}_i$ on asset i is random. Any choice of vector $x' = (x_1, x_2, \ldots, \text{i}x_n)$ that is feasible i.e. $x \geqslant 0$, $e'x = 1$ where e is an n-element column vector with each element unity, is called a portfolio choice or policy with random return $\tilde{z} = \tilde{m}'x$, where $\tilde{m}' = (\tilde{m}_1, \tilde{m}_2, \ldots, \tilde{m}_n)$. If the return vector $\tilde{m}$ has a multivariate normal distribution $N(m, V)$ with means m and covariance matrix V, then the portfolio model solves the following quadratic program:

$$\min_{x \in R} \sigma^2 = x'Vx, \quad R: \{x: \ e'x = 1, \ m'x \geqslant y\} \tag{1.2}$$

where e is a vector with unit elements and the minimal return parameter y, is assumed to be preassigned by the subjective judgment of the decision-maker. Assuming that the set $\theta = (m, V)$ of parameters are known or its suitable estimates are available, the whole set of optimal or efficient portfolios can be determined from (1.2) according to portfolio theory and its various extensions (Szego 1980). Note that this deterministic transformation of the stochastic optimization problem would be very incomplete, if it is not possible to characterize the reliability of the optimal solution recommended. Thus, if an estimate $\hat{\theta}(I)$ depending on the information structure I is used and the optimal solution $x^*(\hat{\theta})$ recommended, what is the probability $P[\hat{m}'x^*(\hat{\theta}) \geqslant y^0]$ of expected return exceeding a target level y^0? What is the form of the probability distribution of the optimal solution vector $x^*(\hat{\theta})$, when the sample estimates $\hat{\theta}$ follow a specified distribution e.g, normal? The loss function in (1.2) is symmetric. It would not be symmetric, if the investor assigns a higher weight to any loss $\hat{m}'x < y$ than otherwise. How would then the optimal solution vector change? These are some of the issues analyzed in stochastic optimization theory, which can be divided into two broad classes: (a) stochastic linear programming (LP) and (b) stochastic linear control.

2. Stochastic Linear Programming

A standard linear programming (LP) model solves for the decision vector c by maximizing a linear function subject to a set of linear constraints i.e.

$$\max_{x \in R} z = c'z, \quad R: \{x: \ Ax \leqslant b, \ x \geqslant 0\} \tag{2.1}$$

where the parameter set $\theta = (A, b, c)$ is assumed to be completely known in the deterministic formulation. For different applications several specialized interpretations of the above LP model may be useful. In production applications, the decision vector x is output, z is profit and the parameters A, b represent the input coefficients and the resource vector respectively. If net returns (c) per unit of output is known or estimated suitably, the firm's decision problem is to maximize profit, given the set θ of parameters.

The LP problem (2.1) above becomes stochastic as soon as one introduces incomplete information in the set θ of parameters. For, if θ is subject to a stochastic generating mechanism, both the objective function and the constraint set R fail to have a deterministic character. Hence one needs to define a suitable deterministic transformation, before optimization can be performed. Three types of deterministic transformation are discussed in the literature. In the first, known as stochastic linear programming a distinction is drawn between passive and active information structure. In the former, the set of realizations of the random vector θ is fed back into the solution structure, whereas in the latter, truncation in the space of distribution of profits is admitted through active allocations of the resource vector, thus changing the original constraint set. In the second, known as chance-constrained linear programming, the probability of feasibility of the solution vector is allowed partially i.e.

$$\text{Prob}(Ax \leqslant b; x \geqslant 0) = u, \quad u = (u_i), \quad 0 \leqslant u_i \leqslant 1$$

so that there is always a cost due to partial infeasibility. If for all inequalities $u_i = 1.0$, then we have no chance constraints, otherwise there is a finite probability of infeasibility. The third approach, known as two-stage programming with recourse starts from an initial guess of some of the parameters in the first stage and then, conditional on the first stage decision specifies a two-facet objective function in the second stage, where the second facet includes a cost due to errors made in the first stage, which are realized now. A comparative analysis of these three approaches is available in the excellent book by Kolbin (1977). Some recent results of stochastic programming theory in relation to estimation of parameters, multiple-criteria decisions and game-theoretic solutions are to be found in the book: Decision Models in Stochastic Programming by Sengupta (1982).

Instead of a general survey, we want to emphasize here the more recent developments in the theory of stochastic linear programming, which are more relevant for economic models and their applications. These developments deal with the following aspects:
(a) Information structure: its asymmetry and the propagation of uncertainty and
(b) minimax and robust decision in a stochastic environment.

2.1. Information Structure Analysis

From an applied viewpoint, the information structure may be classified into two groups: passive vs. interactive and symmetric vs. asymmetric. The passive case assumes the availability of sufficient data to characterize the relevant probability distributions, whereas the interactive case involves sharing or exchange of information, due to its incompleteness and insufficient availability. The symmetry or asymmetry in information structure may be due to the specific form of the loss function or the probability distribution function.

The current theory of stochastic LP ignores for the most part any role of incomplete information structure, either passive or active on the possible solution structure. If the LP model (2.1) is viewed as a method of choosing a vector x, given the set of parameters θ, then the solution $x = x(\theta)$ depends on the prior knowledge of θ. If θ is not given, it has to be estimated from observation.

In contrast to the above view of information structure which is of course passive, an interactive case arises in the LP model when viewed in a game-theoretic context. For this purpose we write the LP model (2.1) in a canonical form e.g.

primal   dual

$$\max z = \sum_{j=1}^{n} p_j \qquad \min w = \sum_{i=1}^{m} q_i$$

subject to   subject to   (2.3)

$$\sum_{j=1}^{n} \alpha_{ij} p_j \leqslant 1 \qquad \sum_{i=1}^{m} q_i \alpha_{ij} \geqslant 1$$

$$p_j \geqslant 0 \qquad q_i \geqslant 0$$

where it is assumed without loss of generality that (b, c) are nonnegative, $\alpha_{ij} = a_{ij}/(b_i c_j)$ for nonzero b_i and c_j and $p_j = \hat{p}_j z$; here $\hat{p}_j$, $1 \leqslant j \leqslant n$ are the mixed strategies of player I with $\sum \hat{p}_j = 1$, $\hat{p}_j \geqslant 0$ and so are $\hat{q}_i = q_i/w$ for player II. By LP duality, the canonical LP models (2.3) define a two-person zero-sum game which can be written in a more compact notation as

player I: $\max_{\hat{p}} \hat{p}' \hat{A} \hat{q}$ s.t. $\hat{p}'e = 1,\ \ \hat{p}'e = 1,\ \ \hat{p} \geqslant 0$

  where $\hat{A} = (\alpha_{ij})$ (2.4)

player II: $\max \hat{p}' \hat{B} \hat{q}$ s.t. $\hat{q}'v = 1,\ \ \hat{q} \geqslant 0$

  where $\hat{B} = (\beta_{ij})$

with $\hat{B} = -\hat{A}$, where e, v are vectors with each element unity and β_{ij} defines the payoff matrix for player II, just as α_{ij} is the payoff for player I. For a cooperative game one may define $C = r\hat{A} + (1 - r)\hat{B}, 0 \leqslant r \leqslant 1$

as a weighted combination of the respective payoffs and set up of a joint maximization problem

$$\max_{\hat{p},\hat{q}} \hat{p}'C\hat{q}$$

subject to $\hat{p}'e = 1 = \hat{q}'v, \quad \hat{p} \geqslant 0, \quad \hat{q} \geqslant 0$

What would happen in this game theoretic framework if the payoff matrices are random i.e. they are $\hat{A}(s)$, $\hat{B}(s)$, $C(s)$ where s belongs to a set S of events with a given probability structure. Two common approaches adopted here are the chance-constrained approach and the parametric approach. In the first, the recognition of randomness of the payoff structure leads to alternative, and in most cases, risk-averse solutions which maximize for example the probability of attaining a given level of expected payoff. The second method attempts to define on the basis of observations, if available, an unbiased estimate of the payoff matrix $\hat{C}$ say and obtain equilibrium solutions of the joint maximization model (2.5). In either case, the same set of observations and an identical amount of information contained in them may lead to different perceptions and different objectives to optimize by the two players. Information when shared cooperatively may have different implications from those not shared or partially shared.

One may present here an illustrative view of these two information structures, one passive when there is one single DM and the other interactive when the LP game has a stochastic payoff matrix with two players. For the passive information structure, consider a simplified example of the LP model (2.1), where only vector c is considered unknown, with A and b being known. Assume that two linear estimates $\tilde{c}$, $\hat{c}$ are made from observations such that they are unbiased i.e. $E\tilde{c} = c = E\hat{c}$ and have variance-covariance matrices $V(\tilde{c})$, $V(\hat{c})$ satisfying a positive definiteness condition i.e.

$$V(\tilde{c}) - V(\hat{c}) = D, \quad \text{a positive definite matrix} \tag{2.6}$$

Denote the optimal solutions of the LP model (2.1) in the two cases of $\tilde{c}$, $\hat{c}$ by $\tilde{x}$ and $\hat{x}$ respectively. Does it necessarily hold that

$$\text{var } \tilde{z} \geqslant \text{var } \hat{z} \tag{2.7}$$

where $\tilde{z} = \tilde{c}'\tilde{x}$, $\hat{z} = \hat{c}'\hat{x}$ for nontrivial optimal decision vectors $\tilde{x}$, $\hat{x}$ which are not necessarily identical? It is not difficult to show that the above variance inequality (2.7) may fail in many cases. However under suitable conditions, the variance inequality (2.7) may hold. For example suppose there exist optimal solutions $\tilde{x}$, $\hat{x}$ corresponding to the linear unbiased estimates $\tilde{c}$, $\hat{c}$ satisfying (2.6) and the following condition

$$V(\tilde{c})(\tilde{x} - \hat{x}) \geqslant 0 \qquad (2.8)$$

then it holds that var $\tilde{z} \geqslant$ var $\hat{z}$, where the inequality is strict if the distributions of $\tilde{c}$, $\hat{c}$ are distinct and nondegenerate. Proof of this proposition follows from the fact that we have

$$\text{var } \tilde{z} - \text{var } \hat{z} = \hat{x}'D\hat{x} + \alpha V(\tilde{c}) + 2\hat{x}'V(\tilde{c})\alpha \geqslant 0, \qquad \text{where} \quad \alpha = \tilde{x} - \hat{x}$$

since $V(\tilde{c})$ is positive semidefinite, D positive definite and α satisfies (2.8). The inequality is strict since $\tilde{V}(\tilde{c})$ cannot be identical with $V(\hat{c})$ by construction.

Consider a second example where the DM minimizes an expected conditional loss function L, given θ

$$L = E\{(\hat{\theta}'\hat{x} - \theta'x)^2 \mid \theta\}; \qquad \hat{x}, x \in R \qquad (2.9)$$

where x is the optimal vector if true θ were known. If $\hat{\theta}$ is conditionally unbiased in the sense $E(\hat{\theta} \mid \theta) = \theta$, then the optimal solution must satisfy

$$\hat{x}^* = [V(\hat{\theta}) + \theta\theta']^{-1}(\theta\theta')x = K_1 x \quad \text{say}$$

where

$$K_1 = [V(\hat{\theta}) + \theta\theta']^{-1}(\theta\theta')$$

and $V(\hat{\theta})$ is the conditional variance given θ. In case $\hat{\theta}$ is not unbiased we get the optimal solution $\hat{x}^0$ as:

$$\hat{x}^0 = [V(\hat{\theta}) + E(\hat{\theta} \mid \theta)\theta']^{-1}E(\hat{\theta} \mid \theta)\theta'x = K_2 x \quad \text{say}$$

where

$$K_2 = [V(\hat{\theta}) + E(\hat{\theta} \mid \theta)\theta']^{-1}E(\hat{\theta} \mid \theta)\theta'$$

The difference between the two optimal decisions $\hat{x}^*$ and $\hat{x}^0$ and their respective expected losses may thus measure the relative gain or loss from accepting an unbiased estimate $\hat{\theta}$ in arriving at an optimal decision. The relative distances of $\hat{x}^*$ and $\hat{x}^0$ from x may be measured by

$$D^2(\hat{x}^*, x) = x'(K_1 - I)'(K_1 - I)x$$

$$D^2(\hat{x}^0, x) = x'(K_2 - I)'(K_2 - I)x$$

from which it is clear that $\hat{x}^* = x$, if $V(\hat{\theta})$ is a null matrix.

If θ is not given but has a prior distribution $p(\theta)$, then using the information function (2.2), posterior optimal decisions can be computed and compared with other solutions when there is no information in the sense that the rank of H is zero in (2.2). Following the method of Chu (1978), one may compare here alternative information structures and arrive at an optimal one. Also, one may characterize a 'sufficient' information structure thus: an information structure H_1 with observations t_1 in (2.2) is defined to be sufficient for another structure H_2 with observations t_2, if regardless of the value of the parameters θ, an observation on t_1 and an auxiliary randomization make it possible to generate a random vector which has the same distribution as t_2. Clearly, if a sufficient information structure is available, it is preferable to others which are not.

If normality of distribution can be assumed, then the value of information available from posterior distributions which incorporate sample information along with prior information can be easily estimated and evaluated. For instance, assume that e is zero in the information function (2.2) and θ is normally distributed $N(\mu_\theta, V_\theta)$, so that the conditional distribution of t given θ is normal $N(H\theta, V_T)$ with mean $H\theta$ and variance V_T, where T observations are used. Maximizing $\log p(\theta\,|\,t)$ with respect to θ, where $p(\theta\,|\,t)$ is the posterior distribution given t, we obtain the optimal value θ^*:

$$\theta^* = \mu_\theta + V_\theta S_T^{-1} t, \quad S_T = HIH' + V_T \tag{2.10}$$

If the loss function (2.9) is written, slightly more generally as:

$$L = \hat{x}'Q\hat{x} + 2\hat{x}'(R\theta + a) \tag{2.11}$$

where $Q > 0$ is positive definite and R, a are suitable constants, then, using the result (2.10) in (2.11) the optimal decision $\hat{x}^*$ is

$$\hat{x}^* = -Q^{-1}(R\theta^* + a)$$

Note that if V_T is a null matrix, $S_T = HH'$ depends on the information matrix H. If H is null (i.e. the case of no information), then the optimal decision vector is

$$\hat{x}^* = -Q^{-1}(R\mu_\theta + a) \quad \text{(null information)} \tag{2.12}$$

If the information structure is complete in the sense that $H = I$ (an identity matrix), then the optimal decision is

$$\hat{x}^* = -Q^{-1}(R\mu_\theta + a) - Q^{-1}RV_\theta\theta \tag{2.13}$$

The value of complete information may thus be measured by the expected reduction in loss by using (2.13) instead of (2.12).

For the interactive information structure we consider the LP game model (2.4) where the two players may or may not share the respective information available to them. It can be easily shown that if more information is valuable, then by not sharing each player would be liable to some cost or loss. We may therefore consider the cooperative case (2.5) where different values of r in its domain constitute different degrees of cooperation. Player I who chooses p observes N rounds of the random payoff game with payoffs $\sum_{j=1}^{m} p_i g_i$, where $g_i = \sum_{i=1}^{n} c_{ij} q_j$ is random due to the randomness of $c_{ij}(s)$. Denote the means and variances of vector $g = (g_i)$ by $\bar{g} = \bar{g}(q)$ and $V_g(q)$. Likewise player II observes the random payoff $\sum_{i=j}^{n} q_j h_j$, where $h_j = \sum_{i=1}^{m} c_{ij}(s) p_i$ has means and variances $\bar{h} - \bar{h}$ $= \bar{h}(p)$, $V_h(p)$ depending on player I's strategy vector p. Let α and β be the risk aversion rates (i.e. the weights on variances of g and h) by the respective players in the sense that they maximize J_1 and J_2:

player I: $\quad J_1 = p'\bar{g}(q) - \dfrac{\alpha}{2} p' V_g(q) p$

subject to $\quad p \geqslant 0, \quad \alpha > 0$

player II: $\quad J_2 = q'\bar{h}(p) - \dfrac{\beta}{2} q' V_h(p) q$

subject to $\quad q \geqslant 0, \quad \beta \geqslant 0$

Assume that player I guesses a value $\tilde{q}$ of q such that $\bar{g}(\tilde{q}) = H_1 \tilde{q}$ and $V_g(\tilde{q})$ is constant and independent of $\tilde{q}$. Likewise for player II with $\bar{h}(\tilde{p}) = H_2 \tilde{p}$ and $V_h(\tilde{p})$ a constant.. Suppose there exist an optimal non-negative pair p^*, q^* consistent with $\tilde{p}$, $\tilde{q}$ i.e. $p^* = \tilde{p}$, $q^* = \tilde{q}$ satisfying $p^{*\prime} e = 1 = q^{*\prime} v$ then the following proposition holds: The optimal pair (p^*, q^*) of strategies defined above satisfies the following complementary eigenvalue problems, provided the matrices V_g, V_h are positive definite

$$\left(H_2 V_g^{-1} H_1 - \alpha\beta V_h \right) q^* = 0, \quad \left(H_1 V_h^{-1} H_2 - \alpha\beta V_g \right) p^* = 0 \qquad (2.14)$$

The proof of this result is due to the fact that by the assumed conditions the objective functions J_1 and J_2 are concave in p and q respectively. Hence the Kuhn–Tucker theorem applies and the optimal vectors p^*, q^* must satisfy the necessary conditions with not all components of p^*, q^* being zero. Hence, taking the positive components only of vectors p^*, q^*, one obtains $\bar{g}(p^*) - \alpha V_g p^* = 0 = \bar{h}(q^*) - \beta V_h q^*$, if necessary by deleting the zero components of p^* and q^*. Then the results follow. Note that if the game is completely mixed in the sense that p^*, $q^* > 0$, then the complementary eigenvalue problems necessarily hold. Also the information matrices H_1 and H_2 may convey unequal amounts of information to the two players except when $H_1 = H_2 = I$ (an identity matrix). In case of equal information $H_1 = H_2 = I$, the eigenvalues associated with problem (2.14) are all nonnegative.

It is clear that learning from past rounds of the play can be easily incorporated in this framework. This may provide some additional rationale for the quadratic term in the objective function of the two players. For instance, let t be the observations on θ which may stand for $(\bar{g}, V_g)$ or, $(\bar{h}, V_h)$. Define an average amount of information by the set of observation ϵ with data t and parameters θ by

$$I(\epsilon) = H_\theta - E_t[H_{\theta|t}]$$

where $H_q = -E_\theta[\log p(\theta)]$, $H_{\theta|t} = -E_{\theta|t}[\log p(\theta|t)]$, $p(\theta) = $ prior probability density (pdf) of θ and $p(\theta|t) = $ posterior pdf of θ, E is expectation, H_θ denotes prior uncertainty about θ, and $E_t[H_{\theta|t}]$ is the expected posterior uncertainty. The objective functions for the two players may then be written as:

player I: $\quad \max_p J_1 = p'\bar{g}_1(q), \quad \bar{g}_1(q) = g(q, I_1(\epsilon))$

player II: $\quad \max_q J_2 = q'\bar{h}_2(p), \quad \bar{h}_2(p) = h(p, I_2(\epsilon))$

$$(2.15)$$

where $I_i(\epsilon) = I_i(\epsilon|N)$ denotes the average amount of information estimated by each player $i = 1$, 2 after N rounds of the play and the functions $\bar{g}_1(q)$, $\bar{h}_2(p)$ represent each player's estimated gain from forecasting the rival's behavior. It is clear that the game model (2.15) would have optimal solutions p^*, q^*, so long as the forecasting functions $\bar{g}_2$, $\bar{h}_2$ are continuous in their arguments. Several special cases of this model may be analyzed for practical applications. First, starting from N equal to zero, one may analyze the sequence of revisions of first stage optimal strategies by each player as N gets larger and $I_i(\epsilon|N)$ gets increased. The value of information conditional on a given round of the play may then be evaluated. Second, if there is a pair (p^0, q^0) of Cournot–Nash equilibrium solutions to this game, the process of learning through information by each player may be evaluated for any N by the distances $(p_N - p^0)$ and $(q_N - q^0)$, where P_N, q_N are the optimal strategies at the N-th round of the play according to (2.15). Third, optimal strategies which are partially controllable, due to constraints on the strategies may be easily analyzed in this framework. The class of non-zero sum games with constraints on the strategies may take several forms e.g., a chance-constrained model has been developed by Charnes, Kirby and

Raike (1968), where the strategies selected by the two players do not in themselves determine the payoffs, but in which random perturbations with known distributions modify the strategy of each player before the actual strategies are implemented. A second approach (Isaacs (1968), Sengupta (1979)) considers the subjective difficulty each player often has in assigning to the states probabilities with which he is completely satisfied and the model with information function must tell the player how much he must perturb his initial probability estimate in order to change his maximum utility alternative from the alternative originally best under the initial estimate. For example, assume that the $\bar{g}_1$ and $\bar{h}_2$ functions in (2.15) take the following form

$$\bar{g}_1 = q_0 - A_1 p - A_2 q, \qquad \bar{h}_2 = p_0 - B_1 p - B_2 q \tag{2.16}$$

where (p_0, q_0) are the initial subjective estimates of each player and A_i, B_i are suitable constant matrices. The expected return $\bar{g}_1$ (or, $\bar{h}_2$) now depends on the estimates of initial and subsequent probabilities of rival's strategies and the best counterstrategy chosen. It may be easily seen that the Cournot–Nash equilibrium solution, if it exists must satisfy the following pair of reaction curves:

$$\begin{aligned}
\left(A_1 + A_1' \right) p^* &= q_0 - A_2 q^* \\
\left(B_2 + B_2' \right) q^* &= p_0 - B_1 p^*
\end{aligned} \tag{2.17}$$

If the components of p^*, q^* are each positive and less than one, then the optimal strategies are completely mixed. If, to each equation of (2.16) we add the errors by a residual term ϵ_1 or, ϵ_2 on the right hand side, then the sequential revision of initial probabilities (q_0, p_0) may be analyzed explicitly. For instance, assume that each player begins with an arbitrarily selected mixed strategy level which he changes from period to period in proportion to the discrepancy between his desired and actual strategies in the preceding period:

$$\begin{aligned}
p_t - p_{t-1} &= K_1\left[R_1(q_{t-1}) - p_{t-1} \right] \\
q_t - q_{t-1} &= K_2\left[R_2(p_{t-1}) - q_{t-1} \right]
\end{aligned} \tag{2.18}$$

where K_1, K_2 are diagonal matrices with positive diagonal elements representing the speed of adjustment or revision, R_1 and R_2 are the reaction functions of players I and II solved from (2.17). Under certain conditions on the matrices K_i, R_i, the characteristic roots of the difference equation system (2.18) may be such that p_t converges to p^* and q_t q^*. In such cases the learning functions proposed in (2.18) are self-convergent to the equilibrium strategies. Otherwise the information structures in (2.18) may be destabilizing in the sense that (p_t, q_t) diverges from (p^*, q^*).

So far we have ignored the problem of asymmetry of information structure. This asymmetry may arise in two ways: either in the preference function, or in the form of departures from normality of the distribution of errors. In the first case, positive and negative deviations are unequally weighted by the decision-maker, whereas in the second case robustness is considered to be a desirable characteristic of an optimal policy in a stochastic environment. We may consider here some simple examples of these two types of asymmetry by assuming that only vector c in the objective function of the LP model (2.1) is random with finite means $\bar{c}$ and variance-covariance matrix V. Let z^0 be the target value the policy-maker seeks to attain and let the stochastic generating mechanism be:

$$\tilde{z} = c'x + \epsilon = \bar{c}'x + \gamma'x + \epsilon \tag{3.1}$$

where γ, ϵ are random errors distributed independently with zero means and variances V and σ^2 respectively. The closeness of $\tilde{z}$ to the target z^0 may be measured in several ways, of which one is the expected weighted distance squared Ed^2:

$$Ed^2 = w^2 E(\tilde{z} - \bar{z})^2 + (1 - w)^2 (\bar{c}'x - z^0)^2 \tag{3.2}$$

where E: expectation, $\bar{z} = E\tilde{z}$ and $0 \leqslant w \leqslant 1$. Viewed as a loss function, the distance function in (3.2) is symmetric, except for the weights, which can be used to characterize a simple type of asymmetry e.g if $w > 0.5$, then the variance term $E(\tilde{z} - \bar{z})^2$ gets more weight than the term $(\bar{c}'x - z^0)^2$. As a matter of fact, for any feasible vector x, the optimal value w^* of w is:

$$w^* = (\bar{c}'x - z^0)^2 \left[x'Vx + \sigma_\epsilon^2 + (\bar{c}'x - z^0)^2 \right]^{-1} \tag{3.3}$$

clearly $Ed^2(w) \geqslant Ed^2(w^*)$ for all w not equal to w^*. Thus preassigning a weight w different from the optimal one has the effect of increasing the expected value of the squared distance Ed^2. Likewise, the symmetric deviations $E(\tilde{z} - \bar{z})^2$ and $(\bar{c}'x - z^0)^2$ may be decomposed into two asymmetric parts:

$$E(\tilde{z} - \bar{z})^2 = k^2 E\{(\tilde{z} - \bar{z})^2 \mid \tilde{z} \geqslant \bar{z}\} + (1 - k)^2 E\{(\tilde{z} - \bar{z})^2 \mid \tilde{z} \leqslant \bar{z}\}$$
$$0 \leqslant k \leqslant 1$$
$$(\bar{c}'x - z^0)^2 = r^2\{(\bar{c}'x - z^0)^+\}^2 + (1 - r)^2\{(z^0 - \bar{c}'x)^+\}^2 \tag{3.4}$$
$$0 \leqslant r \leqslant 1$$

where k and r are scalar weights and $(\bar{c}'x - z^0)^+$ denotes for fixed z^0, only the nonnegative deviations $(\bar{c}'x - z^0) \geqslant 0$. The optimal values $k*$, $r*$ are then

$$k* = E\{(\bar{z} - \tilde{z})^+\}^2 \left[E\{(\tilde{z} - \bar{z})^+\}^2 + E\{(\bar{z} - \tilde{z})^+\}^2 \right]^{-1}$$

$$r* = \{(z^0 - \bar{c}'x)^+\}^2 \left[\{(\bar{c}'x - z^0)^+\}^2 + \{(z^0 - \bar{c}'x)^+\}^2 \right]^{-1}$$

thus selecting a value of $h = 0.5$, $r = 0.5$ arbitrarily, irrespective of the positive or negative deviations of $\tilde{z}$ (or, $\bar{c}'x$) from $\bar{z}$ (or, z^0) would be inoptimal thus suggesting the possibility of gross errors of measurement or control. Two consequences of asymmetry are important. First, it has the effect of truncating the original probability distribution, thus shifting the original parameters. For instance if the deviations $(\tilde{z} - \bar{z})$ are normal, the variable $(\tilde{z} - \bar{z})^+$ has a truncated normal distribution, whose variance is much higher than before. The rate at which the new variance is inflated varies from one distribution to another, due to what is called "outlier proneness" phenomena. Second, the probability of attaining the target value z^0 is affected by asymmetry, so that the degree of closeness to z^0 measured by the squared distance loses much of its value. This can be easily seen from the likelihood $L(\eta)$ of the event $\eta = z^0 - \bar{c}'x$, $\eta = \gamma'x + \epsilon$ when γ and ϵ are assumed to be normally distributed. The log likelihood function is

$$\log L(\eta) = -\tfrac{1}{2} \log(2\pi) - \tfrac{1}{2} \log(x'Vx + \sigma_\epsilon^2)$$

$$- (z^0 - \bar{c}'x)^2 (x'Vx + \sigma_\epsilon^2)^{-1} \tag{3.5}$$

which is to be maximized with respect to vector $x \in R$, when R is $\{x; Ax \leqslant b, x \geqslant 0\}$. Under conditions of asymmetry imposed in (3.4), the log likelihood function in (3.5) is further truncated, so that the region around the maximum becomes very small. Further, if the random components γ and ϵ are not normal, the log likelihood functions become more complicated and so the optimal solution vectors $x*$ are more difficult to compute.

The second type of asymmetry emphasizes the ill-conditioning and nonrobust aspects of an optimal solution computed on the basis of the normality assumption, when the latter may in fact not be true. This can be illustrated by two examples, the first of which is taken from the theory of chance-constrained linear programming (Vajda 1972, Kall 1976). In this theory, only the linear constraints are probabilistic i.e.

$$P\left(\sum_{j=1}^{n} a_{ij}(w)x_j \leqslant b_i(w) \right) \geqslant \alpha_i, \qquad 0 \leqslant \alpha_i \leqslant 1 \tag{4.1}$$

where w indicates the existence of a suitable probability space. Denoting the feasibility set defined by (4.1) by $X_i(\alpha_i)$, where $\alpha \in [0,1]$ it is not true that this set is convex for the case of joint constraints. Thus, the convexity of the restriction set R, which holds in deterministic LP problems may not necessarily hold. However, there are special cases when the feasibility set $X_i(\alpha_i)$ would retain convexity. One such case arises when the random variables $a_{i1}(w)$, $a_{i2}(w),\ldots,a_{in}(w)$, $b_i(w)$ have a joint $(n+1)$-dimensional normal distribution. Then $x_i(\alpha_i)$ is convex for all $\alpha_i \geqslant 0.5$. Hence the intersection of such sets $x_i(\alpha_i)$ is convex under this condition. The convexity of the set $x_i(\alpha_i)$ for $\alpha_i \geqslant 0.5$ follows from the fact that the left hand side of (4.1) can be written as

$$\phi^{-1}(\alpha_i)\sigma_i(x)+\mu_i(x) \leqslant 0 \tag{4.2}$$

where ϕ is the cumulative distribution function (cdf) of a unit normal variate such that $\phi^{-1}(\alpha_i) \geqslant 0$, if $\alpha_i \geqslant 0.5$ and $\mu_i(x)$, $\sigma_i(x)$ are the mean and standard deviation of the random variable $y_i = \Sigma_j(a_{ij}(w)x_j - b_i(w))$. Both the mean $\mu_i(x)$ and the standard $\sigma_i(x)$ are convex functions of vector x and if $\phi^{-1}(\alpha_i)$ is nonnegative, the left hand side of (4.2) is a convex function of x. Hence the set $x_i(\alpha_i)$ is convex. Of course we have to add the nonnegativity on x as an additional condition to be adjoined to the convex sets $x_i(\alpha_i)$.

The above result on the conditions required for convexity of the sets $x_i(\alpha_i)$ has been generalized by Prekopa (1973) to the entire subclass of logarithmically concave distribution functions, which includes the normal distribution as a special case. These logarithmically concave distribution functions have density $f(y)$ in the form

$$f(y) = \gamma \exp(-Q(y))$$

where $Q(y)$ is a convex function of vector y and γ is a positive constant.

As a second example, consider the stochastic LP model where only the vector c is random i.e. $\tilde{z} = \tilde{c}'x$, $x \in R$. If $\tilde{c}$ is normal $N(\bar{c}, V)$ and the policymaker intends to maximize the minimal return level z_0 where

$$P(\tilde{c}'x \geqslant z_0) = \alpha, \quad 0 \leqslant \alpha \leqslant 1 \tag{4.3}$$

then this leads to maximizing

$$\max_{x \in R} z_0 = c'x + \phi^{-1}(1-\alpha)(x'Vx)^{1/2} \tag{4.4}$$

where $\phi^{-1}(1-\alpha)$ is nonpositive if $\alpha \geqslant 0.5$ and then z_0 is a concave function of vector x. However, if $q = \phi^{-1}(1-\alpha)$ is positive, the function

z_0 is not concave and hence a maximum may not necessarily exist. In this case, if we apply the first order condition, we may obtain a minimum rather than a maximum. Thus, in default of knowledge that the underlying distribution is normal, we would have the objective function

$$z_0 = \bar{c}'x + q(x'Vx)^{1/2}, \quad x \in R$$

where q may be either positive or nonnegative. In other words, the probability α in (4.3) cannot be suitably preassigned, in the sense that z_0 becomes a concave function in x, whenever the distribution is not known to be normal.

Instead of maximizing z_0 for fixed α, it may be more appropriate to maximize α itself, for a preassigned z_0 by selecting a vector $x \in R$. This leads to minimizing $\phi(t)$, where $t = (z_0 - \bar{c}'x)(x'Vx)^{-1/2}$ and $\phi(t)$ is the cdf of the random variable t. If $\phi(t)$ is not normal, then it can be expanded in an Edgeworth series in order to evaluate the consequence of departures from normality. For example, if the cdf of t follows a truncated normal distribution with a known truncation point, then the following provides a good approximation to $\phi(t)$:

$$\phi(t) \simeq \frac{1}{2} + \frac{t}{\sqrt{2\pi}} - \frac{t^3}{6\sqrt{2\pi}} \tag{4.5}$$

This leads to the minimization of the expression

$$h(t) = t - \tfrac{1}{6}t^3 \tag{4.6}$$

where the condition $t \leqslant 0$ is required for convexity of the function $h(t)$. Thus, if we ignore the cubic term in (4.6) we obtain the standard normal solution, say x^* and t^*. Let x^{**} and t^{**} be the solutions when the cubic term is not ignored, then the divergences $|t^* - t^{**}|$, $|x^* - x^{**}|$ would provide measures of sensitivity due to nonnormality. If the underlying distribution is not truncated normal but it has a symmetric density $f(t)$ twice differentiable at the origin, then the approximation (4.5), due to the Edgeworth series turns out to be:

$$\phi(t) \simeq \tfrac{1}{2} + tf(0) + \tfrac{1}{6}t^3 f^{(2)}(0), \quad \alpha = \alpha(t) = 1 - \phi(t)$$

where $f^{(2)}(0)$ denotes the second derivative of $f(t)$ evaluated at zero. Note that the convexity of the function $\phi(t)$, which is required for maximizing α, depends on the signs of both t and $f^{(2)}(0)$. In general, $\phi(t)$ being a cubic function may have domains, where it is concave, convex or neither. This shows that greater risks are involved in selecting an optimal solution, whenever normality fails to hold.

2.2. Minimax Solution

Several types of minimax solutions have been recently proposed in the current theory of stochastic programming, of which the following appear to be most important.

(a) mixed strategy solutions when the LP model is viewed as a two-person stochastic game that may be zero-sum or non-zero sum. Here it is assumed that nature chooses a distribution of $\theta(w) = (A(w), b(w), c(w))$ from a certain class and then the decision-maker chooses his strategy vectors $x(w)$ so as to protect himself against the worst that can happen to him (Kolbin 1977, Sengupta 1982).

(b) many population problems, when the probability distribution of random variables $\theta(w)$ is not a single distribution but a class of many distributions. Thus, the single stochastic objective function is replaced by a multicriteria objective function, as a vector instead of a scalar (Whittle 1971, Sengupta 1982).

(c) suboptimal solutions in decision regions, where the two-person game problem is transformed by superimposing a suitable decision region so that the feasible set is convex (Dyson and Swaithes 1978).

To illustrate we consider here two examples, one having a multicriteria objective function with stochastic components (i.e. case (b)) and the other from case (c) involving decision regions. In the deterministic form of the multiple objective LP model we have to maximize a vector function

$$\max_{x \in R} Cx, \quad x \in R: \{x: \quad x \geqslant 0, \quad Ax \leqslant b\} \tag{5.1}$$

where C is a q by n matrix and x is an n-element column vector. A vector $x^0 \in R$ is defined to be an efficient solution for this case, if there does not exist any other feasible vector $\hat{x} \in R$ such that $C\hat{x} \geqslant Cx^0$, where $\hat{x} \neq x^0$ and the vector inequality means that at least in one component i, $C_i'\hat{x} > C_i'x^0$ for $i = 1, 2, \ldots, q$ where C_i' denotes the ith row of matrix C. If such an efficient vector x^0 exists, then it is known from Kuhn–Tucker theory that it would be contained in the set of nondominated extreme point solutions of the equivalent problem having a scalar objective function

$$\max_{x,t} t'Cx, x \in R, t \in T$$

where $\tag{5.2}$

$$T: \left\{ t: \quad t \geqslant 0, \quad \sum_{i=1}^{q} t_i = 1 \right\}$$

with the Lagrangian function $L = t'Cx + \lambda'(b - Ax) + r(1 - e't)$ the necessary conditions of Kuhn–Tucker theory lead to

$$\lambda'A \geqslant t'C \quad x \geqslant 0 \tag{5.3a}$$

$$Ax \leqslant b, \quad t \geqslant 0 \tag{5.3b}$$

$$e't = 1 \tag{5.3c}$$

It is well known that for all values of vector $t = (t_i)$ in the set T, the whole set of nondominated extreme points of the problem can be generated. A nondominated extreme point solution of the LP problem (5.1) corresponds to a basic feasible solution (i.e. vector x_B) of the constraint set. Denoting the nonbasic variables of $x = (x_B \, x_N)$ by vector x, partitioning the matrix C into (C_B, C_N) and substituting $x_B = B^{-1}b - B^{-1}Nx_N$ into the objective function, the programming problem (5.2) can be reduced to:

$$\max_{x \geqslant 0} \quad t'C_B B^{-1}b - \left(t'C_B B^{-1}N - t'C_N\right)x_N \tag{5.4}$$

subject to $\quad t \geqslant 0, \quad e't = 1$

It is well known by Kuhn–Tucker theory that a basic feasible solution (x_B, x_N) of the LP constraint set $x \in R$ is an optimal solution of the derived problem (5.2), if the nonnegative multipliers $t_1, t_2, \ldots, t_1$, not all zero satisfy the condition for all j:

$$\Delta_j = t'C_{N_j} - t'C_B B^{-1}N_j \leqslant 0, \quad j = 1, 2, \ldots, n \tag{5.5}$$

where N_j and C_{N_j} are the column vectors corresponding to variable x_j. It is clear that such optimality conditions would not hold, if some elements of the matrix C are stochastic. In applied models of resource allocation and production decisions, the stochastic variations in the elements of C and b are very important, since the matrix A is more or less fixed by technology. Variations in the elements of C are due to either the subjective differences in the objectives of the q team members, or imperfect information structures and inadequate communication channels. Resource variations in b may be due to the divergence of planned targets from their realizations or due to mismatch of the input-mix. Note that if b and c contain random elements, the necessary conditions (5.3a), (5.3b) hold only probabilistically and the constraint (5.3c) being a normalization condition may be dropped without any loss of generalization. Let the stochastic components in b and C be mutually independent and normally distributed, and policy decisions are made after the stochastic variations are realized. Then, a chance-constrained version of the inequalities (5.3a), (5.3b) would appear as follows:

$$P\left[\frac{c_j - \bar{c}_j}{\sigma(c_j)} \leqslant \frac{\lambda' a_j - \bar{c}_j}{\sigma(c_j)}\right] = F\left(\frac{\lambda' a_j - \bar{c}_j}{\sigma(c_j)}\right) = v_j$$

$$P\left[\frac{a_i' x - \bar{b}_i}{\sigma(b_i)} \leqslant \frac{b_i - \bar{b}_i}{\sigma(b_i)}\right] = 1 - F\left(\frac{a_i' x - \bar{b}_i}{\sigma(b_i)}\right) = u_i$$

$$0 \leqslant v_j, \quad u_i \leqslant 1, \quad c_j = \sum_{i=1}^{q} t_i C_{ij} \sim N(\bar{c}_j, \sigma(c_j)), \quad b_i \sim N(\bar{b}_i, \sigma(b_i))$$

where a_i' and a_j are the ith row and the jth column of matrix A and F is the cdf of a unit normal variate. For retaining convexity of the resulting constraint set one must choose $v_j \geqslant 0.5$ and $u_i \geqslant 0.5$. The chance constraints then become:

$$\lambda' a_j \geqslant \bar{c}_j + \beta_j \sigma(c_j), \quad \beta_j = F^{-1}(v_j) \geqslant 0$$
$$a_i' x \leqslant \bar{b}_i - \alpha_i \sigma(b_i), \quad \alpha_i = -F^{-1}(q - u_i) \geqslant 0 \qquad (5.6)$$
$$\lambda \geqslant 0, \quad x \geqslant 0, \quad \text{all } i = 1, 2, \ldots, m, \quad j = 1, 2, \ldots, n$$

It is clear that the standard deviation term $\sigma(c_j)$ involve the vector t in a nonlinear way; hence the deterministic constraints (5.6) are nonlinear, unless $v_j = u_i = 0.5$, when $\alpha_i = \beta_j = 0$ and we obtain the LP problem:

$$\max \quad \bar{c}'x - \bar{b}'\lambda \qquad (5.7)$$
$$\text{subject to} \quad \lambda'A \geqslant \bar{c}, Ax \leqslant \bar{b}, \lambda \geqslant 0, x \geqslant 0, t \geqslant 0$$

the effects of the nonlinear components $\sigma(c_j)$ when $\beta_j > 0$ are two-fold. First, it shows the sensitivity of the optimal solution obtained from the approximate linear model (5.7). In particular, if a specific set of t_i's are selected (i.e. each t_i equals $1/q$), so that $\sigma(c_j)$ reduces to a constant, one obtains the following primal-dual LP problems:

Primal

$$\max \sum_{j=1}^{n} \{\bar{c}_j + \beta_j \sigma(c_j)\} x_j$$

subject to

$$\sum_{j=1}^{n} a_{ij} x_j \leqslant \bar{b}_i - \alpha_i \sigma(b_i)$$

$$x_j \geqslant 0, j = 1, 2, \ldots, n$$

Dual

$$\min \sum_{i=1}^{m} \{\bar{b}_i - \alpha_i \sigma(b_i)\} \lambda_i$$

subject to

$$\sum_{i=1}^{m} \lambda_i a_{ij} \geqslant \bar{c}_j + \beta_j \sigma(c_j)$$

$$\lambda_i \geqslant 0, i = 1, 2, \ldots, m$$

Let x^*, λ^* be the optimal solutions. Then it is clear from duality that the difference $d^* = \bar{c}x^* - \bar{b}'\lambda^*$ tends to zero from below, as α_i, β_j tend to zero from above. Further we have $\partial d^*/\partial\alpha_i \leqslant 0$, $\partial d^*/\partial\beta_j \leqslant 0$. Second, a complete nonlinear problem can be set up so as to optimize the reliability levels u_i and v_j instead of preassigning them:

$$\text{max} \quad \sum_{j=1}^{n} v_j + \sum_{i=1}^{m} u_i$$

$$\text{subject to} \quad u_i \geqslant 0.5, \quad v_j \geqslant 0.5 \tag{5.8}$$

$$i = 1, 2, \ldots, m, j = 2, 3, \ldots, n$$

Assuming that the optimal solutions here can be computed, a trade-off analysis can then be performed between the system reliability and profits corresponding to the optimal solution denoted by (x^0, λ^0) say. The differences $|x^0 - x^*|$, $|\lambda^- - \lambda^*|$ would then characterize the robustness of the suboptimal or linearized solutions (x^*, λ^*).

A team decision problem under uncertainty leading to suboptimal solutions may arise when the constraint sets impose different decision regions for different members. For instance, assume that we have two decision regions

$$R(k) = \{x: \quad A(k)x \leqslant b(k), \quad x \geqslant 0\}, \quad k = 1, 2$$

one for each team member, such that $R(1)$ (or, $R(2)$) is not known to the second (or first) member. The objective function $z = \tilde{c}'x$, $x \in R_k$ assume $\tilde{c}$ to be random, distributed normally $N(\bar{c}, V)$ with means $\bar{c}$ and covariances V, which are estimable by each member from past realizations of $\tilde{c}$. Assume for simplicity that each member maximizes the following preference function

$$f(x) = \bar{c}'x - \alpha x^* V x, \quad x \in R(k), \quad \alpha > 0 \quad \text{(fixed)} \tag{5.9}$$

to select his optimal solution, $x^*(k)$ say. It is clear that due to lack of knowledge of other member's constraints, optimal solutions $x^*(1)$, $x^*(2)$ are suboptimal. If there were no lack of knowledge and the members could cooperate by pooling their resources a new decision region could be constructed as

$$R = \{x: \quad x \geqslant 0, \quad (\lambda A(1) + (1 - \lambda)A(2))x \leqslant \lambda b(1) + (1 - \lambda)b(2);$$

$$0 \leqslant \lambda \leqslant 1\}$$

Let x^* be the optimal solution maximizing $f(x)$ for $x \in R$. It is clear that the suboptimality of the solutions $x^*(k)$, in relation to the optimal solution x^* can be analyzed in this framework in several ways. First, the conditional distribution of z given $x^*(k)$, which is normal $N(\bar{c}'x^*(k)$,

$x^*(k)'Vx^*(k))$ may be compared with the unconstrained distribution, which is also normal $N(\bar{c}'x^*, x^{*'}Vx^*)$. For example, the differences in their coefficient of variation

$$d = \left| \frac{(x^{*'}Vx^*)^{1/2}}{\bar{c}'x^*} - \frac{(x^*(k)'Vx^*(k))^{1/2}}{\bar{c}'x^*(k)} \right|$$

would indicate their relative variability. If this difference is very large, one might characterize $x^*(k)$ as an outlier relative to x^*. Second, the cdf of two normal distributions F_1, F_2 corresponding to $N(\bar{c}'x^*(k), x^{*'}(k)Vx^*(k))$, $k = 1, 2$ may be analysed to see if they intersect or not. If they intersect, say at t_0 such that $F_1(t) > F_2(t)$ for $t > t_0$ and $F_1(t) \leq F_2(t)$, for $t \leq t_0$, then $F_2(t)$ would dominate $F_1(t)$ to the right of t_0 and vice versa for $t < t_0$. But if for all t in its domain, $F_1(t) \leq F_2(t)$, then $F_1(t)$ would dominate over $F_2(t)$ all throughout and we would have $\bar{c}'x^*(1) \geq \bar{c}'x^*(2)$. It is clear that if the intersection of the two sets $R(1)$, $R(2)$ is not empty, here will be some common points belonging to this nonempty intersection and in this case the two cdfs $F_1(t)$, $F_2(t)$ would overlap in some domain, without dominating one another all throughout. The size of this common domain defined by the nonempty intersections and the associated probability may be very important in many production applications. For instance, assume that the sets $R(1)$, $R(2)$ represent two technologies say old and new methods of producing a crop. For a level of input application $t > t_0$, the new technology may be more efficient in the sense of higher output for identical inputs. The reverse may be true for $t < t_0$. Hence, if the farmer is more confident of his future resource position, so that he assigns a higher probability on $t \geq t_0$, then his preference for the new technology is justified.

A slightly different minimax approach, due to Dyson and Swaithes (1978) is based on the wait and see model of stochastic linear programming. It is argued that the parameter values corresponding to the minimax solution cannot be obtained a priori. Hence it is necessary to specify a plausible region for the parameter values and incorporate this region into the model. One suggestion is that the boundary of this region should be an equi-probability contour of the joint distribution of the random parameters of the right hand side vector say. Thus, with a random resource vector β and a nonstochastic decision vector x, the minimax problem is

$$\min_{\beta} \max_{x} \quad z = c'x$$

subject to $Ax \leq b$ (deterministic)　　　　　　　　　(6.1)

$\qquad\qquad\quad Bx \leq \beta$ (stochastic β)

$\qquad\qquad\quad F(\beta) \leq k,\quad k$ constant

where $F(\beta) \leqslant k$ defines the region of random variations. Note that the constraint set of the minimax problem defined by (6.1) is not necessarily convex and hence the problem may have local optima. The problem is seen to be a non-zero-sum two-person game between player I (nature) and player II (the decision-maker). Once $\hat{\beta}$ has been chosen by player I from the set $\{F(\beta) \leqslant k\}$, player II solves the LP problem:

$$\max\{z = c'x, \quad Ax \leqslant b, \quad Bx \leqslant \hat{\beta}, \quad x \geqslant 0\} \tag{6.2}$$

Likewise, player I solves the programming problem

$$\min_{\beta \in D(\beta)} \left[\max_{x} \{c'x; Ax \leqslant b, Bx \leqslant \beta, x \geqslant 0\} \right]$$

where $\tag{6.3}$

$$D(\beta) = \{\beta: \text{there exists } x \geqslant 0 \text{ for which } Ax \leqslant b, Bx \leqslant \beta, F(\beta) \leqslant k\}$$

Note that (6.3) defines a nonconvex program and hence the problem may have local optima. The set of β values for which a given basis of the LP problem (6.2) is feasible and optimal is called a decision region and suitable decision regions are so imposed that for each decision region, the secondary problem defined by (6.3) is a convex program. Thus there will be one secondary problem of the type (6.3) for each decision region, where the secondary problem consists of minimizing a linear function over a convex region, suitably constructed as above.

If β is distributed as joint normal $N(\bar{\beta}, V_\beta)$ and the region of random variations is assumed to coincide with the equi-probability boundary that contains $(1 - \alpha)$ percent of the joint distribution of the stochastic vector β, then the minimax problem (6.1) can be set up as follows:

$$\min_{\beta} \max_{x} \quad z = c'x$$

$$\text{subject to} \quad Ax \leqslant b, \quad Bx \leqslant \beta, \quad x \geqslant 0 \tag{6.4}$$

$$F(\beta) = (\beta - \bar{\beta})' V_\beta^{-1} (\beta - \bar{\beta}) \leqslant k_\alpha$$

It is clear that it is very difficult to establish a simple analytic relation between k_α and the probability α; but once k_α is determined or subjectively preassigned, the minimax solution becomes well defined in (6.4). Two points are to be noted in this formulation. First, objective functions other than the minimax type can be analyzed, whenever they are meaningful e.g. a maximax solution: $\max_\beta \max_x z$, a maximin solution: $\max_x \min_\beta z$ and a maximal average solution: $\max_x z$, given that $\beta = \bar{\beta}$. Secondly, the last constraint in (6.4) may be related to the prior distribution or information on β and hence a process of successive improvement from the prior to the posterior can be characterized.

A closely related class of minimax solutions arises in LP models with stochastic objective functions: $z = c'x$, $c \in C$, $x \in X$ where C and X are suitable convex sets and the randomness of z may be due to both c and x, although one may be unable to specify completely the probability distributions of c and x. In some situations, it may be reasonable to restrict to conditional probability distribution $F(z \mid x)$ of profits z given x, when the latter can be specified e.g., two allocations $x(1)$, $x(2)$ say are to be compared in terms of the expected value of a suitable utility function $E\{H(c'x)\}$ where H is a concave function and E is expectation over variable c; $x(1)$ is to be preferred to $x(2)$ if the maximum of $E\{H(c'x(1))\}$ over $x(1)$ is greater than that of $E\{H(c'x(2))\}$ over $x(2)$. In other situations when the probability distributions can only be specified very incompletely, one may like to protect oneself against the worst that could happen, by choosing $x \in X$ to maximize $f(x) = \min_c E\{H(c'x)\}$ where the minimum with respect to $c \in C$ is taken over a class of distributions or a set of decision regions denoted by the set C. It is appropriate here to consider a game-theoretic interpretation. Suppose c and x are strategies played by two players N (for nature) and F (for farmer) and w_N, w_F are their respective utility levels or pay-off. If each player assumes the rival to do the worst against him, then the farmer's utility function is

$$F: \quad \max_{x \in X}\left\{ \min_{c \in C} w_F = w_F(c, x) \right\}$$

since the worst utility that N could inflict upon F is $\{\min_{c \in C} w_F\}$. Likewise, nature's utility function is

$$N: \quad \min_{c \in C} \max_{x \in X} w_N = w_N(c, x)$$

If c and x are assumed to be normally distributed i.e. $c \sim N(\bar{c}, V_c)$, $x \sim N(\bar{x}, V_x)$, then following the procedure in (6.4), the convex sets C and X may be specified by equiprobability boundaries as:

$$C: \quad \left\{ c \mid (c - \bar{c})' V_c^{-1}(c - \bar{c}) \leqslant k_\alpha \right\}$$

$$X: \quad \left\{ x \mid (x - \bar{x})' V_x^{-1}(x - \bar{x}) \leqslant k_a, \quad x \geqslant 0 \right\}$$

By suitably interpreting the utility or pay-off functions $w_F(c, x)$, $w_N(c, x)$ the following types of solution, if they exist can be specified in this framework e.g., (a) Cournot–Nash solution, (b) Pareto optimal solution and (c) von Neumann–Morgenstern solution. The structure of such solutions and their implications for application have been analyzed in the current literature (Sengupta 1980).

3. Stochastic Linear Control

Economic applications of control theory have grown extensively over the past decade, ranging from the limit pricing model of the firm (Gaskins 1971, Kamien and Schwartz 1971), monetary fiscal policies using macroeconometric models (Chow 1975, Kendrick 1981) and optimal stabilization policies under nonlinear dynamic models containing disturbances. From an applied viewpoint, one may single out three important trends that have proved most fruitful, yet challenging. These are:
(a) the theory of linear decision rules (LDR)
(b) the methods of adaptive control via learning, and
(c) stochastic differential games
To illustrate some of these trends, one may start with a specific form of the discrete-time control problem, that has been widely used:

minimize $\quad J = EL(x_N, u_{N-1}) = E\left\{ g(x_N) + \sum h(x_i, u_i, \xi_i) \right\}$

subject to $\quad x_{i+1} = f(x_i, u_i, \xi_i), \quad i = 0, 1, \ldots, N-1$

$\qquad\qquad x_0 = \text{constant}, \quad N \text{ fixed}$

$\qquad\qquad R(x_i, u_i) \leqslant 0; \ E: \text{expectation}$

$\qquad\qquad (\text{all } x_i, \xi_i \text{ are } n \text{ by one, all } u_i \text{ are } m \text{ by one vectors})$

Here $i = 1, 2, \ldots, N$ is the index of time, x_i and u_i are the state and control vectors and the functions g, h, f and R which may be nonlinear are assumed to be convex (with f strictly convex), with continuous second derivatives for its arguments and ξ_i is a random vector which must satisfy some regularity conditions of a stationary stochastic process. Define the vectors

$$x' = (x_1, x_2, \ldots, x_N), \quad U' = (u_0, u_1, \ldots, u_N)$$

$$F_1'(x, u, \zeta) = [f(x_0, u_0, \xi_0) - x_1, \ldots, f(x_{N-1}, u_{N-1}, \xi_{N-1}) - x_N]$$

$$F_2'(x, U) = [R(x_0, u_0), \ldots, R(x_{N-1}, u_{N-1})]$$

Then the control model (2.1) can be written as a nonlinear program, where ϕ is a suitable function derived from (7.1) by using the newly defined vectors X, U, ξ:

minimize $\quad J = E\phi(x, u, \xi)$

subject to $\quad F_1(x, u, \xi) = 0, \quad F_2(x, U) \leqslant 0$ $\qquad$ (7.2)

From a stochastic standpoint, some of the simplifying assumptions of this specification need be noted. First, there is no measurement or observation error in the sense that the state vector (x) is identical with the output vector z. If not, then another set of relations

$$z_i = w(x_i, \theta_i)$$

involving the stochastic vectors θ_i have to be incorporated, where z_i's are observable, while x_i's are not. Second, the constraints $F_2(x, u) \leqslant 0$ on X and U do not involve any random component, since only pure strategy solutions are required. Mixed strategy solutions involving randomized decision rules are therefore ignored here. Third, the nonlinear program (7.2) requires for its solvability that the set defined by the constraints is convex. However for some stochastic variations, the set may not be convex. Hence local optimality or lack of optimality may not be excludable. In this sense, the stochastic components in the model impose as it were a penalty or costs due to infeasibility or to local optimality, when our goal is to attain feasible and global optimality. As a matter of fact, the method of computation known as the sequential unconstrained minimization technique utilizes a variety of forms for the penalty function to be adjoined to the objective function of the original program.

Two special cases of the model (7.2) have been widely used in applied economic fields. One is the linear quadratic Gaussian (LQG) model, where J is quadratic in X and U, ξ is normally distributed and additive in $F_1(x, U, \xi) = 0$ and there are no constraints of the type $F_2(x, U) \leqslant 0$. In this case the model may appear in a simplified form as:

minimize $\quad J = E\left[\sum_{i=0}^{N-1} (x_i'Qx_i + u_i'Ru_i) \right]$

subject to $\quad x_{i+1} = Ax_i + Bu_i + \xi_i$

$\qquad\qquad x_0 = c, \quad$ a fixed constant

where it is assumed for simplicity that Q, R, A and B are constant parameters and the random vector ξ is distributed normally and independently of controls u_i with zero means and fixed covariances. For this to define a strictly convex program, where local optimality is also global, we would require the matrices Q and R to be positive definite. In most economic applications, x_i and u_i are measured as deviations $x_i - x_i^0$, $u_i - u_i^0$ from known desired levels x_i^0, u_i^0 and hence Q and R become identity matrices. For $N \to \infty$, a discounted form with $\delta > 0$ has also been widely used:

$$J = E\left\{ \sum_{i=0}^{\infty} (1 + \delta)^{-i} d_i^2 \right\}, \quad d_i^2 = \left(x_i - x_i^0 \right)^2 + \left(u_i - u_i^0 \right)^2 \tag{7.4}$$

Besides computational simplicity, this LQG formulation has a number of attractive features, which would be dealt with later. Certainty equivalence and sequential updating are the two properties most widely invoked. The first emphasizes the point the stochastic model is easily transformed to a deterministic form, by replacing the random variables ξ_i by their zero means. The second allows the conditional mean forecasts $\hat{x}_t$, given the current and past information. These forecasts use a method of filtering called Kalman–Bucy filters applied to sequential estimates of conditional means and variances of x_t.

The second special case of model (7.2) that has been widely applied is called adaptive control. There exist various forms of adaptation and hence several different forms of adaptive control. An excellent survey is given in Wittenmark (1975) and Saridis (1977). Two aspects appear to be most basic in all forms of adaptive control: one is to allow a change of model specification, either in the objective function or the system equations, through a process of information gathering on the system state and control; the second is to allow through learning functions a continuous (or continual) process of simultaneous estimation and regulation. All adaptations are based on the philosophy of reducible uncertainties, which are those that are unknown in the beginning but become reducible as the system evolves and observations are made. Thus, adaptive controls, in relation to LQG models may be viewed as methods for analyzing the robustness of LDR solutions, when some of the required assumptions of the LQG model do not hold.

Consider a simple example of a specific type of adaptive control, with multiplicative uncertainty, where the objective function is given in (7.4) but the state dynamics are:

$$x_{i+1} = \left(\overline{A}_i + \alpha_i \right) x_i + \left(\overline{B}_i + \beta_i \right) u_i + \xi_i$$
$$x_0 = c, \quad \text{a fixed constant} \tag{7.5}$$

which allow time-dependent coefficient matrices $A_i = \overline{A}_i + \alpha_i$, $B_i = \overline{B}_i + \beta_i$, where α_i, β_i represent random disturbances around the deterministic levels $\overline{A}_i$, $\overline{B}_i$. Several economic applications of this type of model are reported in current literature. Some special features of this type of model specified by (7.4) and (7.5) are worth emphasizing. First, one notes the tremendous increase in computational burden, where the stochastic components α_i, β_i enter nonlinearly. The sequential updating and certainty equivalence, the two most desirable properties of LQG models no longer hold and hence great care needs to be exercised in applying the model under evolutionary information structure i.e. when information on the system dynamics and system performance are known to be increasingly available over time. Second, even if $A_i = \bar{A} + \alpha_i$, $B_i = \bar{B} + \beta_i$ with $\bar{A}$ and $\bar{B}$ being time-independent and the random perturbations α_i, β_i are small in a small time-interval, these when associated with large deviation in the state vector or large amplitudes in the control vector may generate worse fluctuations in the optimal trajectory computed on the basis $\alpha_i = \beta_i = 0 = \xi_i$ for all i. For this reason, optimal control solutions restricted to a certain class e.g. linear decision rules of the form $u = u(x, t)$, where U is a linear function of x and t are sought as approximately optimal or suboptimal solutions. Besides LDR, several other types of cautious controls can be formulated by suitably redefining the class to which controls must belong. Third, since adaptivity with respect to past, current and future information about the system dynamics and its performance measure (i.e. the objective function) is most critical to all methods of adaptive stochastic control, it is of great importance to inquire how the twin objectives of estimation (or, learning) and control (or, regulating) are sought to be achieved in various adaptive methods. Following Saridis (1977), the definitions below provide some characterizations:

(a) "Adaptive control" (Gibson's definition): A dynamic system with "adaptive control" must provide continuous information about the state and its performance and thereby initiate a system modification, if necessary so as to drive the system towards the optimum performance or desired goal.

(b) "Learning control" (Fu's definition): The design of controllers which are capable of estimating the unknown information during the system's operation and an optimal control will be determined on the basis of the estimated information, such that the performance of the system will be gradually improved.

(c) "Dual control" (Feldbaum's definition): For systems with incomplete information about state dynamics in the beginning, the dual controls are designed to provide active accumulation of information during the control process, so as to permit subsequent feedback to the controller and easier attainment of desired or optimal states in the future.

(d) "Control as adaptation" (Tsypkin's definition): Adaptation property of a control is considered to be a process of modifying the parameters of the structure of the system and the control actions. The current information is used to obtain a definite, usually optimal state of the system, when the operating conditions are uncertain and time-vary-ing.

(e) "Self-organizing control" (Saridis' definition): A control process is called self-organizing or self-adaptive, if reduction of the a priori uncertainties associated with controlling the system is accomplished through information obtained from subsequent observations of inputs and outputs, as the control process evolves.

It is apparent from these alternative views on adaptive control, that learning through information provides the key to adaptivity. Newer forms of learning e.g. through qualitative information or fuzzy system statistics may thus provide a wider class of adaptive control methods, which provide an active field of research. From this standpoint, Feldbaum's terminology of dual vs. non-dual control seems most appropriate. According to this terminology, a control law is non-dual, if the system performance index takes into account only previous measurements and does not assume that further information will be available; otherwise it is dual. In the latter case, the control vector must be causally related to the state vector as in (7.5) and the dependence of the future observations on control will be specified as the probability distribution of future observations given information up to the actual time.

One important payoff from applying adaptive control methods is the designing of more cautious control policies (much like the minimax solutions of stochastic LP) which are more cautious than the certainty equivalence of the LQG model. A simple example from Wittenmark (1975) of a scalar system with one state and one control may illustrate the point. The system dynamics is

$$x_i - x_{i-1} = bu_{i-1} + e_i$$
$$b: \quad \text{unknown constant}, \quad e_i \sim N(0, \sigma^2), \quad \text{all i} \tag{8.1}$$

and we have to select u_i to minimize the loss or performance function

$$J = E\left\{ x_{i+1}^2 \mid x_i, x_{i-1}, \ldots, x_i(0), \quad u_{i+1}, \ldots, u_0 \right\}$$

From past observations, the unknown parameter b can be estimated by least squares as

$$\hat{b}_i = \left(\sum_{s=1}^{i} u_{s-1}^2 \right)^{-1} \left(\sum_{s=1}^{i} \left[u_{s-1} \{ x_x - x_{s-1} \} \right] \right)$$

with variance

$$v_i(b) = \left(\sum_{s=1}^{i} u_{s-1}^2 \right)^{-1} \sigma^2$$

If b were known in (8.1), then the optimal loss is given as:

$$\text{minimize}_{u_i} J = \min E\left\{(x_i + bu_i + e_{i+1})^2 \,|\, x_i, \ldots, u_{i-1}, \ldots\right\}$$

$$= \min\left\{(x_i + bu_i)^2 + \sigma^2\right\} = \sigma^2 \tag{8.3}$$

Here we have assumed that future errors e_{i+1} are uncorrelated with $(b, x_i, x_{i-1}, \ldots, x_0, u_{i-1}, \ldots, u_0)$ and the optimal control rule is:

$$u_i = -x_i/b \tag{8.4}$$

If the estimated value, $\hat{b}_i$ is used in (8.4) by assuming certainty equivalence, instead of a true value: $u_i = -x_i/\hat{b}_i$, then the optimal loss becomes

$$\min J = (\hat{b}_i^2)^{-1} v_i(b) x_i^2 + \sigma^2 \tag{8.5}$$

which is more than the optimal loss in (8.3) by the term $v_i(b)x_i^2/\hat{b}_i^2$. The control rule $u_i = -x_i/\hat{b}_i$ does not minimize the performance function (8.2). Since

$$J = E\left\{(x_i + bu_i + e_{i+1})^2 \,|\, x_i, \ldots, u_{i-1}, \ldots\right\}$$

$$= \left\{(x_i + \hat{b}_i u_i)^2 + v_i(b)u_i^2 + \sigma^2\right\}$$

the optimal control which minimizes this J is:

$$u_i = \frac{\hat{b}_i x_i}{\hat{b}_i^2 + v_i(b)} \tag{8.6}$$

and the associated optimal loss is

$$\min J = \frac{v_i(b)x_i^2}{\hat{b}_i^2 + v_i(b)} + \sigma^2$$

which is less than that in (8.5), since $v_i(b) \geqslant 0$. It is clear that the optimal control law (8.6) is cautious since it considers the inaccuracy of the estimate of b.

In a more general case the system dynamics may be represented by the mixed autoregressive moving average (ARMA) model:

$$x_i + a_1 x_{i-1} + \ldots + a_n x_{i-n} = b_0 u_{i-1} + b_1 u_{i-2} + \ldots + b_n u_{i-n-1} + e_i$$

which, on using the operators $Ax_i = x_{i-1}$, $Bu_i = u_{i-1}$ and the polynomials

$P(A) = 1 + a_1 A + \ldots + a_n A^n$, $Q(B) = b_0 + b_1 B + \ldots + b_n B^n$ may be expressed as

$$P(A)x_i = Q(B)u_{i-1} + e_i \tag{9.1}$$

where e_i is assumed to be normally independently distributed with zero mean and constant variance σ^2. Denoting the column vector of unknown parameters $(a_1, a_2, \ldots, a_n; b_0, b_1, \ldots, b_n)$ by θ and assuming it to be time-varying, the system dynamics may be reduced to:

$$x_{i+1} = H'_{i+1}\theta_{i+1} + e_{i+1} \tag{9.2}$$

where $H'_{i+1} = [-x_i, -x_{i-1}, \ldots, -x_{i-n+1}, u_{i-1}, \ldots, u_{i-n-1}]$ is the row vector containing past states and controls. The objective in choosing a cautious control is to minimize the loss function

$$J = E\left[(x_{i+1} - x^0)^2 \mid I_i\right] \tag{9.3}$$

where I_i is a vector containing all information available up to time i i.e. $I_i = [x_i, x_{i-1}, \ldots, x_0, u_{i-1}, \ldots, u_0]$. One possible method of solving this problem, known as self-tuning involves two steps. In the first step, the unknown parameters are estimated from (9.1) by using a Kalman filter, which gives the estimates $\hat{\theta}_{i+1}$ and the covariance matrix P_{i+1} say, based on information I_i obtained up to and including time i. Then, in the second step one uses (9.2) and $\hat{\theta}_{i+1}$, P_{i+1} into (9.3), so that the loss function may be written as

$$J = \left(H'_{i+1}\hat{\theta}_{i+1} - x^0\right)^2 + H'_{i+1}P_{i+1}H_{i+1} + \sigma^2 \tag{9.4}$$

Minimizing this loss function leads to the optimal self-tuning regulator, as derived in details by Wittenmark (1975):

$$u_i = \left[\hat{\theta}_{i+1}(n+1)x^0 - \sum_{j=1}^{2n+1}{}' \, [\hat{\theta}_{i+1}(n+1)\hat{\theta}_{i+1}(j) \right.$$

$$\left. + p_{i+1}(n+1,j)] \, H_{i+1}(j)\right]\left[\hat{\theta}_{i+1}^2(n+1) + p_{i+1}(n+1, n+1)\right]^{-1}$$

where Σ' means that the term corresponding to $j = n + 1$ is excluded from summation and $p_i(k, j)$ is the k, jth element of the covariance matrix P_i at time i, $H_{i+1}(j)$ is the jth component of vector H_{i+1} and $\hat{\theta}_i(j)$ denotes the jth component of the vector $\hat{\theta}_i$ of estimates at time i. Note that the

above optimal control clearly incorporates the following types of uncertainties:
(a) uncertainties of the parameter estimates $\hat{\theta}_{i+1}(j)$,
(b) the forecasting errors contained in the elements $p_{i+1}(n+1,j)$ of the covariance matrix P_{i+1}, and
(c) any uncertainty associated with the desired target x^0
These help the controller to adopt a more cautious control action, when the above uncertainties are very large. Thus, the control action can be turned off for some period of time until better estimates can be obtained with reduced uncertainties. Thus, a compromise or balance may be secured between the twin objectives of estimation and regulation.

There exist three other methods for handling this problem of joint estimation and control. One is the direct method proposed by Ljung et al. (1974), where we write the unknown control law as a linear structure

$$u_i = Fx_{i-1} + Ge_i \tag{10.1}$$

where the control rule is not necessarily optimal. This control structure, together with the system equations (9.1) may be incorporated into a simultaneous equations structure

$$u_i = Kx_{i-1} + Me_i, \qquad x_i = Fu_{i-1} + Ge_i \tag{10.2}$$

where $F = P^{-1}(A)Q(B)$, $G = P^{-1}(A)$. If the distribution of each e_i is joint multivariate normal with zero mean and unit variance, joint maximum likelihood estimates of the parameters of this system can be developed. The advantage of this formulation (10.2) is that the feedback control rule (10.1) need not be known beforehand. Two points must be noted in this approach. First, the separation of the two steps, estimation first and then control is not allowed here. In conventional applications of economic policy models (Fox, Sengupta and Thorbecke 1972), an econometric model of $x_i = Fu_{i-1} + Ge_i$ is first estimated from observations and then with parameter estimates $\hat{F}$, $\hat{G}$ treated as constants, a suitable loss function of the policymaker (which need not necessarily be of the form (9.4)) is minimized. In (10.2) it is presumed that the first equation is an approximate specification of a control law which admits of implicit minimization of the policymaker's loss function. Second, this specification (10.2) shows the contrast between optimal control and optimal estimation in a striking fashion. Thus, the first equation may be interpreted, in an LQG framework as a feedback control that is almost optimal, since taking expectations one obtains $Eu_i = Kx_{i-1}$. The second equation however is an typical reduced form, where the endogenous variables x_i are linear functions of the exogenous ones u_{i-1}.

Another method has been proposed by Chow (1975), who recognizes from the outset that some modification of the objective function (9.3) is required to take account of parameter uncertainty. Hence he suggests a modified form of objective function, which for quadratic loss would take the form

$$J = E\left\{ \sum_{i=1}^{T} \left[y_i m_{ii} y_i + \sum_{i<s} y_i m_{is} y_s + n_i y_i \right] \right\} \tag{10.3}$$

where $y_i = x_i - x^0$ and the terms (m_{is}) represent cost weighting placed on correlation between past system weights. It is assumed that the weights m_{ii}, m_{is}, n_i are either known or specified. Minimizing J in (10.3) subject to the second equation of (10.2) leads to an optimal control law, denoted by U^* say and the associated optimal loss becomes $J^* = J(U^*, x^*)$, where x^* denotes the set of optimal x_i^*'s associated with U^*. But since J^* is a highly nonlinear function, Chow approximates this by a suitable quadratic function, which is solved recursively in an iterative fashion, till convergence to optimal controls is achieved. Examples of applications of this method by Chow include typical Keynesian models with government spending and money supply as controls and consumption and investment levels being the target states. The experience from these applications, as emphasized by Chow, is that it is not worth incurring the increased computational burden of joint estimation and control, unless the parameter uncertainties or model specification uncertainties are very large.

A somewhat different type of reconciliation between an econometric model and an optimal control rule has been recently proposed by Klein and Su (1980), where the sensitivity of econometric model is analyzed through a two-stage iterative process. This method would be discussed later, since it has great computational advantages.

We have so far discussed control problems where the controller or policymaker is one rather than several. In the latter case, problems of differential game would arise. Suppose we have two players with control vectors U_1 and U_2 and we rewrite the constraints of model (7.2) as follows, by adding slack variables if necessary:

$$F(x, U, \xi) = F(x, U_1, U_2, \xi) = 0 \tag{11.1}$$

Let $J_k = E\phi(X, U_k, \xi)$, $k = 1$, 2 be the objective functions of the two players and let $J = w_1 J_1 + w_2 J_2$. The two-person game is said to be cooperative if w_1, w_2 are both positive and there exist an optimal pair of vectors U_1^*, U_2^* which maximize J. The game is noncooperative if w_1 and w_2 are opposite in sign; in particular the differential game is zero-sum, if $w_1 J_1 = -w_2 J_2$ so that the value of J at (U_1^*, U_2^*) is zero.

There are several areas of application of this framework of stochastic difference or differential game e.g. (a) the duopoly type market models, where the demand function has additive errors or parameters not completely known to each player, (b) models of limit pricing under uncertain entry and (c) problems of national planning and government policy. Some stochastic applications are reported in Kamien and Schwartz (1971), Levitan and Shubik (1971), Leitman (1975) and Sengupta (1982). This area provides an active field of research for several disciplines and we hope that in the near future there would be seen productive contributions to economic fields.

References

Charnes, A., Kirby, M., and W. Raike. Chance-constrained games with partially controllable strategies. Operations Research 16 (1968), 142–149.

Chow, G.C. Analysis and Control of Dynamic Economic Systems. New York: John Wiley, 1975.

Chu, K.C. Designing information structures for quadratic decision problems. Journal of Optimization Theory and Applications 25 (1978), 139–160.

Dyson, R.G., and G. Swaithes. A global algorithm for minimax solutions to a stochastic programming problem. Computers and Operations Research 5 (1978), 197–204.

Fox, K.A., Sengupta, J.K., and E. Thorbecke. The Theory of Quantitative Economic Policy with Applications to Economic Growth Stabilization and Planning, 2nd ed. Amsterdam: North Holland, 1972.

Gaskins, D., Dynamic limit pricing: optimal pricing under threat of entry. Journal of Economic Theory 3 (1971), 306–322.

Isaacs, H.H. Sensitivity of decisions to probability estimation errors. Operations Research 11 (1963), 536–552.

Kall, P. Stochastic Linear Programming. Berlin: Springer, 1976.

Kamien, M., and N. Schwartz. Limit pricing and uncertain entry. Econometrica 39 (1971), 441–450.

Kendrick, D. Stochastic Control for Economic Models. New York: McGraw Hill, 1981.

Klein, L.R., and V. Su. Recent economic fluctuations and stabilization policies: an optimal control approach, in Klein, L.R., Nerlove, M., and S.C. Tsiang, eds., Quantitative Economics and Development. New York: Academic Press, 1980.

Kolbin, V.V. Stochastic Programming. Dordrecht, Holland: Reidel Publishing, 1977.

Leitman, G. Cooperative and non-cooperative differential games, in J.D. Grote, ed., The Theory and Applications of Differential Games. Dordrecht, Holland: Reidel Publishing, 1975.

Levitan, R., and M. Shubik. Non-cooperative equilibria and strategy spaces in an oligopolistic market, in H.W. Kuhn and G.P. Szego, eds. Differential Games and Related Topics. Amsterdam: North Holland, 1971.

Ljung, L., Gustavsson, I., and T. Soderstrom. Identification of linear multivariable systems operating under linear feedback control. IEEE Transactions on Automatic Control AC-19 (1974), 836–840.

Prekopa, A. Contributions to the theory of stochastic programming. Mathematical Programming 4 (1973), 202–221.

Saridis, G.N. Self-organizing Control of Stochastic Systems. New York: Marcel Dekker, 1977.

86

Sengupta, J.K. Stochastic quadratic games with applications. Working Paper No. 127, Department of Economics, University of California, Santa Barbara, 1979.

Sengupta, J.K. Minimax solutions in stochastic programming, Cybernetics and Systems: An International Journal 11 (1980), 1–19.

Sengupta, J.K. Decision Models in Stochastic Programming. New York: North Holland, 1982.

Szego, G.P. Portfolio Theory. New York: Academic Press, 1980.

Whittle, P. Optimization under constraints. New York: John Wiley, 1971.

Wittenmark, B. Stochastic adaptive control method: a survey. International Journal of Control 21 (1975), 705–730.

Vajda, S. Probabilistic Programming. New York: Academic Press, 1972.

II. Linear quadratic models

3. Informetric analysis of dynamic decision rules in applied economic models: a selective survey

1. Introduction

Dynamic decision rules have been widely applied in economic and socio-economic models of intertemporal optimization, from production scheduling problems of a single enterprise to stabilization policies in a macroeconomic econometric models for the whole economy. The usual conditions required for optimality of these decision rules assume the structure of linear quadratic Gaussian (LQG) models of optimal control, which leads to linear decision rules (LDR), that are optimal against the class of uncertainty postulated. For the LDR, the optimal control vector $u(t)$ – can be expressed as a linear function $u(t) = u(\hat{x}(t))$ of the estimate $\hat{x}(t)$ of the state vector and if the additive errors in the state vector are Gaussian such that its covariances are independent of past controls, then the optimal control law can be expressed as: $u(t) = K(t)$ $m(t)$, where $m(t)$ is the conditional mean forecast of the state vector $x(t)$, given the current information and $K(t)$ is the gain matrix which satisfies a discrete-time Riccati equation. The above control law has several well-known properties (Chow 1975, Hay and Holt 1975, Jacobs 1980, Kendrick 1981, Schneeweiss 1975, Wittenmark 1975), e.g., (a) separability or sequential updating, (b) neutrality or independence from future uncertainty, (c) certainty equivalence or, transformation to a deterministic from with random variables replaced by their means and (d) computational flexibility if suboptimal controllers are desired. By the separability property, the two functions of estimation of the current state $x(t)$ from past observations and of implementing a control law based on the estimate $\hat{x}(t)$ can be separately performed and combined. Since the forecasts or state estimates $\hat{x}(t)$ are conditional means, given the current and past information, the sequential updating of forecasts with additional information permits the optimal LDR to be flexible over the planning horizon. In recent economic applications (Belsley 1969, Sengupta 1981, Zellner 1971), questions have been posed on the appropriateness of this sequential updating or separability property, when the LQG model holds only approximately for the economic system. It has also been emphasized, particularly in production-inventory models (Duffy and

Lewis 1975, Sengupta and Sfeir 1979) and stabilization policy models (Turnovsky 1975, Waud 1976) that the neutrality property may be very restrictive, since it excludes any probing of future uncertainty. Further, the price variables in economic models do not usually follow a Gaussian process and other economic variables are also known to follow non-normal stochastic processes (Lane and Littlechild 1980, ReVelle and Gundelach 1980, Tintner and Sengupta 1972). It is necessary therefore to consider some robustness analysis of the LDR approach, when it is applied to economic and social systems.

Unlike the traditional LDR approach where the stochastic components enter as additive disturbances in the state equations, the problem may arise in detecting signals from measurements and estimating them, and sufficient information may not be available. Two classes of approaches (Kelsey and Haddad 1974, Bar-Shalom and Tse, 1975) are considered in such cases of incomplete information, e.g., minimax and adaptive schemes. A minimax solution to an estimation problem seeks to minimize a given cost function for the worst case values of the unknown statistical parameters, within a certain range of possible parameter values determined from the a priori knowledge. However this approach may turn out to be too conservative. The adaptive scheme on the other hand, depending on the nature of adaptation may build into the decision rule elements that are partly forecast and partly regulatory. However, such schemes generally involve computational complexity and some minimum adaptation time to process enough data so that an acceptable estimate may be generated. It is useful therefore to consider methods for combining these schemes so that an optimal trade-off between regulation and experimentation may be determined.

The payoff or the performance functional in the models is assumed completely specified as a quadratic functional. Here also there may be incomplete information, due to which the payoff may be only partly known. A common example arises in two-person differential games with a nonzero sum and non-cooperative payoff, where each player has to estimate other's strategy before determining his own optimal strategy. In some case, e.g., two-person stochastic quadratic games, where the expected payoff of each player is a suitable quadratic functional and the state equations are linear in the two strategy vectors, this may lead to a pair of optimal LDR, one for each player. However, each optimal LDR must contain a forecast or estimate of the opponent's strategy. Hence, if the mutual forecasts are neither compatible nor realized over time, adaptive adjustments must go on. Role of information here may be stabilizing or destabilizing; in the former case the process of adaptive adjustments is helped by the information sequence to arrive at a converging solution, whereas in the latter case the adjustments are of a diverging nature.

The informetric analysis attempted here seeks to illustrate these and other related aspects of informational implications of linear and nonlinear decision rules, e.g., robustness of these rules, their adaptivity in probing and regulation and their stability in the sense of converging to a game-theoretic solution, e.g., Nash equilibrium. Illustrative cases are drawn from aggregate production planning, where the LDR was first applied by Holt, Modigliani, Muth and Simon [1960] in what is known as HMMS model and macroeconomic stabilization policies (Chow 1975, Prescott 1975) where control-theoretic rules have been most frequently applied and simulated.

2. Robustness of Decision Rules

In this section we discuss two simple methods of robustness of LDR in discrete time models and show how sensitive the optimal LDR may be in respect of simple departures from the assumptions of the LQG model. In the first case, some restrictions are imposed on the additive stochastic component, so that the resulting error distribution is truncated normal, rather than normal. In the second case, the effect of control or instrument variables on the targets is not necessarily normally distributed, so that the conditional variance of the targets, given the control vector is not constant. Hence there is an additional cost of control, depending on the conditional variance and may be equated to cost of probing or experimentation.

The general form of the discrete time control model used here is:

$$\text{minimize} \quad L = \sum_{t=0}^{N-1} \tfrac{1}{2} \left[x'(t)Qx(t) + u'(t)Ru(t) \right] \quad (1)$$

$$\text{subject to} \quad x(t+1) = Ax(t) + Bu(t) \quad (2)$$
$$x(0) = x_0$$

Given the initial point $x(0)$ and the fixed parameters Q, R, A, B, determine a sequence of control or instrument vectors $\{u(0), u(1), \ldots, u(N-1)\}$ which minimizes the cost functional (1) subject to (2), assuming of course the existence of such a control sequence. If N is fixed, Q, R, are time-independent, symmetric positive definite, then it is known that the optimal control sequence and the associated state vectors satisfy the following conditions of Pontryagin's discrete maximum principle:

$$Qx(t) + A'\lambda(t+1) - \lambda(t) = 0, \quad t = 0, 1, 2, \ldots, N-1 \quad (3.1)$$

$$Ru(t) + B'\lambda(t+1) = 0, \quad t = 0, 1, 2, \ldots, N-1 \quad (3.2)$$

$$Ax(t) + Bu(t) - x(t+1) = 0, \quad t = 0, 1, 2, \ldots, N-1 \qquad (3.3)$$

$$\lambda(N) = 0 \quad \text{(Transversality condition)} \qquad (3.4)$$

Since this defines a two-point boundary value problem (3.1) has to be solved backwards starting at the end point $\lambda(N)$, which is zero by (3.4) and $x(t)$ has to be solved forward starting from x_0. Since we have

$$\lambda(t) = Qx(t) + A'\lambda(t+1)$$

$$u(t) = -R^{-1}B'\lambda(t+1)$$

it is clear that the optimal control $u(\tau)$ at any time τ, $1 \leqslant \tau \leqslant N-1$ can be expressed as a suitable linear function of $x(N)$, $x(N-1), \ldots, x(\tau+1)$, $x(\tau)$:

$$u(\tau) = c_0 + C_0 x(\tau) + C_1(\tau+1) + \ldots + C_N x(N) \qquad (3.5)$$

where c_0, C_0, $C_1, \ldots, C_N$ are suitable coefficient terms depending on the original parameters A, B, Q, R. The multiperiod nature of the optimal solution (3.5) even in this deterministic problem must be emphasized. First, even the first-period optimal control $u(1)$ depends on the future states $x(2), \ldots, x(N-1)$, $x(N)$ which may not be completely known in the first period. Second, a perfect forecast of the future shadow prices $\lambda(2), \ldots, \lambda(N-1)$, $\lambda(N)$ must be obtained through solving the complementary difference equations (3.1) and (3.3) after $u(t)$ is eliminated by using (3.2). Third, this process must be repeated for the second, third and later periods in determining optimal controls $u(2)$, $u(3)$, etc. In the LDR model we have additionally the additive stochastic component $\epsilon(t)$ as

$$x(t+1) = Ax(t) + Bu(t) + \epsilon(t+1)$$
$$x(0) = x_0: \quad \text{completely known} \qquad (4)$$

and the objective function is

minimize EL \qquad (5)

where E is expectation over the stochastic component $\epsilon(t)$, which is assumed to be normally independently distributed, i.e., independently of the control vector with zero mean and fixed variance-covariance matrix. In this stochastic case, the optimal control $u(\tau)$ in (3.5) must additionally be a function of the future random variables $\epsilon(\tau+1)$, $\epsilon(\tau+2), \ldots, \epsilon(N)$ or their conditional expectations, i.e.,

$$u(\tau) = f(x(\tau), x(\tau+1), \ldots, x(N); \epsilon(\tau), \epsilon(\tau+1), \ldots, \epsilon(N)) \qquad (6)$$

Hence the optimal decision problem here separates into two parts. First, one calculates forecasts of the disturbance component $\epsilon(t)$ and then one treats the decision problem as a deterministic one, in which of course after each decision period, all forecasts have to be updated. If the future forecasts $\hat{\epsilon}(t)$ are unbiased then $E\hat{\epsilon}(t) = 0$ and hence the LDR (3.5) essentially holds. Note the two most critical assumptions required for this kind of certainty equivalence. First, the conditional variance of $x(t+1)$ given $u(t)$ must be independent of $u(t)$, so that the variance of the stochastic components $\epsilon(t)$, $\epsilon(t+1)$ has no effect on the optimal LDR and second, the knowledge or information about the joint probability distribution $p(\epsilon(0), \epsilon(1), \ldots, \epsilon(N))$ must be complete in the sense that its parameters, say θ are either known or estimable by a set of sufficient statistics $\hat{\theta}$. Since these sufficient statistics $\hat{\theta}$ have the property that the conditional distribution $p(\tilde{\theta} \mid \hat{\theta})$ of any other statistic $\tilde{\theta}$ does not involve the parameter θ, hence any information contained in other estimators $\tilde{\theta}$ cannot offer any improvement over the sufficient statistics $\hat{\theta}$. However the sufficiency requirement must hold for any τ in (6), for otherwise the information structure would be only partial or incomplete. In the latter case adaptive decision rules (Chu 1976, Macrae 1972, Sengupta 1982) of different sorts can be introduced. For instance let us introduce information channels H through a linear relation between the measurements $y(t)$ and the state vector $x(t)$

$$y(t) = Hx(t) + v \tag{7.1}$$

where v is a zero mean Gaussian random vector independently distributed with a constant variance-covariance matrix. In this case if the matrix H is not of full rank, information structure is known to be incomplete. Another important case arises when the measurement space Y of $y(t)$ can be divided into two exclusive and exhaustive regions $Y^{(1)}$, $Y^{(2)}$ such that for $y(t) \in Y^{(i)}$, the estimate $\hat{\theta}_i$, $i = 1, 2$ holds. This case has been applied frequently in economic models of change of regimes (Goldfeld and Quandt 1976). In particular applications to truncated normal distributions have been made by Amemiya (1973). Note that if one could correctly predict which of the two states $Y^{(1)}$, $Y^{(2)}$ are actually realized, then, conditional on this information we could define a "conditional certainty equivalent", a concept used by Keeney and Raiffa (1976) to describe a class of certainty equivalence when the decision-maker's conditional utility (or loss) function given the actual state of the world $Y^{(i)}$ may be incorporated in the original objective function. An example of this situation is now considered with reference to the HMMS model mentioned before, where the probability $\text{prob}[\epsilon(t) \geq 0]$ characterizes one of the two states.

EXAMPLE 1: This model is derived from the empirical HMMS model with the state equations

$$I(t) = I(t-1) + z(t) - x(t) \tag{8.1}$$

$I(t)$, $z(t)$, $x(t)$ are nonnegative for all t and the objective function

$$EQ(N) = \sum_{t=1}^{N} q(t). \tag{8.2}$$
$$q(t) = c(z(t), w(t)) + r(I(t))$$

Here employment, output, inventory and demand rates per unit time t are denoted by $w(t)$, $z(t)$, $I(t)$ and $x(t)$, where $x(t)$ is assumed to contain a random component satisfying the LQG assumptions with the cost functions $c(\cdot)$, $r(\cdot)$ being assumed quadratic and strictly convex. In the HMMS framework, the cost components $c(\cdot)$, $r(\cdot)$ due to production and inventories were estimated by least squares methods from past observations as

$$c(z(t), w(t)) = \hat{c}_1 w(t) + \hat{c}_2 (w(t) - w(t-1))^2 + \hat{c}_3 (z(t)$$
$$- \hat{c}_4 w(t))^2 + \hat{c}_5 z(t) - \hat{c}_6 w(t)$$
$$r(I(t)) = \hat{c}_7 (I(t) - \hat{c}_8 - \hat{c}_9 x(t))^2$$

with the following estimates

$$(\hat{c}_1, \hat{c}_2, \ldots, \hat{c}_9) = (340, 64.3, 0.20, 5.67, 51.2, 281.0, 0.0825, 320, 0.0)$$

and the optimal LDR obtained in the form

$$z(\tau) = \sum_{i=0}^{\tau-1} \hat{a}_i x(\tau + i) + \sum_{i=1}^{\tau-1} \hat{b}_i w(\tau - i) + \sum_{i=1}^{\tau-1} \hat{d}_i I(\tau - i) + \hat{a}_0$$
$$w(\tau) = \sum_{i=0}^{\tau-1} \hat{\alpha}_i x(\tau + i) + \sum_{i=1}^{\tau-1} \hat{\beta}_i w(\tau - i) + \sum_{i=1}^{\tau-1} \hat{\delta}_i I(\tau - i) + \hat{\alpha}_0 \tag{8.3}$$

where terms like $\hat{a}_i$, $\hat{b}_i$, $\hat{d}_i$, $\hat{\alpha}_i$, etc. are functions of the estimated quantities mentioned before. Since these optimal LDR depend on future values $x(\tau + i)$, it is clear that conditional forecasts $\hat{x}(\tau + i \mid y(\tau))$, given the information $y(\tau)$ available up to τ have to be used to update these for each τ, $\tau + 1$, before these rules are applied. It is clear that the error variance of such forecasts will affect the quality of optimality of LDR.

To compare the performance of the LDR (8.3) we constructed alternative linear decision rules of the following feedback form:

$$z(\tau) = \alpha x(\tau - 1) + (1 - \alpha) x(\tau - 2) - \beta I(\tau - 1) - (1 - \beta) I(\tau - 2)$$

where the coefficients α, β are to be within the interval $(0,1)$ in some optimal fashion. The system equations now become

$$\left(1 - \phi_1 B - \phi_2 B^2\right) I(\tau) = -\left(1 - \theta_1 B - \theta_2 B^2\right) x(\tau) \tag{8.4}$$

where B is an operator such that $Bs(t) = s(t - 1)$ and $\phi_1 = 1 - \beta$, $\phi_2 = \beta - 1$, $\theta_1 = \alpha$, $\theta_2 = 1 - \alpha$. However any value of β within the interval $0 \leqslant \beta < 1$ contributes a complex root of the characteristic equation of (8.4) and as β tends to one, the characteristic roots tend to zero. Hence we considered feedback control action of the form

$$z(\tau) = \alpha x(\tau - 1) + (1 - \alpha) x(\tau - 1) + \delta(\tau), \ \tau = 2, 3, \ldots, N$$

which yields the mean and variance functions

$$\bar{z}(\tau) = \alpha \bar{x}(\tau - 1) + (1 - \alpha) \bar{x}(\tau - 2) + \bar{\delta}(\tau)$$

$$\sigma_z^2(\tau) = \alpha^2 \sigma_x^2(\tau - 1) + (1 - \alpha)^2 \sigma_x^2(\tau - 2) + \sigma_\delta^2(\tau)$$

It is clear that the variance function $\sigma_\delta^2(\tau)$ is minimized by a value α satisfying

$$\alpha = \sigma_x^2(\tau - 2) / \left[\sigma_x^2(\tau - 1) + \sigma_x^2(\tau - 2)\right]$$

which however can be realized only if there are no other constraints on the mean and variance of the production process $z(\tau)$ and $x(\tau)$ is statistically independent of the term $\delta(\tau)$. We impose however the probabilistic restriction

$$\text{Prob}\left[I(0) + \sum_{i=1}^{k} (z(i) - x(i)) \geqslant 0\right] \geqslant \epsilon(k), \quad k = 1, 2, \ldots, N$$

where $\epsilon(k)$ is the tolerance level preassigned or determined as a decision variable. This inequality stipulates that we seek optimal decisions in the class which puts a heavy penalty on lost sales and this generates a conditional loss function. The HMMS model now gets transformed as follows:

minimize $EQ(N) = \sum_{t=1}^{N} \Big[(\hat{c}_1 - \hat{c}_6)w(t) + \hat{c}_2(w(t) - w(t-1))^2$

$$+ \hat{c}_3(\bar{x}(t) + \delta(t) - \hat{c}_4 w(t))^2$$

$$+ \hat{c}_5 \delta(t) + \hat{c}_7 \Big(I(0) + \sum_{i=1}^{t} \delta(i) - \hat{c}_8 - \hat{c}_9 \bar{x}(t) \Big)^2 \Big] \qquad (8.5)$$

subject to $\quad I(0) + \sum_{i=1}^{t} \delta(i) \geqslant s(t)a(t)\sigma_x(t)$

$$\delta(t) \geqslant -(\bar{x}(t) - 3b(t)\delta_x(t))$$

where

$$a(t) = \left[1 + (1-\alpha)^2\right]^{1/2} \quad \text{for} \quad t \geqslant 2 \quad \text{and}$$
$$= 1 \qquad\qquad\qquad \text{for} \quad t = 1$$

$$b(t) = 1 \quad \text{for} \quad t \geqslant 3 \quad \text{and}$$
$$= \alpha \quad \text{for} \quad t = 2 \quad \text{and}$$
$$\text{zero} \qquad \text{for} \quad t = 1$$

$$s(t) = F^{-1}(\epsilon(t)),$$

F = cumulative distribution of a unit normal $N(0,1)$ variate

Here a lower bound on the demand variable $x(t)$ has been placed so as to specify nonnegativity of production $z(t)$ for all $t = 1, 2, \ldots, N$. The optimal decision rules derived here are caled quadratic programming (QP) rules and these are compared with the optimal LDR of the HMMS model by means of the following cost functional

$$C(N) = \sum_{t=1}^{N} \Big[(\hat{c}_1 - \hat{c}_6)w(t) + \hat{c}_h(w(t) - w(t-1))^+ + \hat{c}_j(w(t) - w(t-1))^-$$

$$+ \hat{c}_v(z(t) - \hat{c}_4 w(t))^+ + \hat{c}_m(z(t) - \hat{c}_4 w(t))^-$$

$$+ \hat{c}_5 z(t) + \hat{c}_g I^+(t) + \hat{c}_s I^-(s) \Big]$$

where $\hat{c}_j$'s empirically estimated from the HMMS model and the notation q^+, q^- is as follows:

$$q^+ = q, \quad \text{if} \quad q \geq 0 \quad \text{and} \quad \text{zero otherwise}$$

$$q^- = -q, \quad \text{if} \quad q \leq 0 \quad \text{and} \quad \text{zero otherwise}$$

Then a series of pseudo-random numbers was generated from a normal distribution with mean 500 and standard deviation 100 and these were used as random demand for 10 time units for each decision rule separately. The operating costs for the two classes of decision rules were as follows:

	QP rules	LDR
Mean	349650.5	534541.6
Variance	31450.8	310526.5

for which $\alpha = 0.7$, $I(0) = 200$ and $w(0) = 80$. The empirical results were further tested to see if the two classes of decision rules differ in their distributions of operating costs. The nonparametric Kolmogorov–Smirnov test showed the difference to be statistically significant at 1 percent level. Further the optimal value $\alpha = 0.7$ used above turned out to be statistically different from the value $\alpha = 0.5$ which would be generated if there were no other constraints on the decision rule. The effects of truncation in the sample space may partly explain this result, since the variances of production and employment are both increased as α moves away from the value 0 7 in either direction. It is clear that in terms of mean operating cost, the QP rules perform better than the LDR.

Following the line of reasoning in the scheme of feedback controller (8.4), one may propose other types of decision rules. Note that in the original application of HMMS model to production scheduling in a paint factory, the authors estimated the cost functions for output, inventory and employment from past observed data by applying least squares. Then using these parameter estimates, they developed linear optimal control laws in the form of LDR for the future planning period. Since feedback control laws of the form (8.4) provided better results, even when there were inequality constraints, one could consider applying the theory of optimal design (Fedorov 1972, Sengupta 1982) to obtain optimal parameter estimates, when the feedback control coefficients are included. For instance, consider the inventory-output relation (8.1), taking each variable in terms of deviations from respective means and apply the feedback controller as:

$$z(t) = \bar{x}(t) - \alpha_1 I(t-1) + \beta_2 z(t-1)$$

to obtain

$$I(t) = \beta_1 I(t-1) + \beta_2 z(t-1) - e(t), \quad \beta_1 = 1 - \alpha_1, \quad 0 < \beta < 1$$

where $e(t)$ is the white noise error process by assumption and $\bar{x}(t)$ is the mean of the demand process $x(t)$. Following the optimal design theory, we may choose β_1, β_2 by several criteria, e.g., (a) maximize the trace of the information matrix associated with the least squares type estimate, (b) minimize the generalized variance of the estimates of β_1 and β_2, or (c) minimize the sum of the variance of inventory and output. In each case there are several choices available. For example, if we follow the second approach, we have to maximize the determinant

$$D = \begin{vmatrix} E(I^2(t)) & E(I(t)z(t)) \\ E(I(t)z(t)) & E(z^2(t)) \end{vmatrix}$$

where

$$E(I^2(t)) = \sigma_I^2 = \sigma_z^2 \beta_2^2 \frac{1+2k}{1-\beta_1^2} + \frac{\sigma_e^2}{1-\beta_1^2}$$

$$E(I(t)z(t)) = (\sigma_z^2 \beta_2 k)/\beta_1$$

$$E(z^2(t)) = \sigma_z^2,$$

$$k = \sum_{i=1}^{\infty} \beta_1^i r_1 \quad \text{and} \quad r_i = E[z(t)z(t-1)]/\sigma_z^2$$

The value of the determinant D may be written in terms of the variance σ_z^2 of production as

$$D = \frac{\sigma_z^2 \sigma_e^2}{1-\beta_1^2} + \frac{\beta_2^2 \sigma_z^4}{(1-\beta_1^2)^2} - \frac{\sigma_z^4 \beta_2^2}{\beta_1^2}\left[k - \frac{\beta_1^2}{1-\beta_1^2}\right]^2$$

One may now seek solutions with either σ_z^2 fixed or σ_I^2 fixed (or a combination). In the first case, one possible solution is to set $r_i = \beta_1^i$ that is, one has to force the control input $z(t)$ to follow the autoregressive process $(1 - \beta_1 B)z(t) = \epsilon(t)$, $\epsilon(t)$ being a white noise process with variance $\sigma_\epsilon^2 = \sigma_z^2(1 - \beta_1^2)$. In the second case when the variance of inventory, σ_I^2 is fixed, one may maximize D by setting $r_i = (-\beta_1 q)^i$, where $q = \sigma_I^2(\sigma_I^2 - \sigma_e^2)^{-1}$. This forces the control input $z(t)$ to follow the autoregressive process $(1 + \beta_1 q B)z(t) = \epsilon(t)$, where B is the lag operator and $\epsilon(t)$ a white noise process with variance $\sigma_\epsilon^2 = \sigma_z^2(1 - \beta_1^2 q^2)$.

These results emphasize that by dropping the assumption of neutrality, feedback controllers can sometimes be developed, which has been discussed in control theory literature as "self-tuning regulators" (Box and Jenkins 1976, Wittenmark 1975).

There is one additional point about the cost function in the HMMS model, where one component of cost of inventories for instance assumed a quadratic function in terms of deviations from a desired or target level. The fact that such a desired or target level, which is not observable may have to be estimated from observed data leads to a two-stage problem of estimation as pointed out by Kennan (1979) and a similar two-stage view can be adopted in the control period.

EXAMPLE 2: This example (Sengupta and Sfeir 1981) considers the stability of the eigenvalues resulting from the optimal LDR of type (6), when the matrices A, B contain elements that are statistically estimated from observed empirical data. In several empirical studies (Childs 1967, Duffy and Lewis 1975) the reasonableness of the LQG model has been sought to be established by estimating the LDR from aggregate industry data. Thus the model due to Childs (1967) minimizes an intertemporal function over a planning horizon $1 \leqslant t \leqslant N$ which is quadratic in the costs of adjusting three decision variables: production $x(t)$, inventories $H(t)$ and unfilled orders $U(t)$. The resulting optimal decision rules may be written as

$$y(t) = \alpha + Ay(t-1) + \sum_{j=0}^{N} b_j O(t+j) \tag{9.1}$$

where $y(t)$ is a column vector with elements $U(t)$, $H(t)$, $X(t)$ and $O(t+j)$ is the future order rates or demand for which an expected value forecast must be used in empirical application. The elements in vectors b_j, α and the matrix A are the coefficients reflecting various cost adjustments that are to be estimated from observed data. For example the forecast values $\hat{O}(t+j)$ may be obtained as regression functions of past order rates, etc. It is clear however from (9.1) that so long as the forecasts $\hat{O}(t+j)$ have finite error variance, the major source of instability and/or oscillations in the LDR (9.1) would be due to the characteristic roots which enter into the solution of the homogeneous part of (9.1) These roots satisfy the characteristic equation

$$|A - \lambda I| = 0 \tag{9.2}$$

where any complex root containing a nonzero imaginary part contributes to oscillations or sinusoidal fluctuations. Further, it is necessary though not sufficient for stability of the system that the characteristic roots must have their real parts less than unity. Hence if the elements of matrix A are statistically estimated, their standard errors will be available and using these one could test statistically the eigenvalue stability of the LDR. Several empirical studies on aggregate industry data attempted by us confirm in general in high degree of stability of the LDR. In particular, the existence of a futures market tends to impart a strong stabilizing tendency through competitive transmission of market information. This was evident from our LDR estimates of the plywood industry (unsanded variety), where the pre-futures period June 1966 through December 1969 can be clearly distinguished from the futures period January 1970 through June 1975. Statistical tests of eigenvalues through multivariate T^2 and also Chow-tests for sets of regression coefficients confirmed the stabilizing impact of the futures trading by eliminating the oscillatory tendency of the pre-futures era. Further, the LDR estimates of the model (9.1) performed better in terms of R^2 and standard error of the estimated coefficients, when perfect forecasts were used in place of $O(t+j)$; in other words, errors of forecast of the future order rates did affect the precision of the LDR as predictive relations.

3. Value of Information in Decision Rules

Three major sources of inoptimality of linear decision rules may arise in many practical economic applications, e.g., macrodynamic stabilization policy or, the choice of monetary and fiscal policies. These are due to the following:'
(a) the conditional variance $V(y(t)|x(t))$ of the state or the target variable $y(t)$ may not be independent of the instrument or the control variable $x(t)$,
(b) the objective function $J_0 = EJ(y(t), X(t), \theta)$ depending on the set of parameters θ may be more nonlinear than quadratic, e.g., it may be quadratic only for a certain set of values of $x(t)$ and θ and non-quadratic for others, and
(c) some of the parameters like θ, either in the objective function or the system equation may not be completely known, so that some methods of learning may have to be built into any decision rules that are to be practically applied.
The value of information in this framework may be assessed in its positive and negative aspects. Let $\{x^*(t), 1 \leqslant t \leqslant N\}$ be the optimal control sequence derived under the assumption that the above three sources of inoptimality are negligible and let $\{x^{**}(t), 1 \leqslant t \leqslant N\}$ be the optimal policy when the above sources of inoptimality are incorporated. Then if the true state of nature is such that $x^{**}(t)$ is indeed the true

optimal decision rule, then the positive value of information is characterized by any improvement that can be made on $x^*(t)$ so that it can come closer to, or be identical with $x^{**}(t)$. A natural measure would be in terms of improvement of return R

$$R = EJ\big(y^{**}(t), x^{**}(t)\, \theta^{**}\big) - EJ\big(y^*(t), x^*(t), \theta^*\big) > 0$$

where $EJ(\cdot)$ denotes the expected value of return to be maximized. The negative aspect would emphasize the cost of improvement, i.e., the cost of learning or the cost of search for these sources of inoptimality, so that reliability of control can be improved.

Instead of going into the general theory, we would present here some illustrative examples which are relevant for selecting optimal monetary and fiscal policies in a macroeconomic framework. This framework has been most widely discussed in control theory applications to economic policy (Aoki 1976, Chow 1975, Kendrick 1981, Turnovsky 1977).

First, we consider the problem of optimal choice of the monetary m_t or the fiscal instrument r_t, where the equilibrium state equation is either

$$y_t = a_1 y_{t-1} - a_2 y_{t-2} - a_3 m_t + e_t \tag{10.1}$$

or

$$y_t = b_1 y_{t-1} - b_2 y_{t-2} - b_3 r_t + \tilde{e}_t \tag{10.2}$$

Here y_t is real national income, $x_{1t} = m_t$, $x_{2t} = r_t$ are the two instruments, e_t, $\tilde{e}_t$ are the additive stationary disturbances. The objective function for system optimization is the expected loss function

$$L_0 = EL(y, x) = E\big[y_t - y^0 | x_{it}\big]^2 \tag{10.3}$$

conditional on the choice of the instrument x_{it}, $i = 1, 2$ where y^0 is the desired value of the target preassigned exogenously. This simple framework has been discussed by Turnovsky (1975), Poole (1970), Prescott (1972) and others with the simplifying assumption that the bivariate distribution $p(y_t, x_{it})$ is normally independently distributed, i.e., the conditional variance $V(y_t | x_{it})$ is independent of x_{it}. Since

$$L_0 = V\big(y_t - y^0 | x_{it}\big) + \big(Ey_t - y^0\big)^2 \tag{10.4}$$

for any bivariate distribution $p(y_t, x_{it})$, whether normal or not, the assumption of conditional normality implies that the first term on the right hand side of (10.4) is a constant independent of the instrument variable x_{it}, $i = 1, 2$ and hence the optimal control rule satisfies

$$Ey_t = y^0 \tag{10.5}$$

and if the variance $V(y_t - y^0 | x_{1t}) > V(y_t - y' | x_{2t})$ then the second instrument $x_{2t} = r_t$ is chosen to be the optimal; otherwise the first is chosen. The indifference zone arises when the two conditional variances are equal, which of course is most unlikely.

Now relax the normality assumption for the bivariate distribution $p(y_t, x_{it})$. Assume that it has any of the two distributions, e.g., student's t and gamma

$$p(y_t, x_{it}) = \left(\frac{n}{n-2}\right) \frac{1}{2\pi\sigma_1\sigma_2\sqrt{1-\rho^2}}$$

$$\times \left[1 + \frac{1}{(n-2)(1-\rho^2)} \left(\frac{x_{it}^2}{\sigma_1^2} - \frac{2\rho x_{it} y_t}{\sigma_1\sigma_2} + \frac{y_t^2}{\sigma_2^2}\right)\right]^{-1/2(n+2)}$$

$$-\infty < x_{it}, \quad y_t < \infty, \quad n > 0 \tag{10.5}$$

$$Ex_{it} = 0, \quad V(x_{it}) = \sigma_1^2, \quad V(y_t) = \sigma_2^2$$

$$p(y_t, x_{it}) = \frac{a^{m+n}}{\Gamma(m)\Gamma(n)} y_t^{m-1} (x_{it} - y_t)^{n-1} e^{-ax_{it}}$$

$$x_{it} > y_t > 0. \tag{10.6}$$

The first distribution has the property that as the parameter $n \to \infty$, the conditional distribution $p(y_t | x_{it})$ tends to normal. The second distribution is defined on the nonnegative domain and hence is more realistic for economic applications. With the expected loss function (10.4) the optimal LDR now become

$$\frac{\sigma_2(1-\rho^2)}{(n-1)\sigma_1^2} x_{it} - (Ey_t - y^0)\alpha_3 = 0 \quad \text{(t-distribution)} \tag{10.7}$$

$$\alpha_3 = \text{either } a_3 \text{ or } b_3 \text{ according as } i = 1, 2$$

$$\frac{mn}{(m+n)^2(m+n-1)} x_{it} - (Ey_t - y^0)^2 \alpha_3 = 0 \quad \text{(gamma distribution)}$$

$$\tag{10.8}$$

$$\alpha_3 = a_3 \text{ or } b_3 \text{ according as } i = 1 \text{ or } 2.$$

It is clear that as $n \to \infty$ in (10.7), the $t = $ distribution becomes normal and the optimal LDR turns out to be

$$Ey_t - y^0 = 0. \tag{10.9}$$

The three LDR, (10.7) through (10.9) may therefore be compared each time x_{1t} or x_{2t} is selected, through the expected loss function L_0 in (10.3) in particular, the cost of a normal LDR defined in (10.9) may be evaluated in terms of a higher value of expected loss L_0, when the true bivariate relationship is either a gamma or t distribution. Cases involving other distributions and several control variables may be easily incorporated.

Next consider the case when the normality assumption holds but the loss function is more generalized. Let z_t denote $(y_t - y^0)^2$, its mean and variance being $\bar{z}_t$, σ_t^2. Let z_q be the q-quantile of the distribution of z_t. Then z_q indicates the value at which the probability

$$\text{Prob}(z_t \leqslant z_q) = q, \quad 0 \leqslant q \leqslant 1 \tag{11.1}$$

holds. If the quantity $(z_t - \bar{z}_t)/\sigma_t$ is approximately normally distributed, then one could write (11.1) as

$$z_q = \bar{z}_t + r_q \sigma_t, \quad r_q = \phi^{-1}(q), \quad 0 \leqslant q \leqslant 1 \tag{11.2}$$

where $\phi^{-1}(\cdot)$ is the inverse of the cumulative distribution of a unit normal variate. As in (10.3) we may minimize the loss function z_q defined by (11.2) to obtain the optimal decision rules solved from

$$\frac{\partial \bar{z}_t}{\partial x_{it}} + r_q \frac{\partial \sigma_t}{\partial x_{it}} = 0 \tag{11.3}$$

The value of q selected in any decision situation determines the safety level desired. Since under the normality assumption r_q is zero or positive, according as q is equal to or greater than 0.50, therefore with $q = 0.50$ we get back the optimal LDR given by (10.9). Otherwise the optimal decision rule solved from (11.3) is nonlinear and depends on the factor $r_q \sigma_t$, which can be interpreted as penalty for uncertainty. Further, if the quantity z_t is not normally distributed or it converges to normality very slowly, then r_q would not equal zero for $z = 0.50$. Hence the effect of moments higher than the second may be important. Some empirical comparisons are reported in (Sengupta 1972), which show how the performance of nonlinear decision rules may be better than the linear ones.

In the third case we have some parameters like θ are unknown. For example, the loss function may be as

$$L(\alpha, y, x) = \tfrac{1}{2}(\alpha'z - w(\theta^*, z))^2 \tag{12.0}$$

where the output y and control x are subsumed in the vector z and the vector α is assumed to be a stationary multivariate process with a density function $p(\alpha)$. The average risk functional is then

$$R(z) = E_\alpha L(\alpha, z), \quad z \in Z \tag{12.1}$$

where the set Z may be viewed as a set of constraints on control or state and E is expectation over the random components α. Minimization of $R(z)$ in (12.1) will involve the unknown parameter θ^* in the scalar function $w(\theta^*, z)$ and hence the optimal decision rule cannot be completely specified unless some estimate of θ^* is built up from sample observations. Bayesian methods provide updating of prior estimates through additional sample observations, e.g., in the normal case the posterior estimates $\hat{\theta}$ can be explicitly computed. When the scalar function $w(*, z)$ is a polynomial in z of a given degree and the parameters θ^* enter as coefficients in this polynomial, we have to solve a nonlinear program. If there were no constraints on z, the optimal value of θ^* would be obtained from the necessary condition, i.e.,

$$\nabla R(z) = \nabla R(z, \theta^*) = 0 \tag{12.2}$$

This gradient condition (12.2) cannot be specified explicitly, if the probability distribution $p(\alpha)$ of the random component is not known. We have to introduce therefore an algorithm of learning to provide an estimate of $z = \hat{z}(s)$ and the associated value of $\theta^* = \hat{\theta}(s)$ that converge in time to their optimal values z^0, θ^0 say, by using successive observations on $\alpha = \hat{\alpha}(s)$, $\hat{y}(s)$, $\nabla R(\hat{z}(s))$. A suitable discrete algorithm in this case could be defined in terms of a modified gradient algorithm, e.g.,

$$\hat{\theta}(s) = \hat{\theta}(s-1) - h(s) \nabla_\theta L(\hat{z}(s), \hat{\theta}(s-1), \hat{\alpha}(s))$$

with the objective function min $R(z)$ replaced by

$$\min R(\hat{z}(S)) = \hat{R}(\hat{z}(\hat{\theta}(S))) = \frac{1}{S} \sum_{s=1}^{S} L(\hat{z}(s), \hat{\theta}(s), \hat{\alpha}(s))$$

where the search is to be restricted within the set $\hat{z}(s) \in Z$ and the term $h(s)$ above for step length must be appropriately chosen for convergence purposes. Alternative search methods thus provide alternative learning rules (Tsypkin 1973), which require to be compared before one decides the final optimal decision rule. For example, the dual strategy methods proposed by Feldbaum (1963) and Jacobs (1980) for systems where additive disturbances are present along with noise in the control mechanism belong to the class of alternative learning rules. Here the output y_t is different from the state q_t at time t and the control vector x_t has the noise element ϵ_t such that

$$y_t = q_t + \xi_t$$

$$q_t = f(x_t, \epsilon_t)$$

where ξ_t is the output noise. The suggested dual strategy is of the form

$$x_{t+1} - x_t = (x_t - x_{t-1}) \operatorname{sign}(y_t - y_{t-1})$$

This is an incremental hill-climbing strategy which uses the system output in response to exploratory input changes to determine the sign of successive incremental control changes and not the actual position of the peak. Hence the strategy can be applied even when the shape of the hill is unknown or changes with time. The criterion of minimum average loss over successive trials is still used for determining optimal decision rules.

Another class of adaptive decision rules may be defined when there is no distinction between output and the state but the output response $y(j)$ to control $x(j)$ applied at the j-th grid point is specified by

$$y(j) = \hat{\beta}(j)'x(j) + e(j) \tag{13.0}$$

where the row vector $\hat{\beta}(j)'$ is an estimate of the parameter vector β based on all preceeding experiments or observations up to j and $e(j)$ is the additive error independently distributed with zero mean and fixed variance. The average risk function is assumed to be

$$R(y) = x(j)'V(j)x(j) \tag{13.1}$$

subject to $\quad x(j)'x(j) = 1 \tag{13.2}$

where $V(j)$ is the variance-covariance matrix associated with the estimate $\hat{\beta}$ and the cost of search is specified by (13.2). Minimizing (13.1) with respect to the control vector $x(j)$ leads to the eigenvalue problem

$$[V(j) - \lambda I]x(j) = 0$$

where the minimum eigenvalue, $\lambda_0(j)$ and the associated eigenvector $x_0(j)$ have to be taken for each $j = 1, 2, \ldots, J$. Let $\lambda_{00} = \min_{1 \leqslant j \leqslant J} \lambda_0(j)$ and x_{00} be the associated eigenvector. Then the optimal decision rule is specified by x_{00}. When the index j characterizing the state of nature is continuous rather than discrete, the above optimization problem would become

$$\text{minimize} \quad L = \int x'(w)V(x)x(w)dw$$

$$\text{subject to} \quad \int x'(w)x(w)dw = 1$$

(13.3)

where w is the appropriate measure. Since the inverse of the variance-co-variance matrix, V^{-1} may be interpreted as the information matrix associated with an estimate $\hat{\beta}$, one could characterize the optimal decision rule x_{00}, if it exists, as the maximal information decision rule. Note that the optimal decision rule characterization by (13.3) is dependent on the linear model (13.0) and the quadratic risk functional (13.1). These can be generalized however, using the theory of optimal search (Stone 1975). Let $p(w)$ be the multivariate density of the random vector w having a domain W and $r(y(x), w)$ be the probability of detecting the output vector $y = y(w)$ when the state of nature is w; also let the scalar function $c(y(x), w)$ denote the cost of effort. Then the optimal detection rule is specified by the nonlinear optimization problem

$$\underset{x \in X}{\text{maximize}} J = \int_{w \in W} p(w)r(y(x), w)dw$$

(13.4)

$$\text{subject to} \int_{w \in W} c(y(x), w)dw \leqslant K$$

(13.5)

here it is assumed that the conditional probability of detection $r(\cdot)$ is independent of the probability $p(w)$ and K is the upper limit of the cumulative effort cost. If the scalar functions $r(\cdot)$, $c(\cdot)$ are such that $-r(\cdot)$, $c(\cdot)$ are convex and continuous and there exists a finite nonnegative Lagrange multiplier $\lambda \geqslant 0$ such that the left hand side of the constraint (13.5) is finite, i.e.,

$$\int_{w \in W} c(y(x), w)dw < \infty$$

and the set of feasible solutions is not empty, then there must exist an optimal decision rule x_{00}. In particular if x is a scalar, $r(\cdot) = 1 - e^{-x}$ and $c(\cdot) = x$, then it can be shown that the optimal search rule x_{00} satisfies the condition

$$x_{00} = \left[\frac{\log p(w)}{\lambda} \right]^{+}, \quad \text{where} \quad (s)^{+} = \begin{Bmatrix} s, & \text{if} & s \geqslant 0 \\ 0, & \text{if} & s < 0 \end{Bmatrix}$$

It is clear therefore that if loss is defined to be proportional to the conditional probability of detection $L(y(x), w) = -kr(y(x), w)$, $k > 0$, then the objective function (13.4) may be viewed as a generalized loss function, i.e.,

$$\underset{x \in X}{\text{minimize}} \; L = \int_{w \in W} kp(w)r(y(x), w)dw$$

where X is the set of feasible instruments satisfying the cost constraint (13.5). It is clear that the advantage of this formulation is that it can incorporate a two-facet (or dual) objective in its optimal decision rule, one to provide an estimate of the unknown parameter vector and its successive improvement and the other for revising the optimal controls or decisions conditional on the most up-to-date data estimates of the parameter vector.

4. Adaptive Rules in Stochastic Games

In case of games with incomplete information, no player could determine his best strategy, unless he forms a conjectural estimate of the rivals' strategy and their estimate of the future or the unknown parameters. A typical example is provided by an oligopoly model due to Cournot. If there were no uncertainty in total market demand and the Cournot–Nash equilibrium point was acceptable to each player as the best solution, then the sequence of information needed by each player in terms of his forecasts about his rivals' behavior may be stabilizing or destabilizing according as it helps to converge to or diverge from the Cournot-Nash equilibrium solution. Probability of divergence may be large in case, we have in addition additive disturbance term in the total market demand function. We will mention here an illustrative example. Applications to dynamic limit pricing models under stochastic demand are also available (Sengupta 1982).

Consider a linear dynamic demand function for each firm, $i = 1$, $2, \ldots, n$

$$p_i(t) = v_0 - [\beta_0(1 + \gamma_0)]^{-1} \left[\frac{x_i(t-1)}{w_i} + \gamma_0 \sum_{j=1}^{n} x_j(t-1) \right] + u_i(t) \quad (14.0)$$

facing price $p_i(t)$ with output $x_i(t)$ at time t. The fixed parameters v_0, β_0, γ_0 are assumed to be so determined that the above prices are market clearing prices on the average. The stochastic component $u_i(t)$ is independently distributed for all t with fixed mean and variance σ_j^2 and the firms differ only in their parameters w_i, σ_i^2, α_i which are nonnegative constants. It is assumed that each firm maximizes the following risk function

$$f(x_i(t)) = E\pi_i(t) - \frac{\alpha_i}{2} V(\pi_i(t)), \quad \alpha_i > 0 \tag{14.1}$$

where E, V denote expectation and variance respectively of profits $\pi_i(t)$,

$$\pi_i(t) = p_i(t)x_i(t) - (c_i x_i + c_0) \tag{14.2}$$

where c_i, c_0 are known parameters of the cost function. Assuming interior solutions and only two firms, the optimal output would satisfy the linear difference equations

$$\begin{aligned}
x_1(t) &= k_{10} - k_{11}x_1(t-1) - k_{12}x_2(t-1) \\
x_2(t) &= k_{20} - k_{21}x_1(t-1) - k_{22}x_2(t-1)
\end{aligned} \tag{14.3}$$

where

$$\begin{aligned}
k_{i0} &= (v_0 - c_i)/(\alpha_i \sigma_i^2), \quad i = 1, 2 \\
k_{ii} &= (1 + w_i \gamma_0)(\beta_0(1+\gamma_0)w_i \alpha_i \sigma_i^2)^{-1}, \quad i = 1, 2 \\
k_{12} &= \gamma_0 (\beta_0(1+\gamma_0)\alpha_1 \sigma_1^2)^{-1}, \quad k_{21} = \gamma_0 (\beta_0(1+\gamma_0)\alpha_2 \sigma_2^2)^{-1}
\end{aligned} \tag{14.4}$$

This system (14.3) is not ordinarily stable, i.e., the characteristic roots of the associated homogeneous system need not all lie within the unit circle. Even if it does, this holds only under the assumption that output of each firm has no random component and hence there is no error in forecasting rival's output adjustment. Assume however that $x_i(t)$ has an element of randomness and that each firm maximizes a conditional utility function

$$f(x_i(t)) = E[\pi_i(t) \mid x_i(t)] - \frac{\alpha_i}{2} V(\pi_i(t) \mid x_i(t))$$

and that each pair of random variables $x_i(t)$, $x_j(t)$ with $i \neq j$ is distributed such that the conditional variance $V(x_j(t) \mid x_i(t-1))$ is not constant. Then the optimal decision rules for each firm satisfy a set of nonlinear equations, which need not have the stability characteristics of the model (14.3). The role of non-normal distributions, e.g., Pareto, exponential appears in this framework to contribute to nonlinearity of the output adjustment process through terms involving conditional expectations.

It is also clear the even in the linear system (14.4) of difference equations, the parameters σ_i need to be correctly estimated. Any error variance in such estimates would tend to affect the stability of the path of convergence. The role of market information and its transmission in a competitive fashion throughout the industry are therefore essential for ensuring convergence to an equilibrium set of outputs and prices.

5. Other Adaptive Control Rules

As illustrative application of other types of adaptive decision rules in socio-economic models, one may refer to the following approaches. First, in a recent applications Klein and Su (1980) provided a novel method of combining an econometrically estimated model of an economy with an optimal control model in LQG framework. Denote the econometric model as

$$f_i\left(y_t', y_{t-1}', \ldots, y_{t-p}', x_t', z_t'\right) = e_{it}, \quad i = 1, 2, \ldots n \tag{15.1}$$

where y_t' is a row vector with n target variables, x_t' contains m exogenous control variables, z_t denotes other noncontrol variables and e_t are random errors. The objective C of the policy maker is assumed to be a quadratic function of the deviations from their target or desired values, e.g.,

$$C = \sum_{t=1}^{T} \left[w_1\left(y_{1t} - y_1^*\right)^2 + w_2\left(y_{2t} - y_2^*\right)^2 + w_3\left(y_{3t} - y_3^*\right)^2 \right.$$
$$\left. + w_4\left(y_{4t} - y_4^*\right)^2 + p_1\left(x_{1t} - x_1^*\right)^2 + p_2\left(x_{2t} - x_2^*\right)^2 + p_3\left(x_{3t} - x_3^*\right)^2 \right] \tag{15.2}$$

where y_1 is the growth rate of national income, y_2 the rate of inflation, y_3 the rate of unemployment, y_4 the ratio of foreign trade balance to national income, x_1 government expenditure, x_2 an average income tax rate level and x_3 unborrowed reserves. An asterisk over a variable indicates the desired or target levels, w_i's are subjective weights and p_j's are penalties attached to the use of policy instruments. The econometric model used for (15.1) is the Wharton Mark IV quarterly model involving a system of nonlinear simultaneous equations with approximately 450 equations and identities and 200 exogenous variables. The optimum control variables X^0 solved from (15.2) may be written as a linear function of the endogenous variables Y

$$X^0 = -MY \tag{15.3}$$

where the matrix M contains terms involving the derivations dY/dX, in addition to the weights. The solution algorithm consists of an interaction back and forth between solutions to (15.1) and (15.3). The econometric model (15.1) is solved along the base line path by applying the usual Gauss–Seidel method of approximation. Elements of Y are taken from that solution and substituted into the right hand side of (15.3) to obtain a revised estimate of X. The new values of X are then inserted in the second stage into (15.1) to obtain a new solution. A second revised estimate of X is then obtained from (15.3) and so on until the welfare function C does not change from one iteration to the next. The convergence of the solution process is very fast in this specific simulation experiment. Such a method has been applied by Sengupta and Sfeir (1982) in estimating supply response in California agriculture. This application demonstrates how the sensitivity of optimal policy-mixes can be built into the design of a nonlinear econometric model which uses estimates containing different standard errors. Methods of dual control involving simultaneous use of improved estimates and caution in control have also been applied in the current economic literature (Turnovsky 1977). These adaptive methods, of which dual control is a part, depend for their effectiveness on the possibilities for learning, which depend for the most part upon the degree of uncertainty of the policymaker. The greater is his uncertainty, the less is his information and thus the greater is the scope of learning. Hence the need for flexibility and caution in the formulation of economic plans or policies. Three types of uncertainty are clearly distinguished in such cases: (1) the specification errors implied by particular models used for policies, (2) the instrument-instability (Aoki 1976) due to the choice by the policymaker of certain types of control, e.g., derivative, proportional or integral or a mixture of the three, and (3) the estimation uncertainty, when part of the policy model are to be statistically estimated. In case of multiple policymakers two additional sources of uncertainty are due to the possible inconsistency of preferences of different policymakers and the need for exploring compromises (Sandee 1977) and to the unequal degree of sharing of relevant information among the team members.

Second, methods of stochastic control with passive and active learning have been explored for economy-wide models by Kendrick (1981) and others. As a method of passive learning stochastic control, MacRae (1972) formulated the following two-period problem with one unknown parameter which enters in a multiplicative way: find the controls (u_0, u_1) to minimize

$$C = E\left\{ \tfrac{1}{2} \sum_{k=1}^{N} \left(qx_k^2 + ru_k^2 \right) \right\}$$

subject to

$$x_{k+1} = ax_k + bu_k + c + e_k, \quad k = 0, 1$$

x_0 given

$$e_k \sim N(0,Q), \quad b \sim N(\bar{b}, V_b)$$

where the multiplicative parameter b having a normal distribution is unknown. Following the passive learning approach, a procedure for choosing the control is combined with a procedure for updating the parameter estimates. In active control, one has to evaluate the impact of the present choice of control on the future covariances and states. Although various simulation studies (Kendrick 1981) have been made, the computational complexities are still very large.

A third type of adaptation occurs in models of social behavior, where market-oriented variables are not used. For instance, Fox (1981) and Barker (1968) have developed models of behavior settings applicable to communities, where time and money are allocated in the environment to perform certain goals. Two characteristics of this eco-behavioral system appear to be different from the conventional control theoretic models in economic systems. First, the system is self-organizing or self-regulating. Second, the environment as a behavior setting has a number of stable attributes, e.g., one of the stable attributes of a setting is its functional level and another is the optimal number of inhabitants for maintenance of this level. The first requires that some form of adaptation or learning be built into the control law or the decision rule. The second requires that the model specification builds a high degree of aversion towards instability. These two aspects may now be illustrated.

In a simple adaptive control rule, the system's actual performance is compared to the desired performance and the difference is then used first to learn about the unknown components of the environment and then to drive the actual performance towards desired performance. However in many cases total adaptation is not possible, since the environment is incompletely known. Hence the need for developing reinforcement-learning systems in the control law. This control law is self-organizing in the sense that it is able to change as the experience and information about the environment and its functioning become available. An example of such a system has been given by Mendel and McLaren (1970), following the work of Jones (1967).

Denote by $x_i(t)$ the output of the eco-behavioral system, which may be a function of the number of individuals N_i in setting i and the time spent by them t_i. The vector $x(t)$ describes the functioning of the behavior settings as follows:

$$x(t+1) = Mx(t) + hu(t) \quad t = 0, 1, \ldots, T-1$$
$$x(0) \text{ given}$$

(16.1)

where M is the state transition matrix, vector h is the control distribution vector and $u(t)$ is taken to be the scalar control variable, say the total number of inhabitants in the overall system comprising k settings where $i = 1, 2, \ldots, k$. The elements of M and h are constants and the system description (16.1) is linear as a first approximation. Following the linear quadratic model in its deterministic form, the objective function is postulated as

$$J(T) = \sum_{t=0}^{T-1} x(t+1)'Qx(t+1) + ru^2(t)$$

(16.2)

where r is interpreted as the cost (Mohler 1973) associated with control $u(t)$ and Q is assumed to be a constant positive definite matrix. Since both $x(t)$ and $u(t)$ may be measured from some desired or target quantities fixed, the above objective specifies the quadratic cost of deviations over the fixed horizon. Now in a reinforcement-learning control system, the objective (16.2) is desired but since it is known that the objective cannot always be achieved, other objectives or subgoals are introduced to modify the original $J(T)$ in (16.2). One way this may be done is through imposing constraints on the control rule, e.g., let the control $u(t)$ be chosen from a finite set of allowable actions $\tilde{U} = \{u(1), u(2), \ldots, u(s)\}$, i.e., $u(t) \in \tilde{U}$ for $t = 0, 1, \ldots, T-1$. Probabilities are assigned to each element of the set $\tilde{U}$ and the subgoal

$$\tilde{J}(t) = x(t+1)'G(t)x(t+1) + \beta u^2(t)$$

(16.3)

is used in the reinforcement of these probabilities. The decision problem in this reinforcement-learning model is: how should $G(t)$ and β be chosen so that the subgoal $\tilde{J}(t)$ and the overall goal $J(T)$ are compatible? Let the solution of the control model (16.3) and (16.1) be $u^*(t)$, $0 \leqslant t \leqslant T-1$ and that of (16.3) and (16.1) be $u^{**}(t)$, $0 \leqslant t \leqslant T-1$. Compatibility then requires that $u^{**}(t)$ be very close to $u^*(t)$, $0 \leqslant t \leqslant T-1$. In particular, complete compatibility requires that $\beta = r$ and $G(t) = Q + K(T-k-1)$, where the matrix $K(T-k-1)$ has to be so determined, as a function of Q, M, h and time τ such that $u^*(t) = u^{**}(t)$. However, complete compatibility is rare and hence approximate compatibility up to a certain level of tolerance is introduced. Note that since the allowable control action $u(i) \in \tilde{U}$ has an associated probability of being chosen, these probabilities are revised in a sequential fashion

$$p_j^i(t+1) = \theta p_j^i(t) + (1 - \theta) \mid J(t) - \tilde{J}(t)\mid_i \qquad (16.4)$$

where $p_j^i(t)$ denotes the probability that $u(i)$ is chosen at time t, given that the event i has been perceived or observed. Here the set $i = 1, 2, \ldots, I$ is assumed to describe the knowledge about the system environment and for each such event, there are s control actions. The term $\mid J(t) - \tilde{J}(t)\mid_i$ denotes the deviation $(J(t) - \tilde{J}(t))$ in a normalized scale when the event i is estimated or known. Thus the adaptive rule (16.4) prescribes a method of updating the probabilities of choice of control. If the sequence of revisions exists such that asymptotically the control rule $\{u^{**}(t)\}$ converges to $\{u^*(t)\}$, then the learning reinforcement mechanism has stability property very similar to that emphasized by Fox (1981) and Barker (1968).

6. Concluding Remarks

The various methods of characterizing the informational bases of decision rules and improving the latter through empirical application to economic and social systems provide a very active field of recent research. Research work across several disciplines may provide valuable insights into modelling and its suitable applications.

References

Amemiya, T. "Regression Analysis when the dependent variable is truncated normal." Econometrica, 41 (1973), 997–1008.

Aoki, M., Optimal Control and Systems Theory in Dynamic Economic Analysis Amsterdam: North Holland, 1976.

Barker, R.G., 1968, Ecological Psychology (Stanford: Stanford University Press).

Bar-Shalom, Y. and Tse, E., "Value of information in stochastic systems," Proceedings of IEEE Conference on Decision and Control, New York, 1975.

Belsley, D.A., Industry Production Behavior. Amsterdam: North Holland, 1969.

Box, G.E.P. and Jenkins, G.M., Time Series Analysis. San Francisco: Holden-Day, 1976.

Childs, G.L., Unfilled Orders and Inventories. Amsterdam: North Holland, 1967.

Chow, G.C., Analysis and Control of Dynamic Economic Systems. New York: John Wiley, 1975.

Chu, K., "Comparison of information structures in decentralized dynamic systems," in Directions in Large Scale Systems, eds. Y.C. Ho and S.K. Mitter, New York: Academic Press, 1976, pp. 25–39.

Duffy, W. and Lewis, K.A., "The cyclic properties of the production inventory process," Econometrica, 43, (1975) 499–512.

Fedorov, V.V., Theory of Optimal Experiments. New York: Academic Press, 1972.

Feldbaum, A.A., "Dual control theory problems," in Proceedings of Second IFAC Congress, Basle, Switzerland, 1963.

Fox, K.A., The Measurement and Valuation of Social System Outcomes. Unpublished manuscript, Ames, Iowa, 1981.

Goldfeld, S.M. and Quandt, R.E., Studies in Nonlinear Estimation. Cambridge, Massachusetts, Ballinger Publishing, 1976.

Hay, G.A. and Holt, C.C., "A general solution for linear decision rules," Econometrica, 43, (1975), 231–260.

Holt, C.C., Modigliani, F., Muth, J.F. and Simon, H.A., Planning Production Inventories and Workforce. Englewood Cliffs, N.J.: Prentice Hall, 1960.

Jacobs, O.L.R., "The structure of stochastic control laws," in Stochastic Programming, ed. M.A.H. Dempster. New York: Academic Press, 1980.

Jones, J.E., "Sensitivity analysis of control problems," in Proceedings of National Electronic Conference, New York, 1967.

Keeney, R.L. and Raiffa, H., Decisions with Multiple Objectives. New York, John Wiley, 1976.

Kelsey, D.W. and Haddad, A.H., "A method of adaptive control," J. of Franklin Institute, 297, (1974) 29–39.

Kendrick, D., Stochastic Control for Economic Models. New York: McGraw-Hill, 1981.

Kennan, J., "The estimation of partial adjustment models with rational expectations," Econometrica, 47, (1979), 1441–1456.

Klein, L.R. and Su, V., "Recent economic fluctuations and stabilization policies," in Quantitative Economics and Development, eds. L.R. Klein et al. New York: Academic Press, 1980.

Lane, M.N. and Littlechild, S.C., "A stochastic programming approach to weather-dependent pricing for water resources," in Stochastic Programming, op cit. 1980.

Macrae, E.C., "Linear decision with experimentation," Annals of Economic and Social Measurement, 1, (1972), 437–443.

Mendel, J.M. and McLaren, R.W., Adaptive Learning and Pattern Recognition Systems. New York: Academic Press, Chap. 8, 1970.

Mohler, R.R., Bilinear Control Processes with Applications to Engineering Ecology and Medicine. New York: Academic Press, 1973.

Poole, W., "Optimal choice of monetary policy instruments in a simple stochastic macro model," Quarterly J. of Economics, 84, (1970), 197–216.

Prescott, E.C., "The multiperiod control problem under uncertainty," Econometrica, 40, (1972), 1043–1058.

Prescott, E.D., "Adaptive decision rules for macroeconomic planning," in Bayesian Econometrics and Statistics, eds. S.E. Fienberg and A. Zellner, Amsterdam: North Holland, pp. 121–31, 1975.

Revelle, C. and Gundelach, J., "A variance minimizing linear decision rule for reservoir management," in Stochastic Planning, op. cit., 1980.

Schneeweiss, C., "Dynamic certainty equivalents in production smoothing theory," Int. J. Systems Science, 6, (1975), 353–366.

Sengupta, J.K., "Decision rules in stochastic planning under dynamic models," Swedish J. of Economics, 74, (1972), 370–381.

–, Optimal Decisions Under Uncertainty. New York: Springer-Verlag, 1981.

–, Decision Models in Stochastic Programming. New York: Elsevier-North Holland, 1982.

Sengupta, J.K. and Sfeir, R.I., "Short term industry output behavior," Applied Economics, 13, (1981), 1–18.

– and –. "Risk in supply response: An optimal control approach," Working paper no. 192, UC Santa Barbara, 1982.

Stone, L.D., Theory of Optimal Search. New York: Academic Press, 1975.

Tintner, G. and Sengupta, J.K., Stochastic Economics. New York: Academic Press, 1972.

Tsypkin, Y.Z., Foundations of the Theory of Learning. New York: Academic Press, 1973.

Turnovsky, S.J., "Optimal choice of monetary instrument in a linear economic model with stochastic coefficients," J. of Money, Credit and Banking, 5, (1975), 51–80.

–, Macroeconomic Analysis and Stabilization Policies. Cambridge: Cambridge University Press, 1977.

Waud, R.N., "Asymmetric policymaker utility functions and optimal policy under uncertainty," Econometrica, 44 (1976), 53–66.

Wittenmark, B., "Stochastic adaptive control method: a survey," Int. J. of Control, 21, (1975), 705–730.

Zellner, A., An Introduction to Bayesian Inference in Econometrics. New York: John Wiley, 1971.

4. Optimal output inventory decisions in stochastic markets

1. Introduction

Recent economic applications of optimal inventory control models to aggregate industry data (Hay and Holt 1975, Belsley 1969, Sengupta and Sfeir 1979) have been restricted to Linear Quadratic Gaussian (LQG) models and the associated linear decision rules (LDR). For perfect markets with competitive exchange of information, where no individual agent has the monopolistic power to influence the price or the market demand, the LQG model may hold very well as an approximation; this is unlikely to be so for imperfect markets, where imperfection may be due to several sources, e.g., (a) asymmetry in the distribution of market demand, where the third and fourth moments may be as important as the mean and variance, (b) the price may be useable in part as a control variable along with output, (c) the inventory cost function may be partly convex and partly concave and (d) the sensitivity to risk parameters in stochastic demand may modify the LDR and its updating characteristics. Our object here is to formulate in a simplified framework a set of dynamic inventory control models, which incorporates in an approximate sense some of the imperfections of stochastic markets as above. These models are illustrative of the deficiencies of the LDR approach, as they suggest the need for stochastic demand conditions.

2. Imperfect stochastic market

To motivate the decision problem we begin by illustrating two simple stochastic markets, where imperfection is due respectively to (a) the incomplete knowledge of the demand function and (b) the stochastic component in the probability distribution of demand. In the first case, the demand variables are the price $p(t)$ and quantity demanded $d(t)$

117

which are subject to disturbances, such as mistakes or unexpected difficulties in implementing a planned value:

$$p(t) = \bar{p}(t) + \epsilon_1(t), \quad E\epsilon_1(t+k) = 0, \quad k > 0$$
$$d(t) = \bar{d}(t) + \epsilon_2(t), \quad E\epsilon_2(t+k) = 0, \quad k > 0 \tag{2.1}$$

It is assumed that $\epsilon_1(t)$, $\epsilon_2(t)$ are white noise processes with zero means, such that they are realized after the planned values $\bar{p}(t)$ and $\bar{d}(t)$ are selected. Let $x(t)$ be the output rate and $h(t)$ the inventory of unsold goods at the end of period t. Denoting supply of output by $s(t)$ where

$$s(t) = x(t) - (h(t) - h(t-1)) \tag{2.2}$$

and setting it equal to planned demand $\bar{d}(t)$, the decision problem for the firm may be set up by an approximate model, called Model I as one of minimizing a quadratic loss function

$$\min_{s(t), \bar{p}(t)} Ef = -\left[\sum_{t=1}^{N} \left\{ \bar{p}(t)\bar{d}(t) - \frac{\lambda}{2} \left(\sigma_1^2 \bar{d}^2(t) + \sigma_2^2 \bar{p}^2(t) \right. \right. \right.$$

$$\left. \left. \left. + 2\sigma_{12} \bar{p}(t)\bar{d}(t) \right) - c(s(t)) \right\} \right]$$

subject to $\quad \bar{d}(t) = s(t), \quad N$ finite $\tag{2.3}$

where $c(s(t))$ is the cost of supply function and σ_{12} is the covariance of $\epsilon_1(t)$ and $\epsilon_2(t)$. Since the demand function is not known, the dependence of $d(t)$ (or $\bar{d}(t)$) on $p(t)$ (or $\bar{p}(t)$) are unknown, except that $\sigma_{12} = -|\sigma_{12}|$ is known to be negative. This means that around the planned values $\bar{d}(t)$, $\bar{p}(t)$ at least, the covariance σ_{12} is negative. Also λ is the risk-aversion parameter ($\lambda \geqslant 0$) indicating that lower variance of return is preferred by the enterprise. Replacing the negative sign by a positive one in the objective function of (2.3), we obtain a quadratic profit function adjusted for risk aversion. Note that inventories are subsumed in the supply variable $s(t)$, for which the cost function $c(s(t))$ includes both production and inventory costs. This approximation may be plausible when inventories are either a very small part of supply or held as a residual. Assuming a linear cost function $c(s(t)) = \alpha_0 + \alpha s(t)$ and the existence of positive solutions, the optimal values of the control variables $\bar{p}(t)$, $s(t)$ satisfy the necessary conditions for $t = 1, 2, \ldots, N$:

$$-\partial(Ef)/\partial s(t) = \bar{p}(t) - \lambda \left(\sigma_1^2 s(t) - |\sigma_{12}| \bar{p}(t) \right) - \alpha = 0$$
$$-\partial(Ef)/\partial \bar{p}(t) = s(t) - \lambda \left(\sigma_2^2 \bar{p}(t) - |\sigma_{12}| s(t) \right) = 0 \tag{2.4}$$

These imply for the optimal values $s^*(t)$, $\bar{p}^*(t)$ the following impact of uncertainty represented by σ_1^2, σ_2^2, $|\sigma_{12}|$ and λ:

$$s^*(t) = \left(\lambda\sigma_1^2\right)^{-1}\left(\bar{p}(t) - \alpha\right) + \left(\sigma_1^2\right)^{-1}|\sigma_{12}|\bar{p}(t)$$
$$\bar{p}^*(t) = \sigma_2^2 s(t) + \left(|\sigma_{12}| + \lambda^{-1}\right)^{-1}$$

(2.5)

the higher the price uncertainty σ_1^2 in relation to σ_{12}, the lower the optimal supply $s^*(t)$ and the higher the optimal price $\bar{p}^*(t)$. Also, the higher the marginal cost parameter α, the lower the optimal supply. The Hessian matrix associated with the system (2.4) is:

$$H = \begin{pmatrix} -\lambda\sigma_1^2 & 1 + \lambda|\sigma_{12}| \\ 1 + \lambda|\sigma_{12}| & -\lambda\sigma_2^2 \end{pmatrix}$$

from which it is clear that H is negative definite, only if there exist parameter values λ and $|\sigma_{12}|$ satisfying the inequalities:

$$|\sigma_{12}| < \sigma_1\sigma_2 - \lambda^{-1} \quad \text{and} \quad \lambda > \left(\sigma_1\sigma_2\right)^{-1}$$

(2.6)

A sufficient though not necessary condition for strict negative definiteness is to require, for a given $|\sigma_{12}| \geqslant 0$ a value of the risk aversion parameter λ such that

$$\lambda > \left(\sigma_1\sigma_2 - |\sigma_{12}|\right)^{-1} > 0$$

Thus, if the condition (2.6) fails to hold, the profit function $(-f)$ would fail to be concave. This failure of concavity of the profit function (or of convexity of the loss function) has two important implications for industry supply output behavior. First, the stationary values of $s(t)$ and $\bar{p}(t)$ solved from (2.4) would cease to be optimal, hence the enterprises would be better of in not following them. Second, if enterprises comprising the aggregate industry differ in risk aversion, so that some fail to satisfy the inequality (2.6), we would observe an output price behavior different from those expected in (2.5). Indeed in our detailed empirical applications to several manufacturing industries in the U.S. reported elsewhere (Sengupta and Sfeir 1981) we found evidence of divergence from the LDR specified in (2.5) for example.

As a second illustration, consider the steady state version of the output-inventory model originally considered by Mills (1962) and later by Hempenius (1970) and others, where outputs are treated separately from inventories and disequilibrium between demand and supply is explicitly recognised. This model, hereafter called Model II maximizes expected profits

$$Ez = ER(s, p) - c(x) \tag{2.7}$$

defined by expected revenue over production costs where the revenue function is

$$R(x, p) = \begin{cases} pd, & \text{if } d \leqslant x \\ px, & \text{if } d \geqslant x \end{cases} \tag{2.8}$$

and the demand quantity d is stochastic with a known probability distribution function. The enterprise is assumed to face a demand function of the form

$$d = D(p) + e$$

where e denotes a white noise term with a continuous probability density $f(e)$, p is price, a decision variable along with output x and the mean demand function $D(p)$ has a negative slope $\partial D(p)/\partial p < 0$ through the relevant domain. The expected profit function Ez may now be written as:

$$Ez = pD(p) - pI(x, p) - c(x) \tag{2.9}$$

where

$$I(x, p) = \int_{x - D(p)}^{\infty} [e - x + D(p)] f(e) de$$

is the expected level of inventory held. Note that a dynamic model, analogous to the static case can be formulated by incorporating in some sense the effects of current operations on future profitability, e.g., one possible method due to Mills (1962) is to define the total supply at time point t by $s(t) = x(t) + h(t-1)$, where $h(t-1)$ is inventory held at $(t-1)$ and then to introduce a cost function $c(s(t) - x(t))$ for t-th period's inventory $(s(t) > x(t))$ or shortage $(s(t) < x(t))$ and a cost function $c(x(t) - x(t-1))$ for changing production rates between any two consecutive time points. Thus the dynamic profit function for each period t is of the form

$$Ez(t) = \bar{p}(t) D(\bar{p}(t)) - \bar{p}(t) I(s(t), \bar{p}(t)) - c(y(t) - h(t-1))$$

$$+ \int_{-\infty}^{\infty} c(s(t) - D(\bar{p}(t)) - e(t)) f(e) de - c(x(t) - x(t-1))$$

$$\tag{2.10}$$

The long rung objective function may be reformulated as one of maximizing a discounted stream of profits over a fixed horizon

$$\max_{\bar{p}(t),x(t)} \sum_{t=1}^{N} (1+\delta)^{-t} Ez(t); \quad \delta > 0: \quad \text{discount rate.}$$

In the simplified framework of the steady state version (2.9) the enterprise may use either output x or price p or both as decision variables, since the market conditions are imperfect. In terms of economic theory, if perfectly competitive market prevails, then price cannot be used as a decision variable, so that we cannot maximize $Ez(t)$ in (2.10) with respect to $\bar{p}(t)$. In pure monopoly situations on the other hand, it is normally postulated that price and not output is the decision variable. In case of imperfectly competitive market conditions, which are intermediate between perfect competition and pure monopoly, both price and output can be used as control variables. Denoting the optimal values of these decision variables by x^* and p^0, they may be derived from the first order necessary conditions as

$$\frac{m(x^*)}{1 - F(x^* - D(p))} = p \tag{2.11}$$

$$p^0 = \frac{r(p^0) - I(x, p^0)}{(\theta - 1)|\partial D(p^0)/\partial p^0|[1 - F(x - D(p^0))]} \tag{2.12}$$

with

$$\begin{aligned} &x = \theta D(p^0)\theta > 0 \\ &r(p^0) = I(x, p^0) + (\theta - 1)m(x)|\partial D(p^0)/\partial p^0| \\ &\theta > 1 \end{aligned} \tag{2.13}$$

where $m(x^*) = \partial c(x)/\partial x$ is marginal cost evaluated at a positive output level x^*, $r(p^0) = \partial(pD(p))/\partial p$ is marginal revenue evaluated at a positive price level p^0 and $F(x^* - D(p))$ is the probability of shortage at output level x^*. Since output is not used as a decision variable when the optimal price strategy p^0 is followed, we have to add a condition $x = \theta D(p^0)$ requiring that output be proportional to mean demand. Also, it is expected that as the probability of shortage rises and this rise is anticipated, then the optimal price p^0 must increase. From (2.12) this will be true if $\theta > 1$ and $r(p^0) > I(x, p^0)$. Thus the following assumptions are made for economic realism whenever (2.12) or (2.13) are applied:

$$\theta > 1, \quad r(p^0) > I(x, p^0)$$

Denote the simultaneous optimal solution of (2.11) and (2.12) by (p_0, x_0) and assume linear demand $D(p) = a - bp$ and linear cost functions $c(x) = kx$ and we assume the firm to be risk averse so that one can set $x_0 = D(p_0) + q$, q being a positive constant. Then, the Hessian matrix H around the point (p_0, x_0) which satisfies the first order conditions may be written as:

$$H: \begin{bmatrix} \dfrac{-p_0}{2\delta} & \dfrac{\delta - bp_0 - q}{2\delta} \\[2mm] \dfrac{\delta - bp_0 - q}{2\delta} & \dfrac{-b(bp_0 + 2\delta + 2q)}{2\delta} \end{bmatrix} \tag{2.14}$$

where the additive stochastic error e in the demand function is assumed to have a uniform probability density within a finite range $-\delta \leqslant e \leqslant \delta$, for $\delta > 0$, so that δ measures the variability around the mean level zero. Such an assumption has been made for simplicity by Mills and Hempenius and others. It is clear from the Hessian matrix in (2.14)) that H is negative semi-definite if

$$p_0 \geqslant (\delta - q)^2 / (4b\delta) \tag{2.15}$$

Thus the lack of concavity of the expected profit function depends as much on the buffer stock q as on the scale parameter δ. Thus, if q is zero, we need the condition $p_0 > \delta/(4b)$ for strict concavity. Note that a rise in δ, implying increased uncertainty of demand would make it difficult for (2.15) being satisfied. But if p_0 solved from the first order condition does not satisfy this inequality, we would have the Hessian matrix H indefinite. In such cases, it would not be optimal to follow (x_0, p_0) given the first order condition. An analogous result can be derived when the stochastic component e is subject to a nonsymmetrical probability distribution.

A third source of fluctuations in imperfect stochastic market is due to rivalry and dominance of firms in the industry. A typical example is the price fluctuations exhibited in the world coffee market (Sengupta 1982a), where total world demand has been more or less steady and the dominant share of Brazil's supply has been declining over the years. A dynamic model which captures this aspects of interactions by rivals in provided by a limit pricing model (Sengupta 1982a). Denote the quantity supplied by the dominant firm and the rivals by $s(t)$ and $q(t)$ respectively, where supply at t is current output $x(t)$ plus inventory $h(t-1)$ at the end of last period. The market price $p(t)$ of the good obeys the demand function

$$p(t) = \alpha_0 - \alpha_1(s(t) + q(t)) + e(t) \tag{2.16}$$

where the stochastic component $e(t)$ is assumed to be white noise with zero mean and constant variance. If total market demand equals total supply on the average, then the relation (2.16) may also serve as a market clearing condition for equilibrium price determination when $e(t)$ is set equal to zero. The reactions by the rival, who controls the quantity $q(t)$ are specified up to a linear approximation by the entry equation:

$$q(t+1) = \beta_0 q(t) + \beta_1 (p(t) - m(t)) - \beta_2 \tilde{s}(t) + \epsilon(t+1) \qquad (2.17)$$

where $m(t)$ is the minimum level of the price perceived by the rival such that if $p(t) > m(t)$, this acts as a signal for market penetration by the rival; $\tilde{s}(t)$ is the rival's perception of supply by the dominant firm and $\epsilon(t+1)$ is the stochastic component. The objective of the dominant firm is to maximize expected profits over a given horizon;

$$\max_{s(t)} E \sum_{t=0}^{T-1} \pi(t) \quad \text{subject to} \quad (2.16) \text{ and } (2.17) \qquad (2.18)$$

where $\pi(t) = p(t)s(t) - c(s(t))$ and $c(s(t))$ is a convex cost function, which may be assumed to be linear for simplicity, i.e., $c(s(t)) = c_0 + c_1 s(t)$. This is hereafter referred to as Model III.

If the entry equation (2.17) is not known to the dominant firm, except perhaps very imperfectly (Kirman 1975) and a steady state version of the model is used, then we have the expected profit function for the dominant firm:

$$E\pi = (\alpha_0 - \alpha_1 q)s - \alpha_1 s^2 - c_0 - c_1 s \qquad (2.19)$$

where it is assumed for simplicity that $\beta_2 = 0$. About the reactions by the rival, two cases are possible: (i) $\partial q / \partial s \geqslant 0$ and (ii) $\partial q / \partial s < 0$. Also for simplicity, the second-order reaction is ignored so that $\partial^2 q / \partial s^2$ is negligible. In the first case, the first order condition of maximization of expected profits defined in (2.19) leads to the optimal supply (s^*) policy of the dominant firm:

$$s^* = \tfrac{1}{2}(\alpha_0 - c_1) - \frac{\alpha_1}{2}(1 + r_{qs})q \qquad (2.20)$$

where $r_{qs} = (\partial q / \partial s)(s/q)$ is the elasticity of rival's supply reaction in response to that of the dominant firm. However, if condition (i) is replaced by (ii), i.e., $\partial q / \partial s < 0$, and $|\partial q / \partial s| > 2(1 + \alpha_1)^{-1}$, then the supply quantity s^* defined by (2.20) gives the minimum rather than the maximum expected profits. Hence, short of perfect knowledge of the elasticity of the rival's reaction, it may not be optimal to follow the pure strategy solution s^* defined by (2.20), so long as there is a positive probability of not satisfying the condition $\partial q/\partial s \geq 0$. Note that if α_1 very high, e.g., $\alpha_1 = 1.5$, then the conditions $|\partial q/\partial s| > 0.8$ and $\partial q/\partial s < 0$ are sufficient to guarantee the inoptimality of the pure strategy solution s^* defined by (2.20). Thus, for markets characterized by high α_1, a suitable modification of the objective function (2.19) is the adjoin a separate cost component as:

$$z = (\alpha_0 - \alpha_1 q)s - \alpha_1 s^2 - c_0 - c_1 s - c_2 f_1 \tag{2.21}$$

where f_1 is the probability of the event: $\text{prob}(|\partial \gamma/\partial s| > 2(1 + \alpha_1)^{-1}$ and $\partial q/\partial s < 0)$ and the cost component $c_2 f_1$ measures the cost of violating the condition for maximum expected profits for each positive level of f_1. Since subjective probabilities are involved in the definition of f_1, one could generate a conditional expected profits $\{ E\pi \mid f_1$ given by a forecast value $\hat{f}_1 > 0\}$ for every estimate $\hat{f}_1 > 0$ of f_1 by the dominant firm and a series of conditionally optimal policies $s_1^*, s_2^*, \ldots, s_N^*$ may be generated. Associated with this scheme there will be a set of prices $p_1, p_2, \ldots, p_N$ say, characterizing the fluctuations in the stochastic market. Thus, the use of the modified profit function defined in (2.21) helps to generate mixed strategy solutions and a set of conditionally optimal strategies depending on the sequence of forecasts of the probability f_1 of the unfavorable event. Market fluctuations are thus observed and further, any uncertainty of information (e.g., frost damage on coffee production in Brazil) may provide additional sources of instability.

3. Structure of dynamic solutions

In this section we consider the structure of solutions in the three dynamic models presented above and their implications and sensitivity to incomplete information or uncertainty.

For Model I, the cost of supply $c(s(t))$ may be separable into production costs $c(x(t))$ and costs $c(\Delta h(t))$ due to change in stocks $\Delta h(t) = h(t-1) - h(t)$, if inventories are held as buffer stock to meet demand fluctuations. With this change, the necessary conditions for an optimal solution lead to the following decision rules for $t = 1, 2, \ldots, N$:

$$\bar{p}(t) = (1 + \lambda \mid \sigma_{12} \mid)^{-1} [m(x(t)) + \lambda \sigma_1^2 \bar{d}(t)] \tag{3.1}$$

$$\bar{p}(t) = (1 + \lambda \mid \sigma_{12} \mid)^{-1} [m(\Delta h(t)) + \lambda \sigma_1^2 \bar{d}(t)] \tag{3.2}$$

$$\bar{p}(t) = (\lambda \sigma_2^2)^{-1} (1 + \lambda \mid \sigma_{12} \mid) \bar{d}(t) \tag{3.3}$$

where $m(x(t))$, $m(\Delta h(t))$ denote marginal production costs and inventory costs, $\partial c(x(t))/\partial x(t)$ and $\partial c(\Delta h(t))/\partial \Delta h(t)$ respectively and it is assumed that sufficient conditions for optimality are satisfied. By combining (3.1) through (3.3) one may derive further:

$$\bar{p}(t) = m(x(t))\left[1 - \frac{(\lambda \sigma_1 \sigma_2)^2}{1 + \lambda |\sigma_{12}|}\right]^{-1} \tag{3.4}$$

$$m(x(t)) = m(\Delta h(t)) \tag{3.5}$$

$$x(t) = \left(\frac{1 + \lambda |\sigma_{12}|}{\lambda \sigma_1 \sigma_2}\right)^2 - \frac{m_1}{\lambda \sigma_1^2} \tag{3.6}$$

where it is assumed that $m(x(t)) = m_1$, a positive constant. The impact of uncertainty of incomplete information on the optimal price and output behavior may be noted in particular. First of all, the impact of uncertainty can be analyzed through three types of parameters, i.e., σ_i^2 and $|\sigma_{12}|$. An increase (decrease) in λ for example would tend to increase (decrease) price $\bar{p}(t)$ and decrease (increase) output $x(t)$, given that σ_1^2 and $|\sigma_{12}|$ are unchanged. Second, if the covariances σ_{12} are negligible, then by (3.6), every rise (fall) in λ, σ_1 or σ_2 or their product $\lambda \sigma_1 \sigma_2$ leads to a fall (rise) in optimal output. Further, if $\lambda \sigma_1 \sigma_2$ satisfies the second order condition for maximum profits and $\lambda \sigma_1 \sigma_2$ tends to one from below, then $\bar{p}(t) = km(x(t))$ where $k > 1$, i.e., expected price is greater than marginal cost of product. In perfectly competitive markets with no stochastic elements in demand, price equals marginal cost. Hence the extent by which k exceeds one may provide a measure of imperfection of stochastic markets. Third, if the price variable is not used as a strategy variable, and σ_{12} is zero or negligible, then we obtain

$$x(t) = \left(\lambda \sigma_1^2\right)^{-1}\left(\bar{p}(t) - m(x(t)) - \Delta h(t)\right) \tag{3.7}$$

This shows that the higher the price uncertainty measured by σ_1^2, the lower is optimal output. Also, at the optimal level of output, the excess of price over marginal cost of production increases as λ or, σ_1^2 increases.

In many imperfectly competitive markets price is used much less than output as a control variable and firms concentrate on strategies like advertising which emphasize the factors of non-price competition. Costs of adjustment due to a change in prices may be higher than that due to a change in output (Barro 1972, Sengupta 1982c). In such cases, the expected profit function may be well approximated by a quadratic function as follows:

$$Ez(N) = \sum_{t=1}^{N} \left[\bar{p}(t)\bar{d}(t) - \frac{\lambda}{2}\left(\sigma^2(t)\bar{d}(t)^2\right) - c(x(t)) - c(h(t)) \right] \quad (3.8)$$

where

$$c(x(t)) = \tfrac{1}{2}E\left[n_1(x(t) - x^*(t))^2 + n_2(x(t) - x(t-1))^2 \right]$$

$$c(h(t)) = \tfrac{1}{2}E\left[w_1(h(t) - h^*(t))^2 + w_2(h(t) - h(t-1))^2 \right]$$

$\bar{p}(t), \sigma^2(t) =$ mean and variance of price $p(t)$ as a stochastic process

$x^*(t), h^*(t) =$ desired or targeted output and inventories assumed known

This is maximized subject to the state equations

$$h(t) = h(t-1) + x(t) - \bar{d}(t), \quad t = 1, 2, \ldots, N$$
$$h(0) \text{ given} \quad (3.9)$$

The optimal decision rules satisfy the following set of difference equations, assuming that other implicit constraints like nonnegativity of output etc. are satisfied:

$$My(t+1) + Cy(t) - Ky(t-1) = g \quad (3.10)$$

where

$$M = \begin{pmatrix} n_2 & 0 \\ -\lambda\sigma^2(t+1) & w_2 + \lambda\sigma^2(t+1) \end{pmatrix}, \quad y(t) = \begin{pmatrix} x(t) \\ h(t) \end{pmatrix}$$

$$C = \begin{pmatrix} -(n_1 + 2n_2 + \lambda\sigma^2(t)) & \lambda\sigma^2(t) \\ \lambda\sigma^2(t) & -(w_1 + 2w_2 + \lambda\sigma^2(t) + \lambda\sigma^2(t+1)) \end{pmatrix}$$

$$K = \begin{pmatrix} n_2 & -\lambda\sigma^2(t) \\ 0 & w_2 + \lambda\sigma^2(t) \end{pmatrix}, \quad g = \begin{pmatrix} -n_1 x^*(t) - \bar{p}(t) \\ \bar{p}(t) - \bar{p}(t+1) - w_1 h^*(t) \end{pmatrix}$$

The Hessian matrix $H = (h_{ij})$ associated with optimal $x(t)$ and $h(t)$ has elements

$$h_{11} = -(n_1 + 2n_2 + \lambda\sigma^2(t)), \qquad h_{12} = h_{21} = \lambda\sigma^2(t)$$

$$h_{22} = -(w_1 + 2w_2 + \lambda\sigma^2(t) + \lambda\sigma^2(t+1))$$

It is clear that the degree of concavity of the objective function measured by $(-\Delta_1/\Delta_2)$, where $\Delta_1 = h_{11} < 0$, $\Delta_2 = h_{11}h_{22} = h_{12}^2 > 0$ gets increased when the risk aversion parameter λ is positive rather than zero. But if the distribution of the stochastic components in price and demand is completely unknown, then the nonnegativity of λ cannot be assured, in which case the negative definiteness of the Hessian matrix may fail to hold. In such cases again mixed strategy solutions rather than pure strategies may be preferable.

The case of zero risk aversion ($\lambda = 0$) has some interesting implications. First of all, the difference equation system (3.10), for which the determinantal equation is

$$\det(\mu^2 M + \mu C + K) = 0 \qquad (3.11)$$

admits of a decoupled system interpretation in output and inventories, i.e.,

$$\mu^2 - \left(2 + \frac{n_1}{n_2}\right)\mu + 1 = 0, \qquad \mu^2 - \left(2 + \frac{w_1}{w_2}\right)\mu + 1 = 0$$

Since the product of the two roots (μ_1, μ_2) is unity and their sum is positive, it follows that the roots are reciprocal. However such decoupling is not possible when λ is nonzero. Second, if the mean $\bar{p}(t)$ and variance $\sigma^2(t)$ of market price $p(t)$ viewed as a stochastic process are mutually independent, then there exists a domain around $\bar{p}(t)$, where $p(t) = \bar{p}(t) + e(t)$, $e(t)$ being a noise term, where the profit function will be convex. Denote the optimal profit of (3.8) by $z^0(N, \bar{p}(t))$, when the expost or realized value $\bar{p}(t)$ is used and let $z^0(N, \bar{p}(t) + e(t))$ be the optimal profits, when a forecast or estimate of $e(t)$ is made and optimal policies adopted. Then, by Jensen's inequality it must hold

$$Ez^0(N, \bar{p}(t) + e(t)) > z^0(N, \bar{p}(t)) \qquad (3.12)$$

The left hand side denotes optimal profits, when a forecast value of price is used using information structure available up to the point at which forecast is made. The convexity of the profit function around the mean values $\bar{p}(t)$ may be easily seen by considering $n_1 = 0 = \lambda$ and evaluating optimal profit as a function of price, i.e., it turns out that $\partial^2 z^0(\hat{p}(t))/\partial\hat{p}^2(t)$ is positive, where $\hat{p}(t) = \bar{p}(t) + e(t)$ is the forecast price. By continuity it can be shown (Sengupta 1982) that this convexity would be maintained, even when we take a set of positive values of λ and n_2 in a small local neighborhood around zero. The inequality (3.12) assumes that the probability distribution of the stochastic component $e(t)$ is nondegenerate and it shows the value of information in providing a good forecast of prices and determining the quantity accordingly. Third, if the mean $\bar{p}(t)$ and variance $\sigma^2(t)$ of the stochastic price process are not mutually independent, e.g., Poisson or logistic process (Tintner and Sengupta 1972), then there would be domains of both convexity and concavity of the profit function, where (3.12) would hold for the case of convexity and the following

$$z^0(N, \bar{p}(t)) > Ez^0(N, \hat{p}(t))$$
(3.13)

would hold in case of concavity. This would provide the rationale for suppliers in imperfect stochastic markets not to follow average price as the basis of optimal decision-making. To this extent it is a potential source of fluctuations in imperfect stochastic markets.

The dynamic model specified by (3.8) may be interpreted and applied for optimal decision-making under imperfect competition in two other ways, provided price $p(t)$ is not used as a control variable whether due to fear of retaliation or to the low costs of quantity controls. In the first case, we attempt to develop feedback decision rules where the coefficients are chosen so that a weighted linear combination of variance of production and of inventories are minimized. Since the adjustment cost functions $c(x(t))$, $c(h(t))$ may be interpreted as a linear function of their variances if $x^*(t) = \mu_x(t)$, $h^*(t) = \mu_h(t)$, where $\mu_x(t)$, $\mu_h(t)$ are the mean values, this type of policy has an optimal interpretation in terms of the theory of linear decision rules (Hay and Holt 1975), (Sengupta 1982a). The stochastic balance equation used in this theory is

$$h(t) = h(t-1) + x(t) - d(t)$$
(3.14)

where $d(t)$ is the stochastic demand quantity. By summing over $t = 1$ to $t = k$ we get

$$h(k) = h(0) + \sum_{t=1}^{k} x(t) - \sum_{t=1}^{k} d(t)$$
(3.15)

where $h(0)$ is initial inventory. Suppose the distribution of demand is not completely known, although actual demand of previous periods is all realized and known. In this case we cannot completely forecast future demand. In default of this ability to predict, one may consider the following first-order decision rules (DR):

$$\text{DR}_1: \quad x(t) = \bar{d} + \delta_1, \quad t = 1$$

$$= \alpha_1 d(t-1) + (1 - \alpha_1)\bar{d} + \delta_t, \quad t = 2, 3, \ldots, N$$

$DR_2:$ $\quad x(t) = \bar{d} + \delta_1, \quad t = 1$

$\quad\quad = \alpha_2 d(t-1) + (1 - \alpha_2)\bar{d} + \delta_2, \quad t = 2$

$\quad\quad = \alpha_2 d(t-1) + (1 - \alpha_2)d(t-2) + \delta_t, \quad t = 3, 4, \ldots, N \quad (3.16)$

$DR_3:$ $\quad x(t) = \bar{d} + \delta_1, \quad t = 1$

$\quad\quad = \alpha_3 d(t-1) + \alpha_3(1 - \alpha_3)\bar{d} + \delta_2, \quad t = 2$

$\quad\quad = \alpha_3 d(t-1) + \delta_3(1 - \alpha_3)d(t-2) + \delta_t, \quad t = 3, 4, \ldots, N$

$DR_4:$ $\quad x(t) = \bar{d} + \delta_1, \quad t = 1$

$\quad\quad = \alpha_4 d(t-1) + \alpha_5\bar{d} + \delta_2, \quad t = 2$

$\quad\quad = \alpha_4 d(t-1) + \alpha_5 d(t-2) + \delta_t, \quad t = 3, 4, \ldots, N$

Here $\bar{d}$ denotes the mean demand, updated with most recent information available and the parametric coefficients δ_i, α_i (which may be required to be nonnegative) are to be optimally determined by minimizing a linear combination of variances of production and inventories:

$$\min J = w\sigma^2(h(k)) + (1 - w)\sigma^2(x(k)). \quad (3.17)$$

It is clear that if the variance σ_0^2 of demand is assumed to be time-independent, then the variance of production $\sigma^2(h(k))$ and of inventories $\sigma^2(x(k))$ can be explicitly calculated for each of the above four decisions rules in (3.16) as follows:

$DR_1:$ $\quad \sigma^2(x(k)) = 0, \quad t = 1$

$\quad\quad = \alpha_1^2\sigma_0^2, \quad t = 2, 3, \ldots, k$

$\quad \sigma^2(h(k)) = \left\{1 + (1 - \alpha_1)^2(t-1)\right\}\sigma_0^2, \quad t = 2, 3, \ldots, k$

$DR_2:$ $\quad \sigma^2(x(k)) = 0, \quad t = 1$

$\quad\quad = \alpha_2^2\sigma_0^2, \quad t = 2$

$\quad\quad = \left\{\alpha_2^2 + (1 - \alpha_2)^2\right\}\sigma_0^2, \quad t = 3, 4, \ldots, k$

$\quad \sigma^2(h(k)) = \sigma_0^2, \quad t = 1$

$\quad\quad = \left\{1 + (1 - \alpha_2)^2\right\}\sigma_0^2, \quad t = 2, 3, \ldots, k$

$\text{DR}_3:\ \sigma^2(x(k)) = 0, \quad t = 1$

$$= \alpha_3^2 \sigma_0^2, \quad t = 2$$

$$= \left\{ \alpha_3^2 + \alpha_3^2(1 - \alpha_3)^2 \right\} \sigma_0^2, \quad t = 3, \ldots, k$$

$\sigma^2(h(k)) = \sigma_0^2, \quad t = 1$

$$= \left\{ 1 - (1 - \alpha_3)^2 \right\} \sigma_0^2, \quad t = 2$$

$$= \left[1 + (1 - \alpha_3)^2 + \left\{ 1 - \alpha_3 - \alpha_3(1 - \alpha_3) \right\}^2 \right] \sigma_0^2,$$

$$t = 3, 4, \ldots, k$$

$\text{DR}_4:\ \sigma^2(x(k)) = 0, \quad t = 1$

$$= \alpha_4^2 \sigma_0^2, \quad t = 2$$

$$= \left(\alpha_4^2 + \alpha_5^2 \right) \sigma_0^2, \quad t = 3, 4, \ldots, k$$

$\sigma^2(h(k)) = \sigma_0^2, \quad t = 1$

$$= \left\{ 1 + (1 - \alpha_4)^2 \right\} \sigma_0^2, \quad t = 2$$

$$= \left\{ 1 + (1 - \alpha_4)^2 + (1 - \alpha_4 - \alpha_5)^2 \right\} \sigma_0^2, \quad t = 3, 4, \ldots, k$$

It is clear that for DR_1 the inventory variance increases with time and hence this rule is not desirable. If we want to minimize the variance of production as well as of inventory, then the decision rules DR_2 and DR_3 seem to be better. In terms of parsimony of parameters to be optimally determined, DR_2 offers perhaps the most appropriate decision rule which assumes that the decision-maker knows realized demand for two previous time points, before he makes the production decision for the current period. The optimality of such a decision rule was evidenced in (2.5) when compared with rules known as HMMS decision rules (Sengupta 1977). Note that this optimal feedback method could also be applied in principle, when the variances of demand are time-dependent although numerical methods would be necessary to compute the variances.

A second way of viewing the model (3.8) is in terms of a dynamic portfolio model (Szego 1980), which minimizes the total variance subject to an expected return constraint. Setting $x^*(t) = \mu_x(t)$, $h^*(t) = \mu_k(t)$ and denoting the variances of $x(t)$ and $h(t)$ by $\sigma_x^2(t)$ and $\sigma_h^2(t)$, one such formulation is

$$\min \tfrac{1}{2} \sum_{t=1}^{N} L(t)$$

$$\text{subject to} \quad \sum_{t=1}^{N} \bar{p}(t)\bar{d}(t) \geqslant R(N) \tag{3.18}$$

where

$$L(t) = \sigma_x^2(t) + \left(\sigma_x^2(t) + \sigma_x^2(t-1)\right) - 2v_x(1) + \left(\mu_x(t) + \mu_x(t-1)\right)^2$$

$$+ \sigma_h^2(t) + \left(\sigma_h^2(t) + \sigma_h^2(t-1)\right) - 2v_h(1) + \left(\mu_h(t) - \mu_h(t-1)\right)^2$$

and $v_x(1) = \text{cov}(x(t), x(t-1))$, $v_h(1) = \text{cov}(h(t), h(t-1))$ are the autocovariances, assumed to be stationary. A simpler version of this model may be obtained if a supply variable $s(t) = x(t) - (h(t) - h(t-1))$ defined in (2.2) could be used, by combining output and inventory change in one variable. In this case one obtains a standard portfolio model with an intertemporal planning horizon:

$$\min J = \sum_{t=1}^{N} \sigma_p^2(t) s^2(t)$$

$$\text{subject to} \quad \sum_{t=1}^{N} \bar{p}(t) s(t) = R(N) \tag{3.19}$$

Here the autocovariance of prices at different time points is not allowed for. To allow for them one may define the vector $s^* = (s(1), s(2),\ldots,s(N))$ and the matrix $v = (V_{ij})$, $V_{ij} = \text{cov}(p(i), p(j))$, $i, j = 1, 2,\ldots,N$ and write the decision problem as

$$\min_{s} J = s'Vs$$

$$\text{subject to} \quad \bar{p}'s = R(N) \tag{3.20}$$

where $\imath ay' = (\bar{p}(1), \bar{p}(2),\ldots,\bar{p}(N))$. Let $J(s^*(N), R(N)) = J^*$ denote the minimum value of the objective function J in (3.20) for a specified value of expected return $R(N)$. Then the graph of the curve J^* as a function of $R(N)$ specifies the efficiency frontier. Squaring both sides of the equality constraint of (3.20), the above minimization problem can be viewed as an eigenvalue problem:

$$(V - \alpha B)s = 0 \tag{3.21}$$

where $B = (\bar{p}\bar{p}')$ and the minimum eigenvalue α_* and the associated eigenvector s_* have to be used. However, by using the minimax policies in portfolio theory (Sengupta 1982b), other optimal decision rules could be derived and applied sequentially by varying N. In particular, the case $N = 1$ can be compared with the asymptotic case $N = \infty$. Since $\bar{p}(t)$, $\sigma_{(t)}^2$ denote means and variances for future periods, they have to be forecast on the basis of current and past observations. But since k-step ahead forecast for large k will be very unreliable, we may have the replace $\bar{p}(t)$ and $\sigma_p^2(t)$ by $\beta(t)\bar{p}(t)$ and $\gamma((t)\sigma_p^2(t)$ respectively, where $\beta(t)$ is a decreasing function of time and $\gamma(t)$ is an increasing function of time.

The dynamic portfolio models (3.19) and (3.20) could be suitably revised to that we have output $x(t)$ and inventory $h(t)$ as two sets of decision variables and their covariances have some role in determining optimal portfolios. Two major implications howver still remain valid. First, the more uncertain the future, the lower the optimal supply by a risk-averse supplier, since he would estimate higher price variance and lower price means, compared to a risk-neutral decision-maker. Second, he may prefer minimax policies by accepting lower values of minimum expected returns $R(N)$ and lower length of the planning horizon. The latter may call for myopic or short run policies as against steady long rung strategies.

Next we make some comments on Model II defined by (2.9) and (2.10). Since it is highly nonlinear, it is impossible to compute explicit solutions in closed form. Some authors (Mills 1962) have used linear decision rules as suboptimal solutions by considering suitable approximations of the nonlinear model. A series of simulations computed by Fanchon (1982) on the basis of normal, uniform and other nonnegative distribution of errors has shown however that these suboptimal solutions could be considerably improved. The impact of error variance on the optimal solution is far from negligible.

The role of incomplete information in Model II arises mainly through the lack of a reliable estimate of the parameters like δ of the error distribution, which is partly evolving in the future. This lack of knowledge has the consequence that the inequalities (2.13) and (2.15) hold only probabilistically, e.g., there is always a finite positive probability that the inequality (2.15) does not hold. In such cases the cost of uncertainty would be reflected in higher prices, lower outputs or a combination thereof. Likewise, the higher the probability of shortage in any future period, the higher the price and lower the optimal output.

For Model III defined by (2.18), the necessary conditions of optimality are given by:

$$2\alpha_1 s(t) + \alpha_1 q(t) + \left(\beta_2 \frac{\partial \tilde{s}(t)}{\partial s(t)} + \alpha_1 \beta_1 \right) \lambda(t+1) = \alpha_0 - c$$

$$\alpha_1 \beta_1 s(t) + \beta_2 \hat{s}(t) + q(t+1) + (\alpha_1 \beta_1 - 1) q(t)$$

$$= \beta_0 + \alpha_0 \beta_1 - \beta_1 m(t) \tag{3.21}$$

$$\alpha_1 s(t) + (\alpha_1 \beta_1 - 1)\lambda(t+1) + \lambda(t) = 0$$

for $t = 1, 2, \ldots, T-1$

In contrast to the static case (2.20), two additional factors would affect the optimal solution in this case. First is the expected direction of change of the terms $\partial \tilde{s}(t)/\partial s(t)$. This may affect the stability of the solution from (3.21). The divergence of $\tilde{s}(t)$ from the realized value $s(t)$, if wrongly perceived may lead to further propagation of uncertainty. For risk-averse decision-makers it may thus lead to additional costs of adjustment in terms of shifts of the reaction curves of the two players. Second, the form of the bivariate distribution of $s(t)$ and its estimate by the rival assumes some importance, since it may contribute some additional facets of uncertainty. The Bayesian process of learning emphasized by Harsanyi (1967) in his 'tracing procedures' may not always prove to be stabilizing, unless the bivariate distributions assume some convenient form (Sengupta 1978).

4. Concluding remarks

Several features of imperfect stochastic markets are emphasized here in the context of optimal inventory output decisions. These features emphasize among others the role of incomplete information, randomized solution structure and the situations where the costs of adjustment due to inventory may be partly concave and partly convex. The latter may imply in some cases that linear decision rules defined by an approximate LQG model may conceal a high degree of instability measured by variance.

References

Barro, R.J., "Theory of monopolistic price adjustment," Review of Economic Studies, 39, (1972) 17–26.
Belsley, D.A., Inventory Production Behavior: The Order Stock Distinction. Amsterdam: North Holland, 1969.

134

Fanchon, P.F., Inventory Control in Imperfect Markets. Unpublished Ph.D. Dissertation, Santa Barbara: University of California, 1982.

Harsanyi, J.C., "Games with incomplete information played by Bayesian players," Management sci., 14, (1976), 159–171.

Hay, G.A., and Holt, C.c., "A general solution for linear decision rules," Econometrica, 43, (1975), 231–260.

Hempenius, A.L., Monopoly with Random Demand. Rotterdam: University Press, 1970.

Kirman, A.P., "Learning by firms about demand conditions," in Adaptive Economic Models, ed. R.H. Day and T. Groves, New York: Academic Press, 1975.

Mills, E.S., Price Output and Inventory Policy. New York: John Wiley, 1962.

Sengupta, J.K., "Simulation of linear decision rules," International J. of Systems Science, 8 (1977) 1269–1280.

Sengupta, J.K., "Noncooperative equilibria in monopolistic competition under uncertainty," Zeitschrift fur Nationalökonomie 38 (1978), 193–208.

Sengupta, J.K., Decision Models in Stochastic Programming. New York: Elsevier–North Holland, 1982a.

Sengupta, J.K., "A minimax policy for optimal portfolio choice," Int. J. of Systems, Science, 13 (1982b), 39–56.

Sengupta, J.K., "Static monopoly under uncertainty," Working paper No. 204, UC Santa Barbara, 1982c.

Sengupta, J.K. and Sfeir, R.E., "The adjustment of output–inventory process under linear decision rules, "Journal of Economic Dynamics and Control, 1 (1979), 361–381.

Tintner, G. and Sengupta J.K., Stochastic Economics. New York: Academic Press, 1972.

5. A minimax policy for optimal portfolio choice

1. Introduction

The optimal decision problem in portfolio theory considers a decision-maker (DM) who has to optimally invest a proportion of his wealth, x_i, in a risky asset i, where $x_i \geqslant 0$ for $i = 1, 2, \ldots, m$ and $\sum_{i=1}^{m} x_i = 1$ and the return $\tilde{r}_i$ is random. Any choice of vector $x' = (x_1, x_2, \ldots, x_m)$ that is feasible i.e.

$$x \geqslant 0, \quad e'x = 1 \tag{1}$$

where e is an $m \times l$ vector with each element unity and prime denotes transpose, is called a portfolio policy with a random return $\tilde{z}$:

$$\tilde{z} = \tilde{r}'x, \quad \tilde{r}' = (\tilde{r}_1, \tilde{r}_2, \ldots, \tilde{r}_m) \tag{2}$$

With $E(\tilde{r}) = \mu = (\mu_1, \mu_2, \ldots, \mu_m)'$ and $\mathrm{cov}(\tilde{r}) = V = (v_{ij})$, $i, j = 1, 2, \ldots, m$ denoting the mean vector and the variance-covariance matrix of $\tilde{r}$ respectively, the mean and variance of return $\tilde{z}$ on a feasible portfolio policy are, respectively given by

$$E(\tilde{z}) = \mu'x, \quad \mathrm{var}(\tilde{z}) = x'Vx \tag{3}$$

Denoting the set of parameters by $\theta = (\mu, V)$, the traditional optimal solution of the portfolio theory solves the following quadratic programming problem (QP):

$$\min_{x \in R} \ h = x'Vx \tag{4}$$

$$\text{where} \quad R: \left\{ x \mid e'x = 1, \ \mu'x \geqslant M, \ x \geqslant 0 \right\} \tag{5}$$
$$M: \text{a fixed positive number}$$

By varying M parametrically, the whole set of optimal or efficient portfolios is determined according to Markowitz's theory and its various extensions (Szego 1980).

We attempt here a generalization of the QP model (4) in two important directions: (a) How can the DM determine the number m out of

135

n securities $(n > m)$ to include in his optimal portfolio? (b) how is he going to specify his optimal policy, when the parameter set θ is known only by their statistical estimates $\hat{\theta}$? The latter problem has been discussed recently by Lin and Boot (1980) and Lin (1981) in terms of Bayesian theory, when the DM may use sample observations to modify the prior distribution of random return $\tilde{z}$ to a suitable posterior distribution resulting in a new optimal policy. We follow a different approach, using principles of stochastic dominance among a pair of random variables. This approach leads to a new class of optimal solutions which we call minimax policies. These are so called because they minimize the maximum risk associated with selecting a subset k out of m ($k < m$) risky assets. The conditions under which a minimax policy is optimal relative to other policies are characterized by a set of theorems and their implications.

The discussion is presented in four sections. Section 2 formulates several versions of the portfolio choice problem and the associated QPs. Section 3 presents the theorems which characterize the optimality of minimax policies; this is followed by Section 4 indicating the implications of such minimax policies in other stochastic decision models e.g. stochastic linear programming and stochastic bilinear games.

2. Alternative portfolio decision models

The specific decision problem in portfolio theory proposed here has practical relevance (Jacob 1974) for the small investor who has to choose limited diversification portfolios for several reasons. First, he may save on transaction costs by limiting himself to k out of m ($m > k$) securities. Second, he may rationally choose to devote more attention to the selection of a few individual securities, when transaction costs and taxes prohibit frequent changes in decisions. Third, there has been some recent empirical evidence (Jacob 1974) on the relation between risk and return on common stocks suggesting that diversification beyond eight to ten securities may be superfluous.

To consider this selection problem we specify the QP problem (4) and (5) in several reduced forms, according as the parameters are known or estimated. Denote by N the total number of selections of k out of m securities, where for each selection the parameter vectors are denoted by $\mu(s) = (\mu_1(s), \mu_2(s), \ldots, \mu_k(s))'$ and $V(s) = (v_{ij}(s))$, $s = 1, 2, \ldots, N$, where $N = \binom{m}{k}$. For each selection s fixed, we set up a QP problem:

Model A $\quad \min_{x(s) \in R(s)} h(s) = x(s)'V(s)x(s)$ \hfill (6)

where $\quad R(s)$: $\{x(s) \mid \mu'(s)x(s) = 1\}$ $\qquad s = 1, 2, \ldots, N$

where the nonnegativity constraint on $x(s)$ is dropped and the units of $x(s)$ are so chosen that the positive level M in (5) is set to unity without any loss of generality. The nonnegativity restriction is not really necessary. If our optimal solution calls for $x_i(s) < 0$, or $x_i(s) > 1$ we can take this to mean that the optimal action is to go short in one security and take a corresponding long position in the other. This treatment is consistent with modern discussions of portfolio theory.

However, the reduced form model needs to be modified further, if the estimates $\hat{\mu}(s)$, $\hat{V}(s)$ are used in place of the unknown parameters. This leads to the next model in terms of the new decision variables $y(s) = y_1(s)$, $y_2(s), \ldots, y_k(s))'$:

Model B $\quad \min_{y(s) \in R_y(s)} \hat{g}(s) = y(s)' \hat{V}(s) y(s)$ $\qquad\qquad$ (7)

where $\quad R_y(s): \{ y(s) \mid y'(s) y(s) = 1 \}$
$\qquad\qquad y(s) = (y_i(s)), \quad y_i(s) = \hat{\mu}_i(s) x_i(s)$
$\qquad\qquad \hat{V}(s) = \left[v_{ij}(s) / \hat{\mu}_i(s) \hat{\mu}_j(s) \right]$
$\qquad\qquad i, j = 1, 2, \ldots, k; \quad s = 1, 2, \ldots, N$

Note that the constraint $\hat{\mu}'(s) x(s) = 1$ has been replaced here by $y'(s) y(s) = 1$. This may be interpreted in two ways. First, it is an approximation of the earlier constraint squared on both sides i.e.

$$\left(\sum_{i=1}^{k} \hat{\mu}_i(s) x_i(s) \right)^2 = 1$$ $\qquad\qquad$ (8)

which means that all $x_i(s)$ or, all $y_i(s)$ cannot be zero for $i = 1, 2, \ldots, k$ and a fixed $s = 1, 2, \ldots, N$.

A variant of model B results if we use (8) in (7) e.g.

$\quad \min_{x(s) \in R(s)} \tilde{h}(s) = x(s)' \tilde{V}(s) x(s)$ $\qquad\qquad$ (9)

where $\quad R(s): \{ x(s) \mid x'(s) \tilde{M}(s) x(s) = 1 \}$
$\qquad\qquad \tilde{M}(s) = (\hat{\mu}(s) \hat{\mu}'(s)), \qquad \tilde{V}(s) = (\tilde{V}_{ij}(s)); \quad i, j = 1, 2, \ldots, k$

Note that any solution of (9) must necessarily satisfy $\sum_i \hat{\mu}_i(s) x_i(s) = 1$. Second, the constraint on the transformed decision vector $y(s)$ may be viewed in terms of goal programming e.g. if $y(s)$ is a vector of deviations or distance from a desired goal, then the sum of squared distances must be finite and positive, i.e. set equal to one by normalization. The penalty cost of deviations, $C(y) = y'(s)y(s) - 1 = 0$ may be approximated by a quadratic function, as in the theory of linear decision rules (Sengupta 1980b).

Finally, we assume a model where the investor has two stages of selection. In the first stage he selects only those securities, k in number $(k < m)$ for which the covariances $v_{ij}(s)$ are nonnegative for all $i, j = 1, 2, \ldots, k$ and the second stage he determines which selection $s \in S$ to choose, where S is the finite set of N selections, $k = 1, 2, \ldots, N$. In this case the model can be written in terms of the decision vector $y(s)$.

Model C $\quad \min_{y(s) \in \tilde{R}_y(s)} \tilde{g}(s) = y'(s)\tilde{V}(s)y(s)$

where $\quad \tilde{R}_y(s): \{ y(s) \mid y'(s)y(s) = 1, y(s) \geqslant 0 \}$

$\tilde{V}(s)$: variance–covariance matrix in normalized units: $\left(\tilde{v}_{ij}(s) \geqslant 0 \right)$

where the nonnegativity constraint on $y(s)$ has been specifically added, which, by implication would show the cost of losing the option of going short in one subset of securities.

It is clear from the specification (10) that if $\tilde{V}(s)$ is strictly positive definite, then an extreme solution $y^0(s)$ which maximizes rather than minimizes the objective function $\tilde{g}(s)$ must exist such that it satisfies the eigenvalue problem

$$[\tilde{V}(s) - \tilde{\lambda}(s)I] y(s) = 0 \tag{11}$$

where the maximum eigenvalue $\tilde{\lambda}^0(s)$ and the associated eigenvector $y^0(s)$ are both nonnegative. This follows by the Perron–Frobenius theorem on nonnegative matrices.

Since for models A through C, the constraint set is compact for each $s \in S$ fixed, where $S = \{1, 2, \ldots, N\}$ denotes the total number of selections, it is clear that both minimum and maximum solutions exist. Thus, one could define for example the following types of policy for model A:

$$\min_{s \in S} \min_{x(s) \in R(s)} h(s) = h(s_0, x_0) = \min_s \min_x h(s, x)$$

$$\min_{s \in S} \max_{x(s) \in R(s)} h(s) = h(s_0, x^0) = \min_s \max_x h(s, x) \tag{12}$$

$$\max_{s \in S} \min_{x(s) \in R(s)} h(s) = h(s^0, x_0) = \max_s \min_x h(s, x)$$

where the index set S is discrete, as it contains a finite number N of total sections. This allows pure strategy solutions only, viewed in a gametheoretic sense. If we allow mixed strategies in the sense that new parameters $(\bar{\mu}, \bar{V})$ could be meaningfully defined as

$$\bar{\mu} = \sum_{s \in S} p_s \mu(s); \quad p_s \geq 0, \quad \sum p_s = 1$$

$$\bar{V} = \sum_{s \in S} \sum_{t \in S} p_s p_t V_{st}; \quad p_s, p_t \geq 0; \quad \sum p_s = 1 = \sum p_t \tag{13}$$

$$V_{st} = V(s), \quad \text{if} \quad s = t$$

We could redefine the objective function $h(s, x)$ as $h(p, x), p \in P, x \in X$ where P: $\{ p \mid p_s \geq 0, \sum p_s = 1\}$ and X: $\{x \mid \bar{\mu}'x = 1\}$ are suitable compact sets. Thus, the following policies can be defined also:

$$\max_{p \in P} \min_{x \in X} h(p, x) = h(p^0, x_0)$$

$$\min_{p \in P} \max_{x \in X} h(p, x) = h(p_0, x^0)$$

$$\min_{p \in P} \min_{x \in X} h(p, x) = h(p_0, x_0) \tag{13}$$

$$\max_{p \in P} \max_{x \in X} h(p, x) = h(p^0, x^0)$$

It is clear that analogous formulations exist for models B and C, in terms of their respective objective functions. Note however that for model A, the parameters are completely known and hence the best policy is characterized by $h(s_0, x_0) = \min_s \min_x h(s, x)$ in case of pure strategy or, by $h(p_0, x_0)$ in case of mixed strategies. There is no need for considering other policies e.g. minimax policies like $h(s_0, x^0)$ or $h(p^0, x_0)$, which attempt to characterize in some sense a conservative risk averse attitude by choosing a policy which, is in some sense 'best of the worst'. However, when the parameters $\mu(s)$, $V(s)$ are not known, or known incompletely through their sample estimates, the minimax policies defined suitably may prove better than minimin policies, provided certain conditions hold. It would be our purpose to analyze these conditions under which minimax policies would be optimal for portfolio choice.

It is clear that in suitable cases, mixed strategy solutions can be given a game-theoretic interpretation. Consider for example a special case of model A where we have incorporated the constraint in the objective function e.g.

$$\min_{x(s)} h(s) = x(s)'V(s)x(s) - \lambda(s)\mu'(s)x(s)$$

$$= x(s)'V(s)x(s) - \lambda^*\mu'(s)x(s) \tag{14}$$

and the Lagrange multiplier $\lambda(s)$ has been fixed at a preassigned positive value λ^* e.g. this may be determined by a common market index (Jacob 1974). Assume there are two selections $s = 1, 2$ and for simplicity these selections are statistically independent in the sense that V_{st} is zero for $s \neq t$ in (13). Then the optimal solution, $\bar{x}_0$ obtained by minimizing the expression:

$$h = p^2 \sigma_1^2 + (1 - p)^2 \sigma_2^2 - \lambda^*(p\mu_1 + (1 - p)\mu_2)$$

$$\sigma_s^2 = x'(s)V(s)x(s), \quad \mu_s = \mu'(s)x(s)$$

turns out to be

$$\bar{x}_0 = px_0(1) + (1 - p)x_0(2);$$

$$x_0(1) = \frac{\lambda^*}{2p^2}V^{-1}(1)\mu(1), \qquad x_0(2) = \frac{\lambda^*}{2(1 - p)^2}V^{-1}(2)\mu(2)$$

$$p = p_0 = \frac{\lambda^*|\mu_1 - \mu_2|}{2(\sigma_1^2 + \sigma_2^2)} - \frac{\sigma_2^2}{(\sigma_1^2 + \sigma_2^2)} \tag{15}$$

It is clear that a zero value of p, which implies a pure strategy solution is possible, only if $\mu(1) = \mu(2)$ and σ_2^2 is zero i.e. only $x(2)$ is used instead of the mixture defined by $\bar{x}_0$. A completely mixed strategy optimal solution results when the optimal value, p_0 of p satisfies $0 < p_0 < 1$ i.e. when either $|\mu_1 - \mu_2|$ or σ_2^2 is not zero. In the general case when the covariances V_{st}, $s \neq t$ are not zero, the optimal solutions in (15) reduce to the following:

$$p_0 = (\sigma_1^2 + \sigma_2^2 - 2\sigma_{12})^{-1}\left[\frac{\lambda^*|\mu_1 - \mu_2|}{2.0} + (\sigma_2^2 - \sigma_{12})\right] \geq 0$$

$$\begin{pmatrix} x_0(1) \\ x_0(2) \end{pmatrix} = \begin{bmatrix} 2p_0^2 V(1) & 2p_0(1 - p_0)V_{12} \\ 2p_0(1 - p_0)V_{12} & 2(1 - p_0)^2 V(2) \end{bmatrix}^{-1} \begin{pmatrix} p_0\lambda^*\mu(1) \\ (1 - p_0)\lambda^*\mu(2) \end{pmatrix}$$

$$\sigma_{12} = x(1)'V_{12}x(2) = x(2)'V_{12}x(1)$$

Note that we can define a second type of solution by first combining the parameters $\mu(s)$, $V(s)$ over different selections as in (13) with $s = 1, 2$, and then minimizing the expression

$$h(x, p) = x'\bar{V}x - \lambda^*\bar{\mu}'x \tag{16}$$

where $\bar{\mu}$, $\bar{V}$ are defined in (13) for $s = 1$, 2. The optimal solution then becomes:

$$x_0(p) = \frac{\lambda^*}{2} \bar{V}^{-1}\bar{\mu} \tag{17}$$

where a suitable value of p has yet to be determined. How would the two optimal solutions given by (15) and (17) compare? It is clear that if there exists a value of p in (17) such that the variance associated with the solution $x_0(p)$ is much lower than that associated with the mixed strategy solution $\bar{x}_0$, then the action plan $x_0(p)$ would be more robust. However the two solutions $x_0(p)$, $\bar{x}_0$ would be identical if $p_0 = 0.0 = p$ in the two cases (15) and (17) since we would get

$$\bar{x}_0 = x_0(2) = \frac{\lambda^*}{2} V^{-1}(2)\mu(2) = x_0(p)$$

But in general, the two mixed strategy solutions, one $(\bar{x}_0)$ combining separate action plans and the other $(x_0(p))$ combining separate parameters before deciding an optimal action, would give very different results in terms of their expected returns and variances. If, in the second case, the parameters are to be estimated from sample observations, this reduces to the so-called two-arm bandit problems in statistical decision theory (Chernoff 1972), whereas the first case is closely related to bilinear stochastic games involving two players (Sengupta 1980a).

3. Theoretical results

3.1. Allocation under model A

For model A, where knowledge of parameters is assumed available two types of important results can be characterized. One involves the inequalities for the various minimax and minimin policies defined in (12) and (13) respectively and the other involves the decision situations when each of the N selections is viewed as a single multivariate population, so that we have to choose the best among N multivariate distributions. Since the second type of question has been investigated elsewhere we deal here only with the first type of results.

THEOREM 1: *If in model A, each of the N discrete selections $s \in S = \{1, 2, \ldots, N\}$ exist, then the following inequalities hold*:

$$h(s_0, x_0) \leqslant h(s^0, x_0) \leqslant h(s^0, x^0)$$

$$h(s_0, x_0) \leqslant h(s_0, x^0) \leqslant h(s^0, x^0)$$

where the notation of (12) *is used. Furthermore, if the mixed strategy solutions defined in* (13) *exist, then we have also,*

$$\min_{p \in P} \max_{x \in X} h(p, x) \geqslant \max_{x \in X} \min_{p \in P} h(p, x) \geqslant \min_{x \in X} \min_{p \in P} h(p, x)$$

$$\min_{p \in P} \min_{x \in X} h(p, x) \leqslant \max_{p \in P} \min_{x \in X} h(p, x) \leqslant \min_{x \in X} \max_{p \in P} h(p, x)$$

PROOF: The first part follows from the following inequality

$$\max_{x} h(s, x) \geqslant h(s, x) \geqslant \min_{x} h(s, x), \qquad \text{any} \quad s$$

since each of the discrete selections exists. For the second part, we note that by construction $h(p, x)$ is a continuous function defined on the sets P, X which are convex, closed and bounded. Hence

$$\max_{x} h(p, x) \geqslant h(p, x), \qquad \text{any} \quad p$$

or

$$\min_{p} \left[\max_{x} h(p, x) \right] \geqslant \min_{p} h(p, x), \qquad \text{all} \quad x$$

$$\geqslant \max_{x} \min_{p} h(p, x)$$

Again,

$$\min_{x} h(p, x) \leqslant h(p, x) \qquad \text{any} \quad p$$

or,

$$\max_{p} \left[\min_{x} h(p, x) \right] \leqslant \max_{p} h(p, x), \qquad \text{all} \quad x$$

$$\leqslant \min_{x} \max_{p} h(p, x)$$

REMARK 1.1.: If the difference $d(s_0, x^0) = h(s_0, x^0) - h(s_0, x_0)$ is lower than $d(s^0, x_0) = h(s^0, x_0) - h(s_0, x_0)$, then the minimax policy $h(s_0, x^0)$ may be preferable over the maximin policy $h(s^0, x_0)$. In the same sense, the minimax policy $\min_p \max_x h(p, x)$ may be preferable to the maximin policy $\max_p \min_x h(p, x)$, in terms of their relative distance from the first best policy $\min_p \min_x h(p, x)$.

REMARK 1.2.: If the index s in the discrete selection model is allowed to vary continuously, so that N_s times out of $N = \Sigma_s N_s$, the plan $x(s)$ is chosen i.e. N_s/N defines the random probability of selection of a plan $x(s)$, then a two-person non-zero sum game problem can be defined by $\{G_1, G_2; x \in H(x), s \in F(s)\}$, where $G_1 = G_1(x, s)$, $G_2 = G_2(x, s)$ are the payoff functions to players I and II respectively and $H(x)$ is the cumulative distribution function (cdf) of the strategies x used by player I and $F(s)$ is the cdf for strategies s controlled by player II. If $G_i(x, s)$ are continuous functions of their arguments for $i = 1, 2$ and $G_1 = -G_2$, then a saddle point solution exists and the game is zero-sum.

REMARK 1.3.: If player I makes a forecast $\hat{s}$ of player II's strategy based on a distribution $F(\hat{s})$ and similarly by player II, then the optimal reaction or response function of the two players become

$$\min_s u_I = \int_{\hat{s} \in F(\hat{s})} G_1(s, x \,|\, s = \hat{s}) \, dF(\hat{s}) \to R_1(x, \hat{s}) = 0$$

$$\max_s u_{II} = \int_{\hat{x} \in H(\hat{x})} G_2(s, x \,|\, x = \hat{x}) \, dH(\hat{x}) \to R_2(\hat{x}, s) = 0$$

If there exists a pair $(s = s^0 = \hat{s}, x = x_0 = \hat{x})$ which satisfies jointly $R_1(x, \hat{s}) = 0 = R_2(\hat{x}, s)$, then the pair defines a Cournot–Nash equilibrium. By continuity, there must exist neighborhoods $N(x_0)$, $N(s^0)$ of x_0, s^0 respectively. If the set $N(s^0, x_0): N(s^0) \cap N(x_0)$ is nonempty, then the Cournot–Nash equilibrium pair (s^0, x) may be defined to be stable (unstable), if for any point defined by the pair (s, x) belonging to $N(s^0, x_0)$ converges to (diverges from) the point (s^0, x_0) in successive iterations of forecasts and their revisions.

We have to note that the minimax policies characterized by Theorem 1 have to be estimated from observational data, before they could be found practically useful. Writing the random return function $\tilde{z} = \tilde{z}(x)$ as

$$\tilde{z} = \tilde{z}(x) = \tilde{r}'(s)x, \quad x \in R$$

where R is a closed bounded set in k-dimensional space, a linear regression model

$$\tilde{z} = \mu'x + \epsilon, \quad x \in R;$$

with errors ϵ having zero mean and finite variance σ^2, distributed independently of x may be used to obtain linear unbiased estimates $\hat{\mu}$ of the k-dimensional vector μ where $\hat{\mu}'x = 1$ for all $\hat{\mu}$. Since for each selection we have a vector $\hat{\mu}$ of linear unbiased estimates, we have altogether a total of N linear unbiased estimates. How can one evaluate these N unbiased estimates in optimal choice theory? Following the approach in optimal statistical design theory in sequential analysis (Chernoff 1972), we may use three criteria:

(1) Chebyshev or minimax criterion, where we select an allocation policy x to minimize the maximum variance of prediction i.e.

$$\min_{x \in R} \max x' V_{\hat{\mu}\hat{\mu}} x$$

where $V_{\hat{\mu}\hat{\mu}}$ denotes the variance of the estimate $\hat{\mu}'x$,

(2) D-optimality criterion, where we select an allocation policy x to minimize the determinant $|V_{\hat{\mu}\hat{\mu}}|$ of the variance–covariance matrix of the linear unbiased estimates $\hat{\mu}$, and the

(3) A-optimality criterion, according to which we choose an allocation policy x which minimizes the sum of the variances of the components of the estimates $\hat{\mu}$ i.e. minimizes the trace of the matrix $(V_{\hat{\mu}\hat{\mu}})$.

If the allocation policy x can vary continuously within the closed bounded region R, then the following results are known (Chernoff 1972):

(i) If there exists an optimal selection or design x^* which is optimum in terms of the Chebyshev criterion above, then it is also optimum in terms of the D-optimality and A-optimality criteria, and

(ii) if the variance–covariance matrix is positive definite (semi-definite), then the information matrix $I(x^*)$ associated with the optimal allocation policy

$$I(x^*) = \text{inverse (pseudo-inverse) of } V_{\hat{\mu}(x^*)\hat{\mu}(x^*)}$$

is also symmetric positive definite (semidefinite) and hence the design x^* maximizes the trace of the information matrix $I(x^*)$ also.

Note however that the equivalence of the three criteria e.g. Chebyshev, D-optimality and A-optimality need not necessarily hold for discrete selections or designs when x can vary in a discrete sense within the region R. Also, if the rank of $V_{\hat{\mu}\hat{\mu}}$ is k for any optimal allocation policy x^*, one could represent the information matrix $I(x^*)$ as

$$I(x^*) = \sum_{i=1}^{k} p_i X'(i) X(i), \quad p_i \geqslant 0, \quad \sum_{i=1}^{k} p_i = 1$$

where $V_{\hat{\mu}(i)\hat{\mu}(i)} = [X(i)'(X(i)]^{-1}$. Thus, it follows the set of information matrices is convex i.e. for $0 \leqslant \alpha \leqslant 1$, $k = 2$

$$I(x^*) = I(\alpha x^*(1) + (1 - \alpha)x^*(2)) = \alpha I(x^*(1)) + (1 - \alpha)I(x^*(2))$$

3.2. Allocation under model B

Next we consider the optimal allocation decision problem under model B, which optimizes for every $s \in S$ a scalar quadratic function $\hat{g}(s)$ subject to a single normalization condition that is also quadratic. It is clear from the specification of this model in (7) that for any fixed $s \in S$, optimal solutions $\hat{y}_0(s)$, $\hat{y}^0(s)$ exist, which respectively maximize or minimize the objective function $\hat{g}(s)$, if and only if there exist Lagrange multipliers $\hat{\lambda}_0(s)$, $\hat{\lambda}^0(s)$ satisfying the respective eigenvalue problems as follows;

$$[\hat{V}(s) - \hat{\lambda}_0(s)I]\,\hat{y}_0(s) = 0, \qquad [\hat{V}(s) - \hat{\lambda}^0(s)I]\,\hat{y}^0(s) = 0$$

where I is the identity matrix of order k. Since the restriction set $R_y(s)$ is compact and the scalar function $\hat{g}(s)$ is continuous on this compact set, both the multipliers $\hat{\lambda}_0(s)$, $\hat{\lambda}^0(s)$ would exist, if the set $R_y(s)$ is not empty. We may therefore define minimax and other policies as follows:

$$\min_{s \in S} \hat{\lambda}^0(s) \to \left(\hat{\lambda}^0(s_0), \hat{y}^0(s_0), \hat{g}(\hat{y}^0(s_0))\right) = \hat{g}^0(s_0)$$

$$\min_{s \in S} \hat{\lambda}_0(s) \to \left(\hat{\lambda}_0(s_0), \hat{y}_0(s_0), \hat{g}(\hat{y}_0(s_0))\right) = \hat{g}_0(s_0) \qquad (18)$$

$$\max_{s \in S} \hat{\lambda}_0(s) \to \left(\hat{\lambda}_0(s^0), \hat{y}_0(s^0), \hat{g}(\hat{y}_0(s^0))\right) = \hat{g}_0(s^0)$$

It is clear that these eigenvalues $\hat{\lambda}^0(s_0)$, $\hat{\lambda}_0(s_0)$, $\hat{\lambda}_0(s^0)$ are all real and positive, if the estimated variance covariance matrix $\hat{V}(s)$ is positive definite for every $s \in S$. Further for each $s \in S$, the objective functions, $\hat{g}(\hat{y}^0 s))$ and $\hat{g}(\hat{y}_0(s))$ are random quantities, over which a second stage of optimization over the set S can be performed. Let the selection s over the set S be assumed independent and random and denote the cumulative distribution functions of $\hat{g}(y^0(s))$, $\hat{g}(\hat{y}^0(s_0))$, $\hat{g}(\hat{y}^0(s^0))$ respectively by

$$F(t) = \text{prob}\left(\hat{g}(\hat{y}^0(s)) \leqslant t\right), \qquad G(t) = \text{prob}\left(\hat{g}(\hat{y}^0(s_0)) \leqslant t\right)$$

and

$$H(t) = \text{prob}\left(\hat{g}(\hat{y}^0(s^0)) \leqslant t\right)$$

with their densities $f(t)$, $g(t)$ and $h(t)$. Further, denote by $L(z)$ the set of all bounded functions (i.e. loss functions) strictly increasing in z, having continuous derivatives of order one and two at each point z in the interval $[0, \infty]$ such that the first derivatives are finite and positive and the second derivatives are nonnegative over the above interval. Using $L(z)$ as the loss function, the following result can be stated on the expected losses $EL(z)$ under $H(t)$, $F(t)$ and $G(t)$, provided they exist.

THEOREM 2. *For all loss functions $L(z)$ defined above the following inequalities hold for all finite $N \geqslant 2$, where N is the total number of selections*:

$$EL_H \leqslant EL_F \leqslant EL_G \qquad \text{for} \quad t \in [0, \infty]$$

and E is the expectation operator on $L = L(z)$ based on the distribution functions H or F or G.

PROOF: Since we have

$$G(t) = 1 - [1 - F(t)]^N > F(t) \qquad \text{for all finite} \quad N \geqslant 2$$

$$H(t) = [F(t)]^N < F(t) \qquad \text{for all finite} \quad N \geqslant 2$$

hence $G(t) \geqslant F(t) \geqslant H(t)$ and the inequalities are strict for all finite $N > 2$. On integrating by parts,

$$EL_H - EL_F = L(t) [H(t) - F(t)]\Big|_0^{+\infty} - \int_0^\infty \frac{\mathrm{d}L}{\mathrm{d}t}[H(t) - F(t)]\mathrm{d}t$$

$$= \text{zero} - \left[\frac{\mathrm{d}L}{\mathrm{d}t} \cdot \int_0^t [H(\tau) - F(\tau)]\mathrm{d}\tau\right]_0^\infty$$

$$+ \int_0^\infty \frac{\mathrm{d}^2L}{\mathrm{d}t^2} \cdot \left\{\int_0^t [H(\tau) - F(\tau)]\mathrm{d}t\right\}$$

But the second term on the right hand side is zero, since $\lim_{t \to \infty}(\mathrm{d}L/\mathrm{d}t) = 0$, because $L(t)$ is by assumption a decreasing convex function bounded from below and $H(t)$, $F(t)$ have finite means. Again, for all $N \geqslant 2$,

$$\int_0^t [H(\tau) - F(\tau)]\mathrm{d}t \leqslant 0, \quad t \in [0, \infty]$$

and since $\mathrm{d}^2L/\mathrm{d}t^2$ is nonnegative, therefore $EL_H \leqslant EL_F$. By a similar argument, the other part of the inequality could be proved.

REMARK 2.1: By redefining $F(t)$, $H(t)$, $G(t)$ as

$$F(t) = \text{prob}(\hat{g}(\hat{y}_0(s)) \leqslant t), \qquad G(t) = \text{prob}(\hat{g}(\hat{u}_0(s)) \leqslant t)$$

and

$$H(t) = \text{prob}(\hat{g}(\hat{y}_0(s^0)) \leqslant t)$$

one could prove an analogous result:

$$EL_H \leqslant EL_F \leqslant EL_G \qquad \text{for} \quad t \in [0, \infty], \quad N \geqslant 2,$$

where expected losses now refer to the minimum risk solutions $\hat{y}_0(s)$, rather than the maximum risk ones $\hat{y}^0(s)$.

REMARK 2.2. This result implies that under the given conditions on the loss function, a minimax policy $\hat{y}^0(s_0)$ may be preferable to a maximin policy $\hat{y}_0(s^0)$.

REMARK 2.3: Since $G(t) > H(t)$ for all $t \in (0, \infty)$ and all finite $N > 2$, the distribution function $H(t)$ for the maximum stochastically dominates in the first order sense, over the distribution function $G(t)$ for the minimum. This results in $EL_H < EH_G$ for all finite $N > 2$.

THEOREM 3.: *If the random returns vector $\tilde{r}$ is distributed normally $N(\mu, V)$ with V having positive and distinct eigenvalues for each $s \in S$ and $\hat{V}$ is the unbiased estimator of V computed on the basis of T observations $T > k$, then as T increases the sample eigenvalues $\hat{\lambda}^0(s), \hat{\lambda}_0(s), \hat{\lambda}_i(s)$ each tends to a normal distribution with means $\lambda^0(s), \lambda_0(s), \lambda_i(s)$ and respective standard deviations $\sigma^0(s) = \sqrt{2/(T-1)} \ \lambda^0(s), \ \sigma_0(s) = \sqrt{2/(T-1)} \ \lambda_0(s), \ \sigma_i(s) = \sqrt{2/(T-1)} \ \lambda_i(s)$. Let the risk associated with the sample eigenvalues be denoted by the respective ratio of mean to standard deviation i.e.*

$$\alpha^0 = E\hat{\lambda}^0(s)/\sigma^0(s), \quad \alpha_0 = E\hat{\lambda}_0(s)/\sigma_0(s), \quad \alpha_i = E\hat{\lambda}_i(s)/\sigma_i(s).$$

Then, asymptotically for large T, $\alpha^0 = \alpha_0 = \alpha_i$, $i = 1, 2, \ldots, k$ and the minimax and minimin policies defined in (18) have identical risks.

PROOF: Since the unbiased estimate $\hat{V}$ of V has the Wishart distribution and the population matrix V satisfies the determinantal equations $|V - \lambda I| = 0$ with distinct positive eigenvalues $\lambda_i > 0$, the latter can be ordered as $\lambda_0 = \lambda_1 < \lambda_2 < \ldots \lambda_i \ldots < \lambda_k = \lambda^0$. For sufficiently large samples, these eigenvalues λ_i can be approximated by certain of the eigenvalues of $|\hat{V} - \hat{\lambda} I| = 0$. Given that λ_i's are distinct, $\hat{\lambda}_i$'s also will be distinct. Hence the statistic $(\hat{\lambda}_i - \lambda_i)/\sigma_i$ will be distributed like a unit normal variate in the limit. This follows from a result of Girschik (1939). Hence the risks defined by the ratio of mean to standard deviation are identical i.e., $\alpha^0 = \alpha_0 = \alpha_i$, $1 \leqslant i \leqslant k$.

REMARK 3.1.: The minimax $\hat{\lambda}^0(s_0)$ and minimum $\hat{\lambda}_0(s_0)$ policies have the same risk in an asymptotic sense as T becomes large.

REMARK 3.2.: The difference between minimax and minimin policies can be statistically tested by the t-statistic:

$$t \sim \frac{\hat{\lambda}^0(s_0) - \hat{\lambda}_0(s_0)}{\left[\sigma_0^2(s_0) + \sigma^0(s_0)^2\right]^{1/2}}$$

in the asymptotic sense for large T.

REMARK 3.3: The above results may not hold, if either the underlying distribution of returns is not normal, or the asymptotic case of large sample size $T \to \infty$ does not hold.

THEOREM 4: *If the variance–covariance matrix $\tilde{V}$ in the portfolio model (9) is strictly positive definite and there exists a nonzero extreme solution vector $x^*(s)$ which either minimizes or maximizes the objective function $\tilde{h}(s)$, then there must exist a minimax eigenvalue $\tilde{\lambda}^0(s_0)$ that is positive, where $\tilde{\lambda}^0(s_0) = \min_{s \in S} \tilde{\lambda}^0(s)$ and $\tilde{\lambda}^0(s)$ is the maximum eigenvalue of the system*

$$\left[\tilde{V}(s) - \tilde{\lambda}^0(s)\tilde{M}(s)\right]x(s) = 0$$

i.e. $\tilde{\lambda}^0(s) = \max_i \tilde{\lambda}_i(s)$.

PROOF: Since the extreme solution vector $x^*(s)$ must satisfy the necessary condition of optimality, we get the eigenvalue problem

$$\left[\tilde{V}(s) - \tilde{\lambda}(s)\tilde{M}(s)\right]x(s) = 0$$

where both $\tilde{V}(s)$ and $\tilde{M}(s)$ are symmetric, the former being strictly positive definite and the latter positive semidefinite. Hence all the eigenvalues $\tilde{\lambda}_i(s)$, $1 \leqslant i \leqslant k$ are real and nonnegative. But the rank of $\tilde{M}(s)$ is at least one, since we have $x^*(s)'\tilde{M}(s)x^*(s) = 1$ and $x^*(s)$ cannot have all zero as its elements. Hence there must exist at least one eigenvalue that is positive, all others being zero. Denote this positive eigenvalue by $\tilde{\lambda}^0(s)$ for each $s \in S$. Taking minimum over $s \in S$, we obtain the minimax eigenvalue $\tilde{\lambda}^0(s_0)$ and its associated eigenvector $x^0(s_0)$.

REMARK 4.1: If $\tilde{V}(s)$ is strictly positive definite and $\tilde{M}(s)$ has rank one, there may not exist any other positive eigenvalue different from $\tilde{\lambda}^0(s)$. This implies that minimin policies having positive eigenvalues $\tilde{\lambda}_0(s_0)$ may not exist.

REMARK 4.2: If $\tilde{V}(s)$ is strictly positive definite and $\tilde{M}(s)$ positive semidefinite with rank one, then there exists a nonsingular matrix W, such that $\tilde{V}(s) = WW'$ and $\tilde{M}(s) = W\tilde{D}W'$ where $\tilde{D}$ is a diagonal matrix with eigenvalues $\tilde{d}_i = 1/\tilde{\lambda}_i(s)$, where

$$|\tilde{d}_i\tilde{V}(s) - \tilde{M}(s)| = 0 = |\tilde{d}_i I - \tilde{D}|$$

with at least one eigenvalue positive.

REMARK 4.3: Let d^* be the single positive eigenvalue of matrix D in the population and $\tilde{d}^*$ be its approximation in the sample space, given that the underlying population is normal as in Theorem 3. Then the statistic $(\tilde{d}^* - d^*)/\sigma^*$ is distributed like a unit normal $N(0,1)$ variate as the sample size T increases, where $\sigma^* = d^*(2/T)^{1/2}$ is the standard error of $\tilde{d}^*$. This statistic can be used to test the statistical difference between any two d^* values resulting from any pair $s_1, s_2 \in S$ of distinct allocations.

THEOREM 5: *Suppose there exists for every $s \in S$ a nonsingular matrix $W(s)$ which simultaneously diagonalizes $\tilde{V}(s)$ and $\tilde{M}(s)$ in the quadratic programming problem (9). Then the QP problem (9) has a k-dimensional solution vector $\tilde{x}(s)$ if and only if there exists a scalar $\tilde{\lambda}(s)$ and a diagonal matrix $\overline{D}(s)$ having nonnegative elements such that*

$$\tilde{V}(s) - \tilde{\lambda}(s)\tilde{M}(s) - (W^{-1})'\overline{D}(s)W^{-1} = 0 \qquad (i)$$

$$\tilde{x}(s)(W^{-1})'\overline{D}(s)W^{-1}\tilde{x}(s) = 0 \qquad (ii)$$

$$\tilde{x}'(s)\tilde{M}(s)\tilde{x}(s) = 1$$

PROOF: Denote $W^{-1}(s)\tilde{x}(s)$ by $z(s)$. Then, by using simultaneous diagonalization property we get diagonal matrices $\overline{V} = W'(s)\tilde{V}(s)W(s)$, $\overline{M} = W'(s)\tilde{M}(s)W(s)$ and the QP problem (9) becomes

$$\min_{z_i} \sum_{i=1}^{k} \overline{v}_{ii}z_i^2 \quad \text{s.t.} \quad \sum_{i=1}^{k} \overline{m}_{ii}z_i^2 = 1$$

where $\overline{v}_{ii}$, $\overline{m}_{ii}$ are the diagonal elements of $\overline{V}$ and $\overline{M}$ respectively. Denoting z_i^2 by $t_i \geqslant 0$, this reduces to the linear programming (LP) problem

$$\min_{t_i} \sum_{i=1}^{k} \overline{v}_{ii}t_i \quad \text{s.t.} \quad \sum_{i=1}^{k} \overline{m}_{ii}t_i = 1, \quad t_i \geqslant 0$$

The necessary and sufficient conditions for $t_1, t_2, \ldots, t_k$ to solve this LP problem are that there exist a nonzero scalar $\tilde{\lambda} = \tilde{\lambda}(s)$ such that

$$\overline{V} - \tilde{\lambda}(s)\overline{M} - \overline{D}(s) = 0 \qquad (5.1)$$

where the diagonal matrix $\overline{D}(s)$ has nonnegative elements $\bar{d}_{ii}$ where

$$\sum_{i=1}^{k} \bar{d}_{ii} t_i = 0 \qquad (5.2)$$

On premultiplying (5.1) by W^{-1} and postmultiplying by W^{-1} we get the first part (i) of the theorem. Similarly (5.2) reduces to the second part (ii).

REMARK 5.1: The theorem does not necessarily hold if the assumption of simultaneous diagonalizability is dropped. Further, if the rank of $\tilde{M}(s)$ is one for every $s \in S$, then at least for one i, $\bar{m}_{ii}$ is nonzero, with $\bar{m}_{jj} = 0$, for $j \neq i$. Hence the optimal t_i, denoted by t_0^* is given by $t_0^* = \min_{1 \leqslant i \leqslant k}(\bar{v}_{ii}/\bar{m}_{ii})$.

REMARK 5.2: If the minimization objective of (9) is replaced by maximization, everything else remaining the same, then Theorem 5 holds except that part (i) has to be replaced by

$$\tilde{V}(s) - \tilde{\lambda}(s)\tilde{M}(s) + (W^{-1})'\overline{D}(s)W^{-1} = 0$$

However $\tilde{\lambda}(s)$ need not be identical with that of Theorem 5.

In many practical situations however, the distribution of the returns vector $\tilde{r}$ is unknown or nonestimable because of small sample size i.e. underidentification. In this case, a minimax policy may have other advantages. Consider for instance the portfolio decision model as a two-person zero-sum game with player I (the decision-maker) choosing between the finite selections $s = 1, 2, \ldots, N$ and player II (nature) having the choice of k eigenvalues in model (7). Let us take $N = 4$, $k = 3$, where the three values of k denote the minimum ($k = 1$) the maximum ($k = 2$) and the median eigenvalue ($k = 3$). Suppose the payoff (i.e. loss) matrix to player I is

k / s	1	2	3	Worst (max)	Best of Worst (min)
1	3	⑤	4	5	5
2	2	6	4	6	
3	8	10	9	10	
4	1	11	8	11	
min	1	5	4		
max		5			

It is clear from this loss matrix $G = (g_{sk})$ that $s = 4$ is the best policy for player I provided player II selects $k = 1$. But the risk associated with this policy $(s = 4)$ of player I is very great i.e. $g_{42} = 11$. Hence minimin policy may have large risks associated with it. The minimax policy of course recommends the optimal choice $s = 1$ for player I, since it guarantees that the loss is not more than 5, whatever be the opponent's strategy. As a matter of fact $g_{12} = 5$ has the saddle point property, so that it is stable in the usual game-theoretic sense. Extension of this concept in nonzero-sum game cases will be explored elsewhere.

3.3. Allocation under model C

For model C, any extreme solution $y^0(s)$ which maximizes the objective function $\tilde{g}(s) = y'(s)\tilde{V}(s)y(s)$ in (10) must satisfy the eigenvalue problem (11) i.e.

$$\left[\tilde{V}(s) - \tilde{\lambda}^0(s)I\right]y^0(s) = 0$$

where $\tilde{\lambda}^0(s)$ is the maximum of k eigenvalues $\tilde{\lambda}_i(s)$, $1 \leqslant i \leqslant k$, each being positive, since $\tilde{V}(s)$ is assumed to be strictly positive definite for each $s = 1, 2, \ldots, N$. However, the elements $\tilde{v}_{ij}(s)$ of $\tilde{V}(s)$ are nonnegative by assumption. Assume further that the matrix $\tilde{V}(s) \geqslant 0$ is indecomposable in the sense that there does not exist a permutation matrix P such that

$$P^{-1}\tilde{V}(s)P = \begin{bmatrix} V_{11}(s) & V_{12}(s) \\ 0 & V_{22}(s) \end{bmatrix} \quad \text{for every} \quad s \tag{19}$$

where $V_{11}(s)$ and $V_{12}(s)$ are square submatrices. Then the following result holds by Perron–Frobenius theorem.

THEOREM 6. *If for each selection $s = 1, 2, \ldots, N$ the variance–covariance matrix $\tilde{V}(s)$ is nonnegative and indecomposable in the sense of (19), then the minimax policy $\tilde{\lambda}^0(s_0)$, $y^0(s_0)$ exists, where $\tilde{\lambda}^0(s_0) = \min_s \tilde{\lambda}^0(s)$ and $y^0(s_0)$ is the associated eigenvector. The minimax policy has the following characteristics*:

(i) Both $\tilde{\lambda}^0(s_0)$ and $y^0(s_0)$ are positive
(ii) If $w(s_0)$ is any other eigenvalue of $\tilde{V}(s)$ for the selection $s = s_0$, then
$$|w(s_0)| \leqslant \tilde{\lambda}^0(s_0)$$
(iii) The eigenvector $y^0(s_0)$ is unique for every fixed selection s_0.
(iv) The eigenvalue $\tilde{\lambda}^0(s_0)$ increases for every fixed s_0, when any element of $\tilde{V}(s_0)$ increases
(v) $\min_s \max_i \tilde{\lambda}_i(s) \geqslant \max_i \min_s \tilde{\lambda}_i(s)$ where $\tilde{\lambda}_i(s)$ are the k eigenvalues, $1 \leqslant i \leqslant k$ of $\tilde{V}(s)$ for each fixed $s = 1, 2, \ldots, N$.

PROOF: By the Frobenius property, $\tilde{\lambda}^0(s) > 0$, $\tilde{y}^0(s) > 0$, for every selection s. Hence $\tilde{\lambda}^0(s_0)$, $\tilde{y}^0(s_0)$ exist and both are positive, where $\tilde{y}^0(s_0)$ is the eigenvector of $\tilde{\lambda}^0(s_0)$. Parts (i) through (iv) then follow by Perron–Frobenius theorem. Again

$$\max_i \tilde{\lambda}_i(s) \geqslant \tilde{\lambda}_i(s), \qquad \text{any} \quad s = 1, 2, \ldots, N$$

$$\geqslant \min_s \tilde{\lambda}_i(s), \qquad \text{all} \quad i = 1, 2, \ldots, k$$

hence

$$\min_s \max_i \tilde{\lambda}_i(s) \geqslant \max_i \min_s \tilde{\lambda}_i(s)$$

REMARK 6.1: A theorem analogous to Theorem 3 can be stated fro the eigenvalues $\tilde{\lambda}^0(s)$ and $\lambda^0(s_0)$ i.e. for large sample sizes, each of the statistics

$$\frac{\tilde{\lambda}^0(s) - \lambda^0(s)}{\sigma(\tilde{\lambda}(s))}, \quad \frac{\tilde{\lambda}^0(s_0) - \lambda^0(s_0)}{\sigma(\tilde{\lambda}^0(s_0))}$$

tends to a unit normal distribution $N(0,1)$, where $\lambda^0(s)$, $\lambda^0(s_0)$ are population parameters and $\sigma(q)$ denotes the standard error of $q = \tilde{\lambda}^0(s)$ or, $\tilde{\lambda}^0(s_0)$.

REMARK 6.2: Suppose a new security is considered for adding to the existing portfolio having k securities, such that the new matrix $\tilde{V}(s)$ of order $k + 1$ and $s = 1, 2, \ldots, \binom{n}{k+1}$ is still nonnegative and indecomposable, then for large sample sizes, the statistic τ

$$\tau = \left(\tilde{\lambda}^0(s_*) - \tilde{\lambda}^0(s_0)\right)\left(\sigma^2(\tilde{\lambda}^0(s_*)) + \sigma^2(\tilde{\lambda}^0(s_0))\right)^{-1/2}$$

which follows Student's t distribution may be used to test the difference in minimax policies in the two cases, where s_* is the selection over the set $s = 1, 2, \ldots, \binom{n}{k+1}$ and $\sigma^2(q)$ is the variance of the estimate q. If the statistic τ is not significant at a level $\alpha = 0.01$ say, then the new security does not imply any significant difference from the existing minimax policy. But if τ is significant at 1% and τ is negative, the new minimax policy may be better in an asymptotic sense.

REMARK 6.3: The relative cost of imposing the nonnegativity constraint $y(s) \geqslant 0$ in model C may be evaluated in terms of the statistical difference of two eigenvectors $\tilde{y}^0(s_0)$ and $\tilde{y}_0^*(s_0)$, where the latter corresponds to minimin policy with the constraint $y(s) \geqslant 0$ removed. The respective difference in eigenvalues $(\tilde{\lambda}^0(s_0) - \tilde{\lambda}_0^*(s_0))$ would indicate their sensitivity to risk measured by variance.

REMARK 6.4: Let S be the index set $\{s = 1, 2, \ldots, N\}$, where each selection is assumed to be random and independent. Define the following quantities for model C, provided they exist:

$$\text{prob}\left[\max_{s \in S} \tilde{\lambda}^0(s) \leqslant t\right] = H(t), \qquad \text{prob}\left[\min_{s \in S} \tilde{\lambda}^0(s) \leqslant t\right] = G(t)$$

$$\text{prob}\left[\tilde{\lambda}^0(s) \leqslant t\right] = F(t)$$

then $G(t) \geqslant F(t) \geqslant H(t)$ for all $N \geqslant 2.0$ and the inequalities are strict for all finite $N > 2.0$. Thus, a result analogous to Theorem 2 can be stated for suitable loss functions $L = L(\tilde{\lambda}^0(s))$ i.e. $EL_H \leqslant EL_F \leqslant EL_G$ for $t \in [0, \infty]$.

4. Concluding remarks

A few implications of the minimax policies characterized here may now be indicated in brief. First, the minimax policy serves to generalize the concept of risk aversion in the situation when there are N population distributions $\mu(s)$, $V(s)$, $s = 1, 2, \ldots, N$. It is clear that $\lambda^0(s_0)$, $y^0(s_0)$ which characterizes a minimax policy is much less risk averse than the minimin policy specified by $\lambda_0(s_0)$, $y_0(s_0)$. These implications for multivariate risk aversion are indicated elsewhere (Sengupta 1981). Second, consider any two portfolios in model B for $s = s_1$, s_2 having identical mean return but different variances $\hat{V}(s_1)$, $\hat{V}(s_2)$. Then the statistical distance between these two portfolios may be characterized (James 1973) by the concept of geodesic distance D, where

$$D^2 = \sum_{i=1}^{k} (\log \lambda_i)^2$$

and λ_i are the k eigenvalues of the characteristic equation

$$|\hat{V}(s_1) - \lambda \hat{V}(s_2)| = 0$$

Alternatively, if $\hat{V}_1(s_0)$, $\hat{V}_2(s_0)$ are any two unbiased sample estimates of the parameter V when the returns vector $\tilde{r}$ is multivariate normal $N(\mu, V)$ and $s = s_0$ is fixed, then the statistic $\frac{1}{2}kD^2$ where λ_i are the k eigenvalues of the characteristic equation.

$$|\hat{V}_1(s_0) - \lambda \hat{V}_2(s_0)| = 0$$

and D^2 is defined above follows asymptotically the distribution of a chisquare variate with $\frac{1}{2}k(k+1)$ degrees of freedom. Here the variance covariance matrices are assumed to be positive definite.

Third, one may apply the statistical theory of extreme values to the random returns vector $\tilde{r}$ itself. Denote by $\tilde{r}_i(s)$ the return on security $i = 1, 2,\ldots,k$ for selection $s = 1, 2,\ldots,N$. Furthermore, let us define:

$$\tilde{r}_i^0 = \max_s \tilde{r}_i(s); \quad \tilde{r}^0 = \left(\tilde{r}_i^0\right)$$

$$\tilde{r}_{i0} = \min_s \tilde{r}_i(s); \quad \tilde{r}_0 = \left(\tilde{r}_{i0}\right)$$

$$\tilde{r}_{i\alpha} = \alpha \tilde{r}_i^0 + (1-\alpha)\tilde{r}_{i0}; \quad \tilde{r}_\alpha = \left(\tilde{r}_{i\alpha}\right), \quad 0 \leqslant \alpha \leqslant 1$$

Using the extreme value distributions (Sarhan and Greenberg 1962) for example, the mean $\mu(\alpha)$ and variance $V(\alpha)$ of $\tilde{r}_\alpha$ may be estimated in suitable cases to compute an optimal solution from the following QP problem:

$$\min_{x(\alpha)} h(\alpha) = x(\alpha)'V(\alpha)x(\alpha)$$

$$\text{s.t.} \quad x(\alpha)'x(\alpha) = 1$$

A mixed strategy solution for an optimal value α^* of α with $0 < \alpha^* < 1$ can also be defined in suitable cases, following the method indicated in (15). This type of characterization is closely related to the minimax solutions mentioned in the recent discussions of stochastic goal programming and its applications (Kolbin 1977).

Lastly, one must mention that the portfolio models discussed here consider only two sets of parameters e.g. means and covariances of the distribution of returns, which may be appropriate when the underlying stochastic process is either normal or approximately so. In more general cases, higher moments have to be incorporated into the optimal decision rules. In general, this may lead to nonlinear eigenvalue problems. This aspect would be discussed elsewhere.

References

Chernoff, H., Sequential Analysis and Optimal Design. Philadelphia, Pennsylvania. Society for Industrial and Applied Mathematics, 1972,

Girschik, M.A., "On the sampling theory of roots of determinantal equations," Ann. Math. Statist. 10, (1939), 203–224.

Jacob, N.L., "A limited diversification portfolio selection model for the small investor," J. of Finance, 29, (1974), 847–856.

James, A.T., "The variance information manifold and the function on it," in Multivariate Analysis III, edited by P.R. Krishnaiah, New York: Academic Press, 1973.

Kolbin, V.V., Stochastic Programming. Dordrecht: Reidel Publishing, 1977.

Lin, W.T., "A minimum Bayes risk approach to optimal portfolio choice, Int. J. Systems Sci., 12, (1981), 495–509.

Lin, W.T. and Boot, J.C.G., Paper on portfolio choice presented at the ORSA/TIMS Joint National Meeting, Colorado Springs, 1980.

Sarhan, A.E. and Greenberg, B.G., Contributions to Order Statistics. New York: John Wiley, 1962.

Sengupta, J.K., "Stochastic programs as nonzero-sum games," Int. J. Systems Sci., 11, (1980a), 1145–62; "Linear allocation rules under uncertainty," Int. J. Systems Sci., 12 (1980b), 1459–80.

Sengupta, J.K., Multivariate risk aversion with applications. Paper presented at the Third Int. Conference on Mathematical Modeling, Los Angeles, CA, 1981.

Szego, G.P., Portfolio Theory. New York: Academic Press, 1980.

6. A two-period stochastic inventory model

1. Introduction

Even though there is today a multitude of static and dynamic models available to the firm reflecting its perceived economic environment, the number of models including inventories is surprisingly small. These models are roughly divided in two groups: stochastic inventory models, and deterministic inventory models where perfect information is assumed and stochastic functions are replaced by their mean. Formulation of a stochastic inventory model is very dependent upon the specification of the various functions involved, and upon the length of the planning horizon. The demand function usually includes an error term with known stochastic properties. A comprehensive survey of inventory models can be found in Sengupta and Fox (1969). Some simplifying assumptions about the market structure, information available, number of competitors and cost functions have to be made in order to reduce the large number of variables involved, and to obtain some specific results. Among pioneers in the field, Zabel (1970) formulated a model where the demand function has a multiplicative error term, and Mills (1962) formulated a model with an additive error term. We will present in this paper a two period moving horizon (2PMH) model inspired by Mills results, where the demand faced by a firm in each period is uncertain, and where inventories have a dual role; they are held as a buffer against unforeseen fluctuations in demand, and also as an active element in production planning. Mills' model has been compared to the 2PMH model and the results of the simulations illustrate the benefits of extending the planning horizon from one to two periods.

2. Mills' multiperiod model

A firm must decide what are the optimal price (p_t) and level of output (z_t) for the current time period (t), given its initial level of inventory (I_t).

The objective of the firm is to maximize profits over time, and the demand faced is stochastic:

$$x_t = X_t(p_t) + u \tag{1}$$

where u is an additive error term independent of price and with known probability density function $f(u)$, and cumulative density function $F(u)$. The revenue of the firm for period t is:

$$R(I_t, z_t, p_t) = \begin{cases} p_t(I_t + z_t) & \text{if} \quad I_t + z_t < x_t \\ p_t x_t & \text{if} \quad I_t + z_t \geqslant x_t \end{cases} \tag{2}$$

Firms are also assumed to have a subjective estimate of the present value of the effect, a current shortage would have on future profits, and described by the function $\rho(I_t, z_t, p_t)$. The expected profit is given by:

$$E[\pi_t] = \int_{-\infty}^{\infty} (R(I_t, z_t, p_t) + \rho(I_t, z_t, p_t))f(u)\,du - c(z_t) \tag{3}$$

where $c(z_t)$ denotes the production cost function. The first order condition for a maximum lead to two equations giving the optimal price p_t^* and production z_t^* maximizing equation (3). The derivative of equation (3) with respect to output leads to Mills' main result:

$$[1 - F(I_t + z_t - X_t(p_t))]$$

$$= (1/p_t)\left(c'(z_t) - \int_{-\infty}^{\infty} \rho'(I_t + z_t - X_t(p_t))f(u)\,du\right) \tag{4}$$

which translates into: "The optimal price-output vector is such that the probability of having a shortage at time t is equal to the ratio of marginal production cost to price minus a positive term."

3. The proposed model

The following model is an attempt to include explicitly the forecast of future prevailing prices into present decision making, reducing somewhat the degree of subjectivity of the function ρ introduced by Mills, and which is not clearly defined since future demand and profits depend upon the future price. The incertitude surrounding present and future demand affects the functional form of the decision rule adopted by the decision makers, reflecting somewhat his attitude towards risk. In this model, it is assumed that the firm, unable to forecast precisely the possible evolution of demand, and aware that the longer the planning horizon the greater the degree of uncertainty, adopts a cautious attitude and limits its horizon to the current and following periods. The sequence of events can be summarized as follows: At the start of period k, the firm makes a forecast of the demand function it will face during the current and next period, ignoring the possible effect current price could have on future demand. Next, it chooses the price–output vector maximizing the objective function over the next two periods given the known initial level of inventories. Demand is then experienced. However, due to a lack of information or a lack of foresight, the demand experienced might be different from the demand expected. At the end of the first period of its initial forecast, a firm is in a better position to revise the forecast of demand in period $k + 1$, and computes an estimate of the demand in period $k + 2$ using past market information. With this two period moving horizon decision rule, the decision maker looks one period ahead and selects the controls that would be optimal if the next period was the last one. The two period moving horizon decision rule proposed above not only allows a formulation of the problem without specifying a termination time, but also reflects the limiting forecasting ability of the firm as well as an implicit risk aversion of the decision maker. Discounting future profits is omitted since the two period horizon is very short, and even though it could easily be included, it would also greatly complicate the exposition of the proposed model with little insight in return.

The operating costs incurred by the firms can be divided in only two parts; production costs ($c(z)$), and costs associated with holding inventories ($K(I)$). The production process is a continuous one in the sense that infinitesimal amounts of the good can be produced and stored. Production takes place once per time period, at the beginning of each period. The firm knows all the parameters of its non stochastic cost functions, and the marginal costs of production and holding inventories are assumed non decreasing. As a consequence, a firm expecting a large increase in demand might find it advantageous to produce ahead of time to meet the demand. It is assumed throughout this paper that the production cost curve is always above the inventory cost curve, having at most one point in common above the origin. This assumption removes the special cases where storage costs are higher than production costs, rendering the value of inventories equal to zero if the level falls below the point where the two cost curves intersect.

The principal objective of the firm is to maximize the expected sum of profits, using a two period moving horizon. The objective function is: $J = E[\pi_t + \pi_{t+1}]$. A second and simultaneous objective of the firm is to produce efficiently in the sense that it might be more advantageous to produce and store a unit in period t than to produce the same unit in period $t + 1$. This case is likely to occur when, for example, the demand is expected to increase sharply due to a change in the exogenous parameters of the demand function, or due to a decrease in the price of the product relative to the price of possible competitors or to both.

The production solution (z_t^*, z_{t+1}^*) of the two period horizon problem must be such that the cost of meeting the demand is minimal, which implies that marginal production costs plus expected marginal storage costs for the first period must be greater than or equal to the marginal cost of production in the second period, the level of production and inventory being perfectly efficient when equality holds. However the equality constraint cannot always be binding since the level of output solution of the perfectly constrained problem might not be sufficient to meet expected demand during the first period (i.e. period t). The efficiency condition can be written:

$$\frac{\partial}{\partial z_{t+1}} c(z_{t+1}) \leqslant \frac{\partial}{\partial z_t} \left[c(z_t) + K(E[I_{t+1}]) \right] \tag{5}$$

There might also be some situations where carrying over inventories is not advantageous to the firm. Such cases might occur when demand is expected to decrease in the next period. The optimal plan might then be to use the one period horizon described by Mills. Inventories are held for two different reasons: One is that they will act as a buffer to avoid the unsatisfied market that would occur if real demand was to exceed expected demand; the other is that the costs of meeting the expected demand schedules (present and future) might be minimized when inventories are held.

Let $x_t = X_t(p_t) + u$ and $x_{t+1} = X_{t+1}(p_{t+1}) + v$ be the demand functions faced by a firm in periods t and $t+1$, and where u and v are independent additive error terms with zero mean and known probability density functions $f(u)$ and $g(v)$. The revenue to the firm in period t is:

$$R_t = \begin{cases} p_t(z_t + I_t) & \text{if} \quad x_t > z_t + I_t \quad \text{(excess demand)} \\ p_t x_t & \text{if} \quad x_t < z_t + I_t \quad \text{(excess supply)} \end{cases} \tag{6}$$

where z_t and I_t are levels of production and inventory at the start of period t, before the demand is experienced. The expected revenue for period t is:

$$E[R_t] = \int_{-\infty}^{\phi} p_t(X_t(p_t) + u) f(u) du + \int_{\phi}^{\infty} p_t(z_t + I_t) f(u) du \tag{7}$$

where

$$\phi = I_t + z_t - X_t(p_t) \tag{7a}$$

Equation 7 can be reduced to:

$$E[R_t] = p_t X_t(p_t) - p_t \int_\phi^\infty ((u - z_t - I_t + X_t(p_t)) f(u) du \qquad (8)$$

i.e.

$$E[R_t] = p_t X_t(p_t) - p_t D_t(I_t + z_t, p_t) \qquad (9)$$

Similarly, we have for period $t + 1$:

$$E[R_{t+1}] = p_{t+1} X_{t+1}(p_{t+1}) - p_{t+1} D_{t+1}(E[I_{t+1}] + z_{t+1}, p_{t+1}) \qquad (10)$$

where the expected level of inventories at the start of the period $t + 1$ is given by:

$$E[I_{t+1}] = \int_{-\infty}^\phi (z_t + I_t - X_t(p_t) - u) f(u) du \qquad (11)$$

The objective function of the firm using the two period horizon is

$$J = E[\pi_t + \pi_{t+1}]$$

$$\triangleq p_t X_t(p_t) - p_t D_t(z_t + I_t, p_t) - c(z_t) \qquad (12)$$

$$- K(E[I_{t+1}]) + p_{t+1} X_{t+1}(p_{t+1})$$

$$- p_{t+1} D_{t+1}(E[I_{t+1}] + z_{t+1}, p_{t+1}) - c(z_{t+1}) \qquad (12)$$

The first order conditions for a maximum are:

$$\partial J / \partial z_{t+1} = -p_{t+1} D_{t+1}(E[I_{t+1}] + z_{t+1}, p_{t+1}) - c'(z_{t+1}) = 0 \qquad (13)$$

$$\partial J / \partial p_{t+1} = p_{t+1} X'_{t+1}(p_{t+1}) - p_{t+1} D_{t+1}(E[I_{t+1}] + z_{t+1}, p_{t+1})$$

$$+ X_{t+1}(p_{t+1}) - D_{t+1}(E[I_{t+1}] + z_{t+1}, p_{t+1})$$

$$= 0 \qquad (14)$$

$$\partial J / \partial z_t = -p_{t+1} D_{t,z_t}(I_t + z_t, p_t) - c'(z_t) - K'(E[I_{t+1}]) \partial E[I_{t+1}] / \partial z_t$$

$$+ p_{t+1} D_{t+1_{E(It+1)}}(E[I_{t+1}] + z_{t+1}, p_{t+1})(\partial E[I_{t+1}] / \partial z_t)$$

$$= 0 \qquad (15)$$

$$\partial J/\partial p_t = p_t X_t'(p_t) + X_t(p_t) - p_t D_{t_{p_t}}(I_t + z_t, p_t)$$

$$- D_t(I_t + z_t, p_t) - K'(E[I_{t+1}])(\partial E[I_{t+1}]/\partial p_t)$$

$$+ p_{t+1} D_{t+1_{I_{t+1}+1_t}}(E[I_{t+1}] + z_{t+1}, p_{t+1})(\partial E[I_{t+1}]/\partial p_{t+1})$$

$$= 0 \tag{16}$$

where D_{t+1_q} denotes the partial derivative of D_{t+1} with respect to the variable q. Using Leibnitz' rule for the differentiation of integrals, the system of equations (13) to (16) becomes:

$$A \begin{cases} p_{t+1}(1 - G(\psi)) - c'(z_{t+1}) = 0 & (17) \\[2mm] p_{t+1} X_{t+1}'(p_{t+1}) + X_{t+1}(p_{t+1}) - p_{t+1} X_{t+1}'(p_{t+1})(1 - G(\psi)) \\[2mm] \qquad - \int_\psi^\infty (v - \psi) g(v) dv = 0 & (18) \end{cases}$$

$$B \begin{cases} p_t(1 - F(\phi)) - c'(z_t) - K'(E[I_{t+1}])F(\phi) + p_t(1 - G(\psi))F(\phi) = 0 \\[2mm] \hspace{10cm} (19) \\[2mm] p_t X_t'(p_t) + X_t(p_t) - p_t X_t'(p_t)(1 - F(\phi)) - \int_\psi^\infty (u - \phi) f(u) du \\[2mm] \qquad + X_t'(p_t) K'(E[I_{t+1}])F(\phi) = 0 & (20) \end{cases}$$

where

$$\psi = E[I_{t+1}] + z_{t+1} - X_{t+1} - X_{t+1}(p_{t+1}) \tag{21}$$

System A is identical to Mills' one period horizon results where the initial inventory is $E(I_{t+1})$, and the main result he derived still holds, namely that production in the second period should be planned such that the probability of a storage during that period is equal to the marginal cost of production divided by planned price at time $t+1$. System B is somewhat different from the system derived by Mills for the multihorizon problem. If we define the function $\tilde{\rho}(I_t, z_t, p_t)$ by:

$$\tilde{\rho}(I, z, p) \begin{cases} = K(E(I_{t+1})) & \text{when} \quad (I_t + z_t - X_t(p_t)) > 0 \\[2mm] = 0 & \text{when} \quad (I_t + z_t - X_t(p_t)) < 0 \end{cases} \tag{22}$$

Equation (20) is similar to Mills equation for $\partial E(\pi)/\partial \rho = 0$ where $\tilde{\rho}$ is substituted for ρ, and equation (22) is similar to the equation for

$\partial E(\pi)/\partial z = 0$. However since two periods have been considered, the equivalent of the term involving the function ρ takes explicitly into account the planned price and output in the next period, while Mills' original formulation of the problem uses a subjective estimate of the influence of a shortage on future demand, independent of future price; The term

$$\int_{-\infty}^{\infty} \rho'(I + z - X(p) - u)f(u)\mathrm{d}u \tag{23}$$

is replaced by:

$$\left[K'(E[I_{t+1}]) + p_{t+1}[1 - G(\psi)]\right]F(\phi)$$

where $[1 - Q(\psi)]$ is the probability of having a shortage in period $t + 1$ given the expected initial inventory $E[I_{t+1}]$ and the corresponding optimal price-output decisions (z^*_{t+1}, p^*_{t+1}), and $F(\phi)$ is the probability that $E[I_{t+1}]$ will available at the start of period $t + 1$. A result similar to Mills' equation giving the probability of having a shortage (equation (4)) can be derived from equation (19):

$$[1 - F(\phi)] = \frac{c'(z_t) + K'(E[I_{t+1}]) - p_{t+1}(1 - G(\psi))}{p_t + K'(E[I_{t+1}]) - p_{t+1}(1 - G(\psi))} \tag{24}$$

and using equation (17), we can substitute $c'(z_{t+1})$ for $p_{t+1}(1 - G(\psi))$, which yields:

$$[1 - F(\phi)] = \frac{c'(z_t) + K'(E[I_{t+1}]) - c'(z_{t+1})}{p_t + K'(E[I_{t+1}]) - c'(z_{t+1})} \tag{25}$$

The above equation, somewhat different from Mills', carries more information about the behaviour of the firm that were not available with Mills results e.g.,

(a) Since the probability of having a shortage is a non-negative number, the two-period moving horizon model will guarantee that the efficiency condition (equation (5)) is satisfied.

(b) As the marginal cost of holding inventories increases, the possibility of having a shortage in period t increases, and in the limit, a very large marginal inventory cost will yield a near certitude to have a shortage in period t. Firms would then have no incentive to hold inventories, and would revert to a one period model.

(c) Simulation results based on the formulation (25) above appear to show robustness of our optimal decision rules when measured by the variance of profits.

4. Simulation results

The results obtained with Mills' model have been compared with the results of the 2PMH model presented. The numerical solution of the 2PMH model is obtained by using Newton's algorithm to solve the system of equations (17–20) with an accuracy of at least 10^{-4}. The demand and cost functions used in the simulations are identical to the ones presented as an example in Mills' original paper. The demand for the current and future periods are:

$$x_t = a_t - bp_t + u \quad \text{and} \quad x_{t+1} = a_{t+1} - bp_{t+1} + v \tag{26}$$

where u and v are additive error terms independent of price. The cost functions are:

$$c(z) = c_0 + c_1 z + c_2 z^2 \qquad \text{Production cost function} \tag{27}$$
$$K(I) = k_0 + k_1 I \qquad \text{Inventory cost function} \tag{28}$$

The value of the parameters chosen by Mills are $a = 20$, $b = 2$, $c_0 = 0$, $c_1 = 5$, $c_2 = 0$, $k_0 = 0$ and $k_1 = .5$. The function representing the effects of a current shortage on profits is:

$$\rho(I + z - x) = \begin{cases} (c_1 - k_1)(I_t + z_t - x_t) & \text{if} \quad I_t + z_t > x_t \\ k(I_t + z_t - x_t) & \text{if} \quad I_t + z_t < x_t \end{cases} \tag{29}$$

The simulations compare Mills' results to the two period moving horizon model where the true additive error term has a uniform distribution, a normal distribution (the two distributions have equal mean (zero) and variance ($\lambda^2/3$) for each value of tested) and with a distribution skewed to the left, with equation:

$$f(u) = w_1 U(-\lambda, \lambda) + w_2 U(-\lambda, 0) + w_3 U(-\lambda/2, 0) \tag{30}$$

where

$$\text{prob}[w_i = 1] = 1/3, \quad \text{prob}[w_i = 0] = 2/3$$

$$w_i \neq 0 = > w_j = 0, \quad i \neq j \tag{31}$$

and $U(-\lambda, \lambda)$ denotes the uniform distribution on $(-\lambda, \lambda)$. Substitution of the demand functions, probability density functions and function ρ

(eq. (29)) into the first order condition of Mills' model leads to the following two equations (Mills [1962], p. 118–119);

$$\theta(p) = (a - 2bp_t + bc_1)(p_t + k_1 + k - c_1)^2 - k_1 = 0 \tag{32}$$

$$z_t = I_t - a + bp_t - 2\lambda\left(.5 - k_1/(p_t^* + k_1 + kc_1)\right) \tag{33}$$

It should be noted that the price solution quoted by Mills for the multiperiod horizon is not a root of equation (31). In all the simulations below, the correct value of p_t^* was used, computed with an accuracy of at least 10^{-4} using Newton's algorithm. The value of the parameter k, which represents the entrepreneur's subjective estimate of the present value of the future loss in profits due to a current shortage of one unit, is chosen, as in Mills' paper, equal to 2.5 only in the first simulation. It is assumed in all simulations that the entrepreneur postulates that the error term v, affecting future demand, is uniformly distributed on the interval $[-\mu, \mu]$. The value of μ has been arbitrarily fixed at 5. Two sets of simulations have been done: In the first set of simulation, the value of the parameter k (of equation (29)) (representing the entrepreneur's subjective estimate of the present value of the future loss in profits due to a current shortage of one unit) is held constant ($k = 2.5$), and the parameter λ reflecting uncertainty of the entrepreneur for the current period, is varied from 0 to 5 ($\lambda = 0, 0.01, 1, 2, 4, 5$). The first set of simulation considered three types of error distributions: uniform, normal and asymmetrical. Table 1 illustrates the first case. The influence of k on the performance of the model presented was investigated in a separate simulation where instead of holding k fixed and varying the parameter λ of the uniform distribution assumed relevant by entrepreneurs for the current period, k was varied from 0 to 10 and λ was held fixed at 3. One illustrative result of the second set of simulation are given in table 2. The cases of normal and asymmetrical error distributions are not reproduced here.

The first simulation set (where k is fixed and λ varies) confirms what could be expected from the theory: In every case tested, whether the error term was uniformly or normally distributed, the 2PMH model is superior to Mills' model in the sense that mean output and revenue is usually lower in the 2PMH model than in Mills', and the mean profit is always equal or larger in the 2PMH model. Even though the increase in profits is somewhat modest, (less than 3%), it is complemented by a reduction of up to 12% in the variance of profits and revenues. In the case of stationary demand the optimal price is fixed in both models, and the slightly lower price of the 2PMH model could help a firm adopting it to take a greater share of the market. The results of the second simulation set, where k is varied, reveal no difference with the results obtained in the

Table 1
Simulation of the model presented (with $k - 2.5$ and a uniformly distributed error term)

λ	Error	Mills' model					Two period moving horizon model				
		Price	Supply	Output	Revenue	Profit	Price	Supply	Output	Revenue	Profit
0	0	7.5000	5.000	5.000	37.500	12.500	7.500	5.000	5.000	37.500	12.500
		–	–	–	–	–	–	–	–	–	–
0.01	−0.007	7.4999	5.008	4.999	37.494	12.492	7.4999	5.006	4.999	37.494	12.492
	0.00003	–	–	0.0000	0.0016	0.0025	0.00003	–	0.0000	0.0015	0.0024
1	−0.111	7.4979	5.822	4.925	36.651	11.577	7.4930	5.679	4.915	36.598	11.640
	0.3108	–	–	0.3373	17.001	31.349	–	–	0.3032	15.602	28.687
2	−0.026	7.4958	6.644	5.052	37.229	11.169	7.4859	6.358	5.024	37.062	11.271
	1.071	–	–	1.114	56.999	92.64	–	–	0.9698	50.497	81.243
3	0.3148	7.4937	7.466	5.366	39.756	11.873	7.4788	7.035	5.279	39.161	11.888
	3.530	–	–	3.599	192.37	235.05	–	–	3.132	169.03	205.08
4	0.0503	7.4917	8.288	5.494	40.927	12.057	7.4716	7.710	5.411	40.378	12.173
	5.282	–	–	5.083	276.40	363.17	–	–	4.427	245.43	323.59
5	0.2054	7.4896	9.109	5.277	39.141	10.840	7.4644	8.384	5.211	38.750	11.108
	8.826	–	–	9.167	495.11	768.95	–	–	8.335	4.5766	732.39

Table 2
Simulation of the 2PMH model (with $\lambda - 3$, and with a uniformly distributed error term)

		Mills' model					Two period moving horizon model				
k	error	Price	Supply	Output	Revenue	Profit	Price	Supply	Output	Revenue	profit
1	-0.2499	7.4882	7.2713	4.8872	35.4027	9.774	7.4788	7.0351	4.8703	35.308	9.874
	3.3225	-	-	3.2102	171.243	268.472	-	-	3.0425	163.679	259.165
2.5	0.3148	7.4937	7.466	5.366	39.756	11.873	7.4788	7.0355	5.279	39.161	11.888
	3.530	-	-	3.599	192.37	235.05	-	-	3.132	169.03	205.08
5	-0.0521	7.4970	7.6307	4.9489	36.9417	10.856	7.4788	7.0351	4.8914	36.582	11.053
	3.3095	-	-	3.2621	177.258	261.924	-	-	2.7935	156.253	229.450
7.5	0.1380	7.4982	7.7176	5.1484	38.5518	11.525	7.4788	7.0351	5.1113	38.2268	11.708
	2.2175	-	-	2.2537	124.681	225.555	-	-	1.9040	106.498	194.007
10	0.1868	7.4988	7.7714	5.1785	38.8189	11.629	7.4788	7.0351	5.0782	37.979	11.609
	3.8310	-	-	3.7723	211.552	272.477	-	-	3.1143	174.198	239.329

first simulations; the two period horizon model performed better than in Mills' models and the lower the value of k, the closer the performance of the two models. Asymmetry in error structure showed the difference in results of the two models in terms of profit variances, although the difference was not much larger than the normal or the uniform case.

5. Concluding remarks

The 2PMH model presented in this paper is an improvement of Mills' original model in several respects: The subjective estimation of the present value of future loss of profits due to a possible current shortage (represented by ρ in Mills' work) has been removed. The model reconciles the separate roles played by inventories in previous work; Inventories are held as a buffer against fluctuations in demand, and are also an active element in production planning. The model is flexible enough to cover the case where the demand curve shifts over time as a result of a change in customer behaviour or in the actions of a rival, and could be refined by defining more explicitly the way the firm forecasts the demand curve it faces. No specific way to forecast present and future demand is presented and several ways could be investigated in later work. On one hand, one could argue that an entrepreneur with a very good intuition or sense of business might choose a function $\rho(\cdot)$ defined by Mills that might yield better results than the model presented. On the other hand, the two period moving horizon model presented is simple enough to be used by any entrepreneur with or without good intuition. The results of the models seem to agree with the behaviour of many entrepreneurs who decrease their output when demand is uncertain and who seem to prefer small fluctuations in their revenue and profit to larger profits with the potential cash flow problem associated with pure profit maximization.

The entrepreneurs in such a model face a dilemma, since they determine present production and price using the demand parameters of the next period, these parameters being possibly a function of the present decision. This interdependence of control and estimation can be resolved by assuming that the entrepreneurs have a subjective estimate of the best and worst situation they will face during the next period, therefore providing a range for the parameter μ reflecting uncertainty about future demand. However this type of robustness analysis requires much more intensive work than those reported here. Also, since demand cannot be negative, it would be more realistic, in the asymmetric case to assume that the additive error term has an exponential distribution. The derivation of the first order conditions of the 2PMG model might become a lot more complicated, and reducing the resulting system to a simpler one yielding a computable solution will certainly be quite a challenge.

Another line of extension of the 2PMH model, much in line with previous work on linear decision rules for production and inventory scheduling (Sengupta 1977) is to allow chance-constrained solutions into the decision model by requiring that up to a certain probability or tolerance level, the demand constraints and to some extent the constraint imposed by the efficiency condition (5) may be violated.

Any of these modifications contributes however nonlinearities into the optimal solution structure and hence the computational complexity.

References

Fanchon, P., Inventory Control in Imperfect Markets. Unpublished Ph.D. Dissertation, University of California, Santa Barbara, 1982.

Mills, E., Price Output and Inventory Policy. New York: John Wiley, 1962.

Sengupta, J.K. and Fox, K., Optimization Techniques in Quantitative Economic Models. Amsterdam: North Holland, 1969.

Sengupta, J.K., "Simulation of linear decision rules," Int. J. Systems Science, 8 (1977), 1269–80.

Zabel, E., "Monopoly under uncertainty," Review of Economic Studies, 37, (1970), 205–219.

7. Risk in supply response:
an econometric application

1. Introduction

Impact of risk aversion in competitive market models has been analyzed in theory to characterize optimal behavior in different cases from zero to positive levels of risk aversion [1,2,12]. For commodity markets this analysis has important implications for stabilization policies; for, if risk aversion has a significant impact on optimal supply behavior, any policy which reduces risk aversion would also affect optimal supply and therefore suppliers' incomes. The theoretical hypothesis of risk aversion and its impact on demand supply behavior must have empirical plausibility before they can be utilized for policy purposes. With this objective an econometric attempt is made here to provide a quantitative assessment of the incidence of risk on farmers' production decisions for a number of California field crops over the years 1949–70. Risk is measured by several surrogate variables like variance of prices, dummy variables suitably constructed and expectational factors. Reasons for analyzing agricultural supply response to changing risk are two-fold. First, the competitive framework very nearly holds in the agricultural sector, where previous econometric studies [5,7] have emphasized the importance of price and yield variability on farmers' production decisions. Even in less developed countries, where the agricultural sector may not be as competitive as in the developed countries, planted acreages of different field crops have been found to significantly depend on the variances of prices and yields [1,15]. Secondly, a recent study by Richard Just [6,7] has incorporated risk aversion in agricultural supply response in a novel way by generalizing the distributed lag model of adaptive expectations. Thus he includes quadratic lag terms indicative of risk, besides the linear terms as follows:

$$Y_t = A_0 + A_1 Z_t^* + A_2 W_t^* + e_t \tag{1}$$

where

$$Z_t^* = \alpha \sum_{j=0}^{\infty} (1 - \alpha)^j Z_{t-j-1}$$

$$W_{i,t}^* = \beta \sum_{j=0}^{\infty} (1 - \beta)^j \left[Z_{i,t-j-1} - Z_{i,t-j-1}^* \right]^2$$

Here Z_t^*, W_t^* are vectors of explanatory variables, the first of which may represent the decision markers' subjective expectations for the mean prices and yields on which the acreage decisions (i.e., Y_t) are based, while the elements $W_{i,t}^*$ of W_t^* may denote their subjective evaluation of risk measured by variances of prices and yields, i.e. the past observations on risk are geometrically weighted in a way similar to that in which expectations are formed. In this approach, variables representing subjective means and variances are related to observed variables through a Bayesian approach of updating prior means and variances by means of the relevant posterior distribution. We use an alternative specification, which appears to be more direct and economically more relevant to the normative hypothesis that farmers maximize their expected profits in an uncertain world by minimizing their expected adjustments costs. This approach has found successful applications in the linear decision rule (LDR) approach to aggregate output, inventory and price behavior in the industrial sector [13]. In our case, the rule would be modified to quadratic decision rules, since the risk component would be indicated by a variance term or a suitable quadratic component.

Our framework of discussion is as follows: Section Two present the theoretical outline and motivation for the empirical specifications of supply response, which are econometrically estimated in Section Three. This is followed by Section Four dealing with the implications of our estimates for stabilization policies and also for comparison with Just's findings.

2. Alternative specifications of supply response

Under competitive market conditions, one may suggest at least two operational methods of specifying an optimal supply response (x) in terms of prices (p), when the latter follows a probability distribution. One is the quadratic programming approach, where a quadratic expected utility function is maximized leading to an optimal response dependent on the mean prices ($\bar{p}$) and their variances. The second is the adjustment cost function approach, where a quadratic function is postulated for the process of adjustment to short and long-run goals and the expected value of this adjustment cost function is minimized to derive optimal linear decision rules. The quadratic form is of course an approximation to the true adjustment costs, e.g. a cubic adjustment cost function may lead to optimal decision rules that are quadratic.

Quadratic risk programming has been commonly used to analyze the impact of risk aversion on agricultural output in terms of the trade-off between the mean and variance of net income or profits, following the early work of Freund [3,10] who postulated that the optimal decision on output is determined by maximizing the expected value of an exponential utility-of-income function

$$u(z) = a - b \exp(-\lambda z) \qquad \text{for} \quad a, b, \lambda > 0 \tag{2}$$

Under the assumption that the stochastic net income z is normally distributed with mean $\mu = \bar{p}', x$ and variance $c^2 = x'Vx$ where x is the production vector and $\bar{p}$, V are the mean and variance parameters of the distribution of net returns per unit. Maximizing the expected value of $u(z)$ in (2) yields a quadratic objective function

$$f = \bar{p}'x - \frac{\lambda}{2} x'Vx \tag{3}$$

from which the optimal production x can be derived as

$$x = (\lambda V)^{-1} \bar{p}$$

where λ is the risk aversion parameter. Including a vector y of imputed costs or shadow prices for the semi-fixed inputs used in production, the optimal response function (4) may be written more generally as

$$x = (\lambda V)^{-1} [\bar{p} - A'y] \tag{5}$$

where A is the input coefficient matrix and prime denotes transpose. Freund used statistical estimates of $\bar{p}$, V on the basis of observed data and assumed a specific value of λ on a priori basis for specifying the optimal supply response (5). His a priori assumption about the risk aversion parameter λ, as well as the assumption of normality of net incomes z, have been criticized [2,10] on grounds of lack of empirical realism or correspondence with observed behavior. Recently Wiens [15] adopted an ingenious method using the response function (5) to derive an estimate of the risk parameter λ from the two assumptions. The first is that the market input prices are approximately equal to the vector y of imputed costs and the second is that the observed allocative behavior of producers is approximately equal to the optimal behavior derived from the utility function (2) which leads to the objective function (3). Of course, in this case one must have estimates of the parameters $\bar{p}$ and V, possibly through cross-section data. In Wien's case such detailed data were available from a survey of resource allocations among alternative cropping patterns on twenty-one farms in North China over the years 1937–39. It is clear that in most realistic cases such an ideal data situation would not be available. Further, the estimates of the parameters $\bar{p}$ and V have to be made simultaneously with that of λ and other coefficients like A.

However, the general form of the optimal response function

$$x = g(\bar{p}, \lambda, V, y) \tag{6}$$

as a function of the independent variables $\bar{p}$, λ, V, y may be derived from the expected utility function: $Eu(z) = U(\mu, \sigma^2)$ by the optimizing condition

$$\frac{\partial \mu}{\partial x} = \left(-\frac{\partial U/\partial \sigma^2}{\partial U/\partial \mu} \right) \frac{\partial \sigma^2}{\partial x}$$

provided the expected value function $Eu(z)$ is approximated up to quadratic terms by Taylor series expansion. Note however, that the subjective estimates of $\bar{p}$ and V may be derived, at least in principle, from past observations on prices, yields and their variances; but the parameter λ is not directly observable, unless samples are grouped on some a priori basis according to low or high risk aversion. Hence it may be necessary to take an adjusted variance term, $\tilde{V} = \lambda V$ as an explanatory variable and rewrite the optimal response function (6) as:

$$x = g(\bar{p}, \tilde{V}, y) + e \tag{7}$$

where e denotes the additive stochastic component and y stands for all other variables except $\bar{p}$ and $\tilde{V}$ which may affect the dependent variable x. If the risk aversion term $\tilde{V}$ does not change over time and the mean prices $\bar{p}$ are forecast from past prices represented approximately by $p(t-1)$, except for an additive error component, then the linear version of the response function (7) may be expressed as follows:

Model I

$$x_i(t) = a_{i0} + a_{i1} x_i(t-1) + a_{i2} p_i(t-1)$$

$$+ a_{i3} v_i(t) + a_{i4} y_i(t) + \epsilon_i(t) \tag{8}$$

where the subscript i denotes a particular crop, v_i is the diagonal element of matrix $\tilde{V}$, that is assumed to be diagonal for simplicity and the stochastic component $\epsilon_i(t)$ for each time point t is a linear combination of errors in forecasting prices $\bar{p}$, variances $v_i(t)$ and the additive error e_i in (7). Note that the stochastic component $\epsilon_i(t)$ may not be homoskedastic due to linear combination of errors. Furthermore, the incidence of risk aversion is only captured here through the crop-specific variance term, i.e., other forms of risk aversion are not incorporated in this model.

A second approach, which is very similar to the LDR procedure applied to the industrial sector minimizes the expected value of an intertemporal function which is quadratic in costs of adjusting acreage and output. The expected adjustment costs in each year t is

$$C(t) = b_0 + b_1 (A(t) - A^*)^2 + b_2 (A(t) - A(t-1))^2 \tag{9.1}$$

$$A^*: \quad \text{desired level} = f(p(t-1), s(t)) \tag{9.2}$$

where $A(t)$ denotes the acreage planted as the decision variable with A^* as its desired value, the two quadratic cost components $(A(t) - A(t-1))^2$ and $(A(t) - A^*)^2$ are the short and long-run components. The desired or target acreage level for a specific crop depends on the lagged price and a risk factor denoted by $s(t)$. Since it is an adjustment cost model, optimal decisions require staying as close to the desired level as possible, except that the price signals $p(t-1)$ and risk factors $s(t)$ are assumed here to influence the desired levels. The risk factor $s(t)$ may here be captured by several proxy variables, e.g., price variance, dummy variables reflecting regimes of optimistic and pessimistic price changes around the equilibrium and even the price sensitivity factor when government support prices are announced for specific crops.

Minimizing the expected adjustment cost function (9.1) and assuming a linear form of the function $f(\cdot)$ in (9.2), we obtain the following optimal decision rules on acreages for different crops:

Model II

$$A_i(t) - A_i(t-1) = k_i (A_i^* - A_i(t-1)); \quad k_i = \frac{b_{1i}}{b_{1i} + b_{2i}} \tag{10.1}$$

$$A_i^* = c_{i0} + c_{i2} p_i(t-1) + c_{i3} s_i(t) \tag{10.2}$$

$$A_i(t) = \beta_{i0} + \beta_{i1} A_i(t-1) + \beta_{i2} p_i(t-1) + \beta_{i3} s_i(t) \tag{10.3}$$

where

$$\beta_{i0} = k_i c_{i0}, \quad \beta_{i1} = 1 - k_i, \quad \beta_{i2} = k_i c_{i2}, \quad \beta_{i3} = k_i c_{i3}$$

It is clear that if the risk factor $s_i(t)$ is represented by the price variance $v_i(t)$ and the coefficient β_{i3} turns out to be negative in a statistically significant sense, then Model II can be compared with Model I in terms of the different facets of adjustment. Two points may be emphasized in particular. First, the parameters of the model (10.3) are nonlinear, while those of (8) are linear; hence the specification (10.3) is more general. The structural parameter $k_i = 1 - \beta_{i1}$ which indicates the speed of adjustment would show very clearly the relative importance of short and long-run components of adjustment. The more important the crop is, the higher the weightage of the long-run component in terms of higher values of k_i in the domain $0 \leqslant k_i \leqslant 1$. Second, the optimal decision problem under Model II is viewed in two stages, whereas Model I specifies a single stage. The first stage, under Model II, specifies through equation (10.1) the linear adjustment to the desired goal. In a more generalized framework a quadratic component of adjustment could also be incorporated, except at the cost of nonlinearity in specification and estimation. The second stage postulates in (10.2) the various independent variables $p_i(t-1)$, $s_i(t)$ which may affect the desired levels A_i^*. The two stages are assumed to be independent, otherwise the specification would be more nonlinear. We have attempted in our econometric estimates to capture the incidence of the two stages of decision-making on the supply response.

The specifications in Models I and II, however, do share two short-comings. First, each drop is assumed to be independent, so that the covariances of prices are ignored. This is due to problems of multicol-linearity when dealing with empirical data. Second, various government programs on acreage allotment and price supports have affected the production and supply behavior of California field crops over the years 1949–70, which is the period considered by our study. The impact of this price support and other government programs, which may be more effective, the more profitable the crop is, can be analyzed in two alternative ways. One is to compare two sets of linear regression equations, one for the control period 1954–70 and the other for the no control period 1949–53 and perform a Chow-test to analyze if there is any significant difference between the two sets of regressions. This compari-son however would not capture the impact of the covariance of prices for two or more interrelated crops. Hence we perform a test on the difference between the two variance–covariance matrices, one for the post-control period and the other for the pre-control period. Let V_x be the positive-definite variance–covariance matrix of the n-element output vector x, which is approximately normally distributed and let $\hat{V}_x$ be the maximum likelihood estimate of V_x based on N sample observations, then the statistic δ^2 defined by

$$\delta^2 = \frac{N-1}{4} \sum_{i=1}^{n} \left(\log \hat{\lambda}_i - \log \lambda_i \right)^2 \tag{11.1}$$

has for $N \to \infty$ the asymptotic distribution of a chi-square variate with

$1/2n(n+1)$ degrees of freedom, where $\hat{\lambda}_i$ is the i-th eigenvalue of the estimated matrix $\hat{V}_x$ corresponding to λ_i of the matrix V_x. Since under the above assumptions, the sample eigenvalues $\hat{\lambda}_i$ are approximately normally distributed for $N \to \infty$ with expectation $E\hat{\lambda}_i = \lambda_i$ and variance var $\hat{\lambda}_i = 4\lambda_i^2/(N-1)$, a multivariate test known as Hotelling's T^2 may be used to test the difference in means of two sets of eigenvalues:

Model III:

$$T^2 = d'\hat{\Sigma}^{-1}d \tag{11.2}$$

where d' is an n-element row vector with a typical element $d_i = (\hat{\lambda}_i^{(1)} - \hat{\lambda}_i^{(2)})$ denoting the difference in eigenvalues for the two sample periods, and $\hat{\Sigma}$ is the variance–covariance matrix, a diagonal matrix with var $\hat{\lambda}$ in the diagonal. It is assumed in this case that an independent unbiased estimate $\hat{\Sigma}$ is available. In this case, if the null hypothesis is true, i.e. there is no difference between the two sets of eigenvalues, then it is known that asymptotically [4,8] the statistic

$$\frac{N-n}{n}T^2 \sim F(n, N) \tag{11.3}$$

$T^2(N-n)/n$ has a standard F distribution with degrees of freedom n and N. These statistical tests (11.1) through (11.3) provide the framework for Model III used to test the impact of government price support and stabilization policy on two sample sets, one before the control or stabilization program and one after it. Indirectly these tests would show if the gains from stabilization policies and control programs have been effective for farmers' incomes and acreage allocations.

In the next model we consider how important the hypothesis of risk aversion is, if at all, in farmer's decisions, when risk aversion is measured by price variances. But the test of this hypothesis is done in a different way. We define outputs $\hat{x}(t) = \hat{A}(t)\bar{y}(t)$ with means $m(t)$ and variances $\sigma^2(t)$ for the different crops as $m(t) = \bar{p}(t)\hat{x}(t)$, $\sigma^2(t) = \sigma_p^2(t)\hat{x}^2(t)$ where $\hat{A}(t)$ is the acreage predicted by linear regressions on $A(t-1)$ and $p(t-1)$, $\bar{y}(t)$ is the mean yield per acre and $\bar{p}(t)$, $\sigma_p^2(t)$ are the means and variances of observed prices. Predicted acreages $\hat{A}(t)$, mean yields $\bar{y}(t)$ and mean prices $\bar{p}(t)$ are computed successively over the years 1949–66, 1949–67, 1949–68, 1949–69 and 1949–70; then a best fit is made of the curve

Model IV:

$$m(t) = f(\sigma^2(t)) \tag{12}$$

where linear and quadratic functions for $f(\cdot)$ are considered. Note that the predicted acreages $\hat{A}(t)$ are assumed not to depend on an explanatory variable representing risk aversion; hence the slope $\partial m(t)/\partial \sigma^2(t) = \lambda$ of the curve (12), if statistically significant and different from zero would indicate production adjustment due to changes in risk measured by the price variance.

3. Econometric estimates of alternative models

The empirical data used here for estimating the alternative models are for the California field crops for the twenty-two years 1949–70 for the San Joaquin Valley, which has been previously utilized by other researchers [6,7]. Data for the San Joaquin valley was chosen because of its importance in the field crop economy of California. About 90 percent of the state's cotton, California's most important field crop is produced in this valley; further the valley is a major producer of nearly every important California field crop such as corn, sorghum, sugar beets and wheat. The impact of control programs and price support measures are more significantly observable in the data sets. For instance, the cotton program has been the major field crop production in this valley for this period and the effects of variation in cotton controls have been felt in the acreage response of other field crops like rice, sorghum, sugar beets, etc. Next to cotton, wheat was subject to the same allotment pattern as cotton in the 1950's, although price sensitivity of supply response has been very slight in this case, as wheat was not profitable enough to compete with other high-return crops, till 1970 when wheat acreage jumped by more than 60 percent from the 1969 level through the shift toward Mexican varieties. Sugar beet and rice production have also faced government acreage controls through parts of the period 1949–70.

Several features of this data set have been noted by Just [7] in his analysis of the effects of price support and other government programs for these crops. First, cotton and rice have been subject to strict acreage allotment programs, although it has been generally found that strict controls are less effective when the crop is not the most profitable, or not the most important. In San Joaquin Valley, rice is much less important a crop than cotton. Further, the empirical analysis of Just [7] has found the risk factor to be far less important for the rice crop, when the risk sensitivity is measured by price variance. Second, crops like sugar beets are regarded as high risk crops, and due to their importance in profitability, risk sensitivity is likely to be much more significant. Third, the various government programs like acreage control, price support, voluntary restrictions, etc. have not always produced the desirable stabilizing impact. The observed time trend of acreage response of some feedgrain crops like sorghum shows that the impact of government price support policies might have run counter to the acreage-reducing effects of voluntary and other forms of acreage restrictions. Further, the cotton allotment programs have effected the acreage decisions of other crops like rice, sorghum and sugar beets. Hence any risk-reducing effects of government programs on cotton acreages are likely to be transmitted to other crops, through the process of substitution.

The details of the econometric estimates are presented in the various tables grouped according to the four model specifications mentioned above. Two general qualifications must be mentioned. First, the regression estimates presented here were selected from a larger set and the choice was made by considerations of simplicity and ease of interpretation. Second, the estimates were designed to test the reasonableness of the theoretical hypotheses mentioned above. In particular, four specific hypotheses about supply response are tested by our empirical estimates:

H_1: The supply response decisions for the field crops are not significantly affected by risk factors measured by observed price variances.

H_2: The inter-crop variations in output and prices have not changed significantly by the stabilization policy and other government programs pursued during 1954–70.

H_3: Acreage decisions for crops like rice and cotton which are more strictly regulated by government programs are not significantly affected by risk measured through suitable proxy variables representing subjective price variances, etc.

H_4: Response of output rather than acreage for the field crops are not significantly influenced by variance of returns.

The variables in the regression equations reported in this tables are denoted as follows:

$A(t)$: area under a specific crop for year t
$p(t)$: price for a specific crop in year t
$p^\alpha(t)$: adjusted price incorporating yield variations
$p_c(t)$: constructed price: it is equal to lagged price if lagged price is larger than support price and equal to support price if lagged price is less than support price
$p_M(t)$: posterior mean prices computed as the linearly weighted combination of last three years' prices and a prior mean
$v(t)$: variances of crop–specific prices computed on a three-year moving basis
D: dummy variable: it is equal to one if the observed price is less than the mean of the past three observations but zero otherwise.

F: dummy variable for price to incorporate the importance of acreage allotment programs, taking the value -1 if support price is greater and $+1$ if it is less than the market price

The broad pattern of the econometric estimates may be presented in two groups, e.g., the first group relates the results to the four hypotheses and the second group discusses some of the technical aspects of estimation in relevant cases.

3.1. Tests of hypotheses

(i) In respect of hypothesis H_1 it is clear from table 1.1 that except for rice and cotton, the acreage response has negative elasticity with respect to risk measured by observed price variance for all the other crops. However, the variance measure of risk gives equal weights to positive deviations, although for risk aversion it is only the negative deviation that appears important. Hence when a dummy variable D is introduced to emphasize unequal weights, the estimated results in table 2.2 show very uniformly the negative impact of price variance for all the crops including rice and cotton. Similar pattern is borne out by table 2.1, when the lagged price is excluded as an independent variable but the price variance is included.

(ii) The hypothesis H_2 was tested for the impact of price support and acreage restrictions program for four crops: rice, cotton, wheat and sugarbeets. Two sample sets comprising 1949–53 and 1954–70 were used. Due to nonavailability of comparable data for earlier years, the first sample set ($N_1 = 4$) could not be extended. To offset the result to some extent the second sample set were taken either as $N_2 = 4$ or $N_2 = 17$. The hypothesis is tested in terms of the difference of variance–covariance matrices for the two periods for prices V_p, outputs V_x and yields per acre V_y. It is clear from the estimated results in table 3.2 that the two sample sets, one with the control program and the other without it are statistically significant at the 5% level. A t-test based on the difference between only the largest eigenvalues of the two sample sets also produced a significant difference at the 5% level. Note that these statistical tests are made for outputs and yields rather than acreages, since the former are normalized and hence they capture the inter-crop variation in impact.

The observed trend of variances for the two periods reproduced in table 3.1 also shows that variances have been reduced in most cases in the post-control period. For rice and cotton, reduction in price variances has been much more significant than other crops. Note however that this trend in variance ignores the covariances and also the inter-crop variations in output yields.

(iii) For testing hypothesis H_3 for the two crops rice and cotton, which have been more regulated than others, two different methods are used to define suitable proxy variables that may represent subjective variances as risk. One is the Bayesian method of deriving posterior means from prior means and sample means. The second method is to show the impact of the negative deviations in observed price variance trends as being subjectively more important.

Assume that $p(1)$, $p(2),\ldots,p(t)$ follow approximately a normal distribution $N(\theta, \sigma^2)$, with variance σ^2 being known. Further, assume that θ has a prior normal distribution $N(\mu, \tau^2)$, then the posterior mean price $v(t)$ is given by a linear weighted combination of sample mean price $\bar{p} = t^{-1}\Sigma_{k=1}^{t}p(k)$ and the prior mean μ:

$$\mu(t) = \omega\bar{p} + (1 - \omega)\mu; \quad \omega = \frac{t\tau^2}{t\tau^2 + \sigma^2}$$

The proxy variable for the posterior mean $\mu(t)$ is denoted by $p_M(t)$ in table 1.2 and it is computed on a three-year moving basis. For both rice and cotton, the proxy variable $p_M(t)$ has a positive coefficient. However, we have to note that the price series do not follow normality very closely and hence the proxy variable is very approximative. Another alternative is to use the constructed price series $p_c(t)$, which allows the farmers to use their knowledge of support prices. As table 2.3 shows very clearly, the coefficient of $p_c(t)$ is statistically significant at 5% level for both rice and cotton.

For the second method, we consider table 2.2 where a dummy variable D representing higher weightage on the positive deviations of the price variance term, is used along with the price variance. For cotton and rice, this shows for the dummy variable D uniformly negative coefficients, which imply that the pessimistic components of variance (e.g., risk aversion) played a very important role. Further, there is some evidence for cotton [7] that the increase in mean prices have more than offset the reduction in subjective price variances.

Modification of the observed price variance term $v(t)$ by a subjective proxy is also analyzed in tables 2.5 and 2.6, where two stage estimates of $v(t)$ are used as regressors. The negative impact of the subjective risk variables is uniformly observed for rice and cotton.

(iv) For testing hypothesis H_4, linear and quadratic forms of the mean-variance Model IV given by (12) are fitted to observed empirical points. Results of the fit are given in tables 4.1 and 4.2. By the method of derivation used in Model IV, the slopes $\partial m(t)/\partial\sigma^2(t)$ of the linear regressions would not be statistically different from zero, if H_4 were true. The results of table 4.2 indicate otherwise. It appears that farmers' output decisions conform more to the mean-variance efficiency locus of risk-aversion decision-makers than otherwise.

3.2. Technical aspects of estimation

A few technical aspects of the estimation problem may be discussed in brief in this section. One of the most important aspects is the adjustment implicit in the distributed lag framework of Model II. In industrial studies, linear decision rules [13] have proved very useful in empirical specifications of the adjustment process, particularly when data on inventories are available along with output and order rates. In our study here, inventory data of course are not available. Note also that the structural parameters k_i and c_{i1}, c_{i2}, c_{i3} of Model II enter into the response equation (10.3) nonlinearly. However, since $\beta_{i1} = 1 - k_i$ for different crops $i = 1, 2, \ldots, 5$ one could estimate the long-run adjustment coefficient k as in table A.

Since a high value of k, implies through (9.1) a low relative value of b_2, the coefficient of $[A(t) - A(t-1)]^2$, the long-run acreage adjustment is more important for wheat, rice and cotton; hence the short-run factors of price risk are relatively less important for these crops.

The nonlinearity element for the two crops, cotton and rice, has been explored through the two-stage method: in the first stage residuals are calculated from linear regression equations where there is no price variance term; the residuals are then regressed on price variance and in the second stage, estimated residuals are used as regressors. The final estimates are shown in table B.

In case 3 of rice, the time dependence of the price variance term is explicitly recognized in the first stage through the regression equation

$$v(t) = 0.20 + 0.77v(t-1) - 0.04p_M(t-1)$$
$$(5.26) (0.68)$$

$$R^2 = 0.65$$

$$DW = 2.5$$

and it is clear that the value of R^2 increases from 0.65 to 0.90 when the estimated $\hat{v}(t)$ is used as a regressor in the second stage. For cotton a similar increase in R^2 is noted in terms of the estimated residual used as a regressor.

In terms of lagged adjustment over time, price variances have adjusted much faster for rice and cotton than other crops as shown in table C. Hence it is to be expected on a priori grounds that the two-stage estimate of price variance used as regressor would improve R^2 and DW statistic more for rice than for other crops.

Another important technical aspect of our estimation framework relates to the specification of the risk variable as a regressor. It has been clear from our estimation framework that the price variance measure of risk aversion which weights positive and negative deviations around the

Table A

Crop	Estimate of k	
	table 2.1	table 2.2
Wheat	0.92	0.88
Rice	0.73	0.60
Cotton	0.58	0.71
Sugarbeet	0.24	0.38
Sorghum	0.18	0.18

Table B

$A(t)$ for	c	$A(t-1)$	$p(t-1)$	D	Rês	$\hat{v}(t)$	R^2	DW
Rice								
case 1	$-30,425.4$	0.49	11,130.4	–	-1.12	–	0.60	2.09
		(3.14)	(2.18)		(1.94)			
case 2	60,492.7	0.40	$-7,913.8$	-3.29	-0.65	–	0.93	1.62
		(5.25)	(2.37)	(2.63)	(7.48)			
case 3	48,682.8	0.42	$-5,021.0$	0.52	–	$-17,958.0$	0.90	1.8
		ᐧ (4.32)	(1.37)	(7.07)		(1.2)		
Cotton								
case 1	220,341.0	0.51	3,709.4	–	-1.14	–	0.89	1.4
		(5.89)	(3.91)		(5.64)			

Table C

Crop	Dep. variable	c	$v(t-1)$	R^2	DW
Rice	$V(t)$	0.01	0.73	0.64	2.43
			(5.47)		
Cotton	$V(t)$	41.78	0.42	0.42	1.87
			(3.48)		
Wheat	$V(t)$	0.01	0.34	0.11	1.76
			(1.46)		
Sugarbeet	$V(t)$	0.18	0.14	0.02	1.82
			(0.54)		

mean symmetrically equally does not always capture risk sensitivity; in particular it fares worse in case of crops like rice and cotton that have been subject to government control policies more than other crops. We have already emphasized in the estimates of Model II that the use of dummy variables as proxies for subjective risk factors help improve the response equation in terms of R^2 and the appropriateness of the sign (i.e., negative) of the coefficient of the price variance term.

A question however remains if the risk sensitivity of the supply response equation for each crop did change over the period 1949–53 to 1954–70. By risk sensitivity we mean here the coefficient associated with the price variance term $v(t)$, when suitable other regressor variables like $A(t-1), p(t-1), D$ etc. are used. For each crop, most suitable regressor variables are chosen by the criteria of high R^2 and reasonableness of signs of regression coefficients; further since the period 1949–53 provides very few sample observations, the period 1949–70 is compared with 1954–70 by Chow-tests over sets of regression coefficients. The results are in table 4.3., which show that in terms of farmers' risk sensitivity measured by the relative value of the coefficient of the price variance term the acreage response pattern has not changed. The F-values in table 4.3 are not statistically significant at the 5% level. This implies among other things the following: either the price variance measure of risk is a very poor proxy for risk aversion, or that inter-crop adjustments and covariances play a more important role, when price support and acreage control programs are in effect.

4. Concluding remarks

Our econometric estimates broadly reflect negative supply elasticity with respect to price variance and other proxy variables indicative of subjective risk, although in some cases like cotton, there is some evidence that the increase in subjective means of prices have more than offset the reduction in observed price variances. (see table D.)

It is clear that the conditional mean estimate of price given the variance term $v(t)$ is positive in all the above cases except cotton. Further, the estimates $m = \bar{p}/\sqrt{\bar{v}}$ of the ratio of average price ($\bar{p}$) to average standard deviation $\sqrt{\bar{v}}$ turns out to be as follows:

	Cotton	Rice	Sugar Beet	Sorghum
Values of m:	39.23	32.55	31.68	26.21

This implies that in a relative sense, cotton displays the least importance of the price variance term compared to the mean and sorghum, which is mainly a feed crop, displays the highest importance. Hence the response equation for sorghum performs so well for price variance as a risk variable, even when dummy variables are not introduced:

$$\text{Sorghum: } A(t) = \underset{(4.65)}{161.48 + 0.8015\ A(t-1)} + \underset{(0.68)}{26{,}319.9\ p(t-1)}$$
$$\underset{(1.23)}{-1004{,}240\ v(t)}$$
$$R^2 = 0.83; \quad DW = 2.51$$

We have to caution, however, that the expansionary effects of stabilization policy in general and specifically for some crops like rice and feedgrains, though found statistically significant, need to be separated from the effects of acreage reduction programs and these two effects have tended to offset each other for some years. This suggests more caution in separating the two effects, before the supply elasticity as affected by price risks is used as the basis of stabilization programs.

The implications of price risk in the supply function as introduced here in Models I and III in terms of the expected utility function are two-fold. First, it suggests that the notion of equilibrium price as a market clearing price need not have the stabilizing characteristics as ordinarily supposed. Second, the risk associated with the subjective and objective distribution of prices have at least two components, e.g., one measured by the risk aversion parameter and the other by the variance; the first component is more subjective than the second. It is clear that if the two components move in opposite directions, the net result may show up in supply response not responsive to price risk at all. This is more likely to hold when there is an uneven distribution of farm sizes, as Wien's study [15] shows that the risk aversion parameter may vary significantly from small to large farms. The implications for equilibrium price may be briefly indicated through a demand-supply model for one crop with a noisy supply schedule: $S(t)$

Table D

Cotton	$p(t) = 162.26 - \underset{(2.89)}{0.073\ v(t)}$	$R^2 = 0.33$
Rice	$p(t) = 4.64 + \underset{(2.04)}{1.47\ v(t)}$	$R^2 = 0.24$
Sugar Beet	$p(t) = 11.1 + \underset{(2.69)}{4.16\ v(t)}$	$R^2 = 0.30$
Sorghum	$p(t) = 1.19 + \underset{(6.20)}{15.30\ v(t)}$	$R^2 = 0.69$

$$D(t) = a_1 - a_2 p(t)$$

$$D(t) = a_0 + a_3 p(t-1) + a_4 \sigma_p^2(t-1) + \epsilon(t)$$

$D(t) = S(t)$ in equilibrium

where $\epsilon(t)$ is the stochastic component assumed to have zero mean and fixed variance and independent of $\sigma_p^2(t-1)$. Taking expectation over $\epsilon(t)$ and the equilibrium condition, the mean price satisfies the equation:

$$\bar{p}(t+1) = b_0 - b_1 \bar{p}(t) + b_2 \bar{\sigma}_p^2$$

$$b_0 = (a_1 - a_0)/a_3, \qquad b_1 = a_3/a_2, b_2 = a_4/a_2$$

where $\bar{\sigma}_p^2$ denotes the average variance. It is clear that if b_1 is less than unity, the steady state solution $\bar{p}$ of $\bar{p}(t)$ with $t \to \infty$ becomes:
$\bar{p} = \lim \bar{p}(t) = (b_0 + b_2)\bar{\sigma}_p^2/(1 + b_1)$. This shows that the equilibrium price tends not to a constant but to a level which depends on price variance, i.e. the market clearing holds only partially. Also, since b_2 is usually positive, the effect on price deviations in the short-run may be positive or negative depending on whether the short-run variance $\bar{\sigma}_p^2(t)$ exceeds or falls short of the long-run average variance $\bar{\sigma}_p^2$. Hence, any price support program which reduces $\sigma_p^2(t)$ without reducing the long-run variance may fail to have a stabilizing effect if at all. Thus, the welfare gains [14] from price stabilization have to be carefully evaluated when supply responses are sensitive to price risk.

References

1. Behrman, J.R. (1968): Supply Response in Underdeveloped Agriculture. Amsterdam: North Holland.
2. Boussard, J.M. (1969): "The Introduction of Risk into a Programming Model: Different Criteria and the Actual Behavior of Farmers", European Economic Review, Vol. 1, 92–121.
3. Freund, R.J. (1956): "The Introduction of Risk into a Programming Model", Econometrica, Vol. 24, 253–63.
4. Girschik, M.A. (1939): "On the Sampling Theory of Roots of Determinantal Equations", Annals of Mathematical Statistics, Vol. 10, 204–224.
5. Hazell, P.B.R. and P.L. Scandizzo (1974): "Competitive Demand Structures under Risk in Agricultural Linear Programming Models", American Journal of Agricultural Economics, Vol. 56, 235–244.
6. Just, R.E. (1974): "An Investigation of the Importance of Risk in Farmers' Decisions", American Journal of Agricultural Economics, Vol. 56, 14–25.
7. Just. R.E., (1972): "Econometric Analysis of Production Decisions with Government Intervention: The Case of California Field Crops", Unpublished Ph.D. Thesis, University of California, Berkeley.

8. Kshirsagar, A.M. (1972): Multivariate Analysis. New York: Marcel Dekker.
9. Officer, R.R. and A.N. Halter (1968): "Utility Analysis in a Practical Setting", American Journal of Agricultural Economics, Vol. 50, 257–277.
10. Sengupta, J.K. (1972): Stochastic Programming: Methods and Applications. Amsterdam: North Holland.
11. Sengupta, J.K., (1979): "Optimal Resource Allocation Under Stochastic Prices and Yields". Zeitschrift für Nationalökonomie, Vol. 39, 83–104.
12. Sengupta, J.K., (1981): Decision Models in Stochastic Programming. To be published by Elsvier-North Holland, New York.
13. Sengupta, J.K., and R.I. Sfeir (1979): "The Adjustment of Output–Inventory Process under Linear Decision Rules," Journal of Economic Dynamics and Control, Vol. 1, 361–381.
14. Turnovsky, S.J. (1974): "Price Expectations and the Welfare Gains From Price Stabilization", American Journal of Agricultural Economics, Vol. 56, 706–716.
15. Wiens, T.B. (1976): "Peasant Risk Aversion and Allocative Behavior: A Quadratic Programming Experiment", American Journal of Agricultural Economics, Vol. 58, 629–635.

Table 1.1.
Effects of price and its variance on acreages (1949–70): Model I

Crop	Dependent variable	Constant c	$A(t-1)$	$p(t-1)$	$v(t)$	R^2	DW
Rice	$A(t)$	−34057.2 (1.35)	0.49 * (3.14)	11130.4 * (2.18)	30216.1 * (1.94)	0.60	2.09
Cotton	$A(t)$	−291859 * (1.95)	0.51 * (5.89)	3709.41 * (3.91)	517.14 * (5.64)	0.89	1.37
Wheat	$A(t)$	−9317.09 (0.21)	0.76 * (5.08)	775.84 [a] (1.03)	−173003 (0.5)	0.63	1.62
Sugar Beet	$A(t)$	−172883 * (−2.56)	0.66 * (4.67)	17358.6 * (2.84)	−22326.8 (0.63)	0.75	1.6
Sorghum	$A(t)$	161.48 (0.003)	0.8 * (4.65)	26319.9 (0.67)	−0.1E7 (1.23)	0.83	2.5

Note: t-values are in parenthesis, DW denotes Durbin–Watson statistic
[*]: significant at 5% upper tail t-test
[a]: the price is adjusted to reflect yield variations

Table 1.2.
Effects of posterior mean price on acreages (1949–70): Model I

Crop	Dependent variable	Constant c	$A(t-1)$	$p_M(t-1)$	R^2	DW
Rice	$A(t)$	-36358.7	0.33	13989.3	0.37	1.41
		(0.95)	(1.44)	(1.57)		
Cotton	$A(t)$	-206223	0.63 *	2832.0	0.78	1.38
		(0.64)	(4.4)	(1.19)		
Wheat	$A(t)$	4503.12	0.71 *	564.18 [a]	0.47	1.47
		(0.07)	(3.57)	(0.52)		
Sugar Beet	$A(t)$	153280	0.59 *	16018.1	0.68	1.77
		(1.32)	(3.3)	(1.51)		
Sorghum	$A(t)$	8560.54	0.88 *	9176.16	0.80	2.63
		(0.14)	(5.69)	(0.26)		

Note: t-values are in parenthesis, DW denotes Durbin–Watson statistic
*: significant at 5% upper tail t-test
[a]: The price is adjusted to reflect yield variations

Table 2.1.
Effects of price variance and a dummy variable on acreages (1949–70): Model II

Crop	Dependent variable	Constant c	$A(t-1)$	D	$v(t)$	R^2	DW
Rice	$A(t)$	25109.3 * (6.3)	0.42 * (4.87)	−0.51 * (6.99)	−244667.6 (1.7)	0.90	1.13
Cotton	$A(t)$	506518 * (6.46)	0.27 * (2.73)	−0.35 * (5.32)	−131.43 (1.05)	0.93	1.29
Wheat	$A(t)$	96820.3 * (4.2)	0.08 (0.37)	−0.37 * (3.5)	−168350 (0.64)	0.71	1.67
Sugar Beet	$A(t)$	22091.3 (1.55)	0.76 * (4.92)	−1865.96 (0.16)	756.38 (0.02)	0.63	1.97
Sorghum	$A(t)$	31927.5 (1.47)	0.82 * (5.04)	−9169.09 (0.97)	−85164.7 (0.11)	0.81	2.29

Note: t-values are in parenthesis, DW denotes Durbin–Watson statistic
*: significant at 5% upper tail t-test

Table 2.2.
Effects of price, its variance and a dummy variable on acreages (1949–70): Model II

Crop	Dependent variable	Constant c	$A(t-1)$	$p(t-1)$	D	$v(t)$	R^2	DW
Rice	$A(t)$	64167.1 * (3.82)	0.4 * (5.25)	-7913.75 * (2.37)	-0.65 * (7.48)	-35168.3 * (2.63)	0.93	1.61
Cotton	$A(t)$	322854 * (1.89)	0.29 * (2.88)	1072 (1.2)	-0.30 * (4.06)	-45.92 (0.32)	0.94	1.07
Wheat	$A(t)$	101186 * (3.57)	0.12 (0.45)	-4639.14 (0.28)	-0.36 * (3.2)	-165598 (0.61)	0.71	1.73
Sugar Beet	$A(t)$	-170335 * (2.23)	0.62 * (4.33)	17077.2 * (2.56)	7994.49 (0.74)	-14354.7 (0.40)	0.75	1.89
Sorghum	$A(t)$	26593.6 (0.42)	0.82 * (4.79)	4219.77 (0.09)	-9316.5 (0.94)	-154263 (0.14)	0.81	2.3

Note: t-values are in parenthesis, DW denotes Durbin–Watson statistic
  *: significant at 5% upper tail t-test

Table 2.3.
Effect of constructed price on acreages: Model II

Crop	Dependent variable	Constant c	$A(t-1)$	$p_c(t)$	R^2	DW
Rice	$A(t)$	−83366.8 * (2.87)	0.56 * (3.79)	20986.7 * (3.64)	0.60	2.19
Wheat	$A(t)$	59915.1 * (2.14)	0.91 * (6.5)	−24326.8 * (1.54)	0.75	1.90
Cotton	$A(t)$	−520876 * (2.11)	0.44 * (2.96)	5835.89 * (3.85)	0.63	1.47
Sorghum	$A(t)$	26535.6 (0.53)	0.89 * (6.5)	−5919.87 (0.2)	0.83	2.47

Note: t-values in parenthesis and DW denotes Durbin–Watson statistic
  *: significant at 5% upper tail t-test

Table 2.4.
Effects of price and a dummy variable on acreages: Model II

Crop	Dependent variable	Constant c	$A(t-1)$	$p(t-1)$	F	R^2	DW
Cotton	$A(t)$	−458326 * (1.82)	0.47 * (3.15)	5503.04 * (3.65)	31734.9 (0.83)	0.67	0.71
Rice	$A(t)$	−73814.8 * (2.85)	0.33 * (1.93)	21998 * (3.86)	7416.6 * (2.36)	0.64	2.13

Note: t-values are in parenthesis, DW denotes Durbin–Watson statistic
  *: significant at 5% upper tail t-test

Table 2.5.
Effects of price variance on rice acreages by a two-stage method of estimation: Model II

Case 1

$A(t)=$	C −46871 * (1.79)	$A(t-1)$ 0.53 * (3.16)	$p(t-1)$ 14217.6 * (2.72)	R^2 0.51	DW 1.93
Res =	C 3229.21 (1.14)	v −26873.7 * (1.91)	R^2 0.17	DW 2.1	
$A(t)=$	C −30426.4 (1.18)	$A(t-1)$ 0.49 * (3.14)	$p(t-1)$ 11130.4 * (2.18)	Rês −1.12 * (1.94)	R^2 0.60 DW 2.09

Case 2

$A(t)=$	C 48988.3 * (2.62)	$A(t-1)$ 0.37 * (4.14)	$p(t-1)$ −4953.1 (1.34)	D −0.47 * (7.32)	R^2 0.89 DW 1.64
Res =	C −1117.51 (0.78)	$v(t)$ 10695.8 (1.38)	R^2 0.10	DW 1.72	
$A(t)=$	C 60492.7 * (3.69)	$A(t-1)$ 0.4 * (5.25)	$p(t-1)$ −7913.76 * (2.37)	D −3.29 * (2.63)	Rês −0.65 * (7.48) R^2 0.93 DW 1.62

Case 3

$v(t)=$	C' 0.2 (0.72)	$v(t-1)$ (5.26)	$p_M(t-1)$ 0.77 * (0.68)	R^2 0.04	DW 0.65 2.5
$A(t)=$	C −30065.3 (0.99)	$A(t-1)$ 0.41 * (2.06)	$p(t-1)$ 11106.0 * (1.88)	$\hat{v}(t)$ 33575.2 (1.24)	R^2 0.54 DW 2.33
$A(t)=$	C 48682.8 * (2.65)	$A(t-1)$ 0.42 * (4.32)	$p(t-1)$ −5021 (1.37)	$\hat{v}(t)$ −17958 (1.2)	D 0.52 * (7.07) R^2 0.90 DW 1.8

Note: Res denotes residuals, c for the constant term, $\hat{v}(t)$ for the estimated price variance and D for the dummy variable defined earlier.
* significant at 5% upper tail t-test

Table 2.6
Effects of price variance on acreages by a two-stage method of estimation for cotton and sugar beet: Model II

Cotton

Case 1

	C	$A(t-1)$	$p(t-1)$	R^2	DW
$A(t) =$	$-506002\,^*$	$0.49\,^*$	$5579.08\,^*$	0.66	0.88
	(2.09)	(3.38)	(3.74)		
	C	$v(t)$		R^2	DW
Res $=$	$62687.3\,^*$	$-453.28\,^*$		0.58	1.33
	(2.8)	(5.02)			
	C	$A(t-1)$	$p(t-1)$	Rês	R^2	DW
$A(t) =$	-220341	$0.51\,^*$	$3709.41\,^*$	$-1.14\,^*$	0.89	1.37
	(1.44)	(5.89)	(3.91)	(5.64)		

Sugar Beet

Case 1

	C	$A(t-1)$	$p(t-1)$	R^2	DW
$A(t) =$	$-165044\,^*$	$0.65\,^*$	$16361\,^*$	0.74	1.66
	(2.53)	(4.71)	(2.82)		
	C	$v(t)$		R^2	DW
Res $=$	-4083.04	19577.5		0.02	1.6
	(0.52)	(0.63)			
	C	$A(t-1)$	$p(t-1)$	Rês	R^2	DW
$A(t) =$	$-177540\,^*$	$0.66\,^*$	$17358\,^*$	-1.14	0.75	1.6
	(2.56)	(4.67)	(2.84)	(0.63)		

Note: Res denotes residuals and Rês denotes their estimated values; other terms are as defined earlier.
*: significant at 5% upper tail t-test

Table 3.1.
Observed means and variances of prices and acreages for the periods 1949–53 and 1954–70

Variable	Crop	1949–53		1954–70	
		Mean	Variance	Mean	Variance
Price					
	Rice	4.91	0.87	4.67	0.12
	Cotton	172.05	622.43	154.38	324.57
	Wheat	2.12	0.009	1.74	0.07
	Sugarbeet	11.46	0.29	11.98	1.31
	Sorghum	1.64	0.04	1.26	0.01
Acreages					
	Rice	40784.8	0.24E9	44061.7	0.22E9
	Cotton	0.1E7	0.68E11	682062	0.64E10
	Wheat	174386	0.42E9	101675	0.51E9
	Sugarbeet	23354.2	0.12E9	79989.8	0.1E10
	Sorghum	24268.8	0.7E8	119260	0.1E10

Note: En denotes 10^n i.e. E9 $= 10^9$

Table 3.2
Eigenvalue estimates of variance–covariance matrices and the values of T^2 and δ^2 statistics of Model III

	Eigenvalue estimates				δ^2-value
	$N_1 = 4$	$N_2 = 4$	$N_2 = 17$		$N_1 = N_2 = 4$
$V_p V_y$:	0.841	0.067	0.066		8.0
	0.043	0.012	0.024		
	0.0	0.0004	0.003		
	0.0	0.0	0.005		
$V_p V_x$:	93.32E10	3.54E9	6.07E10		35.9
	1.827E10	0.334E9	0.107E10		
	0.0	0.006E9	0.022E10		
	0.002E9	0.0	0.003E10		

Values of T^2

$V_p V_y$;	$N_1 = N_2 = 4$	7.97
$V_p V_y$;	$N_1 = N_2 = 4$	47.97
V_p;	$N_1 = N_2 = 4$	40.51
$V_p V_y$;	$N_1 = 4, N_2 = 17$	6.77
$V_p X_x$:	$N_1 = 4, N_2 = 17$	12.68

Table 4.1.
Estimates of mean $m(t)$ and variance $\sigma^2(t)$ of output: Model IV

Crops	$m(t)$	$\sigma^2(t)$
Rice	76.15E5	70.65E10
	75.17E5	67.02E10
	77.58E5	66.98E10
	93.55E5	92.49E10
	82.28E5	68.16E10
Cotton	160.57E6	222.84E12
	110.35E6	100.66E12
	178.9E6	390.49E12
	111.84E6	200.00E12
	125.19E6	280.00E12
Wheat	37.86E5	22.54E10
	35.97E5	24.03E10
	45.71E5	46.58E10
	47.35E5	53.83E10
	58.82E5	89.59E10
Sugarbeet	23.55E6	1.17E12
	23.09E6	1.54E12
	21.79E6	2.08E12
	31.79E6	5.32E12
	34.24E6	9.44E12
Sorghum	9.43E6	2.44E12
	12.29E6	4.05E12
	11.88E6	3.69E12
	10.7E6	2.85E12
	14.15E6	4.77E12

Table 4.2
Estimates of the mean-variance curve fitted to Model IV

Crop	Dependent variable	Constant	$\sigma^2(t)$	$(\sigma^2(t))^2$	R^2
Rice	$m(t)$	37.55 (2.72)	0.6E-5 (3.28)		0.84
Rice	$m(t)$	383.44 (0.87)	-0.82E-4 (0.73)	0.55E-11 (0.78)	0.90
Cotton	$m(t)$	84.15 (3.09)	0.22E-6 (2.11)		0.60
Cotton	$m(t)$	105.99 (1.45)	0.16E-7 (0.25E-1)	0.42E-15 (0.33)	0.62
Wheat	$m(t)$	30.88 (81.66)	0.31E-5 (48.04)		0.99
Sugarbeet	$m(t)$	23.00 (9.12)	0.13E-5 (3.22)		0.91
Sorghum	$m(t)$	5.01 (8.32)	0.19E-5 (11.39)		0.98

Note: E_n denotes 10^n; t-values in parenthesis.

Table 4.3.
Values of F-statistic of the chow test for acreage response for 1954–70 and 1949–70

Crop	Dependent Variable	Independent Variables	F-Value
Rice	$A(t)$	$A(t-1)$, D, $V(t)$	2.39
Cotton	$A(t)$	$A(t-1)$, $p(t-1)$, D, $v(t)$	1.09
Wheat	$A(t)$	$A(t-2)$, $p^*(t-1)$, $v(t)$	0.32
Sugarbeet	$A(t)$	$A(t-1)$, $p(t-1)$, $v(t)$	1.18
Sorghum	$A(t)$	$A(t-1)$, $p(t-1)$, $v(t)$	0.63

8. Optimal portfolio investment in a dynamic horizon

1. Introduction

The static version of the mean-variance model of optimal portfolio investment has found very wide applications for the investor's decision problem (Lin and Boot 1982, Mao 1969, Sharpe 1970, Ziemba and Vickson 1975). The dynamic version has not been so adequately analyzed in the standard literature, perhaps due to the specification problems of intertemporal variations in mean and variance of portfolio returns. Hillier (1963) attempted a nonlinear programming version of the intertemporal problem of risky interrelated investments with discounted cash flows that have random components over time. Dynamic stochastic programming models have also been considered for the consumer, who has to optimally decide between consumption and investment over his lifetime, when there are risky and also riskless assets (Ziemba and Vickson 1975). These models however, in their steady state, do not necessarily lead to a static mean-variance formulation of the standard portfolio model. Besides, they do not analyze specifically for the investor dealing in n risky assets such decision problems as risk-sensitivity, the length of the planning horizon.

Hence we consider two dynamic formulations of the investor's decision problem regarding optimal portfolio investment in a dynamic planning horizon. The first formulation considers the minimization of a discounted stream of risks measured by variances, subject to the restriction that the discounted stream of expected returns does not fall below a specified level of minimal return. It is shown that a special case of this formulation leads to a control-theoretic model, where the steady state version may be analyzed separately from the transient state. The second formulation seeks to characterize optimality within the class of linear decision rules, where the objective function is to maximize the expected return over a specified time horizon, subject to two sets of probabilistic constraints, e.g., a risk constraint on losses and a capital constraint for liquidity. Since linear decision rules are only approximations, this formulation leads to suboptimal rather than optimal investment decisions.

2. Dynamic portfolio models

The static decision problem in portfolio theory considers a decision-maker (DM) who has to invest a proportion of his wealth, x_i, optimally in a risky asset i, where $x_i \geq 0$ for $i = 1, 2,\ldots,n$ and $\sum_{i=1}^{m} x_i = 1$ and the return $\tilde{r}_i$ is random. Any choice of vector $x' = (x_1, x_2, \ldots, x_n)$ that is feasible i.e. $x \geq 0$, $h'x = 1$, where h is an m-element column vector with each element unity and prime denotes transpose is called a portfolio policy with a random return $\tilde{z}$:

$$\tilde{z} = \tilde{r}'x, \quad \tilde{r}' = (\tilde{r}_1, \tilde{r}_2, \ldots, \tilde{r}_n) \tag{1}$$

Denoting by m and V the mean vector and the covariance matrix of vector $\tilde{r}$, the standard portfolio model solves the quadratic programming (QP) problem:

$$\min_{x \in M} \tfrac{1}{2}\sigma^2 = \tfrac{1}{2}x'Vx \tag{2}$$

where $M: \{ x: h'x = 1, m'x \geq \mu, x \geq 0\}$. By varying μ parametrically, the whole set of optimal or efficient portfolio is determined (Sharpe 1970, Sengupta 1982 a, Szego 1980).

When the investor has a planning horizon of N time points $(1 \leq t \leq N)$ and a constant rate of discount δ is used to discount the future stream of returns and variances on a discounted basis as follows

$$\tilde{z}_N = \sum_{t=1}^{N} e_{t-1}\tilde{q}_t, \quad \tilde{q}_t = \tilde{r}_t'x_t$$

$$E\tilde{z}_N = \sum_{t=1}^{N} e_{t-1}m_t'x_t \tag{3}$$

$$\text{var}(\tilde{z}_N) = \sum_{s=1}^{N} \left(e_{s-1}^2 \tilde{x}_s' R_{ss} x_s\right) + \sum_{s=1}^{N} \sum_{\substack{t=1 \\ t \neq s}}^{N} \left(e_{t-1}e_{s-1}\tilde{x}_t' R_{ts} x_s\right)$$

where $e_t = (1 + \delta)^{-t}$, $\tilde{m}_t' = (m_{1t}, m_{2t},\ldots,m_{nt})$, $\tilde{x}_t' = (x_{1t}, x_{2t},\ldots,x_{nt})$, $R_{ts} = \text{cov}(\tilde{r}_t, \tilde{r}_s)$ and $\tilde{r}_t' = (\tilde{r}_{1t}, \tilde{r}_{2t},\ldots,\tilde{r}_{nt})$. The QP model analogous to (2) may then be formulated as

$$\min \tfrac{1}{2}\sigma_N^2 = \text{var } \tilde{z}_N \tag{4}$$

subject to

$$\sum_{t=1}^{N} e_{t-1} m'_t x_t = \mu_N$$

$$h'_t x_t = 1, \quad t = 1, 2, \ldots, N$$

where $h'_t = (h_{1t}, h_{2t}, \ldots, h_{nt})$ and the nonnegativity constraints on x_{it} are dropped, since the investor can go short in one security and take a corresponding long position in the other. For any fixed level of minimal return μ_N, the minimal value of variance σ_N^2, denoted by σ_{*N}^2 may then be calculated from (4) as:

$$\sigma_{*,N}^2 = \frac{\mu_N^2 - B_N \mu_N}{A_N} + \sum_{t=1}^{N} \left(\frac{e_{t-1}^2}{\gamma_t} \right) - \sum_{t=1}^{N} \left[\frac{e_{t-1} \beta_t (\mu_N - B_N)}{A_N \gamma_t} \right] \tag{5}$$

where

$$A_N = \sum_{t=1}^{N} \left(\frac{\alpha_t \gamma_t - \beta_t^2}{\gamma_t} \right), \quad B_N = \sum_{t=1}^{N} \left(\frac{e_{t-1} \beta_t}{\gamma_t} \right)$$

$$\alpha_t = m'_t R_{tt}^{-1} m_t, \quad \gamma_t = h'_t R_{tt}^{-1} h_t, \quad \beta_t = m'_t R_{tt}^{-1} h_t$$

and the covariance terms R_{ts} are ignored for simplicity. If the covariance R_{ts} are not ignored, σ_{*N}^2 can still be expressed as a nonlinear function of μ_N but would be more complicated. Several implications follow from the result (5). First, if $N = 1$ we have a static model, wherefrom we obtain:

$$\sigma_{*1}^2 = \left(\alpha_1 \gamma_1 - \beta_1^2 \right)^{-1} \left[\gamma_1 \mu_1^2 - 2\beta_1 \mu_1 + \alpha_1 \right] \tag{6}$$

Here it is assumed that R_{11} is positive definite and hence $\alpha_1 > 0$, $\alpha_1 > 0$ and $(\alpha_1 \gamma_1 \beta_1^2) > 0$ (Szego 1980). Since σ_{*1}^2 is a strictly convex function of μ_1, the minimal risk level σ_{*1}^2 can be further optimized if the minimal return parameter μ_1 is not fixed once for all, but varied parametrically over the planning horizon. For instance, if μ_1 has a subjective probability distribution, say normal $N(\mu, v)$ with mean μ and variance v and μ has a prior normal distribution $N(\mu_0, v_0)$ with prior mean μ_0 and prior variance v_0, then the posterior mean of μ, denoted by $\bar{\mu}$ is given by weighted combination of the prior mean μ_0 and the sample mean, $\bar{\mu}_1$, of μ_1 based on T observations say:

$$\bar{\mu} = (1 - w)\mu_0 + w\bar{\mu}_1 \qquad w = \frac{(v/T)^{-1}}{\left(\dfrac{v}{T} \right)^{-1} + v_0^{-1}} = \frac{v^{-1}}{v^{-1} + v_0^{-1}}, \qquad \text{if} \quad T = 1$$

the posterior variance $\overline{V}$ of μ is given by

$$\bar{v} = \frac{1}{\left(\dfrac{V}{T}\right)^{-1} + V_0^{-1}} = \frac{1}{V^{-1} + V_0^{-1}}, \qquad \text{if} \quad T = 1$$

Since we have $\bar{\mu} < \mu_0$, if $\bar{\mu}_1 < \mu_0$, therefore the investor may perform a downward revision of prior mean μ_0, whenever the extraneous information suggests $\bar{\mu}_1 < \mu_0$. The optimal value, $\bar{\mu}_{*1}$ of $\bar{\mu}_1$ in this sequential process may be derived from (6) by setting

$$\left.\frac{\partial \sigma_{*1}^2}{\partial \mu_1}\right|_{\mu_1 = \bar{\mu}_{*1}} = 0 \tag{7}$$

i.e. $\bar{\mu}_{*1} = \beta_1/\gamma_1$ and $\sigma_{**1}^2 = \min \sigma_{*1}^2 = \dfrac{1}{\gamma_1}$

Alternatively, one could introduce an utility function for ranking risky prospects (Mao 1969, Lin and Boot 1982)

$$U = 1 - \exp\left(-\frac{k}{2}\mu_1\right), \quad k > 0$$

where μ_1 has a subjective probability distribution, say normal $N(\bar{\mu}, \sigma_{*1}^2)$ with mean $\bar{\mu}$ and variance σ_{*1}^2. The expected utility function $f(\bar{\mu}) = EU(\mu_1)$ is then quadratic:

$$f(\bar{\mu}) = \bar{\mu} - \frac{k}{2}\sigma_{*1}^2 \tag{8}$$

The optimal value, $\bar{\mu}_{*1}$ of $\bar{\mu}$ may then be derived from (6) by setting $\mu_1 = \bar{\mu}$ and applying the necessary condition:

$$\bar{\mu}_{*1} = \frac{\alpha_1\gamma_1 - \beta_1^2}{k\gamma_1} + \frac{\beta_1}{\gamma_1} \tag{9}$$

Rewriting (8) slightly differently as,

$$f = k_1\bar{\mu} - (1 - k_1)\left(\sigma_{*1}^2/2\right), \quad 0 \leqslant k_1 \leqslant 1$$

One obtains

$$\bar{\mu}_{*1} = \left(\frac{k_1}{1-k_1}\right)\left(\frac{\alpha_1\gamma_1 - \beta_1^2}{2\gamma_1}\right) + \frac{\beta_1}{\gamma_1}$$

from where the result (7) follows if k_1 is set equal to zero.

A second implication of the result (5) is that a "sequential updating" approach (Zellner 1971) can be applied as a decision making process by the investor as follows. For the current period $N = 1$, the optimal vector x_1 is solved from (4). For the second future period ($N = 2$), then DM has observed σ_{*1}^2 and knows the optimal values for x_1, say x_{*1}. Given the realized values m_1^0, R_{11}^0 of the parameters and the known values of x_{*1}, he now solves the QP model

$$\min_{x_2} \tfrac{1}{2}\sigma_{2|1}^2 = \tfrac{1}{2}\left(x_2'R_{22}x_2 + x'_{*1}R_{11}^0 x_{*1}\right)$$

$$= \tfrac{1}{2}x_2'R_{22}x_2 + \text{a constant}$$

subject to

$$m_2'x_2 = \mu_2 - m_1^{0'}x_{*1}$$

$$h_2'x_2 = 1$$

Let the optimal values of $\sigma_{2|1}^2$ be denoted as $\sigma_{*2|1}^2$. If the parameter μ_2 is so preassigned that $e_1\mu_2 = \mu_1$ and further it holds that $\sigma_{*2/1}^2 < \sigma_{*2}^2$, then the sequential updating process would be optimal in the sense of lower risk. Following this argument, the sequential process would be an improvement for any future period $s = 2, 3. \ldots, N$ if it holds

$$\sigma_{*s|s-1}^2 < \sigma_{*s}^2 \quad \text{and} \quad e_{s-1}\mu_s = \mu_{s-1}$$

Note further that for any $N \geqslant 1$, the minimum value of σ_{*N}^2 can be directly computed from (5) by equating to zero the expression $\partial\sigma_{*N}^2/\partial\mu_N$ and obtaining $\mu_N = \mu_{*N} = B_N = \Sigma_{t=1}^N(\beta_t/\gamma_t)$ and $\sigma_{**N}^2 = \min\sigma_{*N}^2 = \Sigma_{t=1}^N(e_{t-1}^2/\gamma_t)$. Thus, the rate of increase (decrease) in risk per unit increase (decrease) in return can be measured for any N by the ratio

$$q_{N+1} = \frac{\sigma_{**N+1}^2 - \sigma_{**N}^2}{\mu_{*N+1} - \mu_{*N}} = \frac{e_N}{\beta_{N+1}} > 0$$

Thus, any increase (decrease) in return of μ_{*N+1} over μ_{*N} is less (more) risky, if it holds that q_{N+1} is less (more) than unity. Thus, any increase of

β_{N+1} over β_N, which may be due among others to an increase of mean, decrease of variances or both would tend to lower q_{N+1} and if q_{N+1} is reduced below unity, it would generate a less risky portfolio.

A slightly different version of the portfolio model (4), more directly related to control theory may be formulated by recasting the decision problem in terms of partly forecasting and partly controlling:

$$\min J = \left[\tfrac{1}{2} \sum_{t=0}^{N-1} (1+\delta)^{-t} x_t' \hat{R}_{TT} x_t \right] \tag{10}$$

subject to

$$x_{t+1}' \hat{m}_{t+1} = \hat{m}_t' x_t + \theta \left(m_t' x_t - \hat{m}_t' x_t \right)$$

$$h' x_t \leqslant 1, \quad \text{cov}(\hat{m}_t, \hat{m}_s) = \begin{cases} \hat{R}_{tt}, & t = s \\ 0, & t \neq s \end{cases}$$

$x_0' \hat{m}_0 = \hat{\mu}_0$ assumed known

$t = 0, 1, 2, \ldots, N-1; \quad < \theta < 1$

Here $\hat{m}_t$ is an estimated vector of returns computed from past data and $\hat{R}_{tt}$ is the matrix of forecasting errors. The state equation may also be written in terms of portfolio returns $\hat{\mu}_t = \hat{m}_t' x_t$ and $\mu_t = m_t' x_t$:

$$\hat{\mu}_{t+1} = \theta \mu_t + (1-\theta) \hat{\mu}_t : \quad 0 < \theta < 1$$

with $\hat{\mu}_t$ being given.

which states that the forecast returns for period $(t+1)$ is a weighted average of last period's forecast and realized returns. The control vector x_t for each t is decided on the basis of the estimated parameters $\hat{m}_t$, $\hat{R}_{tt}$ by minimizing the discounted stream of variances. Here h' is a row vector with each element unity and the covariance of vectors $\hat{m}_t$, $\hat{m}_s$ is assumed for simplicity to be diagonal.

A few comments on the dynamic portfolio model (10) are in order. First, the estimates $\hat{m}_{t+k}$ have to be obtained k periods ahead on the basis of information (I_t) available today i.e. k-step ahead forecast. The larger the k, the higher the variance of forecasting error, hence the need for updating at more frequent intervals. The available information may be a vector of market indices (e.g., representing stock market trends) denoted by I_t. For instance a linear regression model may provide a good starting point (Sharpe 1970, Lin and Boot 1982):

$$m_{t+1} = BI_t + \epsilon_{t+1} \tag{11}$$

where the vector ϵ_t of random disturbances may be assumed to satisfy the usual conditions i.e., $E\epsilon_t = 0$, all t and $E(\epsilon_t \epsilon_s') = Q$, a constant matrix and ϵ_{t+1} is stochastically independent of I_t for all t. The forecast $\hat{m}_{t+1}$ then equals BI_t and the covariance matrix then becomes $B'V_t(I)B + V(\epsilon)$, where $V_t(I)$ and $V(\epsilon)$ denote the variance–covariance matrix of I_t and ϵ_{t+1} respectively and $\bar{I}_t$ represents a mean vector of market indices. In the case of "seemingly unrelated regression" (Zellner 1971), the errors ϵ_{it}, ϵ_{jt} ($i \neq j$) of different securities will be correlated i.e. the matrix $V(\epsilon)$ would not be diagonal. Hence the method of generalized least squares may be applied to estimate $\hat{m}_{t+1}$. Second, the constraint $0 < \theta < 1$ on θ is required for stability, as this generates a process of self-correcting forecasts. In a more general model θ could be made time-varying and also optimally chosen along with the control vector x_t. Also the constraint $h'x_t \leqslant 1$ may not be essential in this model, which has a planning horizon and a state equation representing forecast returns. Lastly, the objective function in model (10) could be viewed more generally as:

$$\min J = E\left[\sum_{t=0}^{N-1} \left\{ (1+\delta)^{-t} \left[\frac{w}{2}(\hat{\mu}_t - \mu^0)^2 - k(1-w)\hat{\mu}_t \right] \right\} \right]$$

where μ^0 is the target return desired by the investor, w is a nonnegative weight $0 \leqslant w \leqslant 1$ and k is a positive scalar which may be parametrically varied so as to generate efficient portfolio (Mao 1969).

The simplified model (10) captures however the most important features of a dynamic model, which involves both forecasting (i.e. updating of parameter estimates) and optimal control (i.e. optimal choice of the control vector sequence $x_1, x_2, \ldots, x_{N-1}$ given the initial value x_0). The necessary conditions for the optimal solution of model (10) may be obtained, in principle, by using the Lagrangian function

$$L = J + \lambda_{t+1}\left((1-\theta)\hat{m}_t'x_t + \theta m_t'x_t - \hat{m}_{t+1}'x_{t+1} \right) + s_t\left(h'x_t - 1 \right)$$

as follows:

$$\frac{\partial L}{\partial x_t} = 0, \quad t = 0, 1, \ldots, N-1$$

$$\frac{\partial L}{\partial \lambda_t} = 0, \quad t = 0, 1, \ldots, N-1$$

$$\frac{\partial L}{\partial s_t} = 0, \quad t = 0, 1, \ldots, N-1 \tag{12}$$

$$\frac{\partial L}{\partial x_N} = 0$$

The case when s_t is zero for all t (i.e. $h'x_t < 1$) leads to $(n + 1)$ unknowns x_t and λ_t as follows:

$$(1 + \delta)^{-t} \hat{R}_{tt} x_t + \lambda_{t+1} b_t - \lambda_t \hat{m}_t = 0$$
$$b_t' x_t - \hat{m}_{t+1}' x_{t+1} = 0$$
(13.1)

where

$$b_t = (1 - \theta) \hat{m}_t + \theta m_t$$

Eliminating x_t from the two equations of (13.1) one obtains a second order difference equation in λ_t with time-varying coefficients as follows:

$$A_{1t} \lambda_t - (A_{2t} + A_{3t}) \lambda_{t+1} + A_{4t} \lambda_{t+2} = 0$$
(13.2)

where

$$A_{1t} = (1 + \delta)^t b_t' \hat{R}_{tt}^{-1} \hat{m}_t, \quad A_{2t} = (1 + \delta)^t b_t' \hat{R}_{tt}^{-1} b_t$$

$$A_{3t} = (1 + \delta)^{t+1} \hat{m}_{t+1}' \hat{R}_{t+1,t+1}^{-1} \hat{m}_{t+1}$$

$$A_{4t} = (1 + \delta)^{t+1} \hat{m}_{t+1}' \hat{R}_{t+1,t+1}^{-1} b_{t+1}$$

It is clear from the characteristic equation of (13.2)

$$A_{40} v^2 - (A_{20} + A_{30}) v + A_{10} = 0$$
(13.3)

that the two roots of (13.3) would both be positive, if the coefficients A_{it} are fixed constants, since A_{10}, A_{20}, A_{30}, A_{40} are all positive. Once the optimal values of λ_t denoted by λ_t^* are computed from (13.2), one could solve for the optimal control sequence:

$$x_t^* = (1 + \delta)^t \hat{R}_{tt}^{-1} [\lambda_t^* \hat{m}_t - \lambda_{t+1}^* b_t]$$
(13.4)

If there is no discounting (i.e. $\delta = 0$) and the steady state value satisfying (13.4) exist, then one obtains:

$$x^* = \theta \hat{R}^{-1} \lambda^* (\hat{m} - m), \quad 0 < \theta < 1$$
(13.5)

where the absence of subscript t denotes the corresponding steady state values. This shows the expected result of static portfolio model: optimal allocation x^* varies directly with $\hat{m}$ but inversely with $\hat{R}^{-1}$; also a higher correction factor θ implies a higher value of control.

Two other implications of the optimal control sequence mentioned in (13.4) may be noted. First, we have

$$\frac{\partial x_t^*}{\partial \theta} = (1 + \delta)^t \hat{R}_{tt}^{-1} \lambda_{t+1}^* (\hat{m}_t - m_t)$$

where the left hand side is positive, zero or negative according as $\hat{m}_t \gtrless m_t$, since the term $\hat{R}_{tt}^{-1} \lambda_{t+1}^*$ would have positive components in practice. Further, if $\theta \to 0$ we have $b_t = \hat{m}_t$ and hence

$$\hat{\mu}_t^* = \hat{m}_t' x_t^* = (1 + \delta)^t \hat{m}_t' \hat{R}_{tt}^{-1} \hat{m}_t (1 - B) \lambda_t^*$$

where B is a forward operator $B\lambda_t^* = \lambda_{t+1}^*$. Hence, if λ_t^* declines over time $t + 1$ i.e. $(1 - B)\lambda_t^*$ is positive then $\hat{\mu}_t^*$ would vary directly with $\alpha_t = \hat{m}_t' \hat{R}_{tt}^{-1} \hat{m}_t$. In this case the optimal sequence of $\{\lambda_t^*\}$ can be explicitly computed as a function of $\hat{\mu}_t / \hat{\sigma}_t^2$, where $\sigma_t^2 = (1 + \delta)^{-t} x_t^{*\prime} \hat{R}_{tt} x_t^*$

$$\lambda_t^* = (1 - \phi B)^{-1} \left(\frac{\hat{\mu}_t}{\hat{\sigma}_t^2} \right)$$

where ϕ is a suitable positive scalar so that $(1 - \phi B)$ is invertible. Thus it is seen that λ_t^* represents in some sense the impact of future mean-variance ratios. Computationally the equation (13.4) for λ_t^* has to be solved backwards, starting with λ_N^*, as in the dynamic programming algorithms.

The case when s_t is not zero for all t i.e., $h' x_t = 1$ holds, we would have to modify equations of (13.1) as follows

$$(1 + \delta)^{-t} \hat{R}_{tt} x_t + \lambda_{t+1} b_t - \lambda_t \hat{m}_t + s_t h = 0$$

$$b_t' x_t - \hat{m}_{t+1}' x_{t+1} = 0$$

$$h' x_t - 1 = 0$$

The steady state equations corresponding to (13.5) would now become:

$$x^* = \theta \hat{R}^{-1} \lambda^* (\hat{m} - m) - s^* h$$

$$s^* = (h' \hat{R}^{-1} h)^{-1} [\theta h' \hat{R}^{-1} (\hat{m} - m) \lambda^* - 1]$$

Also, the steady state variance $\sigma^{2*} = x^{*\prime} R x^*$ would be

$$\sigma^{2*} = \theta (\hat{\mu} - \mu) \lambda^* + (h' \hat{R}^{-1} h)^{-1} [1 - \theta h' \hat{R}^{-1} (\hat{m} - m) \lambda^*]$$

3. Models with risk constraints

A second type of dynamic portfolio model introduces probabilistic constraints on income and capital losses, so that safety-first rules can be adopted. The idea behind putting a lower allowable limit on income and capital losses in each period of a planning horizon is based on the principle of minimizing the probability of ruin. A model with one security and a three-period planning horizon was first applied by Naslund (1967) and discussed by Sengupta (1972), where the individual investor's decisicn problem is one of determining whether to invest his savings in the stock market or to retain it in cash. In each period two types of chance constraints are considered by the individual. First, a risk constraint which sets a tolerance limit on losses below a certain level and second, a capital constraint which stipulates probabilistically that invested capital should be below a limit, which varies according to accumulated capital gains.

A generalized model along this line may involve n securities where the allocations x_{it}, $(i = 1, 2, \ldots, n; t = 0, 1, 2, \ldots, N - 1)$ are to be optimally decided when the element of risk aversion is explicitly incorporated through temporal variances of returns. These considerations lead to the following specification of the intemporal portfolio problem:

$$\max J = \sum_{t=0}^{N-1} (1 + \delta)^{-t} \sum_{i=1}^{n} \left[m_{it} x_{it} - \frac{w}{2} x_t' R_{tt} x_t \right] \tag{14}$$

subject to

$$P(\tilde{m}_{it} x_{it} \geq y_{it}) \geq a_{it}, \quad 0 \leq a_{it} \leq 1, \quad \text{all } t$$

$$P\left(x_{it} \leq k_{it} + \sum_{s=2}^{t} \tilde{m}_{i,s-1} x_{i,s-1} \right) \geq d_{it}, \quad 0 \leq d_{it} \leq 1, \quad \text{all } t$$

where for each $t = 0, 1, 2, \ldots, N - 1$ the variables are as follows:

x_{it} = vector x_t: the accumulated amount in dollars invested in stock $i = 1, 2, \ldots, n$

m_{it} = vector m_t: the mean return on stock i defined as the expectation $E\tilde{m}_{it}$, where $\tilde{m}_{it} = (p_{it}/p_{i,t-1}) - 1$, and p_{it} is the random price of stock i in period t

R_{tt} = variance–covariance matrix of $\tilde{m}_s = \delta_{ts} R_{ts}$, $\delta_{ts} = \begin{cases} 1, & t = s \\ 0, & t \neq s \end{cases}$

y_{it} = vector y_t: the maximum loss the investor is willing to take on security i

a_{it} = vector a_t: tolerance measure preassigned by the investor on the loss constraint for i

d_{it} = vector d_t: tolerance measure preassigned by the investor on the liquidity constraint for i

k_{it} = vector k_t: the capital accumulated in the form of security i which the investor can use for investment either in cash or stocks.

δ: exogenous rate of discount; w: exogenous weight

Note that this dynamic chance-constrained version of the portfolio model leads to a highly nonlinear programming problem, even when one makes the usual simplifying assumptions e.g., $\tilde{m}_{it}$ is normally distributed with constant mean and variance, and y_{it}, k_t, a_{it}, d_{it} are suitably preassigned as constants for all t. Two types of approximate solutions, which are necessarily suboptimal may therefore be considered. One is to seek solutions within the class of linear decision rules as follows:

$$x_{it} = \sum_{s=2}^{t} \beta_{is}(1 + \tilde{m}_{i,s-1}) + \gamma_{it}$$

i.e. (15)

$$x_i = \sum B_s(I + \tilde{m}_{s-1}) + \gamma_t$$

where the coefficients β_{is}, γ_{it} are to be solved for. By assuming y_{it}, k_{it}, a_{it}, d_{it} to be time-invariant and expanding the chance constraints of (14) and ignoring the nonlinear terms one would obtain a QP problem. The sensitivity of this approximate solution to the nonlinear terms in the chance constraints of (14) may be evaluated by repeated linear approximations of the nonlinear terms. Naslund (1967) attempted the unrepeated LP method for the example: $n = 1$, $N = 4$, $y_{11} = -1300$, $y_{12} = -1000$, $y_{13} = -1000$, $a_{1t} = 0.95$, for all t, $d_{1t} = 0.99$ all t, $k_{11} = 7000$, $k_{12} = 5500$, $k_{13} = 9000$, $w = 0 = \delta$ and $m_{1t} = 0.05$ and var $\tilde{m}_{1t} = 0.0225$ for all t. His linear decision rule (LDR) solution may be compared with the repeated LDR and complete nonlinear programming (NLP) solutions from the value of the objective function μ and its variance (σ^2) in shown in table 1.

The last column in this table shows the optimal solution of the NLP model when the tolerance levels a_{it}, d_{it} are not preassigned but optimally chosen along with x_{it} values by the method of reliability programming (Sengupta 1972). It is clear that the suboptimal solutions obtained through linearizing approximations are very close to the complete NLP solution, where the latter is computed by the algorithm of sequential unconstrained minimization technique. Second, one has to note that there is a trade-off between system reliability defined as $S = \sum_{s=1}^{t} \sum_{i=1}^{N} \log u_{it}$, where u_{it} denotes the tolerance measures a_{it} and d_{it} and the expected value of discounted portfolio returns and this trade-off may vary substantially from small N to large N, as the horizon gets increased.

A second way to obtain a simpler version of the nonlinear model (14) is to replace the random variables $\tilde{m}_{it}$ by their means m_{it} and write the constraints as a linear equation system:

$$x_{i,t+1} = k_{it} + m_{it} x_{it}$$

i.e.

$$x_{t+1} = k_t + M_t x_t, \quad M_t : (m_{it}), \quad \text{a diagonal matrix}$$

where the loss constraint is dropped and in the second constraint, the vector k_t is treated as a control variable. The complete model now appears as

$$\max J = \sum_{t=0}^{N-1} \left[(1+\delta)^{-t} \left\{ \hat{m}_t' x_t - \frac{w}{2} x_t' \hat{R}_{tt} x_t - \tfrac{1}{2} (k_t - k^0)' (k_t - k^0) \right\} \right]$$

$$(16)$$

subject to

$$x_{t+1} = k_t + \hat{M}_t x_t$$

x_0 given; $t = 0, 1, 2, \ldots, N-1$

where k^0 is the desired target value of the control vector and $\hat{m}_t$, $\hat{R}_{tt}$ respectively denote the estimates or forecasts for m_t and R_{tt}. As before, the forecast may be made k-step ahead based on the information vector I_t available up to time t; them $\hat{m}_{t+k,t+k|t}$ would replace the estimated quantities for the future k-step ahead. By applying the first order conditions to the Lagrangian function

$$L = J + \lambda_{t+1}' (k_t + \hat{M}_t x_t - x_{t+1})$$

Table 1

	LDR	Repeated LDR	NLP	NLP with Optimal Reliability
μ	807.5	810.2	813.7	756.7
σ^2	$196 \cdot 10^4$	$197 \cdot 10^4$	$199 \cdot 10^4$	$182 \cdot 10^4$
x_1	5900	5907	5909	6581
x_2	5250	5241	5249	3529
x_3	5000	5002	5115	5025

we obtain

$$\frac{\partial L}{\partial x_t} = 0, \quad t = 0, 1, 2, \ldots, N - 1$$

$$\frac{\partial L}{\partial x_N} = 0, \quad T = N \tag{16.1}$$

$$\frac{\partial L}{\partial k_t} = 0, \quad t = 0, 1, 2, \ldots, N - 1$$

These lead to

$$(1 + \delta)^{-1}(\hat{m}_t - w\hat{R}_{tt}x_t) + \hat{M}_t'\lambda_{t+1} - \lambda_t = 0$$

$$k_t + \hat{M}_t x_t - x_{t+1} = 0 \tag{16.2}$$

$$(1 + \delta)^{-t}(k_t - k^0) + \lambda_{t+1} = 0$$

from which it follows that the optimal control sequence $\{k_t^*\}$ and the associated $\{x_{t+1}^*\}$ sequence must satisfy

$$k_t^* = \hat{M}_t^{-1}\left[\frac{k_{t-1}^*}{1 + \delta} - w\hat{R}_{tt}x_t^* + (1 + \delta)^t q_t\right] \tag{16.3}$$

where

$$q_t = (1 + \delta)^{-t}\hat{m}_t - (1 + \delta)^{-(t+1)}k^0 + (1 + \delta)^{-}\hat{M}_t k^0$$

Using this control sequence (16.2) a sequential updating of optimal control k_t^* can be made on the basis of k_{t-1}^* and x_t^*. Since the dynamic model (16) is in the format of an LQG (linear quadratic Gaussian) model, standard methods using Riccati transformation may also be applied. Note that the steady state values, denoted by variables without time subscripts may be easily computed from (16.3) as:

$$k^* = \left(1 + \frac{1}{\delta}\right)\left\{k^0 + \hat{M}^{-1}\left(\hat{m} - \frac{k^0}{1 + \delta}\right) - w\hat{M}^{-1}\hat{R}x^*\right\}$$

This shows that the optimal control vector k^* varies directly with k^0, $\hat{m}$ but inversely with δ, the diagonal elements of $\hat{M}$ and x^*. Further, if the steady state values satisfy (16.2), we would also have for $\delta = 0$,

$$x^* = \frac{1}{w}\hat{R}^{-1}\left[\hat{m} - (I - \hat{M})\lambda^*\right]$$

or

$$\lambda^* = \left[I + \hat{M} + \hat{M}^2 + \ldots \right] (\hat{m} - w\hat{R}x^*)$$

since $\hat{M}$ would have diagonal elements less than unity. Thus x^* would vary inversely with w, $\hat{R}$ and λ^*.

We may mention two other important features of this model. First, one may also seek suboptimal solutions in this case by restricting to LDR of the form

$$k_t = \sum_{s=2}^{t} B_{s-1} x_{s-1} + \gamma_t \tag{17}$$

where the optimal elements of the matrices B_{s-1} and the elements of vector γ_t are to be optimally solved. Since the control variables k_t are unconstrained in this model, a feedback relation of the form

$$k_t^* = -N_t x_t^* + n_t \tag{18}$$

could in principle be derived for the optimal sequence $\{ k_t^*, x_t^* \}$, when the matrix N_t and vector n_t satisfy Riccati-type difference equations. The LDR in (17) could be seen as an approximation of this optimal feedback relation (18).

Second, the dynamic model (16) may be suboptimally solved through a "sequential updating" procedure (Zellner 1971). Given the initial vector x_0 and the parameter estimates $\hat{\theta}_{1|0}$, there $\hat{\theta}_{t|t-1} = (\hat{R}_{tt|t-1}, \hat{m}_{t|t-1}, k^0, w)$ we solve for the first future period:

$$x_1^* = x_1(\hat{\theta}_{1|0}) = -\left(I - w\hat{R}_{11|0}^{-1} \right)^{-1} \left[\hat{m}_{1|0} - k^0 - M_{00} x_0 \right]$$

$$x_1^* = \frac{\hat{R}_{11|0}^{-1}}{w} \left(\hat{m}_{1|0} + k_0^* - k^0 \right)$$

where M_{00} denotes parameters which are already known. For the second future period we have observed x_1^* and know the realized values of M_{11}. Hence the optimal vector for the second future period becomes

$$x_2^* = x_2^*(\hat{\theta}_{2|1}) = -\left(I - w\hat{R}_{22|1}^{-1} \right)^{-1} \left[\hat{m}_{2|1} - k^0 - M_{11} x_1 \right]$$

and so on. Bayesian methods of updating the parameter estimates, discussed by Zellner (1971) may be easily incorporated in this framework. The estimates or forecast values $\hat{m}_{t+1|t}$ may be obtained from market-index models of the type (11) mentioned before by applying the method of generalized least squares or, seemingly unrelated regression as the case may be.

4. Concluding Remarks

We have to emphasize two very basic limitations of our dynamic generalizations. Since only the mean-variance parameters are explicitly considered, the departure from the assumption of normality of distributions would lead to nonquadratic control models with their associated computations complexity. Robustness of an optimal control policy may then be more desirable a property to seek. Methods based on nonlinear Kalman–Bucy type filtering seem to be appropriate. Although the heterogenous structure of covariances $\delta_{ts}\hat{R}_{tw}$ with $\delta_{ts} \neq 0$ for $t \neq s$ can be handled in principle in our dynamic generalizations, problems of near-singularity (i.e. less full rank) and lack of identifiability or estimability may be quite severe (Sengupta 1982b). Further, the steady state solutions, which lead to simpler algebraic equations sometimes, may not be realizable for finite time horizons and hence they may not be very realistic, except as a starting point for further iterative computations. A set of well-structured computer applications to realistic empirical data is needed for resolving some of these problems in a practical context.

References

Hillier, F.S., "Interrelated risky investments," Management Science, 9, (1963), 443–454.

Lin, W.T. and Boot, J.C.G., "A linear decision analysis model of optimal portfolio investments," Int. J. Systems Sci., 13 (1982), 469–490.

Mao, J.C.T., Quantitative Analysis of Financial Decisions. New York: Macmillan, 1969.

Naslund, B., Decisions under Risk. Stockholm: Stockholm School of Economics, 1967.

Sengupta, J.K., Stochastic Programming. Amsterdam: North-Holland 1972. "A minimax policy for portfolio choice," Int. J. systems Science, 13, (1982a), 39–56.

Sengupta, J.K., "Selection and ordering in optimal portfolio choice," Working paper No. 215, UC Santa Barbara, 1982b.

Sharpe, W.F., Portfolio Theory and Capital Markets. New York: McGraw-Hill, 1970.

Szego, G.P., Portfolio Theory. New York: Academic Press, 1980.

Zellner, A., An Introduction to Bayesian Inference in Econometrics. New York: John Wiley, 1971.

Ziemba, W.T. and Vickson, R.G., Stochastic Optimization Models in Finance. New York: Academic Press, 1975.

9. Short-term industry output behavior: an econometric analysis

1. Introduction

Econometric analysis of short-term industry output and inventory behavior has used one of three alternative specifications: (a) the linear decision rule (LDR) approach based on an optimizing hypothesis e.g. cost minimization or profit maximization, (b) the stock adjustment approach based on production variations in response to business cycles, capacity adjustments and seasonality factors and (c) the recursive approach based on a causal-chain interpretation of the dependence of output, inventory and unfilled orders. Thus the LDR approach [2,3,6,9,10] in its different variants has empirical relevance of forecast variables like future order rates along with lagged values of production and inventory level, whereas the stock adjustment approach [1,13] demonstrates the nonlinear relationships between sales fluctuations and production decisions through estimates of piece-wise linear functions showing the effects of cyclical fluctuations and capacity variations. The recursive approach [20] considers however a specific form of the simultaneous equations model containing the endogenous variables: output, inventory and unfilled orders such that the interdependence between the three LDR for output, inventory and unfilled order is limited.

Two major areas have drawn attention in these alternative specifications: (a) the importance of the distinction between production to stock and to order and (b) the pattern of stability or otherwise in production, inventory and other endogenous variables. Thus for finished manufacturing goods, production to stock which implies more or less a continuous production with unchanged set-up costs i.e. a buffer stock model is expected to dominate [4,13], although there is some difference of views on the treatment of backlog of unfilled orders as a separate decision variable along with production and gross finished goods inventory. Also in some phases of business activity it is not unusual for any finished goods manufacturer to produce both to order and to stocks [13] and for nondurable goods as cement, lumber paper etc. output is not unadjustable to errors in anticipation of future orders or sales.

215

The stability of the underlying structure [15] has been discussed most clearly in the LDR approach, where the rules always take the form of the decision variables being a function of initial conditions, past values and forecast of demand in the coming period and, in the more complex structures, of future periods. The stability pattern is usually analysed in terms of the eigenvalues e.g. real or complex and the characteristics of the stochastic component in the decision rules. In general, the estimated linear decision rules tend to indicate a stabilizing behavior [7,18] more so in industries where the futures trading allows a more competitive transmission of market information [18]. However the eigenvalues are functions of the estimated coefficients and have therefore their own standard errors, the impact of which is rarely analyzed; more often it is assumed [4,12] that the standard errors would not alter the presumption about stabilizing behavior derived from the estimated coefficients alone. Moreover in some experiments with simulation of linear decision rules in a quadratic programming contest [16], where future demand is generated by simulating a Gaussian stochastic process it is found that building feedback elements help to improve the performance of linear decision rules in terms of their associated costs.

Our object in this paper is to examine alternative estimates of industry output and inventory behavior for the industries: lumber (southern pine), printing paper, plywood, primary metals, electric machinery and Portland cement. This is done through specification of alternative linear models, their comparison and eigenvalue stability. Except for a few exceptions, the buffer stock model which implies production to stock rather than to order, is observed to dominate the overall pattern of these industries and the linear decision rules observed to be stabilizing in the sense that the real parts of the eigenvalues lie within the unit circle.

The analysis proceeds as follows: Section Two presents the alternative specifications of the LDR, recursive and other models, followed by the empirical estimates and their evaluation in Section Three. Section Four makes some concluding remarks on the supply response behavior at the industry level.

2. Alternative Output–Inventory Models

Assuming production to stock to be more important so that optimal inventories may directly depend on order rates and the absence of aggregation effects, one of the simplest recent models is due to Childs [4], which results from minimizing an intertemporal quadratic function designating the costs of adjusting the rate of production $X(t)$, holding gross inventories $H(t)$ and allowing backlogs of unfilled orders $U(t)$. The model is

$$\text{Model IA:} \quad Q(t) = \alpha + AQ(t-1) + \sum_{j=0}^{N} b_j O(t+j) \qquad (1)$$

where $Q(t)$ is a column vector with elements $U(t)$, $H(t)$, $X(t)$ and $O(t+j)$ is the future order rates for which an expected value forecast is assumed available. The elements in vectors b_j, α and the matrix A are the coefficients reflecting various cost adjustments that are to be estimated from observed data. Since the unbiased forecasts of future order rates [3] are mostly based on their past behavior pattern, an alternative form of model IA is:

$$\text{Model I:} \quad Q(t) = \alpha + AQ(t-1) + \sum_{j=1}^{3} b_j O(t-j) \qquad (2)$$

where only third order lags are utilized. In general the coefficient matrix A is not triangular since the three linear decision rules are expected to be interdependent. However if a recursive model holds good as a valid description of the adjustment behavior, the matrix A would be lower triangular or very nearly so. This implies that short-term production decisions depend on last period's inventory and unfilled order files but inventory and unfilled orders depend only on the order rates and not on lagged production. Denoting the lower triangular coefficient matrix by $\tilde{A}$ the recursive model may be written as:

$$\text{Model II:} \quad Q(t) = \alpha + \tilde{A}Q(t-1) + \sum_{j=1}^{3} b_j O(t-j) \qquad (3)$$

the set of decision rules $(1) - (3)$ above do not include however the price variable characterizing the demand response and the actual shipment or sales which differ from the order rate files.

Assuming a similar framework as the Childs' model except that the decision variables are now production, inventory and prices, we may obtain the following LDR by maximizing an intertemporal profit function as the difference between revenue and costs, where costs are due to adjusting the production rates, holding inventories and due to changing prices:

$$\text{Model IIIA:} \quad R(t) = \alpha + BR(t-1) + \sum_{j=1}^{N} \beta_j S(t+j) \qquad (4)$$

where $R(t)$ is a column vector with elements production $X(t)$, inventories

$H(t)$ and prices $P(t)$ and $S(t+j)$ is the future sales or shipments. In empirical estimates however we have considered $S(t+1)$ and $S(t-1)$ only as the explanatory variables due to reasons of multicollinearity and the ease with which one period forecast $\hat{S}(t+1)$ can be constructed on the basis of current information. Hence the model (4) appears as:

Model III: $\quad R(t) = \alpha + BR(t-1) + \beta_1 S(t+1) + \beta_2 S(t-1)$ (5)

where the elements in vectors α, β_1, β_2 and the matrix B are the coefficients reflecting various adjustments in production, inventories and prices. Model III allows price adjustment through demand functions for an imperfectly competitive system under risk aversion, as Mills [12] has shown in his formulations. A special case of this model arises when the price variable is no longer used as an independent explanatory variable i.e. lagged production and lagged inventories along with shipments determine the current level of $R(t)$. This is called Model IIIB:

Model IIIB: $\quad R(t) = \alpha + \hat{B}R_1(t-1) + \beta_1 S(t+1) + \beta_2 S(t-1)$ (6)

where $R_1(t)$ is a column vector with two elements $X(t)$, $H(t)$ and $\tilde{B}$ is a matrix of order 3×2.

A slightly different version of the LDR arises if the underlying intertemporal profit function is viewed more nonlinear than quadratic and the linear approximations of the optimal nonlinear decision rules are specified for estimation. This method followed by Mills [12] results in the following linear relations:

Model IV: $\quad X(t) = h_1(S^e(t), H(t-1), X(t-1))$
$\qquad\qquad P(t) = h_2(S^e(t), H(t-1), X(t))$ (7)

where h_1, h_2 are linear functions, $S^e(t)$ is anticipated sales which is a function of, among other things, current price. Note that inventory does not play an active role as a separate decision variable; its effects are absorbed in pricing and production decisions which respond to sales and their fluctuations. Using the identity $H(t) = H(t-1) + X(t) - S(t)$ where $S(t)$ is exogenous, short-term production decisions $X(t)$ are assumed to determine the behavior of $H(t)$ as a residual; this may be reasonable if the firms can anticipate demand through $S^e(t)$ more or less accurately.

It is clear that one common element in the specifications (1) through (7) above is the optimization hypothesis with adjustment of production and other decision variables to changing risk in the form of varying sales, orders or anticipated demands. Although a direct test of the optimization hypothesis e.g., maximization of expected profits or minimization of expected costs is not possible on the basis of aggregate data, an indirect test can be made by estimating the linear or linearized decision rules derived from the optimization hypothesis. Such normative decision rules need be distinguished however from other positive econometric relations, two of which have frequently found empirical applications. One is due to Moriguchi [13] who analysed the short-term adjustment in production decisions in terms of the influence of three interactions: capacity interaction, business cycle interaction and seasonality factors. Using linear approximations for these adjustments, we obtain:

Model V: $\quad X(t) = b_1 S(t) + b_2 S^e(t) + b_3 H(t-1)$

$$+ \sum_{i=1}^{N} D(i) + \sum_{j=1}^{N} D(j) \qquad (8)$$

where $S^e(t)$ is anticipated sales used in (7) before i.e.

$$S^e(t) = S^e(t, i) = S(t, i-1) \cdot \frac{\overline{S}(t-1, i)}{\overline{S}(t-1, i-1)}$$

where $\overline{S}(t-1, i)$ designates the average of sales of the i-th month over the past $(t-1)$ years, $S(t, i-1)$ is the actual sales in $(i-1)$th month in the current year. The dummy variables $D(i)$, $D(j)$ in Model IV designate monthly and yearly correlates, which have been found [13] to be most important for Portland cement, where production and inventory stock have a marked degree of seasonality following from construction activity. Normally production and shipment tend to rise from March to June and stay at a high level until October by the end of which winter begins. Inventory stocks of finished cement continue to be accumulated during the off-season period of November to early March. Hence the inventory sales ratio tends to display a definite seasonal pattern, increasing from November to early March and decreasing from late March to end of October every year.

The second type of econometric relation considers supply response behavior as the main dependent variable and the explanatory variables are sought in lagged supply, prices and order rates expected. In commodity market studies [17,19] such supply response estimates have proved very helpful in prediction of supply behavior. Assuming a linear function f, the equation for response of supply $Y(t) = X(t) + H(t-1)$ appears in a general form as follows:

Model VI: $\quad Y(t) = f(y(t-1), P(t), V(t), O(t)) \qquad (9)$

where $V(t)$ is the standard deviation of order rates based on six preceeding months' moving average and $O(t)$ is the order rate. It is clear that prices and order rates are as expected by the suppliers; however separate relations describing the mechanism of expectation formation are not introduced here, since they are subsumed partly in lagged supply $Y(t-1)$ and partly in current prices $P(t)$ and order rates $O(t)$ and its standard deviation $V(t)$ computed over preceeding six months observations. For the industries selected here, the period of six months was chosen for computing $V(t)$, since it appeared approximately to be the average period between two consecutive peaks in the time series of supply.

3. Estimates and their implications

Except for Model V which is applied only for Portland cement, most other models are estimated for the following industries: Southern pine lumber, printing paper, softwood plywood, primary metals, electrical machinery and Portland cement. Weekly data are used for the linear decision rule models in plywood only, where sanded and unsanded varieties are distinguished along with two sample periods: I, June 19, 1966 through December 27, 1969 (pre futures market period) and II: January 3, 1970 through June 27, 1975 (post futures period). Monthly data are used for all other cases: cement (Sample I: July 1927 through December 1941; Sample II: January 1949 through December 1960), lumber (Sample I: January 1933 through December 1940; Sample II January 1961 through December, 1972), printing paper (January 1949 through December 1960), electrical machinery (January 1958 to December 1975) and primary metals (January 1958 to December, 1975). The main source of data is the Statistical Supplement to the Survey of Current Business and the sample periods are chosen either to compare with previous estimates by other researchers or with estimates for more recent periods. Statistical data are not seasonally adjusted and some preliminary calculations using monthly dummy variables did not show results any better, except for cement where the seasonal interaction is found to be most important. Hence seasonal adjustments have not been made.

The least squares estimates of these alternative models which are presented in tables 1–13 are used to answer questions of the following type: (a) Which of the two sectors, production to stock (PTS) or production to order (PTO) dominate in these industries? (b) What are the stabilization and oscillatory characteristics of some of these models in terms of eigenvalues, whether complex or greater than unity in their real parts? (c) How do the recursive models perform compared to the nonrecursive ones? (d) How does the econometric supply response behavior compare with the estimates of normative linear decision rules? and (e) How responsive is the aggregate supply behavior to changing risk, when risk is measured by variance of demand observed in the preceeding months?

Considering the first question it appears there are two ways to determine if the PTO sectors dominate in an industry or otherwise. The first is a priori information and the second is the market characteristics of the product sold [2,4]. For instance, the goods produced by the PTS sectors would tend to be characterized by a continuous, non-intermittent production process which economises changes in set-up costs perhaps at the cost of relatively high finished goods inventory; on the otherhand goods supplied by the PTO sectors would tend to follow closely the demand pattern thereby resulting in intermittent production and relatively lower inventory of finished goods. However in some business cycle phases it may be quite economic for production to adjust to errors in anticipation or to actual developments in current sales for nondurable goods as cement, lumber and paper. It is clear therefore that if the PTS sectors dominate in an industry, the correlation of variations in demand with that of inventories is expected to be positive and more important than that of demand variations with variations in production. Measuring variations in demand, production and inventories by the variances of order rates var O, of gross output var X and of gross inventories var H, the linear relationship is shown in table A. The variances here are computed on a 6-month moving average basis and it is clear that except for lumber Sample II, the demand variability is more closely related to inventory variations and this pattern is retained when a two-stage procedure is followed i.e. by first regressing var H on var O linearly with a coefficient $\hat{\beta}$ and then regressing var $X - \hat{\beta}$ var O on var O at the second stage given the estimate $\hat{\beta}$ from the first stage. However for lumber Sample II covering recent periods, demand variability appears to be more closely related to production variations. The reduced importance of PTS sectors in lumber in the recent period, Sample II has also been noted in other studies [7] For cement this method is inapplicable because of lack of data on order rates. However it may be seen from table 6 that the marginal effect of $H(t-1)$ on $X(t)$ whenever statistically significant is always positive for cement, Samples I and II, and also for paper.

The second question concerning eigenvalue stability is for those models where two or more endogenous variables appear in a system of difference equations e.g. (1) through (6). For any given model, eigenvalues computed from estimated regression coefficients may be analyzed to see if there is any complex eigenvalue, or if the maximum eigenvalue (or maximum real part if it is complex) exceeds unity. The set of complex eigenvalues occurring in different models is shown in tables B1 and B2.

It is clear from tables B1, B2 that complex eigenvalues occurred in few cases only and even in more recent periods the modulus declined for lumber and plywood (unsanded). The detailed analysis for plywood

Table 1
The coefficient estimates and t-values of Model I

Data	Sample	Dependent variable	α	$U(t-1)$	$H(t-1)$	$X(t-1)$	$O(t-1)$	$O(t-2)$	$O(t-3)$	Dummy	R^2	D.W.
Lumber	I	$U(t)$	−29.21 (0.266)	0.858 * (9.47)	0.033 (0.856)	−0.048 (0.537)	0.115 * (1.713)	−0.142 * (2.308)	0.106 * (1.699)		0.72	1.69
		$H(t)$	312.693 * (3.018)	−0.439 * (6.965)	0.881 * (23.949)	0.434 * (5.107)	−0.439 * (6.965)	−0.018 (0.303)	−0.02 (0.342)		0.95	2.24
		$X(t)$	119.598 (0.981)	−0.063 (0.622)	−0.026 (0.592)	0.778 * (7.784)	0.079 (1.064)	0.238 * (3.492)	−0.165 * (2.393)		0.92	2.03
	II	$U(t)$	−58.463 (1.424)	1.042 * (15.801)	0.052 * (2.017)	0.031 (0.411)	−0.034 (0.537)	−0.093 * (2.028)	0.06 (1.313)		0.90	1.61
		$H(t)$	105.753 * (2.925)	−0.051 (0.877)	0.947 * (43.559)	0.294 * (4.421)	−0.337 * (6.109)	−0.043 (1.056)	0.046 (1.132)		0.97	1.78
		$X(t)$	−85.984 (1.635)	0.507 * (5.994)	0.122 * (3.866)	0.309 * (3.193)	−0.064 (0.791)	0.181 * (3.063)	0.152 * (2.594)		0.86	2.03
Printing paper		$U(t)$	−0.082 (0.003)	0.863 * (21.774)	−0.189 * (1.889)	−0.212 (1.328)	−0.006 (0.052)	0.211 * (2.157)	0.268 * (2.489)		0.88	2.05
		$H(t)$	−2.719 (0.382)	0.005 (0.404)	0.979 * (32.214)	−0.042 (0.87)	0.061 (1.627)	−0.039 (1.317)	0.037 (1.126)		0.97	2.63
		$X(t)$	57.548 * (3.956)	0.056 * (2.281)	0.213 * (3.43)	0.102 (1.028)	0.017 (0.219)	0.287 * (4.071)	0.227 * (3.396)		0.85	1.98
Plywood I: unsanded		$U(t)$	55753.9 * (2.686)	0.97 * (44.778)	−0.026 * (1.879)	−0.498 * (3.874)	0.395 * (5.303)	−0.12 (1.564)	−0.076 (1.062)		0.95	1.91
		$H(t)$	26863.6 * (2.865)	−0.005 (0.49)	0.976 * (158.51)	−0.016 (0.275)	−0.101 * (2.984)	−0.055 (1.581)	−0.03 (0.941)		0.99	1.80
		$X(t)$	72628.5 * (6.092)	0.026 * (2.07)	−0.034 * (4.324)	0.483 * (6.541)	0.019 (0.463)	−0.114 * (2.579)	0.039 (0.95)		0.62	1.87

Plywood I: sanded	$U(t)$	128288 (1.136)	0.978* (50.865)	−0.039 (0.815)	−2.431* (2.231)	2.18* (2.721)	−0.284 (0.368)	0.291 (0.391)		0.97	1.74
	$H(t)$	25151.2* (2.592)	−0.001 (0.704)	0.993* (236.255)	0.132 (1.413)	−0.072 (1.043)	−0.01 (0.143)	−0.16* (2.499)		0.99	2.32
	$X(t)$	47780* (6.11)	0.005* (3.887)	0.005 (1.605)	0.448* (5.932)	−0.027 (0.495)	−0.078 (1.465)	0.009 (0.181)		0.35	1.85
II: unsanded	$U(t)$	48021* (3.508)	0.998* (55.63)	0.0004 (0.072)	−0.168* (1.84)	0.0585 (0.938)	−0.0875 (1.604)	−0.003 (0.0652)	7354.9 (1.009)	0.97	1.89
	$H(t)$	36385* (6.168)	0.013 (1.641)	0.994* (397.574)	−0.072* (1.846)	−0.114* (4.233)	−0.037 (1.573)	−0.007 (0.317)	5386.2* (1.715)	0.99	1.97
	$X(t)$	62252* (6.396)	0.075* (5.856)	−0.014* (3.428)	0.394* (6.092)	0.018 (0.416)	0.006 (0.143)	0.039 (1.063)	−6292.7 (1.234)	0.61	1.95
II: sanded	$U(t)$	260814* (2.083)	0.978* (58.116)	−0.059* (1.889)	−3.854* (4.168)	2.351* (3.599)	−0.197 (0.309)	0.758 (1.252)	−9431.7 (0.299)	0.95	2.24
	$H(t)$	4675 (0.666)	0.003* (2.777)	1.001* (567.418)	0.111* (2.134)	−0.095* (2.603)	−0.071* (1.994)	−0.017 (0.494)	−4396.7* (2.485)	0.99	1.85
	$X(t)$	39598* (5.172)	0.004* (3.465)	−0.005* (2.836)	0.488* (8.636)	0.06 (1.502)	0.016 (0.407)	0.069* (1.863)	−2495.4 (1.293)	0.63	2.02
Primary metals	$U(t)$	−89.71 (1.0)	0.97* (69.19)	−0.03* (1.85)	−0.38* (6.01)	0.64* (9.76)	−0.05 (0.55)	−0.06 (0.81)		0.99	1.76
	$H(t)$	−14.4 (0.53)	0.02* (4.45)	0.99* (182.48)	0.06* (2.96)	−0.05* (2.36)	−0.004 (0.14)	−0.007 (0.33)		0.99	1.63
	$X(t)$	149.71 (1.59)	0.05* (3.38)	0.06* (3.32)	0.35* (5.36)	0.2* (2.89)	0.2* (2.19)	0.007 (0.09)		0.95	2.08
Electrical machinery	$U(t)$	−128.9 (3.89)	0.99* (67.49)	−0.12* (5.92)	−0.12 (1.6)	0.21* (3.42)	0.12* (1.89)	0.14* (2.22)		0.99	1.72
	$H(t)$	83.9* (5.34)	0.03* (3.93)	0.9* (89.96)	0.06 (1.62)	−0.05 (1.58)	0.06* (2.07)	0.08* (2.81)		0.99	1.74
	$X(t)$	40.22 (1.37)	0.02* (1.64)	0.003 (0.17)	0.41* (5.99)	0.15* (2.8)	0.19* (3.55)	0.14* (2.62)		0.98	2.23

* Significant at 5% upper tail t-test

Table 2
The Coefficient estimates and t-values of Model IA

Data	Sample	Dependent variable	α	U(t − 1)	H(t − 1)	X(t − 1)	O(t)	O(t + 1)	O(t + 2)	Dummy	R^2	D.W.
Lumber	I	U(t)	142.329 * (1.817)	0.713 * (11.308)	−0.025 (0.872)	−0.259 * (5.784)	0.287 * (6.415)	0.055 (1.19)	−0.062 (1.59)		0.83	1.69
		H(t)	329.147 * (4.273)	−0.289 * (4.668)	0.899 * (32.516)	0.322 * (7.325)	−0.443 * (10.106)	0.099 * (2.19)	−0.016 (0.414)		0.96	1.58
		X(t)	133.377 (1.372)	0.037 (0.48)	−0.061 * (1.755)	0.666 * (12.0)	0.237 * (4.274)	0.029 (0.517)	0.03 (0.618)		0.93	2.17
	II	U(t)	63.143 * (2.019)	0.685 * (13.498)	−0.06 * (2.979)	−0.193 * (4.857)	0.236 * (6.601)	0.051 (1.406)	0.116 * (3.612)		0.94	1.74
		H(t)	140.741 * (3.978)	−0.108 * (1.879)	0.929 * (40.543)	0.137 * (3.053)	−0.275 * (6.795)	0.013 (0.311)	0.097 * (2.669)		0.96	1.37
		X(t)	72.587 * (1.668)	0.211 * (2.983)	−0.004 (0.147)	0.345 * (6.25)	0.462 * (9.276)	−0.033 (0.661)	−0.018 (0.392)		0.90	2.13
Printing paper		U(t)	−29.584 (1.388)	0.869 * (25.425)	−0.279 * (3.25)	−0.182 * (1.716)	0.567 * (6.851)	0.168 * (2.333)	−0.163 * (2.241)		0.91	2.13
		H(t)	−7.602 (1.026)	0.003 (0.303)	0.964 * (32.274)	0.014 (0.373)	0.021 (0.737)	−0.258 (1.034)	0.033 (1.288)		0.97	2.68
		X(t)	37.562 * (3.021)	0.069 * (3.643)	0.163 * (3.246)	0.242 * (3.912)	0.485 * (10.039)	−0.107 * (2.562)	0.083 * (1.941)		0.89	2.08
Plywood	I: unsanded	U(t)	−31575 * (2.346)	0.969 * (78.722)	0.009 (0.812)	−0.471 * (6.497)	0.707 * (16.747)	0.074 (1.601)	−0.032 (0.774)		0.98	1.92
		H(t)	22405 * (2.219)	−0.021 * (2.277)	0.975 * (154.4)	−0.048 (0.88)	−0.139 * (4.398)	0.117 * (3.383)	−0.057 * (1.853)		0.99	1.5
		X(t)	55343 * (4.741)	0.01 (0.939)	−0.032 * (4.393)	0.417 * (6.643)	0.151 * (4.122)	0.039 (0.973)	−0.23 (0.651)		0.68	1.8

Plywood I: sanded	U(t)	-103549 (1.198)	0.95 * (75.032)	-0.098 * (2.82)	-2.795 * (3.749)	6.38 * (11.902)	0.652 (1.183)	-0.75 (1.437)		0.98	1.6
	H(t)	19220 * (1.919)	-0.003 * (1.896)	0.991 * (245.1)	0.126 (1.462)	-0.147 * (2.37)	0.189 * (2.962)	-0.148 * (2.457)		0.99	2.3
	X(t)	33148 * (4.564)	0.002 * (2.107)	0.001 (0.451)	0.389 * (6.213)	0.233 * (5.166)	0.049 (1.066)	-0.043 (0.976)		0.47	1.7
II: unsanded	U(t)	-12761 (1.31)	0.939 * (84.32)	0.007 (1.807)	-0.407 * (7.993)	0.619 * (18.04)	0.024 (0.692)	0.015 (0.451)	12201 * (2.573)	0.98	2.0
	H(t)	28515 * (4.448)	-0.002 (0.209)	0.995 * (396.972)	-0.15 * (4.478)	-0.076 * (3.356)	0.087 * (3.85)	-0.014 (0.656)	7631 * (2.445)	0.99	1.8
	X(t)	34966 * (3.973)	0.0517 * (5.134)	-0.015 * (3.328)	0.29 * (6.295)	0.301 * (9.704)	0.069 * (2.219)	-0.012 (0.412)	-4294 (1.002)	0.73	1.9
II: sanded	U(t)	-255797 * (2.315)	0.974 * (73.377)	0.032 (1.195)	-3.831 * (5.902)	5.538 * (11.495)	-0.317 (0.632)	1.464 * (3.073)	-4884 (0.192)	0.97	2.3
	H(t)	2518 (0.328)	0.002 (2.206)	1.001 * (541.087)	0.035 (0.777)	-0.142 * (4.26)	0.045 (1.315)	0.014 (0.428)	-4177 * (2.372)	0.99	1.7
	X(t)	21962 * (3.01)	0.004 * (3.997)	-0.002 (1.345)	0.487 * (11.376)	0.307 * (9.645)	-0.04 (1.217)	0.008 (0.271)	-2504 (1.492)	0.72	1.9
Primary metals	U(t)	-121.85 * (2.05)	0.96 * (110.32)	-0.068 * (5.34)	-0.39 * (11.17)	0.06 (12.36)	-0.053 (0.94)	0.083 * (1.93)		0.99	1.4
	H(t)	-33.16 (1.24)	0.02 * (4.2)	0.99 * (172.03)	0.04 * (2.21)	-0.009 (0.43)	-0.03 (1.32)	0.004 (0.22)		0.99	1.5
	X(t)	144.79 (1.6)	0.06 * (4.33)	0.06 * (3.19)	0.41 * (7.73)	0.37 * (5.06)	0.05 (0.62)	-0.09 (1.51)		0.96	2.2
Electrical machinery	U(t)	-136.47 * (6.19)	1.01 * (105.68)	-0.12 * (8.79)	-0.28 * (5.86)	0.65 * (16.05)	-0.01 (0.35)	-0.09 (2.45)		0.99	1.5
	H(t)	-77.13 * (4.74)	0.03 * (4.51)	0.9 * (87.93)	0.13 * (3.75)	0.05 * (1.7)	-0.004 (0.15)	-0.04 (1.34)		0.99	1.8
	X(t)	38.38 (1.39)	0.05 * (3.91)	-0.008 (0.44)	0.38 * (6.51)	0.24 * (4.69)	0.12 * (2.45)	0.07 (1.56)		0.99	2.2

* Significant at 5% upper tail t-test

Table 3
The Coefficient estimates and t-values of Model II

Data	Sample	Dependent variable	α	U(t−1)	H(t−1)	X(t−1)	O(t−1)	O(t−2)	O(t−3)	Dummy	R^2	D.W.
Lumber	I	U(t)	50.078 *	0.834 *			0.106 *	−0.156 *	0.072 *		0.72	1.6
			(2.062)	(13.141)			(2.137)	(2.618)	(1.385)			
		H(t)	465.219 *	−0.35 *	0.855 *		−0.237 *	0.042	0.108 *		0.94	1.4
			(4.131)	(4.063)	(20.673)		(4.255)	(0.661)	(1.802)			
		X(t)	119.598	−0.0625	−0.026	0.778 *	0.079	0.238 *	−0.165 *		0.92	2.0
			(0.982)	(0.622)	(0.592)	(7.784)	(.064)	(3.492)	(2.393)			
	II	U(t)	23.308	0.977 *			0.018	−0.089 *	0.046		0.90	1.6
			(1.563)	(16.553)			(0.38)	(1.969)	(1.165)			
		H(t)	128.873 *	−0.059	0.945 *		−0.192 *	−0.006	0.127 *		0.96	1.2
			(3.378)	(0.968)	(40.749)		(4.058)	(0.137)	(3.317)			
		X(t)	−85.984	0.507 *	0.122 *	0.309 *	−0.064	0.181 *	0.152 *		0.86	2.0
			(1.635)	(5.995)	(3.866)	(3.193)	(0.791)	(3.063)	(2.594)			
Printing paper		U(t)	20.727	0.896 *			−0.184 *	0.098	0.148		0.87	1.9
			(1.148)	(24.48)			(1.865)	(1.086)	(1.494)			
		H(t)	−4.874	0.004	0.971 *		0.043	−0.041	0.028		0.97	2.6
			(0.731)	(0.303)	(33.662)		(1.376)	(1.41)	(0.905)			
		X(t)	57.548 *	0.056 *	0.213 *	0.102	0.017	0.286 *	0.227 *		0.85	1.9
			(3.957)	(2.28)	(3.43)	(1.028)	(0.219)	(4.701)	(3.396)			
Plywood	I: unsanded	U(t)	491.554	0.967 *			0.285 *	−0.13	−0.065		0.95	1.6
			(0.039)	(45.697)			(4.005)	(1.641)	(0.907)			
		H(t)	24936	−0.005	0.977 *		−0.104 *	−0.055	−0.029		0.99	1.8
			(4.006)	(0.484)	(204.303)		(3.296)	(1.593)	(0.926)			
		X(t)	72628 *	0.026 *	−0.034 *	0.48 *	0.019	−0.113 *	0.039		0.62	1.8
			(6.092)	(2.071)	(4.323)	(6.541)	(0.463)	(2.579)	(0.95)			

Plywood I: sanded	U(t)	−61229 (0.735)	0.978* (61.115)			1.357* (1.845)	−0.457 (0.592)	0.234 (0.319)		0.97	1.58
	H(t)	33794* (4.474)	−0.0006 (0.399)	0.994* (236.643)		−0.038 (0.559)	−0.007 (0.098)	−0.165* (2.572)		0.99	2.27
	X(t)	47780* (6.11)	0.005* (3.887)	0.005 (1.606)	0.447* (5.933)	−0.027 (0.495)	−0.078 (1.465)	0.009 (0.181)		0.35	1.85
II: unsanded	U(t)	38192* (3.008)	0.993* (57.635)			−0.006 (0.106)	−0.106* (1.985)	−0.027 (0.542)	7256 (0.993)	0.97	1.75
	H(t)	32254* (5.884)	0.009 (1.246)	0.995* (409.387)		−0.139* (6.018)	−0.043* (1.862)	−0.015 (0.677)	5375* (1.704)	0.99	1.98
	X(t)	62252* (6.396)	0.075* (5.856)	−0.014* (3.428)	0.394* (6.092)	0.018 (0.416)	0.005 (0.412)	0.039 (1.063)	−6392 (1.233)	0.61	1.95
II: sanded	U(t)	−61421 (1.142)	0.965* (57.9)			1.412* (2.352)	−0.542 (0.848)	0.502 (0.835)	1294 (0.039)	0.95	2.02
	H(t)	10707 (1.656)	0.003* (3.337)	1.00* (574.391)		−0.064* (1.89)	−0.058 (1.64)	−0.005 (0.155)	−5657* (2.622)	0.99	1.7
	X(t)	39598* (5.172)	0.004* (3.466)	−0.005* (2.836)	0.488* (8.636)	0.06 (1.503)	0.016 (0.407)	0.069* (1.863)	−2495 (1.293)	0.63	2.0
Primary metals	U(t)	−346.65* (3.91)	0.93* (61.83)			0.54* (7.36)	−0.08 (0.77)	−0.23* (3.04)		0.99	1.2
	H(t)	−10.3 (0.37)	0.02* (5.28)	0.99* (203.61)		−0.04* (1.78)	0.0008 (0.03)	0.01 (0.59)		0.99	1.49
	X(t)	149.71 (1.59)	0.05* (3.38)	0.06* (3.32)	0.35* (5.36)	0.2* (2.89)	0.2* (2.19)	0.007 (0.09)		0.95	2.0
Electrical machinery	U(t)	−106.76 (3.0)	0.92* (94.48)			0.18 (2.92)	0.1 (1.57)	0.09 (1.39)		0.99	1.27
	H(t)	−79.5* (5.12)	0.03* (4.07)	0.9* (39.39)		−0.03 (0.98)	0.07* (2.51)	0.09* (3.39)		0.99	1.61
	X(t)	40.22 (1.37)	0.02* (1.64)	0.003 (0.17)	0.41* (5.99)	0.15* (2.8)	0.19* (3.54)	0.41* (2.62)		0.99	2.23

* significant at 5% upper tail t-test

Table 4
Estimated Coefficients and t values of Model IIIB

Data	Sample	Dependent variable	α	H(t−1)	X(t−1)	S(t−1)	S(t+1)	Dummy	R²	D.W.
Lumber	I	H(t)	156.46 *	0.94 *	0.7 *	−0.53 *	−0.22 *		0.94	2.24
			(2.25)	(30.4)	(8.25)	(6.31)	(4.45)			
		X(t)	141.35 *	−0.06 *	0.67 *	0.02	0.27 *		0.93	2.72
			(1.97)	(1.81)	(7.59)	(0.21)	(5.42)			
		P(t)	31.85 *	−0.007 *	0.02 *	−0.0006	−0.008 *		0.58	0.41
			(7.4)	(3.67)	(4.09)	(0.11)	(2.62)			
	II	H(t)	87.81 *	0.96 *	0.59 *	−0.51 *	−0.14 *		0.97	2.34
			(2.86)	(54.45)	(8.09)	(7.73)	(4.6)			
		X(t)	135.95 *	−0.05 *	0.43 *	0.1	0.35 *		0.83	2.93
			(2.55)	(1.74)	(3.39)	(0.88)	(6.42)			
		P(t)	28.25 *	−0.03 *	0.26 *	−0.12 *	0.07 *		0.83	0.71
			(2.24)	(4.03)	(8.68)	(4.5)	(5.59)			
Printing paper		H(t)	−6.18	0.96 *	0.07	−0.07	0.05		0.97	2.71
			(0.89)	(35.1)	(0.38)	(0.43)	(1.31)			
		X(t)	64.03 *	0.23 *	0.2	0.1	0.37 *		0.79	3.0
			(3.92)	(3.56)	(0.49)	(0.26)	(4.1)			
		P(t)	5.62 *	0.02 *	−0.009	0.02 *	0.008 *		0.89	0.48
			(12.57)	(10.13)	(0.88)	(1.76)	(3.33)			
Plywood unsanded	I	H(t)	7229.43	0.99 *	0.1	−0.24 *	0.06		0.99	2.0
			(0.75)	(168.09)	(1.23)	(3.36)	(1.22)			
		X(t)	45396 *	−0.03 *	0.66 *	−0.28 *	0.31 *		0.72	2.55
			(4.56)	(4.18)	(7.56)	(3.84)	(6.67)			
		P(t)	59.22	−0.00005 *	0.0001 *	−0.00008	0.00003		0.51	0.06
			(5.78)	(7.79)	(1.65)	(1.07)	(0.57)			
sanded		H(t)	16067 *	0.99 *	0.27 *	−0.29 *	−0.07		0.99	2.6
			(1.65)	(282.83)	(2.34)	(2.81)	(0.93)			
		X(t)	30082 *	−0.001	0.52 *	−0.08	0.29 *		0.41	2.32
			(4.17)	(0.43)	(6.04)	(1.02)	(5.58)			
		P(t)	−16.44	0.00006 *	0.0008 *	0.0002	0.0005 *		0.24	0.12
			(0.55)	(5.18)	(2.15)	(0.53)	(2.25)			

II unsanded	$H(t)$	24803 * (4.29)	0.99 * (403.79)	−0.09 (1.47)	−0.11 * (2.16)	0.06 * (2.48)	6680 * (2.37)	0.99	1.94
	$X(t)$	33788 * (3.99)	−0.006 (1.59)	0.53 * (5.79)	−0.12 (1.59)	0.42 * (11.33)	5772 (1.39)	0.69	2.83
	$P(t)$	4.79 (0.83)	−0.29E-4 (12.22)	024E-3 * (3.91)	−0.58E-4 (1.14)	0.15E-3 * (5.83)	22.51 * (8.05)	0.69	0.29
sanded	$H(t)$	−2082 (0.29)	1.0 * (561.88)	0.21 * (2.62)	0.21 * (2.72)	0.03 (0.72)	−2976 * (1.67)	0.99	1.93
	$X(t)$	24877 * (3.49)	−0.004 * (2.18)	0.57 * (7.14)	−0.12 (1.6)	0.38 * (8.75)	−1068 (0.61)	0.68	2.67
	$P(t)$	−199.73 * (6.56)	0.13E-3 * (17.76)	0.29E-3 (0.86)	0.6E-3 * (1.87)	0.86E-3 * (4.6)	10.52 (1.4)	0.54	0.16
Primary metals	$H(t)$	−97.52 * (4.15)	0.99 * (170.87)	0.07 * (2.34)	−0.04 (1.08)	0.004 (0.25)		0.99	1.45
	$X(t)$	−82.28 (1.04)	0.026 (1.32)	0.15 (1.42)	0.36 * (3.09)	0.48 * (9.91)		0.95	3.17
Electrical machinery	$H(t)$	−69.33 * (3.62)	0.94 * (104.61)	0.11 * (3.57)	0.04 (0.62)	0.03 (0.76)		0.99	1.57
	$X(t)$	−44.33 (1.39)	−0.05 * (3.15)	0.13 * (2.56)	0.47 * (5.07)	0.52 * (7.97)		0.99	2.72
Cement I	$H(t)$	1.9 * (2.38)	0.92 * (24.59)	0.77 * (11.47)	−0.63 * (9.76)	−0.17 * (4.8)		0.92	2.31
	$X(t)$	1.21 * (1.86)	−0.05 * (1.71)	0.55 * (10.12)	0.78 (1.48)	0.37 * (12.81)		0.96	1.75
	$P(t)$	1.91 * (23.67)	−0.02 * (6.13)	0.03 * (4.15)	0.03 * (4.95)	0.02 * (4.79)		0.23	0.17
Cement II	$H(t)$	2.99 * (3.39)	0.99 * (33.77)	0.63 * (7.68)	−0.49 * (7.22)	−0.27 * (6.74)		0.95	2.41
	$X(t)$	2.52 * (2.6)	0.05 * (1.67)	0.39 * (4.4)	0.24 * (3.27)	0.2 * (4.57)		0.84	2.32

Notes
1. * significant at 5% upper tail t-test
2. E-k denotes 10^{-k}
3. Dummy variable for price reflects the impact of price control in the Sample period II

Table 5
Estimated coefficients and t values of Model III

Data	Sample	Dependent variable	α	$H(t-1)$	$X(t-1)$	$S(t-1)$	$S(t+1)$	$P(t-1)$	R^2	D.W.
Lumber	I	$H(t)$	65.26 (0.77)	0.95 * (29.92)	0.59 * (5.71)	−0.49 * (5.75)	−0.18 * (3.61)	3.13 * (1.85)	0.94	2.17
		$X(t)$	55.34 (0.63)	−0.04 (1.23)	0.56 * (5.24)	0.05 (0.62)	0.3 * (5.72)	2.95 * (1.68)	0.93	2.72
		$P(t)$	5.84 * (2.11)	−0.002 * (2.09)	−0.01 * (3.49)	0.01 * (4.24)	0.001 (0.88)	0.89 * (18.44)	0.91	1.77
	II	$H(t)$	69.67 * (2.33)	0.98 * (55.28)	0.38 * (4.19)	−0.41 * (5.8)	−0.19 * (5.78)	0.71 * (3.56)	0.97	2.34
		$X(t)$	92.94 * (1.86)	−0.009 (0.33)	−0.06 (0.41)	0.35 * (2.99)	0.25 * (4.55)	1.68 * (5.06)	0.86	2.61
		$P(t)$	3.38 (1.16)	−0.004 * (2.24)	−0.02 * (2.78)	0.02 * (3.12)	0.01 * (3.86)	0.97 * (50.0)	0.99	0.9
Printing paper		$H(t)$	−24.46 * (2.44)	0.9 * (25.14)	0.099 (0.58)	−0.14 (0.8)	0.03 (0.64)	3.19 * (2.48)	0.97	2.65
		$X(t)$	5.69 (0.25)	0.04 (0.49)	0.31 (0.78)	−0.09 (0.24)	0.29 * (3.21)	10.17 * (3.44)	0.81	2.72
		$P(t)$	0.06 (0.56)	−0.0001 (0.31)	0.0005 (0.24)	0.0005 (0.24)	0.0005 (1.01)	0.97 * (66.69)	0.99	1.98
Plywood unsanded	I	$H(t)$	2518.13 (0.24)	0.99 * (146.32)	0.09 (1.05)	−0.23 * (3.25)	0.05 (1.17)	81.7 (1.16)	0.99	2.01
		$X(t)$	43278 * (4.0)	−0.02 * (3.36)	0.65 * (7.4)	−0.28 * (3.77)	0.31 * (6.64)	36.72 (0.5)	0.72	3.54

	$P(t)$	2.7 (1.12)	−0.7E-5 (1.09)	−0.8E-4 (0.93)	0.61E-5 (0.37)	0.34E-5 (0.33)	0.98 * (60.27)	0.97	1.26
sanded	$H(t)$	16140 * (1.65)	0.99 * (262.29)	0.27 * (2.26)	−0.29 * (2.8)	−0.07 (0.95)	5.46 (0.22)	0.99	2.61
	$X(t)$	30483 * (4.25)	−0.003 (1.02)	0.5 * (5.68)	−0.08 (1.05)	0.28 * (5.28)	30.334 (1.7)	0.42	2.28
	$P(t)$	−3.48 (0.64)	−0.15E-7 (0.007)	−0.68E-4 (1.04)	0.1E-3 * (1.83)	0.42E-4 (1.06)	0.98 * (72.63)	0.97	1.27
II unsanded	$H(t)$	22537 * (3.97)	−0.99 * (345.3)	−0.11 * (1.66)	0.11 * (2.12)	0.05 * (1.88)	112.25 * (2.06)	0.99	2.0
	$X(t)$	32690 * (4.0)	0.002 (0.5)	0.47 * (5.07)	−0.11 (1.46)	0.39 * (9.99)	261.64 * (3.34)	0.70	2.72
	$P(t)$	0.22 (0.14)	−0.93E-6 (1.12)	0.19E-4 (1.05)	−0.18E-4 (1.23)	0.13E-4 (1.63)	0.96 * (61.6)	0.97	1.71
sanded	$H(t)$	2507 (0.33)	0.99 * (385.63)	0.22 * (2.72)	−0.24 * (3.19)	0.01 (0.24)	26.19 * (1.86)	0.99	1.99
	$X(t)$	31778 * (4.2)	−0.008 * (3.38)	0.56 * (7.16)	0.15 * (2.01)	0.36 * (7.99)	35.9 * (2.59)	0.69	2.61
	$P(t)$	−3.68 (0.53)	0.29E-5 (1.25)	−0.16E-3 * (2.25)	0.73E-4 (1.08)	0.13E-3 * (3.29)	0.98 * (77.18)	0.98	0.98
Cement I	$H(t)$	1.09 (0.61)	0.94 * (22.8)	0.76 * (10.67)	−0.62 * (8.83)	−0.18 * (4.6)	0.43 (0.5)	0.92	2.3
	$X(t)$	0.53 (0.36)	−0.05 (1.38)	0.54 * (9.39)	0.09 (1.56)	0.36 * (11.55)	0.36 (0.51)	0.96	1.75
	$P(t)$	0.07 * (2.06)	−0.002 * (1.85)	0.002 (1.62)	−0.003 * (1.92)	0.31E-4 (0.04)	0.98 * (56.75)	0.97	1.41

* significant at 5% upper tail *t*-test

Note: E-*k* denotes 10^{-k}; also * denotes significant at 5% upper tail *t*-test

Table 6
Estimated coefficients and t values of Model IV

Data	Sample	Dependent variable	α	$S^e(t)$	$X(t-1)$	$X(t)$	$H(t-1)$	$P(t-1)$	R^2	D.W.
Lumber	I	$X(t)$	57.98 (0.79)	0.22 * (4.13)	0.74 * (11.65)		-0.014 (0.47)		0.92	2.34
		$P(t)$	33.78 * (8.24)	0.003 (1.05)		0.006 (1.64)	-0.007 * (4.08)		0.47	0.27
		$P(t)$	6.17 * (2.35)	0.005 * (3.14)		-0.002 (0.91)	-0.002 (2.1)	0.83 * (16.09)	0.88	1.76
	II	$X(t)$	96.02 * (1.98)	0.41 * (8.39)	0.45 * (7.28)		-0.01 (0.45)		0.85	2.59
		$P(t)$	31.68 * (2.29)	-0.016 (0.95)		0.22 * (10.18)	-0.03 * (3.97)		0.8	0.84
		$P(t)$	0.32 (0.11)	0.008 * (2.3)		0.01 * (1.84)	-0.003 * (1.82)	0.93 * (51.32)	0.99	0.77
Printing		$X(t)$	54.14 *	0.72 *	0.03		0.15 *		0.90	2.54

		(1)	(2)	(3)	(4)	(5)	(6)	R²	DW
		(4.63)	(14.49)	(0.06)		(3.63)			
paper	P(t)	7.24 * (16.07)	0.002 (0.74)		0.009 * (2.56)	0.2 * (12.79)		0.88	0.4
	P(t)	0.27 * (1.86)	0.0004 (0.62)		0.0003 (0.38)	0.0003 (0.71)	0.966 * (59.35)	0.99	2.01
Primary metals	X(t)	71.11 (1.31)	-0.01 (0.31)	1.01 * (21.82)		0.005 (0.38)		0.98	1.66
Electrical machinery	X(t)	61.63 (1.61)	0.08 (1.33)	0.87 * (13.36)		0.016 (1.07)		0.98	2.73
Cement I	X(t)	-0.83 (1.47)	0.42 * (14.39)	0.48 * (14.07)		0.07 * (3.07)		0.96	1.17
	P(t)	1.64 * (22.57)	-0.008 (1.336)		0.014 * (1.84)	-0.005 (1.59)		0.05	0.07
	P(t)	0.06 (2.02)	-0.002 (1.5)		0.001 (0.73)	-0.001 * (1.86)	0.98 * (58.05)	0.97	1.42
II	X(t)	3.32 * (3.42)	0.34 * (10.07)	0.47 * (9.64)		0.05 * (2.5)		0.83	2.17

* significant at 5% upper tail t-test

Table 7
Estimated coefficients and t values of Model V

Data: Cement, Sample I								
	$X(t)$	$S(t)$	$S^e(t)$	$H(t_{-1})$	$D(i)$	$D(j)$	R^2	D.W.
Dependent variable		0.74* (0.27)	0.17* (3.44)	−0.098* (2.8)			0.97	0.98

Monthly correlates $D(i)$'s and yearly correlates $D(j)$

	J	F	M	A	M	J	J	A	S	O	N	D	
$D(i)$	8.79* (8.99)	8.5* (8.66)	8.08* (8.65)	7.95* (8.87)	8.57* (11.08)	8.25* (10.59)	7.06* (8.49)	6.62* (7.6)	7.22* (7.83)	7.94* (8.29)	8.85* (8.92)	8.8* (8.9)	
	1928	1929	1930	1931	1932	1933	1934	1935	1936	1937	1938	1939	1940
$D(j)$	0.89* (2.17)	0.75* (2.37)	0.66* (1.9)	−0.89* (2.4)	−3.1 (7.4)	−3.68* (8.26)	−3.05* (7.3)	−2.93* (6.9)	−1.83* (5.23)	−1.31* (3.66)	−1.83* (4.99)	−1.33* (3.96)	−0.85* (2.58)

* significant at 5% upper tail t-test

Table 8
Estimated coefficients and t values of Model V

Data: Cement, Sample II

Dependent variable:	$X(t)$	$S(t)$	$S^e(t)$	$H(t-1)$	$D(ii)$	$D(j)$	R^2	D.W.
		0.87 *	0.1 *	−0.24 *			0.95	1.84
		(12.59)	(2.39)	(2.79)				

Monthly correlates $D(i)$'s and yearly correlates $D(j)$

	J	F	M	A	M	J	J	A	S	O	N	D
$D(i)$	14.09 *	12.68 *	11.39 *	10.33 *	9.6 *	7.17 *	6.29 *	6.05 *	6.06 *	5.77 *	9.71 *	13.6 *
	(4.82)	(3.73)	(3.05)	(2.66)	(2.44)	(1.84)	(1.73)	91.7)	(1.84)	(1.82)	(3.6)	(5.11)
	1950	1951	1952	1953	1954	1955	1956	1957	1958	1959		
$D(j)$	−6.32 *	−4.74 *	−4.75 *	−4.01 *	−4.28 *	−4.25 *	−3.06 *	−1.79 *	−1.29 *	0.99		
	(3.48)	(2.69)	(2.98)	(2.73)	(3.03)	(2.82)	(2.44)	(2.03)	(1.91)	(1.58)		

* significant at 5% upper tail t-test

Table 9
Estimated Coefficients and t values of other regressions for Cement

Data	Sample	Dependent variable	α	$H(t-1)$	$X(t-1)$	R^2	D.W.
Cement	I	$H(t)$	3.87 *	0.87 *	-0.09 *	0.79	0.7
			(4.28)	(24.3)	(2.88)		
		$X(t)$	-3.86 *	0.20 *	0.94 *	0.88	0.89
			(4.8)	(6.21)	(35.48)		
	II	$H(t)$	4.11 *	0.94 *	-0.11 *	0.85	0.67
			(2.92)	(28.38)	(2.01)		
		$X(t)$	2.25 *	0.11 *	0.8 *	0.72	1.66
			(1.98)	(4.19)	(17.86)		

* significant at 5% upper tail t-test

Table 10
Estimated coefficients and t values of other regressions of Cement

Data	Sample	Dependent variable	α	$H(t-1)$	$X(t-1)$	$S(t-1)$	R^2	D.W.
Cement	I	$H(t)$	4.63 *	0.79 *	0.79 *	-0.77 *	0.90	2.0
			(7.51)	(31.66)	(12.14)	(14.14)		
		$X(t)$	-4.33 *	0.25 *	0.4 *	0.48 *	0.91	0.86
			(6.22)	(8.77)	(5.38)	(7.75)		
	II	$H(t)$	0.73	0.85 *	0.91 *	-0.8 *	0.93	1.92
			(0.76)	(37.51)	(10.85)	(13.51)		
		$X(t)$	4.26 *	0.16 *	0.19 *	0.47 *	0.81	1.73
			(4.34)	(7.02)	(2.18)	(7.87)		

* significant at 5% upper tail t-test

Table 11
Estimated Coefficients and t values of other regressions for Cement

Data	Sample	Dependent variable	α	$X(t-1)$	$S(t-1)$	CAP	R^2	D.W.
Cement	I	$X(t)$	0.71 *	-0.04	0.09 *	0.19 *	0.98	0.98
				(6.71)	(1.12)	(3.61)	(37.06)	
	II	$X(t)$	-0.55	0.56 *	0.13	0.09 *	0.77	1.37
			(0.27)	(5.57)	(1.58)	(4.07)		

Note: 1. CAP denotes percentage of capacity utilized for which data are available for cement;
2. * denotes significant at 5% upper tail t-test

Table 12
Estimated coefficients and t values of Model VI

Data	Sample	Dependent variable	α	$Y(t-1)$	$O(t)$	$P(t)$	$V(t)$ [1]	R^2	D.W.
Electrical machinery		$Y(t)$	−65.33 * (2.15)	0.94 * (112)	0.22 * (7.73)		0.08 (0.53)	0.99	2.46
Primary metals		$Y(t)$	6.2 (0.08)	0.94 * (58.38)	0.17 * (4.67)		0.24 (1.51)	0.99	2.52
Printing paper		$Y(t)$	−35.3 * (2.55)	0.75 * (23.2)	0.51 * (8.17)		−0.36 (1.23)	0.95	2.54
		$Y(t)$	−64.46 * (2.54)	0.7 * (10.83)		15.19 * (4.33)	−0.2 (0.61)	0.93	2.67
Lumber	I	$Y(t)$	229.62 * (2.03)	0.91 * (18.7)	0.06 (1.04)		−0.42 (1.56)	0.86	1.44
		$Y(t)$	295.04 * (2.4)	0.93 * (22.2)		−4.13 (1.65)	0.07 (0.28)	0.86	1.61
Lumber	II	$Y(t)$	155.8 * (2.36)	0.88 * (22.59)	0.08 (1.65)		0.31 (1.37)	0.83	1.99
		$Y(t)$	155.78 * (2.3)	0.91 * (24.83)		−0.01 (0.07)	0.22 (0.97)	0.83	2.14
Cement	I	$Y(t)$	2.2 * (2.22)	0.93 * (33.4)		0.09 (0.37)	−10.1 [2] (1.36)	0.88	0.61

[1] $V(t)$ is a 6 month moving average; [2] deviation $V(t)$ here is that of prices
* significant at 5% upper tail t-test

Table 13
Estimated coefficients and t values of Model VI

Data	Sample	Dependent variable	α	$Y(t-1)$	$O(t)$	$P(t)$	$V(t)$ [1]	R^2	D.W.
Printing paper		$Y(t)$	−58.53 *	0.71 *		14.53 *	−0.34	0.93	2.68
			(2.32)	(10.91)		(4.1)	(1.26)		
		$Y(t)$	−32.55 *	0.75	0.51 *		−0.54 *	0.95	2.56
			(2.5)	(23.61)	(8.28)		(2.39)		
Lumber	I	$Y(t)$	283.1 *	0.93 *		−3.79	−0.12	0.86	1.61
			(2.35)	(22.59)		(1.58)	(0.71)		
		$Y(t)$	219.11 *	0.92 *	0.04		−0.39	0.86	1.49
			(1.95)	(18.91)	(0.83)		(1.64)		
	II	$Y(t)$	153.57 *	0.91 *		−0.03	0.22	0.83	2.16
			(2.27)	(25.06)		(0.15)	(1.1)		
		$Y(t)$	152.19	0.89 *	0.07		0.29	0.83	2.01
			(2.3)	(22.910)	(1.64)		(1.46)		
Primary metals		$Y(t)$	−11.168	0.95 *	0.17 *		0.042	0.99	2.51
			(0.12)	(61.22)	(4.55)		(0.25)		
Electrical machinery		$Y(t)$	−64.2 *	0.94 *	0.22 *		0.046	0.99	2.45
			(2.12)	(115.01)	(7.72)		(0.36)		

[1] $V(t)$ is a 4-month moving average and * denotes significant at 5% upper tail t-test

reported elsewhere [18] shows the unmistakable stabilizing impact of the futures market beginning in January 1970. Further, the standard errors of maximum eigenvalues (or maximum of their real parts if complex) which are computed by the method of Neudecker and Van de Panne [14] show that for lumber, primary metals and electrical machinery the maximum eigenvalue is less than one in a statistical sense; for printing paper and plywood (unsanded), the excess of the maximum value over one is statistically not significant. This implies that the source of instability due to complex values and real parts exceeding unity in a statistical sense has become less and less important for the industries in recent times, when

Table A:
Variability of order, output and inventories

Industry	Sample	Dependent variable	Constant intercept	var X	var H	R^2
Lumber	I	var O	3890 *	0.33	0.33 *	0.29
			(5.28)	(1.63)	(4.29)	
	II	var O	433.4	1.57 *	0.12	0.32
			(1.31)	(7.92)	(1.54)	
Paper		var O	432.69 *	0.11	0.34	0.02
			(8.85)	(0.77)	(1.48)	
Primary Metals		var O	68288 *	0.05 *	1.52 *	0.60
			(5.46)	(1.95)	(17.12)	
Electrical Machinery		var O	19771 *	-0.066	0.31 *	0.20
			(8.26)	(1.34)	(7.18)	

* Significant at upper tail 5% level of t-test, t-values in parenthesis

Table B1:
Complex eigenvalues and their modulus

Industry	Model	Sample	Complex eigenvalue		Modulus
			real part	imaginary part	
Lumber	I	I	0.879	0.123	0.888
	IA	I	0.824	0.141	0.836
	IA	II	0.509	0.099	0.519
Plywood (unsanded)	IA	I	0.969	0.026	0.969
Primary Metals	I	–	0.965	0.029	0.9654
	IA	–	0.960	0.029	0.9604
Electrical Machinery	IA	–	0.943	0.053	0.9445

three decision variables: production, inventories and unfilled orders have been interacting. For plywood (unsanded variety for which only futures market prevails), this has meant that market information system has been very efficient in its transmission mechanism; for lumber this provides evidence for increased stabilization over time attributable to a reduction in certain underlying costs; for others like primary metals and electrical

Table B2:
Maximum eigenvalues and standard errors of Model IA

Industry and Sample	Max. eigenvalues or max. real part	Standard error	Normalized eigenvectors	
			left	right
Lumber				
Sample I	0.824 *	0.0165	0.4505	−0.2916
			−0.3096	0.1220
			−0.8370	−0.1143
Sample II	0.939 *	0.026	0.1740	−0.1793
			−0.9457	0.9816
			−0.2743	−0.0661
Paper	0.952	0.082	0.0475	−0.9548
			0.9991	0.2961
			0.0072	0.0230
Plywood				
Sample I: unsanded	0.970	0.032	−0.6244	0.8244
			0.6322	0.5658
			0.4601	−0.1397
Sample II: unsanded	0.995	0.005	−0.1447	0.1520
			0.9815	0.9881
			−0.1255	0.0038
Sample I: sanded	0.995	0.0246	−0.0383	0.8825
			0.9278	−0.4701
			0.3708	0.0117
Sample II: sanded	1.0035	0.009	0.0402	−0.0253
			0.9719	0.7410
			−0.2318	−0.0006
Primary Metals	0.960 *	0.009	0.4451	0.6390
			0.8564	0.7686
			−0.2617	0.0292
Electrical Machinery	0.943 *	0.018	0.0689	−0.8532
			−0.9506	−0.5172
			−0.3027	−0.0675

* Significantly less than 1.0 at 5% upper tail t-test

machinery this suggests that the production inventory and backlog order process exerts a strongly stabilizing effect in the aggregate industrial scene.

The eigenvalues for other models are shown in Table B3.

It is clear that except for cement, Sample I the other eigenvalues have stayed within the unit circle, implying that the stabilizing impact has been more important as regards the response to fluctuations in order or sales.

An alternative way to analyze the set of eigenvalues is to compare two similar models e.g. Models I and II, the simultaneous and the recursive model, using the theory of distribution of eigenvalues in multivariate analysis [8,11]. For this purpose we consider those sample periods where the eigenvalues are all real and denote by $\hat{L}$ the column vector of the eigenvalues. Assume that asymptotically $\hat{L}$ is distributed as a multivariate normal with mean L and variance–covariance matrix M and that an unbiased estimate $\hat{M}$ of M based on N samples is available. The statistic known as Hotelling's T^2, which is analogous to t-test in univariate models may then be used, where T^2 is defined as follows:

$$T^2 = N(\hat{L} - L)'\hat{M}^{-1}(\hat{L} - L) \text{ with } d.f = N - 1$$

Note that the estimates $\hat{M}$ of the variance–covariance matrix M are available from the estimates of standard error of the eigenvalues, which are computed from the regression coefficients as before. For application to two models I and II with a given sample period, we define L as the difference of two sets of eigenvalues and $\hat{M}$ as the sum of two variance–covariance matrix estimates, one for each set of eigenvalues. Since the statistic

$$\frac{N - p}{p} \cdot \frac{T^2}{N - 1} \sim F(p, N - p) \tag{10}$$

is distributed like the standard F distribution with degrees of freedom p

Table B3

Industry Sample	Model	eigenvalues			
		real			imaginary
Lumber: I	II	0.778	0.854	0.834	–
II	II	0.308	0.945	0.977	–
Paper –	II	0.101	0.971	0.895	–
Primary Metals	II	0.353	0.996	0.931	–
Elect. Machinery	II	0.411	0.901	0.918	–
Cement: I	III B	0.490	1.315	–	–
II	III B	0.866	–	–	0.801

and $N - p$, where p denotes the number of eigenvalues, one could perform a comparison of two models by using an F-test. Just as the Chow-test [5] is applied to two sets of regression coefficients, this test (10) is applied to two sets of eigenvalues to determine if they differ significantly. The results of applying this test (10) in an asymptotic sense for the industries here show two very interesting characteristics. First, the difference between the simultaneous (Model I) and the recursive (Model II) models appears to be statistically significant in all comparable cases. Second, the plywood industry has evidenced difference in both varieties, sanded and unsanded although the futures market prevailed only for the latter. This implies that the cost adjustments are better reflected in Model I with three interdependent decision rules, one for each of production, inventories and unfilled order files. Judged by the significance of the regression coefficients, R^2 and other characteristics also, Model I appears to perform better than Model II. In our view this agrees very well with the results of Childs [4], who found that the entrepreneur tends to absorb any fluctuations in demand through optimally varying output, inventory and backlogging of orders.

The next question concerns the estimation of supply response without any specific optimization hypothesis, implicit or explicit. For cement, this method is applied by Moriguchi [13] to analyze the output–inventory adjustment behavior. Our results for cement are in table 6–11 and tables 12–13 show supply response estimates for other industries assuming that supply tends to respond to demand or price and the associated risk of fluctuations in them. A comparison of the estimates for cement from tables 4, 7–8 shows that single equation estimates are not in any way inferior to the optimal linear decision rules. However, the effects of seasonal, capacity and business cycle interaction are probably nonlinear and hence the introduction of monthly and seasonal dummies appear to improve the results. The regression estimates for cement in the recent

Table B4:
Comparison of eigenvalues of Models I and II

Industry	Models	Sample Period	F-value	$F(5\%)$	$F(1\%)$
Plywood	I, II	I, unsanded	9.19	8.53	26.1
		II, unsanded	17.08		
		I, sanded	8.63		
		II, sanded	27.06		
Paper	I, II	–	94.99	8.55	26.2
Electrical					
Machinery	I, II	–	88.83	8.54	26.18
Primary Metals [1]	I, II		25.76	8.54	26.18

[1] The real part of the complex eigenvalues of Model I is considered here, since the imaginary part is very small.

period (Sample II) are very similar to those of Moriguchi for the earlier period (Sample I) except that the impact of lagged inventories appears to be stronger. It is clear from table 6 that the marginal effect $\partial X(t)/\partial H(t-1)$ whenever statistically significant is always positive, implying that the PTS sectors tend to dominate if the actual inventories are on or above their desired levels. Also, the effect on production $\partial X(t)/\partial S^e(t)$ of anticipated sales whenever statistically significant is found to be positive. The supply response estimates in tables 12–13 further confirm the supply elasticity whenever statistically significant, to be positive with respect to order rates or price and negative with respect to their fluctuations. However, the influence of the risk factor is much less visible, as most of the adjustments in production and inventories absorb any anticipated sales fluctuations.

The supply response equations for Models IV and V show not only that anticipated sales $S^e(t)$ is statistically significant in explaning output variations for most of the industries but that the feedback elements $X(t-1)$ are equally important; for cement, lagged inventory $H(t-1)$ is as important an explanatory variable as anticipated sales $S^e(t)$, as is evident from tables 7–8. This behavior pattern agrees with the finding derived from earlier simulation experiments [16] on linear decision rules under quadratic programming that building feedback elements help considerably improve the performance of the decision rules. The observed behavior pattern implies that definite cost advantages exist in relating decisions partly to anticipated sales and partly to the feedback elements designated by output and inventory lagged.

4. Concluding remarks

An empirical analysis is attempted here to quantify the output–inventory adjustment process for the following representative industries: Southern pine lumber, printing paper, softwood plywood, primary metals, electrical machinery and Portland cement. In general the objectives are to quantify and test (i) the sources of instability due to the presence of eigenvalues exceeding unity in their real parts (ii) the possibility of cyclical behavior due to the presence of complex eigenvalue and (iii) the interdependence of three decision variables: output, inventories and unfilled order files. The statistical tests are all limited to the homogeneous parts of the linear difference equation system model, since it was considered reasonable to presume that the other exogenous variables and the stochastic error component would be stable and nonoscillatory.

In general, the applications appear to confirm some of the following adjustment pattern with very minor exceptions: (i) the output–adjustment process has behaved generally in a way conducive to stabilizing and the oscillatory behavior if any, has tended to dampen out in recent periods, (ii) the adjustment process has been marked more by simultaneous adjustments in costs due to varying outputs, inventories and backlogging of orders, than by recursive adjustment in unfilled order, inventories and output in that order, (iii) the adjustment process can be quantified with no less explanatory power by econometric production and/or supply response functions, where anticipated demand plays as crucial a role as lagged output and (iv) the supply behavior, after accounting for order rates and lagged supply has been much less sensitive to risk denoted by demand variance. For plywood, the results show that the futures market has exerted a strong stabilizing force and whatever inventory cycles existed in the pre-futures period have been eliminated by the trading process in the futures market. For cement the output–inventory interaction process has followed a ratchet effect, which has been influenced very strongly by the seasonal elements and anticipated sales. It is difficult in this case to maintain an order–stock distinction which holds in every sample.

It is clear therefore that the output adjustment process in the industrial field can be modelled through either the optimal decision rules or linearized supply response behavior. More applied work is needed before one can discriminate between these alternative models in relation to the aggregate time-series data.

References

1. Abramovitz, M. Inventories and Business Cycles with Special Reference to Manufactures Inventories. National Bureau of Economic Research. New York: The Gallery Press, 1950.
2. Belsley, D.A.: Inventory Production Behavior: The Order Stock Distinction. Amsterdam: North Holland Publishing, 1969.
3. Box, G.P., and G.M. Jenkins: Time Series Analysis: Forecasting and Control. San Francisco: Holden-Day, 1970.
4. Childs, G.L.: Unfilled Orders and Inventories: A Structural Analysis. Amsterdam: North Holland Publishing, 1967.
5. Chow, G.C.: "Test of Equality Between Sets of Coefficients in Two Linear Regressions." Econometrica, 28 (1960), 591–605.
6. Chow, G.c.: Analysis and Control of Dynamic Economic Systems. New York: John Wiley, 1975.
7. Duffy, W., and K.A. Lewis: "The Cyclic Properties of the Production–Inventory Process," Econometrica, 43 (1975), 499–512.
8. Girschik, M.A.: "On the Sampling Theory of Roots of Determinantal Equations," Annals of Mathematical Statistics, 10 (1939), 203–224.
9. Hay, G.A., and C.C. Holk: "A General Solution for Linear Decision Rules: An Optimal Strategy Application Under Uncertainty," Econometrica, 43 (1975), 231–260.
10. Holt, C.C., and F. Modigliani: "Firm Cost Structures and the Dynamic Responses of Inventories, Production, Work Force and Orders to Sales Fluctuations," in Iventoryn-

ventory Fluctuations and Economic Stabilization, Part II. Washington: Joint Economic Committee of the United States, 1961.
11. Kshirsagar, A.M.: Multivariate Analysis. New York: Marcel Dekker, Inc. 1972.
12. Mills, E.S.: Price Output and Inventory Policy: A Study in the Economics of the Firm and Industry. New York: John Wiley 1962.
13. Moriguchi, C: Business Cycles and Manufacturers' Short-Term Production Decisions. Amsterdam: North Holland, 1967.
14. Neudecker, H. and C. Van de Panne: "Note on the Asymptotic Standard Errors of Latent Roots of Econometric Equation Systems," Review of International Statistical Institute, 34 (1966), 43–47.
15. Sengupta, J.K.: "Optimal Stabilization Policy with a Quadratic Criterion Function," Review of Economic Studies, 37 (1970), 127–145.
16. Sengupta, J.K.: "Simulation of Linear Decision Rules," International Journal of Systems Science, 8 (1977), 1269–1280.
17. Sengupta, J.K.: "Economic Policy Simulation in Dynamic Control Models Under Econometric Estimation," in Econometrics and Economic Theory: Essays in Honor of Jan Tinbergen, Ch. 5, pp. 115–138.
18. Sengupta, J.K. and R.E. Sfeir: "The Adjustment of Output–Inventory Process Under Linear Decision Rules." Working Paper, Department of Economics, University of California, Santa Barbara. 1979.
19. Sengupta, J.K: "Risk in Supply Response." Working Paper, Department of Economics, University of California, Santa Barbara. 1979.
20. Wold, H.O.: A Econometric Model Building: Essays on the Causal Chain Approach. Amsterdam, North Holland, 1964.

III. Game theory models
in economics

10. Optimal control in limit pricing under uncertain entry

1. Introduction

The limit pricing theory (Friedman 1979, Gaskins 1971, Kamien and Schwartz 1971) proposes a control theory model of determination of an optimal entry preventing price by a supplier of a market when potential entrants exist and it may not be optimal to maximize immediate or short term profits. The supplier here may be a firm or a cartel comprising a group of tacitly cooperating firms. This is often referred to as a dominant firm, since the potential entrants, sometimes appearing as a composite rival, have in general a smaller share of the total industry market. For the dominant firm or cartel, the optimal policy must balance high short term profits associated with the pursuit of monopoly pricing against the loss of long term profits due to entry of additional suppliers attracted by the high price.

One basic limitation of limit pricing theory is the deterministic view of entry, where a single point or price level divides certain entry from no entry. A probabilistic view of entry helps to relax this limitation. In this paper, we present a reformulation of the optimal control problem in limit pricing under conditions of uncertain entry. One version of the reformulated model is then simulated to compare the sensitivity of the optimal trajectory to certain critical parameters which reflect for example, market growth, demand variance and the entry coefficient. Finally, an empirical application of a modified limit pricing model to the medium-sized computer market in the U.S. is made. The modifications include a short term discrete time version of the limit pricing model, estimated from quarterly data adjusted for quality and price changes, where optimal price and output trajectories are compared with myopic and static decision rules.

2. Uncertain entry

Limit price has been usually defined as the highest common price which the established firms believe they can charge without inducing any entry or market penetration. Thus, in the optimal control due to Gaskins (1971), market entry by rivals is measured by $\dot{x}(t) = dx/dt$, the rate of change of their supply which is positive if the market price $p(t)$ exceeds the limit price $\bar{p}$. hence the entry equation is

$$\dot{x}(t) = h(p(t) - \bar{p}), \quad p(t) > \bar{p} \tag{1.1}$$

where $h(\cdot)$ is a nondecreasing function. The demand function is

$$p(t) = f(x(t), q(t)) \tag{1.2}$$

where $q(t)$ is the quantity supplied to the market by the dominant firm or cartel and the function $f(\cdot)$ normally has a negative slope by the conditions of a standard demand function.

One way to introduce a stochastic view of entry is to reformulate the entry equation (1.1) above by an assumption that the entry probability, given that entry has not yet occurred, is an increasing convex function of output price at time t. This has been the approach of Kamien and Schwartz (1971). Let $F(t)$ denote the probability that entry has occurred by time t, with $F(0) = 0$. Then the conditional probability of entry at time t is $\dot{F}(t)/[1 - F(t)]$, where dot indicates time derivative. The modified entry equation thus becomes

$$\dot{F}(t)/[1 - F(t)] = h(\tilde{p}(t)) \tag{1.3}$$

where $\tilde{p}(t) = p(t) - \bar{p}$ and $h(0) = 0$, $\partial h/\partial p \geq 0$, $\partial^2 h/\partial p^2 \geq 0$. The rationale of the stochastic entry assumption in (1.3) is as follows: since the potential entrants are assumed to be profit maximizers, a higher price level $\tilde{p}(t)$ makes entry more attractive and thereby increases the probability of entry (i.e. shortens expected entry lag), while a lower price has the opposite impact.

This concept of stochastic entry has, in my view two major limitations. First, the conditional probability of entry is not easily estimable from observed data sets on market shares. Further, it is not related to the market demand function (1.2), which specifies the expected price-quantity relationship in the overall market. Second, the fact that anticipated entry may differ from realized entry and such divergence may be due to the errors in the demand function are almost ignored in such a formulation. In game theory models (Friedman 1979, Sengupta 1982), Cournot–Nash type equilibrium solutions emphasize such errors in adjustment through the players' reaction curves and discuss their properties of stability and instability.

We propose in this paper, a second view of stochastic entry, which is more closely related to the stochastic specification of the market demand function. In the demand function (1.2), the price variable is considered to be stochastic and hence the probability prob($p(t) > \bar{p}$) has an impact on the form of the entry equation (1.1). Thus, if an increase in $p(t)$ above the level $\bar{p} > 0$ is interpreted by the potential entrants as an increase in probability of entry, this would enhance the slope $\partial \dot{x}/\partial p(t)$ or the entry coefficient. With a linear form of the entry equation:

$$\dot{x}(t) = k(p(t) - \bar{p}), \quad k > 0 \tag{1.4}$$

the value of the entry coefficient k will thus increase. Since the changes in the mean and the variance of the price and in that of profits may generate a change in entry probability, the entry perceived may differ from actual entry and hence the degree of risk aversion plays an important role in the selection of optimal strategies by the dominant firm and the rivals.

In our view of stochastic entry, the demand function (1.2) contains errors due to incomplete information available to the players. Taking a linear case with additive noise, the demand function becomes

$$p(t) = a - b_1(q(t) + x(t)) + u(t) \tag{1.5}$$

where $u(t)$ is the noise component following a specified stochastic process. Since the price variable $p(t)$ is now random, whereas the quantities $q(t)$, $x(t)$ are not we may modify the linear entry equation (1.4) as follows. By using the probabilistic inequality

$$\text{prob}(p(t) \geqslant \bar{p}) = \epsilon \tag{1.6}$$

and the cumulative distribution

$$F(s) = \text{prob}\left(\frac{p(t) - Ep(t)}{\sigma(t)} \leqslant s\right)$$

We may replace $p(t)$ by ($Ep(t) - \alpha\sigma(t)$), where $Ep(t)$ is the mean and $\sigma(t)$ the standard deviation of the price, and α is usually a positive number $\alpha = -F^{-1}(1 - \epsilon)$, if $\epsilon > 0.50$ and the underlying price distribution is normal. The entry equation is then:

$$\dot{x}(t) = k(Ep(t) - \alpha\sigma(t) - \bar{p}) \tag{1.7}$$

If the variance $\sigma^2(t)$ is independent of the mean price $Ep(t)$, then the stochastic aspect results in raising the floor level p_0 say, where $p_0 = \bar{p} + \alpha\sigma(t)$ i.e. only if $Ep(t)$ exceeds the floor level p_0, we would observe positive entry. This holds good only if the potential entrants are risk-averse. If they are risk-takers however, or do not preassign $\epsilon > 0.50$ because of lack of knowledge of the specific probability distribution of $p(t)$, then the floor level $p_0 = \bar{p} - \alpha\sigma(t)$ becomes lower or the perceived price level, $Ep(t) + \alpha\sigma(t)$ becomes higher than the level $\bar{p}$. In either case, the entry would increase more than the case when α is zero.

But if $\sigma^2(t)$ is not independent of $Ep(t)$ e.g. if $\sigma^2(t) = \alpha_1 Ep(t)$, α_1 a positive scalar then the entry equation (1.7) becomes

$$\dot{x}(t) = k\left(Ep(t) - \alpha\left(\alpha_1 Ep(t)\right)^{1/2} - \bar{p} \right) \tag{1.8}$$

where $E[p(t)\,|\,x(t), q(t)] = a_0 - b_1(q(t) + x(t))$. In this case the transformed entry equation becomes highly nonlinear and as such it may have stability properties very different from the linear entry model.

A second way of using the probabilistic inequality (1.6) in the entry equation (1.4) is through expected penalty cost associated with entry. Assuming the penalty cost to be proportioned to $\dot{x}(t)$, it may be expressed as:

$$\dot{x}(t) = \begin{cases} k_1(p(t) - \bar{p}), & \text{if} \quad p(t) > \bar{p} \\ k_2(\bar{p} - p(t)), & \text{if} \quad p(t) \leqslant \bar{p} \end{cases} \tag{1.9}$$

where k_1, k_2 are nonnegative constants. The expected penalty costs expressed in terms of $E[\dot{x}(t)]$ then reduce to

$$E[\dot{x}(t)] = k_1 \int_{\bar{p}}^{\infty} (p(t) - \bar{p})g(p)\mathrm{d}p + k_2 \int_0^{\bar{p}} (\bar{p} - p(t))g(p)\mathrm{d}p$$

where $g(p)\mathrm{d}p$ is the probability density function of $p(t) = p$, and a nonnegative domain for $p(t)$ is presumed. Since entry in (1.9) is viewed as penalty cost by the dominant firm, the level of the floor price $\bar{p}$, which is also called the limit price (Gaskins 1971) becomes a decision variable to be optimally determined. Like advertisement expenditure, it has a dual role. On the one hand, the higher the level of $\bar{p}$ (the floor price), the lower the entry probability (since the gap $(p(t) - \bar{p})$ is lower); on the other hand, the higher $\bar{p}$ implies increased adjustment cost, due to the market price $p(t)$ falling below $\bar{p}$. Although the optimal value of the limit price $\bar{p}$ has to be determined in terms of the overall profit objective of the dominant firm, its role in minimizing expected entry, $E[\dot{x}(t)]$ may be easily calculated e.g. the value $\bar{p}^*$ of $\bar{p}$ which minimizes $E[\dot{x}(t)]$ is given by

$$G(\bar{p}^*) = \int_0^{\bar{p}^*} g(p)\mathrm{d}p = \frac{k_1}{k_1 + k_2}$$

or

$$\bar{p}^* = G^{-1}(k_0), \quad k_0 = k_1(k_1 + k_2)^{-1}$$

provided this level of $\bar{p}^*$ covers at least the marginal cost of production. This result has several implications. First, the higher the value of the entry coefficient k_1 in (1.9), the lower the optimal limit price $\bar{p}^*$. Likewise, the higher the value of the exit (i.e. negative entry) coefficient k_2 in (1.9), the lower the optimal limit price. Since a dominant cartel may charge temporarily a limit price below its marginal cost of production in order to force exit by other smaller units, the rationale of optimal $\bar{p}^*$ is apparent. Second, net entry is viewed here as the average of positive entry and exit (i.e. negative entry). Hence, if exit is more desirable by the dominant cartel, it may put a low value to the coefficient k_2 and thereby select a very low value of the limit price $\bar{p}^*$. A policy of balancing the loss from positive entry against the gain from exit may also be worked out in this framework.

Defining short run profits of the dominant firm by $\pi(t) = (p(t) - c)q(t)$, where c is constant marginal cost, the objective function may be viewed as the maximization of expected profits over a given horizon i.e.

$$\max V = E \int_0^T \pi(t)\mathrm{d}t \tag{2.1}$$

subject to (1.7) or (1.9)

When the horizon is long i.e. T is infinite, we may have to discount future profits, so that $\pi(t)$ above would be replaced by $e^{-rt}\pi(t)$, where r is the positive rate of discount. Also, the effect of market growth may have to be incorporated in the demand and entry equations.

For a short horizon, though, the profit function V in (2.1) may be reasonably appropriate. In this framework it is useful to compare the implications of stochastic entry as against deterministic ones.

Consider first the deterministic model

$$\max V = \int_0^T [a - b_1(q(t) + x(t)) - c]q(t)\mathrm{d}t$$

subject to

$$\dot{x}(t) = k(p(t) - \bar{p}), \quad p(t) \geqslant \bar{p}, \quad k > 0$$

$$p(t) = a - b_1(q(t) + x(t))$$

where the limit price $\bar{p}$ is determined exogenously. Using $z(t)$ as the adjoint variable and applying the maximum principle, one obtains the optimal trajectory defined by

$$\dot{y}(t) = Ay(t) + \alpha \tag{2.2}$$

where $y'(t) = (z(t)\, x(t))$, α is a vector of constants and the coefficient matrix A is

$$A = \begin{pmatrix} \dfrac{bk}{2} & -\dfrac{b}{2} \\[2ex] \dfrac{bk^2}{2} & -\dfrac{bk}{2} \end{pmatrix}$$

since A is singular, the two eigenvalues are zero and $z(t)$ and $x(t)$ are not independent. It is easy to check that $z(t) = x(t)/k$. Hence the optimal outputs $q(t)$, $x(t)$ of the dominant firm and the entrant are dependent. The optimal quantities, denoted by asterisks turn out to be

$$q^* = (2b_1)^{-1}(a - c) - x^*$$

$$p^* = \tfrac{1}{2}(a + c) - 2b_1 x^* \tag{2.3}$$

$$\pi^* = \frac{(a-c)^2}{4b_1} + 2b_1 x^{*2} - \tfrac{3}{2}(a - c)x^*$$

On the other hand, if the dominant firm ignored the entry equation $\dot{x}(t) = k(p(t) - \bar{p})$ altogether and maximized profits $\pi(t)$ for each time point t, the myopic optimal output and price would be

$$q_M^* = (2b_1)^{-1}(a - c) - \tfrac{1}{2}x_M^*$$

$$p_M^* = \tfrac{1}{2}(a + c) - \tfrac{1}{2}b_1 x_M^* \tag{2.4}$$

$$\pi_M^* = \frac{(a-c)^2}{4b} + \tfrac{1}{4}b_1 x_M^{*2} - \tfrac{1}{2}(a - c)x_M^*$$

Thus, for any forecast $\hat{x}$, the optimal q^* and p^* of the limit price model are lower than the corresponding quantities q_M^*, p_M^* of the myopic model. Also, for large $\hat{x}$, we have higher profits in the limit pricing model.

The impact of uncertainty, either through the error term $u(t)$ in the demand function (1.5) or through the probabilistic entry (1.7) may now be easily evaluated. First of all, this uncertainty may reduce q^* and p^* further due to the risk averse attitude of the dominant firm. Normally, an increase in risk aversion tends to increase price but here it tends to reduce the price as an entry-preventing strategy. Second, the optimal trajectory defined in (2.2) implies that the limit price equals marginal cost i.e. $\bar{p} = c$, whereas in the myopic or monopoly model (2.4) there is no limit price of course. The floor price to which p_M^* may tend to would of course be higher than the limit price, since $p_M^* > p^*$ for any positive value of $\hat{x}$. Third, any error variance in forecasting the entrant's output x would have greater impact an outputs and prices of the limit pricing model. Hence, forecasting and learning are more important for the dominant firm facing uncertain entry. The impact of uncertainty on the variability of short run profits needs however a separate treatment, since it may run counter to the price-reducing effect of uncertain entry.

3. A model of risk aversion

We now propose a dynamic model which allows for risk aversion in the optimization process, along with market growth and discounting of long run profits in the future. The market function now takes the form:

$$p(t) = ae^{nt} - b_1(q(t) + x(t)) + u \tag{3.1}$$

where u is the additive disturbance term with zero mean and constant variance v and the first term on the right-hand side indicates market growth with a proportional rate of growth n which is assumed positive. Since the stochastic component u is assumed to be independently distributed, expected profits $E\pi(t)$ and its variance $\text{var}(\pi(t))$ are:

$$\begin{aligned} E\pi(t) &= [Ep(t) - c]q(t) \\ \text{var } \pi(t) &= vq^2(t) \end{aligned} \tag{3.2}$$

where c is the average total cost of production of the dominant firm, assumed to be constant over time and $q(t)$ is output at time t. By taking a linear combination of expected profits and its variability, the net payoff may be denoted by a present value function

$$V = \int_0^\infty e^{-rt} \big[(ae^{nt} - b_1 q(t) - b_1 x(t) - c)q(t) - mvq^2(t) \big] dt$$

$$= \int_0^\infty e^{-rt} \big[ae^{nt} - b_1 x(t) - b_2 q(t) - c \big] q(t) dt \tag{3.3}$$

where r is the dominant firm's discount rate assumed exogenous, $b_2 = mv + b_1$, where m is a nonnegative constant reflecting risk aversion. The dominant firm thus attempts to maximize V, the net expected payoff, subject to the conditions of entry. The rate of entry of rival producers $x(t)$ is assumed to be determined by their expected rate of return; hence if potential rivals view current output price as a proxy for future price, the rate of entry $\bar{x}(t)$ will be a nondecreasing function of current price. Assuming linearity, the response function of rival entrants would appear as

$$\dot{x}(t) = k\left[ae^{nt} - b_1 q(t) - b_1 x(t) - \bar{p}\right]$$

$$x(0) = x_0, \quad \bar{p} \geq c$$

where $\bar{p}$ is the limit price, x_0 is the initial output of the rival producers and k is a positive response coefficient. The limit price is defined here to be that price level at which net entry is zero, i.e. whenever current expected price $Ep(t)$ exceeds $\bar{p}$, there is some positive entry of rival firms.

Some authors predict a decline in the limit price when total market demand is growing, since they assume a constant price elasticity of demand at the given price. Our model does not make this assumption and hence market growth does not reduce the limit price and hence the limit price is assumed to be the constant without any loss of generality.

The optimal output strategy of the dominant firm is thereby obtained by maximizing net payoff V subject to the restrictions of entry specified by (3.4). It is clear that the dominant firm must make strategic output decisions which measure the trade-off between short-run gains today from a high monopoly price against some loss of market share in the future due to additional entry. Although the entry behavior of rivals indicated by the differential equation in (3.4) is quite standard in limit pricing theory, an explanation of the response coefficient k may be useful here. It reflects in some sense the unwillingness of the dominant firm to give the newcomers any part of the market, thus implying a strong tendency towards output maintenance; it is this output maintenance which partly discourages entry and partly reflects the added cost of idle capacity if the dominant firm were to make room for an entrant. The potential entrants' response coefficient k measures the impact of output maintenance by the dominant firm. The limits of k are $0 < k < 1$ and within this limit, the larger the value of k, the greater the risk of failure for a potential entrant.

Using control–theoretic models we introduce the Hamiltonian function H as:

$$e^{-rt}H = e^{-rt}\left[\left(ae^{nt} - b_1 x(t) - b_2 q(t) - c\right)q(t)\right.$$

$$\left. + kz(t)\left(ae^{nt} - b_1 x(t) - b_1 q(t) - \bar{p}\right)\right] \tag{3.5}$$

where $z(t)$ is the adjoint variable which may be suitably interpreted as the optimal shadow price of new entry to the dominant firm. The optimal output strategy must then satisfy the following necessary conditions:

$$\dot{x}^*(t) = k\left(ae^{nt} - b_1 x^*(t) - b_1 q^*(t) - \bar{p}\right) \tag{3.6.1}$$

$$\dot{z}^*(t) = -\frac{\delta H(x^*, z^*, q^*)}{\delta x^*(t)} + rz^*(t) \tag{3.6.2}$$

$$\lim_{t \to \infty} z^*(t) = 0 \tag{3.6.3}$$

$$\frac{\delta H(x^*, z^*, q^*)}{\delta q^*(t)} = 0 \tag{3.6.4}$$

where the asterisk denotes variables along the optimal trajectory and the Hamiltonian on this trajectory is denoted by $H(x^*, z^*, q^*)$ to indicate its dependence on $x^*(t)$, $z^*(t)$, $q^*(t)$ and t. Since the instantaneous payoff function is a smooth concave function of the dominant firm's output, it is easily shown that the above necessary conditions are also sufficient.

On using the following transformations

$$x(t) = \tilde{x}(t) \, e^{nt}, \quad q(t) = \tilde{q}(t) \, e^{nt}, \quad z(t) = \tilde{z}(t) \, e^{nt} \tag{3.7}$$

We obtain the following two linear differential equations

$$\dot{x}^*(t) = -\left(kb_1 + n - \frac{kb_1^2}{2b_2}\right)\tilde{x}^*(t) + \frac{k^2 b_1^2}{2b_2}\tilde{z}^*(t) + A_1(t) \tag{3.8}$$

where

$$A_1(t) = ka - \frac{ab_1 k}{2b_2} - e^{-nt}\left(\bar{p} + \frac{kb_1 c}{2b_2}\right)$$

$$\dot{\tilde{z}}^*(t) = -\frac{b_1^2}{2b_2}\tilde{x}^*(t) + \left(kb_1 + r - n - \frac{kb_1^2}{2b_2}\right)\tilde{z}(t) + A_2(t) \tag{3.9}$$

where

$$A_2(t) = \frac{ab_1 - cb_1 \, e^{-nt}}{2b_2}$$

Taking the homogeneous parts of these two differential equations, we find the characteristic equations as follows:

$$f(\lambda) = \lambda^2 + (2n - 4)\lambda + \left(n^2 - nr - b_1 kr - b_1^2 k^2 + \frac{rb_1^2 k}{2b_2} + \frac{b_1^3 k^2}{b_2} \right) = 0$$

(3.10)

The two roots are

$$\lambda_1 = -\left(n - \tfrac{1}{2}r\right) + \tfrac{1}{2}\sqrt{a_0}$$
$$\lambda_2 = -\left(n - \tfrac{1}{2}r\right) - \tfrac{1}{2}\sqrt{a_0}$$

(3.11)

where

$$a_0 = 4\left(b_1 kr + b_1^2 k^2 - \frac{kb_1^2 r}{2b_2} - \frac{k^2 b_1^3}{b_2} \right) + r^2$$

Two special cases of the characteristic equation (3.10) may be noted here. First, if there were no risk aversion motive by the dominant fim so that m is zero, i.e. $b_1 = b_2 = b$ say, then the two roots become

$$\lambda_1, \lambda_2 = -\left(n - \tfrac{1}{2}r\right) \pm \tfrac{1}{2}\left(r^2 + 2bkr\right)^{1/2}$$

(3.12)

Since the parameters b, k, r are positive, the optimal trajectory in this case is non-oscillatory and the two roots will be negative if it holds that

$$n > \tfrac{1}{2}r \quad \text{and} \quad n - \tfrac{1}{2}r > \tfrac{1}{2}\left(r^2 + 2bkr\right)^{1/2}$$

(3.13)

Second, if there are no discounting of future profit streams so that $r = 0$ along with $m = 0$ and the necessary conditions (6.1) through (6.3) hold, then the two characteristic roots become identical and negative

$$\lambda_1 = \lambda_2 = -n, \quad n > 0$$

(3.14)

Third, if r and n are both zero, we have $\lambda_1 = \lambda_2 = 0$. However, we should note that conditions such as (3.13) and (3.14) are necessary but not sufficient for convergence to the steady-state. This is so due to the nonhomogeneous terms denoted by $A_1(t)$, $A_2(t)$ in (3.8) and (3.9). Also, even if one of the two roots is positive, e.g.,

$$n > \tfrac{1}{2}r \quad \text{and} \quad n - \tfrac{1}{2}r < \tfrac{1}{2}\left(r^2 + 2bkr\right)^{1/2}$$

(3.15)

when $\lambda_1 < 0$, $\lambda_2 > 0$, the transversality condition (3.6.3) implies that the explosive tendency due to the positive root would be ineffective.

From an applied viewpoint, however, the case (3.12) and (3.13) which preserve conditions of weak convergence to the steady state, provided the nonhomogenous terms are not explosive are the most interesting. By simulation the characteristics of the asymptotic convergence to a steady-state equilibrium may be explicitly determined in this case to show the average time to convergence, their dependence on parameter values and the sensitivity of the four variables: $\tilde{x}(t)$, $\tilde{q}(t)$, $\tilde{z}(t)$, $\tilde{p}(t)$.

In all these cases, the parameter values are so chosen as to satisfy the necessary condition (3.13) of stability without oscillation, the time units are arbitrary and the iterative process of convergence is terminated within 0.01 of the steady state values. Some general characteristics appear very clearly in these model simulations. First, the time to converge to the steady state depends very critically on the assumed initial values of $\tilde{x}^*(t)$, $\tilde{z}^*(t)$ and also the extent by which the absolute value of $(n - \frac{1}{2}r)$ exceeds that of $\frac{1}{2}(r^2 + 2bkr)^{1/2}$. Thus as the initial value of $\tilde{z}^*(t)$ is raised to its value at or near the steady state, the time to convergence is greatly reduced. Similarly, if n is increased to make the absolute value of $(n - \frac{1}{2}r)$ greater than that of $|\frac{1}{2}(r^2 + 2bkr)^{1/2}|$, the faster becomes the convergence to the steady state. Second, the optimal output behavior shows that a variety of phases are possible in the optimal strategy space of the dominant firm, for which output decisions continuously change in response to market growth and the continual threat of entry. The dominant firm can in the long run increase, maintain or reduce its output when the market is growing. The simulated profiles show indeed that in cases where there is a positive market growth, output maintenance loses much of its significance as a means of detering entry. However, the dominant firm can deter entry in spite of market growth by increasing its output capacity through additional investment. Third, the optimal output and price variables are more sensitive to variations in rivals' response coefficient than market growth. Since the response coefficient k indicates the strength of potential entry decisions, whereas market growth depends on timing, the output and pricing policy are found to be much more sensitive to variations in strength parameter but not so much to the variations in the timing parameter. Also, this result is at variance with Gaskins' model where the entry response coefficient is assumed to grow according to an exponential function of time.

Furthermore, it is not difficult to show that the optimal output level $q^*(t)$ will always be above the short run payoff maximizing output $\hat{q}$ at every point along the optimal trajectory. Assuming that the dominant firm has been moving along the optimal trajectory, the short-run payoff is

$$h(q) = \left(ae^{nt} - b_1 x^*(t) - b_2 q(t) - c \right) q(t) \tag{3.17}$$

where $x^*(t)$ denotes that $x(t)$ is one the optimal path. Maximizing this short-run payoff $h(q)$ leads to the myopic optimal output rule $\hat{q}(t)$:

$$\hat{q}(t) = (2s)^{-1}\left[\frac{ae^{nt} - c}{b_1} - x(t)\right]$$ (3.18)

where $b_2 = sb_1$, $s \geqslant 1$. The long run optimal output level $q^*(t)$, on the other hand must satisfy the condition (3.6.3) i.e. maximization of the hamiltonian H at every point on the optimal path. This leads to

$$q^*(t) = (2s)^{-1}\left[\frac{ae^{nt} - c}{b_1} - x^*(t) - kz^*(t)\right]$$ (3.19)

where $z^*(t)$ the shadow price of the additional rival entry is necessarily negative. Since the short run payoff $h(q)$ is a smooth concave function by assumption, we have its second derivative negative at $\hat{q}(t)$. Hence by comparing (3.18) and (3.19) it follows that $q^*(t) > \hat{q}(t)$. Further, the effect of increased risk aversion is to reduce the value of optimal myopic and long run optimal outputs, i.e.

$$\delta\hat{q}(t)/\delta s < 0, \quad \delta q^*(t)/\delta s < 0$$ (3.20)

Since prices are inversely related to output, it would also follow

$$\delta\hat{p}(t)/\delta s > 0 \quad \text{and} \quad \delta p^*(t)/\delta s > 0$$

and

$$\hat{p}(t) > p^*(t)$$

where $\hat{p}(t)$, $p^*(t)$ are myopic and long run optimal prices respectively.

Besides reducing optimal output, increased risk aversion may lead to two other effects. First, the coefficient $b_2 = sb_1$ may rise in the positive domain, thus raising the positive value of a_0 in (3.11), so that one of the roots in (3.11) becomes positive, i.e. $\lambda_1 > 0$, $\lambda_2 < 0$. In this case the general solution of (3.8), (3.9) would appear as

$$\tilde{x}^*(t) = C_1 e^{\lambda_1 t} + C_2 e^{\lambda_2 t} + \alpha_0(t)$$

$$\tilde{z}^*(t) = \alpha_1 C_1 e^{\lambda_1 t} + \alpha_2 C_2 e^{\lambda_2 t} + \alpha_3(t)$$

where the $\alpha_i s$ are known functions of the given parameters of the problem, C_i are suitable functions determined by the boundary conditions by the well-known method of variation of parameters. Now since λ_1

is positive, the transversality condition (3.6.3) cannot be fulfilled unless C_1 is zero and $\alpha_3(t)$ is bounded as $t \to \infty$. Hence we get the following reduced system, in case of apparent instability due to a positive characteristic root:

$$\tilde{x}^*(t) = C_2\, e^{\lambda_2 t} + \alpha_0(t)$$
$$\tilde{z}^*(t) = \alpha_2\, e^{\lambda_2 t} + \alpha_3(t) \tag{3.21}$$

where $\alpha_0(t)$, $\alpha_3(t)$ tend to suitable constants as $t \to \infty$. however, since $\delta a_0/\delta s$ is positive, increased risk aversion leads to a higher absolute value of λ_2 which is negative. This increases the rate of convergence, i.e. the time to converge to the steady state is shorter.

A second way to analyze the system (3.6) is to eliminate $z^*(t)$ and obtain a reduced form system in terms of $\tilde{x}^*(t)$, $\tilde{z}^*(t)$ as follows:

$$\dot{\tilde{x}}^*(t) = -(kb_1 + n)\tilde{x}^*(t) - kb_1\tilde{q}^*(t) + (ka - \bar{p}\, e^{-nt})$$

$$\dot{\tilde{q}}^*(t) = \left(\frac{2kb_1^2 + rb_1}{2b_2}\right)\tilde{x}^*(t) + \left(b_1 k + r - n + \frac{kb_1^2}{2b_2}\right)\tilde{q}^*(t) + A(t)$$

where

$$A(t) = \frac{n - r - b_1 k}{2b_2}(a - ce^{-nt}) - (2b_2)^{-1}\left[kb_1^2 - kab_1 + b_1\bar{p}\, e^{-nt}\right]$$

These cases may be interpreted as the optimal Cournot–Nash type reaction curves of the dominant firm and the potential rivals in differential form. It follows that

$$\frac{\delta\dot{\tilde{x}}(t)}{\delta\tilde{q}^*(t)} = -kb_1 < 0,$$

$$\frac{\delta\dot{\tilde{q}}(t)}{\delta\tilde{x}^*(t)} = b_1 k + r - n + \frac{kb_1^2}{2b_2} > 0$$

whereas in the steady state $\tilde{x}^*$, $\tilde{q}^*$, when $\dot{\tilde{x}}^*(t) = 0 = \dot{\tilde{q}}^*(t)$, we have

$$\frac{\partial\tilde{x}^*}{\delta\tilde{q}^*} < 0 \quad \text{and} \quad \delta\tilde{q}^*/\delta\tilde{x}^* < 0$$

The effect of increased risk aversion at the steady state, much like the increase in market growth, would tend to increase the response of output

$\tilde{q}^*$ following from an increase in $\tilde{x}^*$. Hence, starting in the neighborhood of the steady state $\tilde{x}^*$, $\tilde{q}^*$ and provided the latter is on the optimal trajectory, the rate of convergence to the optimal steady state would be faster, if risk aversion is higher.

If the conditions of dynamic stability are satisfied around the optimal trajectory equations defined by (3.6), then the steady state values of outputs $\tilde{z}^*$, $\tilde{x}^*$ and the adjoint variable $\tilde{z}$ can be computed and using these, the steady state market share $\tilde{S}^*$ and the price $\tilde{p}^*$ may be derived as follows:

$$\tilde{S}^* = \tilde{q}^*(\tilde{q}^* + \tilde{x}^*)^{-1} = (nr - n^2 + bkn)(nr - n^2 + bkr)^{-1}$$

$$\tilde{p}^* = (anr - an^2)(bkr + 2nr - 2n^2)^{-1}$$

then the following comparative static results hold
  (i) $\delta\tilde{S}^*/\delta n > 0$
  (ii) $\delta\tilde{S}^*/\delta k < 0$
  (iii) $\delta\tilde{S}^*/\delta b < 0$
  (iv) $\delta\tilde{S}^*/\delta r < 0$
  (v) $\delta\tilde{p}^*/\delta n < 0$, if $n > \frac{1}{2}r$
  (vi) $\delta\tilde{p}^*/\delta k > 0$, if $n > r$
  (vii) $\delta\tilde{p}^*/\delta r > 0$

These results are self-explanatory. Results (i) and (v) show that with an increase in market size, the dominant firm will tend to increase its market share and the market price will decline. The first result is consistent with Gaskins' model referred to earlier. Likewise it could be shown that at steady-state equilibrium an increase in risk aversion would tend to increase the optimal price and reduce the market share. Results (ii) and (vi) show that an increase in the entry response coefficient reduces the market share and increases the price in steady state equilibrium. This result differs from that of Gaskins' model, which predicts a positive relationship between changes in the market share of the dominant firm and changes in the response coefficient of potential entrants.

Result (iii) implies that the changes in the dominant firm's market share is positively related to changes in the price elasticity of demand, whereas the slope of the inverse demand function is inversely related to the price elasticity of demand. Thus, if uncertainty in demand involves randomness in the parameter b, the dominant firm would react in the steady state as if its market share declined.

4. Application to the U.S. computer industry

In this section we describe an econometric application of the limit pricing model in a simplified version of discrete-time framework. The empirical details and simulation results are reported elsewhere (Sengupta et al. 1981).

For the U.S. computer industry, perhaps the first systematic application of Gaskins-type limit pricing model is by Brock (1975), who estimated a demand equation from yearly data over 1956–65 and an entry coefficient k defined in (3.4) from two observations of IBM's market share in 1963 and 1965. The optimal price and output profiles of IBM as the dominant firm were then simulated for the next 100 years from 1956 through 2056. In the specification and estimation, our application has several significant features which constitute marked improvement over Brock's method. First of all, our data sources are much more disaggregated, improved and the quantity and price variables are adjusted for quality and technical changes by the use of hedonic price indices. Second, the demand and entry equations are estimated both by ordinary least squares and two-stage least squares on the basis of currently available disaggregated quarterly data for 1963IV through 1969I. Third, the suitability of the limit pricing model with IBM as the dominant firm and the composite rival consisting of Burroughs, Control Data, Honeywell, Na-

Table 1
Simulation of optimal trajectories

Time	$\bar{x}^*(t)$	$|\bar{z}^*(t)|$	$\bar{q}^*(t)$	$\bar{p}^*(t)$
0.0	1.0	5.19	140.0	5.51
10.0	10.3	68.2	144.0	5.36
20.0	15.9	111.0	139.0	5.34
30.0	19.3	158.0	134.0	5.41
40.0	21.5	204.0	129.0	5.50
50.0	23.0	249.0	123.0	5.62
60.0	24.2	282.0	117.0	5.75
70.0	25.1	335.0	112.0	5.89
80.0	26.0	377.0	106.0	6.03
90.0	26.7	418.0	101.0	6.17
100.0	27.4	458.0	95.6	6.31
110.0	28.1	498.0	90.3	6.45
120.0	28.8	538.0	85.1	6.59
130.0	29.4	576.0	79.9	6.72
140.0	30.0	614.0	74.8	6.85
150.0	30.6	652.0	69.8	6.99
160.0	31.2	689.0	64.9	7.11
170.0	31.8	725.0	60.1	7.24
180.0	32.4	761.0	55.3	7.37
190.0	33.0	797.0	50.6	7.49
200.0	33.6	831.0	45.9	7.61

Note: Parameters are: $\bar{x}^*(0) = 1.00$, $b = 0.03$, $k = 0.25$, $c = 1.0$, $r = 0.15$, $\bar{p} = 2.0$, $a = 10.0$, $n = 0.055$ Time step size = 10 units, no. of steps = 21, $|\bar{z}^*(t)|$ is the absolute value.

Table 2
Simulation of optimal trajectories

Time	$\tilde{x}^*(t)$	$|\tilde{z}^*(t)|$	$\tilde{q}^*(t)$	$\tilde{p}^*(t)$
0.0	1.00	1.79	149.0	5.49
10.0	8.24	86.4	150.0	5.27
20.0	10.0	107.0	146.0	5.30
30.0	12.2	155.0	140.0	5.47
40.0	12.8	203.0	135.0	5.58
50.0	13.4	251.0	129.0	5.74
60.0	13.4	298.0	122.0	5.91
70.0	14.2	345.0	116.0	6.08
80.0	14.6	392.0	110.0	6.25
90.0	15.0	439.0	104.0	6.42
100.0	15.4	485.0	98.3	6.59
110.0	15.9	532.0	92.3	6.76
120.0	16.3	578,0	86.3	6.92
130.0	16.7	624.0	80.3	7.09
140.0	17.1	670.0	74.4	7.26
150.0	17.5	716.0	68.5	7.42
160.0	17.9	761.0	62.6	7.59
170.0	18.3	806.0	56.7	7.75
180.0	18.6	852.0	50.9	7.91
180.0	19.0	807.0	45.1	8.08
200.0	19.4	941.0	39.3	8.24

Note: Parameters are: $\tilde{x}^*(0) = 1.00$, $b = 0.03$, $k = 0.25$, $c = 1.0$, $r = 0.10$, $\bar{p} = 2.0$, $a = 10.0$, $n = 0.104$, Time step size = 10 units, no. of steps = 21, $|\tilde{z}^*(t)|$ is the absolute value.

Table 3
Regression estimates of demand for computers (Models I and II)

Data and Sample	Dependent variable	Constant	Independent regressors			R^2	DW
			Price	Other I	variables II		
Chow [a] n-11	$\log r$	2.950	− 0.3637 * (2.11)	− 0.2526 * (3.42)	...	0.83	1.77
Brock [a] $n = 10$	$\log r$	9.225	− 1.44 [b]	...	0.147 * (6.08)	0.82	...
Quarterly Sample I $n = 18$	$x + q$	...	− 0.15 * (2.38)	1.00 * (4.62)	...	0.80	2.04
Quarterly Sample II	$x + q$	48098 (11.67)	− 0.26 * (5.33)	...	1.06 * (10.95)	0.88	1.72

Note: 1. a. Price as independent variable is taken in logarithmic form.
  b. Brock used this figure from Chow's estimate and took the dependent variable as $(\log r + 1.44 \log p)$; r denotes rental values.
2. The other variables were: $\log r(t-1)$ for Chow, time t for Brock, proxy variable R_1 for quarterly I estimate and proxy variable R_2 for Quarterly II estimate.
3. r denotes demand in rental value terms.
* denotes significant at 5% level of t-test and DW is Dubin–Watson statistic.

tional Cash Register, Sperry Rand, SDS, General Electric and RCA. Fourth, the quality adjustment was made on the basis of index numbers constructed from quality data in terms of three main characteristics: speed of multiplication, memory size and access speed.

The final form of our quarterly model is taken as follows:

demand: $p(t) = a - b(x(t) + q(t)) + \beta R_i(t), \quad i = 1, 2$

supply: $x(t+1) - x(t) = k(p(t) - \bar{p}) + hR(t)$ \hfill (4.1)

profit: $\pi(t) = (p(t) - c)q(t)$

objective function: $\max_{q(t)} \sum_{t=1}^{T} \pi(t), \quad T$ fixed

Here the exogenous variables are R_i and R denoting inventory and national income and other variables which capture the external environment of the computer industry. The critical parameters are the demand coefficient b, the market penetration (or pseudo-entry) coefficient k and the time horizon T. The estimates of b and k are given in tables 3 and 4

Table 4
Regression and other estimates of rival market penetration in computer industry (Models I and II)

Data and Sample		Dependent variable	Constant	Independent variables		R^2
				Price	Others	
Brock's [a] estimate	1963 and 1965	m	–	0.03	–	
Quarterly [b] Sample I	simultaneous equations	δm	–	0.019 * (8.00)	income proxy and final sales	0.93
Quarterly Sample II	single equation estimate (OLS)	δm	–	0.014 * (2.07)	0.054 (0.76)	0.94
Quarterly Sample III [c]	OLS	δm	142	0.011	0.12 (0.90)	0.92

Note: 1. a. Brock's estimate was not based on any econometric estimation method; he applied an integral equation for two years 1963 and 1965 to estimate the market penetration coefficient 0.03.

　　b. Quarterly estimate I was based on two linear simultaneous equations where two proxy variables for total industry income and final sales were used for identifying the demand–supply equations. For quarterly estimate II an index of expenses was used as explanatory variable.

　　c. Quarterly estimate III was based on single equation regression where lagged inventory of the rival was used as an explanatory variable.

　2. Asterisk denotes significance at 5% level of t-test and δ is a (0,1) dummy variable.

Table 5
Myopic decision rule trajectories (Model III)

x_A	x_O	q_O	q_M	p_O	p_M	Πx_A	Πx_O	Πq_O	Πq_m
386	386	2355	2355	27578	27578	6.01	6.01	36.69	36.39
778	397	2434	2287	28100	27211	11.83	6.39	39.19	34.79
703	413	2514	1786	28630	23881	8.35	6.87	41.81	21.22
1162	429	2597	2614	29179	29386	20.20	7.37	44.61	45.45
845	446	2681	2852	29734	30967	16.03	7.91	47.54	54.09
845	463	2768	2853	30309	20971	16.03	8.48	50.68	54.12
810	481	2857	1511	30897	22046	8.14	9.09	53.99	15.18
510	500	2937	2329	31561	27487	7.90	9.78	57.45	36.07

	Variables					
	x_A	x_O	q_O	q_M	p_O	p_M
Mean	755	439	2643	2323	29498	27441
Std. Dev.	234	40	205	477	1385	3174
Coeff of Variation	31	9	8	21	5	12
Expected loss for $q = 2462.06$;						
for $x = 323.75$; MSE $(q_M, q_O) = 956,639$						

Note: 1. Subscripts A, M, O denote actual, myopic and optimal series for dominant firm output (q), rival output (x), their profits Π and the industry price p.
2. Trajectories are computed from a selected benchmark point at which the actual and the optimal quantity series are most close.

and the time horizon T is parametrically varied to analyze its impact. The values of $b = 0.15$ and $k = 0.011$ are taken as most plausible from our econometric estimates and these are used to compute and compare optimal trajectories with other series. The demand slope coefficient b had an alternative estimate $b = 0.26$, which was used in the simulation Model II. The market penetration coefficient k was also estimated by methods other than ordinary single–equation least squares. The lowest value obtained was 0.0008. This can be compared with brock's calculation via an integral equation; values from his model range from $+0.01$ to -0.005 on a quarterly basis.

The above linear model (4.1) is solved by dynamic programming algorithms by setting up a series of maximizations, where the time horizon T is varied. The results of comparison of the optimal trajectory and the myopic decision (static, one period or two-period), which are reported partly in Tables 5 and 6 show a number of interesting results: [1]
(a) The optimal trajectories of price and output are much more stable in terms of the coefficient of variation than the myopic series; further,

[1] For reasons of space, tables on simulated profiles are not reproduced here. All statistical tables not reproduced here are available from the authors upon request.

profits associated with the optimal trajectory are significantly higher for T exceeding 5

(b) Compared to myopic one period forward (Table 6) and myopic 2-period forward rules (not reproduced in tables here), the optimal trajectory performs much better on the average for $T > 5$, in terms of expected profits and stability measured by the coefficient of variation

(c) Market shares predicted by the optimal series in our quarterly model are on the average better than Brock's, for the years 1963–67 which are common to both models

(d) The stability of the optimal trajectories measured by the coefficient of variation tends to decrease as the time horizon T increases; this implies that the longer the horizon, the greater the probability of fluctuations in the optimal path; also greater becomes the inoptimality of the static short run and myopic decision rules which ignore the

Table 6
Trajectories of optimal vs. myopic I period forward (Model III)

x_A	x_O	q_O	q_M	p_O	p_M	Πx_A	Πx_O	Πq_O	Πq_m
290	290	1853	1853	24260	24260	3.56	3.56	22.72	22.72
1100	301	1920	1796	24700	23941	13.41	3.82	24.38	21.45
707	313	1988	607	25153	16036	2.85	4.12	26.15	2.45
1022	326	2058	1265	25613	20411	8.60	4.44	28.02	10.64
338	339	2130	2169	26089	14425	0.82	4.78	30.01	5.26
386	353	2203	2088	26572	25882	5.36	5.14	32.10	28.99
778	367	2278	2287	27072	27211	11.83	5.53	34.33	34.79
703	382	2355	1787	27578	23884	8.35	5.95	36.69	21.24
1162	397	2434	2614	28100	29386	20.20	6.39	39.19	45.45
422	413	2514	2965	28630	26367	6.06	6.87	41.81	56.97
422	429	2597	2965	29179	26367	6.06	7.37	44.61	56.97
422	446	2681	3965	29734	26367	6.06	7.91	47.54	56.97
422	463	2768	3965	30309	26367	6.06	8.48	50.68	56.97
810	481	2857	1511	30897	22046	8.14	9.09	53.99	15.18
510	500	2937	2329	31561	27487	7.90	9.78	57.45	36.07

	Variables				
	x_A	x_O	q_O	q_M	p_O	p_M
Mean	732	401	2446	2140	28191	25301
Std. Dev.	280	60	310	479	2067	4566
Coeff of Variation	38	15	13	22	7	18

Expected loss for $q = 4247.06$
for $x = 373.77$; MSE $(q_M, q_O) = 1,040,392$

Note: 1. Subscripts A, M, O denote actual, myopic and optimal series for dominant firm output (q), rival output (x), their profits Π and the industry price p.

2. Trajectories are computed from a selected benchmark point at which the actual and the optimal quantity series are most close.

impact of T on long run profits. This pattern was also revealed in the alternative simulated trajectories (not reproduced in tables here). An increase in T tended to increase instability, thus casting some great doubts on the validity of a long-run model for the computer industry; the sensitivity of the market penetration coefficient k is clearly demonstrated by the simulated trajectories. As the value increases from 0.001 to 0.01, rival's production rises much faster and the industry price tend to fall along with the output of the dominant firm. Since IBM's market share has remained steady on or above 65%, a smaller value of the coefficient k is more realistic. Brock's estimate 0.0075 (quarterly) when applied to our model appears to show continuing domination by IBM in the computer market. A set of simulated trajectories of price and output for the parametric values $b = 0.15$, $k = 0.001$, $x(t) \leq 500$ show the net prices and outputs to be continually rising as T gets larger.

Thus, on an overall basis we can conclude the following: the optimal trajectories based on our quarterly econometric estimates differ significantly from the static monopoly and myopic decision rules. They also differ from Brock's optimal profiles in a statistically significant sense. Predictions from our model appear to be significantly better than Brock's in terms of the mean square error.

5. Concluding remarks

It is clear that the limit pricing model here is viewed in terms of the dominant firm alone. With a suitable objective function for the rival entrants, a differential game formulation could be constructed and possibly estimated. One could then compare cooperative and noncooperative solutions to see which type of behavior conforms with the observed patterns in any actual market e.g. computer industry. However for long run applications, an industry where technological innovations are not very rapid may be more appropriate than the computer industry. We are currently developing a model for application to world coffee, where Brazil and Colombia have played a dominant role in the past. The discrete-time version of the generalized model we are using is of the following form

$$\max \quad J = \sum_{t=0}^{N-1} E(1+r)^{-t}\pi(t)$$

$$\text{subject to} \quad y(t+1) = My(t) + N\Delta p(t) + Rw(t)$$

$$y(0) = y_0 \text{ given}$$

where

$$y'(t) = (q(t)p(t)), \quad \Delta p(t) = p(t+1) - p(t)$$

$$Q = \begin{pmatrix} 0 & I \\ I & 0 \end{pmatrix}; \quad \pi(t+1) = p'(t+1)q(t+1) - Cq(t+1)$$

$$M = \begin{pmatrix} A_{11} & A_{12} - C_{12} \\ A_{21} & A_{22} \end{pmatrix}, N = \begin{pmatrix} -(B_1 + B_2) & 0 \\ 0 & R \end{pmatrix}$$

$w(t)$; white noise vector, r: rate of discount

$q(t)$: output vector of the dominant firm

Here the entry equation subsumed in the vector equation for $y(t+1)$ is:

$$x(t+1) = C_{11}x(t) + C_{12}p(t) + B_2\Delta p(t) + \epsilon(t)$$

where $\epsilon(t)$ is the error component. In this model the outputs $q(t)$, $x(t)$ and the prices $p(t)$ may be appropriate vectors, rather than scalars. Similarly the matrices, $\tilde{M}$, N, R may also be time dependent.

Simulated profiles based on the optimal dynamic solution of this type of models are expected to offer valuable tests of the hypothesis that the market power of the dominant suppliers e.g. Brazil and Colombia in world coffee has been significant.

References

Brock, G., The U.S. Computer Industry: A Study of Market Power. Cambridge, Massachusetts: Ballinger Publishing, 1967.

Friedman, J.W., "On entry preventing behavior and limit price models of entry." Applied Game Theory, Wuerzburg: Germany: Physica-Verlag, 1979.

Gaskins, D.W., "Dynamic limit pricing: optimal pricing under threat of entry," J. of Econ. Theor, 3 (1971), 306–322.

Kamien, M.L. and Schwartz, N.L., "Limit pricing and uncertain entry," Econometrica 39, (1971), 441–452.

Sengupta, J.K. and Rifkin, E.J., "Dynamic limit pricing under stochastic demand," Working Paper No. 130, Department of Economics, University of California, Santa Barbara, 1979.

Sengupta, J.K., Leonard, J. and Vanyo, J., "A limit pricing model for U.S. computer industry," Working Paper No. 195, Department of Economics, University of California, Santa Barbara, 1981.

Sengupta, J.K., Decision Models in Stochastic Programming. New York: Elsevier-North Holland, 1982.

11. Game theory models applied to economic systems: their information structure and stability

1. Introduction

Recent applications of game theory models to economic systems have increasingly emphasized the role played by information in microeconomic models of imperfectly competitive markets. This required a more precise description of the demand and supply functions in the market and how signals or messages are processed and conveyed. In contrast to the deterministic models which emphasize a single unchanging price in a static framework, the recent models of markets with imperfect information (Rothschild 1971, Case 1973) have clarified the economic basis of uncertainty which complicates the formulation of the market models and their stability characteristics, e.g., firms have to decide upon the type of information to select, on the frequency of search and on the relative profitability and risk.

We analyze here the role of information, its prior availability and posterior usage in characterizing specific solutions of a class of noncooperative games arising in many applied economic situations. An example is provided by the Cournot model, where there are two suppliers in a market, with demand parameters not completely known. Strategy in this case involves choosing output levels which are in some sense the best for each player. For instance, Cournot–Nash equilibrium solutions define such a class of strategies. Assume that x_1^*, x_2^* denote such a pair of strategies in a Cournot market. However, at any point t of the play, strategies $x_1(t)$, $x_2(t)$ are chosen, based on each player's available information about the state of the demand, about the subjective estimate of the rival's moves and about his own experience of the past history of the play if available. At the next point, $t + 1$ of the play, some of the earlier estimates may be revised in favor of posterior estimates. If the sequential process of information processing by each player is such that $x_1(t) \rightarrow x_1^*$, $x_2(t) \rightarrow x_2^*$, where (x_1^*, x_2^*) is a Cournot–Nash equilibrium point mutually acceptable, then it may be called stabilizing or adaptive, since it helps them converge to the equilibrium solution. It is clear that in many situations the informational process may not be so stabilizing in nature. This is due mainly to three specific factors present in the problem, e.g., (1) knowledge about the unknown stochastic component of the state of nature, i.e., market demand may be very inadequate, (2) the subjective estimates of one player about his opponent's mixed strategies and the associated probability distribution may be revised in ways which may not be favorable to mutual convergence and (3) there may be definite costs associated with search or the trial and error process.

In addition to the above, some additional problem would arise, if the number of players in the above game is increased to N, $N > 2$, e.g., problems of forming coalition of different orders and its stability. However, we would not consider the coalition problems; instead we would examine the team decision problem as an N-player game, where the members may or may not share some common information, e.g., information about the market demand parameters. The role of partial sharing of an information pool or some form of limited cooperation among members of a team as regards common information may then be explicitly shown and its stabilizing or destabilizing characteristics analyzed.

Using static and differential games of the non-cooperative form the above three aspects of the informational process will be illustrated here through applied economic models and their implications analyzed.

2. Information Processing in Cournot–type Models

The duopoly market model of Cournot (Case 1973, Bylka and Komar 1973, Sengupta 1978a) which has been applied in several fields, e.g., ecology provides, in the static case, perhaps the simplest example of the role of information usage in reaching or converging towards an equilibrium solution.

Consider the case of one good with a linear demand function,

$$p = b_0 - b(x_1 + x_2) \tag{1.1}$$

where each duopolist maximizes his own profit function

$$L_i(x_1, x_2) = px_i - c_i x_i - c_0 \quad i = 1, 2 \tag{1.2}$$

subject of course to the condition that at the above price the market clears, i.e., satisfies the total demand (Levitan and Shubik 1971). Ignoring the market clearing condition of equilibrium for the moment, the optimal reaction curves $R_i = R_i(x_1, x_2)$ for each player, assuming he maximizes his own profit with other's output as a given parameter are given by

$$R_1: \quad x_1 = k_{10} - k_1 x_2; \quad k_{10} = \frac{b_0 - c_1}{2b}, \quad k_1 = \tfrac{1}{2}$$

$$R_2: \quad x_2 = k_{20} - k_2 x_1; \quad k_{20} = \frac{b_0 - c_2}{2b}, \quad k_2 = \tfrac{1}{2}$$

(1.3)

Let (x_1^*, x_2^*) be the point at which these two reaction curves intersect and $x^* = (x_1^*, x_2^*)$ is strictly positive. Then, since the slope $\partial x_2/\partial x_1$ along R_1 is steeper than that along R_2, it is clear that starting from any arbitrary point t in the nonnegative orthant of the $x_1 x_2$-space and following the optimal reaction curves, each player's strategy $x_i(t)$ will converge to the optimal x_i^*, $i = 1, 2$. The iterative process of output revision is here stable in the sense that it converges to the equilibrium x^*, which satisfies in the feasibility space:

$$L_1(x_1, x_2^*) \leqslant L_1(x_1^*, x_2^*); \quad x_1 = x_1(t)$$

$$L_2(x_1^*, x_2) \leqslant L_2(x_1^*, x_2^*); \quad x_2 = x_2(t)$$

(1.4)

Note that even when such an equilibrium solution x^* exists, the convergence of the iterative process assumes the availability and usage of three kinds of information, e.g., (1) the parameters of the market demand function (1.1) are known exactly, i.e., there is no stochastic component in the state of nature, (2) the forecast of the opponent's strategy is available with perfect precision, so that x_2 (or x_1) can be taken to be a known parameter in player one's (or two's) reaction curve R_1 or R_2) and (3) there are nil or negligible costs of search associated with the trial and error process, so that the time of iteration could be as large as possible.

Note that if the Cournot–type equilibrium solution x^* does not exist, which can happen in case the two equations in (1.3) are not consistent [8] in this game, there will always exist a saddle point solution in mixed strategies, so long as the strategy choices of each player are finite. This is due to von Neumann's minimax theorem on matrix games. However, a mixed strategy is a probability mixture of pure strategies, i.e.,

$$\tilde{x}_i = \sum_{j=1}^{m} x_i(j) p_i(j), \quad i = 1, 2$$

$$\sum_{j=1}^{m} p_i(j) = 1, \quad p_i(j) \geqslant 0, \quad i = 1, 2$$

(1.5)

where $p_i(j)$ is the probability for the i-th player to choose the j-th pure strategy $x_i(j)$ out of m finite strategies. The plausibility of the von

Neumann solution, say $\tilde{x}^* = (\tilde{x}_1^*, \tilde{x}_2^*)$ depends of course on two hypotheses (McClennen 1978), e.g., (a) expected utility maximization by each player under a certain set of axioms and (b) the knowledge of the probabilities $p_i(j)$ used in the mixing process. In particular the second hypothesis is important from an informational analysis viewpoint, e.g., (a) are there subjective probabilities formed by each player such that they are revised after the outcomes and current play are observed?, (b) are these conjectural in the sense of the reaction curves (1.3) so that player one's probabilities $p_1(j)$ depend on player two's probabilities $p_2(j)$, at least in some domains? and (c) how can one characterize the iterative process of revising either or both the quantities $x_i(j), p_i(j)$ in order that the solution $\tilde{x}^*$ is attained in a finite time span?

The probabilities $p_i(j)$ used to define minimax solutions $\tilde{x}^*$ in (1.5) are interpreted in traditional game theory by a reciprocal reasoning regress. It is assumed at the outset that the players each assign subjective probabilities to the strategy options of the opponent. The regress, or iteration, then proceeds with repeated calculations of best replies (Harsanyi 1975, Bjering 1978) i.e., those strategy responses, which given the opponent's choices, will maximize his own expected payoff. Of course, the regress or iterations can only stop, if the process converges but so long as there is no objective basis utilized by players to modify their own subjective estimates of probabilities $p_i(j)$, it is difficult to see how a general solution can be characterized here. An important contribution here has been made by Harsanyi (1975) who has proposed two tracing procedures, the linear and the linear logarithmic, where each player, instead of treating his opponent's most recently calculated best play as a 'new probability distribution', only uses it to modify an estimate of his opponent's strategy choices. Thus all information, received or available at each level of the regress is 'filtered' in such a way that the equilibrium pint $\tilde{x}^*$ is reached, provided it exists and the information filtering processes are used. An example of linear tracing procedure is as follows:

$$\hat{p}_i = \alpha \bar{s}_i + (1 - \alpha) \bar{p}_i, \quad 0 \leqslant \alpha \leqslant 1, \quad i = 1, 2 \tag{1.6}$$

where $\hat{p}_i$ is player i's subjective or estimated probability distributed (vector) across the rival's strategy choices, $\bar{s}_i$ is the rival's best reply (i.e., his rival's best mixed strategy vector) to his (rival's) estimate of p_i, where p_i is the mixed strategy vector of player i with components $p_i(j)$ and $\bar{p}_i$ is the prior probability distribution (i.e., prior mixed strategy vector) of the opponent; the parameter α characterizes the pathway such that the regress is adaptive and favorable towards the equilibrium point $\tilde{x}$. The surprising and important result of Harsanyi is that, if the players and they can be $N \geqslant 2$ in number, use the information filters provided by the two tracing procedures, then their estimates will always converge onto a unique equilibrium point of the game, provided the latter exists as a mixed strategy vector.

However, there are two basic difficulties with the tracing procedure. One is the problem of choosing a prior distribution, the informative prior or a noninformative prior and how it could be done and the second is the problem of learning the algorithm of the tracing procedure. As we saw in the reaction curves (1.3), the iterative process will converge if the parameters k_1, k_2, k_{10}, k_{20} are known by each player and the stability condition is satisfied. However, as Kirman (1975) has shown, each player's view of the market may be erroneous in at least two ways, e.g. (a) his model of the system may be correct but it may have a false estimate of the parameters, and/or (b) he may have an incorrect model, and may persist in this view, attributing his prediction errors to his incorrect estimation of the parameter. The usual econometric specification assumes, however, a catch-all error term ϵ, so that the demand function (1.1) appears as

$$p = b_0 - b_1 x_1 - b_2 x_2 + \epsilon \tag{1.7}$$

where ϵ is the additive disturbance term assumed to be independently distributed with zero mean and constant variance σ^2 and it is also assumed that b_1, b_2 may or may not be equal to b. In this case however, profit for each duopolist is random and unless we introduce criteria for ordering risky prospects, the reaction curves satisfying profit maximization for each cannot be derived.

A second approach is to allow the specification (1.8)

$$p = b_0 - b_1 x_1 - b_2 x_2 \tag{1.8}$$

but with the interpretation that both x_1, x_2 could be random, i.e., mixed strategies. Sometimes it may be more convenient to let forecasts $\hat{x}_1, \hat{x}_2$ of x_1, x_2 as being random such that $E\hat{x}_i = x_i$, $i = 1, 2$, i.e., forecasts are unbiased or correct on the average and x_1, x_2 are then not random.

A third case, considered by Arrow and Green (1973) analyzes randomness in both the true model and the perceived views by each duopolist, e.g., x_i, $\hat{x}_i$ may both be random, where $\hat{x}_i$ is the forecast of ith player's strategy and also the parameters b_0, b_1, b_2 may be wrongly perceived.

We consider here the first two cases and by way of implications comment on the third case, but in a more simplified framework. In the first case we have the profit functions $L_i(x_1, x_2, \epsilon_i)$, where ϵ_i is the perceived view of the true stochastic component, which is assumed to have zero mean and constant variance σ_i^2, $i = 1, 2$. Assume the profit function to be analytic up to at least quadratic terms and concave in the domain of interest. Then expected profits EL_i and variance, var L_i can be written as:

$$EL_i = (b_0 - c_i) - b_i x_i^2 - b_j x_i x_j + 0_i(\cdot), \qquad i \neq j; \quad i,j = 1,2$$
$$\text{var } L_i = \sigma_i^2 x_i^2 + V_i(\cdot), \qquad i = 1,2 \tag{1.9}$$

where higher order terms are denoted by $0_i(\cdot)$ and $V_i(\cdot)$. Ignoring these higher order terms and maximizing a weighted risk preference function

$$f_i(x_1, x_2) = EL_i - \frac{\alpha_i}{2} \text{ var } L_i \tag{1.10}$$

which is quadratic leads to a new set of optimal reaction curves

$$R_1: \quad x_i = \frac{b_0 - c_1}{2b_1 + \alpha_1 \sigma_1^2} - \frac{b_2}{2b_1 + \alpha_1 \sigma_1^2} x_2$$

$$R_2: \quad x_2 = \frac{b_0 - c_2}{2b_2 + \alpha_2 \sigma_2^2} - \frac{b_1}{2b_2 + \alpha_2 \sigma_2^2} x_1 \tag{1.11}$$

Here α_i is the weight placed on the profit variance by player i. Hence, even if there is no perceived difference in estimates $\sigma_1^2 = \sigma_2^2 = \sigma^2$ of the true parameter σ^2 of error ϵ, the weighted component $\alpha_i \sigma^2$, where $\alpha_1 \neq \alpha_2$ may have a very unequal effect on the slopes of the two reaction curves, e.g., three cases are possible: Case (a): if the perceived values σ_1^2, σ_2^2 of σ^2 are such that

$$\frac{b_1}{2b_2 + \alpha_2 \sigma_2^2} = \left(\frac{b_2}{2b_1 + \alpha_1 \sigma_1^2} \right)^{-1}$$

then the two reaction curves of (1.11) fail to intersect, hence there would be no Cournot equilibrium solution, although for $\sigma_1^2 = \sigma_2^2 = 0$, there was one such solution in (1.3).
Case (b): the perceived values σ_1^2, σ_2^2 lead to another Cournot solution but an unstable one.
Case (c): the perceived values σ_1^2, σ_2^2 lead to another Cournot solution and a stable one.
   Note that in the more general case when higher order terms $0_i(\cdot)$, $V_i(\cdot)$ are not neglected, the optimal reaction curves if they exist must be nonlinear. Linearizing the nonlinear reaction curves along certain grid points may lead to a stable Cournot equilibrium, whereas for another grid point, it may lead to an unstable Cournot equilibrium and for a third grid point it might lead to no equilibrium solution in the nonnegative domain. The collection of grid points which lead only to stable

Cournot solutions of reaction curves is very important in the 'tracing procedure' suggested by Harsanyi, as we have seen before. The role of information processing or learning in this framework is to provide a stabilizing behavior towards convergence to an equilibrium.

It must be noted however that the reaction curves (1.11) present interdependent choices of x_1 and x_2, that are opposed to one another, i.e., if x_2 rises (falls), then x_1 falls (rises). The degree of interdependence depends very critically on the form of the market demand function (1.7). For instance, consider an alternative form

$$p = \tilde{b}_0 + \tilde{b}_1 \tilde{b}_2 (x_1 x_2)^{-1} + \epsilon \tag{1.7}'$$

where the stochastic component ϵ has the same interpretation as in (1.7). The reaction curves analogous to (1.11) now become

$$x_1 = (\tilde{b}_0 - c_1)/(\alpha_1 \sigma_1^2); \quad x_2 = (\tilde{b}_0 - c_2)/(\alpha_2 \sigma_2^2).$$

This has no interdependence at all! Even in the general case of (1.11), it is seen that if the perceived estimates σ_1^2, σ_2^2 are very large, the effect of x_j on x_i for $i \neq j$ may be negligible, so that approximately each duopolist will tend to produce

$$x_i = (b_0 - c_i)(2b_i + \alpha_i \sigma_i^2)^{-1}; \quad i = 1, 2$$

rather than the Cournot equilibrium solution x_i^*, $i = 1, 2$.

The second case where forecasts $\hat{x}_j$ of j's output by i, $i \neq j$ are random but subject to a bivariate form of distribution say $g(x_1, x_2)$, is interesting in that it shows additionally how forecasting errors that affect strategy choices are basically dependent on conditional distributions of strategies of one player assuming the other's strategy to be given. Also, if the bivariate probability distribution is subjective, as in the Bayesian approach of Harsanyi, then the prior estimates of conditional distribution by each player may be revised in favor of posterior estimates. The revision process may be so constrained that the players converge to an equilibrium point suitably defined.

The random demand function (1.8) is now assumed and each player i is assumed to maximize a conditional expected utility function

$$f_i(x_1, x_2) = EL_i(x_i, x_j \mid x_i) - \frac{\alpha_i}{2} \operatorname{var} L_i(x_i, x_j \mid x_i),$$

$$i \neq j; \quad i, j = 1, 2 \tag{2.1}$$

where each player makes a conditional calculation of expected profits and variance of profits thus: first, he computes the conditional expectation and conditional variance of price

$$E(p \mid x_i) = b_0 - b_i x_i - b_j E(x_j \mid x_i), \quad i \neq j$$

$$\text{var}(p \mid x_i) = b_j^2 E\left[x_j - E(x_j \mid x_i) \right]^2 \tag{2.2}$$

$$= b_j^2 \sigma_{x_j \mid x_i}^2; \qquad i \neq j, \quad i,j = 1,1$$

and then the profits as

$$EL_i(x_i, x_j \mid x_i) = E(p \mid x_i) x_i - c_i x_i - c_0$$
$$\text{var } L_i(x_i, x_j \mid x_i) = b_j^2 \sigma_{x_j \mid x_i}^2 x_i^2 \tag{2.3}$$

Using (2.3) in (2.1) we obtain the equilibrium values x_i^* of x_i which maximize (2.1), from the optimal reaction curve equation as follows:

$$2 b_i x_i^* + b_j \left[E(x_j^* \mid x_i^*) + x_i^* \frac{\partial E(x_j^* \mid x_i^*)}{\partial x_i^*} \right]$$

$$+ \frac{\alpha_i}{2} b_j^2 \left(2 x_i^* \sigma_{x_j^* \mid x_i^*}^2 + x_i^{*2} \frac{\partial \sigma_{x_j^* \mid x_i^*}^2}{\partial x_i^*} \right) = (b_0 - c_i);$$

$$i \neq j, \quad i,j = 1,2 \tag{2.4}$$

Note that the forecast values are the conditional expectations $E(x_j \mid x_i)$, $i \neq j$ and the error of forecast results in losses proportional to conditional variance of profits where the weight factor α_i is applied. The two-step procedure used in (2.3) is of course an approximation and a more general, unconditional result can be derived (Sengupta 1978a); but the approximation can be justified on grounds of rationality of reasoning thus: if the rival's expected behavior can be forecast on each given choice x_i by player i, then the expected price resulting in the market can be computed and hence expected profits.

The equation (2.4) is fundamental in two respects. First, it shows that optimal solutions x_i^*, x_j^* depend on conditional expectations and conditional variances and since the latter would vary from one distribution to another, the results on stability associated with different solutions x^* may vary. Second, the bivariate probability distribution $g(x_1, x_2)$ on the basis of which only (2.4) can be computed, may not be fixed once for all. As in the Bayesian theory and adaptive learning models (Sengupta

1978b), the estimates may be revised in favor of a posterior probability distribution and then the conditional expected profits and variance recalculated to update the decision rules, x_i^* derived from (2.4).

Several results can be derived from (2.4) as follows:

PROPOSITION 1: *If the bivariate distribution* $g(x_1, x_2)$ *is such that* x_1, x_2 *are statistically independent and the solutions* x_i^* *satisfying* (2.4) *hold mutually for* $i = 1, 2$ *then the reaction curves are linear but interdependent as follows*:

$$x_i^* = \frac{b_0 - e_i}{2b_i + \alpha_i b_j^2 \sigma_j^2} - \frac{b_j}{2b_i + \alpha_i b_j^2 \sigma_j^2} x_j^*, \quad i \neq j \tag{2.5}$$

Further, if the equilibrium solution x^* *was stable with* $\alpha_1 = \alpha_2 = 0$ *or, with* $\sigma_1^2 = \sigma_2^2 = 0$, *then this stability is preserved by* (2.5) *for finite and positive values of* σ_j^2 *and* α_i.

PROOF: Since $E(x_j | x_i) = Ex_j$, $i \neq j$ and $\text{var}(x_j | x_i) = \sigma_j^2$ where $\sigma_j^2 = \text{var } x_j$, by assumption, the result (2.5) follows directly. Further, if the inequality $2b_1/b_2 > b_1/2b_2$ holds as required by assumption, then $2b_1/b_2 + \alpha_1 b_2^2 \sigma_2^2 > b_1/2b_2 > b_1/2b_2 + \alpha_2 b_1^2 \sigma_1^2$. Hence the result.

PROPOSITION 2: *If the bivariate distribution* $g(g_1, x_2)$ *is normally distributed with a correlation parameter* ρ *and the solutions* x_i^* *satisfying* (2.4) *hold mutually for* $i = 1, 2$, *the the reaction curves are linear and completely independent of each other.*

PROOF: Since $E(x_j | x_i) = \rho \sigma_j x_i / \sigma_i$, $\text{var}(x_j | x_i) = \sigma_j^2 (1 - \rho)^2$ for $i \neq j$, it is clear that the conditional mean $E(x_j | x_i)$ and conditional variance $\text{var}(x_j | x_i)$ are each independent of x_j. Hence the reaction curves x_i^* satisfying

$$\left[2b_i + 2b_j \rho \frac{\sigma_j}{\sigma_i} + \alpha_i b_j^2 \sigma_j^2 (1 - \rho^2) \right] x_i^* = b_0 - c_i, \quad i = 1, 2$$

are mutually independent. Note however that the parameters b_j, σ_j, ρ still influence the optimal strategy x_i^* of player i.

PROPOSITION 3: *If the bivariate distribution* $g(x_1, x_2)$ *has a Beta distribution in a normalized domain for* x_1, x_2 *that is nonnegative*

$$g(x_1, x_2) = \frac{\Gamma(\theta_1 + \theta_2 + \theta_3)}{\Gamma(\theta_1) \Gamma(\theta_2) \Gamma(\theta_3)} x_1^{\theta_1 - 1} x_2^{\theta_2 - 1} (1 - x_1 - x_2)^{\theta_3 - 1}$$

with

$$x_1 \geqslant 0, \quad x_2 \geqslant 0, \quad x_1 + x_2 \leqslant 1, \quad \theta_i \geqslant 0, \quad i = 1, 2, 3$$

and the solutions x_i^* satisfying (2.4) hold mutually for $i = 1, 2$, then the reaction curves are nonlinear, i.e., cubic but completely independent of each other.

PROOF: Since

$$E(x_j | x_i) = \theta_2(1 - x_i)(\theta_2 + \theta_3)^{-1}$$

$$\text{var}(x_j | x_i) = \theta_0(1 - x_i)^2$$

where

$$\theta_0 = \frac{\theta_2 \theta_3}{(\theta_2 + \theta_3)^2(1 + \theta_2 + \theta_3)}$$

in this case, it is seen from (2.4) that none of the terms $E(x_j | x_i)$, $\sigma^2_{x_j | x_i}$ or their partial derivatives can contain x_j. Hence, the reaction curve of player i would be independent of that of j. Also we have,

$$(2b_i - 2b_j\theta_4)x_i^* + \alpha_i b_j^2 \theta_0 x_i^*(1 - x_i^*)(1 - 2x_i^*) = b_0 - c_i - b_j\theta_4$$

where

$$\theta_4 = \theta_2(\theta_2 + \theta_3)^{-1}$$

Note that the conditioning implied by the conditional expectations and conditional variances served to eliminate the interdependence in outputs sold by the two firms. In the case of N ($N \geqslant 2$) players of course this would not be true. However, this suggests the important point that the traditional statistical notion of expected value may not be realistic or relevant in many game situations (Gibbard 1978). An alternative approach would be not to constrain strategy choices from a fixed bivariate distribution. Consider for instance a time point t at which the reaction curves (1.3) appear as

$$x_i(t) = k_{i0} - k_i \hat{x}_j(t), \quad i \neq j \tag{2.6}$$

where $\hat{x}_j(t)$ is the forecast made by player i of the strategy level of j to obtain in the operative time point t. Let the forecasts be made according to decision rules

$$\hat{x}_j(t) = h\big(x_i(t-1), x_i(t-2), \ldots, x_j(t-1), x_j(t-2) \ldots, \ldots\big) \quad (2.7)$$

Choosing different forms of the rules (2.7) will imply different paths of adjustment. Given the available or feasible set of rules, players may learn to follow rules which are adaptive towards an equilibrium point which is mutually acceptable. For example, a linear rule of the form

$$\hat{x}_j(t) = \sum_{i=1}^{2} \lambda_{ij} x_i(t-1), \quad j = 1, 2$$

will lead to a system

$$x(t) = k_0 + Mx(t-1); \quad k_0 = k_{i0}; \quad x(t) = (x_i(t)) \quad (2.8)$$

where the second order matrix M can be built up from the parameters k_i, λ_{ij}. Now suppose that the parameters λ_{ij} are not fixed once for all but each player learns to choose as the environment evolves. Then different learning rules can be evaluated. For instance, one set of rules may be that for which the matrix M has all its eigenvalues real and less than one in absolute value. Then there will be no oscillations along the path or regress which will converge to an equilibrium. Another set of rules is implied by the case when the eigenvalues of M are such that it has a dominant diaponal that is negative. In this case the path will converge but there may be oscillations due to complex roots (Sengupta 1978a).

Another alternative method of learning is provided through search (Stone 1975). Let there be X states indexed by $x_j(k)$ which can be chosen by any player j, where $k = 1, 2, \ldots, K$ and let $p(k)$ be the probability that it is chosen. Let $d_j(k, \zeta_j(k))$ be the conditional probability that the choice $x_j(k)$ is detected by player i after spending resource of amount $\zeta_j(k)$. The two probabilities, that of state $x_j(k)$ revealed and of detecting it by allocating certain resource are assumed independent. The decision model for each player i is now to choose the decision variables x_i and ζ_i so as to maximize the system payoff J_i made up of two components, one $J_i^{(1)}$ denoting the return from search effort and the second $J_i^{(2)}$ denoting profit expected:

$$\underset{x_i, \zeta_i}{\text{maximize}} \, J_i = J_i^{(1)} + r J_i^{(2)} \quad (2.9)$$

subject to

$$\sum_{k=1}^{K} \zeta_j(k) = 1; \quad x_i \geqslant 0, \quad i = 1, 2$$

where

$$J_i^{(1)} = \sum_{k=1}^{K} p_j(k)\left(1 - \exp\left(-\gamma_j \zeta_j(k)\right)\right)$$

$$J_j^{(2)} = \sum_{k=1}^{K} \left[(b_0 - c_i)x_i^2 - b_i x_i^2 - b_j x_i x_j(k)p_j(k)\right] - c_0; \quad i \neq j$$

r = weight on $J_i^{(2)}$

$x_i = x_i(k)$ when $x_j(k)$ is observed with probability $p_j(k)$

Search effort is comparable to promotional spending and the model (2.9) assumes a particular form of the detection function

$$d_j\left(h, \zeta_j(k)\right) = 1 - \exp\left(-\gamma_j \zeta_j(k)\right), \quad \zeta_j(k) \geqslant 0, \quad \gamma_j > 0$$

which is concave and has diminishing returns.

Motivation for formulating this type of model is clear. So long as the forecasts $\hat{x}_j$ of player j's output are unknown to player i, it pays for the latter to invest on searching or detection. The two-arm bandit problems (Rothschild 1974) arise very naturally in this set up.

3. Team decision models and information sharing

The Cournot model discussed so far assumes no cooperation between the players. It is clear however that even limited cooperation, in the form of knowledge about the response coefficients b_0, b_1, b_2 of the demand function would be helpful in the converges process. Cyert and DeGroot (1973) explicitly allowed this in terms of a joint profit function

$$L = L_1(x_1, x_2) + \gamma L_2(x_1, x_2) \tag{3.1}$$

where γ, $0 < \gamma < 1$ is called the coefficient of cooperation, i.e., each duopolist maximizes his own profit plus a fraction of his rival's profit. They argue that by raising his own level of cooperation, the first player hopes to simulate a similar reaction from his rival. This learning process, if repeated by each player in an adaptive fashion may help modify their judgment and move them from a noncooperative equilibrium to a joint maximization position.

The idea of limited cooperation can of course be extended to problems of team decisions, where questions of information sharing become very important. Two cases will be illustrated. The first shows, contrary to common belief, that extra information may not always be valuable in a game situation, i.e., it may not be helpful for arriving at an acceptable solution. The second shows the role of cooperative solutions in optimal team decisions, when information is exchanged.

The first example is due to Ho and Sun (1978), who consider in their simplest case a two-person stochastic zero-sum game with a scalar quadratic performance index

$$J = E\left\{ (\theta + x_1 + x_2)^2 c - ax_1^2 + bx_2^2 \right\} \tag{3.2}$$

where θ is normally distributed, i.e., $N(0, \sigma^2)$ and $a > c > 0$ and x_1, x_2 are scalar control variables of player I and II respectively. Assume that the information obtained by both players is only through public channels, e.g., broadcasting channels. Let $y = i(\theta)$ and $\zeta = i(\theta)$ be such public information for the two players and $i(\theta)$ and θ) are assumed to be jointly normal with means $(i, 0)$ and covariance matrix V:

$$V = \begin{bmatrix} \sigma_i^2 & \sigma_{i\theta} \\ \sigma_{i\theta} & \sigma_\theta^2 \end{bmatrix}$$

Then, the point (x_1^*, x_2^*) defined by

$$J(x_1, x_2^*) \leqslant J(x_1^*, x_2^*) \leqslant J(x_1^*, x_2) \tag{3.3}$$

in the domain of feasible pairs (x_1, x_2) is called optimal strategies in the sense of a saddle point. By direct calculation one can show

$$\begin{pmatrix} x_1^* \\ x_2^* \end{pmatrix} = \begin{bmatrix} a - c & -c \\ c & b + c \end{bmatrix}^{-1} \begin{pmatrix} E\{\theta \mid i(\theta)\} \\ -E\{\theta \mid i(\theta)\} \end{pmatrix}$$

and

$$J^* = J(x_1^*, x_2^*)$$

$$= \left[(b - a) / \{ (a - c)(b + c) + c^2 \} \right] \sigma_{i\theta}^2 (\sigma_i^2)^{-1} + c\sigma_\theta^2. \tag{3.4}$$

Some implications then follow from (3.4). First, if $i(\theta)$ and θ are uncorrelated so that $\sigma_{i\theta} = 0$, then we have $J^* = c\sigma_\theta^2$, the public information $i(\theta)$ has no value at all. Second, if $b > a$ and $\sigma_{i\theta}$ is not zero, then J^* is an increasing function of $|\sigma_{i\theta}|$ and a decreasing function of variance $\sigma_i^2 = \sigma_{i(\theta)}^2$. This implies that the first player would like to have better information due to (3.3) in spite of what the second player will know and $i(\theta)$ is valuable for player I, if $i(\theta)$ is highly dependent on θ. If $i_0 = i(\theta_0)$ denote prior information available to both players about $\theta = \theta_0$ and x_1^0, x_2^0 be their optimal strategies associated with it, the value of information $V_I = J(x_1^*, x_2^*) - J(x_1^0, x_2^0)$, $V_{II} = -V_I$ is given by the difference $J(x_1^*, x_2^*) - J(x_1^0, x_2^0)$. Similarly the two information structures $y = i(\theta)$, $\zeta = i(\theta)$ need not be common, i.e., let $y = i(\theta)$, $\zeta = j(\theta)$ and let (x_1^*, x_2^*) and (x_1^0, x_2^0) be the optimal decision pairs corresponding to the information structures $(i(\theta), j(\theta)$ and $(i_0 = i(\theta), j_0 = j(\theta_0))$ then the value of posterior information $(i(\theta), j(\theta))$ to player is

$$V_I = J\left(x_1^*, x_2^*\right) - J\left(x_1^0, x_2^0\right) = -V_{II}. \tag{3.5}$$

It is clear that if there are costs associated with the collection of such information, they can be easily incorporated in this framework.

A somewhat more general model may involve T performance indices, one for each member τ of a team

$$J(\tau) = m'(\tau)x(\tau) - \tfrac{1}{2}\alpha(\tau)x'(\tau)V(\tau)x(\tau); \quad \tau = 1, 2, \ldots, T \tag{4.1}$$

where the parameter vector $\theta(\tau)$ as perceived by t-th member has mean $m(\tau)$, variance–covariance matrix $V(\tau)$ and $\alpha(\tau)$ is a positive constant indicating risk aversion by each member. Assume that $\alpha(\tau) = \alpha_0$ for all τ, i.e., the weightage on variance denoting risk aversion is common for all members. Then the effect of communication through exchange of information between team members may be analyzed in terms of cooperative sharing of information structures. For instance, one form of such cooperative communication is to define weighted estimates

$$m = \sum_{\tau=1}^{T} w_\tau m(\tau), \quad V = \sum_{\tau=1}^{T} w_\tau V(\tau), \sum_{\tau=1}^{T} w_\tau = 1, \quad w_\tau \geq 0$$

and use them in a team performance index

$$J = m'x - \tfrac{1}{2}\alpha_0 x'Vx.$$

Thus consider $T = 2$ and assume that there is only partial sharing of information in the sense that either $m(1) = m(2) = m$ or, $V(1) = V(2) = V$ but not both. Then the following result holds:

PROPOSITION 4: *If there is partial cooperation in the mean, i.e., $m(1) = m(2) = m$ but not in variance, i.e., $V(1) \neq V(2)$ and $\alpha(\tau) = \alpha_0$ in the performance index maximized by each member, then it follows:*

$$x^0 < wx^0(1) + (1 - w)x^0(2) \qquad \text{for all} \quad w, \quad 0 < w < 1 \tag{4.2}$$

where

$$x^0 = \alpha_0^{-1} [wV(1) + (1-w)V(2)]^{-1} m$$

$$x^0(\tau) = \alpha_0^{-1} wV^{-1}(\tau)m(\tau), \quad \tau = 1, 2$$

Likewise, if there is partial cooperation in variance, i.e., $V(1) = V(2) = V$ but not in the mean, i.e., $m(1) \neq m(2)$, then

$$x^0 \leq [x^0(1) + x^0(2)], \quad \text{if} \quad x^0(\tau) \geq 0 \tag{4.3}$$

where

$$x^0 = \alpha_0^{-1} V^{-1}(wm(1) + (1-w)m(2)), \quad 0 < w < 1$$

$$x^0(\tau) = \alpha_0^{-1} V^{-1} m(\tau), \quad \tau = 1, 2$$

PROOF. Since $V(1)$ and $V(2)$ are positive definite for $0 < w < 1$, we get

$$[wV(1) + (1-w)V(2)]^{-1} \leq wV^{-1}(1) + (1-w)V^{-1}(2) \tag{4.4}$$

with equality holding only if $V(1) = V(2)$. Also, we have from the necessary condition of optimality

$$x^0 = \alpha_0^{-1} [wV(1) + (1-w)V(2)]^{-1} m$$
$$x^0(\tau) = \alpha_0^{-1} V^{-1} m(\tau) = \alpha_0^{-1} V^{-1} m \quad \text{if} \quad m(\tau) = m \tag{4.5}$$

Combining (4.4) and (4.5) we get the result (4.2). The result (4.3) follows by a similar procedure.

The above result has two interesting implications about informational cooperation. First, unless there is complete cooperation in the mean and the variance, i.e., $m(\tau) = m$, $V(\tau) = V$ for $\tau = 1, 2$ the two solutions, x^0 and $(x^0(1), x^0(2))$ would differ. The question of designing an incentive system so that the two solutions do not differ by more than a small amount appears to be very important in this environment. Second, since weights can be interpreted as probability mixtures, one could figure out when a mixed strategy solution will be preferred, e.g., in (4.2), the mixed strategy solution represented by the right hand side leads to a higher output level than x^0, where the latter is computed after modifying the parameter estimates in terms of a weighted average. If $m(\tau)$, $V(\tau)$ are interpreted as estimates and $w(\tau)$ as their relative reliability, then we get another implication: when is it optimal to follow a mixed strategy solution, if the personal estimates of $m(\tau)$, $V(\tau)$ by team member τ have unequal degrees of precision or reliability?

A third case arises in team decision problems, where instead of the parameter estimates, the members revise or modify the probabilities used in their own mixed strategies. This modification is basically due to the subjective difficulty the player as a decision-maker often has in assigning to the states probabilities with which he is completely satisfied; hence he intends to consider a modified model which tells the decision-maker how much he must perturb his initial probability estimate in order to change his maximum expected payoff alternative from the alternative originally best under the initial estimate. These problems lead to a class of nonzero-sum games with partially controllable strategies, which has been treated by Sengupta (1980). The role of information in this setup is to provide knowledge about the constraints of the environment, which are of course partly probabilistic. This provision may or may not be favorable to a saddle point solution, insofar as convergence is concerned. However, in certain situations it may be shown to lead to complementary eigenvalue problems, which arise in stochastic quadratic games.

4. Information structure in differential games

A differential game is a dynamic version of a game, where the state of the system $x(t)$ at time t depends on controls $u_1(t-1)$, $u_2(t-1)$ of two players say chosen at time $t-1$ and perhaps the state $x(t-1)$. The performance index may include costs defined over a period. Time points t are called stages in discrete-time systems. Two cases will be briefly discussed in this section, one arising in nonstochastic two-person two-stage nonzero sum games and the other in a dynamic Cournot model where stochastic components are present in the market demand function. The first case is discussed in more detail in Olsder (1977), whereas the second in Sengupta et al. (1981).

We consider a simple example, due to Olsder (1977), of the following two-person two-stage nonzero-sum game

$$
\begin{aligned}
&x(t+1) = x(t) + u_1(t) + u_2(t), \ t = 0, 1 \\
&x(0) = x_0 \\
&J_1(2,0) = 2x^2(1) + 2x^2(2) + u_1^2(0) + u_1^2(1) \\
&J_2(2,0) = x^2(1) + x^2(2) + u_2^2(0) + u_2^2(1)
\end{aligned}
\tag{5.1}
$$

with scalar state $x(t)$ and control variables $u_1(t)$, $u_2(t)$ for each stage t and the performance index $J_i(2,0)$ of player $i = 1, 2$ is a cost measure depending on stages zero and two. For determining the controls $u_1(t)$, player I for example has access to some information about the value of the state vector $x(t)$ and/or some past values, i.e., $x(\tau)$, $\tau = 0,\ldots,t-1$.

Besides he may have some knowledge of the functional form of the controls $u_2(t)$ chosen by his opponent, either because the rival announces these forms of $u_2(t)$ beforehand, as is the case with a leader in a Stackelberg game (Simaan and Cruz 1974) or from the past history of the play. All these are summarized by the term information structure IS. Here it is assumed that IS is exact, i.e., no measurement noise is possible and three specific cases are illustrated in relation to a Nash–equilibrium solution which is assumed to exist. A Nash–equilibrium solution which is nothing but a Cournot solution (i.e., a Cournot–Nash solution is perhaps a better term) is defined by a pair of control sequences ($\{u_1^*(t)\}$, $\{u_2^*(t)\}$) having the saddle point property, i.e.,

$$J_1(\{u_1^*(t)\}, \{u_2^*(t)\}) \leqslant J_1(\{u_1(t)\}, \{u_2^*(t)\})$$
$$J_2(\{u_1^*(t)\}, \{u_2^*(t)\}) \leqslant J_2(\{u_1^*(t)\}, \{u_2(t)\}) \tag{5.2}$$

with respect to all other feasible pairs of control sequences ($\{u_1(t)\}$, $\{u_2(t)\}$).

The three cases are: (a) a closed loop solution, (b) an open-loop solution, and (c) a Stackelberg solution. In case of an open-loop solutions for the model (5.1), assume that IS consists of only the initial condition x_0 for both players and both stages. To obtain the Cournot–Nash solution with this IS, we express $J_1(2,0)$, $J_2(2.0)$ of (5.1) as functions of x_0, $u_1(t)$ and $u_2(t)$ only:

$$J_1(2,0) = 2[x_0 + u_1(0) + u_2(0)]^2 + 2[x_0 + u_1(0) + u_2(0)$$

$$+ u_1(1) + u_2(1)]^2 + u_1^2(0) + u_1^2(1) \tag{5.3}$$

$$J_2(2,0) = [x_0 + u_1(0) + u_2(0)]^2 + [x_0 + u_1(0) + u_2(0) + u_1(1) + u_2(1)]^2$$

$$+ u_2^2(0) + u_2^2(1) \tag{5.4}$$

Differentiation of (5.3) and (5.4) with respect to $u_1(t)$, $t = 0, 1$ and $u_2(t)$, $t = 0, 1$ respectively and equating to zero yield four linear equations in four unknowns $u_1(t)$, $u_2(t)$. These four solutions are:

$$u_1^*(0) = -\tfrac{10}{19}x_0; \quad u_1^*(1) = -\tfrac{2}{19}x_0$$
$$u_2^*(0) = -\tfrac{5}{19}x_0; \quad u_2^*(1) = -\tfrac{1}{19}x_0 \tag{5.5}$$

In case of closed loop IS, the available information equals the state vector $x(t)$, $t = 0, 1$ for both players. It is assumed that the control has no memory, i.e., at stage 1 the system is at state $x(1)$ and at that stage control $u_j(1) = f(x(1))$, $j = 1$, 2 as a function of $x(1)$ only must be applied by each player. Now the choice of $u_1(1)$ and $u_2(1)$ will only influence the following part of the cost functions

$$J_1(2,1) = 2x^2(2) + u_1^2(1) = 2[x(1) + u_1(1) + u_2(1)]^2 + u_1^2(1)$$

$$J_2(2,1) = x^2(2) + u_2^2(1) = [x(1) + u_1(1) + u_2(1)]^2 + u_2^2(1)$$

Minimization of these functions yields

$$u_1^*(1) = -\tfrac{1}{2}x(1), \quad u_2^*(1) = -\tfrac{1}{4}x(1) \tag{5.6}$$

For obtaining $u_1^*(0)$, $u_2^*(0)$ we substitute the equations (5.6) for stage 1 into $J_i(2,0)$ as required by the dynamic programming algorithm and the minimize $J_i(2,0)$ with respect to $u_i(0)$, $i = 1$, 2. This yields

$$u_1^*(0) = -\tfrac{19}{36}x_0 \quad \text{and} \quad u_2^*(0) = -\tfrac{1}{4}x_0 \tag{5.7}$$

It is clear that the optimal solutions (5.6), (5.7) under closed loop IS differ significantly from the open loop IS ones given by (5.5).

In the Stackelberg case, assume the second player to be the leader following an open loop control policy. Hence $c_2(0) = f(x_0)$, $u_2(1) = g(x_0)$ where f and g are suitable scalar functions. Knowing these functions, player I, the follower solves the optimal control problem: minimize $J_1(2,0)$ in (5.1) subject to $x(1) = x_0 + u_1(0) + f(x_0)$ and $x(2) = x(1) + u_1(1) + g(x_0)$. The optimal solutions are

$$u_1^*(0) = -\tfrac{1}{11}(2x_0 - 2u_2(0) - 6u_2(1))$$
$$u_1^*(1) = -\tfrac{1}{11}(8x_0 - 8u_2(0) - 2u_2(1)) \tag{5.8}$$

Player I, the leader knowing that his rival will choose his strategies according to (5.8) will solve the following control problem: minimize $J_2(2,0)$ subject to $x(1) = x_0 + u_1^*(0) + u_2(0)$ and $x(2) = x(1) + u_1^*(1) + u_2(1)$, where $u_1^*(0)$, $u_1^*(1)$ are given in (5.8). The optimal solution for the leader is therefore

$$u_2^*(0) = f(x_0) = -\tfrac{11}{145}x_0$$
$$u_2^*(1) = g(x_0) = \tfrac{3}{145}x_0 \tag{5.9}$$

These values have to be substituted on the right hand side of (5.8) for the set $(u_j^*(0), u_j^*(1), j = 1, 2)$ to constitute a Stackelberg equilibrium solution.

It is clear that this Stackelberg solution differs significantly from the two solutions mentioned before.

The IS for a stochastic differential game problem involves the knowledge of the process by which the stochastic components are filtered into choices of optimal control sequences. A Cournot–type example is provided by a dynamic limit price model of a dominant firm when the market exhibits exponential growth and the inverse demand function has conjectural error components. The model (Sengupta et al. 1981) assumes that the dominant firm maximizes a discounted payoff function

$$J_1 = \int_0^\infty \exp(-rt)\left[E\pi_1(t) - \lambda \operatorname{var} \pi_1(t)\right]dt \tag{6.1}$$

subject to

$$p(t) = ae^{nt} - b_1(x_1(t) + x_2(t) + \epsilon(t))$$
$$x_1(0) = x_{10}, \quad x_2(0) = x_{20}; \quad \lambda > 0, \quad r > 0 \tag{6.2}$$

where profit of the dominant firm π_1 and its expectation and variance are defined as

$$\pi = (p(t) - c_1)x_1(\quad t = 1, 2,$$

$$E\pi_1 = (Ep(t) - c_1)x_1(t) \tag{6.3}$$

$$\operatorname{var} \pi_1 = \sigma^2 x_1^2(t), \quad \sigma^2 = \text{variance of } \epsilon$$

and the stochastic component $\epsilon(t)$ is assumed to be independently distributed with zero mean and constant variance σ^2. The dynamics of entry is specified by

$$\dot{x}_1 = k\left[ae^{nt} - b_1(x_1(t) + x_2(t)) - \bar{p}\right]$$

$$\bar{p} \geqslant c_1; \quad k > 0; \quad \dot{x}_1 = \frac{dx_1(t)}{dt}. \tag{6.4}$$

which assumes that rival producers with output $x_2(t)$ would enter the market if current price viewed as a proxy for expected return exceeds a limit price $\bar{p}$, which is taken to be constant $\bar{p} \geqslant c_1$ for simplicity. The limit price $\bar{p}$ is here defined to be that price at which net entry is zero (Sengupta and Rifkin 1979).

The optimal strategy for the dominant firm, i.e., $\{x_1(t)\}$ may be obtained by maximizing the performance function J_1 in (6.1) subject to (6.4). Cournot–Nash solutions and even cooperative solutions of the form suggested in (3.1) may be computed in such a framework, since this fits very well into the linear quadratic control models. In particular, the optimal trajectory equations for the model (6.1) and (6.4) may be analyzed for two important characteristics, e.g., how are the steady state solutions affected by some critical parameters like λ, the weight on variance-risks and n, the index of market growth and b_1, the market response? and secondly, how are the stability characteristics associated with the eigenvalues of the optimal trajectory equations? The role of IS is important here in that it may help or hinder the convergence process. For instance, an analysis of the steady state solution of the dominant firm shows that an increase in risk aversion parameter λ would tend to increase the steady state price and output will decline in the steady state. However, since the perceived risks or perceived variance may be higher than what is the true state, such influences may be countered by a suitable information structure.

The role of such informational requirements in the context of stochastic quadratic differential games are discussed by several authors (Clemhout et al. 1973, Sengupta and Rifkin 1979). These applications show that in most cases the stability characteristics of Cournot-type dynamic reaction curves differ significantly according as the information structure is adaptively utilized by the players or not.

For empirical applications to commodity markets like world coffee with Brazil as the dominant supplier or, to the computer industry in the U.S. where IBM has a dominant role (Sengupta et al. 1981) two special cases of the above limit price model (6.1) through (6.4) may appear more relevant. The first case occurs when there is no discounting ($r = 0$) due to the short horizon and absence of market growth ($n = 0$) and no risk aversion ($\lambda = 0$). In this case the optimal trajectory defined by the Hamiltonian co-state equations leads to a degenerate set of linear differential equations in $x_1(t)$ and the adjoint variable $z_1(t)$:

$$\begin{pmatrix} \dot{x}_1(t) \\ \dot{z}_1(t) \end{pmatrix} = \begin{pmatrix} -\dfrac{b_1 k}{2} & \dfrac{b_1 k^2}{2} \\ -\dfrac{b_1}{2} & \dfrac{b_1 k}{2} \end{pmatrix} \begin{pmatrix} x_1(t) \\ z_1(t) \end{pmatrix} \qquad (6.5)$$

where terms not involving $x_1(t)$, $z_1(t)$ are omitted. The coefficient matrix on the right hand side is singular, i.e., of rank one suggesting that the other firms may be dependent on the dominant firm. Of course this holds only when the parameters in the demand function (6.2) and the entry equation (6.4) are known to the firms. Short of such knowledge, the perceived entry equation would differ from the true one, thus implying that there would be no singularity in the system (6.5). Several other cases of uncertain entry have been analyzed by Kamien and Schwartz (1971) and Friedman (1979), by way of extension of the model due to Gaskins (1971).

The second case arises when the variance term $\pi_1(t)$ in the dominant firm's objective function (6.1) is interpreted as conditional variance, depending on the conjectured retaliatory behavior of the rival. Depending on the form of retaliatory behavior, the solutions may not always be stable (Basar 1975, Sengupta 1982, Tabak 1975).

In many practical applications, e.g., world coffee markets, this shows why forms of limited cooperation and market price agreements have limited success whenever there is a dominant firm and the threat of limited entry persists.

5. Applications to other economic models

Of other applications of information structure analysis in game theory models in economic systems, some of the following may be mentioned in particular. The first arises in production–inventory models, where the inventory cost function is partly concave and partly convex, thus requiring a mixed strategy solution in place of a pure strategy one. The role of inventory in this framework may be partly for probing, partly for caution and partly for adjustment due to incomplete information (Crawford 1974, Fromovitz 1965, Kydland and Prescott 1975, Jacobs 1980). The second type of application is in the theory of stochastic programming, in its static and dynamic versions (Dempster 1980, Sengupta 1981), where mixed strategy solutions are contrasted with pure strategy ones, e.g., minimix solutions and the need for optimal use of information emphasized. Thus, a stochastic LP (linear programming) model may be specified in several alternative form depending on the information structure, e.g., the LP model:

$$\max z = c'x, \qquad x \in R_x: \ \{x \mid x \geqslant 0, Ax \leqslant b\} \tag{7.1}$$

$\theta = (A, b, c)$ is the set of parameters and x the decision vector may be viewed conditionally as a method of choosing a vector x, given θ. However, if θ is not given, it has to be estimated from observation vectors $t = t(\theta)$, provided the parameters are estimable. If the function $t(\theta)$ can be expressed as

$$t = H\theta + e \tag{7.2}$$

where e is the stochastic component with zero mean and covariance matrix I, we may call the relation (7.2) an information function. Using such an information function one may construct a suitable estimate $\hat{\theta}$ of θ say, with some desirable properties, e.g., best linear unbiased estimates (blue). This leads to a second view of the stochastic LP model: how to select an optimal vector x, given $\hat{\theta}$? Since the estimates $\hat{\theta}$ have their risk measured by standard errors or variance, the profit vector z associated with optimal x will have its risk measured by its variance. Information on such risk may require modification of the first stage optimal solution vector x. A risk averse decision-maker may thus give higher weightage to profit risks in order to arrive at the final solution in the second stage.

In contrast to the above view of information structure which is of course passive, an interactive case arises in the LP model when viewed in a game-theoretic context. For this purpose we write the LP model (7.1) in a canonical form, e.g.,

primal   dual

$$\max_{p} z = \sum_{j=1}^{n} p_j \qquad\qquad \min_{q} w = \sum_{i=1}^{m} q_i$$

$$\text{s.t.} \quad \sum_{j=1}^{n} \alpha_{ij} p_j \leqslant 1 \qquad \text{s.t.} \quad \sum_{i=1}^{m} q_i \alpha_{ij} \geqslant 1 \tag{7.3}$$

$$p_j \geqslant 0 \qquad\qquad\qquad q_i \geqslant 0$$

where by assuming without loss of generality that (b, c) are nonnegative, we have $\alpha_{ij} = a_{ij}/(b_i c_j)$ for nonzero b_i and c_j and $p_j = \hat{p}_j z$ with $\hat{p}_j$, $1 \leqslant j \leqslant n$ being the mixed strategies of player I with $\Sigma \hat{p}_j = 1$, $\hat{p}_j \geqslant 0$ and $\hat{q}_i = q_i/w$ for player II. By LP duality, the canonical LP models (7.3) define a two-person zero-sum game which can be written in a more compact notation as

player I: $\max_{\hat{p}} \hat{p}'\hat{A}\hat{q}$ s.t. $\hat{p}'e = 1, \quad \hat{p}'e = 1, \quad \hat{p} \geqslant 0$

              and $\hat{A} = (\alpha_{ij})$

player II: $\max_{\hat{q}} \hat{p}'\hat{B}\hat{q}$ s.t. $\hat{q}'v = 1, \quad \hat{q} \geqslant 0$ (7.4)

              and $B = (\beta_{ij})$

with $\hat{B} = -\hat{A}$, where e, v are vectors with each element unity and β_{ij} defines the payoff matrix for player II, just as α_{ij} is the payoff for player I. For a cooperative game one may define $C = r\hat{A} + (1 - r)\hat{B}$, $0 \leqslant r \leqslant 1$ as a weighted combination of the respective payoffs and set up a joint maximization problem

$$\max_{\hat{p}, \hat{q}} \hat{p}'C\hat{q} \quad \text{s.t.} \quad \hat{p}'e = 1 = \hat{q}'v, \quad \hat{p} \geqslant 0, \quad \hat{q} \geqslant 0 \tag{7.5}$$

What would happen in this game theoretic framework if the payoff matrices are random, i.e., they are $\hat{A}(s)$, $\hat{B}(s)$, $C(s)$ where s belongs to a set S of events with a given probability structure. Two common approaches (Sengupta 1981) adopted here are the chance-constrained approach and the parametric approach. In the first, the recognition of randomness of the payoff structure leads to alternative, and in most cases, risk-averse solutions which maximize for example the probability of attaining a given level of expected payoff. The second method attempts to define on the basis of observations, if available, an unbiased estimate of the payoff matrix $\hat{C}$ say and obtain equilibrium solutions of the joint maximization model (7.5). In either case, the same set of observations and the amount of information contained in them may lead to different perceptions and different objectives to optimize by the two players. Information when shared cooperatively may have different implications from those not shared or partially shared.

An important case which has received some attention here arises when the information structure is asymmetrical either in the sense of the relevant probability distribution or in the shape of the payoff function. Incentives for sharing or exchange of information are particularly affected in this framework through diverse attitudes towards risk (Waud 1976, Sengupta 1981).

6. Concluding remarks

Analysis of information structure mainly refers here to two-person games with a finite number of strategies, e.g., (a) use of information helpful for the convergence of player's strategy choices in a Cournot market, (b) sharing and cooperating in informational communication in a team decision, and 9c) the role of information structures in open loop and closed loop solutions. It is clear from our discussion that information can be characterized by the players either in terms of its value or its costs. Value refers to its effect on return or payoff, whereas the cost refers to the errors made due to lack of appropriate information. The role of learning or adaptive behavior, which has been barely mentioned above, emphasizes the fundamental behavioral aspect which is modified or transformed by the information process and the latter need not all be quantitative. The theory of processing and usage of qualitative information structures in decisionmaking is yet to be developed.

This is a most active field of research.

References

Arrow, K. and Green, J., "Noes on expectations equilibria in Bayesian settings," Working Paper No. 33, Institut for Mathematical Studies in Social Sciences, Stanford University, 1973.

Basar, T., "On the uniqueness of the Nash solution in linear quadratic differential games," Int. J. of Game Theory, 4 (1975), 95–108.

Bylka, S. and Komar, J., "Simulation of strategies in nonzero-sum games," in Warsaw Fall Seminar in Mathematical Economics, 1975.

Bjering, A.K., "Conflict and structure in multiple objective decisionmaking systems," in C.A. Hooket er al. eds. Foundations and Applications of Decision Theory, Dordrecht: Reidel Publishing, 1978.

Case, J., "A dynamic version of Cournot's problem," in E.O. Roxin et al. eds. Differential Games and Control Theory, New York: Marcel Dekker, 1973.

Chu, K.C., "Designing information structures for quadratic decision problems," Journal of Optimization Theory and Applications, 25 (1978), 139–160.

Clemhout, S. and Lietman, G. et al., "A differential game model of oligopoly, "Journal of Cybernetics, 3 (1973), 15–26.

Crawford, V., "Learning the optimal strategy in a zero-sum game," Econometrica, 42 (1974), 1052–1063.

Cyert, R. and DeGroot, M., "An analysis of cooperation and learning in a monopoly context," American Economic Review, 63 (1973), 102–112.

Dempster, M.A.H. ed., Stochastic Programming. New York: Academic Press, 1980.

Fromovitz, S., "Nonlinear programming with randomization," Management Science, 11 (1965), 1102–1113.

Gibbard, A. et al., "Rationality in collective choice," in C.A. Hooker et al. eds. Foundations and Applications of Decision Theory, Dordrecht, Reidel Publishing, 1978.

Harsanyi, J.C., "Solution concepts in game theory," International Journal of Game Theory, 5 (1975), 39–54.

Ho, Y.C. and Sun, F.K., "Value of information in two-team zero-sum problems," kn G. Leitmann ed. Multicriteria Decision Making and Differential Games, New York: Plenum Press, 1978.

Jacobs, O.L.R., "The structure of stochastic control laws," in M.A.H. Dempster, ed. Stochastic Programming, New York: Academic Press, 1980.

Kamien, M.L. and Schwartz, N.L., "Limit pricing and uncertain entry," Econometrica, 39 (1971), 441–452.

Kirman, A.P., "Learning by firms about demand conditions," in R.H. Day and T. Groves, eds. Adaptive Economic Models, New York: Academic Press, 1975.

Kydland, F. and Prescott, E.C., "The inconsistency of optimal policy," Norwegian School of Economics Discussion Paper, 1975.

Levitan, R.E. and Shubik, M., "Noncooperative equilibria and strategy spaces in an aligopolistic market," in H. Kuhn and G. Szego, eds., Differential Games and Related Topics, Amsterdam: North Holland, 1971.

McClennen, E.F., "Solution concepts in games," in C.A. Hooker, et al., Foundations and Application of Decision Theory, Dordrecht: Reidel Publishing, 1978.

Rothschild, M., "Models of market organization with imperfect information," Journal of Political Economy, 81 (1973), 1283–1294.

Rothschild, M., "A two-arm bandit theory of market pricing," Journal of Economic Theory, 9 (1974), 185–198.

Sengupta, J.K., "Noncooperative equilibria in monopolistic competition under uncertainty," Zeitschrift fur nationalokonomie 38 (1978), 193–208.

Sengupta, J.K., "Adaptive decision rules for stochastic linear programming," Int. J. of Systems Sci., 9 (1978), 97–109.

Sengupta, J.K. and Rifkin, E.J., "Dynamic limit pricing stochastic demand," Working Paper No. 130, UC Santa Barbara, 1979.

Sengupta, J.K., Optimal Decisions Under Uncertainty. New York: Springer Verlag, 1981.

Sengupta, J.K., Decision Models in Stochastic Programming. New York: Elsevier-North Holland, 1982.

Simaan, M. and Cruz, J.B., jr., "On the Stackelberg strategy in nonzero-sum games," Journal of Optimization Theory and Applications, 11 (1974), 535–555.

Stone, L.D., The Theory of Optimal Search. New York: Academic Press, 1975.

Tabak, D., "Computed solutions of differential games," in J.D. Grote, ed., The Theory of Differential Games. Dordrecht: Reidel Publishing., 1975.

Waud, R.N., "Asymmetric policymaker utility functions and optimal pricing under uncertainty," Econometrica, 44 (1976) 53–66.

12. Stochastic models in dynamic economics: problems of time inconsistency, causality and estimation

1. Introduction

The theory of feedback and optimal control, originally developed for and applied most successfully in physical and engineering systems, has found many applications in dynamic economics for over two decades. Our understanding and analysis of the dynamic economic systems in the form of difference or differential equations in time have been greatly enhanced by developments in control theory, specifically in three particular areas: (a) the theory of economic policy, which deals with the problem of choosing optimal instruments or controls, (b) the method of structural economic analysis in a model, which deals with alternative forms of specification of an econometric model and its implicit and explicit constraints, and (c) the theory of econometric estimation, which seeks to derive in some sense optimal estimates of parameters of dynamic models from given observations.

In recent times [21,22,25] the above control theory perspective in dynamic economics has faced at least three serious challenges, which are most basic and constructive. On the negative side the challenges are basic, because they deny that an optimal economic policy can be meaningfully defined in a traditional econometric model. On the positive side they emphasize that the causal view of control theory (i.e. the instrument or policy is the control input or cause, the effect is the output) may need substantial modification or even replacement by a suitable alternative, when economic systems involving diverse agents who can anticipate and react, are considered in a stochastic environment. Stochastic processes play a much more dynamic role in this environment than the simple additive disturbance terms adjoined to an otherwise deterministic economic model.

Our objective here is to analyze and illustrate these three problems: the inconsistency of optimal policy, the concept of causality in dynamic models and problems of efficient estimation in a multi-agent stochastic framework. We would also consider a few interesting economic applications of different types of stochastic processes. A stochastic process may be viewed as a dynamic counterpart of an ordinary random variable and its probability distribution, since a stochastic process may be defined as a family of random variables depending upon a parameter e.g., time. Thus for a normal distribution characterized by its two parameters, the mean and variance, which are in the ordinary case, assumed fixed for all time t, we obtain a stochastic process known as the diffusion process when we think of a family of normal distributions where the means and variances become functions of time.

2. Optimal control: time inconsistency and separability problems

Consider a dynamic model of an economy as a system of difference equations, where there are N decision agents, each controlling a vector $u_t(i)$ at time t with $i = 1, 2, \ldots, N$.

$$x_{t+1} = f(x_t, u_t(1), \ldots, u_t(N), z_t) \tag{1.1}$$

The state of the economy is here represented by the vector x_t which is not directly observable, so we have to use the output y_t which is observable as:

$$y_t = g(x_t) \tag{1.2}$$

The sequence of variables $\{z_t\}$ over time denotes shocks generated by some stochastic process. It is clear that the system defined by (1.1) and (1.2) may well represent, under suitable qualifications, a typical econometric model of the Keynesian system. For example if both f and g are linear functions, x_t, y_t may, by suitable transformation include higher order lags and the shocks z_t are independent of u_t's with finite means and variances for all t, then this is a traditional econometric model, whose parameters θ can be estimated by least squares (LS) or other suitable techniques.

In an optimal control problem, distinct from the estimation problem the decision agent i chooses the control vector $u_t(i)$ so as to minimize the expected value of a loss function, $E[L_i \mid I_{it}]$ conditional on his information set I_{it}, where

$$L_i = L_i(u_t(i), u_{t+1}(i), \ldots, x_{t+1}, x_{t+2}, \ldots) \tag{1.3}$$

and future control vectors $u_{t+k}(i)$, $k > 1$ are chosen in a similar fashion by minimizing the same criterion. Note that this optimal control problem is dependent on two basic premises: one is that the stochastic processes generating z_t and $u_t(j), j \neq i$ are completely known as of now and for the future. For otherwise the optimal solution $u_t(i)$ would depend on the current information set I_{it} of agent i about the process $P(z, u)$ generating $z_t, u_t(j)$ i.e.,

$$u_t(i) = h_i^0(I_{it}), I_{it} : \{ P(z, u), i \neq j \} \tag{1.4}$$

It is clear therefore that if these generating processes P change any time in future and the agents are aware of it, their optimal control solutions $h_t^0(\cdot)$ would change. This is a basic problem of inconsistency, since in the real economic world models are only approximations and even as approximations future knowledge about the generating process P are far more uncertain. The second premise underlying the optimal control law (1.4) may be understood better if we write the optimal control law more explicitly as dependent on the set of parameters ϕ say:

$$u_t(i) = h_i^0(I_{it}, \phi) \tag{1.5}$$

where ϕ may be called the parameters of the optimal controller $u_t(i)$, which may be distinguished from the parameters θ of the dynamic system representing the econometric model specified in (1.1) and (1.2). For certain types of models known as LQG (linear quadratic Gaussian) control, there exist, under suitable assumptions [18] on the generating process P a mapping from the set θ to ϕ, where a separation principle holds. The separation principle implied by the optimal control rule (1.5) states that it is possible to make a separation between the estimation problem for θ in the econometric model (via maximum likelihood or Kalman-filtering methods of state estimation) and then the determination of the parameters in the optimal controller (1.5), which may be functions of the uncertainties (i.e., standard errors) of the econometric parameters e.g.

$$\phi = \phi(\hat{\theta}, F(\hat{\theta} | \theta)) \tag{1.6}$$

where $\hat{\theta}$ is an estimate based on the information set $I_t = [I_{1t}, I_{2t}, \ldots, I_{Nt}]$ and $F(\hat{\theta})$ is the probability distribution of the estimate $\hat{\theta}$ given the true value θ. Note that the role of information transfer is very critical here; the passage from $\hat{\theta} = (\hat{\theta} | I_t)$ to ϕ in the optimal controller characterizes several forms of the separation principle. Three forms have been most widely used. One is the strong form of separation between estimation and control, also known as the certainty equivalence (CE) principle; the second is the weak form where the uncertainty in the estimate $\hat{\theta}$ is explicitly recognized. The third form uses separation as a principle of approximation of nonlinear models, more nonlinear than the LQG models and suboptimal controllers are used as first approximations which can be later improved with more information. The theory of adaptive control, where various forms of adaptivity and caution are built into, provides in a sense a general operational framework for dealing with cases where the separation principle, in weak or strong forms do not hold. Thus, in adaptive control which is the most active field of applied research in modern control theory there are very few cases where the CE principle is applicable. One exception is when the unknown parameters θ are stochastic variables which are statistically independent between different sampling intervals and other conditions of the LQG model apply. It is easy to show that in default of statistical independence, a simple random parameter model under LQG would fail to uphold the CE principle. Consider for example the following LQG model for one agent:

$$\min L = E_0 \left[\sum_{t=1}^{T} x_t' R_t x_t \right] \tag{2.1}$$

subject to

$$x_t = A_t x_{t-1} + B u_t + \epsilon_t$$

$$x_0 \text{ unknown,} \quad \epsilon_t \sim iid\ N(0, I)$$

where E_0 denotes expectation conditional on all information available up to the end of period zero, A_t, B are random parameters, with A_t t-varying and B time-invariant, R_t is known but time-varying while the stochastic error term ϵ_t is assumed to be identically and independently distributed as $N(0, I)$. We follow the dynamic programming algorithm [6,19] to solve the quadratic problem (2.1) for the last period, given the information up to the end of period $T-1$, i.e., we minimize

$$L_T = E_{T-1} \left[x_T' R_T x_T \right]$$

$$= E_{T-1} \left[x_{T-1} (A_T' R_T) x_{T-1} + u_T' (B' R_T B) u_T \right.$$

$$+ 2 (u_T' B' R_T A_T) x_{T-1} \right] + E_{T-1} (\epsilon_T' R_T \epsilon_T)$$

By setting to zero the first derivative of L_T with respect to the control vector we obtain the optimal decision rule

$$u_T^0 = G_T x_{T-1}; \quad G_T = - \left(E_{T-1} \left[B' R_T B \right] \right)^{-1} \left(E_{T-1} \left[B' R_T A_T \right] \right) \tag{2.2}$$

Following the recursive algorithm we may thus derive the optimal decision rule for any $t > 0$:

$$u_t^0 = G_t x_{t-1}; \quad G_t = \left(E_{t-1} [B'R_t B] \right)^{-1} \left(E_{t-1} (B'R_t A_t) \right) \tag{2.3}$$

where E_{t-1} is expectation conditional on all information available up to the end of period $(t-1)$. Let $\bar{A}_t$, $\bar{B}$ be the expected value of the corresponding random parameters and $\tilde{A}_t = A_t - \bar{A}_t$, and $\tilde{B} = B - \bar{b}$ be the deviations from their respective means. Then, on replacing the random variables by their respective means we obtain for the last period T, from the optimal rule (2.2):

$$G_T = \bar{G}_T = - \left(\bar{B}'R_T \bar{B} \right)^{-1} \left(\bar{B}R_T \bar{A} \right)$$

This is the optimal G_T for the CE principle, if it were correct to apply. However the true optimal rule requires a different G_T as:

$$G_T = - \left[\bar{B}'R_T \bar{B} + E_{T-1} (\tilde{B}'R_T \tilde{B}) \right]^{-1} \left(\bar{B}R_T \bar{A} + E_{T-1} (\tilde{B}'R_T \tilde{A}_T) \right)$$

which indeed gives the correct optimal rule (2.2).

It is of some importance to analyze the various implications of these twin problems of inconsistency and separability for economic theory and policy modeling.

Consider the inconsistency problem first. We have in the optimal control model defined by (1.3) and (1.4) more than one decision agent, where their current decisions depend in part on their expectations of future policy actions. Thus if there are two agents, the private and public sectors for example, the decisions of the private sector would depend in part upon its expectations of future government policies. Unless these expectations are invariant to future policy changes, the optimal control rules calculated as of today would be inappropriate and inconsistent.

(a) This type of inconsistency has been analyzed in some detail by Kydland and Prescott [21], who have shown that in aggregative economic models, where there is usually a lack of details of the micro-structure due to inadequate data, the scope of such inconsistency may be compounded. The standard practice of using econometric models for choosing optimal government policy, in the theory of economic policy in Tinbergen's tradition [17] has followed a two-stage procedure: first one estimates an econometric model and then formally or informally uses optimal control theory to determine optimal policy, e.g., fiscal and monetary policy. But changes in policy induce change in the structure of the model which in turn necessitate reestimation and so on. This iterative process from structure estimation to control and then to reestimation and to control may not always converge. In this case the use of optimal control rules may even increase economic fluctuations rather than decrease them.

(b) When the decision agents are several, the concept of a solution is no longer very precise, since various types of noncooperative solutions of differential games, e.g., Cournot–Nash, Stackelberg, etc. may be considered along with the cooperative solution concept. In the presence of uncertainty, the variety of possible solutions that one may envisage increases considerably. For instance, in a Cournot–Nash type of equilibrium solution, each player may have rational expectations in the sense that the expectation of the others' actions turns out to be the actual outcome, yet in default of appropriate coordination the sequence of revisions of a player's reaction curve may not always converge [17,35]. The iterative process may then be as hazardous as optimal control rules that ignores possible changes in structure through expectations mechanisms.

(c) The optimal plans in the form of open loop control policies for periods 1 through T require a commitment to the given horizon as viewed from the initial position. Thus if one plan at time τ does not turn out to be the same when formulated at $\tau + 1$, then the optimal policy may not be consistent. For instance, $\tau + 1$ may represent the date when new tax on capital gains has been imposed with τ representing the no tax situation. Since policy interventions by the government in the form of new tax would change some of the constraints faced by the private sector, any policy model which calculates optimal policy without taking into account the reaction of the private sector and their constraint changes may be seriously flawed, depending on the magnitude of the intervention of course [22,32]. Note that this type of inconsistency of optimal plans can arise even when the objective function (or the loss function) of the government is identical to that of the private sector in the form of a representative agent.

Next consider the problem of separability of estimation and control. There are two major consequences, when this separability fails to hold. One is that the conditional argument which is used either to forecast any future state given the current information, or to attain a future realizable target through current control, may not hold except perhaps very approximately and even in the latter case, one has to perform robustness and/or sensitivity analysis to test if the results are general. A second implication of the failure of separability is that the optimal estimation problem becomes jointly dependent on the optimal control problem, so that one has to unscramble so to say this interdependence before an optimal controller can be designed or applied. Sometimes this interdependency may be the consequence of lack or normality of the error structure in the dynamic plant equations. For example, consider the dynamic equations in (2.1) but assume that the stochastic process $\{\epsilon_t\}$ is in the form of a nonlinear birth and death process [30,38] satisfying the logistic-type differential equations:

$$\frac{de(t)}{dt} = \left\{ (a+b) \left[\frac{ah_2 + bh_1}{a+b} \cdot e(t) - e^2(t) \right] - (a+b)v(t) \right\}$$

where $e(t) = E(\epsilon_t)$ is the mean function and $v(t) = \text{var}(\epsilon_t)$ is the variance function and a, b, h_i are constant parameters characterizing the stochastic process. In this case we would not have $E(x_t \mid u_t)$ equal to $A_t x_{t-1} + Bu_t$. Thus the linearity of regression following from conditional normality fails to hold and as a consequence the two-step method of estimation first and controlling later becomes very uncertain.

2.1. Methods for resolving inconsistency

From a very practical viewpoint it is important to recognize that there are many situations where the problems of inconsistency associated with the optimal discretionary policies would not be very serious at all. For instance, in stable environments where growth of real income is associated with price stability, expectations of the private sector would not be much affected by the demand management policies of the government sector following a Keynesian strategy. The excellent survey by Eckstein [10] mentions several historical examples to support this view. Again in less developed countries where the assumptions of competitive market structure and price flexibility required by the neoclassical model may fail to hold, interventionism in government policy may have additional justification through the possibility of market failures and other bottlenecks. As Johansen [17] has argued very effectively:

"Consider a government which is about to choose between possible policies $a^{(1)}$, $a^{(2)}$, ... It would be rather artificial to assume that the government could realistically say to itself: "we have to choose between the various possible policies, but regardless of which decision we eventually settle for, our decision has already been anticipated by the rest of the economy ..." Now the theory of rational expectations does not mean that anticipations are necessarily correct, so this way of putting the matter is somewhat strict. However, the theory assumes the deviations between anticipations and realizations to be purely random. This modification does not help very much to make the viewpoint relevant for a government who is pursuing a discretionary policy ...." [17, p. 19].

In recent times several methods have been proposed both by economists and the control theorists to tackle the problem of inconsistency and inseparability. For the control through the physical systems and plant dynamics, these methods are known by their generic name of adaptive control involving self-tuning regulators which are discussed elsewhere. Of several methods of adaptive control, optimal dual controllers are designed to utilize learning and caution along the way where future information is likely to be available for improving the control rule sequentially [19]. However, these methods of adaptive dual control are not very simple to apply and no simple analytic or computational rules are as yet available, except in very simple classroom type examples which are at a great distance from real life situations. The economist's approach to the inconsistency problem has been two-fold. One is to suggest that fixed rules rather than discretionary policies of optimal control are likely to be less hazardous. The second is to allow explicitly in the control model formulation variables and parameters which are "expectational", i.e., they specify mechanisms for formation of expectations of one agent in response to policies adopted or likely to be adopted by the other agents.

The case for fixed rules rather than optimal discretionary policies is justified first by its lack of inconsistency problems and then by its stabilizing influence in restoring competitive equilibrium. If the government sector follows stable policy rules that lead to a stable economic environment, it is more likely that the private sector's response would be more stabilizing and this would make the case for econometric estimation stronger. However the case for fixed rules assumes that the private sector (or other agents) behaves rationally so that it has a learning mechanism quite fast and responsive. However this part of rational expectation theory may not always be realistic, since learning is indeed slow and it takes several years for the society to correctly assess the changes affecting the economic environment.

As an example of modeling interventions through expectational variables, we may consider a linear quadratic and Gaussian version (i.e., LQG version) of Lucas and Prescott's model of investment under uncertainty as discussed by Sargent [32].

EXAMPLE 1 (model of investment under uncertainty): This is a dynamic model of a single competitive industry analyzed through a representative firm, which has to optimally choose its capital stock k_t at time t, given its beliefs about the laws of motion of the random variables not under its control and of the aggregate capital stock K_t.

The representative firm's objective function is taken to be the expectation of discounted profits over an infinite horizon, conditional on all the information known to the firm at t:

$$\max_{\{k_t\}} E_0 \sum_{t=0}^{\infty} \left[P_t y_t - w_t k_t - \frac{d}{2} (k_{t-1} - k_t)^2 \right] \tag{3.1}$$

Subject to given initial capital k_0 the firm has to maximize this criterion (3.1) to determine an optimal contingency plan for k_{t+j}. Here the term $(d/2)(k_{t+1} - k_t)^2$ denotes adjustment costs with d a positive constant, y_t is output given by the production function

$$y_t = fk_t + n^{-1}\epsilon_t, \quad f > 0 \tag{3.2}$$

with f a positive constant and ϵ_t the stochastic shock. P_t is output price given by the demand curve.

$$P_t = A_0 - A_1 Y_t + A_2 D_{1t} + u_t, A_0, A_1 > 0 \tag{3.3}$$

with $Y = ny_t$, $D_{1t} = $ vector of demand shifters $A_i = $ constant and $u_t = $ the stochastic shock. w_t is the rental on capital, being the first element of the vector random process W_t for the industry as a whole, which is assumed to obey the r_w-th order vector autoregression

$$\delta_w(L)W_t = V_t^w \tag{3.4}$$

where $\delta_w(L) = I - \sum_{j=1}^{r_w} \delta_{wj} L^j$ is the vector lag operator and V_t^w is a vector white noise (i.e., a zero mean, constant variance stationary stochastic process) for W_t. Likewise the shocks ϵ_t in (3.2) and u_t in (3.3) are assumed to follow the Markov processes

$$\delta_\epsilon(L)\epsilon_t = V_t^\epsilon \quad \text{(white noise)} \tag{3.5}$$

$$\delta_u(L)u_t = V_t^u \quad \text{(white noise)} \tag{3.6}$$

Also, the demand shifters follow a Markov process:

$$\delta_D(L)D_t = V_t^D \quad \text{(white noise)}$$
$$D_t' = (D_{1t}, D_{2t}), \quad \text{(prime is transpose)} \tag{3.7}$$

and the representative firm believes that the aggregate capital stock K_t evolves according to the dynamic law

$$K_{t+1} = H_0 + H_w(L)W_t + H_D(L)D_t + H_\epsilon(L)\epsilon_t$$

$$+ H_u(L)u_t + H_1 K_t \tag{3.8}$$

where H_0, H_1 are scalars and $H_w(L)$, $H_D(L)$, $H_\epsilon(L)$, $H_u(L)$ are suitable polynomials in lag operators. The firm is assumed to behave competitively so that it acts as a price taker, which is a reasonable assumption if the number of firms, n, is large. The firm's optimization problem would lead to a linear contingency plan of the following form

$$k_{t+1} = h_0 + h_w(L)W_t + h_D(L)D_t + h_\epsilon(L)\epsilon_t$$

$$+ h_u(L)u_t + h_1 K_t + h_2 k_t \qquad (3.9)$$

where h_0, h_1, h_2 are scalars and $h_w(L)$, $h_0(L)$, $h_\epsilon(L)$, $h_u(L)$ are polynomials in lag operator L, provided we make the following simplifying assumptions:

(a) the firm knows the δ's and H's with certainty
(b) the shock variables V_t^ϵ, V_t^u, V_t^D and V_t^w obey normal probability laws so that the least squares predictors of future W, D, ϵ and u's are linear in the conditioning variables.

On multiplying both-sides of the firm's optimal decision rule (3.9) by n and using $K_t = nk_t$ gives

$$K_{t+1} = nh_0 + nh_w(L)W_t + nh_D(L)D_t + nh_\epsilon(L)\epsilon_t$$

$$+ nh_u(L)u_t + (nh_1 + h_2)K_t \qquad (3.10)$$

where all h's are in general functions of both the parameters in the objective function (3.1) and the parameters δ_w, δ_u, δ_ϵ appearing in (3.4) through (3.7) and the H's of the perceived law of motion for aggregate capital (3.8). Equation (3.10) has two interpretations. One is that it is a mapping from the firm's perceived law of motion of aggregate capital (3.8) to the actual law of motion (3.10). Thus for each possible particular perceived law of motion for aggregate capital in the form of (3.8), there is an implied law of motion for aggregate capital of the form (3.10). The notion of rational expectations which requires that the representative firm's perception of (3.8) is correct is satisfied by the equilibrium decision rule (3.10). It is clear that the necessary and sufficient conditions for a rational expectations equilibrium are:

$$H_0 = nh_0; \quad H_w(L) = nh_w(L); \quad H_D(L) = nh_D(L)$$

$$H_\epsilon(L) = nh_\epsilon(L), \quad H_u(L) = nh_n(L), \quad H_1 = (nh_1 + h_2)$$

The second interpretation is that if the representative firm had correct perceptions or perfect foresight of the actual laws of motion of all variables affecting its objective function but beyond its control, then the equilibrium decision rule (3.10) is indeed the optimum.

Two questions immediately arise. First, the firm's perception of the laws of motion of aggregate capital and other variables beyond its control may not be correct and the errors need not be self-correcting over time. Second, the assumption of symmetry underlying the aggregation of optimal linear decision rules of each representative firm may be invalid due to several reasons: difference in risk aversion rates for different firms, which is not allowed for in the objective function (3.1), unequal information structures available to each firm and last of all imperfect knowledge and foresight. To appreciate these difficulties one may look at the first order necessary conditions for the optimum decision rule (3.10):

$$\beta dk_{t+1} - d(1+\beta)k_t + dk_{t-1}$$

$$= \beta w_t - \beta f(A_0 - A_1 fK_t - A_1 \epsilon_t + A_2 D_{1t} + u_t) \quad \text{(Euler equation)}$$

and

$$\lim_{j \to \infty} E_t \beta^{t+j} k_{t+j} = 0 \quad \text{(transversality)}$$

After a little algebra, these can be written as

$$(1-L)k_{t+1} = -d^{-1}\beta \sum_{i=0}^{\infty} \beta^i w_{t+i+1} + \beta f d^{-1} \sum_{i=0}^{\infty} \beta^{-1} P_{t+i+1}$$

$$= -d^{-1}\beta \sum_{i=0}^{\infty} \beta^i E(w_{t+i+1} | \Omega_t)$$

$$+ \beta f d^{-1} \sum_{i=0}^{\infty} \beta^i E(P_{t+i+1} | \Omega_t) \tag{3.11}$$

where L is the lag operator, $\Omega_t = \{W_t, W_{t-1}, \ldots, u_t, u_{t-1}, \ldots, D_t, D_{t-1}, \ldots, \epsilon_t, \epsilon_{t-1}, \ldots, K_t\}$ is the information set and the conditional mathematical expectations $E(w_{t+i+1} | \Omega_t)$, $E(P_{t+i+1} | \Omega_t)$ are to be computed using the laws of motion (3.4) through (3.8). If perfect foresight about the prices w_t, P_t in future is not available, the firm has to replace these by their corresponding conditional expectations $E(w_{t+i+1} | \Omega_t)$ and $E(P_{t+i+1} | \Omega_t)$. However as we have seen this replacement procedure works due to the separation principle which is implicitly assumed here by the concept of random shocks only in white noise forms (i.e., zero mean and constant variance stationarity) and the Gaussian distribution which justified the linear conditional regression procedure, e.g.,

$$w_{t+i+1} = E(w_{t+i+1} | \Omega_t) + \text{error}$$
$$P_{t+i+1} = E(P_{t+i+1} | \Omega_t) + \text{error} \tag{3.12}$$

where the errors are again white noise. For non-Gaussian structure the linearity of the conditional regression (3.12) may not hold and for non-stationary shocks, the rule of forecasting w_{t+i+1} by $\hat{w}_{t+i+1} = E(w_{t+i+1} | \Omega_t)$ may have errors $\epsilon_{t+i+1} = |\hat{w}_{t+i+1} - w_{t+i+1}|$ which diverge as $t \to \infty$.

Two most useful implications of the optimal decision rule (3.9) are that it allows analysis of various hypothetical interventions or changes in the environment and alternative information structures in a local sense when the errors $\epsilon_{t+i+1} = |\hat{w}_{t+i+1} - w_{t+i+1}|$ are small, though divergent for $t \to \infty$. Intervention by government policy may mean here a change in one of the polynomials $\delta_w(L)$, $\delta_u(L)$, $\delta_D(L)$, or $\delta_\epsilon(L)$ that specify the dynamic probabilistic movement of W, u, D and ϵ which affect the market. Quantitative predictions about the impact of such specific interventions e.g. a sales tax on the product would change the coefficients of $\delta_D(L)D_t$, may thus be estimated. Also for small n, a Cournot–Nash type equilibrium can be specifically characterized on the dynamic plane, where the impact of other agents' interventions can be analyzed [15,25].

The role of information structures behind the conditional expectation forecasts (3.12) may be illustrated through two simple examples, one due to Whittle [40], where the certainty equivalence principle fails to hold due to the control framework being non-LQG and the other due to Chu [8], where the dynamic system is decentralized under a set of controllers each having different information and control variables.

EXAMPLE 2 (investment under asymmetric utility): This is a single-stage investment model under uncertain returns, where the investor chooses his consumption , a control variable to decide on his investment $(x - c)$ so as to maximize the utility function

$$U(x, c) = a(c) + b(x - c) \tag{4.1}$$

where

$$a(c) = 1 - \exp(-c), \quad c \geqslant 0$$

$$b(x) = \begin{cases} 0, & x < x_0 \quad x_0: \quad \text{threshold level} \\ b, & x \geqslant x_0 \quad b > 1, \quad x_0 > 0 \end{cases}$$

x_0 is assumed known.

If there were no uncertainty in return from investment x and all parameters were known, the optimal control is

$$c^0 = (x - x_0)^+ = \begin{cases} x - x_0, & \text{if} \quad x \geqslant x_0 \\ -(x - x_0), & \text{if} \quad x < x_0 \end{cases}$$

Now let ϵ be the random variable denoting uncertainty in return from investment with the expected utility function

$$EU(x, c) = a(c) + E[b(x - c - \epsilon)].$$

Let ϵ be exponentially distributed with expectation $E(\epsilon) = \lambda^{-1}$, $g > 0$ being known. Then the optimal consumption becomes

$$c_t^0 = \left[\frac{\lambda(x - x_0) - \log(\lambda b)}{\lambda + 1} \right]_t \tag{4.2}$$

where the subscript t is used to indicate that the parameters are estimable from the information set at t. If we equate (4.2) to

$$c_t^0 = (x - \bar{\epsilon} - x_0)_t$$

where $\bar{\epsilon}$ is the conditional mean forecast of ϵ, we see that instead of the simple linear least squares forecast $\bar{\epsilon} = 1/\lambda$, one has to accept the estimate $\bar{\epsilon}$ as

$$\bar{\epsilon} = \frac{(x - x_0) + \log(\lambda b)}{1 + \lambda}.$$

Thus, if there is uncertainty, the forecast $\bar{\epsilon}$ is both dependent on x and unduly large in value if b is large. This is due to the threshold nature of the utility function, whereby the optimal policy goes to great lengths to avoid the risk of investment falling below the threshold level x_0. Such problems would be compounded when an intertemporal utility maximization is introduced.

EXAMPLE 3 (Value of information structures in teams): Consider a time invariant deterministic dynamic system with N controllers each having a control vector u_i of m_i elements $i = 1, 2, \ldots, N$:

$$\frac{dx}{dt} = Ax + \sum_i B_i u_i; \quad x_0 \text{ given.} \tag{5.1}$$

Here x, an n-element vector is the state variable for the entire system, where the common objective of all the controllers is to minimize the loss function

$$J = \tfrac{1}{2} \int_0^\infty \left[x'Qx + \sum_i u_i' R_i u_i \right] dt \tag{5.2}$$

where Q is positive semidefinite and R_i positive definite and x is measured as deviation from the target level $x = 0$. The information available to controller i at any time is assumed to be

$$y_i = H_i x; \quad i = 1, 2, \ldots, N \tag{5.3}$$

where $H_i \neq H_j$ when $i \neq j$ and H_i has k_i independent rows. The y_i vector in (5.3) includes all information available to controller i through all channels of communication. Further, the control vector u_i is assumed to be a direct linear feedback from y_i, i.e.,

$$u_i = F_i y_i, \quad i = 1, 2, \ldots, N \tag{5.4}$$

where F_i is a time invariant $m_i \times k_i$ matrix. The decision problem is how to optimally choose the feedback gains matrix F_i for all i so that at J in (5.2) is minimized. On using (5.3), (5.4) in (5.1) and solving for $x(t)$ and substituting it in (5.2) we obtain

$$J = \tfrac{1}{2} \operatorname{trace} \left[\int_0^\infty \left\{ e^{D't} M e^{Dt} \right\} dt \right] \tag{5.5}$$

where

$$M = Q + \sum_{i=1}^{N} H_i' F_i' R_i' F_i H_i$$

$$D = A + \sum_i B_i F_i H_i; \quad \text{prime is transpose}$$

D is restricted to be a stable matrix with the sum of all its

eigenvalues having negative real parts.

Two extreme cases of information structures may now be distinguished: (a) complete information and (b) null information. In the first case the information channel matrix H_i in (5.3) has full rank n for all i. By using the Riccati equation [19], the well known optimal control solution is the feedback rule

$$u_{ic}^* = -R_i^{-1} B_i' K_c x, \quad i = 1, 2, \ldots, N \tag{5.6}$$

and the associated value of the loss function is:

$$J_c^* = \tfrac{1}{2} \operatorname{trace} K_c \tag{5.7}$$

where the subscript c stands for complete information and the matrix K_c satisfies the matrix Riccati equation

$$K_c A + A'K_c + Q - K_c \sum_{i=1}^{N} \left(B_i R_i^{-1} B_i' \right) K_c = 0 \qquad (5.8)$$

In case of null information, no controller has access to any information on x, since the information channel matrix H_i has zero rank for all i. The optimal solutions are now:

$$u_{i0}^* = 0, \quad i = 1, 2, \ldots, N$$

$$J_0^* = \tfrac{1}{2} \text{ trace } K_0 \quad \text{and} \quad K_0 A + A'K_0 + Q = 0$$

where subscript zero stands for null information. Generally we would have $J_0^* \geqslant J_c^*$ and the controllers $\{u_{ic}^*\}$ would be more stabilizing than $\{u_{i0}^*\}$. Thus the value of any information structure, intermediate between these two extreme cases can be evaluated in terms of the relative difference $(J_0^* - J_{int}^*)$, where J_{int}^* is the loss function corresponding to any intermediate level control $\{u_{i,int}^*\}$. Two comments may be made about the applicability of this formulation. First, the rank measure associated with H_i, which emphasizes only the degree of nonsingularity of the channel may be easily generalized to represent relative costs associated with noisy measurements of the state. In that case complete information may denote perfect forecasts of the parameters of the optimal controller. Second, the plant dynamics may contain additive shocks ϵ_t in the form of Gaussian white noise process, in which case the common objective function J in (5.2) would be replaced by $E_0 J$ as before conditional on all information available up to time zero. Such stochastic formulations are reported elsewhere [38].

3. Causality in stochastic models

The concept of causality plays a central role in control theory models and its applications. In deterministic theory, inputs may be viewed as causes (or instruments of control) and outputs or state variables (or targets) as effects. The concepts of controllability and observability used in control theory imply in some sense this view of causality. For instance consider the dynamic model in vector-matrix form with $\dot{x}(t)$ denoting dx/dt, $x(t)$ being the output vector and $u(t)$ being the control vector

$$\dot{x}(t) = Ax(t) + Bu(t)$$

$$x(0) \text{ given} \qquad (6.1)$$

the system (6.1) is then said to be completely output (or state) controllable on the time interval $0 \leqslant t \leqslant T$ if for given $t = 0$ and $t = T$, each initial output vector $x(0)$ in its admissible set can be transferred to any final state $x(t)$, using some control $u(t)$ over the closed interval $0 \leqslant t \leqslant T$. The property of observability in control theory, which is akin to estimability in statistical theory, is introduced through a distinction between the state vector $x(t)$ and output vector $y(t)$, where $y(t)$ is observable from past measurements but not $x(t)$. Consider for example the dynamics of (6.1) augmented by

$$y(t) = Gx(t) + H(t) \tag{6.2}$$

where g, H are constant parameters. Now consider (6.1) and assume $u(t)$ to be zero for all t, i.e., the case of no control. This uncontrolled system is said to be completely observable on the interval $0 \leqslant t \leqslant T$, if for given $t = 0$, $t = T$, every unobservable state vector $x(0)$ in its admissible domain can be determined from the knowledge of observations on output $y(t)$ on the interval $0 \leqslant t \leqslant T$ determined by (6.2).

In stochastic control, the existence of one-way feedback between inputs as stochastic processes and outputs as the induced stochastic process implies a similar notion of causality, although care is needed to quantify in some precise manner the one way feedback from the input process $\{u(t, w)\}$ to the output process $\{y(t, \epsilon)\}$, where w, ϵ indicate the randomness of the processes and also the two stochastic processes must satisfy some existence conditions when $T \to \infty$. The latter conditions are usually introduced by assuming that the two processes are mutually jointly stationary. Let $z(t) = (u(t), y(t))$ be a stochastic process, where the random elements are not explicitly shown, i.e., $z(t) = z(t, w)$, $t \in [0, T]$, $w \in W$. The process $z(t)$ is then defined to be strictly stationary if the joint probability distribution of the random variables $z(t_1 + \tau)$, $z(\tau_2 + \tau)$, $z(T + \tau)$ is identical with the joint distribution of the random variables $z(t_1)$, $z(t_2), \dots, \dots, z(t)$. A stochastic process is stationary in the wide sense if the expectations $E[z(t)]$ and $E[z^2(t)]$ exist in the sense of being finite and are independent of t and the covariances $E[z(t)x'(t + \tau)]$ depend only on τ, the time difference.

Now let $I_t(q)$ denote the set of past observed values of any variable q before time t and if q is defined as the set of elements in $z(t)$ without the element $u(t)$, the corresponding observation set is denoted by $I_t(z(t) - u(t))$. Let the mean square errors using the information sets $I_t(z(t))$, $I_t(z(t) - u(t))$ and $I_t(z(t) - y(t))$ be denoted by $\sigma^2(y(t) | I_t(z(t)))$, $\sigma^2(y(t) | I_t(z(t) - u(t)))$ and $\sigma^2(u(t) | I_t(z(t - y(t))))$, respectively. Then in forecasting models, Wiener [39] suggested that one time series $u(t)$ may be said to be causal to the second series $y(t)$, if knowledge of the first series in the form of $I_t(u(t))$ reduces the mean square prediction error of the second series $y(t)$ in a conditional sense, i.e.,

$$\sigma^2\big(y(t)\,|\,I_t(u(t))\big) < \sigma^2\big(y(t)\,|\,I_t(z(t)-u(t))\big). \tag{6.3}$$

For nonexperimental data, where data or measurements cannot be generated by physical experiments (e.g., engineering experiments), one may
need an additional condition for $u(t)$ to be causal to $y(t)$, i.e., the mean
square prediction error of $u(t)$ using $I_t(y(t))$ is more than that of $y(t)$
using $I_t(u(t))$, i.e.,

$$\sigma^2\big(y(t)\,|\,I_t(u(t))\big) < \sigma^2\big(u(t)\,|\,I_t(y(t))\big) \tag{6.4}$$

Granger [13] and others [4,36] have developed this notion of Wiener's
causality for linear systems. Denoting by asterisks the minimum value of
mean square linear prediction error, u is said to cause y, if

$$\sigma_*^2\big(y(t)\,|\,I_t(z(t))\big) < \sigma_*^2\big(y(t)\,|\,I_t(z(t)-u(t))\big). \tag{6.5}$$

In other words, prediction of y using past control measurements u is
more accurate than without using past u. This is one-way feedback from
u to y. Feedback becomes two-way if, in addition to (6.5), the following
holds:

$$\sigma_*^2\big(u(t)\,|\,I_t(z(t))\big) < \sigma_*^2\big(u(t)\,|\,I_t(z(t)-y(t))\big). \tag{6.6}$$

When the dynamic model is in terms of difference equations, one may
easily develop statistical tests for Granger-type causality. By Wold's
theorem it is well known that a full-rank stationary process $z(t) = (y(t),
u(t))$ has an autoregressive representation

$$\begin{pmatrix} y(t) \\ u(t) \end{pmatrix} = \begin{bmatrix} A_{11}(L) & A_{12}(L) \\ A_{21}(L) & A_{22}(L) \end{bmatrix} \begin{pmatrix} y(t) \\ u(t) \end{pmatrix} + \begin{pmatrix} e(t) \\ \epsilon(t) \end{pmatrix} \tag{6.7}$$

where L is the lag operator, i.e., $Ly(t) = y(t-1)$ and the typical elements
of $A_{jk}(L)$ are given by $\sum_{i=1}^{\infty} A_{jki} L^i$ and the $\{e(t), \epsilon(t)\}$ are white noise
processes with zero means and constant variance–covariance matrix.
Now if $u(t)$ does not cause $y(t)$, we must have the coefficients A_{12i} in
$A_{jk}(L) = \sum_{i=1}^{\infty} A_{jki} L^i$ identically zero for all i with $j = 1$, $k = 2$. Thus one
may identify causal relations among economic variables $\{y(t), u(t)\}$ by
fitting a vector autoregressive model in the form (6.7) and checking if
$A_{12i}(L) = 0$ for all i. Note that this is equivalent to checking if the
coefficient matrix $A(L) = (A_{ij}(L))$ is of block-diagonal or recursive
form. Two difficulties may arise in statistically applying this test: one is
that the coefficient matrix $A(L) = (A_{ij}(L))$ on the right hand side of

(6.7) may have near-singularity or less than full rank due to multicollinearity. In this case the autoregressive representation (6.7) is no longer unique and recursiveness may not be sufficient. Second, testing for i greater than 3 may involve arbitrary truncation of the lag terms and the coefficients of variables with higher order lags may be very sensitive to estimate.

For discrete-time dynamic models where Granger-type causality is usually applied, one has to note that this concept emphasizes three important aspects of specification as follows: (a) recursiveness in coefficient structure, (b) cause preceding in time over the effect and (c) asymmetry of relationships or one way feedback. About the first we have already emphasized its importance in (6.7) for Granger-type tests. However, a much broader concept of recursiveness has been emphasized by H. Wold [41] in his "pure causal chain" and "conditional causal chain" models. In these latter models, Wold has argued that in many cases two-way feedback or simultaneous relationships (i.e., non-causal) between $y(t)$ and $u(t)$ may be reduced to one way feedback or causal relationships, by improving the specifications. Thus, the equilibrium condition of demand equals supply may be transformed to an inventory equation with its impact on price.

The implication of cause preceding in time over the effect or state variable is that the proper form of a controllable discrete-time dynamic model is as follows

$$x(t+1) = Ax(t) + Bu(t) \tag{6.8}$$

so that the cause $u(t)$ at time t preceeds the system at time $t+1$. Hence if we have the econometric model in the form

$$x(t) = A_1 x(t-1) - B_1 u(t) \tag{6.9}$$

it is not proper. The causal variables $u(t)$, e.g., government expenditures are contemporaneous with the effect variables $x(t)$, e.g., national income. However one may redefine the system (6.9) in terms of a new vector $y(t) = x(t) - B_1 u(t)$ and obtain a causal system.

$$y(t) = A_1 x(t-1) = A_1 y(t-1) - A_1 B_1 u(t-1) \tag{6.10}$$

that is in proper form and hence controllable. Note however that the parameters in (6.10) enter nonlinearly, i.e., not linearly as in (6.9). Also if any of the parameters A_1, B_1 contain random elements or estimated quantities, the principles of certainty equivalence and separation mentioned before would not hold.

The asymmetry of relationships between the cause and the effect variables is closely related to the distinction in simultaneous models between endogenous and exogenous variables. The exogeneity of the cause variable is exploited in linear econometric models through the reduced form or two-stage methods of estimation. If cause is exogenous, then statistical tests for the exogeneity specification may be developed by following the procedures proposed by Gewek using the results from Granger [14] and Sims [36]. Consider for example the dynamic simultaneous model

$$B(L)y(t) + C(L)u(t) = \epsilon(t) \tag{6.11}$$

where the expectation $E\epsilon(t) = 0$, all t, and the covariance $\text{cov}(\epsilon(T), u(t-s)) = 0$ for all t and all $s \geq 0$ and $\text{cov}(\epsilon(t), y(t-s)) = 0$ for all t and all $s > 0$. The vector of disturbances $\epsilon(t)$ is assumed to be serially uncorrelated and the operators $B(L)$, $C(L)$ are matrix polynomials of the lag operator L, which is defined by $L^s w(t) = W(t-s)$. If the polynomial $B(L)$ has an inverse $B^{-1}(L)$ (I.e., in this case it is said to be stable lag operator), then (6.11) can be reduced to a form:

$$y(t) = -B^{-1}(L)C(L)u(t) + B^{-1}(L)\epsilon(t)$$

which has the following conditional interpretation: Given the current values and the past history of the exogenous variables $u(t)$ and the shocks $\epsilon(t)$, the system (6.11) determines the endogenous variables $y(t)$ completely. However if $B(L)$ is not invertible, i.e., not stable, then this causal interpretation fails to hold. Exploiting this implication, Geweke [14] has developed a simple test for the exogeneity of certain variables in linear dynamic models like $u(t)$ as follows: Let the regression of $y(t)$ on all current and lagged values of $u(t)$ be:

$$y(t) = F(L)u(t) + e(t) \tag{6.12}$$

where $\text{cov}(e(t), u(t-x)) = 0$ for all $s \geq 0$ and $e(t)$ is a white noise stochastic process with autoregressive representation. Let the regression of $y(t)$ on all lagged, current and also future values of $u(t)$ be

$$y(t) = G(L)u(t) + \eta(t) \tag{6.13}$$

where $\text{cov}(\eta(t), u(t-s)) = 0$ for all s and $\eta(t)$ is a white noise stochastic process with autoregressive representation. Then the $u(t)$ variable is exogenous, if and only if in the regression problem (6.13) the coefficients on future values of $u(t)$ are equal to zero.

Two comments are in order. This regression test is no doubt very easy to apply, if the polynomials $B(L)$ did not involve lags higher than two. For higher order lags the estimated coefficients in $B(L)$ may be highly sensitive to multicollinearity and other problems due to errors of observations. Second, if there remains any serial correlation in $e(t)$ and $\eta(t)$ as is most likely, than any method to filter out the serial correlation so to say may transform the problem to a nonlinear one, whereby the linearity of the conditional regression argument cannot be exploited anymore.

4. Estimation and control in differential games

Noncooperative differential games arise very naturally in duopolistic and oligopolistic markets, where rival suppliers choose their strategies over time making some conjectures (i.e., conjectural variation) about their rivals' strategies. Four illustrative examples about such dynamic games are presented here. The first due to Dolezal [9] assumes a two-player zero-sum differential game where it is supposed that the minimizing player selects the values of certain parameters to further decrease the payoff functional at the expense of the maximizing player. In economic situations, the choice of these parameters by the minimizing player may be due to any of several reasons, e.g., specialized private information, initial threat or some form of adaptive behavior. The second model due to Chow [5,7] has two decision makers, the government and the private sector, each choosing its optimal feedback control rules under an LQG framework. This generates a set of observations from which the statistical estimates of various parameters in the system equations and in the objective functions have to be made.

The third model, due to Levhari and Mirman [24] generalizes the implications of the so-called "Cod War" between Iceland and the United Kingdom through a Cournot–Nash equilibrium solution of the differential game between two players, each taking into account the other's actions. In such a framework estimation is not a passive process but an active learning sequence. The fourth model, due to Sengupta and Sfeir [33] discusses in some detail the dominant role of Brazil in the world's coffee economy. To test the plausibility of the dominance hypothesis, three alternative specifications of the differential game are attempted and empirically tested. A comparative evaluation of these three models across two sample periods 1945–61 and 1962–79 (annual data) is performed along with tests for overall predictive power and stability. These tests reveal Brazil's role coming out in sharp focus through such features as cautious behavior and a sharp divergence from the strictly monopolistic strategy.

EXAMPLE 4 (Optimal parameter estimation in zero-sum game): Consider a continuous time dynamic model for the state vector x with two control vectors u and v, one for each player

$$\dot{x} = f(x, u, v, a, t)$$

$$x(0) = x_0, \quad t \in [0, T]. \tag{7.1}$$

The minimizing player (player I) chooses his optimal strategies $u(t)$ and the optimal parameter vector a by minimizing the cost functional (payoff)

$$J(u, v; a) = [S(x, a)]_T + \int_0^T L(x, u, v, a, t) \mathrm{d}t. \tag{7.2}$$

The maximizing player (player II) maximizes the same cost functional $J(u, v; a)$ by using a strategy vector $v(t)$, where both control vectors $u(t)$ and $v(t)$ have constraints such that $u(t) \in U$, $v(t) \in V$, where U and V are closed bounded and convex sets. Also $a \in A$ where A is a closed bounded convex set. These assumptions lead to a simple characterization of the solution of the above differential games as a saddle point, i.e., a strategy pair (u^*, v^*) with $u^* \in U$. $v^* \in V$ for which it holds

$$J(u^*, v; a) \leqq J(u^*, v^*; a) \leqq J(u, v^*; a) \quad \text{where} \quad a \in A. \tag{7.3}$$

Denoting the Hamiltonian by $H = L(x, u, v, a, t) + \lambda' f(x, u, v, a, t)$ the necessary conditions of optimality according to Pontryagin's maximum principle can be written as:

$$\dot{\lambda} = -f_x' \lambda - L_x \qquad t \in [0, T]$$

$$[\lambda - S_x']_T = 0 \quad \text{(transversality)}$$

$$H(u^*, v^*) = \min_{u \in U} H(u, v^*) = \max_{v \in V} H(u^*, v) \tag{7.4}$$

$$\left\{ \int_0^T (\lambda' f_a + L_a) \mathrm{d}t + [S_a]_T \right\} \delta a \geqslant 0$$

where prime denotes transpose, dot is time derivative and subscripts on S, f, L denote partial derivative, e.g., $[S_a]_T$ is $\partial S(a, x)/\partial a$ evaluated at $t = T$. Further ∂a denotes any feasible parameter change. Note that the third equation of (7.4) specifies the saddle-point condition, whereas the last equation determines the optimal value, a^* of a. If the sufficiency conditions are satisfied by the solution of (7.4), then we have to solve a nonlinear two-point boundary value problem of $2n$ differential equations if x has n dimensions. Here one has to apply a numerical method like the modified gradient or conjugate gradient. For the following example

$$\dot{x}_1 = -0.9x_1 + 0.9ax_2 + 0.9v; \quad x_1(0) = 2.0$$

$$\dot{x}_2 = 0.45(x_1 + x_2) + 1.35u; \quad x_2(0) = 2.0$$

$$J = 0.5[x_1 + x_2] + 0.45\int_0^1 (u^2 - v^2)dt.$$

An initial start assumed the values $u(t) = v(t) = 0$ and $a = -0.5$ and after 30 iterations of the first-order gradient algorithm the optimal value of found was $a^* = -1.6357$ with $J(a^*) = 1.4838$. These values were very close to exact values $a^* = -1.338$, $J(a^*) = 1.484$ found previously by Leondes and Siu [23].

Note that this parameter a may be associated with the control strategies u and v and the optimal value a^* may be unknown to the relevant player. The above iterative procedure may then represent learning or adjustment processes. Secondly, if a admits of random variations so that $a = \bar{a} + \epsilon$ with its mean $\bar{a}$ and white noise error ϵ, than an optimal value of $\bar{a}$ may be characterized by the above method. The sensitivity of the cost functional $J(\bar{a}^*)$ and the associated trajectories of the state and adjoint variables may be easily analyzed by numerical procedures. This permits a kind of robustness analysis for the minimax solutions of differential games.

EXAMPLE 5 (Estimation of parameters of optimal control): Consider an LQG model with the quadratic objection function

$$\min J = \sum_{t=1}^{T} \beta^t(y(t) - a_0)K_0(y(t) - a) \tag{8.1}$$

with $y(t)$ as the state vector and $u(t)$ as control having a linear dynamic system with constant parameters

$$y(t) = Ay(t-1) + Cu(t) + b + e(t). \tag{8.2}$$

Here the disturbance vector $e(t)$ is assumed to be normally independently distributed with mean zero and covariance matrix S, a_0 is a constant vector of targets, β is a scalar discount factor (assumed to be known) and K_0 is a constant weighting matrix. Minimizing the expectation of J in (8.1) subject to (8.2) leads to a set of optimal feedback decision rules as we have seen before:

$$u(t) = G(t)y(t-1) + g(t) \tag{8.3}$$

where it is well known that by the recurrence relations of dynamic programming algorithm the coefficients $G(t)$ and $g(t)$ are obtained by solving the following pairs of equations backward in time from $t = T$:

$$(C'H(t)C)G(t) + C'H(t)A = 0 \tag{8.4.1}$$

$$H(t) - K(t) - (A + CG(t+1))'H(t+1)(A + CG(t+1)) = 0 \tag{8.4.2}$$

$$(C'H(t)C)g(t) + C'(H(t)h - h(t)) = 0 \tag{8.4.3}$$

$$h(t) - K(t)a_0 + (A + CG(t+1))'(H(t+1)b - h(t+1)) = 0 \tag{8.4.4}$$

where prime denotes transpose and $K(t) = \beta'K_0$ is such that $H(T) = K(T)$ and $h(T) = K(T)a_0$.

Suppose we have observed the optimal behavior of the decision-makers as revealed in the linear decision rule (8.3), the problem is to statistically estimate the parameters A, C, S, b, K_0, a_0 and others entering into the coefficient matrices $G(t)$ and the vector $g(t)$.

The above estimation problem can be interpreted as a two-person differential game, by letting the control vector $u(t)$ be partitioned into two subvectors $u_1(t)$, $u_{11}(t)$ each under the control of one player. Each player will have his own objective function in the form of (8.1) and his optimal feedback rule in the form of (8.4). The first player (or a group of decision makers) may represent the representative firm in the private sector (or all the aggregate of firms in the private sector) and the second may represent the government (or a group of public agencies). Alternatively the two players may refer to two private firms as in duopoly.

Note that the problem of statistical estimation of the parameters of optimal control rules is complicated by two sources. One is the time varying nature of $G(t)$ and $g(t)$ and the second is the nonlinear nature of parameters entering into the system (8.4) which serve as implicit constraints for $G(t)$ and $g(t)$. To obtain simpler situations, Chow [7] assumes $G(t)$, $g(t)$ to be time invariant $G(t) = G$, $g(t) = g$ and thereby obtains a steady-state approximation of (8.4) as:

$$
\begin{aligned}
&(C'HC)G - C'HA = 0 \\
&H - K - \beta(A + CG)'H(A + CG) = 0 \\
&(C'HC)g + C'(Hb - h) = 0 \\
&[I - \beta(A + CG)']h - K_0a_0 + \beta(A + CG)'Hb = 0
\end{aligned}
\tag{8.5}
$$

where the time subscript has been dropped in H, G, g and h. The steady state form of the optimal feedback rule (8.3) would be reduced to

$$u(t) = GY(t-1) + g + \epsilon(t), \quad \epsilon(t) \sim N(0, V) \tag{8.6}$$

where the random error ϵ, which is a zero mean independent normal with a covariance matrix V, has been added to denote observational errors.

The steady-state statistical problem is how to obtain optimal estimation of the parameters A, C, b and S or, equivalently the parameters K_0 and a_0 of the loss function (8.1) and G, g and V of (8.6) subject to the equality constraints (8.5). Two methods of consistent estimation are presented. One is the maximum likelihood (ML) method, whereby a lagrangian expression (L) combining the log-likelihood of the errors $e(t)$ and ϵ with the equality constraints (8.5) is formed

$$L = \text{constant} - \tfrac{1}{2}n \log|S| - \tfrac{1}{2}n \log|V|$$

$$- \tfrac{1}{2} \text{ tr. } \left[S^{-1}\left(Y' - AY'_{-1} - CU' - bz'\right)\left(Y - Y_{-1}A' - UC' - zb'\right)\right]$$

$$- \tfrac{1}{2} \text{ tr. } \left[V^{-1}\left(U' - GY'_{-1} - gz'\right)\left(U - Y_{-1}G' - zg'\right)\right]$$

$$- \tfrac{1}{2} \text{ tr. } M_1 - \tfrac{1}{2} \text{ tr. } M_2 - \tfrac{1}{2} \text{ tr. } M_3 - \tfrac{1}{2} \text{ tr. } M_4. \tag{8.7}$$

Here Y is an $n \times p$ matrix of endogenous variables, Y_{-1} is an $n \times p$ matrix of observations on the lagged endogenous variables, U is an $n \times q$ matrix of observations on the control variables, z is a vector of n ones and the matrices M_1 through M_4 are Lagrange multipliers associated with the four constraints of (8.5).

The second method, which belongs to the class of two-stage least squares (LS) may be easily illustrated for estimating the parameters of the objective function (8.1) only. In the first step of this method one obtains the LS estimates $\hat{G}$ of the coefficients in the multivariate regression of $u(t)$ on $y(t-1)$ from (8.6). In the second stage, one uses $\hat{G}$ to satisfy the first two equations of (8.5), thus obtaining values of $\hat{H}$ and $\hat{K}$. However there may frequently arise the problem of more equations that unknowns and those methods of normalization which are applied to the case of overidentified structural equations must have to be adopted.

Two types of usefulness of this estimation approach come readily to mind. One is that the government (second player) can form better rules, once it can predict how its decision rule would affect the behavior of the private economic agents (player one). To this extent adaptivity in fixed rules can be built in to take advantage of any unreliability or imprecision in prediction. Secondly, other types of solutions, e.g., Cournot–Nash equilibrium which in effect will modify the conditions (8.5) may be similarly admitted in terms of the ML and two-stage LS.

However, one has to note several theoretical and practical problems in this approach. Practically speaking, iterative numerical methods required by the ML and 2-stage LS may be computationally very expensive and also sensitive due to multicollinearity. Further, the case of time-varying coefficients in (8.4), instead of its steady-state approximation in (8.5) may require the solution of nonlinear equations. The interpretation of estimated coefficients changing in time, in terms of structural economic theory is not very easy, since alternative loss functions or alternative set of constraints on control or state which are generally unobserved are not introduced for comparative purposes.

Theoretically one may raise two basic types of objections. First, there is the specification problem, since there is no reliable way to guarantee for economic data sets that the optimal feedback rules followed by the agents are indeed of the form (8.3), so that only those observations which satisfy (8.3) are utilized in computing the estimates. A class of loss functions leading to a class of decision rules may have to be considered, before one estimation can be recommended. Also, one needs some form of robustness analysis for the estimates; for if the estimates are highly sensitive to outlier observations, the model specification needs to be examined more intensively. Secondly, there are more than one-type of solution which are plausible in game theory models. Chow's method assumes that we know which type of solution is relevant to our observations. In reality of course we do not have such information. As we will see in example 7 on a differential game model for world coffee that even the players may not be always aware of the particular solution worth striving for. A constructive approach in such a situation is to compare alternative specifications, each dependent on a particular type of solution structure and test by the likelihood-ratio tests which particular specification agrees most closely with the given observations. Note also that the steady state approximation in (8.5) may not hold for infinite horizon problems $(T \to \infty)$, if the controlled system, i.e.,

$$y(t) = (A + GC)y(t-1) + b$$

has instability in the sense that any eigenvalue of $(A + GC)$ has its absolute part exceeding unity. Also, if the error processes $e(t)$, $\epsilon(t)$ are nonstationary, the ML and 2-stage LS methods do not hold.

EXAMPLE 6 (Fish war game between two countries): Each country i $(i = 1, 2)$ must decide on the optimal amount of catch c_i of fish, which if uninterrupted, grows according to the biological law

$$x(t+1) = x^\alpha(t), \quad 0 < \alpha < 1 \tag{9.1}$$

It is assumed that this optimal decision is made by each country by maximizing the sum of the discounted utility of fish

$$V = \sum_{t=0}^{\infty} \beta^t u_i(c_i) = \sum_{t=0}^{\infty} \beta_i^t \log c_i, \quad 0 < \beta_i < 1 \tag{9.2}$$

where β_i^t is the discounting function for each country and the utility $u_i(c_i)$ is taken in logarithmic form. If there is a one period horizon and if country 1 assumes country 2's actions as given (e.g., zero conjectural variations in the classical Cournot model), its optimal control rule c_1 is easily found from the maximization problem

$$\max_{0 \leqslant c_1 \leqslant x - c_2} \left\{ \log c_1 + \beta_1 \log\left[\tfrac{1}{2}(x - c_1 - c_2)^\alpha\right] \right\}$$

$$= \max_{0 \leqslant c_1 \leqslant x - c_2} \left\{ \log c_1 + \alpha\beta_1 \log(x - c_1 - c_2) + \beta_1 \log \tfrac{1}{2} \right\} \qquad (9.3)$$

where c_1 is the optimal catch of country 1, given the catch c_2 of country 2, whereas $(x - c_1 - c_2)$ denotes the remaining stock of fish which grows to $(x - c_1 - c_2)^\alpha$ in the next period. The first order condition for the maximum in (9.3) is

$$(1 + \alpha\beta_1)c_1 + c_2 = x \qquad (9.4.1)$$

which specifies the reaction curve of country 1 in the one-period model. Similar arguments gives the optimal reaction curve of country 2 as

$$c_1 + (1 + \alpha\beta_2)c_2 = x \qquad (9.4.2)$$

The equilibrium Cournot–Nash solution $(\bar{c}_1, \bar{c}_2)$ given by the simultaneous solution of (9.4.1) and (9.4.2) is

$$\bar{c}_1 = D^{-1}(\alpha\beta_2)x; \quad D = \left(\alpha^2\beta_1\beta_2 + \alpha\beta_1 + \alpha\beta_2\right)$$

$$\bar{c}_2 = D^{-1}(\alpha\beta_1)x \qquad (9.5)$$

$$y = x - \bar{c}_1 - \bar{c}_2 = D^{-1}\left(\alpha^2\beta_1\beta_2\right)x$$

Next we consider a two-period horizon problem with country 1 still assuming that in future the one period Cournot–Nash solution (9.5) would prevail. The optimal value of the objective function under the one-period Cournot–Nash solution (9.5) is

$$V_1(1) = \log \bar{c}_1 + \beta_1 \log(\tfrac{1}{2}) + \alpha\beta_1 \log(\bar{x} - \bar{c}_1 - \bar{c}_2)$$

$$= (1 + \alpha\beta_1) \log x + A_1$$

where

$$A_1 = \log \frac{(\alpha\beta_2)(\alpha^2\beta_1\beta_2)^{\alpha\beta_1}}{D^{1 + \alpha\beta_1}} + \beta \log(\tfrac{1}{2})$$

Since A_1 is a constant it will have no effect on the optimal policy for the two-year horizon. The objective function of country 1 for the two-year horizon is

$$J_1(2) = \log c_1 + \alpha\beta_1(1 + \alpha\beta_1) \log(x - c_1 - c_2) + A_1.$$

Maximizing this function leads to the reaction curve of country 1

$$\left(1 + \alpha\beta_1 + \alpha^2\beta_1^2\right)c_1 + c_2 = x \tag{9.6.1}$$

Likewise the reaction curve of country 2 is

$$c_1 + \left(1 + \alpha\beta_2 + \alpha^2\beta_2^2\right)c_2 = x. \tag{9.6.2}$$

This process can thus be repeated for an n-period horizon yielding the Cournot–Nash policies

$$\bar{c}_1 = D^{-1}(\alpha\beta_2)\left[\sum_{j=0}^{n-1}(\alpha\beta_2)^j\right]x;$$

$$D = \left(\sum_{j=0}^{n}(\alpha\beta_1)^j\right)\left(\sum_{j=0}^{n}(\alpha\beta_2)^j\right) - 1 \tag{9.6.3}$$

$$\bar{c}_2 = D^{-1}(\alpha\beta_1)\left[\sum_{j=0}^{n-1}(\alpha\beta_1)^j\right]x$$

and the remaining stock is:

$$y = x - \bar{c}_1 - \bar{c}_2 = D^{-1}\left\{\alpha^2\beta_1\beta_2\left(\sum_{j=0}^{n-1}(\alpha\beta_1)^j\right)\left(\sum_{j=0}^{n-1}(\alpha\beta_2)^j\right)x\right\}.$$

It is clear from the above that as $t \to \infty$, the limiting values of $\bar{c}_1$ and $\bar{c}_2$ become

$$\bar{c}_1 = D^{-1}(\alpha\beta_2)(1 - \alpha\beta_1)x; \quad D = 1 - (1 - \alpha\beta_1)(1 - \alpha\beta_2) \tag{9.7}$$

$$\bar{c}_2 = D^{-1}(\alpha\beta_1)(1 - \alpha\beta_2)x \tag{9.8}$$

$$y = x - \bar{c}_1 - \bar{c}_2 = D^{-1}\alpha^2\beta_1\beta_2 x \tag{9.9}$$

To derive the steady-state level of $x(t)$ when the optimal steady state policies (9.7), (9.8) are pursued by the two countries, we consider the growth equation (9.1) under optimal policies for each country. Let $x_0 > 0$ be any initial stock of fish. Under Cournot–Nash equilibrium the growth of fish is governed by the difference equation

$$x(t+1) = [x(t) - c_1(x(t)) - c_2(x(t))]^\alpha. \tag{9.10}$$

At $t = 0$ we get

$$x(1) = [x(0) - c_1(x(0)) - c_2(x(0))]^\alpha$$

$$= x(0)[D^{-1}(\alpha^2\beta_1\beta_2)]^\alpha, \quad D = 1 - (1 - \alpha\beta_1)(1 - \alpha\beta_2).$$

At $t = 1$,

$$x(2) = [x(0)]^{\alpha^2}[D^{-1}(\alpha^2\beta_1\beta_2)]^{\alpha + \alpha^2}$$

At $t = T$

$$x(T) = [x(0)]^{\alpha^T}[D^{-1}(\alpha^2\beta_1\beta_2)]^{\Sigma_{j=1}^T \alpha^j}.$$

Hence as $T \to \infty$, $x(T) \to \bar{x} = D^{-1}(\alpha^2\beta_1\beta_2)^{(1-\alpha)^{-1}\alpha}$. If the discount rates are identical, then the steady state level of fish is

$$\bar{x} = \left(\frac{\alpha\beta}{2 - \alpha\beta}\right)^{\alpha/(1-\alpha)} \tag{9.11}$$

This solution may be compared with the cooperative solution when the two countries combine their catch so as to maximize the discounted sum of both countries' utilities, i.e.,

$$\max \sum_{t=0}^\infty \beta^t\{2u(c(t))\}$$

subject to

$$x(t) + 2c(t) = f(x(t-1))$$

$$x(0) > 0 \text{ given}, \quad f(x) = x^\alpha; \quad u(c) = \log c.$$

The optimal solution in this case must satisfy the necessary condition

$$2\frac{\partial u(c(t))}{\partial c(t)} - 2\beta\frac{\partial u(c(t+1))}{\partial c(t+1)} \cdot \frac{\partial f}{\partial x(t)} = 0$$

from which one obtains the optimal growth equation for $x(t)$ as

$$x(t+1) = [\alpha\beta x(t)]^{\alpha}. \tag{9.12}$$

With an initial stock $x(0) > 0$ given, the steady state solution is

$$\hat{x} = \lim_{t \to \infty} x(t) = (\alpha\beta)^{\alpha/(1-\alpha)}. \tag{9.13}$$

On comparing (9.11) and (9.13) it is seen that $\hat{x} > \bar{x}$, i.e., the Cournot–Nash steady state equilibrium solution implies a smaller quantity of fish than the cooperative solution. Some generalized aspects of the solution structure may be noted here. First, other types of game-theoretic solutions, e.g., Stackelberg's leader–follower model, can be easily envisaged. Second, the linearity of the optimal decision rule in (9.6.3) or in (9.7) and (9.8) suggests, by the analogy of the feedback rule analysed in the LQG model in Example 5, that if there are observational errors in the state variable x where $x = \bar{x} + \epsilon$, ϵ being independent normal with zero mean and constant variance, one could still establish the approximate optimality of $\bar{c}_1$ and $\bar{c}_2$ in (9.7) and (9.8). This is so because x tends to $\bar{x}$ with probability one as the number of observations increases and we get

$$\bar{c}_1 \to k_1\bar{x} \quad \text{and} \quad \bar{c}_2 \to k_2\bar{x}$$

where

$$k_1 = D^{-1}(\alpha\beta_2)(1 - \alpha\beta_1), \quad k_2 = D^{-1}(\alpha\beta_1)(1 - \alpha\beta_2)$$

EXAMPLE 7 (dominant player in world coffee market game): The world coffee market, with its price and quantity fluctuations and the dominant role played by major producers like Brazil has provided an empirical framework uniquely suitable for econometrically testing the applicability of control-theory models and differential game formulations. For testing the dominance hypothesis we have selected three alternative specifications. The common elements of each of which are the use of control variables like output, inventories and price by the major producer (Brazil) and the implicit use of an optimization criterion. The models are as follows:

Model I (Active behavior model)

$$\text{BRUV}(t) = a_{10} + a_{11}\,\text{BRUV}(t-1) + a_{12}\,\text{BRX}(t)$$

$$+ a_{13}\,\text{BRUV}(t+1) + e_1(t)$$

$$BRP(t) = a_{20} + a_{21} \, BRUV(t) + a_{22} \, WOEP(t) + e_2(t) \tag{10.1}$$

$$BRX(t) = a_{30} + a_{31} \, BRUV(t) + a_{32} \, RWXP(t)$$

$$+ a_{33} \, USGNPPC(t) + e_3(t)$$

Model II (Reaction function model)

$$BRP(t) = b_{10} + b_{11} \, BRS(t) + b_{12} \, RWS(t) = e_1(t)$$

$$BRQ(t) = b_2 \, BRQD(t-1) + (1 - b_2) \, BRQ(t-1) + e_2(t) \tag{10.2}$$

$$BRQD(t) = f(RWQ(t-1)) + e_3(t)$$

Model III (Dynamic entry model)

$$WOEX(t) = c_{10} + c_{11} \, BRP(t) + c_{12}t + e_1(t)$$
$$RWEX(t) = RWEX(t-1) + k\left[BRP(t-5) - B\overline{R}P(t-5)\right] + e_2(t)$$

$$\tag{10.3}$$

Here the first two letters in the symbol of a variable stand for the following: BR (Brazil), RW (Rest of the World Excluding Brazil), US (United States of America), WO (World). The rest of the letters are: UV (Unit Value of Exports, X (Exports), P (Real Price), BRP (Real Price of Brazilian Coffee in New York), EP (Exportable Production), XP Percentage of Exports), GNPPC (Gross National Product Per Capita), Q (Production), QD (Desired Output Computed from Optimal Reaction Function), S (Supply Defined as Current Production plus Inventories) and $e_i(t)$ (error at time t).

Econometric estimation and comparative evaluation of performance of these three models are attempted here across two sample periods 1945–61 and 1962–79 with a total of 35 annual observations. The three models have the following dynamic interpretations. The active behavior model (Model I) presumes that Brazil in order to maximize long run profits anticipates the effects of its current actions on future profits and therefore includes in the unit value equation an estimate of the variable BRUV(t + 1) which best represents the state of the future. This is very similar to the linear decision rules of LQG models, which have been very widely applied in explaining industry output–inventory behavior. The reaction function model (Model II) postulates a Cournot–Nash type equilibrium solution, where each player maximizes its own long run profits with a conjectural estimate of the rival's strategy. Thus Brazil's output at time t depends on the actual and desired levels of output in the earlier year, where the desired level is calculated from the optimal reaction curve of Brazil. In contrast to Models I and II, the dynamic entry model (Model III postulates the dominant firm behavior to be sharply different from a single firm monopoly, so that it uses its price as a control variable to maximize long run profits subject to the caution of a rival entry or penetration. The econometric estimates of the three models, which are analyzed in some detail elsewhere [33] suggest a high degree of explanatory power of these models. Since real life applications of game theory models are very few, it is surprising that these alternative models tend to fit the empirical trend satisfactorily. More so, Brazil's role as a dominant supplier comes out in sharp focus through the limit pricing model III. Hence it may be some interest to discuss the application of this model to world coffee. Using the price variable as an entry-preventing strategy by the dominant firm has formed a basic component of the new theory of limit pricing – originally proposed by Bain [3] and later generalized by Gaskins [12] and others [34]. Gaskins in his limit price postulates that the dominant firm maximizes the present value of its future profits

$$V = \int_0^\infty [p(t) - c] Q(p(t), t) e^{-rt} dt$$

where $p(t) =$ price of output, $Q(p(t), t) =$ output sold by the dominant firm, $c =$ average cost per unit of output, $r =$ exogenous rate of discount. here $Q(p(t), t)$ is a residual demand curve, obtained by subtracting the competitive fringe output ($G(t)$, from the total market demand $F(p(t))$:

$$Q(p(t), t) = F(p(t)) - G(t)$$

Rival entry is given by

$$\frac{dG(t)}{dt} = k[p(t) - \bar{p}], \quad G(0) = G_0, \quad \bar{p} \geq c$$

where $\bar{p}$ is limit price and k is a response coefficient indicative of the speed of entry.

On the face of it it seems most likely that the entry model as above would fit the coffee market trend very well. The time series data show very clearly that output and exports of the Rest of the World have been increasing over time, both in percentage and absolute terms. This might be explained through the use of an entry (or market penetration) equation for the Rest of the World as a constraint to the profit maximizing objective of Brazil. It is clear however that Gaskins' model has to be modified in some basic respects to make it more compatible with the coffee market trends. Knowing that high prices today would lead to more planting and thus more output τ years from today, entry by rivals would have to be a function of prices lagged τ years. Various value of τ were tried and $\tau = 5$ was used because it gave the best prediction in terms of high R^2. Second, a discrete-time formulation is needed due to our data being in time-series form. Thus Brazil maximizes the present value of its future profits

$$V = \sum_{t=0}^{\infty} (p(t) - c(t))(F(p) - G(t))(1 + r)^{-t}$$

subject to the entry constraint

$$G(t + 1) - G(t) = k(p(t - 5) - \bar{p}(t - 5)), \qquad G(0) = G_0$$

The Hamiltonian is written as:

$$H = (p(t) - c(t))[F(p) - G(t)](1 + r)^{-t}$$
$$+ z(t)k(p(t - 5) - \bar{p}(t - 5))$$

By Pontryagin's maximum principle, the necessary conditions for a maximum are:

$$[G(t + 1) - G(t)]^* = k(p^*(t - 5) - \bar{p}(t - 5)), \; G^*(0) = G_0 \qquad (10.4)$$

$$[z(t + 1) - z(t)]^* = -\frac{\Delta H(s)}{\Delta G} \qquad (10.5)$$

at

$$s = (G^*(t), z^*(t), p^*(t), t)$$

$$= (p^*(t) - c(t))(1 + r)^{-t}$$

$$H(s) = H(G^*(t), z^*(t), p^*(t), t)$$

$$= \max_{p(t), p(t-5)} H(G^*(t), z^*(t), p(t), p(t - 5), t) \qquad (10.6)$$

where the asterisk denotes optimal points. These necessary conditions are also sufficient since the objective function is strictly concave in $p(t)$. Empirically the market demand is estimated as a function of price and a time trend variable, i.e.,

$$F(p) = \alpha + \beta_1 p(t) + \beta_2 t. \qquad (10.7)$$

By applying the maximum condition (3.3) one obtains

$$\frac{\Delta H}{\Delta p(t)} + \frac{\Delta H}{\Delta p(t-5)}\bigg|_{t+5} = 0$$

which reduces to:

$$\left[F(p) + p(t)F'(p) - G(t) - c(t)F'(p)\right](1+r)^{-t} + z(t+5)k = 0$$

$$(10.8)$$

where prime denotes derivative with respect to p.

On using the equations (10.4) through (10.8) and some algebraic manipulation we finally obtain a difference equation for the optimal control trajectory $p^*(\theta)$ as follows, where $\theta = t + 5$.

$$kp^*(\theta - 10) + 2\beta_1 p^*(\theta - 5) - 2\beta_1 p^*(\theta - 4) + k(1+r)^6 p^*(\theta)$$

$$= \beta_2 - k(1+r)^6 c(\theta) + k\bar{p}(\theta - 10) - \beta_1(c(\theta - 4) - c(\theta - 5))$$

This is a difference equation of the tenth order, from which the time-dependent behavior of the optimal control strategy can be characterized. Also, the dynamic programming algorithm could be applied in principle to solve the two-point boundary value problem characterized by (10.4) through (10.)8. However from a practical standpoint such calculations would not be of significant value. For one thing, the two boundary conditions, the initial and the terminal are not estimated at all. Second, the cost parameters are not empirically identified due to lack of data.

We attempt therefore to characterize two suboptimal solutions in the framework of the limit price model. One is a quasi-monopoly solution derived from the recursive maximization of profits one period at a time. The second is an approximate intertemporal solution based on the replacement of two control variables $p(t)$, $p(t-5)$ by a suitable proxy. The performance of these two suboptimal solution profiles may provide some valuable insight into the usefulness of the dynamic entry model for world coffee.

The estimated parameters of model III for sample I turn out to be as follows:

$$WOEX(t) = 32337.8^* - 209.65^*BRP(t) + 960.82t$$
$$\quad\quad\quad (15.7) \quad\quad\quad (-3.9)$$

$$R^2 = 0.90, DW = 2.8 \quad\quad\quad\quad\quad\quad\quad (10.9.1)$$

$$\text{RWEX}(t) = \text{RWEX}(t-1) + \underset{(1.4)}{44.3} \left(\text{BRP}(t-5) - \overline{\text{BRP}}(t-5) \right)$$

$$R^2 = 0.54, \text{DW} = 1.9 \tag{10.9.2}$$

where $\text{BRP}(t)$ represents the real price of Brazilian coffee in New York and $\overline{\text{BRP}}(t)$ denotes an estimate of limit price based on the cost parameters assumption mentioned before. Using a one-period maximization model, the optimal monopoly solution would require the optimal price $p^*(t)$ for Brazil to be:

$$p^*(t) = \left[c(t)F'(p) + G(t) - F(p) \right] / F'(p) \tag{10.10}$$

where it is assumed that $p(t-5)$ is given recursively in that a succession of one period maximization problem is solved for. If the different variables used in (10.10) are replaced by their estimated values for sample I, this monopoly solution turns out to be more than three times larger than the actual values of the real prices on the average. For the quasi-monopoly solution obtained from the Lagrangian function

$$L = \left[p(t) - c(t) \right] \left(\alpha + \beta_1 p(t) + \beta_2 t - G(T-1) \right)$$

$$- \lambda k \left[p(t-5) - \bar{p}(t-5) \right]$$

the optimal price trajectory, conditional on known values of $p(t-5)$ appears as follows:

$$p^*(t) = (2\beta_1)^{-1} \left\{ c(t)\beta_1 + G(t-1) + k \left[p(t-5) - \bar{p}(t-5) \right] - \beta_2 t - \alpha \right\} \tag{10.11}$$

These values of $p^*(t)$ may be compared with the actual values $p(t)$ for the period 1951–61 as shown in table 1.

The means of $p(t)$ and $p^*(t)$ are 29.98 and 29.19 and their variances turn out to be 73.7 and 6.7. It is clear that the two series do not differ significantly in a statistical sense and the suboptimal series $p^*(t)$ is more stable in terms of much lower variance. It is clear that the suboptimal price trajectory defined by the quasi-monopoly solution (10.11) performed much better than the monopoly solution (10.10) which ignored the threat of actual or potential entry altogether.

The approximate intertemporal solution postulates that the functional relationship between $p(t)$ and $p(t-5)$ can be statistically found by running a linear regression of one on the other. But since in the entry equation it is not the price but the difference between the price and the limit price that is used to explain the change in exports, hence we estimated as follows:

$$\Delta BRP(t) = 25.94^* - 1.1^*\Delta BRP(t-5) - 0.0005^*BRH(t-1)$$
$$\quad\quad\quad (8.6) \quad\quad (-5.6) \quad\quad\quad\quad (-6.7)$$

$$R^2 = 0.84, DW = 1.43$$

where $\Delta PRP(t)$ is the difference between the real observed price and the limit price, $BRH(t)$ is the inventory or stocks held by Brazil. Using this equation one could calculate $\Delta BRP(t-5)$ as a function of $\Delta BRP(t)$ and use this value in the entry equation. For this case the two-point boundary value problem can be explicitly solved in the only one control variable we have, that is the price variable $p(t)$. A comparison of the actual and simulated exports of the Rest of the World, where the latter is based on the suboptimal price trajectory shows very clearly that the empirical correspondence is very close. The mean of the suboptimal price trajectory over 1951–61 turns out to be 32.1 and its variance 12.2. This compares favorably with the mean and variance of the observed price series mentioned before.

Table 1.

Year	$p(t)$	$p^*(t)$	Year	$p(t)$	$p^*(t)$
1951	33.2	33.2	1956	32.4	30.8
1952	43.9	31.5	1957	24.4	24.4
1953	41.5	28.8	1958	21.2	25.7
1954	34.9	32.3	1959	21.3	29.9
1955	37.3	28.2	1960	20.1	28.9
			1961	19.6	27.4

5. Applications of stochastic processes

Recently there has been a substantial increase in the application of various types of stochastic processes in the fields of economics, finance and operations research. A number of books [18,26,38] are now available dealing with such applications. Whereas earlier applications emphasized queuing models, production and inventory control and population growth, recent applications have gone deeper into some of the basic concepts used in economics, e.g., job search, stochastic equilibrium, stabilization and control in a stochastic environment and dynamic portfolio models in finance. Our purpose in this section is to provide an elementary introduction to this field of applied stochastic processes. Gaining some insight rather than mathematical rigor is the object and hence we discuss some recent illustrative applications of stochastic processes in economics with the following questions in mind: (a) What do we gain by replacing the deterministic models by stochastic ones? (b) How to estimate economic models recursively when new information becomes sequentially available? (c) If some process like the Gaussian stochastic process is more applicable as a good first approximation, how can we analyze the implications for stability due to departures from this assumption?

5.1. Introduction to applied stochastic processes

A stochastic process may be viewed in two ways. One is that it is simply a probability process; that is, any process in nature whose evolution can be analyzed successfully in terms of probability, i.e., the transition probability. A second view is that it is a family of random variables denoted by x_t, or, $x(t)$ indexed by $t \in T$. The variation of t over the index set T introduces a dynamical element in the behavior of the random variable, which can be analyzed in two interrelated ways: either in terms of the probability functions dependent on t as t varies, or in terms of the expected value or variance functions of $x(t)$ as t changes. One useful way of division of stochastic processes is in terms of four classes, taking the case where we have one random variable at any particular t: (i) both x and t discrete, (ii) x discrete and t continuous, (iii) x continuous and t discrete and (iv) both x and t continuous. In each of the cases above one can define appropriate probability density functions. Stochastic processes can be classified in several ways depending on the criteria chosen. Three most common criteria are (a) the value taken by the random variable $x(t)$ being in the domain of positive integers or not, (b) the extent of dependence or independence of $x(t)$ on past history or memory and (c) the invariance or otherwise of the joint distribution function of the collection of random variables $x_1 = x(t_1)$, $x_2 = x(t_2), \ldots, x_n = x(t_n)$ under an arbitrary translation of the time parameter.

If the process $x(t)$ is capable of assuming positive integral values only, then it is known as point processes, for in such a case, $x(t)$ can be identified with events or incidences represented as point on the time axis t. Although the parameter t is restricted to play the role of time, the theory of point processes has been generalized to include the multidimensional nature of the parameter t and has been widely applied in ecological problems. A very special class of such processes where the time intervals between successive events are independently and identically distributed are known as renewal processes, that have been most widely studied in statistical literature.

The second criterion introduces the classification of Markovian and non-Markovian processes. For any parametric value t and arbitrarily small $h > 0$, the probability structure of the process corresponding to the parametric value $(t + h)$ may depend only on the probability structure at t. In such a case $x(t)$ is called a Markov process; non-Markovian processes then consist of those processes which do not satisfy the above property of the Markov process known as the Markov property. An alternative way to define Markovian processes is through the joint distribution function of the random variables $X_1 = X(t_1)$, $X_2 = X(t_2), \ldots, X_n = X(t_n)$ for any finite set of $(t_1, t_2, \ldots, t_n)$ of $t \in T$, T being the index set which is denoted as

$$F_n(x_1, t_1; x_2, t_2; \ldots; x_n, t_n)$$

$$= F_{X_1 X_2 \ldots X_n}(x_1, t_1; x_2, t_2; \ldots, x_n, t_n)$$

$$= P\{X_1 \leqslant x_1, X_2 \leqslant x_2, \ldots, X_n \leqslant x_n\} \tag{11.1}$$

where $x_i = x(t_i)$ and P denotes the joint probability. Thus the process $\{X(t), t \in T\}$ is Markovian, if for every n and for $t_1 < t_2 \ldots < t_n$ in the index set T we have

$$F\{x_n, t_n \mid x_{n-1}, t_{n-1}; x_{n-2}, t_{n-2}; \ldots \ldots; x_1, t_1\}$$

$$= F\{x_n, t_n \mid x_{n-1}, t_{n-1}\}. \tag{11.2}$$

If the probability density function f of F exists, then (11.2) is equivalent to

$$f(x_n, t_n \mid x_{n-1}, t_{n-1}; x_{n-2}, t_{n-2}, \ldots \ldots, x_1, t_1)$$

$$= f(x_n, t_n \mid x_{n-1}, t_{n-1})$$

On the basis of this relation an important equation known as the Chapman–Kolmogorov equation can be derived; several economic applications of this equation are discussed in Tintner and Sengupta [38]. Following the concept of memory in Markov property, one could define a memoryless process as one where the random variable $X(t)$ at a given t is independent of the random variables defined by $X(t)$ at all other t.

The invariance criterion classifies stochastic processes into stationary and nonstationary. A process $\{X(t), t \in T\}$ is defined to be strictly stationary if for each n and for every arbitrary τ we have for the distribution function $F_n(\cdot)$ defined in (11.1)

$$F_n(x_1, t_1; x_2, t_2; \ldots \ldots; x_n, t_n)$$

$$= F_n(x_1, t_1 + \tau, x_2, t_2 + \tau; \ldots \ldots; x_n, t_n + \tau) \tag{11.3.1}$$

for $t_j + \tau \in T, j = 1, 2, \ldots, n$ identically. Thus the family of joint probability distributions remains invariant under an arbitrary translation of time. Thus it follows that the distribution function $F_1(x, t)$ is not a function of t and

$$F_2(x_1, t_1; x_2, t_2) = F_2(x_1, x_2; t_2 - t_1). \tag{11.3.2}$$

It is clear from (11.3.2) that if the moments exist we would have

$E\{X(t)\}$ = constant, independent of time

$$E\{X(t)X(t+\tau)\} = R(\tau) = R(-\tau). \tag{11.3.3}$$

A weaker concept than strict stationarity is provided by second-order stationarity. Thus a process $\{X(t), t \in T\}$ is wide-sense, or weakly or covariance, or second-order stationary if

$|E\{X(t)\}| =$ finite constant

and

$$E\{X^2(t)\} < \infty, \quad E\{X(t_1)X(t_2)\} = R(t_2 - t_1).$$

Stationarity can also be defined by a process having a constant spectral density.

In economic applications Markov processes which are stationary in some sense have played very important parts. Reasons are several. First, the practicing econometricians had found very early that autoregressive systems with distributed lags fit very well several kinds of economic behavior, e.g., cobweb cycle, distributed lags, capital-stock adjustment. Second, use of the Chapman–Kolmogorov equation showed that differential equations representing dynamic behavior may be interpreted as dynamic random equations, of which the solutions or trajectories may be interpreted probabilistically. Since the solutions of random differential equations may or may not converge to their steady state equilibrium values, depending on certain conditions, one could obtain a generalized view of stochastic equilibrium or disequilibrium. Thus for instance, a deterministic differential equation may have a convergent solution as $t \to \infty$, while a stochastic analogue may not. Third, the Markovian property is very useful in modelling expectation formations and learning and even for non-Markovian situations the Markovian assumption is a good first approximation, especially when empirical data is very short.

One of the most useful applications of Markov processes is in terms of increment processes, defined over continuous time t. Consider the stochastic process $\{X(t)\}$ for $t \geqslant 0$. Denote the difference $X(t_2) - X(t_1)$ by $X(t_1, t_2)$ where $t_2 > t_1 > 0$, which is termed an increment of $X(t)$ on $[t_1, t_2]$. If for all $t_1 < t_2 < \ldots < t_n$, the successive increments $X(t_1, t_2)$, $X(t_2, t_3), \ldots, X(t_{n-1}, t_n)$ are mutually statistically independent, then the process $\{X(t), t \geqslant 0\}$ is called an independent–increment stochastic process. If for this process the probability distributions of its increments $X(t_1, t_2)$, $X(t_2, t_3), \ldots, X(t_{n-1}, t_n)$ depend only on the parameter differences $t_2 - t_1, t_3 - t_2, \ldots, t_n - t_{n-1}$ then the process $X(t)$ is said to have stationary independent increments. Three important examples of such processes which have found widemost applications are (a) the Brownian motion, named after its discoverer Robert Brown, a botanist; this is also called Wiener process or Wiener–Levy processes that was widely applied by Einstein, (b) the Poisson process, which is most widely applied in queuing, telephone traffic and other fields of operations research and (c) Gaussian stochastic process, which is most frequently applied due to its analytic properties and the fact that the central limit theorem gives it a wider applicability.

More formally a Brownian process $\{X(t), t \geqslant 0\}$, which may now be denoted by $X(t, w)$, $t \in T$, $w \in W$ to indicate its dependence on the sample space W is a process satisfying four conditions: (i) $X(0, w) = 0$ by convention, i.e., the process starts at zero, (ii) stationary independent increments, (iii) the increment $X(t) - X(s)$, $t > s > 0$ has normal Gaussian distribution with zero mean and variance $\sigma^2(t - s)$ and (iv) for each sample index $w \in W$ the process $X(t, w)$ is continuous in t for $t \geqslant 0$. The most significant contribution of Wiener on the development on the theory of Brownian motion is to show that the sample functions $X(t, w)$ viewed as functions of $w \in W$ are continuous but not differentiable [2,37].

The second example of an independent increment stochastic process is the Poisson process. The only difference here is that the process $X(t)$, $t \geqslant 0$ has independent integer-valued increments. Arrival of customers in queue, sequence of production and inventories, spread of impulse noises are modelled by the Poisson process. Estimation of parameters of Poisson processes applied to economic models and its implications are discussed by Tintner and Sengupta [38].

Lastly, a stochastic process $\{X(t), t \in T\}$ is called Gaussian, if for every finite set $t_1, t_2, \ldots, t_n$ the random variables $X(t_1), X(t_2), \ldots, X(t_n)$ have a joint normal distribution with a mean vector $m'(t) = (EX(t_1), EX(t_2), \ldots, EX(t_n))$ and variance–covariance matrix $V = (v_{ij})$, where $v_{ij} = E\{(X(t_i) - m(t_i))(X(t_j) - m(t_j))\}$. In the stationary case the mean vector $m(t)$ is a constant (i.e., time-independent) and the covariance matrix is a function of the time instants only through their differences.

A concept associated with Gaussian processes that is most useful in interpreting random differential equation is the white noise property.

Loosely speaking, a white noise process is defined by the derivative of a Brownian or Wiener process. But a Wiener process is not differentiable in the mean square sense, since by its definition given before we have

$$E\left(\frac{X(t)-X(s)}{t-s}\right)^2 = \frac{\sigma^2}{t-s} \to \infty \quad \text{as} \quad \tau = (t-s) \to 0$$

hence one has to proceed differently. Let $W(t)$, $t \geqslant 0$ denote the Wiener process, which is by definition Gaussian with zero mean and covariance denoted by $\mu(t, s) = 2(t-s)\sigma^2$, where $\sigma^2 = c$ is a finite constant and $t > s$. The formal derivative of $W(t)$, denoted by $\dot{W}(t)$ is clearly Gaussian with mean zero and covariance given by

$$\mu_{\dot{W}(t)}(t, s) = \partial^2 \mu(t, s)/\partial t \partial s$$

$$= 2c\partial^2 \min(t, s)/\partial t \partial s$$

$$= 2c\delta(t-s) \tag{11.4}$$

where

$$\delta(t-s) = \begin{cases} 0, & t < s \\ 1, & t > s \end{cases}.$$

The most important use of Gaussian white noise process is in the theory of random differential equations, where Ito's theorem has to be used for taking account of the nondifferentiability property of the white noise process. Taking the linear scalar case we have the dynamic system

$$\dot{x}(t) = a(t)x(t) + b(t)w(t); \quad x(t_0) = x_0 \tag{11.5.1}$$

where $a(t)$, $b(t)$ are nonrandom time-dependent coefficients and $w(t)$ is Gaussian white noise independent of x_0. One could write (11.5.1) alternatively as

$$dx(t) = a(t)x(t)dt + b(t)dn(t), \quad x(t_0) = x_0 \tag{11.5.2}$$

where we have used $dn(t)/dt = W(t)$ or, on integration

$$x(t) - x(t_0) = \int_{t_0}^{t} a(s)x(s)ds + \int_{t_0}^{t} b(s)dn(s)$$

$$x(t_0) = x_0. \tag{11.5.3}$$

Whereas the first integral on the right-hand side of (11.5.3) is well defined as Riemann integral, the second one may not, since the random variable y_n defined by the partial sum

$$y_n = \sum_{i=1}^{k} x(t_i)(n(t_i) - n(t_{i-1})) \tag{11.5.4}$$

does not converge in the mean square sense to a unique limit. For proof see [37]. Ito's theorem provided a method of selecting the subdivisions t_i, $t_i - t_{i-1}$ so that the limit of y_n in (11.5.4) exists as $\Delta_m \to 0$ where $\Delta m = \max_i(t_{i+1} - t_i)$.

For specific applications of Ito's rules of stochastic calculus to any functional $z(t, x(t))$ defined on $x(t)$ satisfying (11.5.2) we proceed as follows: we define the differential of $Z(t) = z(t, x(t))$ as

$$dZ(t) = \left[z_t + z_x a(t) + \tfrac{1}{2} z_{xx} (b(t))^2 \right] dt + z_x b(t) dn(t) \tag{11.5.5}$$

where $z_t = \partial z(t, x(t)/\partial t$, $z_x = \partial z(t, x(t))/\partial x$ and $z_{xx} = \partial^2(t, x(t))/\partial x^2$. This differential exists under certain regularity conditions. In general if $Z(t) = z(t, x_1(t), x_2(t), \ldots, x_m(t))$ is a continuous function with continuous partial derivatives z_t, z_{x_i} and $z_{x_i x_j}$ and we have in place of (11.5.2) the stochastic differentials on $[t_0, T]$

$$dx_i(t) = a_i(t)dt + b_i(t)dn(t), \quad i = 1, 2, \ldots, m$$

then $Z(t)$ also possesses a stochastic differential in the same interval given by

$$dZ(t) = z_t dt + \sum_{i=1}^{m} z_{x_i} dx_i + \tfrac{1}{2} \sum_{\substack{i=1 \\ j=1}}^{m} z_{x_i x_j} dx_i dx_j \tag{11.5.6}$$

where $dx_i dx_j = b_i(t)b_j(t)dt$, $\quad i, j \leqslant m$

Some examples of applying the Ito differential rules are as follows: Let $Z(t) = x_1(t)x_2(t)$ and

$$dx_1(t) = a_1(t)dt + b_1(t)dn(t)$$

$$dx_2(t) = a_2(t)dt + b_2(t)dn(t)$$

where $dn(t) = W(t)dt$ is the Gaussian white noise. On applying (11.5.6) one gets

$$d(x_1(t)x_2(t)) = x_1(t)dx_2(t) + x_2(t)dx_1(t) + b_1(t)b_2(t)dt$$

$$= \left[x_1(t)a_2(t) + x_2(t)a_1(t) + b_1(t)b_2(t) \right] dt$$

$$+ \left[x_1(t)b_2(t) + x_2(t)b_1(t) \right] dn(t)$$

Take another scalar case where $Z(t) = z(x_0, e^{at})$ where a is a constant and $dx(t) = ax(t)dt$. Then $dZ(t) = z_t dt + z_x dx + \frac{1}{2}z_{xx}dzdx = ax_0 e^{at}dt$.

By applying these rules the solution of the linear scalar random differential equation (11.5.2) taken in a more general form as

$$dx(t) = a(t)x(t) + \sum_{i=1}^{m} b_i(t)x(t)dn_i(t)$$

$$x(t_0) = c, \quad dn(t) = (dn_i(t)) = m\text{-dimensional white noise} \quad (11.6.1)$$

can be explicitly written as

$$x(t) = c \exp\left[\int_{t_0}^{t}\left(a(s) - \sum_{i=1}^{m} b_i(s)^2/2\right)ds + \sum_{i=1}^{m}\int_{t_0}^{t}b_i(s)dn_i(s)\right]$$

if $a(t)$, $b_i(t)$ are constants, then we have

$$x(t) = c \exp\left[\left(a - \sum_{i=1}^{m} b_i^2/2\right)(t - t_0) + \sum_{i=1}^{m} b_i(n_i(t) - n_i(t_0))\right]. \quad (11.6.2)$$

This result (11.6.2) is very useful for application to economic models. For an example consider the proportional feedback rule of government policy analyzed by Phillips [29] under a Keynesian model

$$dy(t) = ay(t) + dg(t) = ay(t) + by(t)dn(t)$$

where $dy(t)$ is deviations of real income from the target level, the government policy intervention $g(t)$ is of the form $dg(t) = by(t)\,dn(t)$, with $dn(t)$ being a white noise Gaussian process and a, b are real constants. The income solution $y(t)$ is now given by

$$y(t) = c \exp\left[(a - b^2/2)(t - t_0) + b(n(t) - n(t_0))\right].$$

Assuming that the law of large numbers holds for the $n(t)$ process, we would have $\lim y(t) \to 0$, as $t \to \infty$ only if $a < b^2/2$; otherwise the controlled system would be unstable. In his original work [29] Phillips argued in terms of only a deterministic differential equation system and showed that in many cases the government policy itself may be destabilizing. Here we find additional stochastic reasons why this may be so.

Next we describe some simple economic applications of these stochastic process.

EXAMPLE 8 (Optimal portfolio selection [27]): Consider the optimal investment allocation problem for an investor; there are two assets, one risk-free with return rate r and the other risky with price $p(t)$ fluctuating according to the stochastic differential equation generated by the Ito-process $n(t)$:

$$dp(t)/p(t) = \alpha dt + \sigma dn(t) \tag{12.1}$$

where α may be interpreted as the instantaneous conditional expected change in price per unit time and σ^2 is the corresponding variance. The parameters α, σ^2 are assumed to be constants. The individual investor who has wealth $W(t)$ at time t must choose the two control variables $w = w(t)$ and $c = c(t)$ so as to maximize the expected discounted total utility

$$J = E\int_0^T e^{-\rho t}V(c(t))dt \tag{12.2}$$

where the utility function $V(c(t)) = (ac(t) + b)^\gamma$ is taken of the form known as hyperbolic risk aversion type. Here $w(t)$ is the fraction of wealth invested in risky assets, where total wealth now fluctuates as

$$dW(t) = (1 - w)Wrdt + wW(\alpha dt + \sigma dn) - cdt.$$

The optimal solutions $c^*(t)$, $w^*(t)$ can be explicitly worked out by dynamic programming algorithms and it turns out that the optimal consumption and investment, the two control variables $c^*(t)$ and $w^*(t)$ $W(t)$ are linear functions of wealth. It is shown that the linearity of these two demand functions hold only for this class of hyperbolic risk aversion type concave utility functions. Thus it is clear that linear optimal decision rules may arise in many non LQG models.

EXAMPLE 9 (Stabilization policy under Phillips' model [38]): It is here assumed that the economy is represented by a multiplier-accelerator model with government expenditure as a control variable. Following Allen [1,29] we adopt the equilibrium version of the Phillips-model as

$$(aD^2 + bD + c)y_t - g_t = \epsilon_t \tag{13.1}$$

where D is the differential operator, g_t is government expenditure and the other constant parameters a, b, c may be related to the multiplier-accelerator mechanisms of Keynesian models and ϵ_t is a white noise stochastic process. Now consider this the second-order model in a slightly different form, when the proportional and derivative policy of government are incorporated:

$$[D^2 + b_2 D + (b_1 + e_{1t})]y_t = e_{2t} \tag{13.1.1}$$

where the fixed coefficients are: $b_1 = (c + k_1)/a$, $b_2 = (b + k_2)/a$ and e_{1t}, e_{2t} (where e_{2t} contains ϵ_t and other shocks due to g_t) are assumed to be a two-dimensional Wiener process with zero mean and finite covariances $E(e_{it}e_{jt}) = 2B_{ijdt}$. It is known that this type of differential equation model satisfies its moment equations in variables $m_{ij}(t) = E\{y_{1t}^i y_{2t}^j\}$ where $y_{1t} = y_t$, $y_{2t} = Dy_t$ and the first-order moments satisfy

$$Dm_{10}(t) = m_{01}(t)$$
$$Dm_{01}(t) = -b_1 m_{10}(t) - b_2 m_{01}(t) \tag{13.2}$$

the second-order moments also satisfy the differential equations

$$Dm_{20}(t) = 2m_{11}(t)$$
$$Dm_{11}(t) = -b_1 m_{20}(t) - b_2 m_{11}(t) + m_{02}(t)$$
$$Dm_{02}(t) = 2(B_{11}m_{20}(t) - b_1 m_{11}(t) - b_2 m_{02}(t) + B_{22} - 2B_{12}m_{10}(t)).$$

$$\tag{13.3}$$

Whereas the solutions for equations (13.2) specify the conditions for stability in the mean, those for (13.3) indicate the conditions for mean square stability. For these terms see the definitions in [37]. It is clear from the characteristic equation of (13.2) that its roots have negative real parts if the coefficients b_1, b_2 are positive, i.e., this result which specifies the requirements for asymptotic mean stability is the same as in the deterministic version. Assuming positive b_1, b_2, we may solve the second-order moment equations (13.3) for analysing the asymptotic stability in mean square. The characteristic equation is

$$\phi(\lambda) = \lambda^3 + 3b_2\lambda^2 + 2(b_2^2 + 2b_1)\lambda + 4(b_1 b_2 - B_{11}) = 0.$$

Applying the Routh–Hurwitz stability criterion, it is clear that the conditions for asymptotic mean square stability are

(i) $b_1 > 0$, $b_2 > 0$,   (which are conditions for mean stability),
(ii) $b_1 b_2 > B_{11}$. $\tag{13.4}$

Thus the second condition of (13.4) implies additional restrictions on the choice of the strength parameters k_1, k_2 of the stabilization policy. Thus under the prescribed control policy, mean income may converge to the target level but not necessarily with decreasing variance.

Now consider a second example where we consider the same model (13.1.1) with some different assumptions, i.e., (i) $e_{1t} = 0$ (ii) the characteristic roots are complex $\lambda = w_0 \exp(\pm i\theta)$ and (iii) the stochastic process

$e_t = e_{2t}$ is continuous in mean square sense and wide-sense stationary with mean zero and correlation function $R_e(\tau)$. In this case the second-order model (13.1.1) may be written as:

$$\left[D^2 + 2\alpha w_0 D + w^2 \right] y_t = e_t,$$

$$\alpha = \cos\theta, \; w_0 = w_0(b_1, b_2), \; \theta = \theta(b_1, b_2).$$

Here the variance of output $\sigma_y^2(t)$ can be explicitly computed from the spectral density function $S_{ee}(w)$ of the stochastic process, where the latter is related to the correlation function $R_e(\tau)$ by

$$R_e(\tau) = \int_0^\infty S_{ee}(w) \cos w\tau \, dw.$$

For a large τ, the variance $\sigma_y^2(t)$ approaches a constant given by

$$\sigma_y^2(t) \to \int_0^\infty |Z(w)|^{-2} S_{ee}(w) dw; \quad Z(w) = w_0^2 - w^2 - 2iww_0\alpha$$

Otherwise the variance of output is in general a function of time t and a wide-sense stationary input e_t may give rise to a nonstationary output in this situation for a finite t. The latter case emphasizes instability due to non-stationarity, which may imply that the long run policy may not be realizable.

If we assume that the spectral density function is a constant $S_{ee}(w) = S_{ee}(w_0)$, then the variance function can be approximately computed for any t as:

$$\sigma_y^2(t) = \frac{\pi S_{ee}(w_0)}{4\alpha w_0^3} \left[1 - \frac{1}{w_1^2} \exp(-2w_0\alpha t) \left\{ w_1^2 + 2(w_0\alpha)^2 \sin^2 w_1 t \right. \right.$$

$$\left. \left. + w_0 w_1 \alpha \sin 2w_1 t \right\} \right] \tag{13.5}$$

where

$$w_1 = w_0(1 - \alpha^2)^{1/2}.$$

It is clear (from 13.5) that the variances when plotted in a graph would sketch an oscillatory pattern and reach a stationary value $\pi S_{ee}(w_0)/(4w_0^3)$ for $t \to \infty$.

It is to be noted that an oscillatory behavior for the variance function $\sigma_y^2(t)$ would imply a feature of instability different from that due to the absence of mean square stability. In multisector growth models and simulation of policy alternatives in nonlinear models, this instability due to the oscillatory behavior of the variance functions has been explicitly recognised. The economic meaning or pay-off of a stable variance function with little or no oscillations remains however an open question to be investigated. On the face of it, it seems that the valuation of the convergence of sample mean to the population mean function as t increase from a small to a large value, becomes more difficult and less precise due to wide oscillations, compared to the steady state estimate when $t \to \infty$.

EXAMPLE 10 (Effect of uncertainty in Kalman–Bucy filters): The analysis here, taken from Pearson [28] and Sage [31] deals with the various types of uncertainty which may affect the Kalman–Bucy filters, that are frequently applied as adaptive control methods in economics [11,18]. We have the plant dynamics in vector-matrix form with time-varying parameters and noisy measurements $y(t)$ of the state $x(t)$, where $u(t)$ is a q-element control vector

$$\dot{x} = A(t, a_1)x(t) + B(t)u(t)$$

$$
\begin{aligned}
&x(t_0) = x_0 \text{ given}; &&\dot{x} = \frac{dx}{dt} : n \times 1 \\
&y(t) = C(t)x(t) + v(t) &&v(t) : r \times 1 \\
&t_0 \leqslant t \leqslant T \text{ given} &&y(t) : n \times 1.
\end{aligned}
\tag{14.1}
$$

Here the policy interventions $\{u(t)\}$ and disturbances $\{v(t)\}$ are assumed to be Gaussian white noise processes with zero means and covariances as follows

$$
\begin{aligned}
&E\{u(t)\} = 0 = E\{v(t)\}, &&\text{all } t \\
&\text{cov}(v(t), v(t_1)) = R(a_3)\delta(t - t_1) \\
&\text{cov}(u(t), u(t_1)) = Q(a_2)\delta(t - t_1) \\
&\text{cov}(v(t), u(t_1)) = 0, &&\text{all } t, t_1 \\
&\delta(t - t_1) = 1 &&\text{for } t = t_1 \text{ and zero otherwise.}
\end{aligned}
\tag{14.2}
$$

Here a_1, a_2, a_3 are time-varying uncertain parameters. The Kalman–Bucy (KB) filter problem is to find a continuous estimate $\hat{x}(t)$ of the state $x(t)$, where $\hat{x}(t)$ is a linear function of the observed measurements $y(\tau)$, $0 \leqslant \tau \leqslant t$ minimizing a squared loss function

$$L = \text{trace}\,(D(t)\gamma(t)) = E\left[(x(t))'D(t)(x(t) - \hat{x}(t))\right] \tag{14.3}$$

where $\gamma(t) = x(t) - \hat{x}(t)$ and $D(t)$ is a symmetric positive definite matrix of weights assumed known. For instance $D(t)$ may be the identity matrix, in which case L denotes the expected sum of squared losses $L = \sum_{i=1}^{n} \gamma_i^2(t)$. Note that this KB filter problem can be given a very generalized interpretation in economic applications. First, one has to identify that as an estimation problem, this is almost similar to the problem illustrated in Example 5, where the parameters of a differential game model are required to be estimated. There is one basic difference however. We do not apply here the methods of ML or, 2-stage LS but a different procedure. For instance, if the noise statistics are all known, and a_1, a_2, a_3 are constants, the KB estimator is defined by the vector differential equation

$$\frac{d\hat{x}}{dt} = F(t)\hat{x}(t) + G(t)y(t)$$

with

$$F(t) = A(t) - G(t)C(t)$$

$$G(T) = \gamma(t)C'(t)R^{-1}$$

where the estimation error $\gamma(t)$ satisfies the matrix differential equation (Riccati equation):

$$\frac{d\gamma(t)}{dt} = A(t)\gamma(t) + \gamma(t)A'(t) - \gamma(t)C'(t)R^{-1}C(t) + B(t)QB'(t)$$

$\gamma(t_0) = \gamma_0$ known.

However, the noise statistics depending on the unknown parameters a_1, a_2, a_3 are not usually known, i.e., $\theta = (a_1, a_2, a_3)$ is uncertain but bounded with known bounds. How are we then to design an optimal KB filter for state estimation? Secondly, for two-player Cournot–Nash games the covariance matrix $R(a_2)$ depending on the unknown parameter a_2 has a natural interpretation in terms of conjectural variation, i.e., one player's conditional expectation of the rival's reaction. The process of learning from past rounds of reactions has been variously modeled in economic system by several authors [23]. Thirdly, one notes that the above KB filter estimates are so designed that any updating through new information can be easily incorporated; also one may replace the above loss function by other forms, e.g.,

$$L(T_1) = \text{trace} \int_{t_0}^{T_1} (D(t)\gamma(t))dt, \quad t_0 \leqslant T_1 \leqslant T$$

in order to emphasize aggregation of some or all information. Several methods for modifying the KB filter in the presence of uncertainty of $\theta = (a_1, a_2, a_3)$ that are available may be briefly described. For this purpose a difference equation analogue is more helpful. Consider the discrete system

$$x(k+1) = \theta(k, a_1)x(k) + B(k)u(k)$$

$$y(k) = C(k)x(k) + v(k).$$

the KB problem is to find a recursive estimate of $x(k)$ denoted by $\hat{x}(k \mid k)$ that is a linear function of observations $y(0), y(1), \ldots, y(k)$ which minimizes the quadratic loss function:

$$L = E\left[(x(k) - \hat{x}(k \mid k))' D(k)(x(k) - \hat{x}(k \mid k))\right].$$

Several methods, outlined below have been suggested on theoretical grounds for quantifying the effects of various uncertainties that may arise but the remedies suggested are very few in practical terms except the vague statement that the existing model specification has to be modified if the uncertainties are large.

(a) The main increase in estimation error due to a bad estimate $\hat{x}(k \mid k)$ is measured by the actual error covariance matrix

$$P_a(k) = E\left[(x(k) - \hat{x}(k \mid k))' D(k)(x(k) - \hat{x}(k \mid k))\right]$$

where $\hat{x}(k \mid$ is the estimate of the state vector $x(k)$ at k-th iteration. If $P_a(k)$ tends to a finite steady state value P_a as $k \to \infty$ but is too large for the estimate to be of any use, the KB method may fail due to apparent divergence. Also it may fail when $P_a(k) \to \infty$ as $k \to \infty$. The latter may be particularly true, when due to faulty measurements the errors may cumulate to produce nonstationarity in the stochastic process.

(b) A second method is to generate at k-th iteration the predicted residual

$$\tilde{y}(k) = y(k) - C(k)\hat{x}(k \mid k - 1)$$

using actual data to test if they have zero mean and white noise properties. If the results indicate otherwise, the model specification has to be modified.

(c) A third method is to bound the estimation error of the KB filter by requiring that the filter gain matrix $K(k)$ in

$$\hat{x}(k+1) = \theta(k, a_1)\hat{x}(k) + B(k)u(k) + K(k)[y(k) - C(k)\hat{x} \mid k]$$

take the following form

$$K(k) = \left(P_{k\mid k-1} + \alpha\right)C'(k)\left[C(k)P_{k\mid k-1}C'(k) + R(k)\right]^{-1}$$

where $P_{k\mid k-1}$ is the variance–covariance matrix of $\hat{x}(k)$ estimated on the $(k-1)$th iteration and α is a constant suitably chosen as the lower bound of acceptable accuracy.

(d) A fourth method due to Sage [31] considers adaptive filtering techniques either by combining traditional methods of estimates like ML with KB filters or introducing Bayesian methods. One technique in the latter case considers maximizing the *a posterior* estimate of the parameters $\hat{\theta}$ say, $\hat{\theta}(y)$ depending on observations y.

Some of these methods are increasingly being applied to economic models. Kendrick [19] has reported some experiences of application to moderate size economic models.

6. Concluding remarks

Our survey of stochastic models in dynamic economics has emphasized three most interesting aspects of the modern trend. First, it has shown that stochastic phenomena in economics may alter in many ways some of our basic thinking in economics viewed in a deterministic fashion. The parallel that immediately comes to mind is the impact of modern stochastic physics and statistical thermodynamics on the classical Newtonian physics. A quote from Hartley's [16] Presidential Address is appropos:

"The mathematician Laplace, in his early life an avid follower of Newtonian mechanics is reputed to have proudly proclaimed something like this: "Once I have discovered the world law, then give me the initial positions and velocities of all particles in this world and I will predict future history." Modern science knows better. Modern science has learned modesty, and has long abandoned the dream of the deterministic outlook. Indeed, the very postulate of Laplace, "... give me the exact initial positions and velocities of all particles," is nowadays ruled out as impossible by the famous Heisenberg Uncertainty Principle in quantum mechanics. So even physics, the leader in the socalled sciences, has had to yield its determinism. Statistics is part of this modern outlook of uncertainty. Its theory can be appropriately described as "the mathematics of uncertainty". The deterministic world law from which all phenomena can be exactly predicted is abandoned as a concept. In place we have laws which do not predict observations with certainty. If I may oversimplify our concepts, our laws may only predict "expectations", and the actual observations may differ from these by "statistical errors". It is the study of these errors that enables us to make predictions under uncertainty. Our mathematics of uncertainty governing these errors is sometimes described as the calculus of probability ... "

Secondly, modelling "expectations", e.g., specifying mathematical relationships so as to explain the process of expectation formation and its modification via learning lead very naturally to methods of adaptive control and the interdependence of multiple stochastic processes. We require more and not less of methods of stochastic control, simply because in economics we have not yet integrated the concepts of expectation formation, learning and adjustment. The causal view of control, a carryover from the deterministic world may not hold in a biological environment where various kinds of adaptivity constantly take place. It is hoped that in future this area would generate fruitful research conclusions.

Thirdly, we have shown that estimation and control, like prediction and their planned realization through policy are most intimately connected in a stochastic view of the time-series. To what extent this will lead to a new type of econometrics is yet to be seen.

References

1. Allen, R.G.D. Macroeconomic Theory: A Mathematical Treatment. Macmillan: London, 1967
2. Arnold, L. Stochastic Differential Equations: Theory and Applications. John Wiley: New York, 1974
3. Bain, J.S. A Note on Pricing in Monopoly and Oligopoly. American Economic Review, 39 (1949), 448–464
4. Caines, P.E. and C.W. Chan. Feedback Between Stationary Stochastic Processes. IEEE Transactions on Automatic Control, 20 (1975), 498–508
5. Chow, G.C. Econometric Analysis by Control Methods. John Wiley: New York, 1981
6. Chow, G.C. Effect of Uncertainty on Optimal Control Policies. International Economic Review, 14 (1973), 632–645
7. Chow, G.C. Estimation and Optimal Control of Models of Dynamic Games, in Deistler, M. et al., eds. Games, Economic Dynamics and Time Series Analysis. Physica Verlag: Wurzburg, Austria, 1982
8. Chu, K. Comparison of Information Structures in Decentralized Dynamic Systems, in Y.C. Ho and S.K. Mitter, eds. Directions in Large Scale Systems. Plenum Press: New York, 1976
9. Dolezal, J. Optimal Parameter Estimation in Two-Player Zero-Sum Differential Games. Transactions of the Eighth Prague Conference on Information Theory, Statistical Decision Functions and Random Processes. D. Reidel: Dordrecht, Holland, 1978
10. Eckstein, O. Economic Theory and Econometric Models, in Kmenta, J. and J.B. Ramsey, eds. Large-Scale Macro-Econometric Models. North Holland: Amsterdam, 1981

11. Fleming, W.H. Optimal Control of Diffusion Processes, in J.B. Keller and H.P. McKean, eds. Stochastic Differential Equations. American Mathematical Society: Providence, Rhode Island, 1972

12. Gaskins, D.W. Dynamic Limit Pricing: Optimal Pricing under Threat of Entry. Journal of Economic Theory, 3 (1971), 306–322

13. Geweke, J. Testing the Exogeneity Specification in the Complete Dynamic Simultaneous Equation Model. Journal of Econometrics, 7 (1978), 163–185

14. Granger, C.W.J. Investigating Causal Relations by Econometric Models and Cross-Spectral Methods. Econometrics, 37 (1969), 424–438

15. Hansen, L. and T. Sargent. Formulating and Estimating Dynamic Linear Rational Expectations Models: Journal of Economic Dynamics and Control, 2 (1980), 7–46

16. Hartley, H.O. Statistics as a Science and as a Profession (Presidential Address). Journal of the American Statistical Association, 75 (1980), 1–7

17. Johansen, L. Econometric Models and Economic Planning and Policy: Some Trends and Problems. Institute of Economics, University of Oslo: Norway, 1982

18. Kendrick, D. Stochastic Control for Economic Models. McGraw Hill: New York, 1981

19. Kendrick, D. Control Theory with Applications to Economics, in K.J. Arrow and M.D. Intriligator, eds. Handbook of Mathematical Economics, Vol. I. North Holland: Amsterdam, 1981

20. Kydland, F. Noncooperative and Dominant Player Solutions in Discrete Dynamic Games. International Economic Review, 16 (1975), 321–351

21. Kydland, R.E. and E.C. Prescott. Rules Rather Than Discretion: The Inconsistency of Optimal Plans. Journal of Political Economy, 85 (1977), 473–491

22. Landsburg, S.E. Algebraic Geometry and the Business Cycle, in P.E. Gaines and R. Hermann, eds. Geometry and Identification. Math Science Press: Massachusetts, 1983

23. Leondes, C.T. and T.K. Siu. Parameter Optimization for Linear Quadratic Differential Games. Trans. ASME 99 (1977), Series G. No. 1, 58–62

24. Levhari, D. and L.J. Mirman. The Great Fish War: An Example Using a Dynamic Cournot–Nash Solution. Bell Journal of Economics, 12 (1981), 57–65

25. Lucas, R.E., Jr. Econometric Policy Evaluation: A Critique, in K. Brunner and A.H. Meltzer, eds. The Phillips Curve and Labor Markets. North Holland: Amsterdam, 1976

26. Malliaris, A.G. and W.A. Brock. Stochastic Methods in Economics and Finance. North Holland: Amsterdam, 1982

27. Merton, R.C. Optimum Consumption and Portfolio Rules in a Continuous Time Model. Journal of Economic Theory, 3 (1971), 373–413

28. Pearson, J.O. Estimation of Uncertain Systems, in C.T. Leondes, ed. Control and Dynamic Systems, Vol. 10. Academic Press: New York, 1973

29. Phillips, A.W. Stabilization Policy in a Closed Economy. Economic Journal, 64 (1954), 290–323

30. Ross, S.M. Stochastic Processes. John Wiley: New York, 1983

31. Sage, A.P. Variational Methods in Adaptive Filtering, in J.S. Rustagi, ed. Optimizing Methods in Statistics. Academic Press: New York, 1971

32. Sargent, T.J. Interpreting Economic Time Series. Journal of Political Economy, 89 (1981), 213–248

33. Sengupta, J.K. and Sfeir, R.E. Control Theory Models in World Coffee: Some Empirical Tests. International Journal of Systems Science, 14 (1983), 811–828

34. Sengupta, J.K., Leonard, J., and Vanyo, J. A Limit Pricing Model for U.S. Computer Industry: An Application. Applied Economics, 15 (1983), 297–308

35. Sheffrin, S.M. Rational Expectations. Cambridge University Press: Cambridge, England, 1983

36. Sims, C. Macroeconomics and Reality. Econometrica, 48 (1980), 1–48

37. Soong, T.T. Random Differential Equations in Science and Engineering. Academic Press: New York, 1973

348

38. Tintner, G. and J.K. Sengupta. Stochastic Economics: Stochastic Processes, Control and Programming. Academic Press: New York, 1972
39. Weiner, N. The Theory of Prediction, in E.F. Beckenback, ed. Modern Mathematics for Engineers (Series I). McGraw Hill: New York, 1956, Chap. 8.
40. Whittle, P. Why Predict? Prediction as an Adjunct to Action, in O.D. Anderson, ed. Forecasting. North Holland: Amsterdam, 1979
41. Wold, H. Construction Principles of Simultaneous Equation Models in Econometrics. Bulletin of International Statistical Institute, 38 (1960), 111-138

IV. Efficiency analysis and risk aversion in economic models

13. Multivariate risk aversion with applications

1. Introduction

Risk aversion has played a fundamental part in applied decision models under uncertainty. The measure which has found wide applications is the Arrow–Pratt (r_A) measure of absolute risk aversion [1,10]:

$$r_A = -\partial^2 u(z)/\partial u(z) \tag{1}$$

defined on the space of real-valued utility functions $u(z)$. Here z may be a scalar i.e. wealth or income, or it may be a vector of goods over which the scalar utility function is defined. If $z = z(\tilde{c}, x)$ represents the consequences of a lottery generated by the random variables $\tilde{c}$ with a probability distribution $F(\tilde{c}|\theta)$ indexed by its parameters θ (e.g. mean, variance), then the decision-maker (DM) has a problem of optimal decision-making under the uncertain environment. Two types of uses are then usually made. One is the notion of certainty equivalence of a lottery which has random outcomes denoted by $\tilde{z}$. For all monotonic utility functions $u(\tilde{z})$ defined on the space of $\tilde{z}$, a DM is said to be risk averse, if he prefers $u(E(\tilde{z}))$ over $E(u(\tilde{z}))$, where E is the expectation operator over the nondegenerate distribution of the random variable $\tilde{z}$ or, of $\tilde{c}$ given θ. If these expectations are finite, then the certainty equivalent (CE) of the lottery is defined by an amount $\hat{z}$ such that

$$u(\hat{z}) = E[u(\tilde{z})]$$

i.e. the DM is indifferent between the lottery and the amount $\hat{z}$ for certain. If the scalar utility function is monotonic increasing, it follows that

$$u[E(\tilde{z}) - \pi] = E(u(\tilde{z})) \tag{2}$$

where π is a positive risk premium

$$\pi = E\tilde{z} - \hat{z}$$

which is unique. It follows that if the scalar utility function is concave

351

(quasi-concave), it implies risk aversion with a positive (nonnegative) risk premium.

A second type of use of the risk aversion concept is in characterizing an efficient vector point in a stochastic system e.g. a stochastic production process. Let x be an n-element output vector and X the set of all output vectors obtainable, where it is assumed that X is convex, closed and bounded. Then, one may define after Peleg and Yaari [9] a concept of efficiency that holds risk aversely. Thus, of two output vectors x, $y \in X$, y dominates x risk aversely if

$$\sum_{i=1}^{n} p_i u(y_i) \geq \sum_{i=1}^{n} p_i u(x_i) \tag{3.1}$$

for all utility functions $u(\cdot)$ belonging to a set $U(\cdot)$ of concave and nondecreasing utility functions and probabilities $p_i \geq 0$, $\Sigma p_i = 1$ and furthermore, there exists an utility function $u^* \in U$ such that

$$\sum_{i} p_i u^*(y_i) > \sum_{i} p_i u^*(x_i) \tag{3.2}$$

Then, the output vector $x^* \in X$ is said to be "risk aversely efficient" (RAE), if there exists no other $x \in X$ that dominates x^*. The importance of this result is due to its implications for a system of efficiency prices. Thus, they have proved that if the output vector $x^* \in X$ is risk aversely efficient, it must have a system of price vectors $\pi = (\pi_i)$ such that

$$x_i^* > x_j^* \text{ implies } \frac{\pi_j}{p_j} > \frac{\pi_i}{p_i}$$

and conversely. Hence the behaviour of risk averters can be analyzed from a set of RAE vector points e.g. cross-section data of risk-averse decision-makers say.

Risk aversion measure (1) has been generalized in theory and applications [3,7,11,13] in several directions e.g. (a) multivariate case when z is a vector and r_A becomes a matrix [4], (b) the utility function $u(\cdot)$ is quasiconcave and specifies asymmetry, (c) the underlying probability distribution of $\tilde{z}$ or of $\tilde{c}$ is other than normal i.e. it belongs to nonsymmetrical class of distributions (d) the information channels (sample observations) are incomplete (not very large), and (e) the case where unequal risk aversion may lead to various degrees of deviation from the level of a Pareto–efficient solution defined in a risk-neutral world. From an applied viewpoint there have been other generalizations [8,12,15] emphasizing the statistical estimation of some of the parameters of the above stochastic decision problem e.g., (f) the estimation of r_A in a situation where it is a constant, due to maximizing expected utility $Eu(z)$ when $u(z) = -\exp(-\alpha z)$ and z is normally distributed with mean μ and variance σ^2, (g) the estimating the mean and variance parameters of the distribution $F(\tilde{c} \mid \theta)$, $\theta = (\mu, \sigma^2)$ from observed data on $\tilde{c}$ in portfolio models, (h) applying Bayesian methods to improve the estimates of mean and variance parameters from sequential observations or through ARIMA (autoregressive integrated moving average) procedures, and (i) building reliability measures for the linear constraints of a stochastic LP model.

Two new generalizations are proposed here in the theory of multivariate risk aversion. The first arises when the utility function $u(z)$ is not a scalar but a vector. This framework is important for example in team decision problems, when each member has an individual utility function e.g. $u_j(z)$ is the utility function of jth member and $U = (z_j(z))$ is a vector of utility functions for the team, where z denotes the random outcome or payoff for the team. Other areas of application of this framework include multicriteria objective functions for a decision problem, stochastic optimization models where there is no knowledge or information about the probability distributions $F(\tilde{c} \mid \theta)$ and situations involving noncooperative games with different payoff functions for different players.

A second approach to multivariate risk aversion considers the situation where the stochastic outcomes z belongs to several population rather than one. Thus, if there are K populations indexed by $F_k(\tilde{c} \mid \theta)$, we have K expected utilities which may contain for example K means and variances (μ_k, σ_k^2), $k = 1, 2, \ldots, K$. This framework is useful in selecting the best population prior to applying the criterion of maximizing expected utility. Other areas of application include stochastic dominance of one distribution over another [6], optimal statistical design theory [16], LP problems with stochastic objective functions having facets subject to a mixture of K population distributions [18], and problems of optimal search and detection, where in the first stage we have to search for the best of the K populations and in the second choose the decision vector which is optimum in some sense.

The framework of our presentation is as follows. Section Two presents the two approaches through some operational examples. This is followed by some theoretical results in Section Three. A few lines of possible applications in applied decision models are indicated in the concluding section.

2. Approaches to multivariate risk aversion

As a characterization of multivariate risk aversion (MRA) we propose the method of variance information manifold, following the approach of James [13] in multivariate statistics. Let $z' = (z_1, z_2, \ldots, z_N)$ be a row vector with N elements, so that $\bar{z}_i = z_i(\theta)$ denotes the payoff for member $i = 1, 2, \ldots, N$ which is assumed to depend on a set of parameters θ through the distribution function $F(\bar{z} \mid \theta)$. The N dimensional vector z has mean μ and variance-covariance matrix V, where V forms a convex cone in $(\frac{1}{2})N(N+1)$ dimensional Euclidean space. Each nonsingular variance-covariance matrix V is associated with an information matrix $J = V^{-1}$. The variance information manifold is then characterized by the space in which each interior point has alternative coordinate matrices V or J^{-1}. The set of singular positive semidefinite matrices when V is singular constitutes part of the boundary of this manifold. A concept of geodesic distance is introduced in this manifold by

$$D = \left[\sum_{i=1}^{N} (\log \lambda_i)^2 \right]^{1/2} \tag{4.1}$$

where λ_i are the N eigenvalues of the characteristic equation:

$$|V_2 - \lambda V_1| = 0 \tag{4.2}$$

where V_1, V_2 are any two positive definite symmetric matrices, representing for example two information structures, available to the team. Note that the vector $\lambda' = (\lambda_1, \lambda_2, \ldots, \lambda_N)$ of eigenvalues of the scalar distance function $D = D(\lambda)$ in (4.1) can be used as a measure of MRA. Thus, if V_1 represents complete information structure (or, complete certainty), whereas V_2 denotes a variance measure of outcomes for incomplete information (or, uncertainty), the above distance measure $D(\lambda)$ or the vector λ' may be used to specify the value of obtaining complete information relative to the no information or less information case. Some other uses of the above concept include the following:

(i) if the column vector z is normally distributed $N(\mu, V)$ where $V = V_1$ in terms of (4.2) and V_2 is the sample estimate obtained by maximum likelihood estimation, then the statistic

$$d^2 = \frac{N}{z} \sum_{i=1}^{N} (\log \lambda_i)^2$$

is asymptotically distributed like a Chi-square variate with $\frac{1}{2}N(N+1)$ degrees of freedom. Using this statistic, one could test the distance of estimates like V_2 from their populations,

(ii) In many agricultural applications the output vector $x' = (x(1), x(2), \ldots, x(N))$ of dimension k say may change due to price support or other stabilization programs which reduce overall risks of price fluctuations; one may then compare through the geodesic distance (4.1) the difference between the two variance–covariance matrices $V_1(x)$ and $V_2(x)$ one before and the other after the price stabilization program,

(iii) If U is the utility vector for an N-member team each with a control vector $x(j)$, $j = 1, 2, \ldots, N$, such that its expected value is concave and differentiable with strict concavity for at least one member j, then the MRA matrix defined by

$$R = -\frac{\partial^2 Eu_j(x)}{\partial x(j)\partial x(j)'} \tag{5}$$

must be positive semidefinite. If the expected utility vector EU is separable in $x(j)$, then one could write up to a second-order approximation

$$Eu_j = \mu_j(x(j)) - \frac{\alpha_j}{2}\sigma_j^2(x(j)); \quad \alpha_j \geqslant 0 \tag{6}$$

where μ_j and σ_j^2 are the means and variances of $\tilde{z} = z(x(j))$ which depend on the control vector $x(j)$ chosen by member j of the team. the optimal decision then is given by $x^*(j)$, if it maximizes Eu_j. Denote the mean vector and variance–covariance matrix of $x^*(j)$ by

$$\bar{x} = N^{-1}\sum_{j=1}^{N} x^*(j), \quad V_x = E_j[(x^*(j) - \bar{x})(x^*(j) - \bar{x})']$$

$$V_j = E_x[(x^*(j) - \bar{x})(x^*(j) - \bar{x})' \mid j \text{ fixed}]$$

If the vector $\alpha' = (\alpha_1, \alpha_2, \ldots, \alpha_N)$ of nonnegative risk aversion increases, what happens to the variance–covariance matrices V_x, V_j which broadly represent dissimilarity from the mean solution $\bar{x}$? How would one measure dissimilarity if the means are equal i.e. $\mu_j = \mu_0$, all j but variances (σ_j) or, risk aversion parameters (α_j) differ across the team? Partial answers to these questions are possible in terms of the geodesic distance D defined in (4.1).

Note however that the distance measure D in (4.1) is defined in terms of variance–covariance matrices. This is necessary when D is viewed as a statistic for testing some empirical hypothesis. In other cases we may not have variance–covariance matrices, but still the distance measure may be defined. Hence we would need to generalize the above concept. To illustrate our generalization we consider the following LP problem:

$$\max_{x \in X} z = c'x; \; X = \{x \mid x \geqslant 0, Ax \leqslant b\}$$

where it is assumed that the elements c_j, a_{ij}, b_i in (c, A, b) are strictly positive. This structure is present in most economic applications where x contains outputs and b denotes available inputs. Denote the set of feasible bases and non-bases by $(B^k, N^k, k = 1, 2, \ldots, K)$ and corresponding outputs by x_B^k, x_N^k respectively. Then we set up the following modified LP model:

$$\max_{1 \leq k \leq K} f_k = c_{B^k}' x_B^k + c_{N^k}' x_N^k + \lambda_k \tag{7.1}$$

s.t. $\quad B^k x_B^k + N^k x_N^k = b$

$\qquad \lambda_k b = x_B^k; \quad (k = 1, 2, \ldots, K)$

where the last constraint has been added to the original LP to stipulate that outputs should be proportional to inputs. If the LP model (7.1) has a solution for each k fixed, then we have an eigenvalue problem

$$\left(B^k - \theta_k I \right) x_B^k = 0, \quad k = 1, 2, \ldots, K \quad \text{and} \quad \theta_k = \lambda_k^{-1}$$

Since B^k is a nonnegative matrix, there exists by Frobenius theorem [22], a real eigenvalue θ_k^* say and its associated eigenvector x_*^k such that they are nonnegative and satisfy the determinantal equations:

$$\left| B^k - \theta_k^* I \right| = 0 \tag{7.2}$$

where θ_k^* is maximal in the sense that it is equal to or greater than the absolute value of any other eigenvalue. Furthermore, if each B^k is indecomposable in the sense that there does not exist any permutation matrix P such that

$$P^{-1} B^k P = \begin{bmatrix} B_{11} & B_{12} \\ 0 & B_{22} \end{bmatrix}$$

where B_{11}, B_{22} are square submatrices, then the maximal eigenvalue θ_k^* and its eigenvector x_*^k is strictly positive. This maximal eigenvalue θ_k^* is unique up to a positive scalar multiple. Denote by θ_0^* the maximum of the Frobenius eigenvalues i.e. $\theta_0^* = \max_{1 \leq k \leq K} \theta_k^*$ and by x_0^* the associated eigenvector. The distance of θ_k^* from θ_k^* from θ_0^* for $k \neq 0$ or, of x_*^k from x_0^* may then indicate the extend of departure from the optimal solution. A numerical example would be helpful. Assume the following:

$$A = \begin{bmatrix} 3 & 1 \\ 1 & 3 \end{bmatrix}, \quad b = \begin{pmatrix} 1 \\ 1 \end{pmatrix}, \quad B^1 = \begin{bmatrix} 1 & 0 \\ 0 & 1 \end{bmatrix}, \quad B^0 = \begin{bmatrix} 3 & 1 \\ 1 & 3 \end{bmatrix}$$

$$c' = (1, 1)$$

where B^1 is the initial basis with all slack variable in the basis and B^0 is the optimal basis. For the initial basis solution the Frobenius eigenvalue is $\theta_1^* = 1.0$ with the eigenvector $(x_*^1)' = (1,1)$ and optimal profit is zero. But for the optimal basis B^0, $\theta_0^* = 4$, $(x_0^*)' = (\frac{1}{4}, \frac{1}{4})$ and the optimal profit is 0.50. The squared Euclidean distance between points (x_*^1) and (x_0^*) is 2.125.

Now consider a weighted combination of the two facets of the objective function of (7.1) i.e. $\hat{f}_k$ replacing f_k as follows:

$$\max_{1 \leqslant k \leqslant K} \hat{f}_k = w\left(c_{B^k}' x_B^k + c_{N^k}' x_N^k\right) + (1-w)\lambda_k \tag{7.3}$$

where $0 \leqslant w \leqslant 1$. If w is set equal to zero, then the prices $c' = (c_B', c_N')$ have no role in determining an optimal output vector. this is exactly the case for many public sector decision making units (DMU), where explicit market prices for its outputs do not exist. However, in such cases the Frobenius eigenvalues would exist and the criterion of maximum positive eigenvalue would determine an optimal solution.

In this framework MRA can be introduced if the elements contained in (c, A, b) are partly stochastic. For instance, consider the LP model for the decision variables, x and λ:

$$\max_{x, \lambda} f = (c \vdots 0)'x + \lambda \tag{8.1}$$

s.t. $(A \vdots I_m)x = b$

$\quad\quad \lambda\begin{pmatrix} b \\ 0 \end{pmatrix} = x$ ~

$\quad\quad x \geqslant 0, \quad b > 0$

where x includes the vector of slack variables and I_m is the identity matrix of order m. Let c be stochastic in the nonnegative domain with c_α^-, c_α^+ denoting lower and upper 5% value when $\alpha = 0.05$. Replacing c in (8.1) by $c_{0.05}^-$ we solve the LP model (8.1) to obtain a risk averse solution and its Frobenius eigenvalues. Likewise, we solve for $c = c_{0.05}^+$. The difference of the two solutions, one more risk averse than the other may then be measured in terms, of the distance of the two Frobenius eigenvalues. If the statistical distribution of the Frobenius eigenvalues and their difference can be derived, one could set up a test statistic to test the difference in impact of increased risk aversion.

When the price vector c is not available, as in the case of public sector DMU's, we adopt a different approach for characterizing efficiency in a risk averse environment. Assume that we have observations on the input and output vector y_j, x_j for j-th DMU, having n and m elements respectively. Assume that x_j is normally distributed with a positive mean vector m_j and variance–covariance matrix S_j, while the input vector y_j is nonrandom. Denote by the scalar quantity μ_j the risk averse level of output value

$$\mu_j = v'm_j - \frac{\alpha}{z} w'S_j w, \quad v \geqslant 0, \quad w \geqslant 0, \quad \alpha \geqslant 0$$

for j-th, DMU, $j = 1, 2, \ldots, N$ where it is assumed that the risk aversion parameter α is identical for all j. Here the vectors v, w are unknown prices to be determined. Define a ratio of weighted outputs to weighted inputs for each j as

$$h_j = \frac{\mu_j}{p' y_j}, \quad j = 1, 2, \ldots, N$$

where p is a vector of nonnegative prices of inputs. Given the cluster of N DMU's, we want to test if a particular DMU is risk aversely efficient or not. Denote the DMU under reference by subscript zero and set up the following nonlinear functional fractional program:

$$\max_{v,w,p} h_0 \quad \text{s.t.} \quad 0 \leqslant h_j \leqslant 1, \quad j = 1, 2, \ldots, N$$
$$w, v, p \geqslant 0 \tag{9.1}$$

If there exists an optimal set w^*, v^*, p^* of nonnegative prices at which $h_0^* < 1$, then the DMU under reference is not risk aversely efficient relative to the cluster. For the cluster to be RAE at the rate of risk aversion α, it must contain only those DMU for which $h_\alpha^* = 1.00$. Note that under these observations (m_j, S_j, y_j) and constraints of (9.1) no other set of common weights other than those (w^*, v^*, p^*) will give a more favorable rating to the DMU under reference (i.e. $j = 0$) relative to the comparison set of N units. Hence if the maximal value of h_0^* is not equal to 1.0 under the optimal set (w^*, v^*, p^*) of nonnegative weights it will not be attained from any other set.

Several specifications of the nonlinear functional fractional program (9.1) may be useful in applied decision situations. First, if there were no risk aversion in the sense that α is zero, we would obtain an LP model from (9.1), provided the price weights for inputs are so normalized that

$$p' y_j = 1 \quad \text{for all} \quad j = 1, 2, \ldots, N \tag{9.2}$$

Also, if there is risk aversion on the input side and we replace the term for weighted inputs by the scalar quantity

$$q_j = p' \bar{y}_j - \frac{\beta}{2} r' \tilde{S}_j r; \quad p, r, \beta \geqslant 0, \quad y_j \sim N(\bar{y}_j, \bar{S}_j)$$

we obtain h_j as:

$$h_j = h_j(\alpha, \beta) = \mu_j/q_j$$

Then we set up the nonlinear fractional program (9.1) for determining an optimal set (v, w, p, r) of weights or prices for measuring efficiency under risk aversion. This approach of measuring efficiency provides a generalization of the efficiency concept developed by Farrell, Charnes and Cooper and others [2,5,17,19]. Second, the impact of risk aversion in the sense of α increasing (or decreasing) from the level $\alpha = \beta > 0$ can be analyzed. Thus if an increase of α (from the level $\beta = 0$ affects each DMU equally, then it follows that if the k-th DMU is RAE (or risk aversely inefficient (RAI)) for $\alpha = 0$ when $k = 0$ in (9.1), then it will remain so for all $\alpha > 0$. In this case α can serve as an overall measure of risk aversion for the team. Third, the nonlinear program (NLP) given by (9.1) reduces to an LP problem in case the variance–covariance matrices S_j, $\tilde{S}_j$ are diagonal with elements $\sigma_{i,j}^2$, $\tilde{\sigma}_{i,j}^2$ in the diagonal. Hence a new set of nonnegative prices u for outputs and t for inputs can be optimally solved for by redefining h_j as follows:

$$h_j = \left(v'm_j - \frac{\alpha}{2}u'\sigma_j \right)\left(p'y_j - \frac{\beta}{2}t'\tilde{\sigma}_j \right)^{-1}$$

$$h_j > 0, \quad h_j \leq 1, \quad \text{all} \quad j = 1, 2, \ldots, N$$

$$p'\bar{y}_j - \frac{\beta}{2}t'\tilde{\sigma}_j = 1 \quad \text{(normalization condition)}$$

$$\sigma_j = \text{diag}\left(\sigma_{i,j}^2\right), \quad \tilde{\sigma}_j = \text{diag}\left(\tilde{\sigma}_{i,j}^2\right)$$

The formal similarity of this formulation with the modified LP problem (8.1) can be directly observed by introducing a scalar positive number λ in the optimization problem associated with (9.3) thus:

max λ

s.t. $\quad 0 \leq v'm_j - \frac{\alpha}{2}u'\sigma_j \leq \lambda$

$\qquad u, v \geq 0, \quad \lambda > 0, \quad j = 1, 2, \ldots, N$ $\qquad\qquad\qquad$ (9.4)

$\qquad \lambda \leq 1.0$

Following von Neumann's concept of efficiency [20,22], we may say that the system (9.4) is efficient if there exists an optimal solution of the above LP problem with v^*, u^*, λ^* such that $\lambda^* \geq 1.0$. The set of nonnegative optimal prices u^*, $v^* \geq 0$ associated with an efficient system may be called efficiency prices, although these need not be unique, unless additional conditions are imposed on m_j and σ_j.

Next we consider the second type of characterization of MRA where we have one DM or a scalar utility function but many population distributions to which the random variable $\tilde{c}$ in $z = z(\tilde{c}, x)$ may belong. To motivate the problem, consider the optimal decision situation in portfolio theory [21], where there are n securities with random return $\tilde{r}_i$ for security $i = 1, 2, \ldots, n$. We minimize the total variance of return

$$\min_x \sigma_z^2 = \sum_{i=1}^{n} \sum_{i=1}^{n} x_i v_{ij} x_j \tag{10.1}$$

s.t. $\quad \displaystyle\sum_{i=1}^{n} m_i x_i \geqslant \mu_z$

$\quad x_i \geqslant 0$

subject to the condition that the expected return be not less than the level μ_2 stipulated by the DM. Thus, if $\tilde{r}_i$ is distributed with mean and variance–covariance parameters m_i and v_{ij} respectively, we have the quadratic program (10.1) in the decision variables $x_1, x_2, \ldots, x_n$. Define a new set of decision variables

$$y_i = x_i - x_i^*$$

measured as deviations from the reference levels x_i^* preassigned and specify, after suitable parameterization and normalization, a reduced version of the portfolio problem as

$$\min_y \sigma_y^2 = y'Vy \tag{10.2}$$

s.t. $\quad m'y = 1$

$\quad V = (v_{ij})$

$\quad m = (m_i)$

For applying this type of model we need to know the parameters m, V exactly and also the reference levels or goals x^*. Also, the DM may be interested in only a subset of n securities, say r in number $r < n$, since the number n may be quite large. Denote by K the total number of selections of r items out of n i.e.

$$\binom{n}{r} = \frac{n!}{r!(n-r)!} = K$$

and let k be any such selection, for which the mean and variance–covariances are $m(k)$, $V(k)$ respectively. On squaring the equality constraint of (10.2) we obtain the final form of the normalized model

$$\min_{y(n)} \sigma^2(k) = y(k)'V(k)y(k) \tag{10.3}$$

$$\text{s.t.} \quad y(k)'M(k)y(k) = 1$$
$$M(k) = (m(k)m(k)')$$

It is clear that the optimal solution $y^*(k)$ of (10.3) would also be optimum for (10.2). Denote the lagrange multiplier associated with the constraint of (10.3) by $\lambda(k)$, then the stationarity condition implies the following eigenvalue problem:

$$[V(k) - \lambda(k)M(k)] y(k) = 0 \tag{10.4}$$

Since $M(k)$, $V(k)$ are symmetric and positive semi-definite, the eigenvalues $\lambda(k)$ are all real and nonnegative and can be ordered. Let $\lambda_*(k)$, $\lambda^*(k)$ be the lowest and the highest eigenvalue with associated eigenvectors $y_*(k)$, $y^*(k)$. The optimal solution of the portfolio problem (10.3) is then given by $(\lambda_*(k), y_*(k), \sigma_*^2(k))$, where

$$|V(k) - \lambda_*(k)M(k)| = 0$$

However there are K selections. Hence other policies can be defined as follows:

$$\lambda_0^* = \min_k \max_\lambda \lambda(k) = \min_k \lambda^*(k) \tag{10.5}$$

$$\lambda_*^0 = \min_k \min_k \lambda(k) = \min_k \lambda_*(k) \tag{10.6}$$

Note that λ_0^* and the associated eigenvector y_0^* denote a minimax policy i.e. best of the worst, whereas λ_*^0, y_*^0 specify a most pessimistic risk averse optimum policy with two facets of risk aversion, one over K selections and the other over r eigenvalues. Note that the K selections can be interpreted as alternative allocations in the active approach of stochastic LP theory [17], conditional on which the expected utility function is defined i.e., net return or profit $\tilde{r}'y$, under the assumption of normality and conditional on the plan $y(k)$ chosen, has the conditional normal distribution with mean $m'(k)y(k)$ and covariance $y'(k)V(k)y(k)$. The concept of geodesic distance introduced in (4.1) may therefore be applied for each k fixed e.g.,

$$D_k^2 = \sum_{i=1}^{r} \left(\log \lambda_i(k) \right)^2 \tag{10.7}$$

where $\lambda_i(k)$ are the r eigenvalues of the system (10.4). Since zero eigenvalues are not excluded, we adopt the convention $\log 0 = 0$ in the distance concept (10.7). Denote the ordered values of D_k^2 as

$$0 \leqslant D_{(1)}^2 \leqslant D_{(2)}^2 \ldots \leqslant D_{(k)}^2$$

then, one may also characterize a risk averse optimal plan $y_{(k)}$ as the one which has the property

$$D_{(k)}^2 = \min_{1 \leqslant j \leqslant K} D_{(j)}^2$$

i.e. it is the selection with the lowest value of D^2. Note that these distance measures are absolute rather than relative. Sometimes the selections may be based on the relative distances. For example, if the K normal populations, one for each selection are homoscedastic i.e. have a common variance one may define the relative distance measures δ as

$$\delta_1 = D_{(1)}^2 - D_{(k)}^2, \quad \delta = D_{(2)}^2 - D_{(k)}^2, \ldots, \delta_k = D_{(k+1)}^2 - D_{(k)}^2$$

Thus, if δ_0 is the threshold value of δ for separating the indifference and preference zones, the DM may choose the k-th ordered selection $y_{(k)}$, if $\delta_{k+1} > \delta_0$. These selection rules may be applied by the DM to statistically test the difference between any two optimal plans $y_{(k)}^{(1)}$, $y_{(k)}^{(2)}$ when independent sample estimates $\hat{m}(1)$, $\hat{m}(2)$ are available under homoscedasticity.

Other applications of the best selection problem for K multivariate normal populations are available in stochastic linear programming theory [14,16,18].

3. Theoretical implications

A few theoretical implications of the MRA concepts will be emphasized in this section.

First we consider the portfolio theory model (10.3) under two different selections $K = 2$ with the modification that we replace $M(k)$ in the normalization condition by $\hat{M}(k) = \hat{m}(k)'\hat{m}(k)$, where $\hat{m}(k)$ denotes a diagonal matrix with elements m_i in the diagonal. This is done to avoid the zero eigenvalues. For each $k = 1, 2$ we choose the minimal eigenvalue $\lambda_*(k)$ of the problem

$$[V(k) - \lambda(k)\hat{M}(k)] y(k) = 0 \tag{11.0}$$

which would be positive if both $V(k)$, $\hat{M}(k)$ are symmetric and positive definite. The eigenvector associated with $\lambda_*(k)$ is denoted by $y_*(k)$. Now define a new mixed strategy

$$y = wy(1) + (1 - w)y(2) = y(w)$$

$$V = w^2 V(1) + (1 - w)^2 V(2) = V(w)$$

$$\hat{m} = w\hat{m}(1) + (1 - w)\hat{m}(2) = \hat{m}(w)$$

$$\hat{M} = (\hat{m}'\hat{m}) = \hat{M}(w), \quad 0 \leqslant w \leqslant 1$$

where it is assumed for simplicity that the random returns vector $\tilde{r}(1)$, $\tilde{r}(2)$ for the two pure strategies are statistically independent. The eigenvalue problem associated with this mixed strategy solution is then

$$[V(w) - \lambda(w)\hat{M}(w)]y(w) = 0 \tag{11.1}$$

DEFINITION 1: The DM is called risk averse if he prefers a mixed strategy solution over the pure strategies in the sense

$$\lambda_*(w) \geqslant \min(\lambda_*(1), \lambda_*(2)) \quad \text{for some} \quad w, \quad 0 \leqslant w \leqslant 1 \tag{11.2}$$

and strictly risk-averse if

$$\lambda_*(w) > \min(\lambda_*(1), \lambda_*(2)), \quad 0 < w < 1 \tag{11.3}$$

where we use the abbreviation

$$\min(\lambda_*(1), \lambda_*(2)) = \begin{cases} \lambda_*(1), & \text{if} \quad \lambda_*(1) \leqslant \lambda_*(2) \\ \lambda_*(2), & \text{otherwise} \end{cases}$$

Using this definition, the following results may be proved. Brief outlines of proof are given in Appendix.

THEOREM 1: *If the matrices $V(k)$, $\hat{M}(k)$ are symmetric positive definite, then there always exists a risk averse solution in the sense of (11.2). The risk averse solution satisfies the generalized eigenvalue problem (11.1) for some w, $0 \leqslant w \leqslant 1$.*

THEOREM 2: *If there is a risk averse solution $\lambda_*(w)$ for some w, $0 < w < 1$, then there must exist a lower and upper value w_*, w^*, of w such that $\lambda_*(w) \geqslant \lambda_*(w_*)$ and $\lambda_*(w) \leqslant \lambda_*(w^*)$.*

REMARK 1: Note that Definition 1 of a risk averse solution is based on the presumption that a risk averse DM always prefers a mixing of two uncertain consequences to the worse of the two alternatives.

REMARK 2: If the means $\hat{m}(1)$, $\hat{m}(2)$ are identical for the two strategies but not the variances, then one may directly apply the concept of geodesic distance (4.1) defined before, in terms of

$$|V(2) - \lambda V(w)| = 0, \qquad |V(1) - \lambda V(w)| = 0$$

to test the difference in distance from a given variance structure $V(w)$.

DEFINITION 2: A strategy is defined to be minimax in terms of the eigenvalue problem (11.0) if there exists a positive eigenvalue λ_0^* satisfying

$$\lambda_0^* = \min_k \lambda^*(k) = \min_k \max_\lambda \lambda(k) > 0 \tag{11.4}$$

The associated eigenvector y_0^* is called the minimax eigenvector.

THEOREM 3: *If the matrices $V(k)$, $\hat{M}(k)$ are symmetric and positive definite, then there always exists a minimax strategy λ_0^* in the sense of (11.4). Furthermore the minimax strategy satisfies the inequality*

$$\lambda_0^* \geqslant \lambda_*(w) \geqslant \min(\lambda_*(1), \lambda_*(2)), \quad 0 \leqslant w \leqslant 1 \tag{11.5}$$

for some w, where $\lambda_*(w)$, $\lambda_*(1)$. $\lambda_*(2)$ are defined in (11.2).

REMARK 1: In the sense in which $\lambda_*(w)$ is a risk averse solution, λ_0^* is strongly risk averse if it holds that $\lambda_0^* > \min(\lambda_*(1), \lambda_*(2))$.

REMARK 2: If for some $\bar{w}$, $0 < \bar{w} < 1$ the inequalities (11.5) hold, then by continuity there must exist a local neighborhood of $\bar{w}$ for which they will hold. This may be used to define local and weak case of risk aversion, to be distinguished from global risk aversion where (11.5) holds for all w in the domain $0 \leqslant w \leqslant 1$.

Next we consider MRA when there are N DMU's each with a common set of input (y_j) and output (x_j) vectors for $j = 1, 2, \ldots, N$ and the nonlinear program (9.1) is used to define risk aversely efficient or inefficient solution for a specific DMU. If the uncertainty elements or noise components in the input vector y_j are negligible, one may reasonably impose the normalization condition (9.2) so that the fractional program (9.1) reduces to a nonlinear program (NLP) for maximizing a quadratic concave function subject to quadratic constraints. For this type of NLP problem, one could prove the following results.

THEOREM 4: *If the k-th DMU is RAE (RAI) according to NLP (9.1) with the normalization condition (9.2) for a specific risk level $\alpha_0 > 0$, then it will* *remain so for all other risk levels* $\alpha \geqslant \alpha_0$. *However, if the k-th DMU is RAE (RAI) for* $\alpha = 0$, *it may or may not remain so for any arbitrary positive levels of* α.)

REMARK 1: The ranking of N DMU's according to efficiency through linear weights (i.e. $\alpha = 0$) may not be invariant for positive levels of risk aversion.

REMARK 2: A similar result analogous to Theorem 4 could be stated in cases where there is risk aversion (β) on the input side only, with normalization applied on the output side ($\alpha = 0$).

THEOREM 5: *Suppose we require the nonnegative weights to be equal,* $v = w$ *for the NLP problem* (9.1) *with the normalization condition* (9.2). *Then the NLP problem has an optimal solution vector* v, *if there exist nonnegative scalars* δ_j, ρ_j, $j = 1, 2, \ldots N$ *not all zero such that*

$$m_k + \sum_{j=1}^{N} (\rho_j - \delta_j) m_j + \alpha \left[\sum_{j=1}^{N} (\delta_j - \rho_j) S_j - S_k \right] v \leqslant 0$$

$$v' m_k + \sum_j (\rho_j - \delta_j) v' m_j + \alpha v' \left[\sum_j (\delta_j - \rho_j) S_j - S_k \right] v = 0$$

$$\delta_j \left[1 - v' m_j + \frac{\alpha}{2} v' S_j v \right] = 0, \quad j = 1, 2, \ldots, N$$

$$\rho_j \left[v' m_j - \frac{\alpha}{2} v' S_j v \right] = 0, \quad j = 1, 2, \ldots, N$$

and the matrix T *is positive semidefinite where*

$$T = \sum_{j=1}^{N} (\rho_j - \delta_j) S_j + S_k$$

REMARK 1: If the nonnegative scalars ρ_j, δ_j satisfy $\rho_j \geqslant \delta_j$ with at least one inequality being strict, then the matrix T is a nonnegative combination of N variance–covariance matrices S_j, each of which is positive semidefinite.

REMARK 2: If there are two DMU's ($N = 2$), each on the risk aversely efficiency boundary satisfying

$$(1 + \rho_1^*) m_1 + \rho_2^* m_2 = \alpha \big((1 + \rho_1^*) S_1 + \rho_2^* S_2 \big) v^*$$

$$v^* > 0, p_2^*, p_2^* \geqslant 0$$

when the optimal weight vector v^* has the following marginal variations:

$$\partial v^*/\partial\alpha < 0, \quad \partial v^*/\partial m > 0, \quad \partial v^*/\partial S < 0$$

where $m = (1 + \rho_1^*)m_1 + \rho_2^* m_2$, $S = (1 + \rho_1^*)S + \rho_2^* S_2$.

Note that the optimal weights v^* are specific to each of N DMU's and hence are not comparable for different DMU's. However, it is clear from the specification of the problem that if the k-th DMU is RAI under its own set of weights, it cannot be RAE under any other set of weights. This leads to the question if one can develop a common set of weights [19]. Although this question is not investigated here, we consider a specific example. Suppose each of N DMU's has an identical mean output vectors $m_j = m_0$, all j but different variance–covariance matrices S_j. Then each DMU is equally efficient at the mean but may not be equally RAE. Hence we set up the following NLP for the k-th DMU:

$$\min_V f(k) = v' S_k v$$

s.t. $\quad v' S_j v \geqslant 1, \quad j = 1, 2,\ldots,k,\ldots,N, \quad v \geqslant 0$

Then, if 1.0 denotes the fully efficient level, the k-th DMU is risk aversely inefficient if at the optimal solution denoted by $v_*(k)$ we have $f(v_*(k)) > 1.0$. However, if we rewrite the constraints of (12.0) in the form

$$\sum_{j=1}^{N} v' S_j v = 1, \quad v \geqslant 0 \tag{12.0}$$

and minimize $f(k)$ defined in (12.0) we obtain N optimal weights $v_*(k)$, $k = 1, 2,\ldots,N$. Of these weight vectors we may select as the reference set any of the following:

(i) $\quad \min_{1 \leqslant k \leqslant 1} f(v_*(k)) = f_*$: $\quad$ most risk averse case

(ii) $\quad \max_{1 \leqslant k \leqslant 1} f(v^*(k)) = f^*$: $\quad$ least risk averse case (where upper asterisk indicates that we are maximizing $f(k)$)

(iii) $\quad wf_* + (1 - w)f^* = f_*^*$: $\quad$ average risk averse case, $0 < w < 1$

where f_*^* denotes an average of the least and the most risk averse cases. For reasons of representativeness and nonparametric robustness, the average should preferably belong to the median class. Denote the reference set chosen by $\bar{v}$, which must satisfy

$$\sum_{j=1}^{N} \bar{v}' S_j \bar{v} = 1 = v'\left(\sum_{j=1}^{N} S_j\right)v$$

This distance of any other optimal solution $v(k)$ may then be analyzed in terms of the eigenvalues problems

$$\left| S_k - \lambda \sum_{j=1}^{N} S_j \right| = 0$$

and the concept of geodesic distance defined before in (4.1) becomes readily applicable.

4. Concluding remarks

Some comments on the various concepts of multivariate risk aversion analyzed before may be in order. First, consider the model (9.1) along with (9.2) where $v = w$. If $v'x_j$ is normally distributed with mean $v'm_j$ and standard deviation $(v'S_jv)^{1/2}$, then there will be a certain probability $u_j > 0.50$ with which the random variable $v'x_j$ will exceed the level $(v'm_j - \alpha(v'S_j \cdot v)^{1/2})$ e.g. the ruin level of probability is $u_j = 0.99$. If for all $j = 1, 2, \ldots, N$ the probability level u_j is the same i.e. $u_j = u_0 > 0.50$, then the risk averse efficiency or inefficiency may be said to hold at probability u_0. This provides some partial link with the concept of Peleg and Yaari.

Second, the notion of a positive risk premium that can be associated with risk aversion in univariate case e.g. (2) may not be uniquely definable in our multivariate cases, although it may be characterized in suitable cases. For instance consider the cases (10.5), (10.6) where minimax and minimin strategies are defined. In a game theoretic sense of a two-person nonzero-sum game, it may be visualized that $\lambda(k)$ for a fixed k is chosen by the second player and the DM is the first player choosing among K selections. If the choice of $\lambda(k)$ is from a stochastic mechanism, we have the case of a two-person noncooperative stochastic game that has been analyzed elsewhere [14,16]. In such a framework the minimax strategy (λ_0^*, y_0^*) may be more robust or more stable than the minimin strategy (λ_*^0, y_*^0). The relative gain from stability or robustness provides a measure of risk premium.

Third, the concept of risk aversion has several facets that require spelling out before one applies such a concept. Even in a univariate case, one may distinguish at least five facets as follows: (i) the form of the utility function $u(z)$ defining the rate of absolute risk aversion in (1), its asymmetry and the scale parameters, (ii) form of the probability distribution $F(\tilde{c}|\theta)$ of $\tilde{c}$ which induces the distribution of z in $u(z)$, its asymmetry and the role of higher moments on and beyond the second, (iii) stochastic game framework, when the selection of $\tilde{c}$ from a chance-mechanism is made by a noncooperative player who is facing the decision maker, (iv) the information available to the DM is incomplete in some sense so that search efforts and costs may have to be incurred and (v) lastly, robust policies in the sense of nonparametric strategies may be called for in an uncertain environment, where by nonparametric strategies we mean those actions which do not depend on specific shapes of utility functions or of probability distributions.

In the multivariate case two other facets may be added e.g. (vi) the utility function $u(z)$ may be a vector as in team decision problems, with the associated game-theoretic structure depending on the degree of cooperation or noncooperation among team members and (v) the parameters may belong to more than one population or more than one information structure. The von Neumann theory of expected utility maximization for uncertain outcomes utilizes the notions of concavity of the utility function and the existence of a meaningful maximum expected utility, none of which may hold under a game theoretic structure of N-person nonzero-sum games e.g., concavity of the individual payoff functions is not required for a mixed strategy solution, expected payoff would depend on the subjective distributions of the players' strategies and the sequence of learning allowed for. These game theoretic aspects would be discussed elsewhere.

Appendix

Brief outlines of proof of Theorems 1–5 are given here.

THEOREM 1: *Since* $\hat{M}(k)$ *is symmetric and positive definite, it can be factored as* $\hat{M}(k) = LL'$ *where* L *is a lower triangular nonsingular square matrix (i.e. otherwise known as Cholesky decomposition). Then the eigenvalue problem* (11.0) *reduces to*

$$L\left[\lambda(k)I - L^{-1}VL'^{-1}\right]q = 0, \quad q = L'y(k)$$

But the matrix $(L^{-1}VL'^{-1})$ *is symmetric and positive definite and hence the eigenvalues* $\lambda(k)$ *are all real and positive and can be ordered from the lowest to the highest. Hence the existence of a risk averse solution.*

THEOREM 2: *Since the eigenvalues* $\lambda(w)$ *are continuous functions of the elements of* $V(w)$, $\hat{M}(w)$, *each of which being continuous functions of* w, *where* w *belongs to the compact set* $0 \leqslant w \leqslant 1$ *we have the existence of* w_*, w^*. *The minimum eigenvalues* $\lambda_*(w_*)$, $\lambda_*(w^*)$, *which must be positive are therefore defined. Hence the result.*

THEOREM 3: *The existence of minimax strategies follows from the arguments given in Theorem 1, since all the eigenvalues are deal and positive.*

THEOREM 4: *If the k-th unit is risk aversely efficient (inefficient), then the necessary conditions of an optimum solution must hold at α_0. For any other level of $\alpha \geqslant \alpha_0$, these necessary conditions remain the same. Hence risk averse efficiency (inefficiency) continue to hold throughout the neighborhood defined by $\alpha \geqslant \alpha_0 > 0$. However, the case $\alpha \neq 0$ differs from $\alpha = 0$, since the former implies a nonlinear program with quadratic constraints, whereas $\alpha = 0$ leads to a linear program.*

THEOREM 5: *The NLP problem defined by (9.1) and (9.2) involves maximization of a concave quadratic function subject to a set of quadratic constraints $0 \leqslant h_j \leqslant 1$. The constraints $C_1 = \{h_j \geqslant 0, v \geqslant 0\}$ defines a convex set C, since each h_j is a strictly concave function of V. However, the set $C_2 = \{h_j \leqslant 1, v \geqslant 0\}$ need not define a convex set, since $(1 - h_j)$ is not a concave function of v. However, if the matrix T defined in the theorem is positive semidefinite, then by the sufficiency conditions of the Kuhn–Tucker theorem, the optimal solution v^* maximizing $h_k(v)$ exists. Hence v^* must lie either in the set C_1 or in the intersection of C_1 with the boundary $h_j(v) = 1$ of C_2. In either case the necessary conditions would characterize the optimal solution.*

References

1 Arrow, K.J., "The Role of Securities in the Optimal Allocation of Risk Bearing," Review of Economic Studies, 31 (1964), 91–96.
2 Charnes, A., W.W. Cooper et al., "Measuring the Efficiency of Decision-Making Units," European Journal of Operations Research, 2 (1978), 429–444.
3 Diamond, P. and J.E. Stiglitz, "increases in Risk and in Risk Aversion," Journal of Economic Theory, 8 (1974), 337–360.
4 Duncan, G.T., "A Matrix Measure of Multivariate Local Risk Aversion," Econometrica, 45 (1977) 895–904.
5 Farrell, M.J. and M. Fieldhouse, "Estimating Efficiency in Production Functions Under Increasing Returns to Scale," Journal of Royal Statistical Society, Series A, part 2, 125 (1962), 252–267.
6 Hadar, J. and W.R. Russell, "Stochastic Dominance and Diversification," Journal of Economic Theory, 3 (1971), 288–305.
7 Kihlstrom, R.E. and L.J. Mirman, "Risk Aversion with Many Commodities," Journal of Economic Theory, 8 (1974), 361–388.
8 Kotz, R. and K. Spremann, "Risk Aversion and Mixing," Discussion Paper in Economics, University of Ulm, Germany, 1981.
9 Peleg, B. and M.E. Yaari, "A Price Characterization of Efficient Random Variables," Econometrica, 43 (1975), 283–292.
10 Pratt, J., "Risk Aversion in the Small and in the Large," Econometrica, 32 (1964), 122–136.

11 Raiffa, H. and R.L. Keeney, Decisions with Multiple Objectives. New York: John Wiley, 1976.
12 Roth, A.E., Axiomatic Models of bargaining. New York: Springer Verlag, 1979.
13 Sengupta, J.K., "Risk Aversion in Decision Models," Working Paper in Economics, University of California, Santa Barbara, July 1980.
14 Sengupta, J.K., "Constrained Games as Complementary Eigenvalue Problems," Journal of Mathematical Analysis and Applications, 73 (1980), 301–314.
15 Sengupta, J.K., Decision Models in Stochastic Programming. New York: Elsevier-North Holland, forthcoming, ca. 1981.
16 Sengupta, J.K., "Problems in Measuring Frontier Production Functions: Some Theoretical Results," paper presented at the TIMS-ORSA Conference in Toronto, Canada, May 4–6, 1981.
17 Sengupta, J.K., Optimal Decisions Under Uncertainty. New York: Springer Verlag, 1981.
18 Sengupta, J.K., "Measuring Frontier Efficiency Without Market Prices," Working Paper in Economics, University of California, Santa Barbara, 1981.
19 Sengupta, J.K. and R.I. Sfeir, "Risk in Supply Response: An Econometric Application," Applied Economics (London), forthcoming, ca. 1981.
20 Stigum, B.P., "Competitive Resource Allocation Under Uncertainty," in Essays on Economic Behavior Under Uncertainty, Chapter 11. Amsterdam: North-Holland, 1974.
21 Szego, G.P., Portfolio Theory. Academic Press, 1980.
22 Takayama, A., Mathematical Economics. Hinsdale, Illinois, 1974.

V. Economic planning and stochastic optimization

14. Uncertainty and economic planning: a selective survey and appraisal

1. Introduction

In recent times economic planning in different countries has increasingly emphasized the role of risk and uncertainty in the planning process. Reasons have differed for different countries. For less developed countries (LDC) with large commodity exports, stabilization policies aimed at reducing income fluctuations have been found very important, along with policies for growth of income and employment; for centrally planned economies (CPE) divergences of actual production and distribution systems from the planned sectoral targets have been related to investment cycles and the need for building safety margins in different sectors has been particularly emphasized. For a developed economy with public and private sectors, the planning process, dependent on the theory of indicative planning ard decentralization of decisions has emphasized the various informational gaps and competing risks which may impede the cooperative framework of the solution. In a noncooperative game-theoretic framework, the need for building consistency in the set of strategies pursued by different players is all the greate₁ in an environment, where the risk perceptions are different for different players.

The theory of economic planning, as district from its practice has increasingly emphasized the various facets of risk and uncertainty in the formulation of a quantitative planning model and its empirical applications. In the specification stage, possible sources of cyclical fluctuations, disequilibria in the adjustment process and unequal risk aversion in different sectors have been frequently stressed. At the optimization stage, multicriteria objective functions with different goals and explicit facets emphasizing fluctuation-aversion have been explored along with probabilistic programming.

Our objective here is to present a selective survey of the state of the arts on economic planning and uncertainty and to illustrate thereby how some specific concepts of risk and fluctuation aversion are built into the various models of economic planning. Our survey is divided into three sections, the first two of which deal with uncertainty and economic planning in CPE and LDC and the third discusses it in the framework of theoretical models of growth and planning in a market framework. This is followed by a general appraisal emphasizing the practical implications.

2. Risk planning in CPE

Recognizing risk as an important element of the planning process and providing a mechanism for reducing it in the modelling phase has found applications in CPE at several different levels, e.g.,

(a) the framework of static and dynamic input–output (IO) models,
(b) the investment cycles generated by misdirection of investments, and
(c) the application of probabilistic programming methods in sectoral planning.

In the IO-models, two stochastic features have been emphasized in particular. First is the case of stochastic supply in plans, where outputs planned may exceed the full employment capacity of the economy [4,40]. This has both short and long run implications, since it may lead to a misdirection of investment funds from capacity expansion to inventory accumulation and thus reduce the real rate of growth of the economy. Second, dynamic IO models have been utilized to specify maximal rates of growth defined in the framework of turnpike theorems [27,43,48], where stochastic oscillations have been explicitly recognized. Sources of such instability may be several, e.g., imperfect knowledge about the constraints on production, uncertain components in consumer behavior and also planner's miscalculations about the plan [21,24,48].

Investment cycles in CPE, reflecting in a large part the malfunctioning of the economy have several features different from those of competitive market economies, e.g., the centralization of investment decisions with its associated rigidities, the tendency to overemphasize targets without checking their feasibility or consistency in a structural sense and the lags in perception in adopting anti-cyclical policies. Average length of investment cycles has varied from 8 years during 1950–65 in Czechoslovakia, Bulgaria and DDR to even longer [8,47].

Methods of probabilistic programming applied to investment planning models have emphasized three important features of the process of planning: (a) building safety reserves in different sectors, (b) allowing tolerance levels for sectoral constraints and (c) providing for multiple objectives in the criterion function. For instance, in the planning model for Hungary [21,22,42] which uses large-scale LP models, it has been explicitly recognized that divergences from the planning solutions can occur in the centralized economy due to errors of information and shortage of critical resources. Appropriate policies are therefore suggested for using the methods of stochastic programming in the planning process [20,37], which includes, among others building suitable degrees of risk-aversion in sectoral programs and providing for flexibility of options through reliability programming.

Applications of probabilistic programming [38,39,41] in micro-levels of planning e.g., optimal planning for water reservoir management, efficient resource allocation for the energy sector and planning for the agricultural sectors have extensively utilized methods of chance-constrained linear programming where the constraints may be jointly dependent due to resource linkages, the methods of linear decision rules applied to multi-stage LP models under uncertainty and also parametric methods of programming, when the information process is evolving sequentially [14,15,18]. Developing an objective function where there are multiple goals has also played a very important role in discussions of optimal resource planning at the various microscopic levels.

Some of the practical aspects of planning resulting from the applications of probabilistic programming may be briefly mentioned. First, the concept of shadow prices, its stability and domain of applicability have been much clarified through comparisons and contrasts with officially set prices. The implicit connection of shadow prices with Pareto optimality has been explored in order to characterize the optimality of decisions of the central planner. Second, the notion of second-best and third-best solutions has been directly admitted into policy discussions, either because the complete solution is not computable or, there are several stochastic components in the parameters of the problem. Third, the implications of setting terminal constraints in five year planning models have been better appraised now in terms of dynamic IO models, where the planning horizon may be much longer. The need for developing suitable compromise at the sectoral levels and reducing inconsistencies at the various stages of the plan, from its formulation to implementation have been explicitly incorporated into the design of the planning process.

3. Optimal allocation under uncertainty in LDC

Models of economic planning in LDC have increasingly used mathematical programming techniques to analyze the optimal pattern of investment allocation between sectors. Usually, some version of the open static or open-dynamic Leontief input-output model is used in such formulations along with an econometric framework for estimating final demand and production coefficients for final inputs like labor and capital. Since this formulation can be viewed as a large-scale linear programming or nonlinear programming model, it is interesting to note that any uncertainty in estimates of the parameters affect the optimal decisions calculated from such models. From a practical standpoint an analysis of such uncertainty is most important for several reasons. First, the planner's objective function must retain some flexibility in the plan in the sense of appropriate responses for likely shortages or oversupply of goods in some sectors. Second, the behavioral response of private producers in a sector under conditions of uncertainty may be far from perfectly competitive in nature, in which case the cost of uncertainty, reflected in market prices and resource allocation processes would lead to inoptimal production and distribution relations. The model must recognize it. Third, for specific sectors like agriculture with a major export crop, fluctuations in agricultural income may build up political pressures for stabilization policies. The latter may not always be stabilizing in a world of uncertainty, unless policies are designed, monitored and implemented properly, since in an imperfectly competitive world, information lags and risk aversion may be very unequally spread between large and small producers.

In some countries, a few of the above types of uncertainty have been explicitly recognized and their effects on the overall plan evaluated. Some planning models have introduced the notion of penalty price to be imposed for meeting average shortages in sectors, where supply falls short of demand. In a project evaluation study for Kenya's agricultural settlement programs [34], where shadow prices were used for computing social profits for various selections, it was found that 57% or more of the variation in social profits is accounted for by fluctuations in input and output prices; further under such market price uncertainty it was found optimal for feedlot projects to carry substantial feed and grain inventories thus reducing the fluctuations in export of grain and stabilizing farm incomes.

In the programming model for Mexican agriculture, Duloy and Norton [12] distinguished between two forms of market equilibrium for agriculture e.g. the competitive case with producers as price takers and the monopolistic case where the sector is assumed to maximize its net income by equating marginal revenue with marginal cost. The latter leads to a quadratic programming formulation, since prices respond linearly to demand. However no distinction in response to uncertainty between a competitive and monopolistic producer is admitted into the model, although there is some empirical evidence that agricultural supply shows risk aversion in international cross-section data.

The response of supply to price or market uncertainty has been explicitly recognized in commodity models and the related stabilization policies. The expected gains from price stabilization policies have been explicitly estimated, when errors or noises are linearly additive to the demand and supply functions and market equilibrium is known. However, if the market is not fully competitive e.g. world coffee market or the suppliers are more risk averse to price fluctuations than demanders, the stabilization policies which assume linearly additive independent errors may have destabilizing impacts.

We may now briefly illustrate how an aversion to fluctuations may be utilized in the various methods of economic planning in LDC. The optimal decision rules derived here admit risk sensitivity and hence the economic problems of risk sharing and risk spreading can be directly introduced into the conventional planning model. For the planner or the policymaker such risk sharing may involve both economic and political costs and these may be viewed as adjustment costs.

3.1. Input-output model under risk aversion

Economic planning applications of open-static input-output model have used in the short run an LP version of minimizing total costs $C = C(L) + C(K) + C(M_n)$ of labor (L), capital (L) and noncompetitive imports (M_n) subject to a demand constraint, i.e.,

$$\min_{x} C = (wa_0 + rb_0 + sc_0)'x \tag{1.1}$$

subject to $\quad (I - A)x \geq \hat{d}, \quad x \leq x^u, \quad x \geq 0$

here a_0, b_0, c_0 are column vectors (prime denotes transpose) of sectoral labor–output, capital–output and intermediate noncompetitive import–output ratios, w, r, s are prices of labor (wage), capital (user cost) and noncompetitive imports (foreign exchange cost). $\hat{d}$ is the vector of final demands net of competitive imports (M_c), which is usually estimated from past time series data e.g. by linear expenditure methods, using the proportions of net national income spend on sectoral demand. Finally, x^u is an upper limit of output i.e. output ceiling permitted by full capacity utilization. For policy purposes it may be convenient to introduce a lower limit x^L also, so that

$$x^L \leq x \leq x^u; \quad x^u > x^L > 0 \tag{1.2}$$

One may interpret $x = x^L$ as the pessimistic variant and $x = x^u$ as the optimistic variant of the output plan, whereas the optimal plan is most likely to be $x > x^L$ and $x < x^u$. Denoting $(wa_0 + rb_0 + sc_0)$ by v and assuming $x^L < x < x^u$, the above LP model may be written as

$$\min_{x} C = v'x \tag{1.3}$$

subject to $\quad Bx \geq \hat{d}; \quad B = (I - A), \quad x \geq 0$

The dual to this LP maximizes national income (Y) as:

$$\max_{p} Y = p'\hat{d} \tag{1.4}$$

subject to $p'B \leqslant v', \quad p \geqslant 0$

Noise or uncertainty components may enter into the above LP models in at least three ways that are important. First, the final demand forecasts $\hat{d}$ may contain errors thus necessitating plan revisions whenever appropriate. At the sectoral level such revisions imply shortages or over-supply which get reflected in the optimal shadow prices p if the market process is competitive. Denote inventories by h_t, which represents excess of supply over demand

$$h_t = Bx_t - d_t \tag{1.5}$$

where t is the time subscript and let $\hat{h}_t$ be the vector of estimated inventories when final demand forecast is $\hat{d}_t$. Any deviation of forecasts from actual demand results in inventories, that may be positive or negative and the planner can associate a cost, $C(h_t)$ with such inventories.

A second source of error is the assumption that the prices implicit in the vector v of the objective function of (1.3) are constant for all output levels. Such an assumption eliminates substitution possibilities between labor and capital and any disequilibrium behavior in the factor markets. Again, at the short run aggregate level, a cost of adjustment function e.g. of the quadratic form

$$C\left(x_t, x_t^D\right) = \bar{v}'x_t + \tfrac{1}{2}\left(x_t - x^D\right)'W\left(x_t - x^D\right)$$

may represent inconsistency due to such errors, where x^D is desired output and W is a matrix of weights, assumed positive definite. If the desired output levels x^D are proportional to lagged output (x_{t-1})

$$x^D = kx_{t-1}$$

then the adjustment cost function would be

$$C(x_t, x_{t-1}) = \bar{v}'x_t + \tfrac{1}{2}(x_t - kx_{t-1})'W(x_t - kx_{t-1}) \tag{1.6}$$

which incorporates in the quadratic term the cost of changes in output levels at different time points. Such adjustment functions have been used very successfully in micromodels of output inventory behavior.

A third source of uncertainty is associated with the shadow prices p in the dual LP model (1.4). If the demand process $\hat{d}_t$ is successively revised in forward time $t + 1$, $t + 2$, ..., the optimal shadow prices p_t, p_{t+1}, p_{t+2}, ... solved from (1.4) successively would be generated thereby. The cost associated with this error-correcting process may be directly incorporated by letting the shadow prices vary in response to demand variability. For instance, if the demand d_t follows a normal stochastic process with a mean vector m and a variance covariance matrix D, for which best statistical estimates from past data are $\hat{m}$ and $\hat{D}$, then the linear objective function of the LP model (1.4) may be transformed as a quadratic:

$$\max_{p} Y_\alpha = \hat{m}'p - \frac{\alpha}{2}p'\hat{D}p \qquad (1.7)$$

subject to $\quad p'B \leqslant v', \quad p \geqslant 0$

where α is a positive (or, nonnegative) constant denoting the intensity of risk aversion.

By the special property or the input–output coefficient matrix A, we know that the inverse matrix B^{-1} has all positive elements and hence the optimal price vector p^* must satisfy the linear decision rule (LDR):

$$p^* = (\alpha\hat{D})^{-1}(\hat{m} - Bx^*) \qquad (1.8)$$

This risk-adjusted LDR has a number of implications for planning. First, the higher the value of α, the lower the optimal price p^*. The sectoral producers interpret this as a signal for lower production. In contrast, player I, the central planner computes an optimal shadow price $\hat{p}^*$ from his risk-less LP model (1.3) which is higher than p^*. The planner's shadow price $\hat{p}^*$ is a signal for higher outputs. The divergence between the two prices, p^* and $\hat{p}^*$ thus generates a disequilibrium system. Second, the optimal risk-adjusted income $Y_\alpha = p^{*\prime}Bx^* + \frac{1}{2}\alpha p^{*\prime}\hat{D}p^*$ is always positive and higher than the optimal value $Y = \hat{p}^{*\prime}\hat{d} = \hat{p}^{*\prime}\hat{m}$ of the planner's objective function in (1.4). Hence the net income $(Y_\alpha - p^{*\prime}Bx^*)$ which equals $\frac{1}{2}\alpha p^{*\prime}\hat{D}\hat{p}$ is strictly positive for player II, the sectoral producers. This net income is like monopoly profits when the producers' perceived demand functions do not agree with those of the planner.

Third, the LDR approach (1.8) may be applied by the second player for updating p^* whenever the mean estimate $\hat{m}$ is revised with additional information about the planner's achievement in realizing output targets. For instance, if the reliability of the estimate $\hat{m}$ can be improved by appropriate stabilization policies, the second player's anticipation of optimal price will improve and given the capacity available it will induce output increase. The sequence of successive revisions of $\hat{m}$ leading to those of p^* may thus reduce the divergence or inconsistency between the two prices in the planning period.

It is clear that for the central planner, the introduction of a quadratic adjustment cost function e.g. equation (1.6) leads to an optimal LDR as follows:

$$\hat{h}_t^* = \frac{1}{\gamma_0}(\lambda_t^* - \lambda_{t+1}^*) + \tilde{\beta}(Ax_t^* + \hat{d}_t)$$

$$x_t^* = [W + \gamma_0 A'\tilde{\beta}\tilde{\beta}A]^{-1}[kWx_{t-1}^* + kWx_{t+1}^* - B'\lambda_t^* \tag{1.9}$$

$$- \gamma_0 A'\tilde{\beta}(\tilde{\beta}\hat{d}_t - \hat{h}_t^*) - \bar{v}]$$

for $t = 0, 1, \ldots, T$, where T is the short run planning horizon. Here it is assumed that inventory costs $C(\hat{h}_t)$ are quadratic:

$$C(\hat{h}_t) = \tfrac{1}{2}\gamma_0[\hat{h}_t - \tilde{\beta}(Ax_t + \hat{d}_t)].$$

$\tilde{\beta}$:   a diagonal matrix with positive elements in the diagonal

$\tilde{\beta}(Ax_t + \hat{d}_t)$:   normal or desired inventories

and the planners objective function is

$$\sum_{t=0}^{T} Q_t, \quad \text{where} \quad Q_t = C(x_t, x_{t-1}) + C(\hat{h}_t) \tag{1.10}$$

with λ_t being the vector of Lagrange multipliers associated with the inventory equation

$$\hat{h}_t = \hat{h}_{t-1} + x_{t-1} - \hat{d}_t$$

It follows from these optimal LDR (1.9) that if $\lambda_t^* = \lambda_{t-1}^*$, then the expected inventories $\hat{h}_t^*$ are at their desired level and the optimal outputs evolve according to the difference equation

$$x_t^* = k(x_{t-1}^* + x_{t+1}^*) - W^{-1}(B'\lambda_t^* + \bar{v}) \tag{1.11}$$

If the coefficient k is a scalar, the characteristic roots of the system (1.11) would be complex if $k^2 > 0.25$. This implies that the optimal output path would be oscillatory even when λ_t^*'s are constant over time. If k is a matrix, then the characteristic equation is

$$|\theta^2 k - \theta I + k| = 0$$

where the roots θ evidently occur in pairs, so that if θ_i is a root, θ_i^{-1} is also a root. Taking the stable roots only, the steady-state solution x^* can be derived as follows:

$$x^* = -(I - 2k)^{-1} W^{-1}(B'\lambda^* + \bar{v})$$

this is quite different from the conventional form of the steady-state equation of the Leontief model, as it includes the policy parameters k, λ^*, W and $\bar{v}$ besides the input–output matrix $B = I - A$. Risk aversion is built into this LDR through these policy parameters. For instance, a rise in the penalty price λ^*, or in the diagonal elements of the inverse weight matrix W^{-1} induces in the steady state a reduction in equilibrium output. A strong aversion to fluctuations in the sense of oscillations may also be secured through damping via the elements of the matrix k e.g. in the scalar case a value of $k < 0.25$ would ensure real roots and hence a non-oscillatory behavior.

It is clear therefore that in the nonsteady state, the planner has to follow the optimal LDR given in (1.9), which involves forecasting λ_{t-1}^* i.e., forecasting shortages or over supply in the next period and plan current output accordingly. Likewise, current optimal outputs x_t^* depend on the forecast of future shortages or oversupply in sectors. An estimation of this error-correcting process should thus form an essential component of models of planning based on static input–output models.

A similar error-correcting process could be defined in terms of the second player's strategy vector p in (1.7).

For an extension of this approach to the case of dynamic I/O models, consider the dynamic formulation [3] where total demand $\hat{d}_t$ is decomposed into consumption $\hat{c}(t) = \epsilon c_T(t) + \bar{c}(t)$ and investment $\hat{j}(t) = k(t + 1) - k(t)$ demand vectors, where $c_T(t)$ is total national consumption, ϵ is the vector of consumption shares by sectors, $\bar{c}(t)$ is the autonomous component:

$$\max c_T(t)$$

subject to $(I - A)x(t) \geqslant \hat{c}(t) + \hat{j}(t)$
$\tilde{a}_0 x(t) \leqslant \bar{l}(t)$
$\tilde{g} H x(t) \leqslant \bar{k}(t)$

Here $\bar{l}(t)$, $\bar{k}(t)$ are sectoral availability limits of labor and capital and $\tilde{a}_0$ is a diagonal matrix of labor requirements and $\tilde{g}$ is a diagonal matrix with diagonal elements g_i indicating the expected growth rate of capital stock $k_i(t)$ in sector i as perceived by the planner; the matrix H denotes the pattern of utilization of the capital stock vector $k(t)$, so that if there is full capacity utilization of capital in the plan period we would have

$$\tilde{g}Hx(t) = \bar{k}(t)$$

since total consumption $c_T(t)$ is positive, the vector of prices $p(t)$ of consumption goods must satisfy the numeraire condition

$$p'(t)'\epsilon = 1$$

and by the duality principle of LP models we must have

$$p'(t)(I - A) = r'(t)\tilde{g}H + w'(t)a_0$$

where $p(t)$, $r(t)$, $w(t)$ are the shadow price vectors associated with the constraints of (2.1) and it is assumed that equality signs hold at the optimal so that the shadow prices are positive.

It is clear that in this dynamic formulation, three sources of error i.e. overestimate or underestimate of net sectoral demand are present e.g. unintended inventories of goods unemployed volume of labor and underutilized level of sectoral capital stocks created. Again costs of adjustment due to these errors may be built into the design of the planning model by taking a quadratic form and deriving an optimal set of LDR.

The planning models [14] which have been explicitly formulated to provide a basis for national investment planning in several LDC's have recognized, to some extent at least. the existence of these errors and sources of inefficiency. Thus, it is recognized [14,15] that the solutions of the macro econometric model are not always consistent with the detailed intersectoral IO tables, unless some consistency checks are made and the design of the planning model suitably revised. Further, in a mixed economy framework, the failure of planned investment allocation by sectors of delivery to equal realized investment may be caused in part, by the divergence of actual from targeted investment by sectors of origin. The latter divergence, insofar as it is generated by the public sector or its lack of perception may have fundamental implications for resource inefficiency for the private sector. The lack of a suitable market test for efficient resource allocation in the public sector and the observed pattern of inefficiency displayed by the experience of several LDC have led some economists to question the value of aggregative planning through well-designed and precisely formulated mathematical models. These concerns have led the experts, in some cases [45,47] to explore the bases of consistency in the planning model or the lack of it and more so in the framework, where income growth and its distribution are both considered simultaneously. Thus, it was found for instance in a study for Colombia [45] that the investment targets planned for are unlikely to be realized or be consistent with the detailed intersectoral framework and the adverse effects on personal income distribution, which were not allowed for in the planning model would be considerable.

In some LDC's, five year plans have postulated, partly through political expediency objectives like price stability and balanced growth without carrying out the possible sources of conflict and inconsistency among these differing objectives or targets. Planning as a process of coordination and compromise through conceived in theory has rarely found an effective implementation in macrodynamic policymaking in LDC [41,42].

3.2. Output planning under imperfect competition

Application of the I/O model for planning implicitly assumes a competitive market structure for outputs and inputs. Thus for the LP model (1.3) if demand d is known with certainty, the optimal shadow prices p^* of output must satisfy the marginal cost rule

$$p^* = wa_0 + rb_0 \qquad (2.1)$$

if noncompetitive imports are ignored. For many LDC such a competitive assumption may not be valid for several sectors. On the cost side, labor is more organized in manufacturing than in agricultural sectors and on the demand side food producing consumer goods industries are less price elastic than non-food durable goods. Two issues therefore appear to be important to the planner. First, he may misspecify the market framework to be competitive, although it is not and thereby overestimate the equilibrium output. Second, the price distortions in monopolistic competition may imply welfare losses for the economy.

Elements of monopolistic competition in the I/O framework have been introduced Negishi, Arrow and Hahn and Nikaido [1,7,28] through the assumption that each sector, behaving as a single decision-making unit uses its price strategy monopolistically to maximize his own profits on the basis of a perceived demand function. This may lead to Cournot–Nash noncooperative equilibrium. Morishima has considered the situation where sectoral profit rates may be neither equal nor zero.

We consider here two types of Cournot–Nash equilibrium solutions, in one the payoff matrix has stochastic components not completely known to each player and in the other each player has to make conjectural estimates of his opponent's strategies. The framework is one of two-person nonzero sum game, where player I is the aggregate of sectors following a monopolistic strategy and the second player is the planner who assumes a competitive market structure and determines his output strategies accordingly.

Player I maximizes total profit π by choosing output strategies (x) when the price response of excess demand in each sector is taken into account:

$$\max_{x} \pi = p'Bx - (wa_0 + rb_0)'x \qquad (2.2)$$

where

$$B'p = \tilde{\alpha}(d - Bx) = \alpha - Cx; \quad \alpha = \tilde{\alpha}d, \quad C = \tilde{\alpha}B$$

$\tilde{\alpha}$ is a diagonal matrix with positive coefficients indicating the intensity of price reaction to excess demand. The optimal solution in terms of output and price vectors is then

$$x_M = \tfrac{1}{2}C^{-1}(\alpha - v)$$

$$p_M = \tfrac{1}{2}B'^{-1}(\alpha + v) \qquad (2.3)$$

$$\pi_M = x_M' C x_M, \qquad \text{where} \quad v = wa_0 + rb_0$$

Player II's competitive solution, under the assumption that the demand function $p = \alpha - Cx$ is correctly forecast is of course

$$x_c = C^{-1}(\alpha - (wa_0 + rb_0))$$

$$p_c = B'^{-1}(wa_0 + rb_0) \qquad (2.4)$$

$$\pi_c = 0$$

If the demand function is not correctly foreseen but unintended excess demands develop, player II may consider the target supply x_0 such that

$$x_0 = B^{-1}d$$

$$p_0 = B'^{-1}(wa_0 + rb_0) \qquad (2.5)$$

$$\pi_0 = 0$$

Since $\alpha > (wa_0 + rb_0)$, it is clear that $x_0 > x_c > x_M$ and $p_M > p_0 = p_c > 0$ since B'^{-1} is a matrix with positive elements. Also $\pi_M > \pi_c = \pi_0$. Thus the consequence of monopolistic competition is to generate lower output, higher price and higher profits compared to competitive situations. It is interesting to note that in some LDC such price and output distortions due to monopolistic competition have been directly estimated [18] and found to be quite substantial.

It is clear from (2.3) and (2.4) that taxing monopoly profits by a proportional tax τ_i on each output x_i so that player I's profits become

$$\pi = (p - \tau)'Bx - v'x, \quad v = wa_0 + rb_0$$

would not induce player I to produce at the competitive level; rather, it would have the reverse effect i.e. it would contract monopoly outputs x_M further thus accentuating the excess demand problem.

Two other features of the trial and error process in this two-person nonzero sum game must be noted. First, the perceived demand functions may include adjustment costs and risk aversion. In particular if player I is risk averse i.e. he thinks that equilibrium targets planned by player II cannot be realized by the market, he would react by producing less equilibrium output, whereas player II by his optimism may be much less risk averse. Thus the gap between two optimal output widens. Second, the cost of noncooperative behavior may be reduced considerably by the two parties agreeing on the plan targets and coordinating their decisions accordingly. It is clear that in this cooperative framework the main concern of the two players would be to forecast the demand function as accurately as possible and then adopt a cooperative payoff function. This is the rationality behind the mixed economy framework of national planning e.g. one such plan may be to let player I (the producers) maximize

$$\pi(x) = \alpha'x - x'Cx - v'x \tag{2.6}$$

subject to $\quad \pi(x) \leqslant \pi_0$

where π_0 is the minimum level of profits determined by the second player (the planner). Note that π_0 must be positive although it may be small; for otherwise there would be no basis of cooperation. It is of course assumed that in (2.6) the forecast of demand, agreed to by both players satisfies the rule

$$B'p = \alpha - Cx$$

given in (2.2). It is clear from (2.6) that optimal output, price and profit (x^*, p^*, π^*) would satisfy

$$x_M \leqslant x^* \leqslant x_c; \quad p_c \leqslant p^* \leqslant p_M; \quad \pi_c \leqslant \pi^* < \pi_M$$

and generally speaking, these inequalities would be strict implying that the welfare loss measured by

$$W = \sum_{i=1}^{n} W_i = \tfrac{1}{2} \sum_{i=1}^{n} (p_{i\mathrm{M}} - p_{ic})(x_{ic} - x_{i\mathrm{M}})$$

would be less in the cooperative plan. If the degree of cooperation is denoted by δ and the welfare loss is viewed as a function $W = W(\delta)$ with a negative slope, an optimal degree of cooperation δ^* may be defined by

$$\partial W / \partial \delta = 0, \quad \partial^2 W / \partial \delta^2 > 0$$

if the welfare loss function is convex around δ^*.

Thus, a planning model based on I–O analysis may necessarily generate welfare losses due to market imperfections, unless the optimal degree of cooperation δ^* is built into the plan. As an empirical illustration, we may refer to a study of investment planning strategy for Colombia which showed that planning by itself would accentuate the degree of inequality of income distribution measured by the share of profits in national income and also the Lorenz coefficient. Similar evidence exists for other LDC [31,44,45]. For instance, Nugent [29] found for the Greek economy that the impact of monopoly elements on IO sectors may be substantial.

The second feature of the trial and error process of the game-theoretic framework involves unequal information structures available to the two players, which lead to divergence of demand expectations and hence to prices. This type of price and output inconsistency calls for two types of coordination at the policy level. First, information about sectoral demand-supply discrepancies must be made available monthly or quarterly in a competitive fashion and the overall five or six year plan should be flexible in terms of quarterly variations. In this sense, flexibility and forecasting of short-term developments of sectoral imbalances must form a basic component of the design of a development planning model. Second, due to the elements of risk-aversion, which may in part be due to expectations about the future performance of the economy and of central planning, any policy which would reduce environmental uncertainty would be most helpful in reducing the price inconsistency. Hence the need for developing an appropriate stabilization policy, especially for strategic sectors like agriculture, power and transport which affect the basic elements of the production distribution process in the economy.

3.3. Stabilization policy under constraints

The framework of stabilization policy in a national planning model in LDC has three interrelated components: (a) commodity price stabilization in sectors which are sensitive to price fluctuations e.g., buffer stock policies, (b) monetary and financial policies aimed at consumption, production and investment decisions, and (c) trade and fiscal policies aimed at stimulating capacity utilization and long-run resource transfer to sectors which contribute most to long-run output growth. The targets in the three cases are: commodity price stability, monetary and financial stability and steady economic growth. Whereas the instruments for (b) and (c) are generally macro-economic e.g. money supply, interest rate and government investment and tax policies, those in case of (a) have emphasized several micro-economic factors, besides the macro ones e.g., (i) expectations that sectoral balances may not be realized (ii) governments' price policy may not be very effective and (iii) there may be considerably lags in adjustment of demand and supply.

In the short-run, commodity stabilization policies are most important for most LDC, since the macroeconomic factors are taken care of in the design of the planning model through I/O and other macroeconometric relations like consumption and investment functions. A second major reason is that in key sectors like agriculture which is sensitive to weather fluctuations and other forms of market uncertainty, such policies if properly designed and implemented may imply substantial welfare gains for the whole economy. For instance, risk aversion may be a major reason why small farmers may fail to produce cash crops that are exportable; they may fail to adopt improved production methods, because of a lack of subsidy in buying new inputs like chemical fertilizers. Lastly, due to lack of appropriate storage and warehouse facilities and the lack of accessible loan markets, the short-run price fluctuations may be far wider than if futures markets prevail.

Thus, the response of agricultural supply, and the extent to which it is affected by risk factors measured by price and yield variance, the existence of price support programs and specific subsidies on specific inputs like chemical fertilizers have been analyzed in some details for underdeveloped agriculture in LDC [40,41]. Applied studies have included some of the following:
(a) the estimation of inefficiency in production functions due to various sources of uncertainty [38],
(b) the risk-sensitivity of agricultural supply measured through quadratic programming [50],
(c) the loss of welfare associated with partial stabilization, when some of the prices are stabilized at the mean by the public authority, without reference to other substitution and income effects [49], and
(d) the various adjustment lags relating market prices to expected prices, where the latter provide the signal to farmers production plans.

Although the incidence of risk aversion on farmers' allocation decisions between cash-crops and food crops has been explicitly recognized, the various institutional processes and mechanisms through which this incidence is transmitted have not been given the required attention. Problems of optimal choice of techniques, optimal pattern of diversification of farms in its process of growth and optimal resource allocations under various conditions of risk and uncertainty are still unexplored in the framework of quadratic and nonlinear programming.

The impact of risk on farmers' resource allocation decisions is important for policy purposes in most LDC for two basic reasons. First of all, risks affect the other constraints of the input–output process including technical knowledge. Second, the inefficiency of the risk-averse behavior, relative to risk neutral ones may not lead to inoptimal resource use and underinvestment, if market organizations and institutional mechanisms exist to provide risk diffusion among a large number of farmers in a costless way or nearly so. The effects of risk constraints on the optimal acreage decisions are found to be significant [36,38] in applications to farm management data in India and other LDC.

4. Risk planning in market economies

The efficiency of the competitive market system under conditions of risk and uncertainty has been extensively discussed under various institutional assumptions e.g. (a) risk allocation in a market with many traders [16], (b) formulation of optimal prices for social insurance [33] and (c) development of two-level prices in the theory of indicative planning, the first level for reducing the informational gap between decision-makers and the second for coordinating the decisions under differing anticipations of the future state of the world [16,26].

At a more practical level, alternative stabilization policies in the form of monetary and fiscal policy-mixes have been evaluated in the framework of econometrically estimated models, usually in a simultaneous nonlinear equations form based on quarterly data [49]. Techniques of statistical simulation and optimal control theory in the form of LDR are frequently applied to test (a) the effectiveness of different policy-mixes, (b) the use of adaptive control through improved information and (c) the robustness of alternative commodity stabilization policies [25,32,49]. In a recent application Klein and Su [19] provided a novel method of combining an econometrically estimated model of an economy with an optimal control model under a linear quadratic framework. Denote the econometric model as:

$$f_i\left(y_t', y_{t-1}', \ldots, y_{t-p}', x_t', z_t'\right) = e_{it}, \qquad i = 1, 2, \ldots, n \tag{4.1}$$

where y_t' is a row vector with n target (i.e., endogenous) variables, x_t'

contains m exogenous control variables, z_t denotes other noncontrol variables, e_t are random errors. The objective or welfare function C of the policy maker, negatively measured is assumed to be a quadratic function of the deviations of the endogenous variables from their targets y_t^* over the planning horizon and also of the values of the control variables that are used to steer the system towards targets. For example, C is taken as

$$C = - \sum_{t=1971:1}^{1975:1} \left[w_1(y_{1t} - y_{1t}^*)^2 + w_2(y_{2t} - y_{2t}^*)^2 \right.$$

$$+ w_3(y_3 - y_{3t}^*)^2 + w_4(y_{4t} - y_{4t}^*)^2 + p_1(x_{1t} - x_{1t}^*)^2$$

$$\left. + p_2(x_{2t} - x_{2t}^*)^2 + p_3(x_{3t} - x_{3t}^*)^2 \right] \tag{4.2}$$

where y_1 is the growth rate of GNP, y_2 the rate of inflation, y_3 the rate of unemployment, y_4 the ratio of foreign trade balance to GNP, x_1 government expenditure, x_2 an average income tax rate level, x_3 unborrowed reserves. An asterisks indicates the desired levels; w_i's are subjective weights attached to target variables and p_j's are the penalties attached to the use of policy instruments. The econometric model used for (4.1) is the Wharton Mark IV quarterly model involving a system of nonlinear simultaneous equations with approximately 450 equations and identities and 200 exogenous variables. The optimum control variables X^0 solved from (4.2) may be written as a linear function of the endogenous variables Y

$$X^0 = -MY \tag{4.3}$$

where the matrix M contains terms involving the deriviations dY/dX, in addition to the weights. The solution algorithm consists of an interaction back and forth between solutions to (4.1) and (4.3). The econometric model (4.1) is solved along the base line path by applying the usual Gauss–Seidel method of approximation. Elements of Y are taken from that solution and substituted into the right hand side of (4.3) to obtain a revised estimate of X. The new values of X are then inserted in the second stage into (4.1) to obtain a new solution. A second revised estimate of X is then obtained from (4.3) and so on until the welfare function does not change from one iteration to the next. The convergence of the solution process is very fast in this specific simulation experiment. This application demonstrates how the sensitivity of optimal policy-mixes can be built into the design of a nonlinear econometric model which uses estimates containing different standard errors. Methods of dual control involving simultaneous use of improved estimates and caution in control have also been applied in the current economic literature [30,49]. These adaptive methods, of which dual control is a part depend for their effectiveness on the possibilities for learning, which depend for the most part upon the degree of uncertainty of the policymaker. The greater is his uncertainty, the less is his information and thus the greater is the scope of learning. Hence the need for flexibility and caution in the formulation of economic plans or policies. Three types of uncertainty are clearly distinguished in such cases: (1) the specification errors implied by particular models used for policies, (2) the instrument instability [18,31] due to the choice by the policymaker of certain types of control e.g. derivative, proportional or integral or a mixture of the three, and (3) the estimation uncertainty, when parts of the policy model are to be statistically estimated. In case of multiple policymakers two additional sources of uncertainty are due to the possible inconsistency of preferences of different policymakers and the need for exploring compromises [32,39] and to the unequal degree of sharing of relevant information among the team members. The implications of the latter case of incomplete information on choice of policies that are suboptimal have been explored in applied decision models for market economies [37,38], although there is scope for further work in this area.

In economy-wide models of investment planning designed for market economies, aversion to fluctuations in target variables e.g. consumption or real output has been specifically built into the model formulation itself. Thus, in the context of the consumption turnpike theorem on optimal growth, Morishima and others [27,43] have emphasized the need for incorporating into the planner's objective function a strong aversion to fluctuations and oscillations in sectoral output by minimizing for every sector j:

$$S_j(T) = T^{-1}\left[\sum_{t=1}^{T}\left(y_j(t) - y_j^*(t)\right)\right] \tag{4.4}$$

the average of deviations of per capita output $y_j(t)$ from its equilibrium (or optimal value calculated separately). This presumes that a more stabilized stream of outputs is preferable to those with fluctuations or oscillations in the presence of complex characteristic roots.

At the sectoral level, the role of uncertainty has been specifically investigated in models [2,9,11] of exploration of nonrenewable resources like oil or other mineral deposits. The problem of optimally managing a nonrenewable resource leads very naturally to optimal control type policies, since the total resource stock is generally uncertain and learning about the true stock size is possible only through the extraction process; also there is some uncertainty about the time at which a suitable substitute becomes available. Let $x_t \geqslant 0$ denote the level of proven reserves of a natural resource at time $t \geqslant 0$ and A denote the set of admissible policies $\pi(\cdot) = (c(\cdot), e(\cdot))$ of consumption $c(\cdot)$ and exploration $e(\cdot)$. Then for each consumption and exploration policy $\pi \in A$, we are interested in the infinite horizon expected discounted return $V_\pi(x)$ as a function of the initial resource level $X_0 = x \geqslant 0$:

$$V_\pi(x) = E_\pi \left\{ \int_0^\infty \exp - (\rho t) \left[u(c(X_t)) - h(e(X_t)) \right] \mid X_0 = x \right\}, \qquad x \geqslant 0$$

then, $\pi^* \in A$ is defined to be an optimal policy if

$$V_\pi^*(x) = \sup_{\pi \in A} V_\pi(x), \quad x \geqslant 0 \tag{4.5}$$

Here $u(c)$ and $h(e)$ respectively denote the utility function for consumption rates and the cost function for exploration rate. The existence of an optimal policy of consumption and exploration, optimality defined in the sense of (4.5) and its properties of stability and instability have been explored under different versions of the utility function $u(\cdot)$ and the exploration cost function $h(\cdot)$. The implications of uncertainty on the choice of optimal policies can then be explored in this framework through several channels e.g. (1) the effect of a high discount rate ρ or, the consequence of truncating the infinite horizon (i.e. problems of utility impatience), (2) the impact of high or low search intensities on the probabilistic exploration rate function $e(X_t)$, (3) the behavior of optimal shadow prices (i.e., optimal values of the adjoint variable in the Hamiltonian of the system) and finally (4) the welfare implications of myopic versus long rung optimal policies. Some empirical applications to the energy sector [5,31] are suggestive of the usefulness of such formulations in practical policymaking.

5. Appraisal and implications

It is useful at this stage to provide a general and non-technical appraisal of the role of risk and uncertainty in the planning process, as applied through quantitative models in the LDC, CPE and other free market economies. Some basic differences between the three economic systems e.g. LDC, CPE and developed countries have, in general influenced the ways through which risk aversion has been allowed for in the policy-making process. Thus, national planning in LDC has stressed on the longrun facets of economic development and redistribution of resources and this has necessarily implied questions of organizational change, technical innovation in production and distribution and self-sustaining process of reinvestment and growth. In many countries, policies towards land reforms, including improved irrigation and cooperative methods of input usages have generated longterm redistribution effects, which are not always beneficial or equitable. For instance, it has been known that land tenure systems as contractual agreements may generate inefficiency in production, under conditions of risk and uncertainty and the longterm implications of such inefficiency may be considerable. Empirical studies [38,39] through sample sets of LP models, based on Farm Management survey data in India for example show that average farm efficiency could be considerably increased through risk reduction in the following stages: tenure conditions, availability of finance, supply of water and fertilizers etc. There are similar experiences in other countries.

The next important area of policymaking in LDC, where the analysis of the role of risk aversion is of fundamental significance concerns the functioning of the public sector in a mixed economy framework. Besides its monopoly role and the power to influence the other sectors of the economy, it has other aspects of rigidity in its decision-making process e.g., it may conceal substantial technical and economic inefficiencies, due partly to the absence of competitive market prices and partly due to the various lags in information processing and utilization. Thus, informational inefficiency may lead to a nonzero-sum game framework in a mixed economy, where the private sector may not operate under forecasts that are considered appropriate by the public sector and vice versa. The costs of adjustment associated with the trial and error process here lead to substantial welfare loss for the economy, as has been stressed in earlier sections. Similar arguments would apply to stabilization policies aimed at reducing price fluctuations of commodities considered to be important for the whole economy, either for export or for general consumption.

The planning process in CPE has concerned itself with determining an appropriate supply of various outputs, on the presumption that demand forecast is either perfect or likely to be so. The experience of applying large-scale LP models under such a framework, in Hungary and other countries [21,47] have shown the implicit costs of such a planning process e.g., (a) the plan calculations tend to fail in sectors like foreign trade and agriculture, where uncertainty of either demand or of supply may be considerable, (b) significant divergences of official prices and the shadow prices calculated from the plan may occur and this may have cumulative multiplier effects on other sectors, and (c) the imbalances of sectoral demand and supply may develop and due to various information lags these may tend to be cumulative. It is clear that planning experts in these countries have increasingly emphasized the need for incorporating some methods of stochastic programming in the design and implementation of investment and production plans.

In contrast to LDC and CPE, the developed market economies have concentrated on large-scale econometric models to forecast cyclical changes in economic indicators. Besides simulation, the aim of these models is to evaluate the impact of (a) policy changes by agencies like Federal Reserve Board, (b) of various energy conservation practices, and (c) the medium-term outlook for economic growth. To the extent that information structure available to the policymaker may be incomplete, this framework may generate sources of inefficiency. Besides, cases of market failure do exist due to the lack of markets for insuring various types of risks. Thus, for public sector agencies and decision-making units, there are no unique criteria of efficiency due to absence of input and output prices. Hence there is scope for significant input and output distortion from an efficient level and more so in a world where the agents have substantial risk aversion. The analysis of macrodynamic policy making in such context has increasingly emphasized the need for adopting adaptive control methods having caution, flexibility and decentralization properties. Linear decision rules and other adaptive methods provide examples as to how aversion to fluctuations in key target variables is built into the model design. However, this field is quite new and considerable scope exists for both theory and applied work.

References

1 Arrow, K.J. and F.H. Hahn: General Competitive Analysis. Holden-Day: San Francisco, 1971.
2 Arrow, K.J. and S.S.L. Chang: "Optimal pricing, use and exploration of uncertain natural resource stocks", in P. Liu (ed.): Dynamic Optimization and Mathematical Economics. Plenum Press: New York, 1980.
3 Blitzer, C.R., P.B. Clark and L. Taylor: Economy-Wide Models and Development Planning. Oxford University Press: London, 1975.
4 Brada, J.C.: "Uncertainty, the structure of production and the pattern of trade of centrally planned economies", Economics of Planning, 13 (1973) 175–185.
5 Carey, M. and others: "The Birmingham energy model: a long term planning model of the British energy sector", Economics of Planning, 15 (1979), 18–50.
6 Chu, K.C.: "Designing information structures for quadratic decision problems", Journal of Optimization Theory and Applications, 25 (1978), 139–160.
7 Cornelisse, P.A.: Price Consistency in Development Planning. Rotterdam University Press: Rotterdam, 1973.
8 Dahlstedt, A.: "Cyclical fluctuation under central planning: an inquiry into the nature and causes of cyclical fluctuations in the Soviet economy", Economics of Planning, 15 (1979), 1–17.
9 Dasgupta, P. and G.M. Heal: "The optimal depletion of exhaustible resources", Review of Economic Studies, 41 (1974) 3–29.
10 Deleau, M., Guesnerie, R. and P. Malgrange: "Planning, uncertainty and economic policy: the optimix study", Economics of Planning, 12 (1972) 79–114.
11 Deshmukh, S.D. and S.R. Pliska: "Optimal consumption model and exploration of nonrenewable resources under uncertainty", Econometrica, 48 (1980), 177–200.

12 Duloy, J.H. and R.D. Norton: "Chac: A programming model of Mexican agriculture", in L.M. Goreux and A.S. Manne, eds., Multilevel Planning: Case Studies in Mexico. North Holland: Amsterdam, 1973.

13 Fandel, G. and T. Gal, eds. Multiple Criteria Decision Making: Theory and Application. Springer Verlag: Berlin, 1980.

14 Fox, K.A., Sengupta, J.K. and E. Thorbecke: The Theory of Quantitative Economic Policy with Applications to Economic Growth, Stabilization and Planning. Second edition. North Holland: Amsterdam, 1972.

15 Fujita, M.: Spatial Development Planning. North Holland: Amsterdam, 1978.

16 Guesnerie, R. and T. de Montbrial: "Allocation under uncertainty: a survey", in J.H. Dreze, ed., Allocation Under Uncertainty. John Wiley: New York, 1974.

17 Heal, G.M.: The Theory of Economic Planning. North Holland: Amsterdam, 1973.

18 Johansen, L.: Lectures on Macroeconomic Planning, Vol. 1–2. North Holland: Amsterdam, 1977, 1978.

19 Klein, L.R. and V. Su: "Recent economic fluctuations and stabilization policies: an optimal control approach," in Klein, L.R., M. Nerlove and S.C. Tsiang: Quantitative Economics and Development. Academic Press: New York, 1980.

20 Kolbin, V.V.: Stochastic Programming. Reidel Publishing: Dordrecht, Holland, 1977.

21 Kornai, J.: Mathematical Planning of Structural Decisions. North Holland: Amsterdam, 1967.

22 Kornai, J.: "A general descriptive model of the planning process", Economics of Planning, 10 (1970), 1–19.

23 Lecomber, R.: "Government planning with and without the cooperation of industry: reflections on British experience", Economics of Planning, 10 (1970), 53–87.

24 Manne, A.S.: "Multi-sector models for development planning: a survey", in Intrilligator, M.D. and D.A. Kendrick, eds., Frontiers of Quantitative Economics, Vol. 2. North Holland: Amsterdam, 1974.

25 Massell, B.F.: "Price Stabilization and Welfare", Quarterly Journal of Economics, 83 (1969), 284–298.

26 Meade, J.E.: The Theory of Indicative Planning. Manchester University press: Manchester, 1970.

27 Morishima, M., Theory of Economic Growth. Clarendon Press: Oxford, 1969.

28 Nikaido, H.: Monopolistic Competition and Effective Demand. Princeton University Press: Princeton, N.J., 1975.

29 Nugent, J.B.: "Linear programming models for national planning: Demonstration of a testing procedures", Econometrica, 38 (1970), 831–855.

30 Preston, A.J.: "Existence, uniqueness and stability of linear optimal stabilization policies," in Pitchford, J.D. and S.J. Turnovsky: Applications of Control Theory to Economic Analysis. North Holland: Amsterdam, 1977.

31 Rausser, G.C.: Dynamic Agricultural Systems: Economic Prediction and Control. Elsevier North-Holland: New York, 1979.

32 Sandee, J.: "Optimum policy alternatives", in Modeling for Government and Business. Martinus Nijhoff Social Sciences Division: Leiden, 1977, 149–164.

33 Sandmo, A.: "Discount rates for public investment under uncertainty," in J.H. Dreze, ed., Allocation Under Uncertainty. John Wiley: New York, 1974.

34 Scott, M.F. and others: Project Appraisal in Practice. Heinemann Educational Books: London, 1976.

35 Sengupta, J.K.: "Economic policy simulation in dynamic control models under econometric estimation", in W. Sellekaerts, ed., Econometrics and Economic Theory. Macmillan: London, 1974, Ch. 5, 115–138.

36 Sengupta, J.K.: "A consistent planning method for income growth and distribution with an application". Working Paper No. 18, Indian Institute of Management, Calcutta; June 1977.

37 Sengupta, J.K.: "Stochastic programming: a selective survey of recent economic applications", in M.A.H. Dempster, ed., Stochastic Programming. Academic Press: London, 1980.

38 Sengupta, J.K.: "Risk aversion in decision models", Working Paper, Department of Economics, University of California, Santa Barbara, 1980.

39 Sengupta, J.K.: Decision Models in Stochastic Programming. To be published by American Elsevier and North Holland, ca. 1981.

40 Sengupta, J.K.: Optimal Decisions Under Uncertainty. Springer–Verlag: New York, 1981.

41 Sfeir–Younis, A., and D.W. Bromley: Decision-making in Developing Countries: Multi-objective Formulation and Evaluation Methods. Praeger Publishers: New York, 1977.

42 Starr, M.K. and M. Zeleny, eds., Multiple Criteria Decision Making. North Holland: Amsterdam, 1977.

43 Stigum, B.P.: "Competitive resource allocation over time under uncertainty," in M. Blach, D. McFadden and S. Wu, eds., Essays on Economic Behavior Under Uncertainty. North Holland: Amsterdam, 1974.

44 Taylor, L: "Theoretical foundations and technical implications", Ch. 3 in Blitzer, C.R., P.B. Clark and L. Taylor, eds., Economy-Wide Models and Development Planning. Oxford University Press: London, 1975.

45 Thorbecke, E., and J.K. Sengupta: "A consistency framework for employment, output and income distribution projections applied to Colombia." Mimeographed Report, Development Research Center, World Bank. Washington, D.C., 1972.

46 Thornton, J. and D.L. Leber: "On the maximizing behavior of a monopoly planner", Economics of Planning, 10 (1970), 159–169.

47 Trezeclawkowski, W.: Indirect Management in a Centrally Planned Economy. North Holland: Amsterdam, 1978.

48 Tsukui, J.: Turnpike optimality in input–output systems. North-Holland: Amsterdam, 1979.

49 Turnovsky, S.J.: Macroeconomic Analysis and Stabilization Policies. Cambridge University Press: Cambridge, 1977.

50 Wiens, T.B.: "Peasant risk aversion and allocative behavior: a quadratic programming experiment", American Journal of Agricultural Economics, 58 (1976), 629–635.

15. Risk aversion in decision models

1. Introduction

Risk aversion has formed an integral part in most applied decision models under uncertainty, where the latter is generated by a probabilistic mechanism. This mechanism is not completely known, so that the environment under which decisions are to be made is random. However, the source of randomness may differ from one application to another, hence the decision-making response may vary. For example, in micro-economic models, consumer's or producer's response behavior is analyzed under conditions of price or cost parameter uncertainty and this behavior is compared with the case when there is no uncertainty. In engineering systems having a number of channels, the reliability levels may vary between channels and the noise elements may vary: the decision problem is one of maximizing the system reliability. In quality control, a sample inspection plan seeks to determine an acceptable quality level (AQL) of a product lot by minimizing the cost of making wrong decisions, where the latter involves producer's risk (α) and consumer's risk (β). The probability that a sampling plan will reject AQL is called the producer's risk α i.e. the Type I error, whereas the probability that the plan will accept fraction-defective levels (FDL) is called consumer's risk β i.e. the Type II error. Usually, if the lot quality is equal to or better than AQL quality, p_a is equal to or greater than $(1 - \alpha)$, where p_a denotes the probability of acceptance which is usually 0.95 i.e. $\alpha = 0.05$. Similarly, if the lot quality is equal to or worse than FDL quality, p_a is equal to or less than β, the Type II decision error and p_a is usually 0.10.

Measures of risk aversion are thus related to the source of uncertainty, the specification of the decision model and the system objective which is optimized. For example, the model may be one of linear programming (LP): max $z = c'x$, $x \in R$ where x is the decision vector and $R : \{x: Ax \leqslant b, x \geqslant 0\}$ is the constraint set and the parameters (c, A, b) are unknown but subject to a probability generating mechanism. This is a stochastic LP model for which suitable equivalent programs can be derived that are deterministic but nonlinear and inclusive of risk aversion measures.

Another example is the linear quadratic Gaussian (LQG) model in stochastic control which leads to linear decision rules under certain conditions. These decision rules have recursive or adaptive properties (e.g. Kalman filters) in the sense that they can be sequentially updated by incorporating posterior knowledge about means and variances when the information sequence is increasing.

The aversion to risk and uncertainty by the decision-maker (DM) may again vary depending on the organizational framework, its hierarchy and the types of information channels and data used. In team decision models of a production-allocation system, the individual and aggregate risks and their perceptions may vary depending on the degree of cooperation or non-cooperation among members. In collective risk theory for an insurance company, the flow of individual premiums and claim payments belonging to different risk classes may be viewed as two continuous and aggregative streams and the company's objective may be to maximize the probability that its aggregate capital S_t at any time t is not zero or negative i.e.

$$\max \text{Pr.} \left(\min S_t \geqslant 0, t = 1, 2, \ldots, T \right)$$

where Pr. denotes probability. In game theory models, mixed strategy solutions may be preferred over pure strategies by a player, when the opponent's reaction functions are incompletely known. In two-person nonzero sum games, mixing pure strategies may be adopted as a policy not to reveal his own reactions to the uncertain environment. Mixed strategies have also been used as randomized solutions in stochastic programming problems e.g. if the objective function is partly concave and partly convex, it may be preferable to use mixed rather than pure strategies as optimal solutions.

Our objective here is to provide a selective survey and critical appraisal of the major concepts of risk aversion as applied to economic and other operational decision models. For convenience of presentation, the measures of aversion to uncertainty and risk due to fluctuations or randomness in the environment may be classified into six groups as follows:

A. Parametric measures e.g., concepts of relative and absolute risk aversion due to Arrow, concepts of conditional and unconditional certainty equivalence, mean-variance characteristics of portfolios etc.
B. Probability-based measures e.g., probability of ruin, stochastic dominance of one distribution over another, Mahalanobis distance and other measures of distance between two or more distributions of the objective function and probability of detection in the search for the true parameter etc.
C. Nonparametric measures e.g., Kolmogorov–Smirnov type distance

functions for comparing alternative distributions, stochastic goal programming based on minimizing Tchebychev–type norms, safety first rules etc.

D. Informational measures e.g., entropy-based concepts, uncertainty of alternative channels of communication and value of information, Kalman filter and other adaptive behavior etc.

E. Measures of risk sharing and diversification e.g., mixing pure strategies in the theory of insurance under collective risk, measures of diversity in distribution of species in ecology and measures of product diversity in monopolistic competition under uncertainty etc.

F. Multivariate measures e.g., size and shape of the distribution of the multicriteria objective function, measures based on informational manifold theory and on multiple classification procedures etc.

1.1. Parametric measures

One of the most important measures that has found wide applications is the Arrow-Pratt measure (r_A) of absolute risk aversion:

$$r_A = -\partial^2 u(x)/\partial u(x) \tag{1.1}$$

which is easily defined, once we accept the existence of a real-valued utility function $u(x)$ defined on x, the wealth or income. A relative measure is obtained by multiplying (1.1) by x. Arrow argues that the absolute measure is a nonincreasing function of wealth and in portfolio model this implies that risky investment is not an inferior good [1,3]. This hypothesis of individual's aversion to income or wealth risks has been applied both empirically and analytically in international trade [3], financial decisions [54], agricultural production [52] and other allocation decisions [40].

Two operational implications of this concept of absolute risk aversion appear to be most important. One is the notion of certainty equivalence of a lottery which has consequences represented by the random variable $\tilde{x}$. For all monotonic utility functions $u(\tilde{x})$ defined on the space of $\tilde{x}$, a decision-maker (DM) is said to be risk averse, if he prefers $u(E(\tilde{x}))$ over $E(u(\tilde{x}))$, where E is expectation over the nondegenerate distribution of the random variable $\tilde{x}$ and it is assumed that it is finite or bounded. The certainty equivalent of the lottery is then defined by an amount $\hat{x}$ such that

$$u(\hat{x}) = E[u(\tilde{x})] \tag{1.2}$$

he is indifferent between the lottery and the amount $\hat{x}$ for certain. If the scalar utility function is monotone increasing, it follows that

$$u(E(\tilde{x}) - \pi) = E(u(\tilde{x})) \tag{1.3}$$

where π is a positive risk premium

$$\pi = E\tilde{x} - \hat{x}$$

and it is unique. If follows that if the scalar utility function is concave (convex), it implies risk aversion (risk proneness) with a positive (negative) risk premium.

Two points may be noted about the certainty equivalence notion. The consequences $\tilde{x}$ of the lottery may be an n-element vector rather than a scalar; the vector π of risk premiums [14] is not unique in this case, although an approximate risk premium vector π with n-elements may be computed as

$$\pi \simeq -\tfrac{1}{2}(u')^- \operatorname{tr}[UV] \tag{1.4}$$

where u' is a row vector with n-elements $u_i = \partial u(x)/\partial x_i$, U is a Hessian matrix $U = \partial^2 u(x)/\partial x_i \partial x_j$ of order n and V is the variance–covariance matrix of the random elements of the problem and $(u')^-$ denotes the generalized inverse of the n-element row vector u'. The absolute risk aversion matrix R_A corresponding to (1.1) now becomes

$$R_A = \left[-u_{ij}/u_i \right]$$

where u_{ij} are the elements of the Hessian matrix U and u_i is an element of the vector u. Note however that the multivariate measure of risk aversion still assumes the existence of a scalar utility function. If the utility function is a vector, as in a team decision problem and each member has a positive risk aversion at different levels, how can one define a risk aversion measure for the aggregate team that will retain some consistency over the preference maps of members? This is an open question for research.

However if the utility vector $u(j)$ of each member $j = 1, 2, \ldots, M$ can be assumed to be multivariate normal $N(m(j), V(j))$ with mean vector $m(j)$ and variance–covariance matrix $V(j)$, then one can characterize the difference $d = u(i) - u(j)$, $i \neq j$ in terms a multivariate statistic D^2 known as Mahalanobis distance:

$$D^2 = \left[\{u(i) - m(i)\} - \{u(j) - m(j)\} \right]' \left[V(i) + V(j) \right]^{-1}$$

$$\left[\{u(i) - m(i)\} - \{u(j) - m(j)\} \right]$$

provided the random utility vectors $u(i)$, $u(j)$ are statistically independent. This distance function D^2 may be applied in the sample or observation space and then this becomes Hotelling's T^2 statistic. For example, assume there are K observations on the random vector $u(j)$ for each member j and we want to test the null hypothesis that $m(i) = m(j)$. We form the T^2 statistic based on degrees of freedom $K - 1$ as follows:

$$\frac{T^2}{K-1} = K\bar{d}'S^{-1}\bar{d} \tag{1.5}$$

where

$$\bar{d} = (\bar{d}_k), \quad \bar{d}_k = K^{-1} \sum_{t=1}^{K} d_{tk}$$

$$S = (S_{ks}), \quad S_{ks} = \sum_{t=1}^{K} (d_{tk} - \bar{d}_k)(d_{ts} - \bar{d}_k)$$

d_{tk} are observations on vector $d = u(i) - u(j)$

this test statistic is related to Fisher's F distribution

$$\frac{K-p}{p} \frac{T^2}{K-1} \sim F_{p,K-p}$$

with degrees of freedom p and $K - p$, where p is the dimension of each utility vector $u(j)$. The critical region will be $T^2 > T^2(f, p, \alpha)$ where $T^2(f, p, \alpha)$ denotes the tabular value of T^2 with degrees of freedom $f = K - 1$ and the level of significance α. If the null hypothesis is rejected at the given significance level α_0 say, then the mean utility vectors for two sample groups i and j are different. The intensity of this difference is then measured by the noncentrality index λ^2, where

$$\lambda^2 = K(m(i) - m(j))'[V(i) + V(j)]^{-1}(m(i) - m(j))$$

thus, a multivariate measure of risk aversion can be developed for the case when $u(j)$ is a random vector for each $j = 1, 2, \ldots, N$ if we just stratify the group into g strata or risk classes such that within a given strata the null hypothesis based on (1.5) is not rejected and then apply to each strata a method of deriving a vector efficient point u^* say. If such a point $u^* \in R$ exists, where R is a suitable convex set assumed to be closed and bounded, then from Kuhn–Tucker theory it follows that there exists nonnegative weights $w_r \geqslant 0$ such that an aggregate utility function

$$u(j) = \sum_{r=1}^{p} w_r u_r(j) \tag{1.6}$$

in a scalar form can be defined for each $j = 1, 2, \ldots, N$ and maximization of $u(j)$ will characterize the vector efficient point u^*. Using this scalar utility function (1.6) for a homogeneous strata defined above, one could develop a measure corresponding to (1.4) and the associated risk premium vectors.

Note that the utility function becomes a profit function when we apply this type of risk aversion model (1.1) in production and resource allocation problems with multi-inputs and multi-outputs. This then leads to stochastic linear and quadratic programming models that have been extensively applied [36,42].

A second point about the risk aversion measure r_A in (1.1) is that it can be used to characterize conditional rather than unconditional certainty equivalence. Thus for any decision or act α, given the state of the world $w \in \Omega$, denote the utility function $u(\hat{x})$ in terms of the conditional variable $u(\tilde{x}_\alpha(w))$. Then the certainty equivalent $\hat{x}_\alpha(w)$ defined by

$$u(\hat{x}_\alpha(w)) = E[u(\tilde{x}_\alpha(w))] \tag{1.7}$$

depends on the fact that the state of the world w or, the action α conditional on w is given. Note that the expectation operator E in (1.7) is over the states of actions α induced by the states of the world $w \in \Omega$.

This concept of conditional certainty equivalence is particularly useful in linear quadratic Gaussian control problems leading to linear decision rules. The latter can be sequentially updated and improved as more and more information becomes available over time [38].

A second important use of the risk aversion measure r_A in (1.1) is the risk preference function for ordering of random lotteries. Let μ and σ be the mean and standard deviation of a random variable x. A scalar function $g = g(\mu, \sigma)$ is called a risk preference function, if for every pair of random variables x_1, x_2 with means μ_1, μ_2 and variances σ_1^2, σ_2^2 it holds that x_1 is preferred or indifferent to x_2 if and only if $g(\mu_1, \sigma_1) \geqslant g(\mu_2, \sigma_2)$. A risk preference function is called rational, according to Neumann–Morgenstern principle if the preference relation it induces on the set of random variables x_1, x_2 can also be induced by a suitably chosen utility function $u = u(x)$. But a (μ, σ) – preference function is determined only up to some strictly increasing transformation. Hence one may restrict to that class of utility functions u which induces the same preference relation as a preference function $g = g(\mu, \sigma)$ if and only if

$$g(\mu, \sigma) = U[Eu(x); x = x(\mu, \sigma)] \tag{2.1}$$

where E is expectation and U is some strictly increasing function. The whole class of utility functions that would be rational in the above sense can then be derived from an elegant result proved by Schneeweiss [35] and developed by others [42]. One of the most commonly used preference function is of the form:

$$g(\mu, \sigma) = \mu - \tfrac{1}{2}\lambda\sigma^2, \quad \lambda > 0 \tag{2.2}$$

which induces a partial ordering among random lotteries in x. The corresponding utility function which satisfies the rationality postulate in the sense of (2.1) is of the exponential form:

$$u(x) = -\frac{1}{\lambda} \exp(-\lambda x), \quad \lambda > 0 \tag{2.3}$$

where λ may be identified as the risk aversion parameter i.e.

$$\lambda = -\frac{\partial^2 u/\partial x^2}{\partial u/\partial x}$$

this parameter λ need not be constant for all levels x e.g. it may be of the form $\lambda(x)$, a nonincreasing function of income or wealth x. In this sense λ is a measure of local risk aversion when the exponential utility function (2.3) holds only approximately.

An interesting extension by Johansen [19,20] considers a linear sum of exponential functions:

$$u(x) = -\sum_{i=1}^{n} B_i \exp(-\beta_i x_i), \quad B_i > 0, \quad \beta_i > 0$$

where the elements x_i of vector x are assumed to be normally distributed with mean $E(x_i)$ and variances σ_i^2. In this case one can write

$$E[u(x; \alpha)] = u[E(x); \tilde{\alpha}]$$

where $\alpha = (B_1, B_2, \ldots, B_n; \beta_1, \beta_2, \ldots, \beta_n)$,

$$\tilde{\alpha} = (\tilde{B}_1, \ldots, \tilde{B}_n; \beta_1, \ldots, \beta_n), \quad \tilde{B}_i = B_i \exp\left(\tfrac{1}{2}\beta_i^2\sigma_i^2\right)$$

It is clear that if some β_i are negative and some positive, it would represent asymmetry in preferences that have been widely applied [51].

An interesting application of the risk aversion concept is in characterizing an efficient vector point in a stochastic production process. Let x be an n-element output vector and X the set of all output vectors obtainable in a random production process such that X is closed, convex and bounded. Then one may define after Peleg and Yaari [31] a concept of efficiency that holds risk aversely. Thus, of two output vectors x, $y \in X$, y dominates x risk-aversely if

$$\sum_{i=1}^{n} p_i u(y_i) \geqslant \sum_{i=1}^{n} p_i u(x_i) \tag{2.4}$$

for all utility functions $u(\cdot)$ belonging to a set $U(\cdot)$ of concave and nondecreasing utility functions and probabilities $p_i \geqslant 0$, $\sum p_i = 1$ and furthermore, there exists an utility function $u^* \in U$ such that

$$\sum_i p_i u^*(y_i) > \sum_i p_i u^*(x_i)$$

Then the output vector $x^* \in X$ is said to be "risk-aversely efficient" if there exists no other $x \in X$ that dominates x^* risk aversely. The importance of this result of Peleg and Yaari is due to its implications for a system of efficiency prices. Thus, if the output vector $x^* \in X$ is risk-aversely efficient, then they have proved that it must have a system of price vectors $\pi = (\pi_i)$ such that

$$x_i^* > x_j^* \quad \text{implies} \quad \pi_j/p_j > \pi_i/p_i$$

and conversely. Hence the behavior of risk-averters can be analyzed from a set of risk-aversely efficient vector points e.g. cross-section data of risk-averse decision-makers say.

To see the importance of the above result consider a deterministic case where the n-dimensional output vector x belongs to a convex set X, that specifies the resource constraints on production. Let X_{min} denote the minimal physical resources required to achieve an output level x^*, where it is assumed that X_{min} is a subset of X and is nonempty. Let x by any other vector point not belonging to X_{min}. The distance from x to the set X_{min} may then provide us with a measure of inefficiency i.e. a coefficient of resource under utilization as has been shown by Debreu [13]. By definition, the vector point $x^* \in X_{min}$ is efficient if there exists no other $x \in X_{min}$ such that $x > x^*$. Then by the convexity of the set X_{min}, there must exist a vector of price $\pi > 0$ such that

$$\pi'(x^* - x) \geqslant 0$$

this implies that

$$\pi'x \leqslant \pi'x^*$$

Denote by x^0 a vector collinear with x and belonging to X_{min}: $x^0 = rx$, then it is clear that

$$\max_{x^* \in X_{min}} \frac{\pi'x}{\pi'x^*} = \frac{1}{r} \max_{x^* \in X_{min}} \frac{\pi'x^0}{\pi'x^*} \leqslant \frac{1}{r}$$

$$= \rho, \quad \rho = \frac{1}{r}$$

since the ratio $\pi'x^0/\pi'x^*$ equals one when $x^0 = x^*$. This coefficient of resource utilization can now be given a "risk-aversely efficient" interpretation by means of concave nondecreasing utility functions $u(x^*)$, $u(x)$:

$$\sum p_i u(x_i^*) > \sum p_i u(x_i) \tag{2.5}$$

where p_i are nondegenerate probabilities. Since the inequality (2.5) can be interpreted as a first order dominance relation (i.e. the average utility or profit of vector x^* is higher than that of x), one could easily define higher order dominance among such portfolios. For example, let $u(x_i) = c'(i)x(i)$ be profit associated with the i-th state of the n-dimensional vector $c(i)$ and associated output vector $x(i)$. A set $x^*(1)$, $x^*(2)$, $\ldots$, $x^*(N)$ is dominant in the second order sense

$$\sum_{i=1}^{N} p_i [c(i)'x^*(i)]^2 > \sum_{i=1}^{N} p_i [c(i)'x(i)^2] \tag{2.6}$$

Here it is assumed that output vectors $x(i)$, $x^*(i)$ belong to the feasible set X for all states $i = 1, 2, \ldots, N$. Note that the second order dominance relation (2.6) along with the first order (2.5) do not necessarily imply

$$\sum p_i [c(i)'x^*(i) - \mu^*]^2 > \sum p_i [c'(i)x(i) - \mu]^2$$

where $\mu^* = \sum p_i c(i)'x^*(i)$, $\mu = \sum p_i c(i)'x(i)$ unless additional restriction are imposed on the utility functions $u(x^*)$, $u(x)$.

The notion of risk-aversely efficient vectors may also be applied to compare efficiency among several decision-making units e.g. N firms say, each with m inputs x_{ij}, $i = 1, 2, \ldots, m$ and n outputs y_{sj}, $s = 1, 2, \ldots, n$; $j = 1, 2, \ldots, N$ where efficiency is measured as the maximum of a ratio of weighted outputs to weighted inputs subject to the condition that similar ratios for every firm be less than or equal to unity. Denote the reference firm by the subscript k and assume that the observed outputs y_{sj} and inputs x_{ij} are positive and nonstochastic. Then the relative efficiency h_k

of the k-th reference firm is specified by the following linear functional fractional program in variables u_s and v_i:

$$\max h_k = \left(\sum_{s=1}^{n} u_s y_{sk} \right) \Big/ \left(\sum_{i=1}^{m} v_i x_{ik} \right) \tag{2.7}$$

subject to $\quad h_j \leqslant 1; \quad j = 1, 2, \ldots, N$
$$u_s, v_i \geqslant 0; \quad s = 1, 2, \ldots, n;$$
$$i = 1, 1, \ldots, m$$

This measure is due to Charnes, Cooper and Rhodes [45], who have shown that it can be solved by an equivalent LP problem:

$$\min g_k = \sum_{i=1}^{m} w_i x_{ik} \tag{2.8}$$

subject to $\quad \sum_{i=1}^{m} w_i x_{ij} \geqslant \sum_{s=1}^{n} \mu_s y_{sj};$
$$j = 1, 2, \ldots, N$$
$$\sum_{s=1}^{n} \mu_s y_{sk} = 1$$
$$w_i = t v_i \geqslant 0, \mu_s = t u_s \geqslant 0$$

where $t = (\sum_{s=1}^{n} u_s y_{sk})^{-1}$ is a positive scalar. Note two very convenient implications of this measure of relative efficiency. First, it provides a scalar dimensionless measure of efficiency in terms of which the N firms which are more or less homogeneous are to be compared and it does not specifically require the technology or the resource constraints to be specified in the model. Second, the efficiency of one number, the k-th is to be rated relative to the others in the reference set of N firms. The optimal choice of weights u_s^*, v_i^* is determined directly from observational data subject only to linear constraints of (2.7):

$$\sum_{s=1}^{n} u_s y_{sj} - \sum_{i=1}^{m} v_i x_{ij} \leqslant 0; \quad j = 1, 2, \ldots, N$$

Under these observations and constraints no other set of common weights will give a more favorable rating to the k-th firm relative to the reference set of N firms. Hence, if the optimal value h_k^* of h_k is not equal to 1.00 under the set u_s^*, v_i^* of nonnegative weights, it will not be attained from any other set. Thus the k-th firm with $h_k^* < 1$ will be less than 100% efficient.

This method of comparing efficiency across firms would not be general however, unless the observed inputs and outputs can be treated as stochastic i.e. being subject to a probabilistic generating mechanism. It is here that the concept of risk-aversely efficient vectors due to Peleg and Yaari can be applied. For example, consider the equivalent LP problem (2.8) and assume that there exist a set of probabilities $p_i \geq 0$, $q_s \geq 0$, $\Sigma p_i = 1 = \Sigma q_s$ such that the vectors $w^* = (w_i^*)$, $\mu^* = (\mu_s^*)$ provide the optimal solution to the following LP problem

$$\min g_k = \sum_{i=1}^{m} p_i w_i x_{ik}$$

$$\text{subject to} \quad \sum_{i=1}^{m} p_i w_i x_{ij} \geq \sum_{s=1}^{n} q_s \mu_s y_{sj}$$

$$\sum_{s=1}^{n} q_s \mu_s y_{sk} = 1$$

$$w_i, \mu_s \geq 0; \quad j = 1, 1, \ldots, N$$

where each of the N firms is assumed to be risk averse. If the optimal value z_k^* of z_k is greater than unity for a given set of nondegenerate probabilities, then the efficient frontier of the production possibility surface has not been attained for the k-th firm at the given set of probabilities. Thus probabilistic ranking of firms according to efficiency may be attempted in this approach. An alternative way of analyzing the stochastic version of the production frontier is to consider a probabilistic version of (2.8):

$$\max \epsilon_k = \text{prob}[g_k \leq g_0] \tag{2.9}$$

$$\text{subject to} \quad \text{prob}\left[\sum_i w_i x_{ij} \geq \sum_s \mu_s y_{sj}\right] = e_j$$

$$\text{prob}\left[\sum_s \mu_s y_{sk} - 1 \geq 0\right] = \tilde{e}_k$$

$$w_i, \mu_s \geq 0$$

where ϵ_k, e_j, $\tilde{e}_k$ are the tolerance levels and g_0 is a small preassigned number. This leads in general to nonlinear programming problems. For example if x_{ij}, y_{sj} are normally independently distributed with means $\bar{x}_{ij}$, $\bar{y}_{sj}$ and variances σ_{ij}^2, γ_{sj}^2, one version of the nonlinear program reduces to the following:

$$\min g_0 = \bar{g}_k + F^{-1}(\epsilon_k)\left[\sum_i w_i^2 \sigma_{ik}^2\right]^{1/2} \tag{2.10}$$

subject to

$$\sum_i w_i \bar{x}_{ij} - \sum_s \mu_s \bar{y}_{sj} = F^{-1}(1 - e_j)\left[\sum_i w_i^2 \sigma_{ij}^2 + \sum_s \mu_s^2 \gamma_{sj}^2\right]^{1/2}$$

$$\sum_s \mu_s \bar{y}_{sk} - 1 = F^{-1}(1 - \tilde{e}_k)\left[\sum_s \mu_s^2 \gamma_{sk}^2\right]^{1/2}$$

$$w_i, \mu_s \geqslant 0; \quad j = 1, 2, \ldots, N$$

where $\bar{g}_k = \sum_i w_i \bar{x}_{ik}$ and $F^{-1}(r)$ denotes the inverse of the cumulative probability distribution of a unit normal variate r. Note that if the terms involving $F^{-1}(\cdot)$ can be neglected in (2.10), we would obtain an LP problem:

$$\min \bar{g}_k = \sum_i w_i \bar{x}_{ik}$$

subject to
$$\sum_i w_i \bar{x}_{ij} - \sum_s \mu_s \bar{y}_{sj} \geqslant 0;$$

$$j = 1, 2, \ldots, N$$

$$\sum_s \mu_s \bar{y}_{sk} \geqslant 1$$

$$w_i, \mu_s \geqslant 0$$

Thus a probabilistic ranking of efficiency may be done through chance-constrained and other versions of stochastic linear programming [42].

1.2. Probability-based criteria

Three types of probabilistic criteria have often been used in characterizing optimal decisions under uncertainty. These may be very simply illustrated through an LP problem: max $z = c'x$, $x \in R$ where only the price vector c is subject to a stochastic mechanism but the restriction set R is convex and nonrandom unless otherwise stated.

The first criterion is the probability of ruin which is easy to apply if the probability distribution $p(z)$ of profits z is normal or approximately so under certain conditions of the central limit theorem. Since we have

$$p(z) = p(c'x \mid x)p(x) = p(c'x \mid c)p(c) \tag{3.1}$$

it is clear that maximizing the probability $p(z)$ is equivalent to maximizing the conditional probability $p(c'x \mid x)$, if only pure strategy solutions are chosen so that $p(x)$ is a constant i.e.

$$p(x) = \begin{cases} 1, & \text{if,} \quad x = x^* \\ 0, & \text{otherwise} \end{cases}$$

where x^* is the optimal pure strategy vector chosen. The ruin level of the conditional probability $p(c'x \mid x)$ in the normal case is given by

$$f = c'x - 3\sqrt{x'Vx} \tag{3.2}$$

where $\bar{c}$, V are the mean and variance–covariance matrix of the random vector c and the ruin probability assumed is 0.001. The optimal decision vector x^* is then found by maximizing f with respect to x subject to $x \in R$. Note however that if mixed strategies are allowed, the above procedure has to be modified [43]. Also when sequential data are available on c_t, $t = 1, 2, \ldots, T$ the conditional distribution $p(c'_t x \mid x)$ can be updated with more information and then the ruin criterion (3.2) applied. Sometimes, Bayesian methods [38,39] may be used to derive the posterior distribution $p(c'x_1 c_t)$ and then one may apply the ruin criterion on the basis of the posterior density.

A second criterion based on the concept of a statistical distance between two random points arises when we consider the problem of choosing the best treatment among a set of treatments, for each of which the response is distributed like a normal distribution say. This leads to the problem of selecting the best from a set of K normal populations say. Several types of optimal decision rules [42] are available here. As an example of one such rule, consider the stochastic LP problem and define a new decision vector $y = x - x_0$, is preassigned and known. Assume that the event

$$y'y \geqslant r, \quad r > 0 \tag{3.3}$$

holds with probability $\alpha > 0$. The stochastic objective function is

$$z = c'y + \epsilon; \quad \epsilon \sim N\left(0, \sigma_\epsilon^2\right) \tag{3.4}$$

where the conditional expectation is $E(z \ y) = \bar{c}'y$ and the stochastic component ϵ is independent of c. The constraint set is now $Y: \{ y: Ay \geqslant b - Ax_0, y + x_0 \geqslant 0\}$ where A, b, x_0 are nonrandom but there is induced randomness in vector y.

Assume that the goal of the decision-maker is to attain the goal z^0 fixed as $z^0 = \bar{c}'y$ as closely as possible. This can be attained by minimizing the average squared distance D^2:

$$D^2(z - z^0) = E[z - z^0]^2$$

conditionally on a vector $y \in Y$ satisfying (3.3). If the constraints $Ay \leqslant b - Ax_0$ are not binding, either due to the choice of x_0 or to the constraint

(3.3) which may be more restrictive, the optimal decision vector y^* can be solved from the eigenvalue problem:

$$[\lambda^* I - V] y^* = 0$$

$$\lambda^*(y^{*\prime} y^* - r) = 0$$

where V is the variance–covariance matrix of vector c, λ^* is the smallest eigenvalue of V with y^* as the associated eigenvector. Clearly the optimal solution $y^* = y^*(\alpha)$ depends on the probability α of the event in (3.3). Since for any other eigenvalue λ and the associated eigenvector y we would have

$$y^{*\prime} V y^* \leqslant y' V y$$

$y^*(\alpha)$ may be referred to as a risk-aversely efficient vector at the probability level α. Extensions to the case when there are K normal distributions $c(1)$, $c(2)$, ..., $c(K)$ for the vector c with a homoscedastic covariance structure may be easily worked out on the basis of a multi-variate distance measure known as Mahalanobis distance [27].

The third criterion for optimal decisions in a random environment is based on maximizing the probability of detection subject to a limit on the cost of search. Consider an idealized search problem in the context of stochastic LP models. Assume that the true value of vector c called the target has the probability p_1 of being in cell one i.e. $c = c(1)$ and the probability $p_2 = 1 - p$, of being in cell two i.e. $c = c(2)$. If $c(1)$ is known, the optimal decision vector is to be $y(1)$ and the reward $z_1 = c(1)' y(1)$. Likewise for $z_2 = x(2)' y(2)$. Assume that search cost is measured in units of z_1 and z_2 and there is a limit on such costs

$$\sum_{i=1}^{2} w_i z_i = 1 \tag{3.5}$$

where w_i is a suitable nonnegative weight. How should search costs be divided between the two cells in order to maximize the probability of detecting the target? Assume the probability of detecting the target $c(i)' y(i)$ to be exponential

$$p(z_i) = 1 - \exp(\alpha_i z_i), \quad z_i \geqslant 0$$

given that it is in cell $i = 1, 2$. The positive coefficient α_i may be an index of intensity of search effort. The total detection probability is therefore $\sum_{i=1}^{2} p_i (1 - \exp(\alpha_i z_i))$ and we maximize this expression with respect to $x(i)$ subject to the limit (3.5) on search costs. In general, when there are

K cells to be searched and the detection probabilities $p(z_i)$ are independent from one cell to another, the optimal search problem is a nonlinear program:

$$\max \sum_{i=1}^{K} p_i p(z_i)$$

subject to (3.5)

where p_i is the probability that the target is in cell i, $i = 1, 2, \ldots, K$.

Two comments may be made about these probability-based measures of risk-aversion. First, they assume specific probability distributions like the normal or, exponential and except for special cases these lead to nonlinear programming problems which raise computational questions. Second, the probabilities may not always be empirical or objective, so that subjective probabilities or weights may also be conceived [39].

1.3. Nonparametric measures

Measures of risk aversion which do not specifically require that we know the specific form of the sampling or population distribution are nonparametric in nature. Their uses can be characterized at three levels e.g. population level, sampling space and the latent or canonical variables.

At the population level, safety first rules [36] of different types have been applied in operational decision models under uncertainty. These rules assert that it is reasonable for an individual to seek to reduce as far as possible the chance of a disaster or ruin, when the outcome is probabilistic. However the relevant probability distribution is not known, hence the probability of ruin criterion cannot be applied. We apply therefore a distribution-free approach. For example, if the DM is concerned that profits z should not be less than z_0, then in default of minimizing the probability $P(z \leqslant z_0)$ we minimize its upper bound given by the Tchebychev inequality

$$P(z \leqslant z_0) \leqslant \frac{\sigma_z^2}{(z_0 - \mu_z)^2}$$

since for stochastic LP problems wth a deterministic constraint set R, profits are $z = c'x$ with mean $\mu_z = \mu_c'x$ and variance $\sigma_z^2 = x'V_c x$, this leads to the nonlinear programming problem:

$$\max_{x \in R} (z_0 - \mu_c'x)^2 (x'V_c x)^{-1} \tag{4.2}$$

This problem could be solved either by methods of nonlinear fractional functional programming or by solving the following saddle-point problem: find vectors x, $x^* \in R$ and scalars λ, $\lambda^* \in L$ where L is assumed to be a closed bounded set such that

$$F(x, \lambda^*) \leqslant F(x^*, \lambda^*) \leqslant F(x^*, \lambda) \tag{4.3}$$

where

$$F(x, \lambda) = (z_0 - \mu_c'x)^2 - \lambda x'V_c x$$

It can be shown that if an optimal solution exists for the problem (4.2), it can be identified by the optimal pair (x^*, λ^*) in (4.3), since the scalar function $F(x^*, \lambda)$ can be shown to be convex and monotonically decreasing function of $\lambda \in L$ for a fixed $x^* \in R$. If the denominator $D(x) = x'V_c x$ is assumed to be positive for all feasible $x \in R$, the convergence of $F(x^*, \lambda)$ to $F(x^*, \lambda^*)$ can be established by the computing sequence $\lambda_{k+1} = N(x_k)/D(x_k)$ where $N(x) = (z_0 - \mu_c'x)^2$ and x_k is the optimal solution vector of the concave program:

$$\max f = N(x) - \lambda_k D(x); \quad x \in R, \quad \lambda_k \in L$$

and as $\lambda_k \to \lambda^*$, $x_k \to x^*$.

Several extensions of the safety-first approaches have been recently made in models of risk programming [36] e.g., (i) use of bounds sharper than the Tchebychev bound, (ii) semi-variance or mean deviation around the median profit level in place of the variance term σ_z^2, (iii) use of reliability bounds from the class of distributions known as IFR (increasing failure rate) and DFR (decreasing failure rate), and (iv) use of bounds based on order statistics like extreme values.

When sample observations are available on vector $c_t = c_{jt}$, say T in number we may compute maximum profits z_t for each t and order them as $z_{(1)} \leqslant z_{(2)} \ldots \leqslant z_{(t)}$. Let $F(z)$ be the cumulative distribution of the random variable z and $F_T(z)$ be the step function:

$$F_T(z) = 0, \quad z < z_{(1)}$$

$$F_T(z) = i/T, \quad z_{(i)} \leqslant z < z_{(i+1)}, \quad 1 \leqslant i \leqslant T - 1$$

$$F_T(z) = 1, \quad z_{(T)} \leqslant z$$

Then, the Kolmogorov–Smirnov statistic D_T:

$$D_T = \sup[F_T(z) - F(z)]$$

has a limiting distribution

$$\text{prob}(D_T \leqslant r) \to 1 - \exp(-2Tr^2), \quad r > 0$$

for large T, which is independent of the population distribution $F(z)$, although it is required to be continuous. Here several choices of r implying different safety-first rules are available e.g. if $r^2 = \sigma_z^2/(z_0 - \mu_z)^2$ as in (4.1) we obtain Tchebycheff type bounds. Applications of nonparametric bounds under cost uncertainty and risk aversion include some of the following aspects: (i) cost implications of deviations from normality [7], (ii) use of relative distance $[F_T(z) - F(z)]/F(z)$ in stochastic programming [48], (iii) reliability analysis where the probability of a large deviation needs to be avoided and (iv) comparing distributions of optimal profits across firms for each of which an LP model is computed [44].

The use of canonical variates as proxy scores for comparing optimal solutions of two or more mathematical programs is generally attempted at two levels, either in the beginning for stratification or screening or at the end when measuring the similarity or dissimilarity of two solution vectors. The first case arises when we have for example a large number of firms` or a large number of activities. Using principal components or similar methods we have to reduce the problem to a smaller dimension. A composite index of resources may thus be constructed in terms of which the efficiency of firms may be evaluated through LP models [42,45]. Secondly, the similarity or dissimilarity of two or more portfolios may be compared e.g. Farrar [16] has compared actual portfolios (x_{ij}) by means of the distance measure

$$d_{ik} = \left[\frac{1}{n} \sum_{j=1}^{n} (x_{ij} - x_{kj}^*)^2 \right]^{1/2} \tag{4.4}$$

where x_{ij} is the i-th actual portfolio's investment in security j ($j = 1, 2, \ldots, n$) where $\sum_j x_{ij} = 1$ and x_{kj}^* is the proportion of k-th optimal portfolio invested in security j where $\sum_j x_{kj}^* = 1$. Note that the distance measure is very similar to the i-th actual portfolio's standard deviation or standard error of estimate when the k-th optimal portfolio is used as the standard of comparison. Simulation data were used to compute d_{ik} in (4.4), where similarity is indicated by a low value and dissimilarity by a high value, when rank order correlation is computed on the basis of these values.

Another example is from the brand loyalty model used in marketing literature in various forms [50]. Assume there are three brands of a product with $y_j(t)$ denoting the proportion sold of brand j at time point t. Let p_{ij} be the transition probability for a switch from brand i to brand j, assumed to be constant. The brand switching model is of the form

$$y_j(t) = \sum_{i=1}^{3} p_{ij} y_i(t-1) + \epsilon_j(t) \tag{4.5}$$

where $\epsilon_j(t)$ is the stochastic component assumed to be independently distributed with zero mean and constant variance and $\sum_j p_{ij} = 1$, $p_{ij} \geqslant 0$. Given the observed data on $y_j(t)$, the regression estimates $\hat{p}$ of p_{ij} may be used to test the hypothesis of brand loyalty e.g. if the inequality $\hat{p}_{11} > \hat{p}_{12} + \hat{p}_{13}$ holds with a significance level 0.95 or more, then the diagonal element $\hat{p}_{ii}$ has a row dominance; likewise we test $\hat{p}_{11} > \hat{p}_{21} + \hat{p}_{31}$ for column dominance.

Note that in (4.4) and (4.5) no specific distributional assumption is made and to that extent they provide only a measure of similarity or dissimilarity. In the transition probability model (4.5), the observed proportions $y_j(t)$ are scores which may approximate the probability of N customers choosing brand j in a random experiment. This idea can be easily applied to stochastic LP models [42]. For example, assume that the constraint set R to which the output vector x must belong has three extreme points as basic feasible solutions. Denote these points by vector x_i, $i = 1, 2, 3$. Let the random vector c in the objective function $z = c'x$ change over time from $c(t-1)$ to $c(t)$. Due to this change, the optimal solution vector may change from x_i^* to x_j^* or remain the same. If p_{ij} is the transition probability of switch, then one can write

$$x_j^*(t) = \sum_{i=1}^{3} p_{ij} x_i^*(t-1) + \epsilon(t)$$

where x_j^* is an optimal vector given the observation $c(t)$ at time t. It is clear the robustness of specific optimal vectors x_k^* may be directly estimated from the transition probability matrix p_{ij} once these are estimated either from observed time-series data on $c(t)$ or equivalent simulation data.

1.4. Informational measures

From an applied viewpoint three types of informational measures appear to be important e.g. (a) entropy and related concepts, (b) value of information channels, and (c) Kalman–Bucy filters in linear quadratic Gaussian models of stochastic control.

The entropy and related information theoretic measures use a function

$$H = -k \sum_{i=1}^{n} p_i \log p_i \tag{5.1}$$

(or its continuous analogue) where k is a suitable positive constant used for normalization and p_i is the probability of state i of a scalar random variable x. If x is a continuous n-dimensional vector with a multivariate density $p(x)$, then entropy is defined as

$$H = -\int_{-\infty}^{\infty} p(x) \log p(x) dx \tag{5.2}$$

If the multivariate density $p(x)$ is normal $N(\mu, V)$ with mean vector μ and a positive definite variance–covariance matrix V, then (5.2) reduces to

$$H = \tfrac{1}{2} n(1 + \log 2\pi) + \tfrac{1}{2} \log |V|$$

where $|V|$ denotes the determinant of V. Further, if we define a linear transformation from the n-element vector x to an m-element vector y by means of a constant matrix A of dimension m-by-n:

$$y = Ax$$

then the entropy $H(y)$ of y becomes

$$H(y) = \tfrac{1}{2} m(1 + \log 2\pi) + \tfrac{1}{2} \log |AVA'|$$

An information measure $I = I(f_1, f_2)$ related to this entropy concept and known as Kullback–Leibler information (KL) number is often used in multivariate statistics:

$$I = I(f_1, f_2) = \int \log \frac{f_1(x)}{f_2(x)} \cdot f_1(x) dx \tag{5.3}$$

to separate or discriminate between two distributions having densities $f_1(x)$, $f_2(x)$ which may have generated the random observations on vector x. If the density functions $f_i(x)$ are each n-variate normals with mean μ_i and variance–covariance matrix V_i, then (5.3) reduces to

$$I(f_1, f_2) = \tfrac{1}{2} \left[\delta' V_2^{-1} \delta + \log |V_1^{-1} V_2| - n + \mathrm{tr.}\left(V_2^{-1} V_1 \right) \right] \tag{5.4}$$

where tr. denotes the trace and $\delta = \mu_1 - \mu_2$ is the difference of the two mean vectors. Thus, if the KL number is very small (large), the two distributions are (are not) very close.

The informational measures have been used in applied and empirical work in at least four different ways:

(i) as a criterion of choice or discrimination among probability distributions [4,11] e.g. as a design criterion in optimum feature extraction and image processing problems, as a forecasting principle in econometrics, or as statistical distance for measuring the affinity of two distributions of a particular species in two ecological environments.

(ii) as a measure of the rate of information acquisition or transmission when specific communication channels are used [12] e.g., an optimal channel capacity may be defined for a decision-maker in terms of his maximizing an objective function W:

$$W = \sum_{j=1}^{M} q_j \sum_{i=1}^{N} p_{ij} U\left[a_i(j)x_i - cr\right]$$

where the channel has a rate of transmission r, c is the cost of channel capacity per unit, M messages can be conveyed in the channel with q_j, $j = 1, 2, \ldots, M$ as the unconditional probability that the j-th message is transmitted and p_{ij} is the conditional probability that the (random) state of the world is i, if the message transmitted is j; $a_i(j)$ is the action taken for state i and message j and x_i is the associated reward in state i and $U(\cdot)$ is concave utility function, assumed to be logarithmic.

(iii) as a measure of average amount of information. Thus, Lindley [25,26] defines the averages amount of information provided by an experiment e with data x and parameters θ by

$$I(e) = H_\theta - E_x\left[H_{\theta|x}\right] \tag{5.5}$$

where

$$H_\theta = -E_\theta[\log p(\theta)], \quad H_{\theta|x} = -E_{\theta|x}[\log p(\theta|x)]$$

$p(\theta) = $ prior probability density of parameter θ

$p(\theta|x) = $ posterior density of θ

This measure $I(e)$ evaluates the sampling experiment x as prior uncertainty (entropy) minus expected posterior uncertainty. It is clear from (5.5) that if θ and x are statistically independent i.e. $p(x, \theta) = p(x)p(\theta)$, then $I(e)$ is zero; otherwise $I(e)$ is nonnegative. Hence this measure, like Shannon's concept of information channel capacity cannot allow misrepresentation through faulty experiments. Let d_t denote the terminal decision and $u(e, x, d_t, \theta)$ be the utility associated with the event (e, x, d_t, θ) such that it is decomposable into two parts: u_s: sampling utility and u_t: terminal utility as:

$$u(e, x, d_t, \theta) = u_s(e, x) + u_t(d_t, \theta)$$

Then a cost of sampling: $c_s(e, x)$ can be associated with the pair (e, x) and a value of information can be defined as follows by u^0 in case of no information and by u^∞ in case of perfect information:

$$u^0 = u(e_0, x_0, d_t(0), \theta) = u_t(d_t(0), \theta) - \text{zero},$$

$$u^\circ = u(e_\infty, x_\infty, d_t(\theta), \theta) = u_t(d_t(\theta), \theta) - c_s(e_\infty, x_\infty)$$

where $d_t(0), \, d_t(\theta)$ are defined as

$$\int u_t(d_t(0), \theta) p(\theta) d\theta = \max_{d_t} \int u_t(d_t, \theta) p(\theta) d\theta$$

and

$$u_t(d_t(\theta), \theta) = \max_{d_t} u_t(d_t, \theta)$$

thus the terminal opportunity loss of a decision $d_t(0)$ with no information is given by the nonnegative quantity: $u_t(d_t(\theta), \theta)$. This is the value $V(\theta)$ of perfect information resulting from the event $(e_\infty, x_\infty, d_t(\theta), \theta)$. The expectation of this value of perfect information, $E_\theta[v(\theta)]$ taken over the prior density $p(\theta)$ thus defines the a priori value of a message conveyed by the state of nature θ say. Thus

$$EVPI = \int v(\theta) p(\theta) d\theta \geqslant 0 \tag{5.6}$$

It is clear that the expected value of any information structure intermediate between null information and perfect information may likewise be evaluated through expressions analogous to (5.6).

(iv) as a measure of efficiency of an estimate e.g. Fisher's information matrix associated with the maximum likelihood method of estimation. Thus, if L is the likelihood function for estimating two or more parameters θ_i of a set of observations the information matrix $I = (I_{ij})$ is defined as

$$I_{ij} = \left\{ E\left[\frac{1}{L} \frac{\partial L}{\partial \theta_i} \cdot \frac{1}{L} \frac{\partial L}{\partial \theta_j} \right] \right\}$$

This is widely used in the theory and applications of optimal design [10], which consider rules of allocating samples so that a scalar function of information matrix is maximized in some sense e.g. the trace or determinant of this matrix is maximized.

The applications of informational measures in Kalman filters and information channels of a team decision are extensively discussed in control theory literature [12]. The information structure for a quadratic problem arises as follows: a scalar quadratic objective function $f(u, x)$ is to be minimized by the choice of the control vector u, when the state vector x is not completely known due to incomplete information on the environment. One introduces an informational channel through the transformation H

$$y = Hx$$

where H is an m by n matrix, y is an m-element vector and x and n-element vector. Under incomplete information, the original objective function has to be modified e.g. we may minimize the expected value, $E[f(u, x) \mid y]$ for any given channel matrix. If the rank of H is zero, the information structure is null. But if the rank is n and $m = n$, then the information structure evolves over time i.e. increases or decreases, one could define sequentially optimal decisions. Also one can compare the two cases of null and complete information structures.

It is clear that risk aversion is introduced in the field of informational measures by several ways e.g., (a) through accepting estimates of parameters which are best in the sense of maximizing the information matrix as defined, (b) by decisions which maximize the average amount of information (5.5), (c) by selecting transmission of messages in a channel by maximizing a logarithmic utility function and (d) by adopting Kalman filter and other adaptive methods of sequential controls which updates successive controls using posterior data and information etc.

1.5. Measures of diversity

Measures of diversity have been widely used in market structure analysis in economics and ecological distribution of species in natural environments. Concentration of firms with an industry or of a particular brand among several brands in a market have been analyzed as a measure of dominance and its effects on market performance e.g. price-spreads or advertising discussed. Product diversification or market segmentation by brands has been analyzed as a risk averse attitude to cope with the uncertainties of duopolistic and monopolistic competition [24,47].

In ecology, indices of dominance in a many-species community have been analyzed in order to consider its effects on the structure and evolution of such a community. For example an index due to Simpson [32]

$$H_\alpha = (1 - \alpha)^{-1} \log \sum_{i=1}^{\infty} p_i^\alpha, \quad \alpha > 0$$

where p_i is the probability that the species belongs to a particular class-size x_i, $\Sigma p_i = 1$ leads to a measure of concentration H_2 for $\alpha \to 2.0$

$$H_2 = -\log \lambda, \quad \lambda = \Sigma p_i^2 \tag{6.1}$$

where λ describes the probability that any two individuals selected at random will belong to the same species. The index of diversity is $(1 - \lambda)$ or, the function H_2 itself. For a finite collection of species, an appropriate index is

$$H = N^{-1} \log \frac{N!}{\prod_{i=1}^{n} N_i}$$

where N_i is the number of individuals of the i-th species and N is the total in the whole collection. This index is empirically analyzed if the behavior of species is in equilibrium in a distributional sense, where the term behavior means the total interaction between a species and its environment that results in a given spatial and temporal distribution. Sources of disequilibrium are traced to (a) crowding or clumping, (b) random removal of individuals, thus affecting the size and shape of the original distribution (c) partial migration and (d) truncation in the pattern of interaction between two or more species in their natural distributions [30]. The equilibrium distributions found in some natural environments evidence stability in population dynamics, where stability measured the tendency that the scale parameter e.g. variance of the species distribution remains more or less constant. Indirectly this reflects a risk averse behavior in species distributions, since migration and other natural tendencies tend to reinforce the state of the equilibrium distribution.

For to or more species distributions within a community, the diversity measure may be related to measures of distance or entropy. For example, denote by F_1, F_2 two cumulative distributions over the nonnegative integers with associated probabilities p_{ij} i.e., $\Sigma_{j=0}^{\infty} p_{ij} = 1$, $i = 1$, 2 then the following two measures have been frequently applied in statistical ecology:

$$C_\lambda - \text{measures: } 2 \sum_{j=0}^{\infty} p_{1j} p_{2j} / \left(\sum_j p_{1j}^2 + \sum_j p_{2j}^2 \right)$$

$$\rho - \text{measures: } \sum_{j=0}^{\infty} (p_{1j} p_{2j})^{1/2} \tag{6.2}$$

These measures have continuous analogues, although infrequently used in ecology. Based on the C_λ measure the quantity $\lambda_i = \sum_{j=0}^{\infty} p_{ij}^2$, often termed by ecologists a measure of clumping has been mentioned before in (6.1), where $1 - \lambda_i$ is a measure of diversity. The ρ-measure specifies the correlation between the two species distributions.

The pattern of ecological species distributions, which evidence risk-averse behavior in maintaining equilibrium may be closely related to the index of concentration in the size distribution of firms in an industry. Denote by s_i the share of firm i in total industry sales of a product, then the index $\sum_i s_i^2$, $i = 1, 2, \ldots, n$ used to measure diversity in market structure [50] is seen to be nothing other than the λ measure of concentration mentioned in (6.1).

A more interesting measure of diversity in consumer choice is provided by the existence of several brands of a product sold in a market, that is either spatially separated or monopolistically competitive [24]. In either case, it has been argued that product differentiation and the associated advertising strategies for building brand loyalties are normally expected behavior for producers who are averse to risks due to fluctuations in sales and profits. Sources of such risk-averse optimizing behavior have been traced however to different factors e.g., (a) the existence of specific distribution like Beta for the brand loyalty parameter in consumer purchases, although the market share of the brand remains constant [34], (b) the profitability of the practice of price discrimination in a case where fixed costs are not negligible [47], (c) the varying price elasticities of demand for different spatial boundaries of a product market [24], (d) the need for diversification and risk spreading in the financial and market portfolio structure of firms [53].

The absence of perfectly competitive markets for contingent claims due to the nonexistence of appropriate insurance schemes for risk spreading may lead however to adverse selection and distribution of risks among individuals or firms. This may give rise to skewness in risk distribution requiring policy interventions and improved social insurance schemes [53].

1.6. Multivariate measures

Risk-aversion measures discussed before are all univariate, because they are either scalars or may be reduced to scalars e.g. entropy or distance measures. Multivariate measures are needed when risk aversion is measured by a vector or a matrix. For instance, let R be the variance–covariance matrix, also called risk matrix [22] of the standard least squares estimate $\hat{\beta}$ of the linear regression equation $y = X\beta + e$:

$$R = E\left[(\hat{\beta} - \beta)(\hat{\beta} - \beta)' \right] \tag{6.3}$$

where $R = (X'X)^{-1}$. Suppose the observations $x(i)$, $i = 1, 2, \ldots, g$ are grouped into g strata with N_i observations in group i and $N = \sum_{i=1}^{g} N_i$, then the overall mean $\bar{x}$ which corresponds to mean response

$$\bar{y} = \bar{x}'\beta; \quad N\bar{y} = \sum y(i), \quad N\bar{x} = \sum x(i)$$

satisfies the relation

$$\bar{x} = \sum_{i=1}^{g} \left(\frac{N_i}{N} \right) x(i)$$

where each $x(i)$ is a k-variate column vector and there are k response parameters in vector β. The risk matrix R now becomes a function $R(p_1, p_2, \ldots, p_g)$ of the allocation proportions $p_i = N_i/N$. If these proportions are decision variables how should they be chosen in some optimal sense? This question has several implications for optimizing behavior under risk e.g.,

(i)   in optimal design theory [10], the allocations p_i which are called the spectrum of the design are so selected that a suitable scalar function of the risk matrix is minimized e.g. trace of the risk matrix.

(ii) in item selection problem, the allocation p_i may be chosen by the additional condition that only $k_1 < k$ of the total k items are to be selected by an optimizing criterion e.g. in the active approach of stochastic linear programming, the DM may have chosen to produce m out of n ($m < n$)outputs.

(iii) minimum norm quadratic unbiased estimates for $\hat{\beta}$ may be used [42]; other estimators known as James and Stein type minimax estimators [22] may also be considered when the response coefficients β are not all nonrandom.

A multivariate measure of risk aversion is needed very naturally in a team decision problem, when the different members of a team have different risk preference functions e.g.

$$u(i) = m(i)'x(i) - r_i x(i)'V(i)x(i)$$

where there are N members $i = 1, 2, \ldots, N$ in a team, each with a risk aversion parameter $r_i > 0$. The perceptions of the mean $m(i)$ and variance–covariance $V(i)$ of the state vector $c(i)$ are different and hence their optimal decision vectors $x^*(i)$ will be different. Cases of complete cooperation may be compared with no cooperation in information structures, where the former may imply for example a common value r, a common mean m and a common variance–covariance matrix V. Risk pooling and risk spreading may be discussed very naturally in the context of this type of multicriteria decision problems under risk [39]. Note however that risk aversion characteristics are now indicated in terms of the closeness of r_i, $V(i)$, $m(i)$ to r, V, m where the latter is the risk averse behavior under complete sharing of information structures.

A very different type of characterization of multivariate risk aversion may be proposed by following the approach of James [18], which uses the variance information manifold. Let $z' = (z_1, z_2, \ldots, z_N)$ be a vector with N elements, so that $z_i = z_i(\theta)$ denotes the payoff for member $i = 1, 2, \ldots, N$ which is assumed to depend on a set of random parameters θ. The N dimensional vector z has a mean μ and variance V, where the variance–covariance matrix V forms a convex cone in $\frac{1}{2}N(N+1)$ dimensional Euclidean space $R^{1/2N(N+1)}$. Each nonsingular variance covariance matrix V is associated with an information matrix $J = V^{-1}$. The variance information manifold is then characterized by the space in which each interior point has alternative coordinate matrices V or J^{-1}. The set of singular positive semidefinite matrices when V is singular constitutes part of the boundary of this manifold. A concept of geodesic distance is introduced in this manifold by:

$$D = \left[\sum_{i=1}^{N} (\log \lambda_i)^2 \right]^{1/2} \tag{6.5}$$

where λ_i are the N characteristic roots of the determinantal equations

$$|V_2 - \lambda V_1| = 0 \tag{6.6}$$

where V_2, V_1 are any two positive definite symmetric matrices, representing here the variance–covariance matrices of the team. Several implications of this distance concept are useful in applied decision models under uncertainty e.g.,

(i) If V_1 represent complete information structure, whereas V_2 is for any other information structure, the above distance measure would specify the value of complete information,

(ii) If the vector z is normally distributed $N(\mu, V)$, $V = V_1$ and V_2 is the sample estimate obtained by maximum likelihood, then the statistic

$$d^2 = \frac{1}{2}N \sum_{i=1}^{N} (\log \lambda_i)^2 \tag{6.7}$$

is asymptotically distributed as a Chi-square variate with degrees of freedom $N/2(N+1)$. Using this statistic, one could test the similarity or dissimilarity of alternative estimates like V_2,

(iii) If the output vector $x' = (x(1), x(2), \ldots, x(N))$ of dimension k varies due to unequal risk aversion r_i, then one may compare in terms of this geodesic distance any two variance–covariance matrices $V_1(x)$, $V_2(x)$, and

(iv) a complementary set of bilinear stochastic programming problems may be set up and analyzed [41].

2. Risk aversion in economic models

From an applied viewpoint, risk aversion hypotheses have played important roles in the specification and empirical estimation of economic models and the decision rules following therefrom. At the general level some of the following tendencies may be clearly identified:

A. Economic theory

(a) risk aversion in consumer and producer behavior in static and dynamic contexts and its comparison or contrast with deterministic equilibrium and its stability [1,42].

(b) adjustment costs and lags due to divergence of equilibrium and fluctuations of demand or other parameters of the environment e.g. inventory adjustments [42].

(c) incomplete information and learning behavior, particularly in dynamic contexts when myopic or short run optimality may differ from long run optimality.

(d) gains from policies aimed at reducing uncertainties and fluctuations in the environment e.g. commodity price stabilization policies.

(e) gains from optimal diversification of risk-bearing securities through competitive allocation and distribution arrangements e.g. efficiency in Arrow–Debreu markets for contingent claims.

B. Planning models

In economy-wide models of investment planning [44], aversion to fluctuations in demand and other conditions of uncertainty and bottlenecks in different sectors has been specifically built into the planning models through safety reserves and policies designed to stabilize the system. Thus in the context of the consumption turnpike theorem [29] on optimal growth, Morishima has suggested the need for incorporating into the objective function a strong aversion to fluctuations in sectoral output by minimizing for every sector j:

$$S_j(T) = T^{-1} \left[\sum_{t=1}^{T} \left\{ \frac{y_j(t)}{l_j(t)} - \frac{\bar{y}_j}{\bar{l}_j} \right\} \right]$$

the average of derivations of per capita output $y_j(t)/l_j(t)$ from its equilibrium or optimal value. This of course assumes that a more stabilized stream of outputs is preferred to those with fluctuations.

Sharing of the risk of fluctuations as between sectors becomes more critical, when the planning model has regional breakdowns and the framework is a mixed economy.

C. Supply response

Recent econometric studies [23] have emphasised the importance of price and yield variability on farmer's production decisions and risk elements have been directly introduced through indicators such as price and yield variance. Thus Richard Just [23] has generalized the econometric form of a supply function in the framework of an adaptive expectations distributed lag model by including quadratic lag terms indicating risk aversion. Thus supply at time t, y_t is of the form

$$y_t = a_0 + \sum_i a_i x_{it}^* + \sum_{i=1}^{k} b_i w_{it} + e_t$$

where

$$x_t^* = \alpha \sum_{j=0}^{\infty} (1 - \alpha)^j x_{t-j-1}$$

$$w_{it}^* = \beta \sum_{j=0}^{0} (1 - \beta)^j \left[x_{i, t-j-1} - x_{i,t-j-1}^* \right]^2$$

Here x_t^*, w_t^* are vectors of explanatory variables, the first of which may represent the decision makers' subjective expectations about the mean prices and yields on which the decisions on production or acreage allocation i.e. y_t are based, while the element w_{it}^* of w_t^* may denote his subjective evaluation of the variances of prices and yields.

Empirical applications [40] of such risk averse supply functions in agriculture show several interesting features e.g., (a) risk aversion may be partly subjective and partly objective, the latter being derived from the variance of past observed prices, (b) risk aversion parameter may vary significantly from small to large farms, and (c) corp diversification and acreage substitution reflect the risk averse behavior more strongly, when the intensity of price fluctuations is more severe.

D. Production allocation behavior

Linear and quadratic programming problems have been widely applied in determining optimal resourcemix and output-mix in production and allocation models [42]. Quadratic models have specified in their objective functions a quadratic component indicating risk aversion either explicitly through a parameter λ in the risk preference function (2.2) or, implicitly through adjustment costs reflecting price response under conditions of imperfect competition. For LP models however, risk aversion is implicitly observed through output–diversification e.g. change from one optimal basis to another. To see this, assume that there are N LP models: $\max z(k) = c'(k)x(k)$, $x(k) \in R_k$ where the optimal solutions $x^*(k)$ preserve the same optimal basis in the sense

$$x^*(k) = Mb(k)$$

Clearly, if the resource vector $b(k)$ can be written as $b(k) = b + e(k)$, where the error component $e_i(k)$ is independently distributed with zero mean and variance unity, then the linear regression model

$$x^*(k) = Mb + \epsilon(k), \quad \epsilon(k) = Me(k)$$

may be estimated by Aitken's generalized least squares. Now assume that the N farms can be divided into two groups. For each group the optimal basis equation is

$$x_1^* = M_1 b + \epsilon_1, \quad N_1 \text{ observations}$$

$$x_2^* = M_2 b + \epsilon_2, \quad N_2 = N - N_1 \text{ observations}$$

Let D be a diagonal matrix of order m with d_j in the diagonal such that

$$d_j = \begin{cases} 0, & \text{when the farms belong to the first group} \\ 1, & \text{when they belong to the second group} \end{cases}$$

Then the combined regression equation becomes

$$x^* = (I - D)M_1 b + DM_2 b + w$$

where

$$w = (I - D)\epsilon_1 + D\epsilon_2$$

Here x_2^* may represent a solution more risk-diversified than x_1^* depending on the variance–covariance matrices of ϵ_1 and ϵ_2. Alternatively, x_2^* may be more close to the optimal solution x_Q^* of a quadratic programming model in terms of the distance function

$$D^2(x_2^*, x_Q^*) = (x_2^* - x_Q^*)'(x_2^* - x_Q^*)$$

E. Shadow price evaluation

Shadow prices computed from LP or quadratic programming models have been frequently used in efficiency evaluation. For specific resources like water, the shadow prices have been compared with administered prices [46]; for other resources shadow prices have been compared with market prices to imply the optimal direction of adjustment in resource planning. Quadratic risk programming has been commonly used to analyze the impact of risk aversion on optimal production decisions in farm planning. These models have used a quadratic risk preference function

$$f(x) = \bar{c}'x - \frac{\lambda}{2}x'Vx, \quad \lambda > 0$$

where $x \in R$: $\{x: x \geq 0, Ax \leq b\}$ is the decision vector, e.g., production or acreage allocation for different crops and $\bar{c}$, V are means and variance–covariance matrices of net prices. It is clear that if an optimal solution x_0 exists which corresponds closely with the actual behavior of farmers, then the shadow prices y^0 can be approximated by

$$A_i' y^0 = \bar{c}_i - \lambda^0 V_i x^0$$

where $\bar{c}_i$ is the i-th element of the mean price vector $\bar{c}$, V_i, A_i' are the i-th rows of matrices V and A respectively and λ^0 is that level of risk aversion which corresponds to x^0. It is clear that shadow prices $y^0(k)$ of different farms may differ, yet their average $N^{-1} \sum_{k=1}^{N} y^0(k)$ would be approximately close to y^0, so long as the farms are classified into relatively homogeneous groups [37].

It is clear that the above method can be applied to estimate the risk aversion parameter λ^0 from a cross-section data of N homogeneous farms, each having a quadratic programming model with approximately the same degree of risk aversion. In this case we have to assume, as Wiens [52] did that the optimal shadow prices y^0 are approximately equal to the market prices (y) and then the risk aversion parameter λ^0 can be estimated as an average relation from

$$\lambda^0 = A_i' y / V_i x$$

thus the empirical plausibility of a particular set of shadow prices and response of the decision makers to the gap $(y - y^0)$ between the two prices may be tested against empirical cross-section data on resource allocation and production. It is here that econometric testing of LP and quadratic programming solutions become very important [42].

3. Applications in other models

Applications of risk-aversion hypothesis in other fields, besides economics have ranged from an explicit specification in market research studies to the need for variance reducing techniques as a basis of reliable estimation. We attempt here a selective survey.

A. Market research

Models of brand choice and the need for reliable estimates of consumers' purchasing attitude have been heavily dependent in market research studies on optimal classification and cluster analysis techniques [42], which may be based on some of the concepts of multivariate distance we have introduced in earlier sections. For instance, suppose it has been known that people can be grouped into several types on the basis of some information regarding their attitudes and buying habits. Let the scores for an individual on the variables of interest be denoted by a vector x. Then the squared distance from an individual to a group mean u_i for group i is

$$D^2 = (x - u_i)'C^{-1}(x - u_i)$$

where C is the common covariance matrix. Under the null hypothesis that this individual is truly a member of group i, this statistic is distributed as Chi-square, if u_i, C are known. Accordingly, one can estimate the probability of an individual being this dissimilar to each group mean, given that he is truly a member of that group. By allocating individuals in proper categories we can thus maximize the response from say a direct mailing campaign.

A similar procedure is followed in optimal pattern recognition schemes and learning algorithms. For example, there are K category regions, each represented by a n-dimensional random vector x assumed to be normally distributed. An unknown vector is encountered and we have to assign it to a category region so that it has minimum probability of error, assuming equiprobable categories. In this case the optimal classification rule is to assign the unknown vector x to that category having the largest likelihood function i.e. to that category k for which $p_k(x)$

$$p_k(x) = (2\pi)^{-n/2}|V_k|^{-1/2} \exp\left[-\tfrac{1}{2}(x - \mu_k)'V_k^{-1}(x - \mu_k)\right]$$

is largest, where μ_k is the mean vector and V_k is the variance–covariance matrix.

B. Reliability analysis

Risk aversion enters into reliability analysis for a multicomponent series at several levels e.g., (a) concept of reliability used for the whole system,

(b) provision of standby component and its relation to component reliabilities and (c) the procedure of maintenance or inspection activities. Models of geometric programming which attempt to maximize system reliability take a stochastic character [49] when some parameters of the failure distribution of components are probabilistic and optimal standby provisions may vary depending on which k items out of n $(k < n)$ are selected. Sampling or inspection error aspects are most common in quality control [49]. As an example consider a case where defectives in both the sample and rejected lots are repaired. Then the cost of the decision to accept a lot containing u defectives after n items are sample and x defectives found is,

$$T_a = c_i n + c_r x + c_a u$$

where c_i is the cost of inspecting an item, c_r the cost of repairing and c_a the cost of accepting a defective item. The cost of the decision to reject a lot is given by

$$T_r = c_i S + c_r(u + x), \quad S = \text{lot size}$$

when inspection error is present, the above expressions become

$$T_a = (c_i + c_r e_1)n + (c_r \epsilon + c_a e_2)x + c_a u$$

$$T_r = (c_i + c_r e_1)S + (c_r \epsilon + c_a e_2)X + (c_a e_2 + c_r \epsilon)u$$

where

$$\epsilon = 1 - e_1 - e_2, \quad e_1 = \text{error type I}, \quad e_2 = \text{type II error}$$

Depending on the probability distribution of errors, optimum inspection plan for minimizing the expected cost of the sampling plan can be determined.

C. Insurance business

Here the criteria of probability of ruin and minimax credibility [6] are used for minimizing actuarial risks. As an example of the latter, consider a quantity x_{ij} as the performance of risk j ($j = 1, 2, \ldots, N$) in year i ($i = 1, 2, \ldots, n$), which is of interest for an insurance company which can classify risks into different classes j. The probability distribution $F_\theta(x)$ of x_{ij} is not determinate but depends on an unknown parameter θ. The decision problem for the actuary is to estimate the risk performance for risk k by a linear estimator $(\gamma Y + \delta)$ where $y_k = (1/n)\sum_{i=1}^{n} x_{ik}$ is a typical element of Y and $y_1, y_2, \ldots, y_N$ are assumed to be distributed with a common distribution function $G_\theta(x)$. Note that θ is to be chosen by nature, the second player and we denote the joint density functions of λ and θ by $dP(y, \theta)$. Then the decision problem can be recast as a game of the actuary against nature with a quadratic loss function

$$r(P, A) = \int [\gamma y + \delta - \mu(\theta)]^2 dP(Y, \theta)$$

$$= \gamma^2 v + (1 - \gamma)^2 + [(1 - \gamma)m - \delta]^2$$

where

$$v = E[\sigma^2(\theta)], \quad w = \text{var}[\mu(\theta)], \quad m = E[\mu(\theta)]$$

$$\mu(\theta) = \int x \, dF_\theta(x), \quad \sigma^2(\theta) = \int x^2 \, dF_\theta(x) - [\mu(\theta)]^2$$

Nature's strategies are $P = (v, w, m)$

Actuary's strategies are $A : (\gamma, \delta)$

It can be easily shown that

$$\inf_A r(P, A) = (vw)(v + w)^{-1}$$

$$L = \sup_P \inf_A r(P, A) = \frac{v_{max} w_{max}}{v_{max} + w_{max}}$$

$$U = \inf \sup r(P, A) = \frac{v_{max} \tilde{w}}{\tilde{w} + v_{max}},$$

$$\tilde{w} = \left[w_{max} + \frac{w_{max} - w_{min}}{2} \right]^2$$

Since $U > L$, the two-person game does not have a saddle point equilibrium in pure strategies. Hence a randomized strategy $(\tilde{\gamma}, \tilde{\delta})$ for the actuary may be recommended as follows:

$$\tilde{\gamma} = \frac{\tilde{w}}{v_{max} + \tilde{w}}, \quad \tilde{\delta} = (1 - \tilde{\gamma}) \left(\frac{m_{max} + m_{min}}{2} \right)$$

A minimax randomized strategy pair allows risk diversification, when the opponent (i.e. nature) chooses the strategies (v, w, m) from a parametric family $G_\theta(x)$.

4. Selected empirical applications

Three selected applications are briefly reported here to show the empirical plausibility of the risk aversion hypothesis: (a) the role of the risk parameter in a quadratic programming model of allocation, (b) risk aversion in supply response for selected field crops in California and (c) optimal output-mix under incomplete information.

The first example [46] maximizes a risk preference function of the form

$$f(x) = \bar{c}'x - \frac{\lambda}{2}x'Vx, \quad \lambda > 0 \tag{7.0}$$

subject to linear constraints: $Ax \leqslant b$, $x \geqslant 0$ and the empirical data for six crops in the Oxnard Plain, Ventura Country over 1960–77 are utilized to test the hypothesis: Do the quadratic programming solutions correspond more closely to the observed allocative behavior than the LP optimal solutions? Denote the distance measure between vectors x and $\bar{x}$:

$$D^2(x, \bar{x}) = (x - \bar{x})'(x - \bar{x})$$

where the reference level output vector $\bar{x}$ is the observed average behavior computed over the years 1974–77 and the other output vector x may denote the LP optimal solutions x_L or the quadratic programming solutions x_Q. Then for a value of $\lambda = 2.0$ the distance statistic takes the value 0.1154 for x_Q but 0.4314 for the LP solution. Further in terms of total variance we observe $x_L'Vx_L > x_Q'Vx_Q$.

The second example [40] uses an optimal output response derived from (7.1) as:

$$x = (\lambda V)^{-1}[\bar{c} - A'y] = g(\bar{c}, \lambda, V, y) \tag{7.2}$$

where y is the shadow price vector which may be approximated by their average market prices for inputs. Assuming that observed variances $\tilde{V} = \lambda V$ are inclusive of the effect of risk aversion, the optimal supply relation (7.2) can be linearly approximated by

$$x_i(t) = a_{i0} + a_{i1}x_i(t-1) + a_{i2}p_i(t-1) + a_{i3}v_i(t-1) + a_{i4}y_i(t) + e_i(t)$$

where $p_i(t)$ are prices of crop i in year t, $\sigma_i^2(t)$ are variances computed on a three year moving average basis, and $x_i(t)$ are the areas under crop i. Five major crops: cotton, rice, wheat and sugar beets and sorghum for the San Joaquin Valley in California are considered for the years 1949–60. The estimates turned out as follows:

$$x_1(t) = -198842 + 0.56\, x_1(t-1) + 31303.8\, p_1(t)$$

$$+ 302.50\, \sigma_1^2(t-1) - 36156.7\, z_1(t-1)$$

$$R^2 = 0.866$$

$$x_2 = -9317 + 0.76\, x_2(t-1) + 775.8\, p_2^*(t-1) - 173003\, \sigma_2^2(t-1)$$

$$R^2 = 0.631$$

$$x_3(t) = -20567 + 0.40\, x_3(t-1) + 9079.1\, p_3(t-1) + 43619\, \sigma_3^2(t-1)$$

$$- 1377.2\, z_3(t-1)$$

$$R^2 = 0.491$$

$$x_4(t) = -172883 + 0.66\, x_4(t-1) + 17358.6\, p_4(t-1)$$

$$- 22326.8\, \sigma_4^2(t-1)$$

$$R^2 = 0.750$$

$$x_5(t) = 161 + 0.80\, x_5(t-1) + 26319.9\, p_5(t-1) - 1004240\, \sigma_5^2(t-1)$$

$$R^2 = 0.830$$

Here $z_i(t)$ are dummy variables for the mean price to reflect higher weightage for the positive deviations of price above the mean price and p_1^* is the adjusted price to reflect substantial yield effect for rice. It is clear that except for cotton and rice, the supply response estimates have negative elasticity with respect to price risk measured by variance. For cotton, there is some evidence that the mean prices have more than offset the reduction in price variances. Note that the dummy variables $z_1(t-1)$, $z_3(t-1)$ uniformly show negative coefficients, reflecting the fact that the optimistic components of variance played an important role. Using a more detailed set of weights and dummy variables to reflect acreage control programs, Richard Just [23] found negative supply elasticity with respect to price risk measured by variance for all the crops above.

In the third example [45] we have computed LP solutions, one for each of twenty agricultural farms from the farm management data for Burdwan, India (1972–73). Twenty farms were selected by first arranging 72 farms in terms of principal component indices, so that they are relatively homogeneous. There are nine crops and six major resources for each farm. Denote by z_i^*, z_i the optimal and actual net income (objective function) for each farm $i = 1, 2, \ldots, 20$. A linear regression over these values shows the result:

$$z^* = -216.7 + 1.158z, \quad R^2 = 0.96; \quad DW = 2.18$$
$$\quad (-1.19) \quad (20.5)$$

where the t-values are in parentheses. It is clear that $\partial z^*/\partial z = 1.158$ i.e. optimal exceeds the actual on the average by 1.158 times. When we compute a second set of 20 LP models, on the assumption that a standard set of technologies based on all 20 farms (i.e. a new input–output matrix A^*) is available to each farm, besides its own input–matrix (A_i say) the regression result is as follows:

$$z^{**} = 860.8 + 1.566z, \quad R^2 = 0.62, \quad DW = 1.86$$
$$\quad (0.92) \quad (5.41)$$

where z^{**} is the new values of the objective function. This shows that information and availability of new technology may improve the output efficiency to a considerable extent. Further, it was found that the empirical distribution function of z^*, z and z^{**} are normal by Shapiro–Wilk test and hence the null hypotheses $H_0 : \bar{z}^* = \bar{z}$, $H_0 : \bar{z}^{**} = \bar{z}$, where bar denotes average values were econometrically tested by the t-test and each were rejected at 1% level. This shows that standard econometric tests may be applied in suitable cases to optimal solutions computed from a cross-section sample of LP models.

References

1. Amihud, Y: "On the Consumer Demand Theory Under Uncertainty", in R. Henn and O. Moeschlin, eds.: Mathematical Economics and Game Theory: Essays in Honor of Oskar Morgenstern. Springer–Verlag: Berlin, 1977
2. Arrow, K.J.: "Value and Demand for Information", in K.J. Arrow: Essays in the Theory of Risk Bearing. North Holland: Amsterdam, 1971
3. Batra, R.N.: The Pure Theory of International Trade Under Uncertainty. John Wiley: New York, 1975
4. Behara, M.: "Entropy and Utility", in G. Menges, ed. Information, Inference and Decision. Reidel Publishing: Dordrecht, Holland, 1974, pp. 145–154
5. Binswanger, H.P.: "Risk Attitudes of Rural Households in Semi-Arid Tropical India", Economic and Political Weekly, June 1978, 49–62
6. Buhlmann, H.: "Minimax Credibility", in P.M. Kahn, ed. Credibility: Theory and Applications. Academic Press: New York, 1975, pp. 1–18
7. Bury, K.V.: "Design Optimization Under Cost Uncertainty and Risk Aversion", Infor, 14 (1976), 250–258

.8 Charnes, A., Cooper, W.W. and D.B. Learner: "Constrained Information Theoretic Characterizations in Consumer Purchase Behavior", Journal of Operational Research, 29 (1978), 833–842

9. Charnes, A., Cooper, W.W. and E. Rhodes: "Measuring the Efficiency of Decision-Making Units", European Journal of Operational Research, 2 (1978), 429–444

10. Chernoff, H.: "Sequential Analysis and Optimal Design", Society for Industrial and Applied Mathematics: Philadelphia, 1972

11. Chernoff, H. "Some Measures for Discriminating Between Normal Multivariate Distributions with Unequal Covariance Matrices", in P.R. Krishnaiah, ed. Multivariate Analysis III. Academic Press: New York, 1973, 337–344

12. Chu, K.C.: "Designing Information Structures for Quadratic Decision Problems", Journal of Optimization Theory and Applications, 25 (1978), 139–160

13. Debreu, G.: "The Coefficient of Resource Utilization", Econometrica, 19 (1951), 273–292

14. Duncan, G.T.: "A Matrix Measure of Multivariate Local Risk Aversion", Econometrica, 45 (1977), 895–904

15. Fama, E.F. and M.H. Miller: The Theory of Finance, Holt, Renehart and Winston: New York, 1972

16. Farrar, D.E.: The Investment Decision Under Uncertainty, Prentice-Hall: Englewood Cliffs, N.J., 1962

17. Hanoch, G.: "Risk Aversion and Consumer Preferences", Econometrica, 45 (1977), 413–426

18. James, A.T.: "The Variance Information Manifold and the Functions on It", in P.R. Krishnaiah, ed., Multivariate Analysis, Vol. 3, Academic Press: New York, 1973

19. Johansen, L.: "Targets and Instruments Under Uncertainty", in H.C. Bos, H. Linnemann and P. de Wolff, eds., Economic Structure and Development: Essays in Honor of Jan Tinbergen. North Holland: Amsterdam, 1973

20. Johansen, L.: "Parametric Certainty Equivalence Procedures in Decision-Making Under Uncertainty". Memorandum of Institute of Economics, University of Oslo, September 1979

21. Johnson, R.M.: "Multiple Discriminant Analysis: Marketing Research Applications", in J.N. Sheth, ed., Multivariate Methods for Market and Survey Research. American Marketing Association: Chicago, 1977

22. Judge, G.G. and M.E. Brock: The Statistical Implications of Pre-Test and Stein-Rule Estimators, in Econometrics. North Holland: Amsterdam, 1978

23. Just, R.E.: "An Investigation of the Importance of Risk in Farmers' Decisions", American Journal of Agricultural Economics, 56 (1975), 14–25

24. Lancaster, K.: Variety, Equity and Efficiency. Columbia University Press: New York, 1979

25. Levin, R.D. and M. Tribus, eds.: The Maximum Entropy Formalism. MIT Press: Cambridge, 1978

26. Lindley, D.V.: "On a Measure of Information Provided by an Experiment". Annals of Mathematical Statistics, 27 (1956), 986–1005

27. Mardia, K.V.: "Mahalanobis Distance and Angles", in P.R. Krishnaiah, ed., Multivariate Analysis, IV. North Holland: Amsterdam, 1977

28. Marschak, J.: "Elements for a Theory of Teams", Management Science, 1 (1955), 127–137

29. Morishima, M.: Theory of Economic Growth. Clarendon Press: Oxford, 1969

30. Patil, G.P. and Others: Statistical Ecology, Vol. 1: Spatial Patterns and Statistical Distributions. Pennsylvania State University Press: Pennsylvania, PA 1971

31. Peleg, B. and M.E. Yaari: "A Price Characterization of Efficient Random Variables, Econometrica, 43 (1975), 283–292

32. Pielou, E.C.: Ecological Diversity. John Wiley: New York, 1975

33. Pratt, J.: "Risk Aversion in the Small and in the Large", Econometrica, 32 (1964), 122–136

34. Pyatt, G.: "A Model of Brand Loyalties", in M.G. Kendall, ed., Mathematical Model Building in Economics and Industry. Second Series. Charles Griffin: London, 1970

35. Schneeweiss, H.: "On the Consistency of Classical Decision Criteria", in Inference and Decision. Toronto University Press, Toronto, 1973

36. Sengupta, J.K.: Stochastic Programming: Methods and Applications. North Holland: Amsterdam, 1972

37. Sengupta, J.K.: "Regression and Programming: Overview of Linkages", IIMC Working Paper No. 16, Calcutta, 1976

38. Sengupta, J.K.: "Adaptive Decision Rules for Stochastic Linear Programming". International Journal of Systems Science. 9 (1978), 97–109

39. Sengupta, J.K.: "Multiple Criteria Decisions Under Risk", Working Paper in Economics #132. University of California, Santa Barbara, 1979

40. Sengupta, J.K. and R.I. Sfeir: "Risk in Supply Response", Economics Working Paper, University of California, Santa Barbara, 1979

41. Sengupta, J.K.: "Constrained Games as Complementary Eigenvalue Problems". Journal of Mathematical Analysis and Applications, 73 (1980), 301–314

42. Sengupta, J.K.: Decision Models in Stochastic Programming. To be published by Elsevier-North Holland: New York, ca 1980

43. Sengupta, J.K.: "Constrained Nonzero-Sum Games with Partially Controllable Strategies". Journal of Optimization Theory and Applications, 31 (1980), July

44. Sengupta, J.K.: "Stochastic Programming: A Selective Survey of Recent Economic Applications", Chap. 30, Stochastic Programming, ed. by M.A.H. Dempster. Academic Press: London, 1980

45. Sengupta, J.K. and Subhash C. Ray: "Efficiency in Activity Analysis Models: Econometric Measurements and Tests". Department of Economics, University of California, Santa Barbara, 1980

46. Sengupta, J.K. and R.E. Sfeir: "Allocative Behavior Under Risk Aversion Through Quadratic Programming Experiments". To be published in Applied Economics, ca 1981

47. Spence, M.: "Product Selection, Fixed Costs and Monopolistic Competition". Review of Economic Studies, 43 (1976) 217–236

16. Risk aversion, robustness and adaptive information in decision models

1. Introduction

Optimal decision making under risk and uncertainty has provided one of the most active fields of current research on applied economic models. A number of excellent surveys [26,34] are now available on the role of probabilistic economics and its use in characterizing optimal decision rules under uncertain environments. The object here is two-fold. One is to analyze selected illustrative examples to relate the concepts of risk and uncertainty to different information structures available and to ask how agents or decision-makers adapt to uncertainty through learning. Learning of course may take several forms, depending on the decision and the environment. We would concentrate however on specific forms of learning, as discussed in current models of economics and other decision sciences especially engineering and control theory.

Most often we would concentrate on the concept of risk as it relates in some sense to the probability distribution of relevant economic variables in the environment, although at a deeper level, other philosophical issues may be raised. Only decision models that are operational in some sense would be considered in our selected examples, which purport to illustrate the various implications and consequences of riskiness or risk-aversion on the part of decision-makers (DM).

In the economic theory of decision-making under uncertainty, as distinct from the theory of econometrics, the property of robustness associated with optimal decisions is not usually discussed. It is clear however that if the DM follows an adaptive behavior through learning situations, robustness emphasizes a very desirable goal in several ways. First, it helps the DM characterize and build elements of caution and flexibility in the decision finally chosen. Second, it allows a sequential way of viewing the information structure, when the latter is evolving over time or sample realizations. Thus, deferring decisions to a later stage may be particularly helpful in some situations of dynamically optimal policies, when the current information flows are too inadquate or too incomplete in some sense. Third, if the parameters of the probability distribution

associated with the relevant decision variables are not known but estimated from sample observations, then the estimates depend specifically
and sometimes very significantly on the form of distribution of errors
that is assumed. Hence any optimal decision based on a specific set of
estimated parameters may, at times, be very sensitive to large departures
from the assumed error distribution. If this sensitivity is quite large, the
estimates are said to be non-robust and any optimal decisions based on
such non-robust estimates may themselves be non-robust and therefore
be of very limited applicability. In recent advances of control theory,
robustness is increasingly emphasized [10,17] as a desirable property and
its trade-off with the optimality property of optimal control analayzed.
This trade-off analysis is particularly valuable in two situations: (a) when
there are nonlinear elements in the control policies and/or (b) the
control model used is only approximately linear. Designing stabilization
policies for commodity markets frequently present such situations as
above. In the area of natural resources for example, optimal management
of fisheries as renewable resources presents a similar problem, where
robustness of optimal control is frequently emphasized [39].

2. Risk attitudes and information structures

Three types of characterization of risk attitudes have been frequently
used in economic models e.g., (a) measures of relative and absolute risk
aversion due to Arrow and Pratt [2,30], (b) riskiness in the form of mean
preserving spreads due to Rothschild and Stiglitz [32], and (c) cautious
and probing behavior in adaptive control models [23,40].

The Arrow-Pratt measure (r_A) of absolute risk aversion

$$r_A = -\partial^2 u(x)/\partial u(x) \tag{1.1}$$

is easily defined, once we accept the existence of a real-valued utility
function $u(x)$ defined on x, the wealth or income. A relative measure is
obtained by multiplying (1.1) by x. Arrow argues that the absolute
measure is a nonincreasing function of wealth and in portfolio model this
implies that risky investment is not an inferior good. This hypothesis of
individual's aversion to income or wealth risks has been widely applied
both empirically and analytically in international trade, financial decisions, agricultural production, and other allocation decisions.

Two operational implications of this concept of absolute risk aversion
appear to be most important. One is the notion of certainty equivalence
of a lottery which has consequences represented by the random variable
$\tilde{x}$. For all monotonic utility functions $u(\tilde{x})$ defined on the space of $\tilde{x}$, a
decision-maker (DM) is said to be risk averse, if he prefers $u(E(\tilde{x}))$ over

$E(u(\tilde{x}))$, where E is expectation over the nondegenerate distribution of the random variable $\tilde{x}$ and it is assumed that it is finite or bounded. The certainty equivalent of the lottery is then defined by an amount $\hat{x}$ such that

$$u(\hat{x}) = E[u(\tilde{x})] \tag{1.2}$$

he is indifferent between the lottery and the amount $\hat{x}$ for certain. If the scalar utility function is monotone increasing, it follows that

$$u(E(\tilde{x}) - \pi) = E(u(\tilde{x})) \tag{1.3}$$

where π is a positive risk premium

$$\pi = E\tilde{x} - \hat{x}$$

and it is unique. It follows that if the scalar utility function is concave (convex), it implies risk aversion (risk proneness) with a positive (negative) risk premium.

Two points may be noted about the certainty equivalence notion. The consequences $\hat{x}$ of the lotterymmay be an n-element vector rather than a scalar; the vector π of risk premiums [11] is not unique in this case, although an approximate risk premium vector π with n-elements may be computed as

$$\pi = \simeq -\tfrac{1}{2}(u')^{-} \, \mathrm{tr}.[UV] \tag{1.4}$$

where u' is a row vector with n-elements $u_i = \partial u(x)/\partial x_i$, U is a Hessian matrix $U = \partial^2 u(x)/\partial x_i \partial x_j$ of order n and V is the variance–covariance matrix of the random elements of the problem and $(u')^{-}$ denotes the generalized inverse of the n-element row vector u'. The absolute risk aversion matrix R_A corresponding to (1.1) now becomes

$$R_A = \left[-u_{ij}/u_i\right]$$

where u_{ij} are the elements of the Hessian matrix U and u_i is an element of the vector u. Note however that the multivariate measure of risk aversion still assumes the existence of a scalar utility function.

A second point about the risk aversion measure r_A in (1.1) is that it can be used to characterize conditional rather than unconditional certainty equivalence. Thus for any decision or act α, given the state of the world $w \in \Omega$, denote the utility function $u(\tilde{x})$ in terms of the conditional variable $u(\tilde{x}_\alpha(w))$. Then the certainty equivalent $\hat{x}_\alpha(w)$ defined by

$$u(\hat{x}_\alpha(w)) = E[u(\tilde{x}_\alpha(w))] \tag{1.5}$$

depends on the fact that the state of the world w or, the action α

conditional on w is given. Note that the expectation operator E is (1.5) is over the states of actions α induced by the states of the world $w \in \Omega$.

This concept of conditional certainty equivalence is particularly useful in linear quadratic Gaussian control problems leading to linear decision rules. The latter can be sequentially updated and improved as more and more information becomes available over time.

A second important use of the risk aversion measure r_A in (1.1) is the risk preference function for ordering of random lotteries. Let μ and σ be the mean and standard deviation of a random variable x. A scalar function $g = g(\mu, \sigma)$ is called a risk preference function, if for every pair of random variables x_1, x_2 with means μ_1, μ_2 and variances σ_1^2, σ_2^2 it holds that x_1 is preferred or indifferent to x_2 if and only if $g(\mu_1, \sigma_1) \geqslant g(\mu_2, \sigma_2)$. A risk preference function is called rational, according to Nieumann–Morgenstern principle if the preference relation it induces on the set of random variables x_1, x_2 can also be induced by a suitably chosen utility function $u = u(x)$. But a preference function $g(\mu, \sigma)$ is determined only up to some strictly increasing transformation. Hence one may restrict to that class of utility functions u which induces the same preference relation as a preference function $g = g(\mu, \sigma)$ if and only if

$$g(\mu, \sigma) = U\left[Eu(x); x = x(\mu, \sigma) \right] \tag{2.1}$$

where E is expectation and U is some strictly increasing function. The whole class of utility functions that would be rational in the above sense can then be derived from an elegant result proved by Schneeweiss [33] and developed by others [34]. One of the most commonly used preference function is of the form:

$$g(\mu, \sigma) = \mu - -\tfrac{1}{2}\lambda\sigma^2, \lambda > 0 \tag{2.2}$$

which induces a partial ordering among random lotteries in x. The corresponding utility function which satisfies the rationality postulate in the sense of (2.1) is of the exponential form:

$$u(x) = -\frac{1}{\lambda} \exp(-\lambda x), \quad \lambda > 0 \tag{2.3}$$

where λ may be identified as the risk aversion parameter i.e.

$$\lambda = -\frac{\partial^2 u/\partial x^2}{\partial u/\partial x}$$

this parameter λ need not be constant for all levels x e.g. it may be of the form $\lambda(x)$, a nonincreasing function of income or wealth x. In this sense λ is a measure of local risk aversion when the exponential utility function (2.3) holds only approximately.

An interesting extension by Johansen [20] considers a linear sum of exponential functions:

$$u(x) = - \sum_{i=1}^{n} B_i \exp(-\beta_i x_i), \quad B_i > 0, \quad \beta_i > 0$$

where the elements x_i of vector x are assumed to be normally distributed with mean μ_i and variances σ_i^2. In this case one can write for the expected value of $u(x)$:

$$E[u(x)] = - \sum_{i=1}^{n} \left\{ B_i \exp\left[-\left(\beta_i \mu_i - \tfrac{1}{2} \beta_i^2 \sigma_i^2 \right) \right] \right\}$$

This leads to a parametric certainty equivalence procedure. The asymmetry of preferences can be easily handled by an objective function consisting of both positive and negative exponential functions as follows:

$$u(x) = - \sum_{i} \left(B_i \exp(-\beta_i x_i) + C_i \exp(\gamma_i x_i) \right)$$

$$B_i, C_i > 0, \quad \beta_i, \gamma_i > 0$$

when we obtain:

$$Eu(x) = \sum_{i} \left(\tilde{B}_i \exp(-\beta_i \mu_i) + \tilde{C}_i \exp(\gamma_i, \mu_i) \right)$$

where

$$\tilde{B}_i = B_i \exp\left(\frac{\beta_i^2 \sigma_i^2}{2} \right), \quad \tilde{C}_i = C_i \exp\left(\frac{\gamma_i^2 \sigma_i^2}{2} \right)$$

This general formulation, used in some decision context by Keeney and Raiffa [21] permits the degree of risk aversion to change with the value of the argument instead of being constant.

The concept of riskiness as mean preserving spread is easily defined by a stretching of the original density function. Let $z(x)$ and $\hat{z}(x)$ be the random returns on two different production or investment policies indexed by x. Then the return $z(x)$ is said to be more risky than $\hat{z}(x)$, if there exists a random noise term $\epsilon(x)$ with zero conditional expectation $E[\epsilon(x) | \hat{z}(x)] = 0$ for all x, such that

$$z(x) = \hat{z}(x) + \epsilon(x) \tag{3.1}$$

Thus the two random returns $z(x)$ and $\hat{z}(x)$ have the same mean but $z(x)$ has more weight in the tails than $\hat{z}(x)$. Given $E[\hat{z}(x)] \geqslant E[z(x)]$ every risk-averter prefers the less risky prospect $\hat{z}(x)$ to $z(x)$, since his expected utility $E[u(\hat{z}(x))]$ with the former is equal to or higher than $E[u(z(x))]$ for all utility functions $u(\cdot)$ concave in its argument. Two simple types of use of the concept of mean-preserving spread come readily to mind. One is in stabilizing schemes which preserve mean quantity of supply rather than mean price [28], by transferring by buffer stock operations a unit of output from a date at which price is low to a date when price is high. Thus if $p_i = p_i(x)$ is the price at date i when quantity demanded is x and if $p_1 > p_2 > 0$, the price distribution $F(p)$ generated by

$$
x_i = \begin{cases} x_i, & i \neq 1,2 \\ x_1 + \delta x, & i \doteq 1 \\ x_2 - \delta x, & i = 2 \end{cases} \tag{3.2}
$$

is less disperse than the original distribution, $F_0(p)$ say, provided the quantity change δx is small and demand at i is independent of price at j, $j \neq i$. If the representative consumer has a concave utility function $u(x)$ and is risk averse, he will prefer the less disperse distribution $F(p)$ over $F_0(p)$. Thus the gains from such partial stabilization schemes and the associated storage policies can be unambiguously measured. One could also characterize, in an appropriate dynamic context, optimal levels of commodity transfers or storage δx.

The second type of use of the concept of more riskiness is the role of learning in modifying or adapting the utility or objective function of an economic agent in a world in which uncertainty prevails. Cyert and DeGroot [8] have utilized Bayesian analysis as a means of modeling this learning process. For the firms learning in oligopolistic market situations, this framework leads to more flexible and sometimes more cautious behavior than if the world were certain and there was no need for learning. Similar arguments hold for the multiperiod utility maximization problem of a consumer, who would consume less of the known or certain commodity and more of the commodity about which is uncertain and risk-averse than he would in a one-period problem.

The notion of mean-preserving spreads can be most directly related to information–theoretic measures e.g., entropy which uses a function

$$
H = -k \sum_{i=1}^{n} p_i \log p_i \tag{4.1}
$$

(or its continuous analogue) where k is a suitable positive constant used for normalization and p_i is the probability of state i of a scalar random variable x. If x is a continuous n-dimensional vector with a multivariate density $p(x)$, then entropy is defined as

$$H = - \int_{-\infty}^{\infty} p(x) \log p(x) \mathrm{d}x \qquad (4.2)$$

If the multivariate density $p(x)$ is normal $N(\mu, V)$ with mean vector μ and a positive definite variance–covariance matrix V, then (4.2) reduces to

$$H = \tfrac{1}{2}n(1 + \log 2\pi) + \tfrac{1}{2} \log |V|$$

where $|V|$ denotes the determinant of V. Further, if we define a linear transformation from the n-element vector x to an m-element vector y by means of a constant matrix A of dimension m-by-n:

$$y = Ax$$

this may represent an information channel; then the entropy $H(y)$ of y becomes

$$H(y) = \tfrac{1}{2}m(1 + \log 2\pi) + \tfrac{1}{2} \log |AVA'|$$

An information measure $I = I(f_1, f_2)$ related to this entropy concept and known as Kullback–Leibler information (KL) number is often used in multivariate statistics:

$$I = I(f_1, f_2) = \int \log \frac{f_1(x)}{f_2(x)} \cdot f_1(x) \mathrm{d}x \qquad (4.3)$$

to separate or discriminate between two distributions having densities $f_1(x)$, $f_2(x)$ which may have generated the random observations on vector x. If the density functions $f_i(x)$ are each n-variate normals with mean μ_i and variance–covariance matrix V_i, then (4.3) reduces to

$$I(f_1, f_2) = \tfrac{1}{2}\left[\delta' V_2^{-1} \delta + \log |V_1^{-1} V_2| - n + \mathrm{tr.}\left(V_2^{-1} V_1 \right) \right] \qquad (4.4)$$

where tr. denotes the trace and $\delta = \mu_1 - \mu_2$ is the difference of the two mean vectors. Note that δ is zero for mean preserving spreads. Thus, if the KL number is very small (large), the two distributions are (are not) very close.

The informational measures have been used in applied decision models in at least four different ways:

(i) as a criterion of choice or discrimination among probability distributions [6] e.g. as a design criterion in optimum feature extraction and

image processing problems, as a forecasting principle in econometrics, or as statistical distance for measuring the affinity of two
distributions of a particular species in two ecological environments.

(ii) as a measure of the rate of information acquisition or transmission
when specific communication channels are used [7] e.g., an optimal
channel capacity may be defined for a decision-maker in terms of his
maximizing an objective function W:

$$W = \sum_{j=1}^{M} q_j \sum_{i=1}^{N} p_{ij} U\left[a_i(j)x_i - cr\right]$$

where the channel has a rate of transmission r, c is the cost of
channel capacity per unit, M messages can be conveyed in the
channel with $q_j, j = 1, 2, \ldots, M$ as the unconditional probability that
the jth message is transmitted and p_{ij} is the conditional probability
that the (random) state of the world is i, if the message transmitted
is j; $a_i(j)$ is the action taken for state i and message j and x_i is the
associated reward in state i and $U(\cdot)$ is a concave utility function,
assumed to be logarithmic.

(iii) as a measure of average amount of information. Thus, Lindley [25]
defines the average amount of information provided by an experiment e with data x and parameters θ by

$$I(e) = H_\theta - E_x\left[H_{\theta|x}\right] \tag{4.5}$$

where

$$H_\theta = -E_\theta[\log p(gq)], \quad H_{\theta|x} = -E_{\theta|x}[\log p(\theta)|x]$$

$p(\theta) =$ prior probability density of parameter θ

$p(\theta|x) =$ posterior density of θ

This measure $I(e)$ evaluates the sampling experiment x as prior
uncertainty (entropy) minus expected posterior uncertainty. It is
clear from (5.5) that if θ and x are statistically independent i.e.
$p(x, \theta) = p(x)p(\theta)$, then $I(e)$ is zero; otherwise $I(e)$ is nonnegative.
Hence this measure is like Shannon's concept of information chan-
nel capacity, and

(iv) as a method of quantifying an optimal control policy under incomplete information. Here an objective function $f(u, x)$ is to be maximized by the choice of control vector u, when the state vector x is
not completely known due to incomplete information on the en-

vironment. One introduces an informational channel through the transformation H

$$y = Hx$$

where H is an m by n matrix, y is an m-element vector and x and n-element vector. Under incomplete information, the original objective function has to be modified e.g. we may maximize the expected value, $E[f(u, x) \mid y]$ for any given channel matrix. If the rank of H is zero, the information structure is null. But if the rank is n and $m = n$, then the information structure evolves over time i.e. increases or decreases, one could define sequentially optimal decisions. Also one can compare the two cases of null and complete information structures [7].

The next type of characterization of risk attitudes arises most frequently in stochastic and adaptive control theory, where the concept of optimality may not be very unique and trade-offs of optimality against robustness may need to be explicitly incorporated; also other elements of risk aversion due to caution and probing may have to be examined when current decisions have future impacts which are incompletely known. From the viewpoint of applying economic policy, the following aspects of stochastic adaptive control are most important: (i) "*caution*" introduced by the fact that only the estimates $\{\hat{\theta}\}$ of the unknown parameters $\{\theta\}$ may be available when one chooses an optimal control, (ii) "*flexibility*" admitted into the optimal sequential decision by letting some control actions as probing in order to improve the estimates of unknown parameters, especially when several future periods lie ahead over which new information will become available, and (iii) "*robustness*" built into the control policy, either through modification of the system performance index, or through trade-off analysis of suboptimal policies depending on different information structures. We follow Wittenmark's excellent survey [40] of stochastic adaptive control to illustrate these three aspects in a very simple framework. Three basic elements are distinguished by Wittenmark. One is the information structure I, which may include e.g., the estimates $\{\hat{\theta}\}$ of the unknown parameters, or the estimates and their uncertainty or error $\{\hat{\theta}, P(\hat{\theta})\}$. If the uncertainties or errors of the estimates denoted by $P(\hat{\theta})$ are allowed to affect the choice of optimal control, it is "cautious"; otherwise it is not. A second element is the extent to which future information and its availability are allowed to influence optimal decision as of current date. Feldbaum [13] made a very useful distinction here between "dual" and "non-dual" controls. If the system performance index only allows previous measurements and does not assume that further information will be available, then the resulting controller is said to be nondual, otherwise it is dual. Thus, the minimization of a loss function one step ahead gives a non-dual controller, while minimization several steps ahead generates a dual controller, which must necessarily strike a balance between good control and good estimation. Thus for a dual controller it might be worthwhile to take some control actions in order to improve the estimates of the unknown parameters.

The third element emphasizes the need for adaptivity in cases of non-dual controllers, when the parameters estimated before active control is applied differ from those that may prevail afterwards. One of the basic objections to the conventional model of economic policy by the rational expectations theorists is that the assumption of parameter invariance fails to hold when active control policies are applied. Reasons are that the economic agents build expectations, the policies tend to have announcemental impacts and those underlying constraints which are unobservable and yet affect the choice of optimal policy may change the environment for determing future optimal policies. Thus in a stochastic world of many future periods it may be difficult if not impossible to follow fine-tuned optimal controllers; it may be more worthwhile as it were to follow simple fixed rules that have some robustness features. However one may conceive of different concepts of robustness here. For economic policy and national planning, Hughes Hallett and Rees [18] considered several measures of robustness through sensitivity of optimal control in respect of information errors, shocks in parameters and most of all incomplete specification of the performance measure as an index of welfare loss. Their simulation analysis for Dutch economic policy over 1976–80 slowed that the uncertainty in an open loop optimal control is nine times more damaging than in a closed loop one. A second type of robustness, found useful in applications to electric power systems by Petkovski and Athans [29] consider ways of building robustness through linear feedback controls applied to nonlinear dynamic models, which have a specified degree of stability in the sense of linear differential equations i.e. eigenvalue having negative real parts. A third type of robustness in the sense of minimizing the norm of control along with the system loss function hass been surveyed by Doyle and Stein [10]. A simple example of cautious control considered by Wittenmark is in terms of the following scalar system with $y(t)$ as state or output and $u(t)$ as input or control:

$$y(t) = y(t-1) + bu(t-1) + e(t) \tag{5.1}$$

where the error component $e(t)$ is independently identically distributed as normal with zero mean and constant variance $N(0, \sigma^2)$ for all t. The objective is to minimize the loss function

$$L = E\left\{ y(t+1)^2 \mid y(t), y(t-1), \ldots, y(0), u(t-1), \ldots, u(0) \right\} \tag{5.2}$$

The least squares (LS) estimate of b based on past observations is denoted by $\hat{b}$ and its conditional variance by $\hat{v}$. If b was known without any error, the optimal control is

$$u^0(t) = -y(t)/b \tag{5.3}$$

In case when b is unknown and the LS estimate $\hat{b}$, given the information structure $I(t)$, is used, the optimal control turns out to be:

$$u^*(t) = -\left[\hat{b}^2(t) + \hat{v}(t)\right]^{-1}\{\hat{b}(t)y(t)\} \tag{5.4}$$

where $\hat{b}(t) = \{\hat{b} \mid I(t)\}$, $v(t) = \{\hat{v} \mid I(t)\}$ and $I(t) = \{y(t), y(t-1),\ldots,y(0); u(t-1), u(t-2),\ldots,u(0)\}$. If instead of the cautious controller $u^*(t)$ given in (5.4), a controller of the form

$$\tilde{u}^0(t) = -y(t)/\hat{b}(t) \tag{5.5}$$

is used by following the certainty case (5.3), the value of the loss function L becomes

$$\tilde{L}^0 = \left(\hat{b}^2(t)\right)^{-1}\left(\hat{v}(t)y^2(t)\right) + \sigma^2 \tag{5.6}$$

In case of optimal cautious control $u^*(t)$, the loss function becomes

$$L^* = L(u^*(t)) = \left[\hat{b}^2(t) + \hat{v}(t)\right]^{-1}\left(\hat{v}(t)y^2(t)\right) + \sigma^2 \tag{5.7}$$

It is clear the L^* is less than $\tilde{L}^0$, since $\hat{v}(t)$ is positive.

More generally, the scalar system dynamics (5.1) may be considered with lags of order n:

$$y(t+1) = H(t+1)\theta(t+1) + e(t+1)$$

with

$$e(t) \sim iidN(0, \sigma^2)$$

$$\theta(t+1) = F\theta(t) + w(t); \quad w(t) \sim iid\, N(0, R) \tag{6.2}$$

where

$$H(t+1) = \left[H_1(t+1), H_2(t+2),\ldots,H_{2n+1}(t+1)\right]$$

$$= \left[-y(t), -y(t-1),\ldots, -y(t-n+1),\right.$$

$$\left. u(t-1),\ldots,u(t-n-1)\right]$$

$\theta(t+1) =$ parameter vector modeled by the stochastic process above where the vector of errors $w(t)$ is assumed to be normally independently distributed with zero mean vector and constant covariance matrix R.

The loss function to be minimized by optimal control may be taken slightly generally as

$$L = E\left[(y(t+1) - y^*)^2 \mid I(t)\right] \tag{6.3}$$

where y^* is the desired or target level preassigned and $I(t)$ is the information set containing observations obtained up to and including time t. The optimal control problem is now solved in two stages. In the first stage, the unknown parameters F in (6.2) are estimated by using Kalman filter. This gives the estimates $\hat{\theta}(t+1)$ and their variance–covariance matrices $V(t+1)$ conditional on the information set $I(t)$. Then at the second stage one minimizes the loss function

$$L = \left[H(t+1)\hat{\theta}(t+1) - y^*\right]^2 + H(t+1)V(t+1)H'(t+1) + \sigma^2 \tag{6.4}$$

where prime denotes the transpose. The optimal controller $u^*(t)$, which is analogous to (5.4) is now obtained by minimizing L in (6.4):

$$u^*(t) = \left[\hat{\theta}^2(t+1) + v(t+1)\right]^{-1}_{n+1} \left[\hat{\theta}(t+1)y^* - C\right] \tag{6.5}$$

where the correction factor C is given by

$$C = \sum_{\substack{i=1 \\ i \neq n+1}}^{2n+1} \left[\hat{\theta}(t+1)\hat{\theta}_i(t+1) + v(t+1)\right] H_1(t+1)$$

$v_{ij}(t) =$ the (i, j) element of the variance–covariance matrix $V(t)$ estimated in first stage. Several features of the optimal control $u((t)$ in (6.5) are to be noted. First, it has cautious elements through the variance $v(t+1)$ of the estimates $\hat{\theta}(t+1)$ obtained in the first stage. A high variance means less reliable estimates of $\hat{\theta}(t+1)$, which in turn implies less use of the control. For very poor estimates, the control can be unintentionally turned off for some period of time until the observations of the system (6.2) permit better and more reliable estimates. This "turn-off phenomenon" is basically due to the fact that the optimal control rule (6.5) minimizes the loss function only one step ahead and not for several future periods, so that the control action is not rewarded if it could spend some time and effort to obtain better estimates of $\theta(t+1)$ which can be utilized to improve the control in future steps. The latter is precisely the objective of dual control strategies emphasized by Feldbaum and others.

Three simple steps are often suggested for protection against the so-called "turn-off" phenomenon of control, especially when the unknown parameters are strongly time-varying. One suggestion, due to Wittenmark [40] is to modify the loss function (6.3) and adjoin a separate constraint on control as follows:

$$\min L = E\left\{ (y(t+1) - y^*)^2 + \lambda f(V(t+2)) \mid I(t) \right\}$$

and (6.6)

$$u(t) = \begin{cases} u_c(t) & \text{if} \quad |u_c(t)| \geqslant M \\ M & \text{if} \quad \text{otherwise} \end{cases}$$

where λ is a nonnegative weight on the scalar function f depending on the elements of the variance–covariance matrix of the estimates $\hat{\theta}(t+2)$ and $u_c(t)$ is given by the cautious control rule defined by (6.5). Note that the loss function in (6.6) offers a compromise between good control and good estimation. Further, the threshold level M has to be properly chosen so that the implicit cost associated with control remains bounded. The link with the robustness concepts of control is readily apparent.

A second method is to convert the loss function to a multiperiod form and then apply a sequential Bayesian procedure [24]: the problem here is one of minimizing the loss function

$$L = \int_{-\infty}^{\infty} E_\theta \left\{ \sum_{t=1}^{T} (y(t) - y^*)^2 \right\} d\pi(\theta) \tag{6.7}$$

where $\pi(\theta)$ is a prior distribution of the unknown parameters $\theta = \theta(t)$. The Bayes solution can in principle be obtained by dynamic programming and backward induction. However computation complexities may be quite burdensome.

A third method proposed by Anderson and Taylor [1] considers a sequential rule of the form:

$$u(t+1) = \begin{cases} M_1: & \text{minimum threshold preassigned} \\ u^0(t), \quad t \geqslant 2 & \text{if} \quad u^0(t) > M_1 \\ M_2: & \text{maximum level preassigned} \end{cases}$$

where in terms of the first order plant dynamics (5.1), $u^0(t) = -\hat{b}^{-1}(t)[y(t) - y^*]$, where $\hat{b}(t)$ is the LS estimate conditional on the information set $I(t)$ containing available data up to and including t. Anderson and Taylor call this rule the least squares certainty equivalence

(LSCE) and performed some simulation experiments to establish its convergence. Further results derived by Lai and Rabbins [24] show that the convergence results do not ordinarily hold and hence the LSCE rules are only suboptimal and not optimal in multiperiod context.

Two other features of the non-dual cautious optimal control rule (6.5) may be noted. The assumption of normality of the disturbance terms $e(t)$ and $w(t)$ implies that only the variance $v(t)$ of the estimates $\hat{\theta}(t)$ enter into the cautious optimal control. Any departure from normality may have to be allowed for through more robust estimates of $\theta(t)$. This generally leads to more nonlinearities in both phases, the estimation phase and the controlling phase. Second, note that the correction factor C in (6.5) tends to build up through summation when the order of the lag n increases. This emphasizes the complexity of the optimal control problem in higher dimensions. If in addition, the loss function included more than one step ahead, this would have led to problems of instability and divergence referred to before.

3. Information adaptivity in economic models

In this section we discuss selected examples of optimizing economic models which allow adaptivity to various information structures. Selections here emphasize those operational aspects of adaptivity, which are most interesting and most easily applicable in several areas.

EXAMPLE 1 (Dual control in Fisheries Management): This is a model of decision-making for fisheries, due to Walters [39] where annual catches $u(t)$ are to be optimally determined, when the fish population $x(t+1)$ dynamics is given by a stock-recruitment model:

$$\ln x(t+1) = \ln(x(t) - u(t)) + \alpha - \beta(x(t) - u(t)) + \epsilon(t) \tag{7.1}$$

with disturbance terms $\epsilon(t) \sim N(0, \sigma^2)$ and the covariance terms $\text{cov}(\epsilon(t), \epsilon(t+k)) = 0$ for $k = 1, 2, \ldots$ If the parameters α, β are known, then the variance term $\text{var}(\ln x(t+1)) = \sigma^2$ a positive constant independent of t. But if only the LS estimates of α, β are only available with covariance matrix $\hat{V}(t)$, then

$$\text{var}(\ln x(t+1)) = s(t)'\hat{V}(t)s(t) + \sigma^2 \tag{7.2}$$

where prime denotes transpose and

$$s(t) = \begin{pmatrix} 1 \\ -(x(t) - u(t)) \end{pmatrix}, \quad \hat{V}(t) = \begin{bmatrix} \sigma_{\hat{\alpha}}^2 & \sigma_{\hat{\alpha}\hat{\beta}}^2 \\ \sigma_{\hat{\alpha}\hat{\beta}}^2 & \sigma_{\hat{\beta}}^2 \end{bmatrix}$$

It is easily verified (e.g. by Kalman filtering equations) that the covariance matrix $\hat{V}(t)$ satisfies the difference equation

$$\hat{V}(t+1) = \hat{V}(t) - \left[\sigma^2 + s(t)'\hat{V}(t)x(t)\right]^{-1}\left\{\hat{V}(t)s(t)s's\,\hat{V}(t)\right\}$$

It is clear that the error variance $\sigma_{\hat{\alpha}}^2$ of $\hat{\alpha}$ is reduced more rapidly when the control action $u(t)$ is very large, while $\sigma_{\hat{\beta}}^2$ is most quickly reduced if $u(t)$ is set to zero. Thus if the target is to reach the population size giving maximum average production in the shortest possible time, we have to apply dynamic programming algorithms.

This is a problem in dual control, since the probability distribution of the outcome $x(t)$ conditional on any control policy $u(t)$ will evolve through time and explicit analytic solutions may not be tractable. Hence Walters sought an approximately optimal solution i.e. a suboptimal policy in the class of constrained feedback policies as follows:

$$u(t) = x(t+1) - x(t) \quad \text{with} \quad k_1 \leqslant u(t) \leqslant k_2 \tag{7.3}$$

where the control action becomes an incremental change, where the limits $k_1 = -0.01$, $k_2 = 0.06$ put some tolerance factors on the cost of control.

A further ingredient of caution was introduced in this adaptive policy by the following requirement followed in numerical simulation: combinations of $x(t)$ and $x(t+1)$ are so chosen that the expected value: $E[x(t+1) - x(t)]$ is zero if $u(t)$ is close to zero. The effects of varying the tolerance limits k_1 and k_2 were also found to be significant for this type of approximate version of dual control.

EXAMPLE 2 (Futures Market Equilibrium): The futures market model, due to Danthine [9] has two classes of agents, the producers and speculators who are assumed to maximize their expected utility given their information sets; also the expectations held by the agents are assumed to be in equilibrium i.e. the probability distribution of market price $\tilde{p}$ is correctly identified by them in terms of the function $p(p^f, \eta)$ where p^f is the unit price of a futures contract promising delivery of one unit of commodity in period two and η is a random shift parameter of the random market demand $Y_d = D(\tilde{p}, \tilde{\eta})$.

Assume a two period model, where at the start of period one, when the planting decision has to be made, the period two market price $\tilde{p}$ is unknown. However farmers have the opportunity in the first period to trade futures contracts at a unit price p^f. Assuming a strictly concave production function $y = y(x)$ relating single output y and single input x with input price set equal to unity, the optimizing objective of an expected utility maximizing, price taking farmer is taken as

$$\max_{x \geqslant 0, f} J_1 = E\left[U\left((y-f)\tilde{p} + p^f f - x\right) \mid p^f\right] \tag{7.4}$$

where f is the number of unit futures contracts bought and sold by the representative farmer (it can be positive or nonnegative) and $U(\cdot)$ is a strictly concave, von Neumann–Morgenstern utility function of income, assumed to be identical for all farmers and E is the expectation operator taken with respect to the conditional subjective distribution of the spot price $\tilde{p}$ given p^f. Assuming the existence of an interior optimal solution for (7.4), the optimal inputs x^* and the optimal supply of futures contracts f^* can be obtained as:

$$x^* = x(p^f) \quad \text{and} \quad f^* = f(p^f) \tag{7.5}$$

with

$$\partial x^*/\partial p^f = -\left[p^f \partial^2 y/\partial x^2\right]^{-1}(\partial y/\partial x) > 0$$

It is clear from (7.5) that since $y^* = y(x^*) = y(p^f)$, farmers' optimal output supply depends only on the futures price p^f and the input price of x which is unity by assumption here. There is no influence of risk aversion, nor any impact of the probability distribution of the outcome summarizing his expectations.

Assuming a fixed number N of farmers the aggregate spot market equilibrium is sepcified by

$$Y_s = Ny(x) = Ny\big(x(p^f)\big) \tag{7.5}$$

$$Y_d = D(\tilde{p}, \tilde{\eta}), \quad \tilde{\eta} \sim N\big(0, \sigma_\eta^2\big) \tag{7.6}$$

where the aggregate market demand function Y_d is assumed to be continuously differentiable with $\partial D/\partial p < 0$ and $\partial D/\partial \eta > 0$ where p and η are any realization of the random variables $\tilde{p}$ and $\tilde{\eta}$ respectively. Setting $Y_s = Y_d$ and assuming the existence of a solution for some realizations of the random variables, one derives the equilibrium spot price p as a function of the futures price and the realized value of the stochastic term $\tilde{\eta}$:

$$p = p(p^f, \tilde{\eta}) \tag{7.7}$$

Next consider the optimal behavior of speculators, M in number say, each of whom is identical except for his information set. Speculator $i = 1$, $2, \ldots M$ has to optimally decide on the number of future contracts b_i to buy on the basis of his expectation of the spot-futures price differential $(\tilde{p} - p^f)$, given his attitude towards risk. The expected utility J_2 of risk-averse price-taking speculator is:

$$\max_{b_i} J_2 = \int W\big[(p(p^f, \tilde{\eta}) - p^f)b_i\big] g(\eta/v_i, p^f) \, d\eta \tag{7.8}$$

where W is the strictly concave von Neumann–Morgenstern utility function common to all speculators and $g(\eta \mid v_i, p^f)$ is the conditional probability distribution of $\tilde{\eta}$ given v_i and p^f. Here speculators are assumed to be rational in the same sense as farmers are, except that each speculator i is assumed to observe some unbiased approximation v_i of the true value of the random variable $\tilde{\eta}$ i.e. $v_i = \eta + \tilde{w}_i$, where the $\tilde{w}_i$'s are *iid* $N(0, \sigma_w^2)$. On maximizing (7.8) we obtain the optimal demand for b_i by speculator i:

$$b_i = b^*\left(p^f, v_i\right) \tag{7.9}$$

Combining (7.5) and (7.9) leads to the market clearing equilibrium for future contracts:

$$Nf^* = \sum_{i=1}^{M} b^*\left(p^f, v_i\right) \tag{7.10}$$

Assuming solvability, p^f can be solved from (7.10) as

$$p^f = h(v_1, \tilde{v}_2, \ldots, v_M) \equiv h(\mathbf{v}) \quad \text{say,} \tag{7.11}$$

which expresses the equilibrium futures price as a function of speculators' individual elements of information. Thus the concept of an equilibrium future price p^f in competitive markets requires the satisfaction of (7.5), (7.9), (7.10) and (7.11) given that there exist $\mathbf{v} = (v_1, v_2, \ldots, v_M)$, $p = p(p^f, \eta)$ and $g(\eta)$.

A simple example constructed by Danthine is as follows: $y(x) = \alpha x^{1/2}$, $\alpha > 0$; $D(p, \eta) = a - cp + \eta$, $a, c > 0$, $\tilde{\eta} \sim N(0, \sigma_\eta^2)$. Then the equilibrium spot price is $p = A - Bp^f + \eta/c$, $A = a/c > 0$, $B = N\alpha^2/2c > 0$. The representative farmers profit is

$$\tilde{\pi} = \left(\frac{\alpha^2}{2} p^f - f\right)\left(A - Bp^f + \frac{\tilde{\eta}}{c}\right) + p^f f - \frac{\alpha^2}{4}\left(p^f\right)^2$$

while speculator i's profit is

$$\tilde{z}_i = \left[A - (B+1)p^f + \frac{\tilde{\eta}}{c}\right] b_i$$

with utility functions $U(\pi) = -e^{-\xi \pi}$, $W(z) = -e^{-kz}$, $\xi, k \geqslant 0$ the optimal (f^*, b_i^*) and the associated p^f are:

$$f^* = -\frac{c^2}{2\xi \operatorname{var}(\tilde{\eta} \mid p^f)}\left[E(\tilde{p} \mid p^f) - p^f\right] + \frac{\alpha^2}{2} p^f$$

$$b_i^* = -\frac{c^2}{2k\,\text{var}(\tilde{\eta}\,|\,v_i,p^f)}\left[E(\tilde{p}\,|\,v_i,p^f)-p^f\right]$$

$$p^f = h(v_1,\ldots,v_M) \tag{7.12}$$

$$= K_0\left\{\frac{Nc^2}{2\xi\,\text{var}(\tilde{\eta}\,|\,p^f)}\left[A + c^{-1}E(\tilde{\eta}\,|\,p^f)\right]\right.$$

$$\left. +\frac{c^2}{2k\,\text{var}(\tilde{\eta}\,|\,v,p^f)}\left[nA + c^{-1}\sum_{j=1}^{M}E(\tilde{\eta}\,|\,v_j,p^f)\right]\right\}$$

where

$$K_0 = \left[\frac{Nc^2(B+1)}{2\xi\,\text{var}(\tilde{\eta}\,|\,p^f)}+\frac{N\alpha^2}{2}+\frac{Mc^2}{2k\,\text{var}(\tilde{\eta}\,|\,v,p^f)}\right]$$

Three aspects of this example are worth noting. First, the future price p^f above may be used as a "sufficient statistic" for the information available to the market in the form of the vector $v=(v_1,v_2,\ldots,v_M)$ or in the sum of the v's, Σv_i which is the sufficient statistic for v. In this case knowledge of p^f is equivalent to the knowledge of Σv_i and farmers' and speculators' expectations coincide. Second, the futures price is not an unbiased estimate of the future spot price. Thus the speculators expected profits are positive. From (7.12) it follows that at the level $E(\tilde{p})=p^f$ farmers still prefer trading for hedging purposes but the speculators do not; this implies that there is a transfer from farmers to speculators as compensation for risk allocation as follows:

$$E\left[(\tilde{p}-p^f)b\right] = \left(2k\,\text{var}(\tilde{\eta}\,|\,p^f)\right)^{-1}\left[c^2E\left[\tilde{p}-p^f\,|\,p^f\right]^2\right] > 0$$

as long as

$$E\left(\tilde{p}-p^f\,|\,p^f\right)^2 > 0$$

provided M does not tend to infinity, since uncertainty then disappears. Third, the variance of the spot price with a futures market can be easily shown to be smaller than the variance of the spot without futures trading if it holds

$$\sigma_\eta^2/\sigma_w^2 \geqslant 1/M$$

Thus for any ratio σ_η^2/σ_w^2 there exists a number M of speculators for which this inequality will be satisfied. This emphasizes the stabilizing role of competitive speculation.

EXAMPLE 3 (Robustness in Portfolio Selection): One of the main reasons for testing optimal portfolio choice for robustness is the presence of estimation risks associated with the statistical estimates of the mean variance parameters from sample observations. The asymmetry associated with estimation risks has been strongly emphasized by Black and Scholes [5] to show that variances estimated from past data inflated the actual spread in the variances; thus, the mean variance model using noisy estimates of variance tends to overprice options on high variance securities and underprice options on low variance securities. Several aspects of building robustness with the portfolio policy of an investor have been discussed by Sengupta [36], of which the following is a typical example.

Suppose an investor chooses the following quadratic model discussed by Szego [38] to select the optimal allocation vector x with k elements for k securities

$$\min_{x} \sigma^2 = x'Vx \tag{8.1}$$

subject to $m'x = c, \quad e'x = 1$

where e' is a row vector with each element unity and the portfolio return $y = \tilde{r}'x$ is distributed with expectation $m'x$ and variance $(x'Vx)$; m is the mean return vector and V the variance–covariance matrix of returns. Denote the given set of solutions of this problem by S_0 and let S_1 be a comparison set. Then one may define robustness as the property of optimality of a portfolio in S_0 relative to the comparison set S_1. Such robustness considerations may arise very naturally when for instance the investor has to revise the given portfolio by adding a new security chosen from outside the given set S_0. It is clear from (8.1) that the optimal allocation vector x_* and the associated minimal variance σ_*^2 can be expressed as functions of the parameters $\theta = (m, V, c)$ as follows:

$$\begin{aligned} x_* &= \left[(\alpha\gamma - \beta^2)V\right]^{-1}\left[(m\gamma - \beta e)c + (\alpha e - m\beta)\right] \\ \sigma_*^2 &= (\alpha\gamma - \beta^2)^{-1}(\gamma c^2 - 2\beta c + \alpha) \end{aligned} \tag{8.2}$$

where $\alpha = m'V^{-1}m$, $\beta = m'V^{-1}e$, $\gamma = e'V^{-1}e$. (It will be assumed that β is ordinarily positive). Note that in the presence of estimation error, m and V would be replaced by $\hat{m}_t$, $\hat{V}_t$ where t may represent the sample size and hence we would have $\hat{\alpha}_t = \hat{m}'_t V_t^{-1}\hat{m}_t$, $\hat{\beta}_t = \hat{m}'_t \hat{V}_t^{-1}e$, $\hat{\gamma}_t = e'\hat{V}_t^{-1}e$. Since minimal variance σ_*^2 is a strictly convex function of c, it can be minimized further by choosing a value c_* of c such that σ_*^2 is minimized i.e.

(no error case): $\quad c_* = \beta/\gamma, \quad v_* = \min \sigma_*^2 = 1/\gamma$

(with error): $\qquad \hat{c}_* = \hat{\beta}_t/\hat{\gamma}_t, \quad \hat{v}_* = 1/\hat{\gamma}_t$
$$\tag{8.3}$$

Now consider adding a new security j from the comparison set S_1. Let the optimal solutions be now denoted by

$$\sigma_*^2(j) = \delta_j^{-1}\left(\gamma_j c^2 - 2\beta_j c + \alpha_j\right) \equiv f_j(c)$$

(no error) $\hfill (8.4)$

$$c_*(j) = \beta_j/\gamma_j; \quad v_*(j) = 1/\gamma_j$$

$$\hat{\sigma}_*^2(j) = \hat{\delta}_j^{-1}\left(\hat{\gamma}_j c^2 - 2\hat{\beta}_j c + \hat{\alpha}_j\right) \equiv f(c)$$

(with error) $\hfill (8.5)$

$$\hat{c}_*(j) = \hat{\beta}_j/\hat{\gamma}_j; \quad \hat{v}_*(j) = 1/\hat{\gamma}_j$$

where it is assumed that δ_j, $\hat{\delta}_j$ are positive: $\delta_j = \alpha_j \gamma_j - \beta_j^2$ and $\hat{\delta}_j = \hat{\alpha}_j \hat{\gamma}_j - \hat{\beta}_j^2$. Suppose the set S_1 of new selections is such that for all $j \in S_1$ it holds

(no error) $\quad \sigma_*^2(j) > \sigma_*^2, \quad v_*(j) > v_*$ $\hfill (8.6a)$

or,

(with error) $\quad \hat{\sigma}_*^2(j) > \hat{\sigma}_*^2, \quad \hat{v}_*(j) > \hat{v}_*$ $\hfill (8.6b)$

then the reference portfolio say $P_k \in S_0$ is robust relative to S_1. However the conditions (8.6) may not hold for all selections j in S_0. This provides the incentive to revise the given portfolio and thereby we are led to examine the conditions under which the given portfolio may be robust in some sense. For example consider the following situation:

Let $\alpha_j > \alpha$ and $\gamma < \gamma_j$ then the two risk-return curves $\sigma_*^2(j) = f_j(c)$ and $\sigma_*^2 = f(c)$ intersect at least once, if they are not coincident in any interval of c. Let (c_0, σ_0^2) be any such intersection point. Then it can be proved that there must exist a local neighborhood around c_0, throughout which it holds that $\sigma_*^2(j) < \sigma_*^2$. A similar result holds for the case with estimation error. The implications of departures from normality in the probability distribution of the returns vector can be discussed in such a framework.

EXAMPLE 4 (Monopolistic Strategy under Stochastic Demand): Problems of optimal decision-making by the monopolist facing demand uncertainty have been examined by several authors, of which the contributions by Barro [4] and Mills [27] are examined here; Barro's model deals with a perishable product which cannot be stored, while Mills' model allows excess demand and excess supply to affect monopolist's profits. Only the static case is considered here for simplicity.

Two cases of Barro's model are analyzed. In one, the linear demand function with an additive error e is assumed to arise through a conditional regression model

$$E(x_d \mid \hat{p}) = a - b\hat{p}, \quad a, b > 0 \tag{9.1}$$

with

$$x_d = E(x_d \mid \hat{p}) + e \tag{9.2}$$

where the joint distribution $f(x_d, p)$ of demand (x_d) and price (p) is bivariate normal with a population coefficient ρ which is negative. Although bivariate normality is not essential to the argument, it is assumed for convenience so as to permit the conditional linear regression interpretation of the stochastic demand function. Also, such an assumption utilized by Baron [3] was considered most plausible in several types of imperfectly competitive markets. Note that the two parameters a, b of the linear demand function (9.1) can be related to the population parameters $\theta = (\mu_p, \mu_x, \sigma_p^2, \sigma_x^2, \rho)$ of the bivariate normal density $f(x_d, p)$ as follows:

$$a = \mu_x - \rho \frac{\mu_p \sigma_x}{\sigma_p}; \quad b = -\rho \sigma_x / \sigma_p \tag{9.3}$$

Barro's model assumes that the parameters in θ, i.e., a, b are known to the monopolist, whose demand and profit functions are as follows:

$$x_d = a - bp + e$$

$$\pi = (p - c)x \tag{9.4}$$

$$x \leqslant x_d$$

The marginal cost parameter c of the linear cost function is assumed to be a fixed nonrandom quantity known to the monopolist.

In the second case we analyze the firm is assumed to have partial ignorance of some of the parameters contained in θ, e.g., the correlation parameter ρ or, the unconditional mean price μ_p, which is different from the conditional mean price $E(p \mid \hat{x})$, may not be completely known in the sense that only forecasts or estimates are available. This line follows the suggestion of Kirman [23] that in an uncertain environment an imperfectly competitive firm tends to adapt its behavior through a Bayesian process of revision of parameter estimates.

In terms of the linear stochastic model specified by (9.4) along with (9.2), Barro uses price as the control variable and distinguishes between two types of price adjustments, i.e., continuous adjustment and constrained adjustment. In the case of continuous adjustment of price to variations in the error component, the firm solves the quadratic programming model

$$\max \pi = (p - c)x \tag{10.1}$$

subject to $x \leqslant x_d$

where

$$x_d = a - bp + e$$

Note that this is a nonstochastic programming problem so long as it is assumed that the random component e is perfectly forecast with zero forecasting error. This model (10.1) leads of course to the familiar optimal rule: marginal revenue equals marginal cost at the optimal price. On using the stochastic demand curve (9.2) the impact of changes in e on optimal profit (π^*) can be easily evaluated. Thus if e is varied from an initial value zero to a final value $u > 0$ for example, the corresponding change in optimal profits denoted by $\Delta\pi_{(0,u)}$ turns out to be:

$$\Delta\pi_{(0,u)} = \int_0^u \left(\frac{d\pi^*}{de}\right) de = \frac{a - bc}{2b} u + \frac{u^2}{4b} \tag{10.2}$$

The above change in profit can be compared to that which would occur if the firm did not adjust price as e varied. The latter case is termed 'constrained adjustment' when e is set to zero and the monopolistic firm fixes a price $\hat{p}$ at a level which equates marginal revenue to marginal cost with e constrained to be zero. In this case the optimal output (x) is solved from the linear programming model

$$\max \pi = (\hat{p} - c)x \tag{10.3}$$

subject to $x \leqslant x_d$

where

$$x_d = a - bp$$

The change in optimal profits in this case denoted by $\Delta\hat{\pi}_{(0,u)}$ turns out to be

$$\Delta\hat{\pi}_{(0,u)} = \frac{a-bc}{2b}u \qquad (10.4)$$

Thus the gain from optimal price adjustment is given by the difference

$$\Delta\pi_{(0,u)} - \Delta\hat{\pi}_{(0,u)} = \frac{u^2}{4b} > 0 \qquad (10.5)$$

This result has two important implications. First, it is clear from (10.5) that if price could be adjusted instantaneously at zero costs and no delays in perception were involved, the firm is unlikely ever to forego the extra profits indicated in (10.5).

A second implication of the result (10.5) which quantifies the relative gain in forecasting the environment and adjusting optimal prices continuously, is that it is not dependent on any specific distributional assumption for the error component e. Thus, any skewness or asymmetry in the distribution of e has no effect on the result; also it is immaterial whether price or output is used as the control variable, since at the optimal level they both lead to identical expected profits and identical profit variance. To see the implications of the latter point more clearly, consider the inverse demand function as:

$$p = a_1 - b_1 x_d + e_1 \qquad (10.6)$$

where

$$a_1 = a/b, \quad b_1 = 1/b, \quad e_1 = e/b$$

Set the output level $x = x_d$ without any loss of generality and maximize expected profits, $E(\pi \mid x)$ by choosing the output level x. At the optimal output level x^*, the expected profit $E(\pi \mid x^*)$ and variance of profit $V(\pi \mid x^*)$ reduce to

$$E(\pi \mid x^*) = \frac{(a-bc)^2}{4b} + \frac{(a-bc)E(e)}{2b}$$

$$V(\pi \mid x^*) = \left(\frac{a-bc}{2b}\right)^2 \sigma_e^2 \qquad (10.7)$$

If price is used as the control variable instead of output and the stochastic demand function used is of form (9.2), then at the optimal price $p*$ we get

$$E(\pi \mid p*) = E(\pi \mid x*)$$
$$V(\pi \mid p*) = V(\pi \mid x*)$$

(10.8)

In other words the firm is indifferent between the two strategies, a result identical with the case when the demand function is deterministic with no stochastic components anywhere. However this result (10.8) is very deceptive and it may not hold very generally. For one thing, the demand function (10.6) requires the random term e to be independent of x, which is impossible in the specification (9.2). Second, if the parameters a, b of the demand functions are estimated by linear regression with empirical data, it is well known that $\hat{b}_1 \neq 1/\hat{b}$, where $\hat{b}_1$ is estimated from the regression of p on x, and $\hat{b}$ from that of x on p. Third, it is clear that none of the two optimizing models of Barro in (9.1) and (9.3) explicitly allows for risk aversion or risk preference in the objective function. Profit rather than expected profit is used in the objective function in both cases, justified in (9.1) by a perfect forecast of e with no error and in (9.3) by constrained adjustment imposed by setting e to zero. The realism or validity of any of these justifications cannot be made unless one introduces a discrimination function for choosing between the two regression models:

$$E(x \mid p) = a - bp$$
$$E(p \mid x) = a_1 - b_1 x$$

(10.9)

Under the bivariate normality assumption, the two conditional demand functions (10.9) appear as follows:

$$E(x \mid \hat{p}) = \mu_x - |\rho|\sigma_x(\hat{p} - \mu_p)/\sigma_p$$

(11.1)

$$E(p \mid \hat{x}) = \mu_p - |\rho|\sigma_p(\hat{x} - \mu_x)/\sigma_x$$

(11.2)

where $|\rho|$ is the absolute value of the correlation coefficient ρ, which is negative since we deal here with a normal good. The parameters a_1, b_1, in (10.9) are here given as

$$a_1 = \mu_p + |\rho|\sigma_p\mu_x/\sigma_x, \quad b_1 = |\rho|\sigma_p/\sigma_x$$

Some features of the two conditional demand functions (11.1), (11.2) may be noted. First, it is clear that the parameters b_1 cannot equal $1/b$ unless $|\rho| = 1$, i.e., $b^{-1} > b_1$ for all nonzero $|\rho| < 1$. The case $|\rho| = 1$ is unimportant since the two strategies would then become indistinguishable. For all other relevant cases, i.e., $0 < |\rho| < 1$, the firm faces the choice problem: to choose $\hat{p}$ as the strategy, $\hat{x}$ as the strategy or some combination of them. If the parameters (a, a_1, b, b_1) are completely known to the firm, as is assumed in Barro's formulation, then it chooses that strategy which offers the highest expected profits. Let $\hat{p}^*$, $\hat{x}^*$ be the levels of price and output which maximize respectively the conditional expected profits $E\pi(x|\hat{p})$ and $E\pi(p|\hat{x})$. Assuming the existence of positive interior solutions, the optimal expected profits are:

$$E\pi(x|\hat{p}^*) = \tfrac{1}{4}\left[2\mu_x(\mu_p - c) + \frac{|\rho|\sigma_x}{\sigma_p}(\mu_p - c)^2 + \frac{\mu_x^2\sigma_p}{|\rho|\sigma_x}\right] \tag{11.3}$$

with

$$\hat{p}^* = \tfrac{1}{2}\left[\mu_p + c + \frac{\mu_x\sigma_p}{|\rho|\sigma_x}\right] \tag{11.4}$$

$$E\pi(p|\hat{x}^*) = \tfrac{1}{4}\left[2\mu_x(\mu_p - c) + \frac{\sigma_x}{|\rho|\sigma_p}(\mu_p - c)^2 + \frac{\mu_x^2\sigma_p|\rho||e|}{\sigma_x}\right] \tag{11.5}$$

with

$$\hat{x}^* = \tfrac{1}{2}\left[\mu_x + \frac{(\mu_p - c)\sigma_x}{|\rho|\sigma_p}\right] \tag{11.6}$$

It is clear that

$$E\pi(p|\hat{x}^*) \gtrless E\pi(x|\hat{p}^*) \tag{11.7}$$

according as

$$\mu_p \gtrless c + \sigma_p\frac{\mu_x}{\sigma_x}$$

Since it is more likely that $\mu_p > c$, i.e., price exceeds marginal cost, the monopolistic firm would choose output ($\hat{x}^*$) as control rather than price ($\hat{p}^*$) with $E\pi(p|\hat{x}^*) > E\pi(x|\hat{p}^*)$. However, this decision may no longer hold if the parameters μ_p and $|\rho|$ for example are not completely known to the monopolistic firm. This lack of knowledge may be formalized through the subjective probability distributions held by the monopolist as in Kirman [23], or through two-person zero-sum games where the other player is Nature choosing the strategies μ_p say in a randomized fashion.

In the latter case, a saddle-point or minimax strategy becomes particularly relevant. Let y denote any of the two strategies $\hat{x}$ or, $\hat{p}$ with Y as their domain of feasible variations; let u be the set of feasible variations of Nature's strategies μ_p, with $\phi(y, \mu_p)$, $y \in Y$, $\mu_p \in u$ as the payoff function of the monopolistic firm. By von Neumann's minimax theorem, a saddle-point solution (y^*, μ_p^*) must exist, if the sets Y and u are compact and nonempty. But since $\phi(y, \mu_p) = (E\pi(p \mid \hat{x}), E\pi(x \mid \hat{p})$, for any $\mu = \mu_p$ is strictly convex in μ_p for any fixed and feasible $y \in Y$, there exists an optimal pure strategy μ_p^* for Nature. A Bayesian solution can easily be defined in such a framework. For example, assume Nature chooses a mixed strategy

$\mu = \mu_1$ with probability q

$\mu = \mu_2$ with probability $(1 - q)$

such that $E\pi(x \mid \hat{p}, \mu) > E\pi(p \mid \hat{x}, \mu)$ for $\mu = \mu_1$, while $E\pi(p \mid \hat{x}, \mu) > E\pi(x \mid \hat{p}, \mu)$ for $\mu = \mu_2$. Then it may be optimal for the firm to play a mixed strategy in terms of a combination of y_1 and y_2, rather than a pure strategy.

Note that imperfect knowledge about the parameters need not be restricted to the unconditional mean prices μ_p only. A more general way to introduce partial ignorance or imperfect knowledge is to postulate the stochastic components in demand only implicitly, i.e., the stochastic demand function is

$$h(\tilde{p}, \tilde{x}) = 0 \tag{12.1}$$

where prices $\tilde{p}$ and quantities $\tilde{x}$ are random quantitis and the function $h(\cdot)$ is not separable. The firm does not know if quantity $\tilde{x} = \tilde{x}(\tilde{p})$ is a function of price, or price $\tilde{p} = p(\tilde{x})$ is a function of quantity. Short of this knowledge the firm has to specify optimal strategies in the situation where profits π are random. Following Leland [10] it may be assumed that the firm is risk averse and it maximizes an expected utility function $z = E[U(\pi)]$ of the form:

$$z = E\pi - \frac{\lambda}{2} \operatorname{var} \pi, \quad \lambda \geqslant 0 \tag{12.2}$$

where $\pi = \tilde{p}\tilde{x} - T(\tilde{x})$, $T(\tilde{x})$ is the cost function and λ is a nonnegative parameter denoting risk aversion. Two cases of the cost function are considered e.g.,

$$T(\tilde{x}) = c\tilde{x}, \quad c \text{ known} \tag{12.3}$$

$$T(\tilde{x}) = c\tilde{x} + \tfrac{1}{2}k\tilde{x}^2; \quad c, k \text{ known} \tag{12.4}$$

which represent without loss of generality the linear and quadratic cost functions. In the linear case (12.3), the positive constant c may be subsumed in the definition of price as net price, so that profit may be redefined as

$$\pi = \tilde{p}\tilde{x} \tag{12.5}$$

In case of quadratic costs (12.4), profit is

$$\pi = \tilde{p}\tilde{x} - \tfrac{1}{2}k\tilde{x}^2 \tag{12.6}$$

where price $\tilde{p}$ is gross return per unit of output sold.

For this risk-averse model defined by (12.2) and (12.5), the competitive firm cannot use price as a control variable. But a monopolistic firm may use either price or quantity or both. It may however still choose a constrained strategy in the sense defined before. Thus, the random or mixed strategies $\tilde{p}$, $\tilde{x}$ may be viewed as

$$\tilde{p} = \bar{p} + \epsilon_1, \quad \tilde{x} = \bar{x} + \epsilon_2 \tag{12.7}$$

where $\bar{p}$, $\bar{x}$ are mean strategies and ϵ_1, ϵ_2 are zero-mean random variables with covariance σ_{12}. It is clear that the mean controls $\bar{p}$, $\bar{x}$, which are pure strategies in a game-theoretic sense can be used as constrained strategies, if the parameters $\sigma_i^2 = \text{var } \epsilon_i$, $i = 1, 2$ and σ_{12} are observable on the basis of past experience. Define the strategy sets M: $(\tilde{p}, \tilde{x})$, N: $(\tilde{p}, \tilde{x})$ for the two players with a payoff function $z = z(\tilde{p}, \tilde{x})$ in a two-person zero-sum game $G = G(M, N; Z)$. Then the following results can be stated.

THEOREM 1: *A mixed strategy solution always exists for this two-person game* $G = G(M, N; Z)$ *of the monopolistic firm against the market. Further, there exists a unique pure strategy optimal solution for the firm, if any of the following three conditions are satisfied*:
(a) *the covariance term* σ_{12} *is either zero or very small or negligible, and*
$$\lambda\sigma_1\sigma_2 > 1$$
(b) λ *satisfies the inequality*

$$\lambda > (1 - |\rho|)^{-1}(\sigma_1\sigma_2)^{-1}, \quad 1 \geqslant |\rho| > 0$$

where ρ *is the correlation of* ϵ_1 *and* ϵ_2
(c) ρ *satisfies the inequality*

$$|\rho| < 1 - (\lambda\sigma_1\sigma_2)^{-1}, \quad 0 < |\rho| \leqslant 1.0$$

PROOF: Since the strategy sets M and N are subsets of finite two-dimensional nonnegative Euclidean space, they are convex compact sets in finite dimensions and the payoff function is continuous in $\tilde{p}$ and $\tilde{x}$. Hence by von Neumann's minimax theorem, a mixed strategy minimax solution must exist. Further, the payoff function z can be shown to be directly concave at the point $(\bar{p}, \bar{x})$, if any of the three conditions above hold. This is so because the Hessian matrix H evaluated at $(\bar{x}, \bar{p})$ is then negative definite:

$$
H: \quad \begin{bmatrix} -\lambda\sigma_1^2 & 1 - \lambda\sigma_{12} \\ 1 - \lambda\sigma_{12} & -\lambda\sigma_2^2 \end{bmatrix}
$$

where $\sigma_{12} = -|\sigma_{12}|$ and $\rho = -|\rho|$, since price and quantity are inversely related in the stochastic demand function. Hence the point $(\bar{p}, \bar{x})$ constitutes the optimal pure strategy solution for the monopolistic firm.

Now we consider Mills' model where inventory is explicitly allowed. We follow here Mills' notation and write demand x_d as x, output x as z and the stochastic demand curve as

$$
x = X(p) + u \tag{13.1}
$$

where u is a random variable assumed to be distributed independently of p. The cost function $c(z)$ is assumed convex and differentiable and total revenue $R = R(x, z, p)$ is of the form:

$$
R = \begin{cases} px, & \text{if} \quad x \leqslant z \quad \text{(excess supply)} \\ pz, & \text{if} \quad x \geqslant z \quad \text{(excess demand)} \end{cases} \tag{13.2}
$$

One may interpret Mills' model in three different ways depending on the choice of strategies, e.g., price, output and inventories, the knowledge of the parameters of the underlying distribution and the extent to which the implicit costs of excess supply or excess demand are incoporated in the firm's objective function. In Mills' original formulation, price (p) and output (z) are taken to be nonrandom, so that the only stochastic variable is demand (x) which has the additive random component u in (13.1). Expected total revenue therefore depends only on the statistical distribution of u; also the costs of excess supply or unfilled demand are not explicitly introduced in the net profit function $\pi = \pi(x; p, z)$:

$$
\pi = R(x; p, z) - c(z) \tag{13.3}
$$

The expected profit is:

$$
E\pi = pX(p) - pD(z, p) - c(z) \tag{13.4}
$$

where

$$D(z, p) = \int_{z-X(p)}^{\infty} [u - z + X(p)] f(u) du$$

and $f(u)du$ denotes the probability density of the random variable u. Note that inventories are held only as buffer stocks to meet the variability of demand around its mean level and the term $D(z, p)$ expresses here the expected amount of unfilled demand. Applying the first order conditions on $E\pi$ with respect to output and price one obtains for the optimal z^0, p^0:

$$1 - F(z^0 - X(p)) = m(z^0)/p \tag{13.5}$$

and

$$M(p^0) = D(z, p^0) - \alpha\eta X(p^0) \tag{13.6}$$

where $\alpha = 1 - F(z^0 - X(p))$ is the probability of shortage (i.e., excess demand), $m(z^0)$ is marginal cost evaluated at output level z^0 and $M(p^0)$ is marginal expected revenue $\partial[ER(x, p)]/\partial p$ evaluated at p^0 and η is the absolute value of price elasticity of mean demand. The first marginal condition (13.5) says that marginal expected revenue (αp) equals marginal cost at the optimal output level. The second relation (13.6) shows that at the optimal price strategy, marginal expected revenue varies directly with the mean level of unfilled demand but inversely with the probability of shortage and the elasticity of demand.

A second interpretation of the Mill's model is that the monopolist produces z prior to demand x. If demand is less than output z, the quantity sold equals demand and the excess supply $(z - x)$ is assumed to perish. If on the other hand, demand exceeds output, the excess demand $(z - x -$ gos unfilled. However in Baron's interpretation, output is a deterministic decision variable but price is not; hence the monopolist consider the bivariate density $f(x, | \hat{p})$ of demand conditional on the choice of the control variable $\hat{p}$ in computing expected profit $E\pi$ and maximizing it first with respect to $\hat{p}$ and then to z.

$$E\pi = E\pi(\cdot \mid \hat{p}, z)$$

$$= \int_0^z \hat{p} x f(x \mid \hat{p}) dx + \int_z^{\infty} \hat{p} z f(x \mid \hat{p}) dx - c(z) \tag{13.7}$$

The first order conditions are:

$$\frac{\partial E\pi}{\partial x}\bigg|_{x=z} = 0 = \hat{p}\left(1 - F(z\,|\,\hat{p})\right) - m(z) \tag{13.8}$$

$$\frac{\partial e\pi}{\partial p}\bigg|_{p=\hat{p}} = 0 = E(x\,|\,\hat{p}) + \hat{p}\,\frac{\partial E(x\,|\,\hat{p})}{\partial\hat{p}}$$

$$- \int (x-z)\left[f(x\,|\,\hat{p}) + \hat{p}\,\frac{\partial f(x\,|\,\hat{p})}{\partial\hat{p}}\right] dx \tag{13.9}$$

Hence $F(\cdot)$ is the cumulative distribution function corresponding to density $f(\cdot)$ and demand is assumed to have the range from zero to infinity. Note that these two conditions (13.8) and (13.9) collapse into (13.5) and (13.6) respectively, if either the pricing strategy is stochastically independent of demand, or if both output and pricing strategies are deterministic. It is clear therefore that the optimal solutions $\hat{p}^*$, z^* from (13.8) and (13.9) would be different from those p^0, z^0 in (13.5) and (13.6), so long as x and p are not statistically independent. Note however that the derivations in 913.8) and (13.9) are not completely general. First, the quantity variable z may contain random elements, as much as the price variable p; in this case we have to replace the density function for demand $f(x\,|\,\hat{p})$ as $f(x\,|\,\hat{p}, \hat{z})$, and z as $\hat{z}$ in the profit function $E\pi(\cdot\,|\,\hat{p}, \hat{z})$, whence both $\hat{p}$ and $\hat{z}$ are decision variables to be optimally determined. Two economic interpretations of the conditional density $f(x\,|\,\hat{p}, \hat{z})$ and the associated mean demand $E(x\,|\,\hat{p}, \hat{z})$ can be given. One is that the conditioning strategy $\hat{p}$ cannot be independently chosen of the output strategy $\hat{z}$, because inventories may not be costless in the firm's perception. Second, price (p) may be as much a function of quantity $q = \min(x, z)$ in the unconditional case, as the quantity of price and we have seen before in (11.7) that a profit-maximizing monopolist need not be indifferent to using the quantity as a decision variable.

Note also that in the marginal rule (13.9) for the price strategy $\hat{p}$, there is no role of the cost function $c(z)$, since if they are not independent and $c(z) = cz$ with constant marginal cost and the demand function is linear under the conditional normality, then a third term would have to be added on the right hand side of (13.9) as $cE(z\,|\,\hat{p}, \hat{z}) = cE(x\,|\,\hat{p}, \hat{z})$ where the condition $x = \hat{z}$ holding in (13.8) is assumed. This is similar to our earlier derivation (11.4) noted before, where it was assumed that $x = z$, no inventories were held and the optimal pricing strategy $\hat{p}$ satisfied

$$\left(E(x\,|\,\hat{p}) + (\hat{p} - c)\frac{\partial E(x\,|\,\hat{p})}{\partial p}\right.$$

A third generalization of the Mill's model, due to Fanchon and

Sengupta [12] assumes that the firm is unable to forecast precisely the true parameter values of present and future demand and hence of the conditional distribution $f(x \mid \hat{p}, \hat{z})$; also inventory costs are explicitly introduced. However inventories cannot be fully treated in one-period model, since they are held partly as buffer-stocks in the current period and partly as active decision variables. Hence a two-period model is considered, where the optimal solution is characterized by maximizing expected profits over two periods with an additive error in the linear demand function having a known prior density in the form of normal and uniform distributions. Simulations of the solution profiles in terms of price, output and inventories reported in [12] show that the variance of profits are sharply reduced to the extent of 50% or more, compared to the Mills' model which assumed fixed parameters; also the simulation profiles uniformly showed a negative correlation of uncertainty and output, which the firm can utilize to revise its forecast of next period demand in a moving horizon two-period model.

The process of learning through adaptive revision of forecast of the parameters of the demand function may be illustrated in an approximate sense in terms of Mills' original model specified by (13.5) and (13.6). Whereas a competitive firm facing price uncertainty has only output as the only decision variable to be optimally chosen, a monopolistic firm has three choices: either output, or price or both. The last case, i.e., both price and output optimally chosen appears particularly appealing, when as we saw before in (11.7) the true parameters of the demand distribution are unknown to the monopolist and Nature plays a mixed strategy.

To illustrate the optimal choice problem for the monopolist firm, we make a specific assumption like Mills [27] that the random component in (13.1) has a uniform probability density within the finite range $-\delta \leqslant u \leqslant \delta$ for $\delta > 0$, so that δ measures the spread or variability around the mean level zero. Also it is assumed that the mean demand function $X(p) = a - bp$ is linear and the marginal cost $c'(z) = c$ is a positive constant known to the firm. We first examine the situation where like the competitive firm, the monopolist optimally chooses output as the only decision variable, using a price forecast [1] denoted by $\tilde{p}$. Then the following result holds.

THEOREM 2: *Let $\tilde{p}$ be any positive price associated with the optimal and positive output level z^0 satisfying the first order condition (13.5), such that*

---

[1] If $\tilde{p}$ is such that $\tilde{p} < c$, the firm would not produce anything; hence $\tilde{p} > c$ is a condition required for viable output policies. Also, if as in Barro's formulation the price forecast is perfect in the sense of no error of forecasting and the firm can make continuous adjustment of output, then the optimal expected profits $E\pi(z^0, \tilde{p})$ would be reached with probability one and there would be zero variance of profits.

the following inequality holds

$$\tilde{p} > c(2\delta/a)^{1/2} \tag{14.1}$$

Then the optimal expected profits $E\pi(z^0; \tilde{p})$ is strictly convex in $\tilde{p}$ in the neighborhood $N_{\tilde{p}}$ defined by (14.1). Furthermore, if the forecast price $\tilde{p}$ is less than perfect in the sense that the error variance of forecast is positive, then the monopolistic firm would gain in terms of extra profits, if it follows an adaptive process of revising forecasts as demand is successively realized and its parameters become known with increased precision. The extra profits is given by

$$\Delta\pi = E_{\tilde{p}}\{E\pi(z^0; \tilde{p})\} - \pi(z^0; \bar{p}) > 0 \tag{14.2}$$

where $\bar{p} = E_{\tilde{p}}\tilde{p}$ is the fixed forecast determined once and for all with no adaptivity to increased information and $E_{\tilde{p}}$ is expectation over the forecast prices $\tilde{p}$.

PROOF: Under the assumed conditions the optimal output z^0 and the associated expected optimal profits are

$$z^0 = \left(\delta - \frac{2c}{\tilde{p}}\right) + a - b\tilde{p}$$

$$E\pi(z^0; \tilde{p}) = \tilde{p}(a - b\tilde{p}) - \tilde{p}\frac{(\delta - z^0 + a - b\tilde{p})^2}{4\delta} - cz^0$$

It follows that

$$\frac{\partial^2 E\pi(z^0; \tilde{p})}{\partial \tilde{p}^2} = \frac{1}{\tilde{p}}\left(a - 2b\tilde{p} + \frac{2c^2\delta}{\tilde{p}^2} - \alpha\right) > 0 \quad \text{if} \quad \tilde{p} > \left(\frac{2\delta}{a}\right)^{1/2}c$$

Since the optimal profit $E\pi(z^0; \tilde{p})$ is strictly convex in $\tilde{p}$ for all $\tilde{p} \in N_{\tilde{p}}$, we have by Jensen's inequality

$$E_{\tilde{p}}\{E\pi(z^0; \tilde{p})\} > \pi(z^0; E_{\tilde{p}}\tilde{p})$$

Two remarks may be made about these results.

First, if the parameters (a, δ) defining the neighborhood $N_{\tilde{p}}$ in (14.1) are not known to the firm, then the extra gains from adaptive forecasts may not be realizable. Since the optimal profit function $E\pi(z^0; \tilde{p})$ may not necessarily be convex for arbitrary neighborhoods, extra losses are as much likely as extra gains. This provides a rationale for the firm to use an active price policy along with the output policy.

Second, if $\bar{p}$ in (14.2) is interpreted as prior mean according to the subjective (forecasting) density of the firm, and $\pi(z^0; \bar{p})$ as prior optimal profits, then the result (14.2) says that the posterior optimal profits exceeds prior optimal profits. For specific forms of prior densities, e.g., conjugate family of distributions, the extra profits given in (14.2) can be calculated. Thus a Bayesian learning process can be easily incorporated as in Kirman [23] and others.

EXAMPLE 5 (Statistical Learning Model): Consider the decision rule defined by (11.7) for choosing optimal price and quantity strategies by the monopolistic firm under demand uncertainty. Let $\theta = \mu_p - c - \sigma_p\mu_x/\sigma_x$ be the parameter which divides the parameter space into two classes θ_1: $\{\theta \mid \theta > 0\}$ and θ_2: $\{\theta \mid \theta < 0\}$. If θ were known to be θ_1 then the monopolistic firm would choose output (x) rather than price (p) as the control variable, since expected profits $E\pi(p \mid x^*)$ would be higher than $E\pi(x \mid \hat{p}^*)$. But the firm has available only a set of estimates $\hat{\theta}_i$, which has a conditional density $f_i(\hat{\theta}) = \text{prob}(\hat{\theta}_i \mid \theta_i)$. This conditional density may be subjective or empirical. Taking the negative or profits, let us define a loss function $L(\theta_i, y_j)$ associated with θ_i and the strategy y_j = output or price

$$L(\theta_i, y_j) = v_{ij} \tag{15.1}$$

The conditional loss for $\hat{\theta} = \hat{\theta}_i$ for given θ_i is then

$$l(\theta_i, y) = \int_{S(\hat{\theta})} L(\theta_i, y) f_i(\hat{\theta}) d\hat{\theta} \tag{15.2}$$

where $S(\hat{\theta})$ denotes the space of random variations of $\hat{\theta}$ such that if $\hat{\theta} = \hat{\theta}_j$, then $y = y_j, j = 1, 2$. Let w_i be the *a priori* probability of θ_i ($i = 1, 2$), then the average loss W may be written as

$$W = w_1 l(\theta_1, y_1) = w_2 l(\theta_2, y_2)$$

$$= \int_{S(\hat{\theta})} \{L(\theta_1, y) f_1(\hat{\theta}) w_1 + L(\theta_2, y) f_2(\hat{\theta}) w_2\} d\hat{\theta} \tag{15.3}$$

Now define two kinds of estimation error for the states of the world θ_i:

$$\alpha = \int_{\theta_2} f_1(\hat{\theta}) d\hat{\theta}: \quad \text{conditional error probability of the first kind}$$

$$\beta = \int_{\theta_1} f_2(\hat{\theta}) d\hat{\theta}: \quad \text{conditional error probability of the second kind}$$

Then it is clear from (15.3) that the average loss W can be expressed as

$$W = w_1 \{ v_{11}(1 - \alpha) + v_{12}\alpha \} + w_2 (v_{21}\beta + v_{22}(1 - \beta)) \tag{15.4}$$

where one would normally expect $v_{11} < v_{12}$ and $v_{22} < v_{21}$ since ir is more costly for mismatching. Several statistical learning algorithms may now be presented.

A. Bayes rule

This requires minimization of the average loss W in (15.3) for any observation or estimation $\hat{\theta}$. Thus one chooses the following rule:

$$u = u_1 \quad \text{if} \quad v_{11}f_1(\hat{\theta})w_1 + v_{21}f_2(\hat{\theta})w_2 < v_{12}f_1(\hat{\theta})w_1 + v_{22}f_2(\hat{\theta})w_2$$

and

$$u = u_2 \quad \text{if} \quad \text{otherwise}$$

This rule can also be written as:

$$y = \begin{cases} y_1, & \text{if} \quad \lambda(\hat{\theta}) > h \\ y_2, & \text{if} \quad \lambda(\hat{\theta}) < h \end{cases} \tag{15.4}$$

where $\lambda(\hat{\theta})$ is the likelihood ratio $\lambda(\hat{\theta}) = f_1(\hat{\theta})/f_2(\hat{\theta})$ and h is the threshold level where

$$h = \frac{(v_{21} - v_{22})}{v_{12} - v_{11}} \cdot \frac{w_2}{w_1} \tag{15.5}$$

B. Mixed decision rule

If the v_{ij}'s are such that $v_{11} = v_{22} = 0$ but $v_{12} = 1$ and $v_{21} = s > 0$, then the average loss W becomes

$$W = \alpha w_1 + s\beta w_2 \quad \text{and} \quad h = sw_2/w_1.$$

If we interpret $h = sw_2/w_1$ as the Lagrange multiplier, then this decision rule minimizes the conditional error probability α of the first kind subject to a constant error probability of the second kind. This corresponds to the Neyman–Pearson rule in statistics.

C. Minimax rule

If the a priori probabilities w_1, w_2 are not known, one possible approach is to optimize the worst case. This leads to the minimax rule, which can be interpreted as a "game with nature", where nature chooses the a priori probabilities that maximize the average risk. For instance take the case $v_{11} = v_{22} = 0$. The optimal Bayes rule is then determined by minimizing the average loss

$$W = v_{1w}\hat{w}_1\alpha + v_{21}(1 - \hat{w}_1)\beta$$

where w 5_1 is an estimate of the a priori probability w_1. The optimal rule is identical with (15.4) and (15.5) except that $\hat{w}_1$ replaces w_1 e.g.,

$$h = \text{threshold} = \frac{v_{21}}{v_{12}} \frac{(1 - \hat{w}_1)}{\hat{w}_1} \qquad (15.6)$$

and the error probabilities α, β would be functions of the estimates $\hat{w}_i$ instead of w_i. If the actual value of w_1 is w_1^0 then the above decision rule with the threshold value (15.6) leqds to the following deviation between the actual average loss and its estimated optimal value:

$$\Delta W(\hat{w}_1, w_1^0) = [v_{12}\alpha(\hat{w}_1) - v_{21}\beta(\hat{w}_1)](w_1^0 - \hat{w}_1) \qquad (15.7)$$

We choose $\hat{w}_1$ to minimize this maximum deviation $\Delta W(\hat{w}_1, w_1^0)$ for obtaining the minimax rule. It is clear that the minimax rule satisfies the condition

$$v_{12}\alpha(\hat{w}_1) - v_{21}\beta(\hat{w}_1) = 0 \qquad (15.8)$$

Although the minimax decision rule derived from (15.7) and (15.8) may not always be easy to compute analytically for given conditional densities, it has the robustness property in the sense of securing the best of the worst in some sense.

EXAMPLE 6 (Information Aggregation in Competitive Markets): This model developed by Hellwig [16] analyzes the aggregation of information through the price in a large competitive market, where individual agents are price takers. In this competitive framework of a large market the relative importance of information I_i available to agent $i = 1, 2, \ldots, n$ depends on his preferences, so that the more important I_i is, the less risk averse agent i is. This veiw is very different from that of Grossman [14–15] who argued in a capital market model that the equilibrium price aggregates the available information perfectly, so that any aspect of the information vector $I = (I_1, I_2, \ldots, I_n)$ that is not reflected in the price is not worth communicating due to noise; further the aggregation of information though market price depends only on the statistical properties of the information vector I and is independent of agents' preferences.

In this model each agent i allocates his initial wealth w_{0i} between a riskless asset yielding unit return and a risky asset with unit random returns $\tilde{x}$. For an agent i holding z_i units of the risky asset with price p, his portfolio return is

$$\tilde{w}_{1i} = w_{0i} + z_i(\tilde{x} - p)$$

Agent's preference satisfy the following three assumptions:

A1. Each agent i maximizes the expected utility $E_i u_i(\tilde{w}_{1i})$, where the utility function u_i is assumed to have constant absolute risk aversion $\lambda_i > 0$. Under this assumption the agent i's demand for risky asset $z_i = z_i(p, I_i)$ depends only on the price and the information I_i entering through the expectation operator E_i and not on the initial wealth w_{0i}. The information I_i consists of the market price p and his private information y_i, where the latter is a realization of a random variable $\tilde{y}_i$, which communicates the true return $\tilde{x}$ perturbed by some noise $\tilde{\epsilon}_i$:

$$\tilde{y}_i = \tilde{x} + \tilde{\epsilon}_i \tag{16.1}$$

Let Z be the realization of the random market supply $\tilde{Z}$ of the risky asset. We have the market clearing condition for equilibrium

$$z = \sum_{i=1}^{n} z_i(p, I_i) \tag{16.2}$$

A2. The random vector $(\tilde{x}, \tilde{z}, \tilde{\epsilon}_1, \tilde{\epsilon}_2, \ldots, \tilde{\epsilon}_n)$ has a normal distribution with mean $(\bar{x}, \bar{z}, 0, \ldots, 0)$ and variance–covariance matrix $P = (\sigma^2, \delta^2, s_1^2, \ldots, s_n^2)$.

A3. Each agent i is assumed to know the actual joint distirbution of the triple $(\tilde{x}, \tilde{y}_i, \tilde{p})$, where the price p is a realization of the random variable $\tilde{p}$. Thus it implies that for any information $I_i = (y_i, p)$, each agent can compute the expectation operator E_i from the actual conditional distribution of $\tilde{x}$ given y_i and p. This is a rational expectations assumption.

The determination of an equilibrium price under these three assumptions can be treated as a fixed point problem. Under assumptions A1 and A2 this fixed-point problem is shown to have a linear solution as follows. Consider an arbitrary linear relation

$$\tilde{p} = \pi_0 + \sum_{i=1}^{n} \pi_i \tilde{y}_i - \gamma \tilde{z} \tag{16.3}$$

Let $\pi = \sum_{i=1}^{n} \pi_i$. Then the triple $(\tilde{x}, \tilde{y}_i, \tilde{p})$ has a normal distribution with mean $(\bar{x}, \bar{x}, \pi_0 + \pi\bar{x} - \gamma\bar{z})$ and variance–covariance matrix V_i:

$$
v_i = \begin{bmatrix}
\sigma^2 & \sigma^2 & \pi\sigma^2 \\
\sigma^2 & \sigma^2 + s_i^2 & \pi\sigma^2 + \pi_i s_i^2 \\
\pi\sigma^2 & \pi\sigma^2 + \pi_i s_i^2 & \gamma^2\delta^2 + \sum_i \pi_i^2 s_i^2
\end{bmatrix}
$$

By the assumption of normality, the posterior distribution of $\tilde{x}$ given a realization (y_i, p) is again normal, with mean and variance of the form

$$E(\tilde{x} \mid y_i, p) = \alpha_{0i} + \alpha_{1i} y_i + \alpha_{2i} p \tag{16.4a}$$

$$\operatorname{var}(\tilde{x} \mid y_i, p) = \beta_i \tag{16.4b}$$

where the values of α_{0i}, α_{1i}, β depend on the matrix V_i.

If expectations are based on the linear relation (16.3), normality of distribution implies that the asset demands under expected utility maximization depend only on the posterior mean and variance of returns given in (16.4a), and (16.4b). In case of constant absolute risk aversion, this demand function is:

$$
\bar{z}_i(p, y_i; \pi_0, \pi_1, \ldots, \pi_n, \gamma) = \lambda_i \operatorname{var}\left[(\tilde{x} \mid y_i, p)\right]^{-1} \left[E(\tilde{x} \mid y_i, p) - p\right]
$$

$$
= \frac{\alpha_{0i} + \alpha_{1i} y_i + (\alpha_{2i} - 1) p}{\lambda_i \beta_i}
$$

Substituting this relation into the market clearing condition (16.1) viewed as

$$z = \sum_{i=1}^{n} \bar{z}_i(p, y; f) \tag{16.1a}$$

where f is a function determining the conditional distribution of $\tilde{x}$, given any realization $I_i = (y_i, p)$ one obtains for the equilibrium price

$$p = \left[\sum_{i=1}^{n}\left(\frac{1 - \alpha_{2i}}{\lambda_i \beta_i}\right)\right]^{-1}\left[\sum_{i=1}^{n} \frac{\alpha_{0i} + \alpha_{1i} y_i}{\lambda_i \beta_i} - z\right] \tag{16.1b}$$

Expectations defined by (16.3) are rational if and only if the coefficients

π_0, π_i, γ in (16.3) are identical with the corresponding coefficients in (16.1b). Thus:

$$\gamma = \left[\sum_i (\lambda_i \beta_i)^{-1}(1 - \alpha_{2i}) \right]^{-1}$$

$$\pi_i = \gamma \alpha_{1i}/(\lambda_i \beta_i), \quad i = 1, 2, \ldots, n \qquad (16.5)$$

$$\pi_0 = \gamma \sum_{i=1}^{n} (\lambda_i \beta_i)^{-1} \alpha_{0i}$$

The coefficients $\alpha_{ij}(j = 0, 1, 2)$ and β_i can be explicitly computed from the formulas for the conditional mean and variance of $\tilde{x}$ given y_i, p assuming V_i to be nonsingular:

$$\alpha_{1i} = \frac{\sigma^2}{b_i} \left[\sum_{k=1}^{n} \pi_k^2 s_k^2 + \gamma^2 \delta^2 - \pi_i \pi s_i^2 \right]$$

$$\alpha_{2i} = \frac{\sigma^2}{b_i}(\pi - \pi_i)s_i^2$$

$$\alpha_{0i} = \bar{x}\frac{s_i^2}{b_i} \left[\sum_{k=1}^{n} \pi_k^2 s_k^2 + \gamma^2 \delta^2 - \pi_i^2 s_i^2 \right] - \alpha_{2i}(\pi_0 - \gamma \bar{z})$$

$$\beta_i = \frac{\sigma^2 s_i^2}{b_i} \left[\sum_{k=1}^{n} \pi_k^2 s_k^2 + \gamma^2 \delta^2 - \pi_i^2 s_i^2 \right]$$

$$b_i = \left(\sigma^2 + s_i^2 \right) \left[\sum_{k=1}^{n} \pi_k^2 s_k^2 + \gamma^2 \delta^2 - \pi^2 s^2 \right] + \sigma^2 s_i^2 (\pi - \pi_i)^2$$

Under assumptions A1 through A3, two important propositions have been proved by Hellwig.

PROPOSITION 1:

(a) If $\lambda_i \geqslant \lambda_j$ and $s_i^2 \geqslant s_j^2$, then $\pi_i \leqslant \pi_j$

(b) If $\lambda_i \geqslant \lambda_j$ and $s_i^2 = s_j^2$, then $\lambda_i \pi_i \geqslant \lambda_j \pi_j$

(c) If $\lambda_i = \lambda_j$ and $s_i^2 \geqslant s_j^2$, then $s_i^2 \pi_i \leqslant s_j^2 \pi_j$

If one of the inequalities in the statements of (a) through (c) is strict, the inequality in the corresponding conclusion is also strict.

This proposition shows very clearly the dependence of the ratios π_i/π_j on the risk aversion parameters λ_i, λ_j and the variances s_i^2, s_j^2 of the noise elements $\tilde{\epsilon}_i$ and $\tilde{\epsilon}_j$ in the private information functions $\tilde{y}_i$ and $\tilde{y}_j$ defined by (16.1). In particular the first part of the proposition implies that a precise signal available to a risk neutral agent affects the price more than an imprecise signal available to a risk averse agent. This is because the sensitivity of agent i's demand to the signal y_i increases with the precision of the signal and decreases with the agent's risk aversion.

PROPOSITION 2:
If δ^2 tends to zero, then
(a) the equilibrium price converges to

$$\tilde{p}_0 = (\sigma^2 C + 1)^{-1} \left[\bar{x} + \sigma^2 \sum_{i=1}^{n} \frac{\tilde{y}_i}{s_i^2} - \frac{\sigma^2 \bar{z}}{A} \right]$$

where

$$A = \sum_{i=1}^{n} \frac{1}{\lambda_i}, \quad C = \sum_{i=1}^{n} \frac{1}{s_i^2}$$

(b) the conditional expectation and variance of $\tilde{x}$ given $I_i = (y_i, p)$ converges as follows:

$$E(\tilde{x} \mid I_i) \to p + \left[A(\sigma^2 C + 1) \right]^{-1} \sigma^2 \bar{z}$$

$$\mathrm{var}(\tilde{x} \mid I_i) \to \sigma^2 (\sigma^2 C + 1)^{-1}$$

Two implications of this result are most important. First, we note that as the supply-induced noise δ^2 becomes small, market price becomes a more reliable predictor of the return $\tilde{x}$, both because it reveals $\Sigma \pi_i y_i$ more precisely and because with the disappearance of the risk aversion coefficient λ_i from the weights π_i, $\Sigma \pi_i y_i$ becomes a more efficient predictor of $\tilde{x}$. In the limit $\delta^2 \to 0$, the equilibrium price of the risky asset reveals $\Sigma \rho_i y_i$ perfectly and moreover, $\Sigma_{i=1}^{n} \pi_i y_i$ becomes a sufficient statistic for the vector $(y_1, y_2, \ldots, y_n)$ in the sense that given $\Sigma \pi_i y_i$, no other aspect of their own information is worth looking into by each agent. This result is basically similar to that of Grossman [15].

Second, this result shows that in competitive markets with small supply-induced noise, market price may provide a good aggregator of information, provided there are many price-taking agents with many independent sources of information. In such a case the so-called noise $\tilde{\epsilon}_i$ in the private information $\tilde{y}_i$ available to any individual agent is filtered out and hence has no effect on the equilibrium price.

Hellwig has also extended his results for a sequency of competitive market economies where the weights π_i, risk aversion λ_i and other parameters like γ may be viewed dependent on n, so that the implications of the limits $\pi_i(n)$, $\lambda_i(n)$, $\gamma(n)$ when $n \to \infty$ can be analyzed.

4. Concluding remarks

By the very selective nature of our survey it has not been possible to include several other uses of adaptive information in decision models that are somewhat broader than economic models. First, one may mention game-theoretic models, where in non-cooperative situations, sharing of information may not always be stabilizing. Although self-fulfilling or rational expectations solutions can be proposed in such a framework under suitable restrictions [31], the generality of such proposals is yet to be established. Second, the characterization of information in a qualititative sense, as distinct from its quantitative content is important for many areas like new technology with unknown rates of obsolescence, new products with unknown quality and new research investment with uncertain yields. Third, the role of asymmetry, heterogeneity and near-singularity of quantitative information structures in adaptive models of stochastic control are increasingly being researched and investigated in learning and pattern recognition, search theory and remote sensing. Psychological processes associated with learning emphasize many aspects of fuzzy systems theory that are relevant here.

References

1. Anderson, T.W. and J.B. Taylor, "Some Experimental Results on the Statistical Properties of least Squares Estimates in Control Problems," Econometrica, 44 (1976), 1289–1302.
2. Arrow, K.J., Essays in the Theory of Risk Bearing. North Holland: Amsterdam, 1971.
3. Baron, D.P., "Demand Uncertainty in Imperfect Competition," International Economic Review, 12 (1971), 196–208.
4. Barro, R.J., "A Theory of Monopolistic Price Adjustment," Review of Economic Studies, 39 (1972), 17–26.
5. Black, R. and M. Scholes, "The Valuation of Option Contracts and a Test of Market Efficiency," Journal of Finance, 27 (1972), 399–417.
6. Chernoff, H., "Some Measures for Discriminating Between Normal Multivariate Distributions with Unequal Covariance Matrices," in P.R. Krishnaiah, ed., Multivariate Analysis 111. Academic Press: New York, 1973.
7. Chu, K.C., "Designing Information Structures for Quadratic Decision Problems," Journal of Optimization Theory and Applications, 25 (1978), 139–160.
8. Cyert, R.M. and M.H. DeGroot, "Learning Applied to Utility Functions," in A. Zellner, ed., Bayesian Analysis in Econometrics. North Holland: Amsterdam, 1980.

9. Danthine, J., "Information, Future Prices and Stabilizing Speculation," Journal of Economic Theory, 17 (1978), 79–98.

10. Doyle, J.C. and G. Stein, "Multivariable Feedback Design: Concepts for a Classical/Modern Synthesis," IEEE Transactions on Automatic Control, 26 (1981), 4–16.

11. Duncan, G.T., "A Matrix Measure of Multivariate Local Risk Aversion," Econometrica, 45 (1977), 895–904.

12. Fanchon, P. and J.K. Sengupta, "A Two-Period Stochastic Inventory Model," International Journal of Systems Science, 13 (1982), 869–879.

13. Feldbaum, A.A., Optimal Control Systems. Academic Press: New York, 1965. (English translation)

14. Grossman, S., "On the Efficiency of Competitive Stock Markets Where Traders Have Diverse Information," Journal of Finance, 31 (1976), 573–585.

15. Grossman, S., "Further Results on the Informational Efficiency of Competitive Stock Markets," Journal of Economic Theory, 18 (1978), 81–101.

16. Heelwig, M.G., "On the Aggregation of Information in Competitive Markets," Journal of Economic Theory, 22 (1980), 477–498.

17. Hipel, K.W., "Geophysical Model Discrimination Using the Akaike Information Criterion," IEEE Transactions on Automatic Control, 26 (1981), 358–378.

18. Hughes–Hallett, A. and H. Rees, Quantitative Economic Policies and Interactive Planning. Cambridge Press: Cambridge, England, 1983.

19. James, A.T., "The Variance Information Manifold and the Functions on It," in P.R. Krishnaiah, ed., Multivariate Analysis, Vol. 3. Academic Press: New York, 1973.

20. Johansen, L., "Parametric Certainty Equivalence Procedures in Decision-Making Under Uncertainty," Zeitschrift fr nationlökonomie, 40 (1980), 257–279.

21. Keeney, R.L. and H. Raiffa, Decisions with Multiple Objectives: Preferences and Value Trade-Offs. John Wiley: New York, 1976.

22. Kendrick, D., "Control Theory with Applications to Economics," in K.J. Arrow and M.D. Intriligator, eds., Handbook of Mathematical Economics, Vol. I. North Holland: Amsterdam, 1981.

23. Kirman, A.P., "Learning by Firms about Demand Conditions," in R.H. Day and T. Groves, eds., Adaptive Economic Models. Academic Press: New York, 1975.

24. Lai, T.L. and H. Robbins, "Adaptive Design and the Multiperiod Control Problem," in S.S. Gupta and J.O. Berger, eds., Statistical Decision Theory and Related Topics III, Vol. 2. Academic Press: New York, 1982.

25. Lindley, D.V., "On a Measure of Information Provided by an Experiment," Annals of Mathematical Statistics, 27 (1956), 986–1005.

26. Lippman, S.A. and J.J. McCall, "The Economics of Uncertainty: Selected Topics and Probabilistic Methods," in K.J. Arrow and M.D. Intriligator, eds., Handbook of Mathematical Economics, Vol. 1. North Holland: Amsterdam, 1981.

27. Mills, E.S., Price Output and Inventory Policy. John Wiley: New York, 1962.

28. Newbery, D.M.G. and J.E. Stiglitz, The Theory of Commodity Price Stabilization: A Study in the Economics of Risk. Clarendon Press: Oxford, 1981.

29. Petkovski, D. and M. Athans, "Robustness of Decentralized Output Control Designs with Application to an Electric Power System, in J.E. Marshall, et al., eds., Third IMA Conference on Control Theory. Academic Press: New York, 1975.

30. Pratt, J., "Risk Aversion in the Small and in the Large," Econometrica, 32 (1964), 122–136.

31. Prescott, E.C. and R.M. Townsend, "Equilibrium Under Uncertainty: Multiagent Decision Theory," in A. Zellner, ed., Bayesian Analysis in Econometrics. North Holland: Amsterdam, 1980.

32. Rothschild, M. and J.E. Stiglitz, "Increasing Risk I: A Definition," Journal of Economic Theory, 2 (1970), 225–243.

33. Schneeweiss, H., "On the Consistency of Classical Decision Criteria," in Inference and Decision. Toronto University Press: Toronto, Canada, 1973.
34. Sengupta, J.K., Decision Models in Stochastic Programming. North Holland: Amsterdam, 1982.
35. Sengupta, J.K., "Static Monopoly Uncertainty," Working Paper in Economics, University of California at Santa Barbara, 1983.
36. Sengupta, J.K., "A Theory of Portfolio Revision: Robustness and Truncation Problems," to appear in International Journal of Systems Science.
37. Stiglitz, J.E., "Symposium on Economics of Information: Introduction," Review of Economic Studies, 44 (1977), 389–392.
38. Szego, G.P., Portfolio Theory. Academic Press: New York, 1980.
39. Walters, C.J., "Some Dynamic Programming Applications in Fisheries Management," in M.L. Puterman, ed., Dynamic Programming and Its Applications. Academic Press: New York, 1978.
40. Wittenmark, B., "Stochastic Adaptive Control Method: A Survey," International Journal of Control, 21 (1975), 705–730.

INDEX

478

480

ADVANCED STUDIES IN THEORETICAL AND APPLIED ECONOMETRICS
VOLUME 4

1. J.H.P. Paelinck (ed.) Qualitative and Quantitative Mathematical Economics, 1982.
   ISBN 90 247 2623 9.
2. J.P. Ancot (ed.) Analysing the Structure of Economic Models, 1984.
   ISBN 90 247 2894 0.
3. Dr. A.J. Hughes Hallett (ed.) Applied Decision Analysis and Economic Behaviour
   ISBN 90 247 2968 8.
4. Jati K. Sengupta Information and Efficiency in Economic Decision
   ISBN 90 247 3072 4.